Data Structures & Their Algorithms

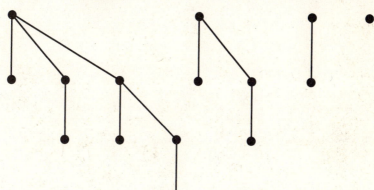

Data Structures & Their Algorithms

Harry R. Lewis
Harvard University

Larry Denenberg
Harvard University

HarperCollins*Publishers*

Sponsoring Editor: Don Childress
Project Editor: Janet Tilden
Art Direction: Julie Anderson
Cover Design: Matthew J. Doherty
Production Administrator: Beth Maglione
Printer and Binder: R. R. Donnelley & Sons Company
Cover Printer: Phoenix Color Corp.

Data Structures and Their Algorithms

Copyright ©1991 by Harry R. Lewis and Larry Denenberg

Library of Congress Cataloging-in-Publication Data

Lewis, Harry R.
    Data structures and their algorithms / Harry R. Lewis, Larry Denenberg.
        p.   cm.
    Includes bibliographical references and index.
    ISBN 0-673-39736-X
    1. Data structures (Computer science)   2. Algorithms.
    I. Denenberg, Larry. II. Title.
    QA76.9.D35L475   1991
    005.7'3--dc20   90-23290
                                                                 CIP

94 9 8 7 6 5 4 3

To Eunice and Norman Denenberg, and to Elizabeth and Anne Lewis

Contents

10

MEMORY MANAGEMENT   341

11

SORTING   379

Preface

Like all engineering activities, computer programming is both craft and science. Building a bridge or a computer program requires familiarity with the known techniques for the overall design of similar artifacts. And making intelligent choices among the available techniques and designs requires understanding of the mathematical principles governing their performance and economy. This book is about methods for organizing, reorganizing, moving, exploring, and retrieving data in digital computers, and the mathematical analysis of those techniques. This subject is a theoretical foundation of the useful art of computer programming in the same way that the statics and dynamics of physical systems lie at the heart of mechanical engineering.

A few simple principles have governed our choice of topics. First, we have chosen only practically useful techniques. We omit treatment of some theoretically excellent algorithms that are not practical for data sets of reasonable size. Second, we have included both classical and recently discovered methods, relying on inherent simplicity, wide applicability, and potential usefulness as the criteria for inclusion rather than any preconceived exhaustive catalogue. For example, Chapter 6, List and Tree Implementations of Sets, includes both the classical algorithm for construction of optimal binary search trees on static data, and the newer skip list structures for dynamic data. In other chapters there are sections on splay trees, extendible hashing, grid files, and other elegant newly developed methods. Third, we have included an analysis of almost every method we describe. One of our major objectives has been to present analyses that are relatively brief and nontechnical but illuminate the important performance characteristics of the algorithms. As in mechanical engineering, one of the crucial lessons to be taught is about scalability: a method that is satisfactory for a structure of one size may be unsuitable for a structure ten times as large.

We omit unnecessary syntactic detail from the presentations. Our subject matter is algorithms, not the expression of algorithms in the syntax of particular programming languages, so we have adopted a pseudocode notation that is readily understandable to programmers but has a simple syntax. It is assumed that the reader will have had a first course in computer programming in a language like Pascal or C, and will therefore be able to translate our pseudocode into such a language without difficulty, by introducing appropriate identifier declarations, **begin–end** blocking, and the like. To simplify one of the messiest coding problems in dynamic tree algorithms—how to alter pointers that have already been traversed during a search process—we have introduced *locatives*, a new programming device. We have been able to present precise and complete pseudocode throughout, using no more than one page per algorithm.

In the same way, we give detailed analyses of the algorithms, but avoid mathematical techniques that are likely to be inaccessible to college sophomores. Logarithms, exponentials, and sums of geometric series play a central role in many analyses, so we give some elementary examples of these topics in Chapter 1. Naïve probabilistic reasoning is also essential, and the book has a self-contained introduction. On the other hand the differential calculus is used in only a few spots (the integral calculus not at all), and precalculus readers can simply skip to the conclusion of those arguments.

Each chapter ends with problems and references. The problems are split up into sections that correspond to the main sections of the text of that chapter. Within those sections the problems range from straightforward simulations of the algorithms on small data sets, to requests for completion of arguments whose details were omitted in the text, to the design and analysis of new or extended data structures and algorithms. The references cite publications that are of historical significance or present good summaries of a particular set of topics.

Chapter 13 is a collection of synthetic and open-ended exercises in data structure design and analysis. Some of these problems are amenable to paper-and-pencil answers of a page or two; others to programming projects that might take a semester to do properly. What they have in common is that they are phrased not as problems about particular data structures, but as problems about computational situations where there can be more than one approach to the design of data structures and it may not be possible to make a selection on the basis of a clean mathematical analysis. It is our hope that through these exercises students will get realistic experience with the engineering of efficient computational methods.

Acknowledgements   We want to thank the many people who have given us advice and corrections over the years this book has been in preparation. Paul Bamberg, Mihaly Gereb, Victor Milenkovic, Bernard Moret, and Henry Shapiro have taught courses using drafts of the book and have given us valuable feedback. Our thanks to Danny Krizanc for pointing out an error in the analysis of Quick Sort, and to Bob Sedgewick for his advice on fixing it. Marty Tompa gave a late draft of the book a careful reading and helped remove many errors. Mike Karr provided a very helpful critique of locatives. Bill Gasarch and Victor Milenkovic supplied a great many problems and references that have been incorporated into the text. David Johnson helped us with a problem on memory management. Stephen Gildea was our dance consultant. BBN Communications provided a supportive environment for the second author while this work was in progress. Joe Snowden of Chiron, Inc. always responded promptly and professionally to our typesetting demands. This book emerged from a course taught at Harvard, Computer Science 124 (originally Applied Mathematics 119); a large number of talented teaching assistants have contributed over the years to our understanding of how to present the material, as well as to our inventory of exercises. Among those teaching fellows are David Albert, Jeff Baron, Mark Berman, Marshall Brinn, David Frankel, Adam Gottlieb, Abdelsalam Heddaya, Kevin Knight, Joe Marks, Mike Massimilla, Marios Mavronicolas, Ted Nesson, Julia Shaffner, Ra'ad Siraj, Dan Winkler, and Michael Yampol; thanks to all. Alex Lewin deserves special thanks for his detailed proofreading. One anonymous reviewer provided valuable improvements to several of our analyses.

Marlyn McGrath Lewis provided boundless encouragement and support as this project dragged on, and sage advice about how to get it finished.

This book was typeset using Donald Knuth's T$_E$X; we want to thank him for having made possible so much of its form as well as its substance.

1

Introduction

1.1 PROGRAMMING AS AN ENGINEERING ACTIVITY

A program is a solution to a problem. The problem might be very specific and well-defined—for example, to calculate the square roots of the integers from 1 to 100 to ten decimal places. Or the problem might be vast and vague—for example, to develop a system for printing books by computer. Large, ill-defined problems are, however, best solved by breaking them down into smaller and more specific problems. As a part of the problem of printing books by computer, for example, we might need to determine the places where a word could be hyphenated if it had to be split across two lines. Our subject matter is programming problems that are specific enough that we can describe them in a few words and can judge readily what is a solution and what isn't, but are common enough that they come up over and over again in the solution of larger programming problems.

Even for problems that can be described very exactly in a few words, however, there can be many possible solutions. Of course one can always get different *programs* by changing variable names, translating from FORTRAN to Pascal, and the like. But there can be solutions that differ in more fundamental ways, that use quite different approaches or methods to solve a problem. Consider, for example, the problem of finding a word K in a sorted table of words. Here are three approaches.

A. Start at the beginning of the table and go through it, comparing K to each word in the table, until you find K or reach the end of the table.

Of course that way doesn't take advantage of the fact that the table is sorted. Here's a slightly more intelligent variation:

B. Start at the beginning of the table and go through it as in (A), stopping when you find K or another word that should come after K in the table, or when you reach the end of the table.

Changing the stopping condition in this way eliminates some unnecessary work done by method (A). If we're looking for aardvark, for example, chances

1

are we won't have to look long if we use method (B). But there is a better way yet.

C. Start in the middle of the table. If K is the middle word in the table, you're done. Otherwise, decide by looking at that middle word whether K would be in the first half of the table or the second, and repeat the same process on one half of the table. On subsequent iterations search a quarter, an eighth, ... of the table in the same way. Stop when you find K or have shrunk to nothing the size of the table you're searching.

Method (C) is called **binary search** and is generally the fastest of the three. (It's also the trickiest to program correctly. Actually, this description leaves out a lot of important details; for example, which element is in the "middle" of a table of length 10?) We'll get to a detailed account of binary search in Chapter 6, but for now there are a few morals to be drawn from the example. First, (A), (B), and (C) are different *algorithms* for the same problem. None of them is a program, since the language used to describe them isn't a programming language. But any programmer would understand these descriptions, and would understand that FORTRAN and Pascal implementations of (C) embody the same algorithm, whereas Pascal implementations of (A) and (C) embody utterly different algorithms.

An **algorithm** is a computational method used for solving a problem. The goals of this book are to teach you some of the most important algorithms for solving problems that come up over and over again in computer programming, and to teach you how to decide which algorithm to use when you have a choice (as you almost always do).

We might choose one algorithm over another becauses it is always faster, or because it is usually faster, or because it uses less memory. Or we might choose an algorithm because it is easier to program, or because it is more general and we want to anticipate the possibility that the problem we are solving might change in the future. For our purposes in this book, however, we will mostly be looking at the speed of algorithms, and how much memory they use.

Of course we are not going to determine the speed of an algorithm by writing a program and then timing it. The numbers obtained in this way would depend too much on the quality of the programmer and the speed of the particular computer to be of general interest or applicability. Instead, we'll try to think in more abstract, mathematical terms. If the table has length n, then method (A) takes time proportional to n; double the size of the table and the algorithm will take roughly twice as long. Method (C), on the other hand, takes time proportional to the base 2 logarithm of n at worst (since that is the number of times you can divide a table of length n in half before it is reduced to a single element).

We'll spend a good deal of time in Chapter 2 on this business of **algorithm analysis**, but again a few simple morals will suffice for now. We want to use mathematical tools for analyzing the algorithms we consider, since the right mathematical tools will give us conclusions that hold for *all* implementations. To develop those mathematical tools, we have to come up with mathematical **models** for the situations we are trying to understand. For example, to conclude that method (A) takes time proportional to the length of the table, we need assume only that it always takes the same amount of time to get from any element of the table to the next. That is true for a great many ways of implementing tables, so from a weak assumption we can draw a conclusion of quite general applicability.

Programming is an engineering activity. It isn't pure science, or pure mathematics either; when we write programs, we can't ignore annoying details of practical importance, and we're not working in an environment where there's only one right answer. Engineers make design decisions based on an understanding of the consequences of alternative choices. That understanding comes from a knowledge of laws, usually stated in mathematical terms, that cover a broad variety of situations. An engineer decides what kind of bridge to build to span a river at a particular spot by sizing up the parameters of the situation (how long? how much weight to be borne?) and applying the general laws that characterize the behavior of various kinds of bridges. An engineer will also bring to bear the wisdom of experience accumulated by witnessing the construction of the things that have been designed. Programmers should think the same way; they need both an understanding of the general laws that govern the performance of algorithms, and the practical wisdom that comes from having attempted to implement them.

1.2 COMPUTER SCIENCE BACKGROUND

Memory and Data in Von Neumann Computers

The computers we are thinking about when we discuss our algorithms are called "von Neumann" machines.* Such a computer has a single processor, which is connected to a large block of memory. This memory is binary, that is, it ultimately consists of single bits, but those bits are organized into larger units or **cells**. A cell might contain a single integer, character, floating-point number, or element of some other basic data type; in our terminology the size of a cell can depend on the kind of data stored in it, so a cell need not correspond to a byte, word, etc. Indeed, contiguous cells can be grouped together to store several

---

* Virtually all digital computers that have been built to date are von Neumann machines. In the last few years a number of machines that are not of the von Neumann type have for the first time begun to appear; for example, machines with dozens or even thousands of processors, scattered through the memory and interconnected in complicated ways. Programming such machines requires a new style of algorithmic thinking (see the references at the end of this chapter).

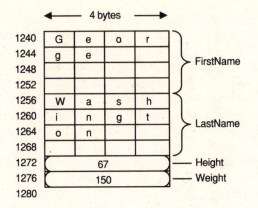

Figure 1.1 Layout of a data record in memory. The record has four fields, of 16, 16, 4, and 4 bytes.

data items as a single **record**, which is really just a memory cell containing a logically structured object. In this case the individual components of a record are called its **fields**. For example, a record designed to contain the first and last name and the height and weight of an individual might look as illustrated in Figure 1.1; it contains two 16-byte fields for the first and last names, and two four-byte integer fields for the height (in inches) and weight (in pounds), so the whole record is 40 bytes in length.

Each individual memory cell has a numerical **address**; when a datum is to be brought to the processor, it must be referred to by the address where it is stored. These addresses are typically in units of the smallest possible cell size, such as the eight-bit byte. For example, in the example of Figure 1.1, the record begins at byte address 1240; the first address after the end of the record is 1280.

A series of memory cells of the same type can be packed together at equal intervals in a contiguous block of memory. Such a memory organization we call a **table**: the addresses of the individual memory cells $C_0, C_1, \ldots, C_{n-1}$ differ by a fixed amount, which is the size of the cell (Figure 1.2). Hence if X is the memory address of the beginning of the table and c is the size of a single cell, then cell C_i is located at address $X + c \cdot i$. For example, in Figure 1.2, $c = 40$ and $X = 1240$, so C_i is at address $1240 + 40 \cdot i$.

Within records of a given type, the fields are defined by their sizes and their distances from the beginning of the record. For example, in the record structure of Figure 1.1, if a record is located at address X,

- the FirstName field is 16 bytes long and begins at address X;
- the LastName field is 16 bytes long and begins at address $X + 16$, right after the end of the FirstName field;
- the Height field is four bytes long and begins at address $X + 32$; and
- the Weight field is four bytes long and begins at address $X + 36$.

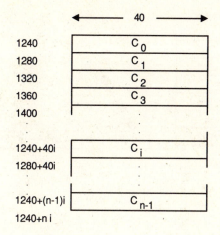

1240	C_0
1280	C_1
1320	C_2
1360	C_3
1400	

| 1240+40i | C_i |
| 1280+40i | |

| 1240+(n-1)i | C_{n-1} |
| 1240+n i | |

Figure 1.2 Layout of a table in memory.

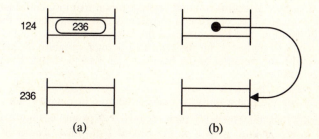

(a)   (b)

Figure 1.3 Addresses and pointers. (a) The situation inside the computer: the cell at address 124 contains the number 236. (b) A logical representation: regarded as containing an address, the cell at 124 points to the cell at 236.

To refer to the various fields of a particular record located at address X, we use the notations such as FirstName(X), LastName(X), and the like. We can also give a name to the record type as a whole—Person, say, in the present example.

The memory is **random-access**, which means for our purposes that it takes the same amount of time to retrieve from, or to store into, any address in memory, independent of the address (though it may, of course, take longer to read or store a larger datum or record than a smaller one). This means in particular that given a table of records $C_0, C_1, \ldots, C_{n-1}$ as in the example just given, the time required to access the ith record is constant, independent of i.

Addresses, being mere numbers, can themselves be stored in memory cells. A cell containing the address of another cell acts as a reference or **pointer** to that cell, and we use an arrow to illustrate the connection between the cell where an address is stored and the cell whose address it contains (Figure 1.3).

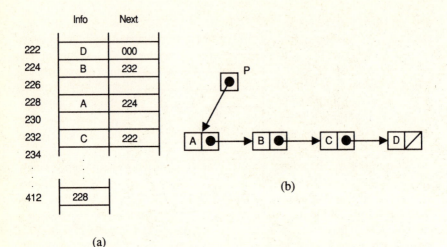

Figure 1.4 Linked lists. (a) Internal representation; (b) graphic illustration. In this example Λ is represented by address 000 in memory in the left-hand illustration, and by a diagonal line through a pointer field on the right. The cell named P on the right is a pointer variable, located at address 412 and pointing to the beginning of the linked list, which is at address 228.

This creates the opportunity to build structures in memory with complex patterns of internal references between records. For example, Figure 1.4 shows a memory structure known as a **singly linked list**. Each record of a singly linked list has one or more fields for storing arbitrary data (the Info field of Figure 1.4), and a Next field which contains an address. The record structure as a whole is usually called a Node. Although the actual numerical addresses of the records in a linked list may fall into no pattern whatsoever, the nodes are logically organized as a sequential list, since we can start from one node, move to the node whose address is in its Next field, then to the node whose address is in *its* Next field, and so on. The end of such a list is indicated by a distinguished address Λ in the Next field; this is depicted in our illustrations by drawing a diagonal line through that field. A solid black circle at the tail of an arrow represents another pointer value. In Figure 1.4(b) there are cells of two kinds: linked list records consisting of an Info field (shown here as containing a letter A, B, C, D) and a pointer variable P (shown here as pointing to the beginning of the linked list).

A singly linked list, like a table, can be used to represent a sequence of data items of the same type. The representation is less economical in memory usage, since every node must bear the overhead of a pointer field to link it to the next node in the list. And it does not enjoy the pleasant property of tables that referring to a cell by its index in the sequence takes time independent of that index; in general, to find a node in a singly linked list, one must trace through all of the preceding nodes from the beginning of the list. On the other hand certain operations, such as inserting a record in the middle of the sequence or removing a record from the sequence, would require major shuffling of data in a table but can be achieved with only a couple of pointer movements in a linked list. It is because linked structures so readily support such dynamic structural reorganizations that they are at the heart of many efficient algorithms. Another major advantage to linked lists is that they can be used when the amount of memory to be required is not known in advance, whereas tables must be preallocated at their maximum size.

We write **p** for the number of bits needed to store a pointer; thus a singly linked list has an overhead of **p** bits per cell. In many cases it is not necessary to store a full machine address to achieve the effect of a link or pointer field. If all the records in the data structure are in a table of length n beginning at a known address, then to refer to any one of those cells it is enough to store an index in the range from 0 to $n - 1$, and this may well require many fewer bits than would be needed for a general pointer. Gains achieved in this way are, however, somewhat offset by the need to perform an arithmetic calculation to determine the machine address of a cell from its index, and by the need to take into account the base address of the particular table in which a record is located when following its link field.

As a general matter, the design of data structures often involves such compromises or **tradeoffs**: we would like a data structure that is superior in several different ways that cannot all be realized simultaneously, so we accept somewhat poorer characteristics of some kinds in order to achieve better characteristics of other kinds. For example, using table indices instead of pointers into a table trades speed for memory usage, and using tables instead of linked lists trades memory usage for speed of insertion or deletion.

Notation for Programs

Today most programs are written in higher-level programming languages. Such languages offer a number of advantages over lower-level machine and assembly languages for the description of algorithms. Higher-level programming languages provide mechanisms for talking about data aggregates as wholes, without reference to how they are represented in memory. For example, the Pascal two-dimensional array A: **array**$[1 .. 10, 1 .. 10]$ **of real** consists of 100 **real**s distributed somehow in memory. As Pascal programmers we do not need to know how; we need only be assured that each time we refer to, say, $A[5, 7]$, we get the same element, though not necessarily the same value. If we want to consider in detail the performance of an algorithm, however, we may need to have tighter control over the organization of memory than the semantics of higher-level languages allow us to assume. For this reason we distinguish sharply between a **data type**, which is a programming-language notion, and a **data structure**, which is a logical organization of computer memory, generally exploiting patterns of addresses of memory cells.

---

procedure *SinglyLinkedInsert*(**pointer** P, Q):
{Insert the cell to which P points just after the cell to which Q points}
    Next(P) ← Next(Q)
    Next(Q) ← P

Algorithm 1.1 Insertion of node in a singly linked list.

With the increase in expressiveness provided by higher-level languages come a few other disadvantages. Languages such as Pascal have "strong types," meaning that every variable and every data object has a data type, and a value can be assigned to a variable only if both are of the same type. Some algorithms, which manipulate data representations at a lower level or use the same memory cells at different times for different kinds of data objects, cannot be implemented efficiently in languages like Pascal. Another problem comes with the manipulation of addresses by algorithms. Some languages do not have address or "pointer" data types at all; others have such types but enforce strong typing with respect to the type of the datum pointed to (so that a pointer to a record and a pointer to its first component must be objects of different types, even though they correspond to the same machine address).

We use a sort of compromise notation in describing algorithms. We write $T[a..b]$ to denote a table with indices running from a to b (both integers). $T[i]$ stands for the ith element of the table T, provided that $a \leq i \leq b$. Tables are assumed to occupy contiguous memory. *Arrays*, which are indexed in the same way as tables and are discussed at length in Chapter 5, come with no such guarantees about how the entries are stored, or how much time it takes to access an element.

We also use higher-level notation for record types and their fields, and freely use the assignment operator (←) between any variable or field of a variable and a value of the appropriate type. If P is a pointer to a record which has a field by the name of F, we write F(P) for the F field of the record pointed to by P. For example, Algorithm 1.1 inserts the node to which P points in a singly linked list immediately after the node to which Q points (Figure 1.5).

As an extension to the assignment notation, we use a "column vector" notation to denote the *simultaneous* assignment of several values to several variables. For example, the notation

$$\begin{pmatrix} X \\ Y \\ Z \end{pmatrix} \leftarrow \begin{pmatrix} Y \\ Z \\ X \end{pmatrix}$$

represents "rotating" to the left the values of the three variables X, Y, and Z; X gets the old value of Y, Y gets the old value of Z, and Z gets the old value

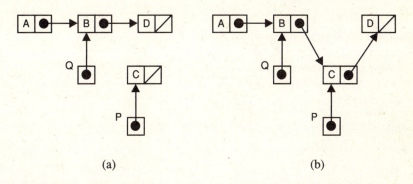

(a)   (b)

Figure 1.5 Inserting the node to which P points in a singly linked list just after the node to which Q points.

of X. We abbreviate the commonly used form $\begin{pmatrix} X \\ Y \end{pmatrix} \leftarrow \begin{pmatrix} Y \\ X \end{pmatrix}$ by $X \leftrightarrow Y$, that is, exchange the values of X and Y. In most programming languages, these assignments could not be written without introducing a wholly extraneous "temporary" variable whose only purpose is to permit time sequencing of the two or more individual assignments.

Other notations will be introduced from time to time as they are convenient. However, we attempt to get by with the minimum of necessary notation; if it is easier to say something in English than to invent a special notation for it, we are apt to say it in English, trusting that as an experienced programmer you are able to imagine how it could be rendered in the syntax of your chosen programming language.

For the control part of our algorithms we adapt the "**if** ... **then** ..." and "**if** ... **then** ... **else** ..." constructions from languages such as Pascal, and also the "**while** ... **do** ..." and "**for** ... **do** ..." loops. A loop of the form "**repeat forever** ... " causes its body to be repeated indefinitely; the body should contain some statement, such as one that returns from a subroutine, that will eventually cause an exit from the loop. We dispense with Pascal's **begin**s and **end**s, preferring to use indentation to indicate grouping of statements. Also, we regard each subprogram as either a **procedure** (a subroutine executed solely for its effect on memory or on the input-output behavior of a program) or a **function** (a subroutine executed in order to obtain a value). We use the construct **return** to cause a procedure to return immediately, and **return** x to return the value x immediately as the value of a function. If the subprogram is to be called from elsewhere, we give it a name and list its parameters in an informative way in the first lines, together with one of the terms "**procedure**" or "**function**." At the end of the first line of a function definition, we also list the type of the value it returns. Explanatory **comments** are enclosed in {braces like these}. For example, Algorithm 1.2 is a more formalized version of algorithm (A) on page 1.

---

function *SequentialSearch*(**table** $T[0 .. n - 1]$, **key** K): **integer**
{Return position of K in table T, if it is present, otherwise -1}
    for i **from** 0 **to** $n - 1$ **do**
        if $T[i] = K$ **then return** i
    return -1

Algorithm 1.2 Search sequentially in table $T[0 .. n - 1]$ for key K.

Our algorithms deal with the common atomic data types, such as **integer**s and **boolean**s, and tables of these types. Values of type **pointer** are addresses. Occasionally (as above), when the details of a type are unimportant, we use a generic name such as **key**. In some higher-level languages (such as Pascal) **key** would have to be a particular data type, such as **integer**; in other languages it might be possible to code *SequentialSearch* as a generic function that works for any data type. In our notation we aim to convey just enough information to enable an experienced programmer to translate the algorithm into a program, but we do not attempt to be so explicit that the translation could be done automatically.

A boolean expression of the form "*Condition1* **and** *Condition2*" is true in case both *Condition1* and *Condition2* are true. However, evaluation of the second condition is **short-circuited**: if *Condition1* is false, we are guaranteed that *Condition2* will not be evaluated. Thus we can write a conditional such as "**if** $P \neq \Lambda$ **and** $\mathsf{F}(P) \neq \Lambda$ **then** $...$," confident that no attempt will be made to find the F field of P if P is actually Λ. (The C and Lisp languages use short-circuited evaluation of boolean expressions, but Pascal does not.) Similarly, in "*Condition1* **or** *Condition2*," if *Condition1* is true then *Condition2* will not be evaluated.

A subprogram can call itself; such a call is said to be **recursive**. The recursive style of programming often contributes greatly to expository clarity, and many highly efficient algorithms are best described recursively. However, there are some hidden costs in implementing recursive programs. In particular, a stack is used to keep track of the values of variables and parameters during recursive calls; since this data structure is not apparent to the programmer, who makes no reference to it in the source code, it is easy to forget that it may occupy significant amounts of memory when the program is run. We shall return to this point on page 79. Algorithm 1.3 is another example of our notation for programs, this time a recursive description of binary search (algorithm (C) on page 2).

We have changed the calling conventions a bit from our description of the sequential search algorithm. Since we wish to specify arbitrary lower and upper bounds a and b on the index of the table that is passed as an argument, we

---

function *BinarySearch*(**table** $T[a..b]$, **key** K): **integer**
{Return position of K in sorted table T, if it is present, otherwise -1}
    if $a > b$ **then return** -1
    middle $\leftarrow \lfloor (a+b)/2 \rfloor$
    if $K = T[middle]$ **then**
        return *middle*
    else if $K < T[middle]$ **then**
        return *BinarySearch*($T[a..middle-1], K$)
    else {$K > T[middle]$}
        return *BinarySearch*($T[middle+1..b], K$)

Algorithm 1.3 Binary search to locate key K in sorted table $T[a..b]$.

---

include those bounds as part of the description of the table. (Since a returned value of -1 is used to indicate that the search has failed, a and b should be nonnegative.) It is even possible for the lower index to exceed the upper index, in which case the table has no elements at all. Indeed, if the item sought is not in the table, then eventually *BinarySearch* is called to search a table $T[a..a-1]$, and it is this case that causes the recursion to terminate.

We have also introduced a useful notation $\lfloor x \rfloor$, the **floor** of x, which stands for *the largest integer that is less than or equal to* x; for example, $\lfloor 3.4 \rfloor = 3$, $\lfloor 3 \rfloor = 3$, and $\lfloor -3.4 \rfloor = -4$.* This resolves the question we asked earlier, about what is the "middle" element of a table $T[0..9]$; according to the algorithm, it is element $\lfloor (0+9)/2 \rfloor$, that is, element 4. If K is not found as $T[4]$ then *Binary-Search* is called recursively, with either $T[0..3]$ or $T[5..9]$ as an argument.

A data structure is said to be **dynamic** if it is possible to increase or decrease the amount of data it represents after the structure has been created; it is said to be **static** if the amount of data cannot be changed without recreating the structure from scratch. Thus linked lists are dynamic structures, while tables must generally be regarded as static. For dealing with dynamic structures like linked lists we assume the existence of a routine *NewCell* that magically delivers on demand a new cell of any desired type. The type desired is specified as the argument; thus *NewCell*(Node) returns the address of a block of memory the right size to hold a Node. The memory management component of the support environment for many programming languages provides just such a routine (e.g., Pascal's *new* and C's *malloc*). In practice, these routines parcel out chunks of a finite "storage pool," which definitely can become exhausted. Though we ignore that possibility in describing our algorithms, we do study in Chapter 10 the storage allocation problem itself in some detail.

---

*This notation has a sister $\lceil x \rceil$, the **ceiling** of x, which is *the smallest integer that is greater than or equal to* x; for example, $\lceil 3.4 \rceil = 4$, $\lceil 3 \rceil = 3$, and $\lceil -3.4 \rceil = -3$.

---

function *NewNode*(**key** K, **pointer** P): **pointer**
{Return address of a new cell of type **Node** containing key K and pointer P}
    $Q \leftarrow NewCell(\textsf{Node})$
    Key$(Q) \leftarrow K$
    Next$(Q) \leftarrow P$
    return Q

Algorithm 1.4 Create a new linked list cell of type **Node** and initialize its two fields.

Locatives

Many algorithms that alter linked structures must deal with the inconvenient reality that once a pointer has been followed, it is too late to change the value of the pointer itself; one can change only the value in the cell to which the pointer points. To illustrate the problem, let us return to the example of inserting an item in a linked list. The difficulty can be described by saying that "you can't insert before an item in a linked list, only after an item." To be concrete, assume that our records have two fields, a **Key** field that contains values of some linearly ordered data type like numbers or strings, and a **Next** field that contains the address of the next record in the list. The routine *NewNode*(K, P) (Algorithm 1.4) creates a new record of type **Node** and sets its **Key** and **Next** fields to K and P, respectively.

In the linked list insertion algorithm itself, the variable *list* points to the first record in the list; if the list is empty, *list* $= \Lambda$. We wish to keep the list in order (so that search time is reduced), and we want a function *LLInsert* that takes a key value K as its argument and modifies the list by adding a list cell containing that key value. If such a cell is already in the list when the function is called, the function does nothing; otherwise it creates a new linked list cell by calling *NewNode* and splices it into its appropriate position in the list so that the list nodes remain ordered by their key values. The naïve approach is to search the list using a pointer P to access successive list cells; if P eventually points to a record with **key** K, then the function returns. But if K is not in the list then this is discovered only when P becomes Λ or points to a record whose **Key** value comes after K. To insert the new record for K we need, in effect, the value of P one iteration earlier, and the usual approach is to use a second variable S to save P's previous value (Algorithm 1.5).

Quite aside from the inelegance of using two variables where it would seem that one should do, the coding of Algorithm 1.5 is unpleasant for two other reasons. First, the final **if** statement has different code for two cases that are really quite parallel; it is annoying to have to make a special check on each insertion just to cover the case in which K becomes the first key in the list. Second, the code contains a reference to the global variable *list*; this

procedure *LLInsert*(**key** K):
{Insert a cell containing key K in *list* if none exists already}
    $S \leftarrow \Lambda$
    $P \leftarrow list$
    while $P \neq \Lambda$ **and** Key$(P) < K$ **do**
        $S \leftarrow P$
        $P \leftarrow$ Next(P)
    if $P \neq \Lambda$ **and** Key$(P) = K$ **then return**
    if $S = \Lambda$ **then**   {Put K at the beginning of the list}
        $list \leftarrow NewNode(K, list)$
    else   {Insert K after some key already in the list}
        Next$(S) \leftarrow NewNode(K, P)$

Algorithm 1.5 Insertion of a key value in an ordered linked list. The global *list* contains the address of the first cell in the list.

---

variable cannot be passed as a parameter because its value may have to be changed.* Consequently, a program that uses several linked lists either has to have a separate insertion routine for each list, or else must have a single insertion routine that uses a variable of the awkward type "pointer to a pointer to a list element."

Two other approaches to this problem are commonly seen. A "dummy" or "header" node can be created; this node contains no key value but its Next field points to the true beginning of the list. Thus a list containing no keys consists of just the header node. Under this approach the two branches of the **if** statement at the end of Algorithm 1.5 can be coded identically. But it is still necessary to use two pointers that move in step with each other, or to have an equally clumsy proliferation of field references. Alternatively, if the programming language supports it, the algorithm can be recoded to handle explicitly the address of the *list* variable and the address of the Next field of a record. This is impossible in Pascal; it can be done in C using the "address-of" (&) and "dereference" (*) operators, though the code becomes rather tangled.

In this book we use a new data type **locative** to make the coding of such algorithms smoother. A locative behaves exactly like an ordinary variable in most contexts; if P is a **locative** that points to a linked list node, for example, then we can extract the Key and Next fields using Key(P) and Next(P). However, when a locative is given a value by an assignment statement, it remembers not only the value but *the place in memory where that value came from*. For example, suppose that P is a locative whose current value is 1000,

---

*In Pascal, *list* could be passed as a **var** parameter.

---

procedure *LLInsert*(**key** K, **locative** P):
{Insert a cell containing key K in list P if none exists already}
　　while $P \neq \Lambda$ **and** $\text{Key}(P) < K$ **do**
　　　　$P \leftarrow \text{Next}(P)$
　　if $P \neq \Lambda$ **and** $\text{Key}(P) = K$ **then return**
　　$P \Leftarrow NewNode(K, P)$

Algorithm 1.6 Insertion of a key value in an ordered linked list, using a locative. The variable *list* that points to the beginning of the linked list is passed to the procedure as its second parameter.

---

which is the address of a linked list node; and suppose that the Next field of this node is at address 1002 and contains the value 400. Then the assignment $P \leftarrow \text{Next}(P)$ assigns the value 400 to P, but also remembers that this value came from address 1002. We call this secondary piece of information associated with P its **locative value**; in this example, P's ordinary value is 400 and P's locative value is 1002.

Only one construct uses the locative value. An assignment $P \Leftarrow Q$, where P is a **locative**, assigns the value of Q to the place in memory that is *the locative value of P*. To see how useful this is, consider Algorithm 1.6, which recodes Algorithm 1.5 using a locative. In essence, Algorithm 1.6 proceeds by running P through the list as though it were responsible only for searching, and not for inserting as well. When the time comes to insert, however, the locative value of P is used to alter the appropriate cell.

Note that in Algorithm 1.6 the address of the beginning of the list is received as a parameter, rather than being retrieved from a global variable. This illustrates another characteristic of a locative: when a call is made to a function or procedure that has a locative as its formal parameter, the locative value as well as the ordinary value is established as though an ordinary assignment had been made from the actual parameter to the formal parameter. For example, if Algorithm 1.6 were called by *LLInsert*(K, *list*), the effect would be the same as if the body of the algorithm began with the assignment $P \leftarrow list$; that is, P's ordinary value becomes the value of *list*, while P's locative value becomes the address of the variable *list*. In this way the final assignment $P \Leftarrow Q$ produces the correct effect, whether the locative value of P is the address of the variable *list* or the address of the Next field of one of the list cells.

There are three more important points about the behavior of locatives. First, if one locative is assigned to another, or passed to a subroutine that has a locative as its formal parameter, then both the ordinary value and the locative value are transferred from one to the other. Second, any assignment of the form $P \Leftarrow Q$, where Q is a locative, changes the ordinary value of P to that of Q. Finally, the locative assignment operator $\Leftarrow$ acts like the ordinary assignment operator $\leftarrow$ if the thing being assigned to is not a locative.

Although locatives may seem unfamiliar, programs using them can easily be translated into many conventional higher-level programming languages by using pointers to variables rather than associating two values with each locative. Appendix A discusses the semantics and implementation of locatives in complete detail.

Abstract Data Types

A fundamental principle of programming is to understand clearly what you are trying to accomplish before you set about to accomplish it. A common instance of this rule has to do with the selection of data representations: figure out what are the operations to be performed on your data *before* you choose a representation for the data.

To take an example, we began this chapter with three algorithms for finding an entry in a sorted table. These might have been, for instance, alternative implementations of a program module in our hypothetical publication system— a module that tries to find a word in a lexicon to see if it is a word known to some part of the system. These algorithms are among the most plausible for this purpose—*if* it is assumed that the lexicon is to be stored as a sorted table. Whether that is the most reasonable implementation of the lexicon depends, however, on what other operations the lexicon module must support. If, for example, the system were required to support insertions into the lexicon as well as searches of the lexicon, a tree representation might be superior; on the other hand, if the lexicon doesn't change at all, the table in contiguous memory might be the most appropriate representation.

Stepping back even a bit further, we realize that most of the algorithms that come to mind for searching a table are essentially the same, whether we are looking up a word in a lexicon, or finding a number in a set of numbers, or searching for data of any other variety. For algorithms (A)–(C) or any of a variety of other data structures and algorithms to work, we need make only the following assumptions:

1. The data we are dealing with are of some data type **key**. Data of type **key** are **linearly ordered**, that is, there is an ordering relation $<$ on data of type **key** such that for any two elements u and v of type **key**, either $u < v$, or $v < u$, or $u = v$.

2. We have a set S of data of type **key**, and we want to be able to answer questions of the form, is $u \in S$?

A sorted table and any of algorithms (A)–(C) constitute a correct implementation of (1) and (2). Many other implementations are possible as well, and might be preferred if we were required to implement additional operations, such as

3. In addition to answering questions of type (2), we want to be able to add an element u to S if u is not already in S.

A set of specifications such as (1) and (2), or (1), (2), and (3), make up an **abstract data type**. An abstract data type consists of two parts.

- One or more **domains**, that is, classes of mathematical objects. In the example we have a class **key** of objects with a linear order, and the class of finite sets of **key**s.
- One or more mathematical **operations** on elements from the domains. In the example, one operation is to provide a true or false answer to a question of the form "$u \in S$," where $u \in$ **key** and S is a finite set of **key**s. Another could be to construct $S \cup \{u\}$ from S and u.

An abstract data type is neither a data structure (though an abstract data type can be *implemented* by means of a data structure), nor a data type (though in an implementation of an abstract data type in a particular programming language the domains may become data types).

By thinking in terms of abstract data types, attention can be focussed as long as possible on the essential features of the situation to be captured, and away from characteristics that might be suggested by a particular implementation. As long as a program refers only to abstract operations—and not lower-level operations on the particular data structure that happens to have been chosen to implement the abstract data type—the implementation of the abstract data type can be changed without affecting the correctness of the program.

To see how "higher-level" programs can be written in terms of abstract operations, consider the abstract data type which we shall call a **priority queue**. (Priority queues are discussed at some length in Chapter 9.) The domains for this abstract data type are the same as those in the example just given: a priority queue is a set of items drawn from a linearly ordered data type **key**. But in a priority queue the general set-membership operation "$u \in S$?" is not supported; instead only these four operations are available for a priority queue S:

1. Create $\emptyset$ (the empty set).
2. Determine whether $S = \emptyset$.
3. Given any $u \in$ **key**, add u to S.
4. Remove and return the smallest element of S.

There are a great many ways to implement priority queues, from simple lists in contiguous memory to complicated tree structures. But any priority queue implementation automatically gives rise to a sorting algorithm. The following procedure outputs the elements of the set X in sorted order by using the priority queue operations (1)–(4).

procedure *PriorityQueueSort*(**set** X):
   $S \leftarrow \emptyset$
   foreach $x \in X$
      add x to S
   while $S \neq \emptyset$
      remove and output the smallest element of S.

We shall see that certain efficient implementations of the priority queue operations give rise to very efficient sorting methods.

We have described the elements of abstract data types as mathematical objects—linearly ordered sets and the like—but in one respect they are not, at least in the way we are using them. Mathematical objects are timeless and do not change; if I say that $S = \{1, 2, 3\}$, then in mathematics I can't say a little later that 1 should be removed from S so that S becomes $\{2, 3\}$. (Though of course I can define a new set $S' = S - \{1\} = \{2, 3\}$.) But in mathematics we don't have to store objects in memory and pay for what it costs to manipulate those representations, while in computer science we do. So when we say that S is a particular abstract data type (a priority queue, let's say), we really mean that S is a *representation* of such an abstract object; then it makes sense to talk about *changing* S, since we are really changing S so that it represents something else.

How should the behavior of abstract operations be specified? We follow the practice of appealing, whenever possible, to familiar mathematical notions to describe abstract operations. For example, we assume you are familiar with the mathematical notion of a set, so nothing more needs to be said to explain what it means for an object to be a member of a set, or to form a new set by adding an object to another set, or the like. An alternative approach is to describe the abstract operations **axiomatically**, that is, in terms of how they interact with each other. For example, if S is formed by adding x to an existing set, then "$x \in S$" must be true. With a sufficiently complete collection of such axioms, the relevant behavior of the abstract operations can be characterized completely, and the correctness of an implementation of the abstract data type can be verified formally. As our objective is expository rather than formalistic, we shall content ourselves with more informal accounts of the effect of the operations of an abstract data type.

1.3 MATHEMATICAL BACKGROUND

The level of mathematical maturity needed to read this book is not high. A few facts from the calculus are useful, but even with a solid high-school mathematics background you should be able to follow most of the arguments given here. The next few pages bring together most of the basic facts that are needed.

Finite and Infinite Series

We shall need several times to compute the value of sums of the form $a_1 + a_2 + \cdots + a_k$, where the terms a_i follow some regular pattern. For example, what is $1 + 2 + 4 + 8 + \cdots + 2^n$, where each term is twice the preceding term? What about $1 + \frac{1}{2} + \frac{1}{4} + \cdots + 2^{-n}$, where each term is *half* the preceding term? Any sum of successive powers of some constant is called a **geometric series**; its value can be calculated using the following formulas:

■ **THEOREM** *(Geometric Series)* For any real number c and any integers k and l such that $k \le l$,

$$\sum_{i=k}^{l} c^i = \begin{cases} \dfrac{c^k - c^{l+1}}{1-c}, & \text{if } c \ne 1 \\[2ex] l - k + 1, & \text{if } c = 1. \end{cases} \tag{1}$$

Also, if $|c| < 1$, then

$$\sum_{i=k}^{\infty} c^i = \frac{c^k}{1-c}. \tag{2}$$

In particular, $\sum_{i=0}^{\infty} c^i = 1/(1-c)$.

PROOF The second case of Equation (1) is obvious, since if $c = 1$ then $\sum_{i=k}^{l} c^i$ is just the sum of $l - k + 1$ copies of 1. To prove the first case, let S represent the sum on the left-hand side. Multiplying it by c and subtracting,

$$S = c^k + c^{k+1} + \cdots + c^l$$
$$cS = \qquad c^{k+1} + \cdots + c^l + c^{l+1}$$
$$S - cS = c^k \qquad\qquad\qquad - c^{l+1}.$$

Since $c \ne 1$ we can divide both sides by $1 - c$ and Equation (1) follows. Equation (2) can be established by similar reasoning (though a bit of care is required when handling infinite series). □

To wrap up the examples with which we started,

$$1 + 2 + 4 + 8 + \cdots + 2^n = \sum_{i=0}^{n} 2^i = \frac{1 - 2^{n+1}}{1 - 2} = 2^{n+1} - 1,$$

and

$$1 + \frac{1}{2} + \frac{1}{4} + \cdots + 2^{-n} = \sum_{i=0}^{n} \left(\frac{1}{2}\right)^i = \frac{1 - 2^{-(n+1)}}{1 - \frac{1}{2}} = 2 - 2^{-n}.$$

Note also the infinite version of the second example:

$$1 + \frac{1}{2} + \frac{1}{4} + \cdots = \frac{1}{1 - \frac{1}{2}} = 2.$$

Another sum that comes up all the time is $1 + 2 + 3 + \cdots + n$, whose value is

$$\sum_{i=0}^{n} i = \frac{n(n+1)}{2}.$$

To see this, add two copies of the sum together, one in ascending order and the other in descending order:

$$
\begin{array}{ccccccccc}
S & = & 1 & + & 2 & + & \cdots & + & n \\
S & = & n & + & n-1 & + & \cdots & + & 1 \\
2S & = & (n+1) & + & (n+1) & + & \cdots & + & (n+1) & = & n(n+1),
\end{array}
$$

so

$$S = \frac{n(n+1)}{2}.$$

Logarithms, Powers, and Exponentials

Let b be any real number greater than 1, and let x be any real number greater than 0. Then the **logarithm** to the base b of x, denoted $\log_b x$, is defined to be that number y such that

$$b^y = x.$$

Thus $\log_b 1 = 0$ (since $b^0 = 1$ for any b), $\log_b x > 0$ if $x > 1$, $\log_b b = 1$, and $\log_b x < 0$ if $0 < x < 1$. We call any function from reals to reals of the form $f(x) = \log_b x$ a **logarithmic function**, or a function that is **logarithmic in** x. Any logarithmic function is a **monotone increasing** function of its argument, that is, $\log_b x_1 > \log_b x_2$ provided that $x_1 > x_2$. For example, doubling the argument increases the base 2 logarithm by 1, that is, $\log_2 2x = \log_2 x + 1$, since

$$2^{\log_2 x + 1} = 2^{\log_2 x} \cdot 2 = 2x.$$

More generally,

$$\log_b(x_1 \cdot x_2) = \log_b x_1 + \log_b x_2,$$

$$\log_b(x_1/x_2) = \log_b x_1 - \log_b x_2, \quad \text{and}$$

$$\log_b x^c = c \log_b x.$$

Suppose a and b are both greater than 1; what is the relation of $\log_a x$ to $\log_b x$? Since $x = a^{\log_a x}$,

$$\log_b x = \log_b(a^{\log_a x})$$

$$= \log_a x \cdot \log_b a.$$

Thus any two logarithmic functions differ only by a constant factor.

For the most part we'll be using logarithms to only two bases: $\log_e$, where $e = 2.71828\ldots$, the so-called **natural logarithm**; and $\log_2$, the **binary logarithm**. We write $\ln x$ for $\log_e x$ and $\lg x$ for $\log_2 x$. For example, the number of bits in the usual binary notation for the positive integer n is $\lfloor \lg n \rfloor + 1$. We'll also have occasion to write simply $\log x$, but we'll do that only when it doesn't matter what the base is (for example, "$\log x$ is an increasing function of x").

Any function from reals to reals of the form $g(x) = x^\alpha$, for some constant $\alpha > 0$, is called a **simple power**. Thus any simple power is also an increasing function of its argument (we are excluding negative powers to ensure this). An **exponential function** is one of the form $h(x) = c^x$ for some constant $c > 1$ (again, we want to consider only increasing functions, so we exclude $c \leq 1$). Thus x^2, x^3, and $\sqrt{x} = x^{1/2}$ are simple powers, while 2^x and 100^x are exponential functions of x.

These three classes of functions—logarithms, powers, and exponentials—will come up repeatedly. Though all are increasing functions, logarithms increase "less rapidly" than powers, and powers increase "less rapidly" than exponentials. This intuition can be formalized as follows. Let f and g be functions from reals to reals. Then f **dominates** g if the ratio $f(n)/g(n)$ increases without bound as n increases without bound; that is, if for any $c > 0$ there is an $n_0 > 0$ such that $f(n) > cg(n)$ for all $n > n_0$.

For example, the function $f(n) = n^2$ dominates the function $g(n) = 2n$ since for any c, $n^2 > c \cdot 2n$ whenever $n > 2c$. But $f(n) = 10n$ does not dominate $g(n) = 2n$ since the ratio $f(n)/g(n)$ is never larger than 5. The general rule relating functions of these kinds is given by the following Theorem (see Problem 18 for the proof).

■ **THEOREM** (*Exponentials, Powers, and Logarithms*) Any exponential function dominates any simple power, and any simple power dominates any logarithmic function. □

Some functions dominate all the exponential functions. For example, 2^{n^2} dominates all the exponential functions; and even this function is dominated by 2^{2^n}. A function intermediate between the exponentials and 2^{n^2} is the **factorial** function

$$n! = 1 \cdot 2 \cdot 3 \cdot \ldots \cdot n;$$

according to a formula called Stirling's approximation, $n!$ is roughly

$$e^{-n} n^n \sqrt{2\pi n} = \sqrt{2\pi} \cdot e^{(n+\frac{1}{2})\ln n - n}.$$

The factorial function of n is the number of permutations of n distinct objects, where a **permutation** is an arrangement of objects in a particular order. For example, the six permutations of $\{1, 2, 3\}$ are 123, 132, 213, 231, 312, and 321.

More generally, if we know that $(n-1)!$ is the number of permutations of $n-1$ objects, then $n \cdot (n-1)! = n!$ must be the number of permutations of n objects, since there are n possibilities for the first object and for each of these n choices the remaining $n-1$ objects can be arranged in $(n-1)!$ different ways.

To close our discussion of logarithms and powers, let us look at the sum of another series in which logarithms arise rather unexpectedly. What is the sum of successive *reciprocals* of the integers? That is, we want to know the value of

$$H_n = 1 + \frac{1}{2} + \frac{1}{3} + \cdots + \frac{1}{n}.$$

H_n is called the nth **harmonic number**. Although the values of the H_n increase more slowly as n increases, the series does not converge; any fixed bound x is exceeded by all harmonic numbers from some point on (Problem 19). In fact, H_n grows with n in a logarithmic fashion; to be precise $H_n \approx \ln n + \gamma$, where $\gamma = 0.577\ldots$ is a number called **Euler's constant**. The quality of this approximation gets better as n gets larger.

Order Notation

The notion of domination is too strong a way of comparing functions for some purposes. For example, we would like to be able to say in some precise way that two functions are "roughly equal" to each other, but need not be exactly equal for all values of their argument. This would be the case, for example, if neither dominates the other, but the difference between them is always in the range between -1 and $+1$, or they are always within 10% of each other. Even when the ratio of one function to another is very far from 1, we may consider the two functions to be more similar than they are different. Consider, for example, for $n \geq 1960$,

$f(n) =$ the cost, in dollars, of a can of tuna fish in year n

$g(n) =$ the cost, in cents, of a can of tuna fish in year n.

Then the difference $g(n) - f(n)$ might become arbitrarily large, but the two functions tell the same story about the *trend* in the cost of tuna fish over time because their ratio is bounded. It is this notion of the **growth rate** of functions in which we are particularly interested.

The comparison of growth rates of functions can be made precise by means of "big-O notation." Let **N** be the set of nonnegative integers $\{0, 1, \ldots\}$, let **R** be the set of real numbers, and let $\mathbf{R}^*$ be the set of nonnegative real numbers. Let g be a function from **N** to $\mathbf{R}^*$. Then $O(g)$ is the set of all functions f from **N** to $\mathbf{R}^*$ such that, for some constants $c > 0$ and $n_0 \geq 0$,

$$f(n) \leq cg(n) \qquad \text{for all } n \geq n_0.$$

In other words, f is in $O(g)$ if the value of f is bounded from above by a fixed multiple of the value of g for all sufficiently large values of the argument.

For any f it is the case that $f \in O(f)$. Indeed any constant multiple of f is in $O(f)$, as is the sum of f and any constant. For example, the function $f(n) = 13n + 7$ is in $O(n)$, since $13n + 7 \leq 14n$ whenever $n \geq 7$ (so the definition is satisfied with $c = 14$, $n_0 = 7$). Likewise $1000n \in O(0.0001n^2)$, since we can take $c = 10^7$ and $n_0 = 0$ in the definition of $O(\ )$.

On the other hand $10^{-4}n^2 \notin O(10^3 n)$. For suppose $10^{-4}n^2 \leq c \cdot 10^3 n$ for some constant c and for all $n \geq n_0$. Then $n \leq 10^7 c$ for all $n > n_0$, which is impossible since c is a constant.

We have used in this example a notation that is extremely convenient. We use any expression containing the variable n to stand for the *function* from natural numbers to reals that has the value indicated by the expression for any value of n. That is, when we write "$1000n \in O(0.0001n^2)$," the "n" does not refer to any particular number, but to the independent variable in a formula defining a function. If we wanted to be excruciatingly proper, we would say instead, "Let $f(n) = 1000n$ for all $n \in \mathbf{N}$ and $g(n) = 0.0001n^2$ for all $n \in \mathbf{N}$; then $f \in O(g)$."

The definition of $f \in O(g)$ requires that f and g be defined and nonnegative for all $n \in \mathbf{N}$, but it is convenient to relax this requirement a bit. If $f(n)$ or $g(n)$ is negative or undefined for certain $n < n_0$, but only for such n, then it still makes sense to say that $f \in O(g)$ provided that there is some constant $c > 0$ such that $f(n) \leq cg(n)$ for all $n \geq n_0$. In this way we can talk, for example, about the class $O(\log n)$, or a big-O class containing $\log n$, even though the function $\log n$ is undefined for $n = 0$. To recapitulate, the notation $f \in O(g)$ makes sense provided that $f(n)$ and $g(n)$ are defined and nonnegative for all but a finite number of nonnegative integers n.

Another point of usage: we sometimes say "f is $O(g)$," rather than "f is in $O(g)$." This permits us to say things like, "the sum of two $O(n^2)$ terms is also $O(n^2)$." (See the references at the end of this chapter for more discussion of big-O notation.)

Related to the big-O classes are the little-o classes: for any function g, $o(g)$ is the set of all functions that are dominated by g, that is, the set of all f such that for each constant $c > 0$ there is an $n_c > 0$ such that

$$f(n) \leq cg(n) \qquad \text{for all } n > n_c.$$

For example, if g is any simple power then $o(g)$ contains all the logarithmic functions. More generally, the following Theorem summarizes the important little-o and big-O properties of the exponential, power, and logarithmic functions:

■ THEOREM *(Growth Rates)*

1. The power n^α is in $O(n^\beta)$ if and only if $\alpha \leq \beta$ $(\alpha, \beta > 0)$; and n^α is in $o(n^\beta)$ if and only if $\alpha < \beta$.
2. $\log_b n \in o(n^\alpha)$ for any b and α.
3. $n^\alpha \in o(c^n)$ for any $\alpha > 0$ and $c > 1$.

4. $\log_a n \in O(\log_b n)$ for any a and b.

5. $c^n \in O(d^n)$ if and only if $c \le d$, and $c^n \in o(d^n)$ if and only if $c < d$.

6. Any constant function $f(n) = c$ is in $O(1)$.

PROOF These follow either directly or from the Exponentials, Powers, and Logarithms Theorem; we prove just part (1) by way of example. If $\alpha \le \beta$ then $n^\alpha \le 1 \cdot n^\beta$ for all $n \ge 0$, so $n^\alpha \in O(n^\beta)$; and if $\alpha > \beta$ then for any c, $n^\alpha > cn^\beta$ whenever $n > c^{1/(\alpha - \beta)}$, so $n^\alpha \notin O(n^\beta)$. As for the little-$o$ relations, if $\alpha < \beta$ then for any c, $n^\alpha \le cn^\beta$ whenever $n \ge c^{\beta - \alpha}$; but if $\alpha \ge \beta$ then $n^\alpha \ge 1 \cdot n^\beta$ for all $n \ge 0$, so $n^\alpha \notin o(n^\beta)$. This completes the proof of part (1).

Also, part (6) deserves some comment. We are treating 1 as the function that has the value 1 for all n. Since $f(n) = c \le c \cdot 1$ for all n, $f \in O(1)$. $\square$

Big-O notation and little-o notation are transitive; for example, if $f \in O(g)$ and $g \in O(h)$, then $f \in O(h)$. Big-O notation behaves rather like "$\le$," since $O(\ )$ is reflexive (that is, $f \in O(f)$ for any f). On the other hand $o(\ )$ is not reflexive, so little-o notation behaves more like "$<$."

The following Theorem summarizes a variety of general facts about big-O notation. The proof is left as an exercise (Problem 26).

■ **THEOREM** (*Big-O*) For any functions f, f', g, and g',

1. $o(f) \subseteq O(f)$;

2. if $f \in o(g)$, then $O(f) \subseteq o(g)$;

3. if $f \in O(g)$, then $o(f) \subseteq o(g)$;

4. if $f \in O(g)$, then $f(n) + g(n)$ is also in $O(g)$;

5. if $f \in O(f')$ and $g \in O(g')$, then $f(n) \cdot g(n) \in O(f'(n) \cdot g'(n))$;

6. $kf(n) + c \in O(f)$ for any constants k and c, provided that there are some $d > 0$ and some integer $n_0 \ge 0$ such that $f(n) \ge d$ for all n greater than or equal to n_0. $\square$

Parts (4) and (6) in particular are valuable because they permit us to discard distracting information. For example, to see that $0.001n^2 + 32n + 17 \in O(n^2)$, take $f(n) = 32n + 17$ and $g(n) = 0.001n^2$ in (4) to get $0.001n^2 + 32n + 17 \in O(0.001n^2)$; clearly $0.001n^2 \in O(n^2)$ by (6); then use the transitivity of big-O.

More generally, let us define a **polynomial of degree** d, where d is a nonnegative integer, to be any function of the form

$$f(n) = \sum_{i=0}^{d} a_i n^i$$

where the a_i are reals and $a_d > 0$. Then it follows from (4) and (6) that *any polynomial of degree* d *is in* $O(n^d)$.

A **linear function** is a polynomial of degree 1, that is, a function of the form $f(n) = a_0 + a_1 n$ for some a_0 and some $a_1 > 0$; this function is said to be **linear in** n. A **quadratic function** is a polynomial of degree 2, and a **constant function** is a polynomial of degree 0.

Big-O notation provides only an **upper bound** on the growth rate of a function. For example, it is true that $17n^2 \in O(n^2)$, but it is also true that $17n^2 \in O(n^{37})$ and $17n^2 \in O(2^n)$. In order to talk about the "tightest bound" g such that $f \in O(g)$, we need a complementary notation for **lower bounds** on the growth rate of functions. So let g be a function from $\mathbf{N}$ to $\mathbf{R}^*$. Then $\Omega(g)$ is the set of all functions f from $\mathbf{N}$ to $\mathbf{R}^*$ such that, for some constants $c > 0$ and $n_0 \geq 0$, $f(n) \geq cg(n)$ for all $n \geq n_0$.

Thus big-Ω notation is exactly the converse of big-O notation; $f \in \Omega(g)$ if and only if $g \in O(f)$. (As mentioned for big-O notation, it is convenient here as well to allow the functions to be undefined or negative for a finite number of argument values.) Just as $f \in O(g)$ implies that f grows *at most* as quickly as g, so $f \in \Omega(g)$ implies that f grows *at least* as quickly as g. Finally, we have a third notation to indicate that two functions are big-O of each other: $\Theta(f) = O(f) \cap \Omega(f)$. We say that the set of functions $\Theta(f)$ is the **order** of f. For example, $n^3 + 135n + 100 \in \Theta(77n^3)$ and, of course, $77n^3 \in \Theta(n^3 + 135n + 100)$. More generally, all polynomials of the same degree have the same order.

Let us apply these notions to generalize the fact that $\sum_{i=1}^{n} i = n(n+1)/2$. What is the sum of n consecutive squares or cubes? Exact formulas can be derived with some ingenuity, but if we are willing to be content with establishing the *growth rate* of such a sum, as a function of n, the task is much easier.

■ **THEOREM** (*Sum of Successive k^{th} Powers*) For any $k \geq 0$,

$$\sum_{i=1}^{n} i^k \in \Theta(n^{k+1}).$$

For example, the sum of the first n squares is in $\Theta(n^3)$. (The exact formula turns out to be $\sum_{i=1}^{n} i^2 = n(n+1)(2n+1)/6$.) Note that since n is regarded as a variable and k as a constant in the statement of this Theorem, the constant implicit in Θ-notation can depend on k.

PROOF Let k be fixed, and let $S_k(n) = \sum_{i=1}^{n} i^k$. To get an upper bound on $S_k(n)$, note that each term in the sum is less than or equal to n^k, so

$$S_k(n) = \sum_{i=1}^{n} i^k \leq \sum_{i=1}^{n} n^k = n \cdot n^k = n^{k+1},$$

so $S_k(n) \in O(n^{k+1})$. To get a lower bound on $S_k(n)$ we add together two copies as was done on page 18 for the $k = 1$ case. Then

$$2S_k(n) = \sum_{i=1}^{n} i^k + \sum_{i=1}^{n} (n - i + 1)^k$$

$$= \sum_{i=1}^{n} (i^k + (n - i + 1)^k)$$

$$\geq \sum_{i=1}^{n} \left(\frac{n}{2}\right)^k \qquad \text{since either } i \text{ or } n - i + 1 \text{ is at least } \frac{n}{2},$$

so

$$S_k(n) \geq \frac{1}{2^{k+1}} n^{k+1} \in \Omega(n^{k+1}).$$

Then $S_k(n) \in \Theta(n^{k+1})$ since $S_k(n)$ is in both $O(n^{k+1})$ and $\Omega(n^{k+1})$. $\qquad \square$

Recurrence Relations

A **recurrence relation** is an equation or inequality that relates the value of a function to values of the same function for smaller arguments. For example, the sum of the first n integers can be described recursively as the sum of the first $n - 1$ integers, plus n. So if we let $f(n)$ be the sum of the first n integers, then the following is a simple recurrence relation for f:

$$f(n) = \begin{cases} 1, & \text{if } n = 1; \\ f(n - 1) + n, & \text{if } n > 1. \end{cases}$$

The first clause defines the value of the function for the smallest value of the argument n; the second clause describes how the value can be calculated for larger n, given that the values have been determined for smaller n. This pair of conditions—the first is called the **base case**, while the second is called the **recursive case**—uniquely determine the value of the function for all n. In this particular example it is easy to work out a nonrecursive formula for the function f:

$$f(n) = f(n - 1) + n$$

$$= f(n - 2) + (n - 1) + n$$

$$= \cdots$$

$$= f(1) + 2 + \cdots + (n - 1) + n$$

$$= \sum_{i=1}^{n} i = \frac{n(n + 1)}{2}.$$

We call such an explicit, nonrecursive formula a **solution** of the recurrence relation. In general, recurrence relations are not as easy to solve as this one. In this section we describe some techniques that will be useful in solving a variety of cases that come up in practice.

A simple recurrence relation with an exponential solution is

$$T(0) = 1$$
$$T(n) = 2T(n - 1), \quad \text{if } n > 0,$$

which has the solution $T(n) = 2T(n - 1) = 4T(n - 2) = \cdots = 2^n T(0) = 2^n$. Sometimes a recurrence cannot be "expanded" as easily as these to infer a closed formula for the solution, but it is still possible to derive a reasonable estimate of the solution. A good example is the recurrence for the **Fibonacci numbers**, each of which is the sum of the previous two:

$$F(0) = 0$$
$$F(1) = 1$$
$$F(n) = F(n - 1) + F(n - 2), \quad \text{if } n \geq 2.$$

This sequence of numbers (usually we write F_n instead of $F(n)$) begins 0, 1, 1, 2, 3, 5, 8, 13, 21, ...; it has many beautiful properties and surprising applications, some of which will be encountered in this book. For our purposes it will suffice to derive big-O and big-Ω estimates of the function's behavior. Certainly it is easy to show by induction that $F(n)$ is a **monotone nondecreasing*** function of n; therefore, for all $n \geq 2$, it follows that $F(n) = F(n-1) + F(n-2) \leq 2F(n-1)$. Since $F(1) = 1$, it follows from the example just given that $F(n) \leq 2^{n-1} \in O(2^n)$. By the same token $F(n) = F(n-1) + F(n-2) \geq 2F(n-2)$, from which it follows (since $F(1) = F(2) = 1$) that $F(2n + 1) \geq 2^n$ and $F(2n + 2) \geq 2^n$ for all n. Therefore

$$F(n) \geq 2^{(n-1)/2} \quad \text{for odd } n \geq 0$$
$$F(n) \geq 2^{(n-2)/2} \quad \text{for even } n > 0.$$

Hence in any case

$$F(n) \in \Omega(2^{n/2}) = \Omega((\sqrt{2})^n).$$

Because $F(n) \in \Omega((\sqrt{2})^n) \cap O(2^n)$ we might guess that there is a number ϕ, somewhere between $\sqrt{2} = 1.414\ldots$ and 2, such that $F(n) \in \Theta(\phi^n)$; in fact such a number exists, though methods beyond those presented here are needed

---

*That is, $F(m) \leq F(n)$ provided that $m \leq n$.

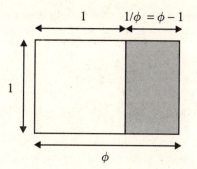

Figure 1.6 The golden ratio ϕ is the length of the whole rectangle, if its height is 1. The small shaded rectangle, formed by removing a 1 by 1 square, has the same proportions as the whole; the whole is 1 high and ϕ long, while the shaded rectangle is $\phi - 1$ wide and 1 high, so ϕ satisfies $1/\phi = (\phi - 1)/1$.

to discover it. It turns out that if we let

$$\phi = \frac{1 + \sqrt{5}}{2} = 1.6180\ldots$$

$$\hat{\phi} = \frac{1 - \sqrt{5}}{2} = -0.6180\ldots,$$

then

$$F_n = \frac{1}{\sqrt{5}}(\phi^n - \hat{\phi}^n) \in \Theta(\phi^n).$$

The number ϕ is the **golden ratio** of ancient Greek mathematics; a ϕ by 1 rectangle has the same proportions as the rectangle that is left when a unit square is removed (Figure 1.6). Consequently ϕ satisfies the identity

$$\phi - 1 = \frac{1}{\phi},$$

which leads to a quadratic equation with the solution as stated (the negative number $\hat{\phi}$ is the other solution).

Divide-and-Conquer Recurrences   Recurrence relations arise naturally when we attempt to determine the running time of a recursive algorithm. For example, let us consider the behavior of Algorithm 1.3 on page 11. The algorithm does a small initial calculation, and returns quickly if the table is empty; it then carries out a slightly longer calculation, and returns if the search is successful at this point; then on the basis of a comparison, it calls itself recursively on either a lower or an upper subtable. Roughly speaking, each of the possible recursive calls searches about half the table. To get a sharper picture of the behavior of the algorithm, let n denote the size of the table to be searched (that is, $n = b - a + 1$), and for simplicity assume that n is 1 less than a power of 2, for example, 1, 3, 7, or 15. If we let $n = 2^k - 1$, then $b = 2^k - 2 + a$ and on the first recursive call

$$middle = \lfloor(a + b)/2\rfloor = \lfloor(a + 2^k - 2 + a)/2\rfloor = a + 2^{k-1} - 1.$$

Therefore the first recursive call is on a table of length $middle - 1 - a + 1 = 2^{k-1} - 1$, and the second recursive call is on a table of length $b - middle = n + a - 1 - (a + 2^{k-1} - 1) = 2^k - 1 - 2^{k-1} = 2^{k-1} - 1$. Therefore the two alternative recursive calls are on subtables of the same size. Now let us imagine what is the *largest* amount of time this algorithm might take when called to search a table of fixed size; the worst-case scenario is when the table does not contain the key and the algorithm calls itself recursively until it is called on an empty table. If we let $T(n)$ be the maximum possible running time of the algorithm on a table of length n, we therefore have that for some constants c and d,

$$T(2^k - 1) = \begin{cases} c, & \text{if } k = 0; \\ d + T(2^{k-1} - 1), & \text{if } k > 0. \end{cases}$$

Here c is the time simply to execute the first line of the algorithm, while d is the time to execute the body of the algorithm, except for a recursive call; $T(2^{k-1} - 1)$ is the time to execute either of the recursive calls. Then for any k,

$$T(2^k - 1) = d + T(2^{k-1} - 1)$$
$$= 2d + T(2^{k-2} - 1)$$
$$= \cdots$$
$$= kd + T(0)$$
$$= kd + c.$$

If $n = 2^k - 1$ then $k = \log_2(n + 1)$ and hence $T(n) = d\lg(n + 1) + c$ when n is 1 less than a power of 2.

This takes care of analyzing the complexity of the algorithm in case n is one less than a power of 2, but of course n might actually be any nonnegative integer. The analysis in the general case is only slightly more complicated. The two recursive calls in Algorithm 1.3 on page 11 split a table of length n into two tables, one of length $\lfloor(n - 1)/2\rfloor$ and one of length $n - 1 - \lfloor(n - 1)/2\rfloor = \lceil(n - 1)/2\rceil$. Therefore

$$T(n) = \begin{cases} c, & \text{if } n = 0; \\ d + \max(T(\lfloor(n - 1)/2\rfloor), T(\lceil(n - 1)/2\rceil)), & \text{if } n > 0. \end{cases} \quad (3)$$

This recurrence relation is awkward to analyze exactly because of the "floor" and "ceiling" functions, but for practical purposes we need only an upper bound on the value of $T(n)$, not an exact formula. First, it is easily shown by induction on n that $T(n)$ is a monotone nondecreasing function, that is, that $T(n) \leq$

procedure *MergeSort*(**table** $T[a..b]$):
{Recursively sort T so that $T[i] \leq T[i+1]$ for $a \leq i < b$}
   if $a \geq b$ **then return**
   middle $\leftarrow \lfloor (a+b)/2 \rfloor$
   MergeSort($T[a..middle]$)
   MergeSort($T[middle+1..b]$)
   Merge($T[a..middle], T[middle+1..b]$)

Algorithm 1.7 Merge Sort algorithm. The *Merge* procedure merges two contiguous sorted tables into the space they collectively occupy. In general it is necessary to copy one of the arguments into an auxiliary table before carrying out the merge, but *Merge* can be implemented in time proportional to the size of its arguments. (See also Problem 15 of Chapter 11.)

$T(n+1)$ for all n (Problem 35). It follows that $T(n)$ cannot exceed $T(u(n))$, where $u(n) < 2n$ is the next number of the form $2^k - 1$ that is greater than or equal to n. But we already have an exact formula for $T(u(n))$, namely, $T(u(n)) = d \lg(u(n) + 1) + c$. Therefore for all n,

$$T(n) \leq T(u(n))$$

$$= d \lg(u(n) + 1) + c$$

$$< d \lg(2n + 1) + c.$$

In particular, $T(n) \in O(\log n)$.

This example is a special case of a more general class of recurrence relations that arise commonly in the analysis of recursive algorithms. In the general case of a so-called **divide-and-conquer algorithm**, a problem of size n is reduced to $a \geq 1$ similar problems, each of which is roughly the same size n/b. The subproblems are solved recursively using the same method, unless they are so small that they can be solved directly. The solutions to the subproblems are or can be combined to yield the solution to the larger problem. For example, in the case of Algorithm 1.3 on page 11, $b = 2$ (the table is split in half, more or less) and $a = 1$ (only one of the two halves is searched recursively). Another familiar example is Merge Sort (Algorithm 1.7), which sorts a list by splitting it in half, sorting the two halves recursively, and then merging the two sorted sublists into one. In Merge Sort $a = 2$ (two sublists to sort) and $b = 2$ (each half as long as the original); in addition the analysis must take into account the cost of merging.

To get a handle on the approximate behavior of this kind of algorithm, we model its behavior by the recurrence relation

$$T(n) = \begin{cases} c, & \text{if } n = 1 \\ aT(n/b) + d(n), & \text{if } n > 1, \end{cases} \tag{4}$$

which defines a value for $T(n)$ provided that n is an exact power of b. Here $d(n)$ is a function of n that represents the time required to split the problem into its subproblems and to combine the solutions to those subproblems back together to yield the solution to the larger problem. In case of binary search, $d(n)$ is a constant, denoted by d in the analysis above; in the case of Merge Sort, $d(n)$ is a linear function of n, since it takes time proportional to the sum of the lengths of two sorted lists to merge them together. If $n = b^k$, then the recursive case of this recurrence relation expands into

$$
\begin{aligned}
T(n) &= aT(n/b) + d(n) \\
&= a(aT((n/b)/b) + d(n/b)) + d(n) \\
&= a^2 T(n/b^2) + ad(n/b) + d(n) \\
&= a^3 T(n/b^3) + a^2 d(n/b^2) + ad(n/b) + d(n) \\
&= \cdots \\
&= a^k T(n/b^k) + \sum_{j=0}^{k-1} a^j d(n/b^j) \\
&= ca^k + \sum_{j=0}^{k-1} a^j d(b^{k-j}).
\end{aligned}
$$

The first term represents the cost of solving the smallest subproblems; there are a^k of them, and each takes time c to solve. Since $n = b^k$, this term can be written as

$$
ca^k = ca^{\log_b n} = cn^{\log_b a} \in O(n^{\log_b a}),
$$

that is, a polynomial in n of degree $\log_b a$. For example, if $a = b$, then this term is cn—there are n smallest subproblems, each of which costs c to solve. The other term (the extended summation) represents the time required for all the splitting and combining of subproblems. To simplify this summation, let us assume that $d(n)$ is polynomial in n, in fact that $d(n) = c'n^e$ for some constants c' and e. (In the binary search example, $e = 0$ and $c' = d$; in the Merge Sort example, $e = 1$.) Then

$$
\sum_{j=0}^{k-1} a^j d(b^{k-j}) = c' \sum_{j=0}^{k-1} a^j b^{e(k-j)} = c' b^{ek} \sum_{j=0}^{k-1} \left(\frac{a}{b^e}\right)^j, \tag{$*$}
$$

which is the sum of a geometric series. Depending on the relation between a and b^e, there are three cases to distinguish.

1. $a < b^e$, that is, $e > \log_b a$. Then

$$
(*) = c'b^{ek}\left(\frac{1 - (a/b^e)^k}{1 - (a/b^e)}\right) = c'\frac{b^{ek} - a^k}{1 - (a/b^e)} \in O(b^{ek}) = O(n^e),
$$

Recursion Level

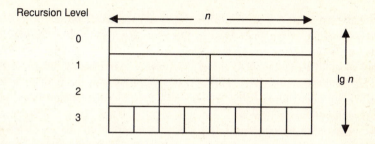

Figure 1.7 Illustration of the total time taken by a divide-and-conquer algorithm in case $a = b = 2$ and $e = 1$ (Merge Sort is like this). On the outermost call there is only one block of data and the time taken (aside from the recursive calls) is proportional to its size n. There are two first-level recursive calls, each on half as much data, and each takes time proportional to the size of its argument, so the total time for the nonrecursive processing at the first level is again proportional to n. The same holds at each subsequent level of recursion. After $\lg n$ levels the argument is small enough that the algorithm solves the problem directly within a constant time bound rather than making a further recursive call, so the total time for all levels is proportional to $n \log n$.

so $T(n) \in O(n^{\log_b a} + n^e) = O(n^e)$. In this case the cost of splitting and combining exceeds the cost of solving the smallest subproblems.

2. $a > b^e$, that is, $e < \log_b a$. Then

$$(*) = c' \frac{a^k - b^{ek}}{(a/b^e) - 1} \in O(a^k) = O(n^{\log_b a}).$$

In this case the cost of solving the smallest subproblems is of the same order as the cost of splitting and combining, and $T(n) \in O(n^{\log_b a})$.

3. $a = b^e$, that is, $e = \log_b a$. Then

$$(*) = c' b^{ek} \cdot k = c' n^e \log_b n,$$

so $T(n) \in O(n^{\log_b a} + n^e \log_b n) = O(n^e \log n)$. This is the case that applies to Merge Sort, with $a = b = 2$ and $e = 1$, so Merge Sort runs in time $O(n \log n)$ on lists of length n. In this case each level of recursion has the same total cost (Figure 1.7).

If n is not an exact multiple of b then Equation (4) on page 29 does not really represent the behavior of a divide-and-conquer algorithm, since the quantity n/b is not an integer. Thus the recurrence relation must be modified to reflect accurately the effect of an "uneven division" when an algorithm splits a problem into subproblems of nearly but not exactly equal sizes. A related difficulty in applying Equation (4) is that we have characterized a divide-and-conquer algorithm as one that calls itself recursively until the argument is of size 1; only the size 1 arguments are solved by a nonrecursive method. The byproduct of this view is that Equation (4) has the base case $n = 1$. In practice it may well make sense to use an alternative, nonrecursive algorithm if the size of the argument is "small" but larger than 1. For example, the Merge Sort algorithm (Algorithm 1.7) works more efficiently if tables of five or ten items are sorted by another method, even a method that for larger n would require time quadratic in n. The problem, intuitively, is that the time required to split up and rearrange small amounts of data and the overhead for recursive subroutine calls might well be significant for small n.

To accommodate algorithms that do "uneven splitting" of problems into subproblems and stop their recursion on arguments of size at most n_0, which may be greater that 1, the following more general version of Equation (4) is often more useful:

$$\begin{aligned} T(n) &\leq c, & \text{if } n \leq n_0; \\ T(n) &\leq aT(\lceil n/b \rceil + n_0') + d(n), & \text{if } n > n_0. \end{aligned} \quad (5)$$

Equation (5) differs from Equation (4) in three respects. First, the equalities in both the base and the recursive cases have been replaced by inequalities, to reflect the fact that each expression on the right-hand side represents only an upper bound on the running time of the algorithm, not an exact time. Second, the **cut-off** point at which the algorithm switches from a recursive to a non-recursive method may be any size n_0, not necessarily 1. Finally, the sizes of the subproblems need not be n/b exactly, but anything up to $\lceil n/b \rceil + n_0'$; that is, about $1/b$ of the original size, rounded up, and possibly larger than that by a small additive constant n_0'. (For this recurrence relation to make sense as a model for the behavior of an algorithm, n_0' must be small relative to n_0; otherwise repeatedly dividing n by b and adding n_0' might never reduce the value of n below n_0. See Problem 40.) Then by reasoning like that used in the special case of binary search (page 29), $T(n)$ falls in one of the three big-O classes as just analyzed for the case in which $n = b^k$ (Problem 41). In sum, we have the following:

■ **THEOREM** *(Divide-and-Conquer Recurrences)* For any integer constants $a \geq 1$, $b \geq 2$, $c \geq 0$, $c' \geq 0$, $e \geq 0$, $n_0 \geq 1$, and $n_0' \geq 0$ such that $n_0' \leq \lfloor ((b-1)n_0 - 1)/b \rfloor$, the recurrence relation

$$\begin{aligned} T(n) &\leq c, & \text{if } n \leq n_0; \\ T(n) &\leq aT(\lceil n/b \rceil + n_0') + c'n^e, & \text{if } n > n_0 \end{aligned}$$

has the solution

$$T(n) \in \begin{cases} O(n^e), & \text{if } e > \log_b a; \\ O(n^e \log n), & \text{if } e = \log_b a; \\ O(n^{\log_b a}), & \text{if } e < \log_b a. \end{cases} \quad \square$$

Algorithm 1.7 can easily be adapted to stop the recursion before the argument is of size 1; we need simply replace the first line, which currently reads "**if** $a \geq b$ **then return**", by

$$\textbf{if } b - a < n_0 \textbf{ then } NonRecursiveSort(T[a..b]),$$

where *NonRecursiveSort* is some direct sorting algorithm to be used in case the argument is of size less than or equal to n_0. For example, *NonRecursiveSort* might be Insertion Sort or some other algorithm whose time complexity increases more rapidly with n than does Merge Sort, but which is more efficient for small n. Then by choosing the cut-off value n_0 appropriately, the efficiency of the algorithm as a whole can be improved (Problem 44).

Naïve Probability Theory

We are interested in assessing the *expected* behavior of certain sequences of events that individually cannot be predicted with certainty. Such a desire is not unique to computer science; gamblers want to do this all the time. To get some of the basic notions out, let us consider a gambling situation.

The Computer Science Department runs a raffle to raise money for student scholarships. One thousand tickets are sold for $1 each, and each ticket bears a different number between 1 and 1000. At the drawing the department chairman draws 100 tickets out of a bin containing 1000 similarly numbered tickets. To the holders of the first ninety numbers drawn go prizes of $5; to the holders of the next nine numbers drawn go prizes of $10; and to the holder of the last number drawn goes a prize of $100. The others who bought tickets get nothing, except the satisfaction of knowing they have supported a worthy cause.

A few things about this situation are certain. It is certain that the department will take in $1000 from ticket sales, and pay out $90 \cdot \$5 + 9 \cdot \$10 + 1 \cdot \$100$ or a total of $450+\$90+\$100 = \$640$. (It will therefore be able to contribute $360 to its scholarship fund.) The situation of a ticket buyer is, of course, not so clear. A person who buys one ticket can win a maximum of $100, and a minimum of nothing; to go beyond this level of analysis we need to use the language of probability. Since 100 of the 1000 tickets will win something, we say that the *probability of holding a winning ticket is* $\frac{100}{1000}$, *or* .1. The probability of holding a $5 ticket is $\frac{90}{1000}$, or .09; of holding a $10 ticket, $\frac{9}{1000}$, or .009; and of holding the unique $100 ticket, $\frac{1}{1000}$, or .001. And, of course, the probability of holding a losing ticket is $\frac{900}{1000}$, or .9. In general,

- Let $E_1, \ldots, E_k$ be events, one of which *must* occur, and no two of which can both occur. If $p_1, \ldots, p_k$ are the probabilities of these events, then $0 \leq p_i \leq 1$ for each i, and $\sum_{i=1}^{k} p_i = 1$. The probability that one of several of the events occurs is the sum of their individual probabilities; thus in particular the probability of an event that is certain to occur is 1.

In our example, the four "events" are holding a $5 ticket, holding a $10 ticket, holding a $100 ticket, and holding a losing ticket; they have probability .09, .009, .001, and .9, respectively, and these numbers sum to 1. The probability of holding a winning ticket (that is, a ticket that wins $5, $10, or $100) is .09 + .009 + .001 = .1.

A **probability distribution** assigns probabilities to individual events that are mutually exclusive and together exhaust all possibilities. We have just used a distribution whose domain is a set of four events. At another level, this lottery situation can be modelled by a distribution that assigns a probability of 0.001 to each of the 1000 tickets. Such a distribution is said to be **uniform**, that is, there are k possible events for some $k > 0$ and each has probability $1/k$. To take another case of uniform distribution, it is usually fair to assume that the events of rolling the different faces of a single die have uniform distribution, that is, each has probability $\frac{1}{6}$. Of course the 11 possible totals when two dice are rolled do *not* have uniform distribution (Problem 47).

Returning to the lottery example, suppose now that a similar lottery is held the next day, and I buy tickets both days. What is the probability that I will hold winning tickets *both* days? *Neither* day? *At least one* of the two days?

There are $1000 \cdot 1000$ combinations of tickets I might buy on the two days. Of these, $100 \cdot 100$ are pairs that consist of a winning ticket on the first day, *and* a winning ticket on the second day. So the probability of holding winning tickets for both lotteries is $\frac{100 \cdot 100}{1000 \cdot 1000}$, or .01. But this result can be derived more directly from the probability of winning a single lottery.

- If E_1 and E_2 are independent events (that is, neither affects or influences the other) of probability p_1 and p_2 respectively, then the probability that both E_1 and E_2 occur is $p_1 \cdot p_2$.

So in our example, the probability of winning a single lottery is .1, and the outcome of one lottery does not affect the other, so the probability of winning both lotteries is $.1 \cdot .1 = .01$. Similarly, the probability of losing on the first day and losing again on the second is $.9 \cdot .9 = .81$.

Since I win on at least one day just in case I don't lose on both days, the probability of winning on at least one day must be $1 - .81 = .19$. This too can be derived more directly.

- Let E_1 and E_2 be independent events of probability p_1 and p_2, respectively. Then the probability that at least one occurs is $p_1 + p_2 - p_1 \cdot p_2$, that is, the sum of the probabilities of the events minus the probability that both occur.

The reason for subtracting the probability that both events occur from the sum of the individual probabilities is that in the sum $p_1 + p_2$ the possibility that both E_1 and E_2 occur is in effect being counted twice, once as part of p_1 and once as part of p_2.

In our example, the probability of winning on at least one day is determined in this way from the two events of "winning on the first day" and "winning on the second day" as $.1 + .1 - (.1 \cdot .1) = .19$.

The most important probabilistic notion for us is that of **expected value**. If we had to assign a single dollar value to our lottery ticket (before the drawing, of course), what would it be? We know that it might be worth $100, or (more likely) it might be worth $0; so the actual value ought at least to be somewhere in between. The value we are looking for is the amount that a perfectly rational gambler would be willing to pay for the ticket. That value is $0.64, a figure that can be arrived at in either of two ways. First, we know that a total of $640 is to be distributed to ticket holders, and there are 1000 tickets, so each must be worth $\frac{\$640}{1000}$ or $0.64. Equivalently, we can take each possible value a ticket might have, multiply that value by the probability that a ticket has exactly that value, and add these "weighted values" together to obtain the expected value. That is,

$$\text{Expected value of ticket} = \$0 \cdot \text{probability ticket is worth } \$0$$
$$+ \$5 \cdot \text{probability ticket is worth } \$5$$
$$+ \$10 \cdot \text{probability ticket is worth } \$10$$
$$+ \$100 \cdot \text{probability ticket is worth } \$100$$
$$= \$0 \cdot 0.9 + \$5 \cdot 0.09 + \$10 \cdot 0.009 + \$100 \cdot 0.001$$
$$= \$0 + \$0.45 + \$0.09 + \$0.10$$
$$= \$0.64.$$

In general,

- Let Q be a quantity that has value v_1 with probability $p_1, \ldots,$ and value v_k with probability p_k. Then the **expected value** of Q is $\sum_{i=1}^{k} p_i \cdot v_i$.

Notice that the "expected value" of something does not need to be any of its possible actual values. There are no lottery tickets that pay off $0.64, yet this is exactly the expected payoff from a ticket. Those new to probabilistic reasoning sometimes are distressed by this apparent anomaly, particularly when the "quantity" is something for which noninteger values would be meaningless. Suppose we watch cars going by on the highway in an effort to determine the expected number of occupants of a vehicle. After long observation, we conclude that a car has one occupant with probability $\frac{1}{4}$, two occupants with probability $\frac{3}{8}$, three with probability $\frac{1}{4}$, and four with probability $\frac{1}{8}$. Then the expected number of occupants is

$$1 \cdot \tfrac{1}{4} + 2 \cdot \tfrac{3}{8} + 3 \cdot \tfrac{1}{4} + 4 \cdot \tfrac{1}{8} = \tfrac{1}{4} + \tfrac{3}{4} + \tfrac{3}{4} + \tfrac{1}{2} = 2\tfrac{1}{4}.$$

The fact that there aren't any quarters of people is irrelevant; if we give a dollar to each person that is in a car, then after n cars have gone by we expect to have given out about $n \cdot 2\frac{1}{4}$ dollars.

One further example illustrates how expected values can be computed even over an infinite set of possible outcomes. Suppose I flip an ordinary coin until it comes up heads, and I am paid k dollars if it comes up heads for the first time on the kth toss. How much money should I expect to win? The probability of getting heads on the first toss is $\frac{1}{2}$; the probability of not getting heads on the first toss, but getting heads on the second toss, is $\frac{1}{2} \cdot \frac{1}{2}$, or $\frac{1}{4}$; the probability of getting tails on each of the first two tosses, and then heads on the third toss, is $\frac{1}{2} \cdot \frac{1}{2} \cdot \frac{1}{2}$, or $\frac{1}{8}$; and in general the probability of getting heads for the first time on the kth toss is $1/2^k$. My expected winnings are therefore

$$1 \cdot \frac{1}{2} \;+\; 2 \cdot \frac{1}{4} \;+\; 3 \cdot \frac{1}{8} \;+\; 4 \cdot \frac{1}{16} \;+\; \cdots \;+\; k \cdot \frac{1}{2^k} \;+\; \cdots$$

$$= \quad \frac{1}{2} \;+\; \frac{1}{4} \;+\; \frac{1}{8} \;+\; \frac{1}{16} \;+\; \cdots \;+\; \frac{1}{2^k} \;+\; \cdots$$
$$+\; \frac{1}{4} \;+\; \frac{1}{8} \;+\; \frac{1}{16} \;+\; \cdots \;+\; \frac{1}{2^k} \;+\; \cdots$$
$$+\; \frac{1}{8} \;+\; \frac{1}{16} \;+\; \cdots \;+\; \frac{1}{2^k} \;+\; \cdots$$
$$+\; \frac{1}{16} \;+\; \cdots \;+\; \frac{1}{2^k} \;+\; \cdots$$
$$\vdots$$

But the first row sums to 1, and each subsequent row is half the preceding row, so the sum of all the rows is $1 + \frac{1}{2} + \frac{1}{4} + \frac{1}{8} + \cdots = 2$.

Problems

1.1   **1.** The table search in algorithm (A) terminates when either K is found in the table or the end of the table is reached. Each of these conditions must be checked every time around the loop. (In Algorithm 1.2 on page 10, the more formal description of algorithm (A), the first test is $T[i] = K$ and the second test is implicit in the **for** loop, where we must always check whether $i \leq n - 1$.) Find a simple improvement to algorithm (A) that avoids testing whether the end of the table has been reached. (You may assume that table position $T[n]$ is available for your use.)

2. We said that algorithm (B) is slightly more intelligent than algorithm (A). For exactly which words K does algorithm (B) compare fewer pairs of words than algorithm (A)?

1.2   **3.** Suppose that $T[0 .. n - 1]$ is a table of records with the structure shown in Figure 1.1 on page 4. If T begins at address X, what is the address of Weight($T[i]$)?

4. A **Frob** is an object that is available in three different sizes, and has front, middle, and back parts, each of which (independently) can be painted any of ten colors, or can be left unpainted.

   a. Design a record structure with four fields that can be used for representing Frobs. What is the minimum number of bits for each field, and for the entire record structure?

   b. It is possible to represent a Frob uniquely by using only 12 bits. Explain how to encode the size and three color values to produce the encoded representation of a Frob, and how to decode the representation of a Frob to extract its size and three color values.

5. There are two basic kinds of **Froobs**, fragrant and frumious. Fragrant Froobs come in 35 varieties, each of which can be found in four different colors; frumious Froobs come in another 17 varieties, each of which can be found in fifteen different colors. Devise an encoding of Froobs in as few bits as possible so that it is easy to tell, by using ordinary computer operations, whether a Froob is fragrant or frumious, and what its variety and color are.

6. Write the procedure *SinglyLinkedDelete* that complements procedure *SinglyLinkedInsert* of Algorithm 1.1 on page 8. It should take as its argument a pointer P and should delete the cell just after the one to which P points. Be sure to handle the possible error condition in some appropriate way.

7. **a.** Write a procedure *Append* that adds a new element to the end of a linked list represented as in Figure 1.4 on page 6. The call *Append*(K, *list*) should create a new record with key value K and add it just after the last element in *list*. You may use the procedure *NewNode* of Algorithm 1.4 on page 12, and use of a locative will be handy.

   b. Write the same procedure without locatives. *Append* should now take only one argument, and may refer to *list* as a global variable (in case *list* has no elements).

8. Suppose T is a table of ten numbers with $T[i] = i$ for $0 \le i \le 9$. What are the values of a, b, and *middle* on successive calls to *BinarySearch* (Algorithm 1.3) starting with *BinarySearch*($T[0..9], 3$)?

9. Write a routine *LLMember*(K, P), which takes a key K and a linked list P and returns **true** or **false**, depending on whether K is in the list. You should assume that the list has been constructed using Algorithm 1.5 or 1.6, so that the keys are in order in the list.

10. This problem concerns the notation for simultaneous assignment, for example $\begin{pmatrix} X \\ Y \end{pmatrix} \leftarrow \begin{pmatrix} Z \\ W \end{pmatrix}$.

a. We abbreviated the special case $\begin{pmatrix} X \\ Y \end{pmatrix} \leftarrow \begin{pmatrix} Y \\ X \end{pmatrix}$ by $X \leftrightarrow Y$. Write code for this swap using only simple assignment statements and a temporary variable T.

b. Generalizing part (a), suppose we want to rotate the values of n variables $X_1, \ldots, X_n$ as follows:

$$\begin{pmatrix} X_1 \\ X_2 \\ \vdots \\ X_{n-1} \\ X_n \end{pmatrix} \leftarrow \begin{pmatrix} X_2 \\ X_3 \\ \vdots \\ X_n \\ X_1 \end{pmatrix}.$$

Write code for this operation using only simple assignments and as few temporary variables as possible.

c. Suppose we need to translate the notation

$$\begin{pmatrix} X_1 \\ \vdots \\ X_n \end{pmatrix} \leftarrow \begin{pmatrix} \alpha_1 \\ \vdots \\ \alpha_n \end{pmatrix}$$

into a programming language that does not provide these simultaneous assignments. Translate this simultaneous assignment into code that uses only simple assignments, again using as few temporary variables as possible. (The α_i are arbitrary expressions.)

d. Now suppose that we are working in a language where simultaneous assignments are not available, but there is a primitive swap operation $X \leftrightarrow Y$ that exchanges the values of X and Y. Solve parts (b) and (c) again.

11. Which of the following are true for any real numbers x and y? Explain or give a counterexample.

a. $\lfloor x + y \rfloor \geq \lfloor x \rfloor + \lfloor y \rfloor$

b. $\lfloor \lceil x \rceil \rfloor + 1 = \lceil \lfloor x \rfloor \rceil$

c. $\lfloor |x| \rfloor = |\lfloor x \rfloor|$

12. Show that the relationship

$$\left\lfloor \frac{\lfloor x/y \rfloor}{z} \right\rfloor = \left\lfloor \frac{\lfloor x/z \rfloor}{y} \right\rfloor$$

does not always hold for real numbers x, y, and z, but that it does hold for integers x, y, and z.

13. Show that if m and n are integers and $m \neq 0$ then

$$\lceil n/m \rceil \leq (n-1)/m + 1.$$

Under what conditions does equality hold? What if m or n is not an integer?

1.3   **14.** Evaluate the following sums:

    a. $\sum_{i=0}^{k} i2^{i}$

    b. $\sum_{i=0}^{k} i2^{-i}$

15. Show that for any integer $n > 0$, the length of the binary notation for n is $\lfloor \lg n \rfloor + 1$.

16. How would you convert binary logarithms to natural logarithms?

17. a. What is the relation between $\log_{b} a$ and $\log_{a} b$?

    b. If $a > b > 0$, how does $\log_{a} x$ compare with $\log_{b} x$?

    c. Let $c \geq 0$ and $b > 1$. Show that there is a number $d \geq 0$ such that $\log_{b}(n + c) \leq \log_{b} n + d$ for every $n \geq 1$.

18. Prove the Exponentials, Powers, and Logarithms Theorem. (Hint: To show that any exponential function dominates any simple power, let $f(x) = c^{x}$ and $g(x) = x^{\alpha}$, where $c > 1$ and $\alpha > 0$. Apply L'Hôpital's rule repeatedly.)

19. Show that the harmonic numbers are unbounded; that is, show that for any $x > 0$ there is an n such that $H_{n} > x$. (Hint: Show that $H_{2^{k+1}} - H_{2^{k}} > \frac{1}{2}$ for any k.)

20. Show that for any $\alpha > 1$ and $b > 1$, $\log_{b}(n^{n}) \in O(n^{\alpha})$. On the other hand, show that $\log_{b}(n^{n}) \notin O(n)$.

21. Is it true that if $\log f(n) \in O(\log g(n))$, then $f(n) \in O(g(n))$? Why or why not?

22. Which of the following are true and which are false, and why?

    a. $\sqrt{n^{5}} \in O(n^{2})$

    b. $\lg(n^{3}) \in O(n \log n)$

    c. $\sqrt{n} \lg \sqrt{n} \in O(n)$

23. Which of the following are true and which are false, and why?

    a. $2/n + 4/n^{2} \in \Theta(1/n)$

    b. $n \log_{10} n \in \Theta(n \log_{2} n)$

    c. $\log_{2} \sqrt{n} \in \Theta(\log n)$

    d. $\sqrt{\log_{2} n} \in \Theta(\log n)$

    e. $\min(700, n^{2}) \in \Theta(1)$

24. Prove that if $f \in O(g)$ and $g \in O(h)$ then $f \in O(h)$. What are the n_{0} and c for f and h, in terms of those for f and g, and g and h?

25. Show that if $f(n)$ and $g(n)$ are positive for all n, then $O(f + g) = O(f) + O(g)$, where the sum of two sets of functions is the set of functions that can be expressed as the sum of one function from each set. Does the same hold if addition is replaced by subtraction? Why or why not?

26. Prove the Big-O Theorem.

27. Some authors prefer the following definition: $f \in \Omega(g)$ if and only if there is a c such that $f(n) > cg(n)$ for infinitely many n. Show that this definition amounts to something different from ours, because there are cases in which $f \in \Omega(g)$ according to this definition but not according to ours. Also, show that under this definition $\Omega(\ )$ is not transitive: there are functions f, g, and h such that $f \in \Omega(g)$ and $g \in \Omega(h)$ but $f \notin \Omega(h)$. Finally, we prefer our definition because it is transitive; but show that the alternative definition has the advantage that for any f and g, either $f \in o(g)$ or $f \in \Omega(g)$.

28. Show that $f \in \Theta(g)$ if and only if $g \in \Theta(f)$. (Thus Θ actually partitions the class of all functions into equivalence classes.)

29. In each case, prove that the statement is true for all functions f and g, or give a counterexample.
   a. $f \in o(g)$ if and only if $f \in O(g)$ and $f \notin \Theta(g)$.
   b. $f \in \Theta(g)$ if and only if $f \in O(g)$ and $f \notin o(g)$.

30. Suppose that f and g are functions such that $f \in o(g)$. Find a function h such that $f \in o(h)$ and $h \in o(g)$. That is, show that between any two functions that are related by little-o a third can be interpolated. (Technically, this means that the ordering defined by little-o is **dense**.)

31. For any function f, we have defined classes $O(f)$, $o(f)$, and $\Omega(f)$. There ought to be a fourth class $\omega(f)$ that bears the same relation to $\Omega(f)$ that $o(f)$ bears to $O(f)$. Define $\omega(f)$, and explain the class in ordinary English.

32. Find, as a function of k, that constant c_k such that

$$\sum_{i=1}^{n} i^k = c_k n^{k+1} + f_k(n),$$

where $f_k(n) \in O(n^k)$.

33. Show that $F_n = (1/\sqrt{5})(\phi^n - \hat{\phi}^n)$, where F_n is the nth Fibonacci number and ϕ and $\hat{\phi}$ are as defined on page 27.

34. Show the following facts about the Fibonacci numbers F_n, where $\gcd(a, b)$ denotes the greatest common divisor of a and b:

a. $F_{m+n} = F_m F_{n+1} + F_{m-1} F_n$

b. F_n and F_{n+1} have no common factors other than 1

c. $\gcd(F_m, F_n) = \gcd(F_m, F_{n-m})$ for $n \geq m$

35. Show that the function $T(n)$ defined by Equation (3) on page 28 is monotone nondecreasing.

36. For each of the following recurrence relations, assume that $T(1) = 1$, and find the order of the function $T(n)$. (You may also assume that n is a power of the divisor, 2 or 3.)

a. $T(n) = 3T(n/2) + n$

b. $T(n) = 3T(n/2) + n^2$

c. $T(n) = 8T(n/2) + n^3$

d. $T(n) = 4T(n/3) + n$

e. $T(n) = 4T(n/3) + n^2$

f. $T(n) = 9T(n/3) + n^2$

37. For each recurrence relation in Problem 36, give an *exact* form for $T(n)$, including the multiplicative constant and any lower-order terms.

38. Let $G(n)$ be defined by the conditions that $G(0) = G(1) = 0$, $G(2) = 1$, and

$$G(n) = G(n-3) + G(n-2) + G(n-1)$$

for all $n \geq 3$. Find constants α and β, as accurately as you can, such that $G(n) \in \Omega(\alpha^n) \cap O(\beta^n)$.

39. a. Find an exact form and the order of the solution to the recurrence relation

$$T(1) = 1$$

$$T(n) = 2T(n/2) + n \lg n \qquad \text{if } n \geq 2 \text{ is a power of 2.}$$

b. Find an exact form and the order of the solution to the recurrence relation

$$T(2) = 1$$

$$T(n) = \sqrt{n} T(\sqrt{n}) + n \qquad \text{if } n > 2 \text{ is of the form } 2^{2^k}.$$

40. Explain why the statement of the Divide-and-Conquer Recurrences Theorem includes the provision that $n_0' \leq \lfloor ((b-1)n_0 - 1)/b \rfloor$.

41. Complete the proof of the Divide-and-Conquer Recurrences Theorem by showing that recurrence relation of the Theorem has a solution in the big-O classes as stated.

42. Find the exact solution (in terms of n, c, a, c', and e, not a big-O answer) to the recurrence relation

$$T(1) = c$$

$$T(n) = aT(n/b) + c'n^e, \qquad \text{if } n > 1.$$

(This is a simplified form of the relation of the Divide-and-Conquer Recurrences Theorem, with inequalities replaced by equalities.) Make any assumptions you find convenient about the form of n, but state those assumptions.

43. Consider a recurrence of the form

$$T(n) \leq \begin{cases} c, & \text{if } n < n_0 \\ \sum_{i=1}^{k} T(\lfloor \alpha_i n \rfloor), & \text{if } n \geq n_0, \end{cases}$$

where $n_0 \geq 0$ and the α_i are constants in the range $0 < \alpha_i < 1$. Show that if $\sum_{i=1}^{k} \alpha_i < 1$ then $T(n) \in O(n)$. Is this still true if "$\lfloor \alpha_i n \rfloor$" in the recurrence is replaced by "$\lceil \alpha_i n \rceil$"?

44. This problem explores the choice of the optimal cut-off value n_0 below which Merge Sort should switch to a nonrecursive sorting method, as proposed on page 33. Suppose that the time complexity of *NonRecursiveSort* is given by the formula $T(n) = c_2 n^2 + c_1 n$ (all the commonly used nonrecursive sorting algorithms, such as Insertion Sort and Bubble Sort, fit this pattern reasonably well). Also assume that the total time required for k levels of *MergeSort*, starting with a table of size n, is $dn \cdot k$ for some constant d (if *MergeSort* were used all the way down to subtables of a single element, we would have $k = \lg n$).

   a. Write a formula for the total cost of sorting a table of size n by using *MergeSort* recursively until the subtables are of size n_0, and then using *NonRecursiveSort* for tables of that size. (You may assume that n/n_0 is a power of 2.)

   b. By taking the derivative with respect to n_0 of the formula from part (a), find the value of n_0 that minimizes the total cost.

45. a. A single die is thrown. What is the expected value of the number that comes up on top?

   b. A date between January 1, 1901 and December 31, 2000 is selected at random. What is the expected value of the day of the month?

46. Assume a uniform distribution on the permutations of $\{1, \ldots, n\}$. What are

   a. the probability that a randomly chosen permutation will be monotone increasing or monotone decreasing?

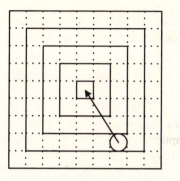

Figure 1.8 A circular bug lands on a random square of a 9×9 square board and crawls to the center square, traversing 3 rings in the process. (See Problem 50.)

    b. the probability that a randomly chosen permutation will begin with 1?

    c. the probability that a randomly chosen permutation will begin with an even number?

    d. the probability that two randomly chosen permutations will begin with the same number?

47. When two ordinary dice are rolled the total can be any number from 2 to 12. What is the probability distribution of these eleven possible events?

48. Suppose that n^2 different numbers are distributed at random in an n by n square. What is the probability that the smallest number is at a corner or along one of the edges?

49. Lottery tickets cost $1 each. What is the expected profit (or loss) by the lottery organizers if, of the tickets sold,

    90% are losers;
    5% win one free ticket;
    3.5% win $10;
    1.3% win $20;
    0.15% win $100;
    0.04% win $250;
    and 0.01% win $1000?

50. A $(2n+1) \times (2n+1)$ square board is partitioned by a series of concentric square "rings" around the center square, indicated by the solid lines in Figure 1.8. A bug lands on a random square of the board and crawls straight to the center square. What is the expected number of rings that it crosses? (Count the border of the center square as a ring.)

51. It is a simple matter to make a fair two-way choice using a fair coin: assign one choice to "heads" and the other to "tails," and toss the coin.

  a. Show how to make a fair three-way choice using a fair coin.

  b. Generalize part (a), finding a procedure for making a fair n-way choice using a fair coin.

  c. Show how to make a fair two-way choice using a coin that is not known to be fair, that is, where "heads" occurs with unknown (but fixed) probability. (Hint: It is unnecessary to determine the probability of "heads.")

  d. Prove that none of parts (a)–(c) can be solved by any procedure that always terminates in a number of steps that can be determined in advance, except in the case of certain values of n in part (b).

52. You are playing *Let's Make a Deal!* with Monty Hall. He shows you three doors labelled A, B, and C. Behind one of the doors is a new computer worth \$65,536, behind another is a slide rule, and behind the third is a box of punched cards. Monty offers you your choice of doors, and you pick door A. Monty, who knows where each prize is located and always keeps the computer hidden, now opens door C to reveal the slide rule.

  a. As he always does, Monty now offers you the option of switching to the remaining unopened door, door B. Should you do it? Does it matter if Monty offers you \$1000 to switch? What if you have to pay Monty \$1000 to switch?

  b. Suppose that after you pick door A, Monty pulls out a wheel of fortune with A, B, and C represented equally. He says, "Let's open a door!" and spins the wheel. While the wheel is spinning, Monty tells you that if the wheel lands on A you'll get whatever is behind door A and the game will be over. But the wheel lands on C, door C is opened, and the slide rule is behind it. Now Monty offers you the option to switch. Answer part (a) under these new circumstances.

References

The classic books on data structures, algorithms, and the mathematical analysis of the efficiency of computer programs are

D. E. Knuth, *The Art of Computer Programming, Vol. I: Fundamental Algorithms,* Addison-Wesley Publishing Company, 1968 (First Edition) and 1973 (Second Edition), *and*

D. E. Knuth, *The Art of Computer Programming, Vol. III: Sorting and Searching,* Addison-Wesley Publishing Company, 1973.

These books contain a wealth of mathematical background and historical references which we urge the interested reader to consult. Moreover many of the analyses presented in this textbook have their origins in Knuth's work. Another book that has been extremely influential is

A. V. Aho, J. E. Hopcroft, and J. D. Ullman, *The Design and Analysis of Computer Algorithms,* Addison-Wesley Publishing Company, 1974.

Two other good sources for information about data structures and their analysis are

T. A. Standish, *Data Structure Techniques,* Addison-Wesley Publishing Company, 1980,

and

G. H. Gonnet, *Handbook of Data Structures and Algorithms,* Addison-Wesley Publishing Company, 1984.

An interesting example of a computer design that is not of the von Neumann variety is described in

W. D. Hillis, *The Connection Machine,* MIT Press, 1985.

A very readable presentation of the design and analysis of some algorithms for this type of parallel computer is given in

W. D. Hillis and G. L. Steele, "Data Parallel Algorithms," *Communications of the ACM* **29**, 12 (1986), pp. 1170–1183.

Big-O notation and its relatives have a very long history in mathematical writing. Until recently it has been the universal practice to write "$f = O(g)$" instead of "$f \in O(g)$," that is, to treat the relation between f and g as a kind of equation, although it is really more like an inequality or a "one-way" equation (the notation "$O(g) = f$" being meaningless). Recently the trend has been to treat $O(g)$ as a set of functions; not only is this mathematically precise, but it justifies the use of standard notations like "$\in$" in association with "$O(\ )$." But some of the old way of talking is convenient and efficient, too. For discussions of big-O notation and its relatives, see

D. E. Knuth, "Big Omicron and Big Omega and Big Theta," *SIGACT News* **8**, 2 (1976), pp. 18–24

and

G. Brassard, "Crusade for a Better Notation," *SIGACT News* **17**, 1 (1985), pp. 60–64.

We follow Brassard's proposals in this book. A classic but still excellent work on probability theory is

W. Feller, *An Introduction to Probability Theory and its Applications (Third Edition),* John Wiley and Sons, 1968.

2

Algorithm Analysis

2.1 PROPERTIES OF AN ALGORITHM

An algorithm is a computational method to be used for solving a problem. Among the important properties of an algorithm are *effectiveness*, *correctness*, *termination*, *efficiency*, and *program complexity*.

Effectiveness

To say that a process is **effective** is simply to say that it can be rendered as a computer program—it can be understood without leaps of imagination and utilizes only operations that can be performed by a computer in some obvious way. If an algorithm is presented in a conventional programming language, its effectiveness is guaranteed automatically. But we shall use English a good deal to describe algorithms, since it is easier to understand than most programming languages. We must therefore take care that our descriptions are reasonably unambiguous, and can be translated into concrete code without difficulty.

For example, consider some problems about prime numbers. A number is **prime** if it is divisible only by 1 and by itself; for example, 7 is prime but 9 is not. There are many effective ways to tell if a number n is prime, the most obvious of which is to try dividing it by each number from 2 to $n - 1$; note that an effective method does not have to be particularly efficient. Given such a method for testing primality, the direction "let p be the smallest prime number greater than n" is reasonably effective, since there is at least one obvious way to implement it (start counting up from $n + 1$, testing each number to see if it is prime). But "let p be the prime number that is closest to a multiple of n" is not effective; it seems to ask for that prime number p that minimizes $|p - m \cdot n|$, over all possible values of m. Since there are infinitely many possible m (as well as infinitely many possible p), how could we be sure that we have found one for which $m \cdot n$ is as close as possible to a prime? And what are we supposed to do if there are two numbers m_1 and m_2 such that $m_1 \cdot n$ and $m_2 \cdot n$ are equally close to prime numbers p_1 and p_2? Perhaps these questions can be resolved by mathematical methods, but as stated the directions for finding p are insufficiently precise.

Correctness

An algorithm must not give the wrong answer. Ever.* Thus consider the following approach to determining whether a number $n > 1$ in binary notation is prime. The number n is prime if it is not divisible by any integer less than or equal to $\sqrt{n}$, and $\sqrt{n}$ has about half as many bits as n. So we might try:

1. A b-bit number is prime if and only if it is not divisible by any number greater than 1 with $b/2$ or fewer bits.

This works for the four-bit number $1001_2 = 9$, which is divisible by the two-bit number $11_2 = 3$; it also works for the four-bit number $1011_2 = 11$, which is prime and is not divisible by any of the numbers $10_2 = 2$, $11_2 = 3$ of two bits. But it fails for the five-bit number $11001_2 = 25$, which is not prime and is not divisible by any number with fewer than $5/2 = 2.5$ bits. For this number we must also check at least some of the possible three-bit divisors, such as $101_2 = 5$. Thus a correct version of the test would be:

2. A b-bit number is prime if and only if it is not divisible by any number greater than 1 with $\lceil b/2 \rceil$ or fewer bits.

Perhaps this is what was meant all along; small consolation to the person who took (1) literally and got the right answer for more than 99%—but not 100%—of the numbers between 1 and 1000!

Termination

It is not enough to be confident that the answer is correct, when you get it; you must be sure to get an answer at all. Some pieces of code that "look like" algorithms are not known to terminate with all possible inputs; a famous example is Algorithm 2.1. If this function computes a value on input m, that value is surely m; but despite the efforts of many mathematicians, we cannot rule out the possibility that there are some m for which the **while** loop never exits!

The assurance that an algorithm terminates is often taken for granted as part of its correctness, but sometimes it is helpful to treat termination separately. From the fact that $n^2 = (n - 1)^2 + 2n - 1$ for any integer n we might be tempted to believe the following recursive algorithm for computing n^2:

$$\text{sqr}(n) = \begin{cases} 0, & \text{if } n = 0; \\ \text{sqr}(n - 1) + 2n - 1, & \text{if } n \neq 0. \end{cases}$$

This gives the correct answer for $n \geq 0$, but does not terminate for $n < 0$, even though the formula on which it is based is correct for negative n as well.

---

*We are not considering so-called **probabilistic algorithms**, which used randomized methods (a kind of coin-flipping by computer) to produce results that may, with extremely low probability, be incorrect. Such methods can be practically useful but are beyond the scope of this book.

---

function *OddEven*(**integer** m): **integer**
    $n \leftarrow m$
    while $n > 1$ **do**
        if n is even **then**
            $n \leftarrow n/2$
        else
            $n \leftarrow 3n + 1$
    return m

Algorithm 2.1 A mysterious "algorithm." Does this piece of code compute the identity function? Or is there some positive integer m that causes it to go into an infinite loop?

Efficiency

This is the concept that motivates most of this book. Algorithms that are equally correct can vary widely in their utilization of computational resources; it is a critical part of the engineering of complex systems to be able to predict how they would behave when used under a range of possible conditions. For our purposes, the relevant resources are **time** and **memory**. A program that is too slow is likely not to be used, and for some applications (for example, where real-time response is required) may not be suitable at all. A program that demands too much memory may not even be executable on the machines that are available. Nonetheless, the rapid decline in cost of all kinds of memory has made memory efficiency less critical in many applications than it once was. Our main emphasis will therefore be on the time efficiency of algorithms.

The time efficiency of an algorithm will be measured by analyzing how the *running time* varies with the *size of the input* to the algorithm. We naturally expect that in most situations of practical interest the time to solve a problem will increase with the size of the problem to be solved; for example, any sorting algorithm tends to take more time to sort bigger tables. What will be important, however, is to measure the *rate* at which the running time increases with the size of the input—for example, linearly, quadratically, or exponentially. This measure of the efficiency of an algorithm focuses attention on intrinsic characteristics of the algorithm, rather than incidental factors such as the speed of the computer on which the algorithm is running and fine-grained local optimizations of the code implementing the algorithm.

Program Complexity

Sometimes simple methods are preferred to more ingenious but more complex methods, even when the more ingenious methods are also more efficient in their use of machine time. The reason, of course, is that the programmer's time is valuable too. Also, no real program is forever static—programs are regularly repaired and adapted to changed requirements and operating environments, often by individuals other than the original programmer. Straightforward design and simple algorithms are valued highly by those who have to make such changes.

Unlike the other properties of algorithms discussed above, program complexity is entirely qualitative—simplicity is in the eye of the beholder. The related notion of **program size** can be characterized formally, but we shall not be concerned with size alone.

2.2 EXACT VS. GROWTH-RATE ANALYSIS

To introduce techniques for the mathematical analysis of algorithms, in this section we consider two algorithms to solve the same problem, one of which is simpler and more familiar but generally slower than the other. We shall derive formulas for the running times of the algorithms, and then return to draw some general lessons from this example.

The problem we consider is the familiar one of integer multiplication; from integers x and y, calculate their product $z = x \cdot y$. As computer programmers we usually think of this as a "built-in" machine operation, but such computer instructions work only on numbers of fixed size; here we want to think about algorithms for multiplying integers of unlimited size. To be precise, we assume that the numbers x and y are nonnegative integers presented to us in binary notation, and we wish to produce the binary numeral for their product. (All the methods discussed below work with little modification if the base is a number other than 2.) The inputs to the algorithm are two tables $X[0 \mathinner{\ldotp\ldotp} n - 1]$ and $Y[0 \mathinner{\ldotp\ldotp} n-1]$ containing two binary numerals of n bits each, representing x and y. The length n is part of the input, and the multiplication algorithm must work correctly for all $n \geq 1$. The table entry $X[i]$ is the ith bit of x, where $X[0]$ is the **least significant** (rightmost) bit of x and $X[n - 1]$ is the **most significant** (leftmost) bit of x; and similarly for y and Y. Thus each entry in X and Y is 0 or 1 and

$$x = \sum_{i=0}^{n-1} X[i] \cdot 2^i$$

$$y = \sum_{i=0}^{n-1} Y[i] \cdot 2^i.$$

The largest possible value of x or y is $2^n - 1$ (when all of the bits are 1), so the largest possible value of $z = x \cdot y$ is $2^{2n} - 2 \cdot 2^n + 1$; therefore $2n$ bits are sufficient (and necessary—see Problem 3) to represent the product z.

$$
\begin{array}{r}
y\ \ 11101 \\
x\ \ 01011 \\
\hline
11101 \\
11101 \\
00000 \\
11101 \\
00000 \\
\hline
0100111111
\end{array}
$$

$$
\begin{array}{l}
i{=}0 \\
i{=}1 \\
i{=}2 \\
i{=}3 \\
i{=}4
\end{array}
$$

$$j=9876543210$$

Figure 2.1 Grade school multiplication algorithm for two numbers x and y of n bits; here $n = 5$ and the product is $11 \times 29 = 319$, or, in binary, $01011 \times 11101 = 0100111111$. The ith partial product is either y or 0, depending on the ith bit of x (counting from the right), and is shifted left i bits.

Algorithm 1: Grade School Algorithm The multiplication method we all learned in grade school for integer multiplication is quite serviceable, and it becomes even simpler when the factors are represented in binary (Figure 2.1). To multiply y by x, write down n rows, with the ith row representing the product $y \cdot X[i]$ shifted left i bit positions. Then, for each column from rightmost to leftmost, add up the bits in the column to produce a sum S, record $S \bmod 2$ as the next bit of the answer,* and carry $\lfloor S/2 \rfloor$ into the sum of the next column.

In practice it is unnecessary to produce all the products $y \cdot X[i]$ before adding them up; instead we can calculate any bit of any partial product at the time we need it while adding up a column. Thus the algorithm (Algorithm 2.2) is controlled by an outer loop whose index j represents a column number, or equivalently, a bit position in the result z; thus j runs from 0 to $2n - 1$. The inner loop index i runs through the rows, or equivalently, the bit positions of x. The bit in the ith row and the jth column is then $X[i] \cdot Y[j - i]$, provided that $0 \le j - i \le n - 1$; otherwise the position in row i and column j is empty. Of course the multiplication $X[i] \cdot Y[j - i]$ is just the product of two bits and is determined without a recursive call on the multiplication algorithm!

Now let us fix a particular programming language, compiler, and computer, and derive an expression for the running time of this algorithm as a function of n. For $1 \le i \le 8$ let T_i be the time required to execute line (i) of Algorithm 2.2 once. (In the case of lines (2) and (3) these are the times required to initialize or increment the loop index and to test the loop exit condition.) Lines (1) and (8) are executed once each. Lines (2), (6), and (7) are executed $2n$ times each. Lines (3) and (4) are executed n times for each execution of line (2), or $n \cdot (2n)$ times in all; and line (5) is executed at most $n \cdot (2n)$ times. If we let $T_{\text{GradeSchool}}(n)$

---

*Here $a \bmod b$ ("a modulo b") is the nonnegative remainder when a is divided by b. Thus $S \bmod 2$ is 0 or 1, depending on whether S is even or odd.

---

function *GradeSchoolMult*(**table** $X[0 .. n - 1], Y[0 .. n - 1]$): **table**
{Multiplication of two nonnegative binary numerals X and Y of n bits}
{The result Z is a table of length $2n$}

$\quad S \leftarrow 0$	(1)
$\quad$**for** j **from** 0 **to** $2n - 1$ **do**	(2)
$\quad\quad$**for** i **from** 0 **to** $n - 1$ **do**	(3)
$\quad\quad\quad$**if** $0 \leq j - i \leq n - 1$ **then**	(4)
$\quad\quad\quad\quad S \leftarrow S + X[i] \cdot Y[j - i]$	(5)
$\quad\quad Z[j] \leftarrow S \bmod 2$	(6)
$\quad\quad S \leftarrow \lfloor S/2 \rfloor$	(7)
$\quad$**return** Z	(8)

Algorithm 2.2 Grade school algorithm for multiplication of two nonnegative integers x and y represented in binary. X and Y are tables containing the bits of the numbers to be multiplied, with $X[0]$ being the least significant bit of x.

---

denote the maximum amount of time taken by the grade school algorithm to multiply any two numbers of n bits each, then by multiplying the time to execute each line by the number of times that line is executed we have

$$(T_1 + T_8) + (T_2 + T_6 + T_7) \cdot (2n) + (T_3 + T_4) \cdot n \cdot (2n)$$

$$\leq T_{\text{GradeSchool}}(n)$$

$$\leq (T_1 + T_8) + (T_2 + T_6 + T_7) \cdot (2n) + (T_3 + T_4 + T_5) \cdot n \cdot (2n).$$

It follows that $T_{\text{GradeSchool}}(n) \in \Theta(n \cdot (2n)) = \Theta(n^2)$.

Algorithm 2: Simple Block Multiplication Algorithm   Can divide-and-conquer be used as the basis for an integer multiplication algorithm? Split x and y in half, as nearly as possible, and call x_L and x_R the left and right halves of x, and y_L and y_R the left and right halves of y. To be precise, let $m = \lceil n/2 \rceil$, and let

$$x = x_L \cdot 2^m + x_R$$

$$y = y_L \cdot 2^m + y_R,$$

where x_L and y_L are numbers with $n - m = \lfloor n/2 \rfloor$ bits, and x_R and y_R are numbers with m bits. Then

$$xy = (x_L \cdot 2^m + x_R) \cdot (y_L \cdot 2^m + y_R)$$

$$= x_L y_L \cdot 2^{2m} + (x_L y_R + x_R y_L) \cdot 2^m + x_R y_R. \qquad (1)$$

If we can calculate the four products $x_L y_L$, $x_L y_R$, $x_R y_L$, and $x_R y_R$, then shifting them (to implement multiplication by powers of 2) and adding them (by the straightforward algorithm for addition of two integers, Problem 4) can be done in $O(n)$ time. Some work might also be required to do the "splitting" before the numbers are multiplied, but the time for this work is also linear in the size of the numbers. Let us write $T_{\text{Block}}(n)$ for the time required, in the worst case, to multiply two n-bit numbers using this recursive "block multiplication" algorithm. Since the four products involve numbers with at most m bits each, if we use the same method recursively to calculate those products, the total time needed for this algorithm to multiply two n-bit numbers is described by a recurrence of the form

$$T_{\text{Block}}(n) \leq c, \qquad\qquad \text{if } n \leq n_0$$

$$T_{\text{Block}}(n) \leq 4T_{\text{Block}}(\lceil n/2 \rceil) + c'n, \qquad \text{if } n > n_0,$$

where n_0 is the "cut-off" value such that a nonrecursive algorithm, such as the grade school algorithm, is used for numbers of n_0 bits or shorter. To solve this recurrence we can use the Divide-and-Conquer Recurrences Theorem, with $a = 4$, $b = 2$, and $e = 1$; by the Theorem, $T(n) \in O(n^2)$, the same bound as we calculated for the grade school algorithm. So the answer seems to be that divide-and-conquer is applicable, but does not gain us anything over the simpler algorithm.

Algorithm 3: Clever Block Multiplication Algorithm We can rewrite Equation (1) using only three recursive multiplications rather than four by noting that

$$x_L y_R + x_R y_L = (x_L + x_R) \cdot (y_L + y_R) - x_L y_L - x_R y_R.$$

That is, if we calculate just the three products

$$p_1 = x_R y_R$$

$$p_2 = x_L y_L$$

$$p_3 = (x_L + x_R) \cdot (y_L + y_R),$$

then the value of $x_L y_R + x_R y_L = p_3 - p_1 - p_2$ can be calculated from them by using subtraction only.

Algorithm 2.3 shows the code for this clever algorithm. The functions *Add* and *Sub* return the sum and difference of two integers represented as tables of bits; it is assumed that *Add* returns a table of length one greater than the length of its longer argument, and *Sub* returns a table of length equal to that of its first argument (Problem 4(a,c)). In this algorithm *Sub* is never called with arguments that would produce a negative result, so we can avoid specifying its behavior under such circumstances. *Accum*(P, Q) is a procedure that adds its first argument *into* its second (Problem 4(d)); again, overflow cannot occur under the conditions of this algorithm.

---

function *CleverMult*(**table** $X[0..n-1], Y[0..n-1]$): **table**
{Multiplication of two nonnegative binary numerals X and Y of n bits}
{The result Z is a table of length $2n$}
{Tables P_1, P_2, and P_3 have lengths $2\lceil n/2 \rceil$, $2\lfloor n/2 \rfloor$, and $2\lceil n/2 \rceil + 2$}

$\quad m \leftarrow \lceil n/2 \rceil$ (0)

$\quad$ **if** $n \le 3$ **then return** *GradeSchoolMult*(X, Y) (1)

$\quad P_1 \leftarrow$ *CleverMult*$(X[0..m-1], Y[0..m-1])$ (2)

$\quad P_2 \leftarrow$ *CleverMult*$(X[m..n-1], Y[m..n-1])$ (3)

$\quad P_3 \leftarrow$ *CleverMult*$(Add(X[0..m-1], X[m..n-1]),$

$\qquad\qquad\qquad Add(Y[0..m-1], Y[m..n-1]))$ (4)

$\quad D \leftarrow Sub(Sub(P_3, P_1), P_2)$ (5)

$\quad Z[0..2m-1] \leftarrow P_1$ (6)

$\quad Z[2m..2n-1] \leftarrow P_2$ (7)

$\quad Accum(D[0..2m+1], Z[m..2n-1])$ (8)

$\quad$ **return** Z (9)

Algorithm 2.3 Block multiplication algorithm for integers, using only three recursive multiplications rather than four.

To get this algorithm to work correctly some care must be taken with the sizes of the tables. The recursive multiplication method can't be used for integers of three bits, so in line (1) the grade school algorithm is used on integers of that size or smaller (Problem 8). Each quantity $x_L + x_R$ and $y_L + y_R$ is the sum of an integer of length $\lfloor n/2 \rfloor$ and an integer of length $\lceil n/2 \rceil$, so each sum requires $\lceil n/2 \rceil + 1 = m + 1$ bits in the worst case. Therefore the product table P_3 requires $2m + 2$ bits; so does the difference $p_3 - p_1 - p_2$, which is stored in the table D in line (5). Since the product $x_R y_R = p_1$ takes $2m$ bits and the product $x_L y_L$ is to be shifted exactly this many bits, these products are "assembled" into Z by copying P_1 into the low $2m$ bits of Z (line (6)) and copying P_2 into the high $2n - 2m$ bits (line (7)). Then $p_3 - p_1 - p_2$, which should be shifted by m bits in computing the final result, is added in by aligning bit 0 of table D with bit m of Z—roughly speaking D is aligned with the "middle half" of Z.

Let us once again fix some computer system and investigate $T_{\text{Clever}}(n)$, the time required to execute Algorithm 2.3 on two integers of n bits each. Let $T_i(n)$ be, for $0 \le i \le 9$, the time required to execute line (i); then $T_{\text{Clever}}(n) = \sum_{i=0}^{9} T_i(n)$. Certain of these functions depend on the time used by the functions *Add*, *Sub*, and *Accum*. If we let $T_{\text{Add}}(h)$, $T_{\text{Sub}}(h)$, and $T_{\text{Accum}}(h)$ denote the time required for these operations when run on arguments of length at most h bits, we know (Problem 4) that each of these functions is linear in h. Likewise $T_{\text{Copy}}(h)$, the time required to copy a table of length h from one place to another, is a linear function of h. By examining the lengths of the various tables, we find the following expressions for the $T_i(n)$:

$$T_0(n) = c_0$$

$$T_1(n) = c_1$$

$$T_2(n) = T_{\text{Clever}}(m)$$

$$T_3(n) = T_{\text{Clever}}(\lfloor n/2 \rfloor) \leq T_{\text{Clever}}(m)$$

$$T_4(n) = 2T_{\text{Add}}(m) + T_{\text{Clever}}(m + 1)$$

$$T_5(n) = 2T_{\text{Sub}}(2m + 1)$$

$$T_6(n) = T_{\text{Copy}}(2m)$$

$$T_7(n) = T_{\text{Copy}}(2n - 2m)$$

$$T_8(n) = T_{\text{Accum}}(2n - m)$$

$$T_9(n) = c_9.$$

(Here c_0 is the constant time to divide n by 2, c_1 is the maximum time to check the value of n and to run the grade school algorithm on numbers of at most three bits, and c_9 is the time to execute line (9), which does not depend on the value of n.)

Everything except $T_2(n)$, $T_3(n)$, and $T_4(n)$ is bounded by a linear function of n, and the three recurrences on T_{Clever} involve arguments less than or equal to $m + 1$. Therefore, for suitable constants c and c', a recurrence correctly describing T_{Clever} is

$$T_{\text{Clever}}(n) \leq c, \qquad\qquad\qquad \text{if } n \leq 3$$

$$T_{\text{Clever}}(n) \leq 3T_{\text{Clever}}(\lceil n/2 \rceil + 1) + c'n, \qquad \text{if } n > 3.$$

By the Divide-and-Conquer Recurrences Theorem, this recurrence has the solution $T_{\text{Clever}}(n) \in O(n^{\log_2 3}) = O(n^{1.59\cdots})$.

In sum, we have established that

$$T_{\text{GradeSchool}}(n) \in \Theta(n^2) \tag{2}$$

$$T_{\text{Clever}}(n) \in O(n^{\log_2 3}). \tag{3}$$

We want to draw the conclusion that the clever algorithm is better, since $\log_2 3 < 2$. But some care and caution is in order.

First of all, in comparing these two algorithms it is crucial that the relation for $T_{\text{GradeSchool}}(n)$ involves a *lower bound*, not merely an upper bound. That is, the important fact is that $T_{\text{GradeSchool}}(n) \in \Omega(n^2)$, which is half of what is implied by Equation (2). This statement implies that there is some sequence of inputs, at least one pair of inputs for each value of n, such that the time actually used by the grade school algorithm on these inputs increases quadratically with n. This phenomenon would be unaffected by efforts to speed up the grade school algorithm for certain inputs—for example, by checking if one of the arguments represents 0 and if so returning the representation of 0 immediately; any such simple modification would still have running time in $\Omega(n^2)$.

In fact, merely from knowing two *upper* bounds—that $T_{\text{GradeSchool}}(n) \in O(n^2)$ and $T_{\text{Clever}}(n) \in O(n^{\log_2 3})$—nothing at all would follow about the superiority of one algorithm over the other; $T_{\text{GradeSchool}}(n)$ might be constant and $T_{\text{Clever}}(n)$ might be linear! But from a lower bound and an upper bound— $T_{\text{GradeSchool}}(n) \in \Omega(n^2)$ and $T_{\text{Clever}}(n) \in O(n^{\log_2 3})$—we can conclude (Problem 9) that

$$T_{\text{Clever}}(n) \in o(T_{\text{GradeSchool}}(n)), \tag{4}$$

and this implies that for sufficiently large n the worst-case performance of the clever algorithm will beat the worst-case behavior of the grade school algorithm. Indeed, for sufficiently large n the clever algorithm will beat the grade school algorithm, even if the grade school algorithm is implemented on the world's fastest computer and the clever algorithm on the world's slowest, and the grade school algorithm is coded in assembly language by the world's best programmer and the clever algorithm is coded in a higher-level language by a grade school student. Such considerations affect only the constants implicit in big-O notation, and not the relation between the growth rates of these functions. In other words, the superiority of the clever algorithm *will survive any technological change*. It is this kind of comparison that we want to make when studying algorithms.

Principles of Mathematical Analysis

Let us summarize some of the basic principles that emerged during consideration of the integer multiplication example.

- Measure resource usage as a function of input size.

In the integer multiplication example, the value of n—the length of the numbers in bits—is a natural measure of the size of the problem to be solved. (Generally, the **size** of a problem is something that measures the amount of paper it takes to write down the question we want answered; thus in the case of numerical algorithms, the size is the number of bits, not the actual values of the numbers in question.) As the size of a problem increases, the amount of time generally increases as well. There is no point in trying to measure the time needed to solve a problem on any fixed set of data, since we can always build a program that works very quickly on those data by table-lookup. For example, it is pointless to compare integer multiplication algorithms by their performance on one or two fixed and supposedly "hard" inputs, since we can always "soup up" any algorithm to work very fast on those particular inputs by building the answer into the program itself.

Algorithm analysis becomes interesting and profitable only when an algorithm can handle all possible inputs, of potentially unbounded size.

- Measure the worst-case performance for all inputs up to a given size.

There are variations on the grade school algorithm that work well for certain inputs, for example, when one input is 0 or a power of 2. In fact in everyday life we remember and use such tricks to avoid unnecessary labor. But when measuring worst-case performance, whittling away a case here and a case there does not change our overall assessment of an algorithm's quality, which measures its performance on all inputs of size less than or equal to a given bound n.

- When measuring time, ignore constant factors.

We have already mentioned the justification for this principle—it means that variations in coding style, compiler performance, and machine power can be ignored. Of course all those things are important in practice, but this principle gives us a way of studying the algorithms themselves in a way that does not depend on those factors.

All principles have their limitations, and this one is no exception. In the example of the integer multiplication algorithms, if the running time of the grade school algorithm on numbers of up to n bits were no more than $10^{-10}n^2$ and the running time of the clever algorithm might be as much as $10^{10}n^{1.59\cdots}$, would we really ignore the twenty-order-of-magnitude difference in the constants because the clever algorithm was guaranteed to be better for *extremely* large n? Probably not. In fact in the real world the data on which we run our algorithms are not of unbounded size, and we must sometimes determine the crossover point at which a theoretically superior algorithm is really preferable. (If we never want to multiply numbers bigger than a machine word, we should not use any of the multiplication algorithms explained here—we should just invoke the computer's multiplication instruction!) When a computer scientist says that a certain algorithm is "of only theoretical interest," what is usually meant is that it is superior to other algorithms in the sense of growth-rate analysis, but because of the constant factors involved and the size of the inputs that are likely to be encountered in practice, it is not in fact superior in ordinary use. We shall see a few of these algorithms in this book, but most of the methods we present are useful in practice as well as in theory.

This rule is restricted to measurement of *time*—not memory—because there is a natural intrinsic unit of memory on a digital computer—the **bit**—but there is no correspondingly natural unit of time. Thus if an algorithm uses $3n$ bits of memory to process a data set of size n, it can probably be programmed to use $3n$ bits on any computer. Questions of word size and the ease with which fields can be packed and unpacked may have to be considered as well, but in most cases it *does* make sense to compare algorithms in terms of *exactly* how much memory they use.

- Compare the functions that measure the time complexity of algorithms by their growth rate; use big-O notation for giving estimates of upper bounds and big-Ω notation for estimates of lower bounds.

This is more or less a restatement of the previous point. Once constant factors are ignored, the difference between $T_{\text{GradeSchool}}$ and T_{Clever} is that the one is in $\Omega(n^2)$, while the other is in $O(n^{\log_2 3})$; the latter growth rate is "slower" since $n^{\log_2 3} \in o(n^2)$.

Expected-Case and Amortized Analysis

Worst-case analysis is not the only reasonable basis for evaluating the efficiency of an algorithm. A natural alternative is **expected-case analysis** (or, as it is often called, **average-case analysis**). An expected-case analysis would yield, as a function of the input size n, the time expected to be used by the algorithm—averaged over all possible inputs of size n. This might be a reasonable approach to studying a sorting algorithm, for example—there are a great many possible data sets of size, say, 100, and if the algorithm were slow on only a few of them we might weigh those bad cases in proportion to their frequency.

Unfortunately, expected-case analysis has several drawbacks.

1. We must be sure that we are taking the "average" in the same way that the users of the algorithm would do it. Suppose, for example, that of the $n!$ permutations of n numbers, our sorting algorithm is fast except on about 1% of them—the 1% where the numbers are nearly in order already. And suppose that the algorithm is being used in an environment in which 99% of the data sets that are actually sorted fall in that 1% of cases that are nearly in order. The algorithm might be fast in theory, but not in any practical sense. Thus to do an expected-case analysis properly one must know the distribution of the data on which the algorithm is actually used.

2. Expected-case analysis is in most cases more difficult mathematically than worst-case analysis. Thus we shall sometimes avoid it simply because it is too hard.

3. In some applications expected-case analysis is simply not appropriate. For example, consider an air-traffic control system that must complete a section of code that sorts 100 numbers within 1 second in order to avoid causing a catastrophic collision. It would be small comfort to know that the expected running time for that code was only 0.1 second, without having any guarantee about the worst-case running time!

Yet another alternative to worst-case analysis is **amortized analysis**. Amortized analysis gives guarantees about running time that are less strong than a worst-case analysis might provide, but stronger than an expected-case analysis. It provides an absolute guarantee of the total time taken by a sequence of calls on the algorithm. The bound on the total time for the sequence of calls provides a bound on the average time for each call in the sequence, but gives no guarantee about the time required for any individual call; some single calls may be very expensive, if there are enough inexpensive calls so that the total time is within the bound. Of course, in order for amortized analysis to be applicable, some data must persist from one call to the next, so that information about the condition of the data at the end of one call helps bound the time needed for a subsequent call.

As an example, consider the problem of counting in binary: 0000, 0001, 0010, 0011, 0100, ... Imagine that the bits are stored in separate memory cells, and we wish to calculate the total number of cells that must be accessed as a k-bit integer is incremented $2^k - 1$ times starting from 0 up to the largest k-bit value $11...1$. Consider any point in this process, and let v denote the value currently in the counter. If v is even, then only the low-order bit is changed, from 0 to 1. If the two low-order bits of v are 01, then there is a carry and these two bits are changed to 10. In general, if the l low-order bits are 0 followed by $l - 1$ bits which are 1, then these l bits, but no others, are changed. Of the 2^k patterns of k bits, 2^{k-1} of them have the low-order bit 0, 2^{k-2} of them have the low-order bits 01, and in general 2^{k-l} of them have the l low-order bits of the form $011...1$. Hence the total number of bit positions changed during a sequence of $2^k - 1$ incrementing operations is

$$2^{k-1} \cdot 1 + 2^{k-2} \cdot 2 + 2^{k-3} \cdot 3 + \cdots + 1 \cdot k.$$

This sum can be evaluated by methods like those used on page 36; the total is $2^{k+1} - k - 2$ (Problem 13). Thus the average number of bits changed during a single call in such a sequence of incrementing operations is guaranteed to be (Problem 14)

$$\frac{2^{k+1} - k - 2}{2^k - 1} < 2,$$

although the worst-case number of bits changed is k (when $011...1$ changes to $100...0$). If the sequence of operations is viewed as a whole, the cost of such expensive incrementing operations is spread out, or "amortized," over the more numerous less expensive calls.

Notice the difference between this analysis and an expected-case analysis. If we imagine a series of calls of the incrementing algorithm on *random* k-bit numbers, then the *expected* number of bits changed in any single call would again be a little less than 2. However, the expected-case analysis could not guarantee that during some unlucky sequences of calls the cost per call might not be much higher—we might by bad luck get a long sequence of calls to increment the "worst" number $011...1$. The conditions for the amortized analysis rule out this possibility, and therefore make it possible to establish a stronger result. A *worst-case* analysis would yield less information yet: all that can be said in the worst case is that incrementing a k-bit number changes at most k bits.

2.3 ALGORITHM PARADIGMS

Algorithms that solve very different problems sometimes bear a strong family resemblance to each other. For example, the general strategy of Divide-and-Conquer underlies Binary Search, Merge Sort, and the clever integer multiplication algorithm, as well as useful algorithms for many other problems. It is worth keeping the general idea of Divide-and-Conquer in mind when faced with new problems to solve. In this section we will give examples of several other general strategies for the design of algorithms.

Brute-Force and Exhaustive Search

In many algorithmic problems the objective is to find something: the object that best fits some criterion, or is least costly, or smallest, or largest. Determining whether a number is prime can be solved by finding a factor, or failing to do so. In the famous **Travelling Salesman Problem**, we are given a set of cities and all the distances between pairs of them, and are asked to design a tour through all the cities of minimal total length. (By a **tour**, we mean a trip that visits each city once and returns at the end to its starting point.)

The strategy of first invention, or last resort, is often to look through all the candidates until the desired object is found. We call such a strategy **brute-force search** or **exhaustive search**. For example, the most naïve algorithm for determining whether a number n is prime uses a brute-force strategy; it checks all the numbers from 2 to $n - 1$ in search of one that divides n. The term "exhaustive search" suggests a method that searches through all candidates, even after the right one has been found, because the right one cannot be recognized as such until all the possibilities have been checked. For example, an exhaustive-search strategy for the Travelling Salesman Problem would be to calculate the length of every possible tour through the cities, and choose the ordering of the cities for which the tour length is the shortest.

Such strategies are, almost by definition, to be avoided if possible; the goal of algorithm design is often to find ways of reducing the number of candidates that must be checked, since this number imposes a lower bound on the speed of any algorithm that searches through them all. For example, in the case of the Travelling Salesman Problem, there are

$$(n - 1)! \in \Omega(2^n)$$

possible tours for the travelling salesman through n cities; the exhaustive-search strategy is prohibitively expensive even for small n.

Exhaustive-search algorithms often take time that is exponential or worse in the size of the answer being sought. For example, if the answer consists of n numbers, and there are m possible values for each number, then there are m^n possible answers to check. To get a feel for how quickly an exponential search would get out of hand, consider Figure 2.2, which shows, for some small values of n, the values of several functions that commonly arise in algorithm analysis.

n	1	2	5	10	20	50
$\lceil \lg n \rceil$	0	1	3	4	5	6
$\lceil n \lg n \rceil$	0	2	12	34	87	283
n^2	1	4	25	100	400	2500
n^3	1	8	125	1000	8000	125000
2^n	2	4	32	1024	1048576	1.13×10^{15}
$n!$	1	2	120	3628800	2.43×10^{18}	3.04×10^{64}

Figure 2.2 Values of various functions for small values of the argument. By contrast with the size of the number in the lower right-hand corner of this table, consider that the number of instructions that could have been executed on the world's fastest computer is only 10^{27}—even if it had been running continuously since the birth of the universe!

Greedy Algorithms

A **greedy algorithm** is based on the following simple principle: when called on to make a sequence of choices to develop a solution to a problem, always make the choice that has the lowest immediately visible cost; don't try to look ahead to see if that choice might turn out to be more costly in the long run. The first thing to note about greedy algorithms is that, for most problems (as in most real-life situations!), they do not work. For example, a greedy strategy for the Travelling Salesman Problem would always choose to visit next the unvisited city that is nearest to the last city visited. It is easy to come up with examples in which this myopic strategy leads to a decidedly suboptimal tour; optimal tours often visit a more distant site before returning to a nearer one.

However for certain problems the greedy strategy actually does yield the correct result. As a first simple example, suppose we are presented with piles of coins of identical size but different monetary values (for example, some coins are gold, some silver, some copper, and so on, but all coins have the same physical dimensions). We also are given a knapsack, which can hold only so many coins, and are told that we can take away whatever we can carry in the knapsack. How should we fill the knapsack in order to maximize our winnings? Clearly a greedy strategy works. We should start by taking as many coins as we can of the maximum value; if we can fill the knapsack with these we are done. Otherwise, if we run out of coins of maximum value before we run out of room in the knapsack, we should follow the same strategy with the next most valuable coins, and repeat this method with successively lower denominations until the knapsack is filled.

Any other choice of coins must be suboptimal, since any other choice would have to include at least one less coin of some value v and omit at least one more coin of some value u, where $u > v$. Then simply substituting a coin of value u for a coin of value v would increase the total value by $u - v > 0$.

Another example in which the greedy strategy is successful arises in the domain of "job-shop scheduling." Imagine that n cars arrive at a gas station simultaneously, but there is only one pump, so the cars must line up and each car must wait for all the cars ahead of it in line to finish before it can be served. Suppose that we know in advance the time that is going to be needed by each car once it actually reaches the pump; say these times are $t_1, t_2, \ldots, t_n$, where $t_1 \leq t_2 \leq \cdots \leq t_n$. So the total time that will be required to serve all the cars is fixed; it is $t_1 + \cdots + t_n$. Still, the service station may be able to increase the "general happiness" by *minimizing the average time per car spent at the service station.* For example, if there are only two cars, and car 1 will need only one minute but car 2 will need ten, it makes sense to schedule car 1 first, since then the average waiting time will be $(1+11)/2 = 6.0$; in the other order the average would be $(10+11)/2 = 10.5$. Notice that, since the number n of cars is fixed, minimizing the average time spent by the cars really amounts to minimizing the sum of the times spent by all cars.

In general, the best strategy is to serve the cars in order of the time they will require, from smallest to largest; this is a greedy approach. Once again, any other ordering would be suboptimal. For in any other approach there would have to be two successive cars in line, say car A and car B, whose required service times are t and u, respectively, where $t > u$ even though car A is in line just before car B. Then swapping those two cars in the ordering would not affect the time spent by any of the cars before car A or after car B. But it would reduce the time spent by car B by t while increasing the time spent by car A by u; since $t > u$, this is a net reduction of $t - u > 0$ in the total time spent by all cars.

Dynamic Programming

A **dynamic programming** algorithm is based on a strategy of solving limited subproblems, saving the results, and then reusing those results several times when the same partial result is needed more than once in solving the main problem. By means of a dynamic programming strategy it is sometimes possible to turn a problem that seems to require exponential time into one of more manageable complexity.

Dynamic programming is often based on a recursive formula for solving larger problems in terms of smaller problems. A simple example of this strategy is the calculation of values of the Fibonacci function, defined on page 26 by the equations

$$F(0) = 0$$

$$F(1) = 1$$

$$F(n) = F(n-1) + F(n-2), \qquad \text{if } n \geq 2.$$

If these equations are used directly to calculate $F(n)$ from larger n to smaller by recursive substitution, it would take $\Omega(F(n)) = \Omega(\phi^n)$ time to calculate $F(n)$, since in the end $F(n)$ values of 1 must be added together to get the result. On the other hand if a table of length $n+1$ is set up to hold the values $F(0), \ldots,$ $F(n)$, and the values of $F(i)$ are calculated in the order $i = 0, 1, \ldots,$ then each value takes constant time to compute and the whole calculation takes time $O(n)$.

This example illustrates the basic characteristics of all dynamic programming algorithms: problems are solved from smaller to larger, so that the time taken by the algorithm depends on the number of subproblems and the time required to compute the answers to larger problems from the answers to the subproblems. In the case of the Fibonacci function, to compute $F(n)$ requires solving just $n+1$ problems, the first two of which are given—the values of $F(0)$ and $F(1)$—and the last $n-1$ of which take constant time to determine from the previously answered subproblems—a single addition of two known values is needed to determine $F(n)$ from $F(n-1)$ and $F(n-2)$.

0–1 Knapsack   As a more substantial example, consider the following variation on the knapsack problem, called the **0–1 Knapsack Problem**. Instead of coins of identical size but differing values, we are presented with a set of objects that vary in both size and value. What is the maximum value we can carry away, and how should we fill up our fixed-capacity knapsack in order to achieve that maximum value? (This is essentially the television "supermarket shopping spree" problem, in which contestants are allowed to take out of the store as much as they want that will fit into a shopping cart.)

This version of the Knapsack Problem has characteristics that were not present in the first version. Using a greedy strategy based on the value of items, or the value per unit size, does not work; it may be better to leave a valuable item behind if including it leaves some empty space in the knapsack that is too small to be used for anything else. A little experimentation with such anomalies suggests that an exhaustive-search strategy may be the only hope; but exhaustive search might be very expensive, since there are 2^n combinations of n items that might have to be checked. However, things might not be as bad as that.

Suppose that the n objects have sizes $s_1, \ldots, s_n$ and values $v_1, \ldots, v_n$, and that the knapsack has capacity C. We will assume that C and the v_i are all positive integers.

To solve this specific problem we begin by generalizing it. If $0 \leq i \leq n$ and $A \leq C$, let us define $V(k, A)$ to be the maximum value that can be carried in a knapsack of capacity A, given that we can choose the contents from among the first k objects. Thus $V(n, C)$ is the maximum value that can be carried in the original knapsack when we can choose from among all the items; we wish to determine $V(n, C)$, and how it can be achieved. Then $V(k, A) = 0$ if $k = 0$ or $A \leq 0$, and for any k the $V(k, A)$ are related to the $V(k-1, A')$ by the following recurrence relation:

$$V(k, A) = \max(V(k-1, A), V(k-1, A-s_k) + v_k). \qquad (5)$$

Equation (5) says that in solving the Knapsack Problem for k objects there are two choices for object number k; we can include it or leave it out. If we leave it out we can do the best job possible of filling our capacity of A from among the first $k - 1$ items. If we include it we can add its value to the value of the best set of choices from among the remaining $k - 1$ objects; but now the knapsack capacity is reduced to $A - s_k$. The best that can be done for the first k objects and capacity A is whichever of these two alternatives is superior.

Unfortunately, if we try to solve for $V(n, C)$ by recursive substitution using Equation (5), we find that two values of $V(n - 1, A)$ must be determined for different A, four values of $V(n - 2, A)$, and so on; since the number of values to be determined doubles at each level, it seems that determining $V(n, C)$ will require $\Omega(2^n)$ steps, no improvement over exhaustive search. However, many of these values are likely to be the same, if C is small by comparison with 2^n. So let us try starting from the other end, and calculating all the values of $V(0, A)$ for $A \leq C$, then all the values of $V(1, A)$, and so on. As these values are calculated, we store them in a table of $n + 1$ rows and C columns. As already noted, $V(0, A) = 0$ for all A; then once $V(k - 1, A)$ is known for all A, Equation (5) can be used to determine any $V(k, A)$ in constant time. So the total time to fill in the table is proportional to its size, that is, in $O(nC)$. When we are done filling in the table we simply check the value of the single entry $V(n, C)$. Unless we must solve instances of the problem in which C is exponential in n, this approach will be more efficient than the exhaustive-search or "top-down recursive" method.

Of course, we wanted to know not only the maximum value that can be put in the knapsack, but also which objects should be included to achieve that value. We can retain this information as well by letting $X_i(k, A)$ (where $1 \leq i \leq k$) be 1 or 0, depending on whether or not item i is included when the Knapsack Problem is solved for the first k objects and a knapsack of capacity A. A table of the values of $X_i(k, A)$ can also be calculated iteratively from the $X_i(k - 1, A')$ as Equation (5) is used to calculate the $V(k, A)$. The values of $X_i(n, C)$, where $1 \leq i \leq n$, answer the question of which objects to include and which to omit. (This is why the problem is called the "0–1 Knapsack Problem.")

Travelling Salesman Problem   It was noted earlier that there are $\Omega((n - 1)!)$ tours that would have to be checked in an exhaustive-search attack on the Travelling Salesman Problem; but if each were checked separately there would be many partial tours that would be rechecked many times. To be specific, let us number the cities from 1 to n, and (since tours are cyclical) let us consider just tours that begin and end at city 1. Let us write $d(i, j)$ for the distance from city i to city j. Then for any b, where $1 \leq b \leq n$, and for any set $S \subseteq \{1, \ldots, n\} - \{1, b\}$, let $D(b, S)$ be the length of the shortest path that starts at city b, then visits all the cities in S in some order, and then ends at city 1. Thus we want ultimately to determine $D(1, \{2, \ldots, n\})$, and the order of the cities that achieves it. We will calculate the $D(b, S)$ in order of the size of the set S, utilizing the fact that an optimal path from b through the cities in S to city 1 must consist, after its first step, of an optimal path from one of the cities in S, through the remainder of the cities in S, to city 1.

So let us try calculating these optimal paths, and their lengths, from the "bottom up." The $D(b, S)$ can be determined by the recurrence

$$D(b, S) = \min_{a \in S}\{d(b, a) + D(a, S - \{a\})\}, \tag{6a}$$

with the base case

$$D(b, \emptyset) = d(b, 1). \tag{6b}$$

That is, if the path is to start from b and visit all the cities in S it must begin with one of them, call it a; there is a unique value of the optimum length of the path starting with a, passing through the remainder of the cities, and ending at city 1, and that optimum does not depend on b.

Equation (6) can be used to calculate all the $D(b, S)$ by induction on the size of S, starting from the case in which S is empty and proceeding upwards until $S = \{2, \ldots, n\}$. There are at most $n \cdot 2^{n-1}$ values of $D(b, S)$ to determine, since there are n values of b and S is a subset of a set of size $n - 1$. Applying Equation (6a) once takes time that is $O(n)$ since the minimum of $|S| < n$ values must be found, and each value can be found in constant time if all the $D(b, S)$ are stored in a table. Thus the whole procedure takes time

$$O(n^2 2^{n-1}) \subseteq o(2^{(n-1)\lg n}),$$

so the dynamic programming method presents an improvement over exhaustive search. (Nonetheless, time $O(n^2 2^{n-1})$ is too large to permit efficient solution of the Travelling Salesman Problem for large n.) As in the case of the 0–1 Knapsack Problem, it is easy to modify this method so that it keeps track of the optimal paths at each stage as well as the lengths of those paths.

NP-Completeness

This book is dedicated to the development of efficient algorithms for a variety of computational problems; by ingenuity and analysis it is often possible to pass from an impractically slow algorithm to one that solves a problem with useful efficiency. But it is important not to hope for too much: there are some problems for which algorithms exist, but for which we know that no efficient algorithm can exist. We don't consider an algorithm to be "efficient" unless it runs in **polynomial time**, that is, time $O(n^k)$ for some fixed value of k. Certainly we consider an algorithm to be inefficient if its running time is $\Omega(2^n)$ on problems of size n, since the running time of such an algorithm would double or more, in the worst case, every time the input increases in size by adding 1. It has been mathematically proven (not simply observed as the result of repeated failed efforts) that for certain problems, *every* possible algorithm runs in time that increases at least exponentially with the size of the input.

Between the problems that admit efficient solution and the problems that are known to have no efficient algorithms are a variety of mysterious problems for which no efficient algorithms have been discovered, but for which efficient algorithms are not known to be impossible. The most famous problems of this type are the **NP-complete** problems, a class which includes both the Travelling Salesman Problem and the 0–1 Knapsack Problem (with no restriction on the size of the numbers involved, so that the dynamic programming algorithm does not lead to an efficient method). All NP-complete problems have the common characteristic that they can be solved by brute-force search through an exponentially large set of candidate solutions. For example, in the case of the Travelling Salesman Problem the candidate solutions are the tours (there are $(n - 1)!$ of them), and in the case of the Knapsack Problem the candidate solutions are selections of items (there are 2^n of them). Of course, there are also many easy problems that can be solved by exhaustive search; what distinguishes the NP-complete problems is that no essentially better algorithm is known for any of them. Moreover all of them are in a certain precise sense computationally equivalent to each other: finding a polynomial-time algorithm for any of them would imply the existence of polynomial-time algorithms for all of them. As no such efficient algorithm has been discovered for any NP-complete problem, all are believed to be computationally intractable. But this has not been proved, in spite of extensive research, and remains one of the great open problems of computer science.

Problems

2.1   **1.** For what numbers less than 1000 does the test (1) on page 47 give the wrong answer?

2. Find the smallest input m such that the value of n exceeds 100 during the execution of Algorithm 2.1 on page 48.

2.2   **3. a.** For what values of n, if any, is it true that *every* product of two n-bit integers is an integer of *fewer* than $2n$ bits?

b. For what values of m and n, if any, is it true that *every* product of an m-bit integer and an n-bit integer is an integer of *fewer* than $m + n$ bits?

4. a. Write the grade school algorithm for the addition of two nonnegative integers in binary notation. The algorithm should take as arguments two tables of bits, not necessarily of the same length, and return a table of bits one longer than the length of its longer input.

b. Show that this algorithm runs in time linear in the length of the longer of its arguments.

    c. Repeat parts (a) and (b) for subtraction of two integers. Assume that the value of the first argument is greater than or equal to the value of the second argument, so that there is no possibility of producing a negative answer.

    d. Write the procedure $Accum(A[0..m-1], B[0..n-1])$, which adds the value represented by A into the table B. (You may assume that $n > m$ and that overflow is impossible.)

5. Rewrite the grade school multiplication algorithm so that it works on decimal (base 10) integers.

6. Program the grade school and clever integer multiplication algorithms, and determine empirically for what size integers, if any, the clever algorithm is in practice faster than the grade school method. Does the choice of base affect the threshold value?

7. Rewrite the grade school multiplication algorithm so that it takes as arguments two integers of different sizes, say m and n bits. Try to make the algorithm as efficient as possible; what is the order of the time complexity of your version, as a function of m and n?

8. Why does the clever multiplication algorithm switch to a nonrecursive method to multiply integers of three or fewer bits? What happens if line (1) is replaced by "**if** $n \leq 2$ ..."?

9. Carefully derive Equation (4) on page 55 from Equations (2) and (3) and the Big-O Theorem.

10. Show that if n-bit numbers x and y are split into 3 parts x_L, x_M, x_R and y_L, y_M, and y_R, the product $x \cdot y$ can be computed with the aid of the 5 recursive products $x_L \cdot y_L$, and $(x_L + e \cdot x_M + x_R) \cdot (y_L + e \cdot y_M + y_R)$ and $(x_L + e \cdot 2x_M + 4x_R) \cdot (y_L + e \cdot 2y_M + 4y_R)$ for $e = \pm 1$. What is the time complexity of the resulting algorithm?

11. This problem concerns calculation of the **greatest common divisor** $\gcd(m, n)$ of two positive integers m and n, that is, the largest number that divides both evenly. For example, $\gcd(28, 42) = 14$. We consider algorithms that take the numbers m and n themselves as inputs (rather than tables representing the binary notations of these numbers).

    a. The simplest approach to finding the greatest common divisor is simply to search for it, starting from the smaller of m and n and counting down. Write this algorithm, and analyze its time complexity.

    b. A better method, called **Euclid's algorithm**, has been known since antiquity (Algorithm 2.4). Trace the operation of Euclid's algorithm on inputs 28 and 42; on inputs 200 and 99; and on inputs 111 and 191.

function *Euclid*(**integer** m, n): **integer**
{Return greatest common divisor of positive integers m and n}
> $a \leftarrow m$
> $b \leftarrow n$
>   **while** $b \neq 0$ **do**
> $$\begin{pmatrix} a \\ b \end{pmatrix} \leftarrow \begin{pmatrix} b \\ a \bmod b \end{pmatrix}$$
>   **return** a

Algorithm 2.4 Euclid's algorithm for the common divisor of two positive integers.

---

    c. Show that *if* Euclid's algorithm terminates, it must produce the true greatest common divisor. (Hint: Show that each iteration of the loop does not change $\gcd(a, b)$.)

    d. Show that Euclid's algorithm terminates, by showing that the value of b decreases on each iteration.

    e. Part (d) shows that Euclid's algorithm runs in time $O(n)$, but in fact it terminates much more quickly than that, as the examples of part (b) suggest. Show that in fact the algorithm terminates in time logarithmic in the smaller of its arguments. (Hint: Show that if a_0, b_0 and a_1, b_1 are the values of a and b on two successive iterations of the loop and $a_0 > b_0$, then either $a_1 < \frac{2}{3} a_0$ or $b_1 < \frac{2}{3} b_0$.)

    f. Give as exact a formula as you can for the running time of Euclid's algorithm, in terms of constants representing the time required to execute each of the five lines of Algorithm 2.4.

12. This problem continues Problem 11 on algorithms for finding the greatest common divisor. Define $a \operatorname{smod} b$ to be the integer r with the smallest absolute value such that $a - r$ is divisible by b. For example, $10 \operatorname{smod} 3 = 10 \bmod 3 = 1$, but $11 \operatorname{smod} 3 = -1$. Show that if we replace "mod" with "smod" in Euclid's algorithm, the algorithm still terminates and correctly computes the greatest common divisor. Determine the running time of this modified Euclid's algorithm.

13. Show that the sum on page 58 has the value $2^{k+1} - k - 2$.

14. Show that, for all $k > 0$,

$$\frac{2^{k+1} - k - 2}{2^k - 1} < 2.$$

2.3 **15.** Let $T(n)$ be the running time of *Fum(n)*. Find the order of T (that is, find a function $f(n)$ such that $T \in \Theta(f)$). (Assume that real arithmetic is carried out exactly, and is not subject to floating-point roundoff errors.)

> **procedure** *Fum*(**integer** n):
>   **for** i **from** 1 **to** n **do**
> $\delta \leftarrow 1/i$
> $x \leftarrow i$
>   **while** $x > 0$ **do**
> $x \leftarrow x - \delta$

16. Let $T(n)$ be the running time of *Foo(n)*. Find the order of T.

> **procedure** *Foo*(**integer** n):
>   **for** i **from** 1 **to** n **do**
> $x \leftarrow n$
>   **while** $x > 0$ **do**
> $x \leftarrow x - i$

17. Let $T(n)$ be the running time of *Mystery(n)*. Find the order of T.

> **procedure** *Mystery*(**integer** n):
>   **for** i **from** 1 **to** $n - 1$ **do**
>   **for** j **from** $i + 1$ **to** n **do**
>   **for** k **from** 1 **to** j **do** $x \leftarrow x + 1$

18. Let $T(n)$ be the running time of *Peculiar(n)*. Find the order of T.

> **procedure** *Peculiar*(**integer** n):
>   **for** $i \leftarrow 1$ **to** n **do**
>   **if** i is odd **then**
>   **for** j **from** i **to** n **do** $x \leftarrow x + 1$
>   **for** j **from** 1 **to** i **do** $y \leftarrow y + 1$

19. Let $T(n)$ be the running time of *What(n)*. Find the order of T.

> **procedure** *What*(**integer** n):
>   **for** i **from** 1 **to** $\lfloor \sqrt{n} \rfloor$ **do**
>   **for** j **from** 1 **to** $\lfloor \sqrt{n} \rfloor$ **do**
>   **for** k **from** 1 **to** $\lfloor \sqrt{n} \rfloor - j + 1$ **do** $x \leftarrow x + 1$

20. Let $T(n)$ be the running time of *Puzzle(n)*. Find the order of T.

> **procedure** *Puzzle*(**integer** n):
>   **for** i **from** 1 **to** n **do**
>   **for** j **from** 1 **to** 10 **do**
>   **for** k **from** n **to** $n + 5$ **do** $x \leftarrow x + 1$

21. Devise a simple example in which the greedy strategy for the Travelling Salesman Problem does not work. You don't need to write any numbers; it should suffice just to arrange six dots on a piece of paper and to give an explanation.

22. How much *memory* is used by the dynamic programming algorithm for the Travelling Salesman Problem?

23. Explain how the dynamic programming algorithm for the Travelling Salesman Problem can be modified to return the optimal path as well as the length of that path.

24. Here is a "divide-and-conquer" style algorithm for the Travelling Salesman Problem that takes more time, but much less memory, than the dynamic programming algorithm. (It takes *less* time than the brute-force, exhaustive-search method.) Consider some instance of the Travelling Salesman Problem with n cities and with $d(i, j)$ being the distance from city i to city j. If $n \leq 3$ the problem can be solved directly, so assume $n > 3$. If $a, b \in S$, let $D(S, a, b)$ be the minimum length of a path that starts at a, visits each city in S exactly once, and ends at b. We calculate the minimal cost of a tour by finding the minimum value of $D(\{1, \ldots, n\}, 1, j) + d(j, 1)$ for $2 \leq j \leq n$. To find $D(S, a, b)$, where S has more than 3 elements, we proceed as follows. Let c be any city in $S - \{a, b\}$ (c will be in the "center" of the path from a to b), let $T = S - \{a, b, c\}$, let A be any subset of T of size $\lfloor |T|/2 \rfloor$, and let $B = T - A$. Calculate $D(A \cup \{a, c\}, a, c)$ and $D(B \cup \{c, b\}, c, b)$ recursively, and let $D(S, a, b)$ be the minimum of the sums $D(A \cup \{a, c\}, a, c) + D(B \cup \{c, b\}, c, b)$, for all such choices of c and A.

a. Explain why this algorithm always finds the cost of the minimal-cost tour.

b. If $T(n)$ is the running time of this algorithm on problems with n cities, show that $T(n) \in O(n^c 2^{2n})$ for some constant c.

c. Show that the amount of memory required by this algorithm is linear in n. (Hint: This requires explicitly managing the stack implicit in the recursive description of the algorithm. It also requires using a bit vector representation of sets such that if $S_1 \subseteq S_2 \subseteq \cdots \subseteq S_k = \{1, \ldots, n\}$ and each S_i is about half as big as S_{i+1}, then S_k does not need to be represented at all, S_{k-1} is represented as a bit vector of length n, and each S_i for $1 \leq i < k - 1$ is represented by a bit vector about half as long as that representing S_{i+1}.)

25. Consider the problem of multiplying two $n \times n$ matrices A and B to produce an $n \times n$ matrix $C = AB$ as the result. The usual algorithm calculates each entry of C as the dot product of a row of A and a column of B:

$$c_{ij} = \sum_{k=1}^{n} a_{ik}b_{kj}.$$

Since one dot product takes n multiplications, this method uses n^3 multiplications in all, and the time complexity of the multiplication algorithm is therefore $O(n^3)$. However, if n is even then C can also be computed by breaking A and B into square quarters and recursively "block multiplying" those quarters:

$$\begin{pmatrix} A_{11} & A_{12} \\ A_{21} & A_{22} \end{pmatrix} \begin{pmatrix} B_{11} & B_{12} \\ B_{21} & B_{22} \end{pmatrix} = \begin{pmatrix} C_{11} & C_{12} \\ C_{21} & C_{22} \end{pmatrix},$$

where $C_{ij} = A_{i1}B_{1j} + A_{i2}B_{2j}$ for $1 \leq i \leq 2$ and $1 \leq j \leq 2$.

a. Assume for convenience that n is a power of 2. Show that this recursive matrix multiplication algorithm takes n^3 multiplications.

b. Remarkably, the four quarters of C can be calculated with the aid of only *seven* matrix multiplications, instead of the eight that seem to be required. Let

$$M_1 = (A_{21} + A_{22} - A_{11})(B_{22} - B_{12} + B_{11})$$

$$M_2 = A_{11}B_{11}$$

$$M_3 = A_{12}B_{21}$$

$$M_4 = (A_{11} - A_{21})(B_{22} - B_{12})$$

$$M_5 = (A_{21} - A_{22})(B_{12} - B_{11})$$

$$M_6 = (A_{12} - A_{21} + A_{11} - A_{22})B_{22}$$

$$M_7 = A_{22}(B_{11} + B_{22} - B_{12} - B_{21}).$$

Show that each C_{ij} can be calculated by adding and subtracting certain of the M_k.

c. Show that using this method, called **Strassen's algorithm**, multiplication of $n \times n$ matrices can be done in time $o(n^3)$.

26. Write a function *FastExp* such that $FastExp(x, n) = x^n$ for any real number x and for any $n \in \mathbf{N}$ and such that $FastExp(x, n)$ performs at most $2 \lg n$ multiplications.

References

The "3n + 1 problem" (the question of whether Algorithm 2.1 terminates for all inputs) has been in circulation at least since the early 1950s, though its exact origin is obscure. It has stimulated much research, but remains a great puzzle. The mathematician Paul Erdös commented that "Mathematics is not yet ready for such problems." For a good survey, see

J. C. Lagarias, "The $3x + 1$ problem and its Generalizations," *American Mathematical Monthly* **92** (1985), pp. 3–23.

The integer multiplication algorithm described on page 51 was first presented in

A. Karatsuba and Y. Ofman, "Multiplication of Multidigit Numbers on Automata," *Doklady Akademii Nauk SSSR* **45** (1962), pp. 293–294.

This method can be extended to produce, for any k, an $O(n^{\log_k(2k-1)})$ time multiplication algorithm for n-bit numbers (see Problem 10), and can be extended yet further, by using the Fast Fourier Transform, to give an algorithm that runs in time $O(n \log n \log \log n)$. See

A. Schönhage and V. Strassen, "Schnelle Multiplikation Grosser Zahlen," *Computing* **7** (1971), pp. 281–292.

The dynamic programming algorithm for the Travelling Salesman Problem (page 64) was first described in

R. Bellman, "Dynamic Programming Treatment of the Travelling Salesman Problem," *Journal of the ACM* **9** (1962), pp. 61–63.

The space-efficient algorithm for the Travelling Salesman Problem given in Problem 24 is from

Y. Gurevich and S. Shelah, "Expected Computation Time for Hamiltonian Path Problem," *SIAM Journal on Computing* **16** (1987), pp. 486–502.

Strassen's matrix multiplication algorithm (Problem 25) is from

V. Strassen, "Gaussian Elimination Is Not Optimal," *Numerische Mathematik* **13** (1969), pp. 254–356.

Many improvements in the exponent for matrix multiplication have been made since Strassen's discovery, and as of this writing the best algorithm has time complexity $O(n^{2.376\cdots})$. However, the multiplicative constant hidden by the big-O notation is so enormous that the conventional method is superior for calculations of realistic proportions.

A classic of computer science is

M. R. Garey and D. S. Johnson, *Computers and Intractability: A Guide to the Theory of NP-Completeness,* W. H. Freeman and Company, 1979.

This book is mainly devoted to the study of the NP-complete problems and contains very readable sections on their history and characteristics. However, the book also has some material of a more positive character; for example, it presents in §4.2 the method we describe on page 62 for the 0–1 Knapsack Problem. More information on the classification of computational problems can be found in

H. R. Lewis and C. H. Papadimitriou, *Elements of the Theory of Computation,* Prentice-Hall Publishing Company, 1981.

3

Lists

3.1 LIST OPERATIONS

Abstractly, a **list** L is simply an ordered sequence of elements $\langle x_0, \ldots, x_{n-1} \rangle$. The **length** of the list L is denoted by $|L|$; thus $|\langle x_0, \ldots, x_{n-1} \rangle| = n$. The length can be any nonnegative integer, including 0; if the length is 0, L is the **empty list** $\langle \rangle$. We use the notation $L[i]$ for the ith element of list L, provided that $0 \le i < |L|$.

We shall discuss representations of lists in general in order to consider alternative implementations of the abstract data types that can be viewed as lists. In general, all imaginable operations can be implemented using even the simplest of list representations. However, the efficiency of some of the operations can be improved substantially by using more sophisticated representations.

Although we shall not define a single abstract data type of "lists," the following list operations will be used, in various combinations, to define abstract data types of special kinds of lists:

$Access(L, i)$: Return $L[i]$. (An error results if i is out of range, that is, less than 0 or greater $|L| - 1$. In general we shall not specify the result of such illegal operations.)

$Length(L)$: Return $|L|$.

$Concat(L_1, L_2)$: Return the result of concatenating L_1 with L_2; that is, if $L_1 = \langle x_0, \ldots, x_{n-1} \rangle$ and $L_2 = \langle y_0, \ldots, y_{m-1} \rangle$, then $Concat(L_1, L_2)$ returns the combined list

$$\langle x_0, \ldots, x_{n-1}, y_0, \ldots, y_{m-1} \rangle.$$

$MakeEmptyList()$: Return the empty list $\langle \rangle$.

$IsEmptyList(L)$: Return **true** if $|L| = 0$, **false** otherwise.

Applications requiring all these operators in full generality are unusual. However, two special types of lists are of great importance. A **stack** is a list that can be modified only by adding and removing items at one end; we picture a stack as a pile of data items, which can be changed only at the top. Adding a

73

new item to the top of a stack is called **pushing** the item, and removing the top item is called **popping** it. Stacks are also referred to as **last-in-first-out** (**LIFO**) lists, since the item removed at any point is the last item inserted that has not already been removed. As we shall see, the importance of stacks emanates from the fact that they are the fundamental data structure used to implement recursion. Thus a recursive algorithm may require a stack as an implicit data structure, which may not be visible at first. The abstract operations for the stack abstract data type are:

Top(L): Return the last element of L; same as $Access(L, |L| - 1)$. (An error results if L is empty.)

Pop(L): Remove and return the last element of L; that is, return $Top(L)$ and replace L by $\langle L[0], \ldots, L[|L| - 2] \rangle$. (An error results if L is empty.)

Push(x, L): Add x at the end of L; that is, replace L by $Concat(L, \langle x \rangle)$.

MakeEmptyStack( ): Return the empty list $\langle \rangle$.

IsEmptyStack(L): Return **true** if $|L| = 0$, **false** otherwise.

The operation *Push(x, L)* modifies the list L; thus it is not a mathematical function, like *Length* or *Concat*. Likewise, *Pop(L)* both returns a value and modifies L as a side-effect. Note that some of these operations are simply re-namings of general list operations; for example, *MakeEmptyStack* is a synonym for *MakeEmptyList*.

A **queue** is a list that can be modified only by removing items from one end (the front) and by adding them to the other end (the back). Queues are also called **first-in-first-out** (**FIFO**) lists, since the item removed at any point is the earliest item inserted that has not already been removed. The abstract operations for a queue data structure are:

Enqueue(x, L): Add x at the end of L; that is, replace L by $Concat(L, \langle x \rangle)$.

Dequeue(L): Remove and return the first element of L; that is, replace L by $\langle L[1], \ldots, L[|L| - 1] \rangle$ and return $L[0]$. (An error results if L is empty.)

Front(L): Return the first element of L; that is, return $L[0]$. (An error results if L is empty.)

MakeEmptyQueue( ): Return the empty list $\langle \rangle$.

IsEmptyQueue(L): Return **true** if $|L| = 0$, **false** otherwise.

By using these abstract operators, programs manipulating stacks and queues can be written without making reference to whether the "top," "bottom," or "front" is the end with the small indices or that with large indices, whether the list is stored in computer memory as a contiguous table or some kind of linked structure, and the like. Indeed, the internal structure of the stack or queue can be changed simply by changing the implementations of the abstract operations, without changing the program that invokes those operations.

3.2 BASIC LIST REPRESENTATIONS

Two kinds of internal representations are natural for lists and their special varieties: contiguous-memory representations and linked representations. In a **contiguous-memory representation**, the list elements are stored in a table whose size is fixed and greater than or equal to the maximum length of the list to be represented. Adjacency in the table represents (more or less directly) adjacency in the list; a fixed amount of additional information (including, for example, the size of the representation of a single list element) is needed to specify exactly the correspondence between list positions and table positions. By contrast, in a **linked representation**, the list elements can be scattered arbitrarily in memory; list elements carry with them pointers to one or both of their neighbors. Linked representations are more flexible than contiguous-memory representations, because only the pointers need to be adjusted in order to insert or delete elements, and because the maximum size of a list is bounded only by the total memory available, whether or not it forms a single contiguous block; but contiguous-memory representations are more efficient than linked representations, in bytes required per list element, because the memory for pointers is not needed.

Let us look at natural representations of stacks and queues in contiguous memory. In these and all subsequent algorithms in this chapter, we assume that the items to be kept in the list are of a data type **info**; we make no assumptions about the size, nature, or internals of these objects. The list itself is created by the functions *MakeEmptyStack* and *MakeEmptyQueue* and is passed to the other routines as a pointer L. Depending on the implementation, this pointer might point to the first node of a linked list, or to a special record structure that captures important information about the extent of the list.

Stack Representation in Contiguous Memory

Given a stack $L = \langle x_0, \ldots, x_{n-1} \rangle$ and a table $A[0 \ldots N-1]$, we can store x_i in $A[i]$, so that the stack occupies $A[0 \ldots n-1]$, with the bottom stack element at $A[0]$ and the top stack element at $A[n-1]$. In addition to the table A itself, we need to keep track of the location of the top of the stack, or equivalently, the size n of the stack. That is to say, the stack is represented as a record with two components: the table $A = \mathsf{Infos}(L)$ and its current length, an integer $n = \mathsf{Length}(L)$. The stack is empty if $n = 0$, and is full if $n = N$. Then the stack operations can be implemented as shown in Algorithm 3.1. With this implementation each stack operation uses $\Theta(1)$ time, independent of the size of the stack, since an operation changes only one or two memory cells.

Queue Representation in Contiguous Memory

Since additions and removals occur at opposite ends of a queue, if the position of an element remains stationary from the time it is enqueued until it has been dequeued then the queue as a whole will seem to "crawl" gradually in memory.

---

function *MakeEmptyStack*( ): **pointer**
    $L \leftarrow NewCell(\text{Stack})$
    $\text{Length}(L) \leftarrow 0$
    return L

function *IsEmptyStack*(**pointer** L): **boolean**
    return $\text{Length}(L) = 0$

function *Top*(**pointer** L): **info**
    if *IsEmptyStack*(L) **then error**
    else return $\text{Infos}(L)[\text{Length}(L) - 1]$

function *Pop*(**pointer** L): **info**
    if $\text{Length}(L) = 0$ **then error**
    else
        $x \leftarrow Top(L)$
        $\text{Length}(L) \leftarrow \text{Length}(L) - 1$
        return x

procedure *Push*(**info** x, **pointer** L):
    if $\text{Length}(L) = N$ **then error**
    else
        $\text{Length}(L) \leftarrow \text{Length}(L) + 1$
        $\text{Infos}(L)[\text{Length}(L) - 1] \leftarrow x$

Algorithm 3.1 Contiguous-memory implementation of stack operations. The stack is represented by a pointer L to a record with two components: a table $\text{Infos}(L)$ and its current length $\text{Length}(L)$. The maximum length N is a constant.

We could move the whole queue each time an item is removed to keep one end anchored against the end of the table, but this would require $\Theta(|L|)$ work each time an element was dequeued. Instead we picture the table as circular, with the first element immediately following the last element; such a structure is sometimes called a **ring buffer** (Figure 3.1). Again let $A[0..N-1]$ be a table. To keep track of the position of the queue elements in the ring buffer, we can remember F (for *Front*), the position in the table of x_0, and $n = |L|$. Thus $x_0, x_1, \ldots, x_{n-1}$ are stored in $A[F]$, $A[(F+1) \bmod N]$, $A[(F+2) \bmod N]$, $\ldots, A[(F+n-1) \bmod N]$. There are N different representations for the empty queue, but from the standpoint of our abstract operations this fact is hidden. The queue itself is a record of the three components $A = \text{Infos}(L)$, $F = \text{Front}(L)$, and $n = \text{Length}(L)$, and the operations are implemented as shown in Algorithm 3.2. Each queue operation takes $\Theta(1)$ time in this implementation.

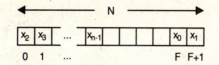

Figure 3.1 Ring buffer implementation of a queue. The queue currently has n elements; element x_i is located at position $(F + i) \bmod N$.

---

function *MakeEmptyQueue*( ): **pointer**
   $L \leftarrow NewCell(\text{Queue})$
   Front(L) $\leftarrow 0$
   Length(L) $\leftarrow 0$
   return L

function *IsEmptyQueue*(**pointer** L): **boolean**
   return Length(L) $= 0$

function *Dequeue*(**pointer** L): **info**
   if *IsEmptyQueue*(L) **then error**
   else
       $x \leftarrow$ Infos(L)[Front(L)]
       Front(L) $\leftarrow$ (Front(L) $+ 1$) mod N
       Length(L) $\leftarrow$ Length(L) $- 1$
       return x

procedure *Enqueue*(**info** x, **pointer** L):
   if Length(L) $= N$ **then error**
   else
       Length(L) $\leftarrow$ Length(L) $+ 1$
       Infos(L)[(Front(L) $+$ Length(L) $- 1$) mod N] $\leftarrow x$

procedure *Front*(**pointer** L):
   if *IsEmptyQueue*(L) **then error**
   else return Infos(L)[Front(L)]

Algorithm 3.2 Ring buffer implementation of queue operations. Each Queue has three components: a table Infos, an integer Front, and an integer Length.

Stack Representation in Linked Memory

A stack can be implemented as a linked list of nodes with a single pointer in each node; the top of the stack corresponds to the beginning of the linked list (Figure 3.2). Thus following the pointer chain would correspond to going *down* into the stack, and pushing an element corresponds to adding a new node to the beginning of the list. The linked list nodes have two fields, Next for the

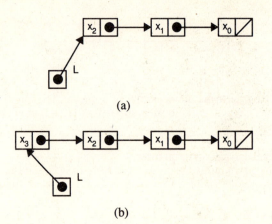

(a)

(b)

Figure 3.2 Linked list implementation of a stack. (a) Stack containing x_2, x_1, and x_0, with x_2 on top and x_0 on bottom; L points to top of stack. (b) Stack of part (a) after $Push(x_3, L)$.

---

function *MakeEmptyStack*( ): **pointer**
    return Λ

function *IsEmptyStack*(**pointer** L): **boolean**
    return $L = \Lambda$

function *Top*(**pointer** L): **info**
    if *IsEmptyStack*(L) **then error**
    else return Info(L)

function *Pop*(**locative** L): **info**
    if *IsEmptyStack*(L) **then error**
    else
        $x \leftarrow Top(L)$
        $L \Leftarrow \text{Next}(L)$
        return x

procedure *Push*(**info** x, **locative** L):
    $P \leftarrow NewCell(\text{Node})$
    Info(P) $\leftarrow x$
    Next(P) $\leftarrow L$
    $L \Leftarrow P$

Algorithm 3.3 Linked list implementation of stack operations. The stack is represented as a the address of the linked list cell containing the top element of the stack, or Λ if the stack is empty.

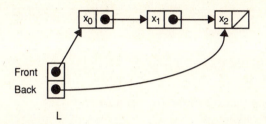

Figure 3.3 Linked queue representation. The queue is passed as a pointer to a record of type Queue, which has pointers to both the first and the last elements in the queue; the queue is empty if both these pointers are Λ.

pointer and Info for the stack entry itself. The stack operations can then be implemented as shown in Algorithm 3.3. The variable L points to the first cell in the linked list, and is Λ if the list is empty. This variable is passed to certain of the routines as a locative so that the state of the list can be altered from inside the routines. A linked list node (with Info and Next fields) is a record of type Node. We shall follow the convention in the future of always using Node as the name of the record from which a dynamic data structure is constructed.

Of course one may wonder why a linked representation would ever be used; since the relative order of items deep in a stack cannot be changed, there would seem to be no need for the flexibility that a linked representation provides. But with a linked implementation a stack can be used without knowing its maximum size in advance. Linked stacks can also be used to help search a data structure by temporarily altering the data structure itself; Algorithm 4.7 on page 115 and Algorithm 10.2 on page 348 illustrate this technique.

Queue Representation in Linked Memory

A queue can also be represented by a linked list, but the list header record is a record with two fields: Front(L) points to the first record in the list and Back(L) points to the last record in the list (Figure 3.3). If the list is empty then both are Λ. An element is dequeued from the front of the list by ordinary linked list deletion; an element is enqueued at the end of the list, with the Back pointer advancing to point to the new last element. With this implementation all operations take constant time (Algorithm 3.4).

3.3 STACKS AND RECURSION

The use of recursion adds considerable expressive power to the language we use for describing algorithms. It is important to realize, however, that this power generally does not come without some cost. When recursion is implemented on a von Neumann computer, a stack is used to do the bookkeeping about how far

---

function *MakeEmptyQueue*( ): **pointer**
    $L \leftarrow NewCell$(Queue)
    Front(L) $\leftarrow$ Back(L) $\leftarrow \Lambda$
    return L

function *IsEmptyQueue*(**pointer** L): **boolean**
    return Front(L) $= \Lambda$

procedure *Enqueue*(**info** x, **pointer** L):
    $P \leftarrow NewCell$(Node)
    Info(P) $\leftarrow x$
    Next(P) $\leftarrow \Lambda$
    if *IsEmptyQueue*(L) **then** Front(L) $\leftarrow P$
    else Next(Back(L)) $\leftarrow P$
    Back(L) $\leftarrow P$

function *Dequeue*(**pointer** L): **info**
    if *IsEmptyQueue*(L) **then error**
    else
        $x \leftarrow$ Info(Front(L))
        Front(L) $\leftarrow$ Next(Front(L))
        if Front(L) $= \Lambda$ **then** Back(L) $\leftarrow \Lambda$
        return x

function *Front*(**pointer** L): **info**
    if *IsEmptyQueue*(L) **then error**
    else return Info(Front(L))

Algorithm 3.4 Linked list implementation of queue operations. A Queue record has two fields, Front and Back, which point to linked list nodes; the queue is empty when these pointers are both Λ.

---

the execution has proceeded and what remains to be completed after the current invocation of the subprogram is finished. Since the size of the stack increases with the depth of recursion, algorithm analysis that takes memory usage into account must remember to measure the size of this "hidden" data structure.

The reason that a stack is the appropriate structure for keeping track of recursive invocations of subprograms is that *subprogram invocations end in the opposite order from their beginning*; that is, at any point in time, if an invocation of a subprogram finishes, the one that finishes is the last one that began but has not already finished. This is exactly the "last-in–first-out" property of stacks.

To be more precise, we sketch below how we could transform a recursive algorithm into a nonrecursive algorithm that uses a stack. (Programming language compilers do something like this, though a good deal more cleverly and

procedure *MergeSort*:
{Sort $T[a .. b]$ by the merge sort algorithm}
{On entry, T, a, b, and the return address are on the stack}
 Leave space on the stack for the local variable *middle*
 if $a \geq b$ **then goto** *CommonExit*
 middle $\leftarrow \lfloor (a + b)/2 \rfloor$
 {First recursive call}
 Push(return1, S); *Push(T, S)*; *Push(a, S)*; *Push(middle, S)*
 goto *MergeSort*
return1 :
 {Second recursive call}
 Push(return2, S); *Push(T, S)*; *Push(middle + 1, S)*; *Push(b, S)*
 goto *MergeSort*
return2 :
 Merge(T[a .. middle], T[middle + 1 .. b], T[a .. b])
 {This turns into more pushes and a branch to *Merge*}
CommonExit :
 Discard the local variables and arguments from the stack
 Pop and branch to the return address

Algorithm 3.5 The Merge Sort algorithm, recoded iteratively by using a stack.

systematically than this sketch suggests.) To take a concrete example, let us focus on Merge Sort (page 29). The call *MergeSort(T[a .. b])* results either in an immediate **return**, if $a \geq b$, or in two recursive calls, *MergeSort(T[a .. middle])* and *MergeSort(T[middle + 1 .. b])*, where *middle* is the value $\lfloor (a + b)/2 \rfloor$ (followed by an implicit **return** at the end of the algorithm). In general, the text of a recursive algorithm has certain places where it or other algorithms are *called*, and certain places where it *returns*. To transform the recursive algorithm into an iterative, stack-based algorithm, both the calls and the returns must be replaced by stack operations.

 Each *call* is replaced by statements to push a return address onto the stack, to push the arguments onto the stack, and then to branch to the beginning of the called algorithm. Conversely, each *return* is replaced by a statement that pops the arguments off the stack and discards them, and then pops the return address off the stack and branches to that return address. Algorithm 3.5 shows the translation.

 Local variables, such as *middle* in *MergeSort*, also occupy space on the stack; this is because if there are several nested invocations of *MergeSort* that have not been returned from, then the value of *middle* associated with each invocation will be needed later. Space for such variables is allocated on the stack after the procedure has been entered.

---

function *BinarySearch*: **integer**
{Search $T[a..b]$ for key K and return its index}
{On entry, T, a, b, and K are on the stack}
    Leave room on the stack for *middle*
    if $a > b$ **then**
        ReturnValue $\leftarrow -1$
        goto *CommonExit*
    middle $\leftarrow \lfloor (a+b)/2 \rfloor$
    if $w = T[middle]$ **then**
        ReturnValue $\leftarrow$ *middle*
        goto *CommonExit*
    if $w < T[middle]$ **then**
        Push(CommonExit, S)
        Push(T, S); *Push(a, S)*; *Push(middle − 1, S)*; *Push(K, S)*
        goto *BinarySearch*
    else
        Push(CommonExit, S)
        Push(T, S); *Push(middle + 1, S)*; *Push(b, S)*; *Push(K, S)*
        goto *BinarySearch*
CommonExit:
    Discard values of local variables and arguments from stack
    Pop and branch to the return address

Algorithm 3.6 Binary search algorithm compiled into iterative code using a stack.

In Algorithm 3.5 there are references to the variables, such as T, a, and *middle*, which are actually not stored in fixed locations in memory but instead exist in multiple versions on the stack. What makes the stack work in this situation is that the algorithm needs to see only one copy of these variables at a time, namely, the set that was most recently put on the stack. Therefore a compiler, knowing where the stack pointer is kept and in what order the variables have been pushed on the stack, can replace references to the variables by name ("T", "*middle*", etc.) with references to the locations where they are stored *relative to the current position of the top of the stack*. In our example, the first five items on the stack are, from the top down, *middle*, b, a, T, and the return address.

In a similar way any recursive algorithm can be implemented with the aid of a stack. However, use of a stack is not always necessary. For example, Algorithm 3.6 is the result of translating the Binary Search Algorithm (page 11) into a stack-based algorithm.

---

function *BinarySearch*: **integer**
{Search $T[a..b]$ for key K and return its index}
    if $a > b$ **then**
        ReturnValue $\leftarrow -1$
        goto *CommonExit*
    middle $\leftarrow \lfloor (a+b)/2 \rfloor$
    if $w = T[middle]$ **then**
        ReturnValue $\leftarrow$ *middle*
        goto *CommonExit*
    if $w < T[middle]$ **then**
        $b \leftarrow$ *middle* $- 1$
    else
        $a \leftarrow$ *middle* $+ 1$
    goto *BinarySearch*
CommonExit:
    Pop and branch to the return address

Algorithm 3.7 Binary search, with tail recursion eliminated.

At a typical point during the execution of Algorithm 3.6, several sets of arguments, local variables, and the return address will be on the stack, but only the current set of data will be accessed by the algorithm, exactly as in the case of *MergeSort*. However, unlike in the case of *MergeSort*, all the return addresses are the same, namely, *CommonExit*. It follows that once the return value has been determined, the algorithm will loop through its last four lines until the stack has been emptied and the original return address—from somewhere outside the algorithm itself—is uncovered. This phenomenon is traceable in the original, recursive code for *BinarySearch* to the fact that *the first instruction executed after returning from the recursive call on BinarySearch is a* **return**. A recursive call with this property is said to be **tail-recursive**, and a recursive routine in which all the recursive calls are tail-recursive is said to be a tail-recursive routine. Evidently, there is no need to preserve local variables or argument values before a tail-recursive call, since they will not be needed once that call has completed. Similarly, there no need to stack the return address; instead of returning only to carry out another **return** statement, the *Push* and the corresponding *Pop* may as well both be omitted. When this optimization has been carried out on the *BinarySearch* routine, all that is left is the code of Algorithm 3.7; the new values of the arguments simply replace the old, which do not even need to be on the stack. (The code beginning at *CommonExit* is still required, of course, to handle *non*recursive calls on *BinarySearch*, from outside.)

Thus in the case of a tail-recursive routine the implicit stack needed to implement recursion can be dispensed with completely. (The space to hold the

---

procedure *Traverse*(**pointer** P):
{Visit nodes of a singly linked list, beginning with cell that P points to}
    while $P \neq \Lambda$ **do**
        Visit(Key(P))
        $P \leftarrow$ Next(P)

Algorithm 3.8 Forward traversal from beginning to end of a singly linked list.

---

single set of arguments does not need to be on a stack; it could be in fixed memory locations.) Some compilers are clever enough to carry out such a transformation automatically, in an effort to save stack space at run time; we shall, in any case, note some cases in which savings could be realized in this way.

3.4 LIST REPRESENTATIONS FOR TRAVERSALS

The singly linked list representation is useful because it permits insertion or deletion of the item following any given item in the list in $\Theta(1)$ time. A price is paid for this added flexibility over the contiguous-memory representation, however; $Access(L, i)$ cannot be implemented in $O(1)$ time. It is still true, however, that given a particular item in the list, the *next* item in the list can be found in $O(1)$ time. For many applications no more is needed, since a list of length n can then be traversed from the beginning to the end in time $\Theta(n)$ (Algorithm 3.8). By **traversal** of a list L, we mean performing a specified operation *Visit* on some or all of the elements of L in a specified order. When we reckon the time to perform a traversal, we omit the time required for carrying out *Visit* itself, since *Visit* is completely arbitrary.

For example, the algorithm on page 14 illustrates a very simple kind of linked list traversal, used to keep the elements of the list in order by their Key values. For the purposes of the following illustration, let us assume that the keys are actually English words and that the order being maintained is the usual alphabetical order. (Technically, this is called **lexicographic order**.)

The singly linked list structure can be adapted to a variety of circumstances for which it might at first seem that a more elaborate structure is needed. In the context of the list of words in lexicographic order, suppose we want to find, given a word w, the last word in L that alphabetically precedes w and ends with the same letter as w. (For example, if

$$L = \langle \text{canary, cat, chickadee, coelacanth, collie, corn, cup} \rangle$$

---

function *FindLast*(**pointer** L, **key** w): **key**
{Find the last word in list L ending with the same letter as w}
{Return Λ if there is no such word}

    $P \leftarrow L$
    $Q \leftarrow \Lambda$
    while $P \neq \Lambda$ **and** Key(P) $< w$ **do**
        if Key(P) ends with the same letter as w **then** $Q \leftarrow P$
        $P \leftarrow$ Next(P)
    if $Q = \Lambda$ **then return** Λ **else return** Key(Q)

Algorithm 3.9 In a linked list, find the last word preceding w that ends with the same letter as w.

---

and $K =$ crabapple, then the answer we are looking for is collie.) A "brute-force" approach to solving this problem would use backward pointers, so that we could pass in $\Theta(1)$ time from any list element to its predecessor; we might then search forward from the beginning of the list to the position where w ought to occur, and then backward for the first word that ends with the same letter as w. But it is equally easy (and more efficient) to use a singly linked representation and to keep a second pointer that always points to the last word that has been seen that ends with the same letter as w (Algorithm 3.9).

Sometimes this kind of forward-backward condition can be too complicated to implement by remembering a fixed amount of information during the forward traversal. Imagine, for example, that a number is stored with each word in the list; and we want to find, given a word w in the list associated with a number n, the word that precedes w in the list by n positions. This specification suggests an algorithm that searches forward in the list for the word w and then backs up in the list by n positions; we call an algorithm that moves back and forth in a list like this a **zig-zag scan**. As long as a zig-zag scan always begins from the beginning of the list, it can be implemented by stacking pointers to all the cells during the forward traversal, and popping those pointers to effect the backward traversal. The stack takes no more memory than storing extra pointers in the cells themselves, but the memory is used only during the traversal.

One final and drastic variation on this train of ideas implements a zig-zag scan of a singly linked list without using any additional memory at all by a method known as **link inversion**. The stack of pointers is stored in the linked list itself, "turning around" the Next pointers of the cells through which we advance so that they point to the previous cell in the list. This operation temporarily destroys the linked list. At any point during the scan we need two pointers, P and Q, to keep track of our whereabouts (Figure 3.4). Q points to the first unvisited cell in the remainder of the list; following Next fields starting

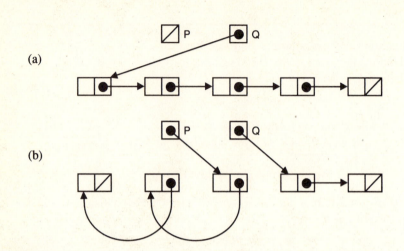

(a)

(b)

Figure 3.4 Link inversion of a singly linked list. (a) Before traversal;
(b) after traversing the first three list cells.

with Q will take us in the forward direction, as usual, through the tail end of L from some point on: $x_i, x_{i+1}, \ldots, x_{n-1}$. P, on the other hand, points to the cell containing x_{i-1}, but its Next field has been changed so that it points to the cell containing x_{i-2}, and so on. That is, following Next pointers starting with P essentially takes us down the pointer stack described just above, towards the *front* of the list.

The operations of starting a traversal at the beginning of the list, moving one step forward in the list, and moving one step back in the list (while undoing the damage done when moving forward) are achieved by these three routines:

$$StartTraversal(L):$$
$$\binom{P}{Q} \leftarrow \binom{\Lambda}{L}$$

Forward(P, Q):

$$\begin{pmatrix} P \\ Q \\ \text{Next}(Q) \end{pmatrix} \leftarrow \begin{pmatrix} Q \\ \text{Next}(Q) \\ P \end{pmatrix}$$

Back(P, Q):

$$\begin{pmatrix} P \\ \text{Next}(P) \\ Q \end{pmatrix} \leftarrow \begin{pmatrix} \text{Next}(P) \\ Q \\ P \end{pmatrix}$$

This method must be used with extreme caution, where it is applicable at all. Restoring the list to its original state requires backing out completely. Also, no other use of the list can be accommodated while this traversal is in progress; in particular, this method is inapplicable if several concurrent processes require simultaneous access to a data structure. In spite of its apparent limitations, this basic idea is at the heart of a number of algorithms to be discussed in Chapter 10.

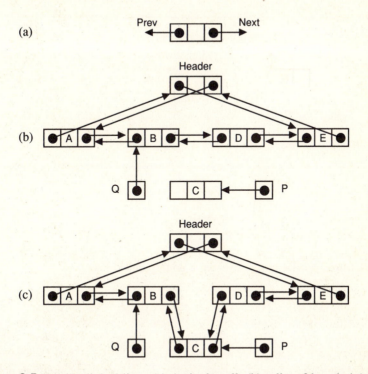

Figure 3.5 Doubly linked lists. (a) A single cell; (b) a list of length 4 (plus a header cell); (c) the same list, with C inserted after the cell pointed to by Q.

3.5 DOUBLY LINKED LISTS

Sometimes we need to traverse a list freely in both directions starting from any point. A **doubly linked list** consists of nodes with two pointer fields, Next and Prev, which point to the following and preceding nodes in the list, respectively. The Next field of the last node and the Prev field of the first node can either be Λ, or can point to a special header node whose Key field is unused; the latter representation is generally more convenient, since then Prev(Next(P)) and Next(Prev(P)) are both always defined for any node P, and are always equal to P. We therefore assume the latter convention (Figure 3.5).

With a doubly linked list, traversal in the forward direction, the backward direction, or any intermixture can be implemented with ease. Moreover it is easy to perform an insertion either just before or just after an item, given only the node containing the item itself. This is because it is easy to get from a node to its predecessor or successor, whichever needs to be changed to insert the new item. For example, Algorithm 3.10 inserts a node pointed to by P after the cell pointed to by Q (Figure 3.5(b,c)).

---

procedure *DoublyLinkedInsert*(**pointer** P, Q):
{Insert node pointed to by P just after node pointed to by Q}
$$\begin{pmatrix} \text{Prev}(P) \\ \text{Next}(P) \\ \text{Next}(Q) \\ \text{Prev}(\text{Next}(Q)) \end{pmatrix} \leftarrow \begin{pmatrix} Q \\ \text{Next}(Q) \\ P \\ P \end{pmatrix}$$

Algorithm 3.10 Insert a node into a doubly linked list.

---

procedure *DoublyLinkedDelete*(**pointer** P):
{Delete cell P from its doubly linked list}
$$\begin{pmatrix} \text{Next}(\text{Prev}(P)) \\ \text{Prev}(\text{Next}(P)) \end{pmatrix} \leftarrow \begin{pmatrix} \text{Next}(P) \\ \text{Prev}(P) \end{pmatrix}$$

Algorithm 3.11 Delete a cell from a doubly linked list.

Inserting before a given node is, of course, symmetrical. A cell can be *deleted* from a doubly linked list with only two pointer operations, and only the address of the node itself need be known (Algorithm 3.11). In fact, one of the most common reasons for using doubly linked lists is the ability to delete a node, knowing only the node and not its predecessor.

The disadvantage of doubly linked lists is, of course, that they require two pointers in each cell, so the "overhead" needed to hold the list together is twice as great as for a singly linked list of the same length. Surprisingly, there is a way around this drawback. That is, there is a structure that uses only as much space per list element as would be needed to hold a single pointer, and yet supports all of the following in $\Theta(1)$ time: from any list element x,

- to move forward in the list to the item after x;
- to move backward in the list to the item before x;
- to insert an item before or after x;
- to delete x.

A first inkling that such a list representation might be possible arises when one notices that in the pointer fields of doubly linked lists every pointer value appears twice; if X is the address of the list node representing a particular list element, then X appears as the value of the pointer fields Next(Prev(X)) and Prev(Next(X)), that is, in the Next field of the node before X and the Prev field of the node after X. Although there are $2n$ pointers in a doubly linked list of length n, there are only n values of those pointers, since every value that occurs is duplicated at a list position two ahead of or behind its other occurrence. The "trick" of our representation will be to compress into a single pointer-sized field

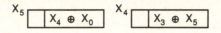

Figure 3.6 Exclusive-or coded doubly linked list representing the list $\langle A, B, C, D \rangle$ of length $n = 4$. X_4 and X_5 are the header nodes.

in each node a composite of the addresses of the preceding and succeeding list nodes, that is, the two pointers that would be within that node in an ordinary doubly linked list. Although such an amalgam of bits could not be deciphered if it were encountered in isolation, together with the address of an adjacent node it can be used to reconstruct the address of the node on the other side. Therefore this representation can be used instead of storing two pointer fields in each node, but only if the list is always entered from one end or the other, and nodes in the middle are reached only by traversing the list from one of the ends; if it is necessary to be able to enter the list abruptly at any node in the interior, an ordinary doubly linked representation must be used.

The **exclusive-or** $a \oplus b$ of two bits a and b is 1 if and only if the two bits are different; that is, $1 \oplus 0 = 0 \oplus 1 = 1$, and $0 \oplus 0 = 1 \oplus 1 = 0$. The exclusive-or of two bit strings is computed bitwise, that is, $a_1 a_2 \ldots a_k \oplus b_1 b_2 \ldots b_k = c_1 c_2 \ldots c_k$, where $c_i = a_i \oplus b_i$ for $1 \leq i \leq k$. The important properties of $\oplus$ for our purposes are two:

1. $\oplus$ is commutative and associative; that is, $a \oplus b = b \oplus a$ and $(a \oplus b) \oplus c = a \oplus (b \oplus c)$, so it does not matter in what order bit strings are combined with $\oplus$.
2. For any bit string a, $a \oplus a = 0$ (that is, the bit string of all 0's), and $a \oplus 0 = a$. Together with (1), this means that in any exclusive-or of several bit strings in which the same term appears twice, two occurrences can be dropped without changing the value.

Now we can explain the representation of list $L = \langle x_0, x_1, \ldots, x_{n-1} \rangle$. Each node has a Key field and a single additional field, called Link, which is the same size as a pointer field. Let the addresses of the cells containing $x_0, x_1, \ldots, x_{n-1}$ be $X_0, X_1, \ldots, X_{n-1}$, and let X_n and X_{n+1} be the addresses of two additional nodes to be used as headers. Then the Link field of each node in the list contains the exclusive-or of the addresses of the nodes before and after it in the list, with the header nodes deemed to be before X_0 and after X_{n-1} (Figure 3.6). That is,

$$\text{Link}(X_i) = X_{(i-1) \bmod (n+2)} \oplus X_{(i+1) \bmod (n+2)}.$$

To traverse a list represented in this way, we need pointers P and Q to two adjacent nodes X_i and $X_{(i+1) \bmod (n+2)}$. If P and Q have this property, then the operations of moving both pointers forward and backward in the list can be implemented as follows:

Forward(*P*, *Q*):

$$\begin{pmatrix} P \\ Q \end{pmatrix} \leftarrow \begin{pmatrix} Q \\ P \oplus \text{Link}(Q) \end{pmatrix}$$

Back(*P*, *Q*):

$$\begin{pmatrix} P \\ Q \end{pmatrix} \leftarrow \begin{pmatrix} \text{Link}(P) \oplus Q \\ P \end{pmatrix}$$

To see why these routines work, recall that P and Q point to successive nodes in the list. Let N be the cell before P and R the cell after Q. Then $\text{Link}(Q) = P \oplus R$ and $\text{Link}(P) = N \oplus Q$. Therefore

$$P \oplus \text{Link}(Q) = P \oplus (P \oplus R) = (P \oplus P) \oplus R = R$$

and

$$\text{Link}(P) \oplus Q = (N \oplus Q) \oplus Q = N.$$

Finally, to insert a new node pointed to by C between those pointed to by P and Q,

$$\begin{pmatrix} \text{Link}(P) \\ \text{Link}(Q) \\ \text{Link}(C) \\ Q \end{pmatrix} \leftarrow \begin{pmatrix} \text{Link}(P) \oplus Q \oplus C \\ \text{Link}(Q) \oplus P \oplus C \\ P \oplus Q \\ C \end{pmatrix}.$$

Initially $\text{Link}(P) = N \oplus Q$, where N is the address of the node before P in the list. Consequently $\text{Link}(P) \oplus Q \oplus C = N \oplus C$, which is what $\text{Link}(P)$ should become when P is between N and C.

This representation is both economical of memory and easy to manipulate, but the operations on the Link fields are so low-level that they are likely to be impossible in some strongly typed higher-level programming languages. That is, even if manipulation and storage of pointers to cells are supported by the language, the operation of forming the exclusive-or of two pointers may be impossible, even though almost every computer could support such an operation at the machine-language level. However, these "bitwise" operations are possible in the C programming language, and even the strongly typed languages Modula-2 and Ada leave loopholes that may make such operations possible.

Problems

3.1   **1.** Using abstract operations only, write a routine that takes as its argument a list of lists and returns the concatenation of all the component lists.

3.2   **2.** A **run** in a list $L = \langle x_0, \ldots, x_{n-1} \rangle$ is a pair of indices $\langle i, j \rangle$, $i \le j$, such that $x_i = x_{i+1} = \cdots = x_j$. A **run-length encoding** of L represents L as a table $A[0..k-1]$ of records with two fields, Count and Value; if $\langle i_0, i_1 - 1 \rangle$, $\langle i_1, i_2 - 1 \rangle$, $\ldots$, $\langle i_{k-1}, i_k - 1 \rangle$ are runs of L, with $i_0 = 0$ and $i_k = n$, then L is represented by setting Count($A[j]$) = $i_{j+1} - i_j$ and Value($A[j]$) = x_{i_j} for $0 \leq j < k$.

a. Give an algorithm for $Access(L, i)$ with this representation.

b. Give necessary and sufficient conditions for this representation to use less memory than the ordinary contiguous-memory representation of L. (Assume that the Count field is C bits, and the Value field is V bits.)

3. Describe the implementation of *two* stacks in a single table, in the style used on page 75 to describe the implementation of the stack operations for a single stack in contiguous memory.

4. Susan decides to implement a queue of maximum length N in a table of size N by keeping track of the positions of the first and last elements of the queue, rather than the position of the first element and the length of the queue; she figures this will save her some modular arithmetic and the code will be clearer. Unfortunately, she can't seem to get her code to work; why not? What alternatives will work correctly?

5. A **deque** (pronounced "deck") or **double-ended queue** is a list abstract data type such that both additions and deletions can be made at both ends. Present representations of deques in both contiguous and linked memory.

6. A **pseudo-random number generator** is a function of no arguments that returns, when called repeatedly, a sequence of values that appears to be random and uniformly distributed over a range $\{0, \dots, N - 1\}$. (The value of N is typically 2^k, where k is the computer word length in bits; $N = 2^{32}$, for example.) In particular, a **lagged Fibonacci generator** for the range $\{0, \dots, N - 1\}$ returns the values $x_n = (x_{n-r} + x_{n-s}) \bmod N$, where r and s are integer constants of the algorithm ($0 < r < s$) and the initial "seed" values $x_0, \dots, x_{s-1}$ are determined in some other way. (The values $r = 5$ and $s = 17$ are recommended, because they result in a sequence $x_0, x_1, \dots$ that does not repeat a value for a very long time.) Explain how to implement a lagged Fibonacci generator using list abstract data types. What representation would be most appropriate?

7. One difficulty with the linked representation of lists is the space required; unless the Info field of each record is large compared with the size of a pointer, each list will have a great deal of memory overhead for pointers compared to the amount of "real" data. **Cdr-coding** is one way of overcoming this problem. The idea is to have two different types of list records, say LargeNode and SmallNode. Each has

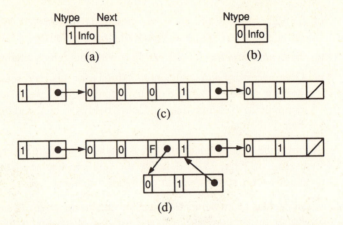

Figure 3.7 Cdr-coded lists. (a) A LargeNode. (b) A SmallNode. (c) A list with seven elements. (d) The result of inserting a new element after the third element of the list in (c).

an Info field as usual plus a one-bit field **Ntype** that distinguishes one type from the other. (It is quite often possible to "steal" an otherwise unused bit from a storage location, especially if the location is known to contain a pointer.) Each **LargeNode** contains 1 in its **Ntype** field and contains a **Next** field as usual. Each **SmallNode** contains 0 in its **Ntype** field and has no **Next** field at all. Instead, the next record in the list follows immediately in memory, as though in a table; that is, each **SmallNode** has an implicit **Next** pointer that points just beyond itself in memory. Figure 3.7(c) shows an example of a cdr-coded list.

a. Write the routine *Access(L,i)* that finds the ith element of a cdr-coded list *L*. Assume that $N + smallnodesize$ gives the address of the record immediately succeeding record N in memory when N is a **SmallNode**.

b. Write a routine *CopyList* that makes a copy of a cdr-coded list, ensuring that the new list is represented as compactly as possible. Assume that consecutive calls on *NewCell* are guaranteed to return nodes that are adjacent in memory.

8. It is not a simple matter to insert a new record into a cdr-coded list, since if we wish to insert a new record just after a **SmallNode** there may be no place to put the relevant information! To obviate this difficulty we create yet another type of node called a **ForwardingAddress**. (The **Ntype** field must now be expanded to two bits; we use F for the bit sequence identifying a **ForwardingAddress**.) Other than the **Ntype** field, each **ForwardingAddress** has exactly the same structure as a **SmallNode**—in particular, they are necessarily the same size

in memory. The Info field of a ForwardingAddress N contains a pointer to another record, which is the record that *really should be located at N's address.* (We assume that the Info field is at least as large as a pointer.) Any routine that encounters a pointer to N must retrieve Info(N) to find the "real" record; foresighted routines will update pointers to N to point to Info(N), thus speeding up the next access. Figure 3.7(d) illustrates how to use a ForwardingAddress to insert into a cdr-coded list.

a. Write insertion and deletion routines for cdr-coded lists like those for doubly-linked lists on page 88.

b. Update the *Access* and *CopyList* routines written for Problem 7 to respect forwarding addresses.

c. Only three of the four possible values of the Ntype field are used. One possibility for a fourth type of node will permit us to save one more pointer in each list. Define this new node type and update the list-manipulation routines as necessary.

3.3   **9.** Give a version of the clever integer multiplication algorithm (Algorithm 2.3 on page 53) showing explicitly the stack manipulations needed to implement the recursive calls.

3.4   **10.** Show that link inversion during list traversal can be avoided if we know that we never look more than K positions behind the position probed, where K is a constant fixed before the algorithms are implemented. That is, imagine that the record structure for a list L has, among others, a component Finger(L) that points to the item most recently accessed. Show how to implement the procedures *StartTraversal*(L), which initializes the traversal, and *Forward*(L), which advances one position in the list, and the function *Before*(L, k), where $k \leq K$, which returns the Key field of the cell k before Finger(L). What other components need to be added to L? What is the time required by these algorithms, as a function of K?

11. On page 85 we described the problem of finding the word in a singly linked list that precedes a word w by an associated distance n. The record for w has fields Key(P) = w and Dist(P) = n, as well as Next(P). Write algorithms for this problem using

a. two pointers that move only forward in the list;

b. a "zig-zag" scan with a stack of pointers;

c. link inversion.

3.5   **12.** What is the representation of the empty list when using

a. ordinary doubly linked lists with header cells?

b. exclusive-or coded lists?

13. Give the algorithm for deleting the cell with address P from an exclusive-or coded list, given that Q points to the next cell in the list.

14. Give an algorithm for deleting the ith cell $(0 \leq i \leq n - 1)$ from an exclusive-or encoded list with n cells plus header cells, given the addresses of the header cells. You should reject as illegal attempts to delete a cell with index larger than the length of the list (and, of course, you should not delete the header cells themselves).

15. Show how to represent a doubly linked list with only **p** extra bits per cell, using the operations of ordinary addition and subtraction instead of exclusive-or.

16. Suppose that lists are used to represent sets of items, so that the order of items in a list is irrelevant. Moreover, suppose that no item belongs to more than one set. Devise a representation that permits the following two operations to be implemented: to traverse, from any item, all of the other items in the same set with it, in time linear in the number of those items; and to form in constant time, from two items belonging to different sets, a set consisting of the union of those two sets.

References

The use of stacks to implement recursion is now so commonplace that we can almost forget that the idea was ever invented. In fact the relation of stacks to recursion was first clarified in the context of the development of a compiler for the programming language ALGOL 60. Like many other important innovations in computer science, this one is due to Edsger Dijkstra:

E. W. Dijkstra, "Recursive Programming," *Numerische Mathematik* **2** (1960), pp. 312-318. In S. Rosen, ed., *Programming Systems and Languages*, McGraw-Hill Book Company, 1967.

Any book on programming languages or compilers contains a more complete explanation of the implementation of recursion than that given in §3.3. Lagged Fibonacci generators (Problem 6) are discussed in

G. Marsaglia and L.-H. Tsay, "Matrices and the Structure of Random Number Sequences," *Linear Algebra and its Applications* **67** (1985), pp. 147–156.

Cdr-coding (Problem 7) was described in

W. J. Hansen, "Compact List Representation: Definition, Garbage Collection, and System Implementation," *Communications of the ACM* **12** (1969), pp. 499–507

and

D. W. Clark, "An Empirical Study of List Structures in Lisp," *Communications of the ACM* **20** (1977), pp. 78–87, *and has been implemented in hardware in certain computers called "Lisp machines." The name "cdr-coding" comes from the name of one of the primitive operators in the Lisp programming language, which in turn was derived from the name of the machine instruction ("contents of the decrement part of the register") used to implement that operator on the IBM 704 computer. For the original (and still highly readable) account of list processing in Lisp, see*

J. McCarthy, "Recursive Functions of Symbolic Expressions and Their Computation by Machine," *Communications of the ACM* **3** (1960), pp. 184–195.

4

Trees

4.1 BASIC DEFINITIONS

Whenever information is classified by breaking a whole into parts, and repeatedly breaking the parts into subparts, it is natural to represent the classification by a tree structure. For example, Figure 4.1 shows a small part of the contemporary scientific classification of the animal kingdom; structures like this have been used to analyze the realm of living things at least since Aristotle. Each category is divided into the subcategories shown below it in the diagram. Such a diagram is called a tree because this process of subdivision resembles the branching structure of a living tree. Just as the branches of a living tree do not grow back together, so each item in a tree structure belongs to only one category at the next higher level.

Trees are an important object of study in computer science, because so much of computer science deals with ways of organizing information to make it easily accessible. Tree structures have long been used to make information more tractable. For example, library classification systems, such as the Dewey Decimal system and the Library of Congress system, were designed to make it easy to find a book quickly given a modest amount of information about its content (Figure 4.2). Answering a series of questions (is it about Religion? History? Science?) and subquestions (is it about Botany? Astronomy?) leads through a series of branching points to the book's exact classification. (Ambiguities of classification exist because knowledge is not perfectly tree-structured; does computer science properly belong under Q, Science, or T, Technology?) This organization persists even within a book: for example, this book is divided into chapters, the chapters into sections, most sections into subsections, and so forth.

All tree structures have the following general characteristics in common. A tree has a single starting point called the "root" of the tree—"ANIMALIA," in Figure 4.1. In general an element is related to particular elements at the next lower level (as a parent is related to children in a family tree; for example, Metazoa is the parent of Mollusca, Chordata, Annelida, and Arthropoda in

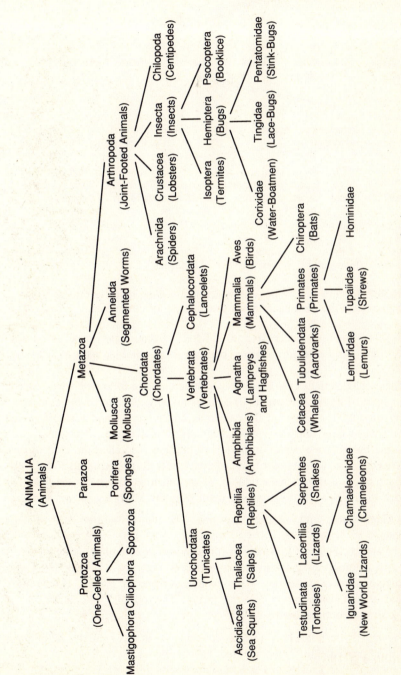

Figure 4.1 Scientific classification of the animal kingdom (very incomplete).

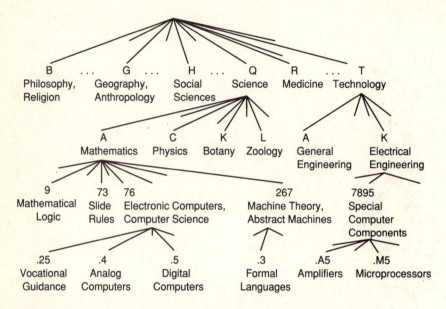

Figure 4.2 Library of Congress classification system, much abridged, showing some of the sections relevant to the study of computers.

Figure 4.1). Some elements have no children. Because the branches do not merge, from every element of a tree one can trace a unique path back to the root.

These characteristics can be defined abstractly in the following way. A **tree** is composed of **nodes** and **edges**. The nodes are any distinguishable objects at all, for example, the names of the categories in Figure 4.1 and Figure 4.2. In general nodes will be illustrated in our diagrams as small circles. A distinguished node—the one that we depict at the top of the tree—is called the **root** of the tree. An edge is an ordered pair $\langle u, v \rangle$ of nodes; it is illustrated by an arrow with its tail at node u and its head at node v, so we call u the **tail** and v the **head** of the edge $\langle u, v \rangle$. Specifically, trees are defined by the following recursive rules:

1. A single node, with no edges, is a tree. The root of the tree is its unique node.
2. Let $T_1, \ldots, T_k$ ($k \geq 1$) be trees with no nodes in common, and let $r_1, \ldots, r_k$ be the roots of those trees, respectively. Let r be a new node. Then there is a tree T consisting of the nodes and edges of $T_1, \ldots, T_k$, the new node r, and new edges $\langle r, r_1 \rangle, \ldots, \langle r, r_k \rangle$. The root of T is r, and $T_1, \ldots, T_k$ are called the **subtrees** of T.

Figure 4.3 illustrates how a tree is constructed via this recursive definition. The crucial provision in (2) that the trees have no nodes in common ensures that the composed object really is a tree, and not a structure with loops or multiple parents for a single node.

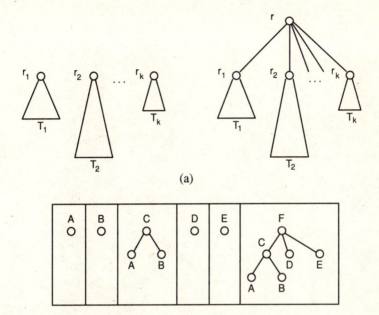

(a)

(b)

Figure 4.3 Recursive definition of trees. (a) Illustration of the general definition; (b) construction of a six-node tree in six steps.

In part (2) of this definition, r is called the **parent** of $r_1, \ldots, r_k$, which are the **children** of r and the **siblings** of each other. Node v is a **descendant** of node u if $u = v$ or v is a descendant of a child of u. In terms of our illustrations, v is a descendant of u if one can get from u to v by following a sequence of edges down the tree, starting with an edge whose tail is u, ending with an edge whose head is v, and with the head of each edge but the last being the tail of the next. Such a sequence of edges is called a **path** from u to v (Figure 4.4). Note that every node is a descendant of itself, since the path need not have any edges at all; when we want the descendants of a node, other than the node itself, we shall refer to the **proper** descendants of a node. Node u is an **ancestor** of node v just in case v is a descendant of u; of course there are proper ancestors as well as proper descendants.* A **leaf** is a node with no children. Any tree has one more node than edge, since each node, except the root, is the head of exactly one of the edges.

The **height** of a node in a tree is the length of the longest path from that

---

*Tree terminology in computer science is an odd mixture of botanical and genealogical metaphors. When interpreting the botanical metaphor, remember to turn the tree upside down; the node referred to as the "root" is invariably drawn at the top of the tree. And when interpreting the genealogical metaphor, think of a tree of your descendants, not of your ancestors.

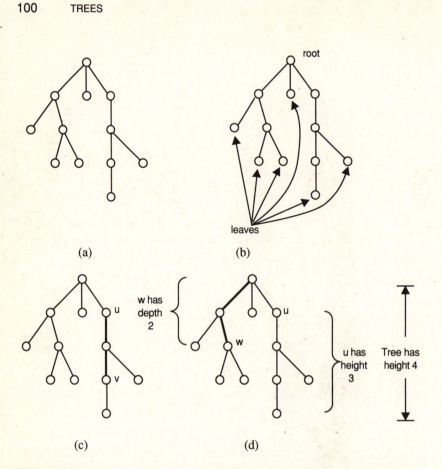

Figure 4.4 (a) A tree with 12 nodes; (b) its root and leaves; (c) a path from u to v, showing that u is an ancestor of v; (d) height and depth of nodes.

node to a leaf; thus all the leaves have height 0. The height of the tree itself is the height of the root. The **depth** of a node is the length of the path (there is exactly one) from the root of the tree to the node. Thus the height of a tree can also be described as the maximum of the depths of its nodes.

4.2 SPECIAL KINDS OF TREES

Several special kinds of trees can be distinguished either because they have additional structural properties, beyond those possessed by all trees, or because their shapes are restricted in one way or another.

An **ordered tree** is a tree with a linear order on the children of each node. That is, in an ordered tree the children of a node have a designated order: one

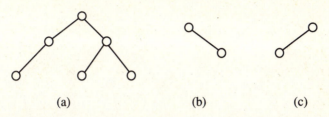

(a)   (b)   (c)

Figure 4.5 Binary trees. Note that (b) and (c) are different binary trees; the
root of (b) has only a right child, while the root of (c) has only a left
child.

can refer unambiguously to the first, second, ..., k^{th} child of a node that has k
children. Most of the trees we deal with are ordered trees, but occasionally trees
without an ordering of the children constitute the right model; for emphasis we
refer to them as **unordered** trees.

A **binary tree** is an ordered tree with at most two children for each node;
moreover when a node has only one child, that child is distinguished as being
either a **left child** or a **right child**. When a node has two children, the first is
also called the left child and the second is called the right child. In our diagrams
a left child is to the southwest of its parent, and a right child is to the southeast
(Figure 4.5). Note that while there is only one ordered tree with two nodes,
there are two different binary trees with two nodes: one consisting of a root and
a left child, and one consisting of a root and a right child.

It turns out to be convenient to extend the notion of a binary tree to include
an **empty binary tree** which has no nodes; we write Λ to denote this binary
tree. The definition of a binary tree can then be reformulated more gracefully as
follows: a binary tree is either Λ; or is a node with left and right subtrees, each
of which is a binary tree. (It is understood that if a subtree is nonempty then
there is an edge joining the root to it.) By this definition the tree of Figure 4.5(b)
consists of a root with an empty left subtree and a right subtree which is a node
with two empty subtrees. (Of course Λ is *not* a tree; for example, it violates
the rule about trees having one more node than edge.)

A nonempty binary tree is said to be **full** if it has no nodes with only one
child; that is, if each node is a leaf or has two children. In a full binary tree
the number of leaves is one more than the number of nonleaves; this is easily
proved by induction (Problem 6).

A **perfect** binary tree is a full binary tree in which all leaves have the same
depth. A perfect binary tree of height h has $2^{h+1} - 1$ nodes, of which 2^h are
leaves and $2^h - 1$ are nonleaves. These numbers are easily derived by induction
on the height of the tree. In the base case, when $h = 0$, the perfect height-zero
tree consists of a single node and no edges; thus it has $2^{0+1} - 1 = 1$ node,
$2^0 = 1$ leaf and $2^0 - 1 = 0$ nonleaves. In the inductive case, the subtrees of the
root of a perfect tree of height $h + 1$ are two perfect trees of height h, so if a
perfect tree of height h has 2^h leaves and $2^h - 1$ nonleaves, then a perfect tree

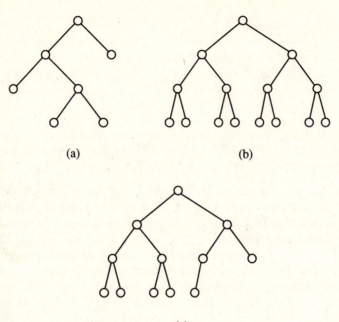

(a)   (b)

(c)

Figure 4.6 Binary trees: (a) full; (b) perfect; (c) complete.

of height $h+1$ has $2^h + 2^h = 2^{h+1}$ leaves and $(2^h - 1) + (2^h - 1) + 1 = 2^{h+1} - 1$ nonleaves.

A *complete* binary tree is the closest approximation to a perfect binary tree when the number of nodes is not exactly one less than a power of two. To be precise, the **complete** binary trees are defined inductively as follows. A complete binary tree of height 0 is any tree consisting of a single node; and a complete binary tree of height 1 is a tree of height 1 with either two children or a left child only. For $h \geq 2$, a complete binary tree of height h is a root with two subtrees satisfying one of these two conditions: either the left subtree is perfect of height $h - 1$ and the right is complete of height $h - 1$, or the left is complete of height $h - 1$ and the right is perfect of height $h - 2$. More informally, a complete tree of height h is formed from a perfect tree of height $h - 1$ by adding one or more leaves at depth h; these leaves must be filled in at the leftmost available positions (Figure 4.6). Thus for any n there is only one complete binary tree with n nodes; the shape is fully determined by the number of nodes.

Our interest in perfect and complete binary trees arises from the need to minimize the height of a tree with a given number of nodes; in many contexts the height of a tree determines the worst-case running time of an algorithm that follows a path in the tree. Of all binary trees with n nodes, none has lesser height than the complete binary tree with n nodes. Since the number of nodes, n, in a complete binary tree of height h satisfies $2^h \leq n \leq 2^{h+1} - 1$, the height of the complete binary tree with n nodes is exactly $\lfloor \lg n \rfloor$, which is therefore the minimum height of any n-node binary tree.

A **forest** is a finite set of trees. In the case of ordered trees, the trees in the forest must have a distinguishable order as well. For example, the subtrees of an ordered tree form an ordered forest.

4.3 TREE OPERATIONS AND TRAVERSALS

Many of the terms defined so far in this chapter are natural candidates for abstract operations on trees; we mention just a few possibilities here. It will be convenient to restrict attention to the situation in which a node belongs only to a single tree; then the node's children and parent in the tree are uniquely determined by the node itself. We follow this convention and use nodes, rather than trees, as arguments to the abstract operations.

Parent(v): Return the parent of node v, or Λ if v is the root.

Children(v): Return the set of children of node v (the empty set, if v is a leaf).

FirstChild(v): Return the first child of node v, or Λ if v is a leaf.

RightSibling(v): Return the right sibling of v, or Λ if v is the root or the rightmost child of its parent.

LeftSibling(v): Return the left sibling of v, or Λ if v is the root or the leftmost child of its parent.

LeftChild(v), *RightChild*(v): Return the left (right) child of node v (Λ if v has no left or right child).

IsLeaf(v): Return **true** if node v is a leaf, **false** if v has a child.

Depth(v): Return the depth of node v in the tree.

Height(v): Return the height of node v in the tree.

Some of these operations make sense only for ordered trees, others only for binary trees. If trees are regarded as belonging to forests—still under the hypothesis that a node cannot belong to more than one tree—most of these abstract operations retain their same meanings. But it may make sense, in the case of an ordered forest, to define the *RightSibling* and *LeftSibling* of a root to be the root of the next or previous tree in the forest.

In practice, trees are often represented by associating with a node a collection of pointers to its children, in a way that mimics exactly the recursive definition on page 98. In that case a pointer to a node can serve to identify the subtree rooted at that node, and operations such as *LeftChild* can be implemented readily as field references to the record addressed by that pointer. For this reason trees are passed as **pointers** in the discussion below—trees are identified with pointers to their roots.

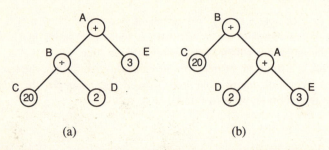

Figure 4.7 Expression trees. Tree (a) represents the expression $(20 \div 2) + 3$, while tree (b) represents the expression $20 \div (2 + 3)$. Parentheses are omitted from these trees, since their structure captures the same information.

It will be helpful in discussing the use of these operations to focus on a specific application of trees: the representation of arithmetic calculations. The sort of calculation we have in mind are those involving numbers and the arithmetic operations of addition ("+"), subtraction ("−"), multiplication ("×"), and division ("÷"). In describing these calculations we also use parentheses to indicate grouping; for example, $(20 \div 2) + 3$ means one thing, but $20 \div (2 + 3)$ means something quite different. "Mathematical English" has a particular set of conventions that determine the implied location of parentheses, when they are omitted; thus $20 \div 2 + 3$ means the same as $(20 \div 2) + 3$, since multiplications and divisions take place before additions and subtractions, if there are no parentheses to indicate otherwise. Expressions such as $20 \div 2 + 3$ and $20 \div (2 + 3)$ are called **infix** arithmetic expressions; the operators are written in between the things on which they operate.

The calculations represented by infix arithmetic expressions can be described quite naturally by full binary trees, where the leaves are labelled with numbers and the nonleaves are labelled with the operators (Figure 4.7). If T has subtrees T_1 and T_2, then the implied value of the whole tree T is the result of combining the values of the subtrees T_1 and T_2 by means of the operator that labels the root of T. This is a recursive rule that applies in the same way to the subtrees of T_1 and T_2; and the value of a leaf is the value of the number that labels the node.

Algorithm 4.1 evaluates such an "expression tree"; it is presented in terms of suitable abstract operations on the tree. We assume that for any node v, Label(v) is the number or operator that labels that node, and that $ApplyOp(op, x, y)$, where x and y are numbers and op is one of "+," "−," "×," and "÷," computes the sum, difference, product, or quotient of x and y.

Let us trace the evaluation of the tree of Figure 4.7(a); in the trace, the node names A, B, etc. are used to refer to the entire subtrees rooted at those nodes. Notice how this graphic illustration of what happens within each call to

function *Evaluate*(**pointer** P): **integer**
{Return value of the expression represented by the tree with root P}
    if *IsLeaf*(P) **then return** Label(P)
    else
        $x_L \leftarrow$ *Evaluate*(*LeftChild*(P))
        $x_R \leftarrow$ *Evaluate*(*RightChild*(P))
        $op \leftarrow$ Label(P)
        return *ApplyOp*(op, x_L, x_R)

Algorithm 4.1 Evaluating an expression tree.

---

procedure *Postorder*(**pointer** P):
  foreach child Q **of** P, in order, **do**
    Postorder(Q)
  Visit(P)

Algorithm 4.2(a)

procedure *Preorder*(**pointer** P):
  Visit(P)
  foreach child Q **of** P, in order, **do**
    Preorder(Q)

Algorithm 4.2(b)

Evaluate reflects the shape of the tree itself.

$$Evaluate(A) \begin{cases} Evaluate(B) \begin{cases} Evaluate(C) \Rightarrow 20 \\ Evaluate(D) \Rightarrow 2 \\ ApplyOp(\div, 20, 2) \Rightarrow 10 \end{cases} \\ Evaluate(E) \Rightarrow 3 \\ ApplyOp(+, 10, 3) \Rightarrow 13 \end{cases}$$

Any well-defined ordering of the visits to the nodes of a tree is called a **traversal** of the tree. In our example, the nodes are visited in the order C, D, B, E, A, and their labels in this order are 20, 2, $\div$, 3, +. (We count as a "visit" to a node only an inspection of its Label, not the check of whether it is a leaf on the descent through the node.) As a general matter, when evaluating an expression tree it is not necessary to look at the label of a node which is not a leaf until after its subtrees have been completely visited. This is the defining characteristic of one of the basic traversals of an ordered tree, the **postorder traversal**: a node is considered *after* its children have been considered. We shall say that a node is **visited** at the time when the information in its label is considered; in a postorder traversal, a node is visited after its children. Schematically, a postorder traversal which applies the procedure *Visit* to each node of the tree has the form shown in Algorithm 4.2(a).

In this algorithm the phrase "**foreach child** Q **of** P ..." is a shorthand for code involving the abstract operation *Children*(P) and iteration over the resulting set. A postorder traversal of the tree of Figure 4.7(a) which lists the

---

procedure *PostorderEvaluate*($e_1, \ldots, e_n$)**:**
    for i **from** 1 **to** n **do**
        if e_i is a number **then** push it on the stack
        else
                Pop the top two numbers from the stack
                Apply the operator e_i to them,
                        with the right operand being the first one popped
                Push the result on the stack.

Algorithm 4.3 Finding the value of a postfix arithmetic expression.

---

names of the nodes as it visits them produces the list C, D, B, E, A; for the tree of Figure 4.7(b) the list C, D, E, A, B is produced.

If the labels, rather than the names, of the nodes are listed, a postorder traversal of Figure 4.7(a) produces 20, 2, ÷, 3, +, while from Figure 4.7(b) the list 20, 2, 3, +, ÷ is produced. These enumerations of numbers and operators can be defined formally as follows: A **postfix expression** is a number, or the concatenation, in order, of two postfix expressions and an operator. For example, since "2" and "3" are postfix expressions, so is "2, 3, +"; and since "20" is also a postfix expression, so is "20, 2, 3, +, ÷". Postfix expressions are commonly used instead of infix expressions as the command language for electronic calculators, since they represent calculations unambiguously without parentheses, and since they can be evaluated by the simple stack-based method of Algorithm 4.3. This algorithm begins with an empty stack and leaves the value of the expression as the sole item on the stack after processing all the numbers and operators that make up the expression. The behavior of the stack during evaluation of a postorder expression is essentially the same as the behavior of a stack that implements the recursive postorder traversal of the corresponding expression tree; the values of the local variables x_L and x_R of Algorithm 4.1, which are stacked during the recursion on subtrees, correspond directly to the values pushed on the stack during the execution of Algorithm 4.3.

Dual to the postorder traversal of a tree is the **preorder traversal**, in which a node is visited *before* its subtrees are traversed (Algorithm 4.2(b)). This might be called "outline order," since an outline of a paper or book is really a way of representing tree-structured information, and the outline lists the contents of that tree in preorder. For example, the outline of Figure 4.8(b) is a preorder traversal of the ordered forest of Figure 4.8(a); the tree shows each subsection as a descendant of the more major section of which it is a part.

A third type of traversal is relevant only to *binary* trees. The **inorder traversal** of a binary tree visits the root *after* visiting the left subtree, and *before* visiting the right subtree (Algorithm 4.4). Both the binary trees in Figure 4.7 have the inorder traversal $CBDAE$ or, in terms of the labels instead of

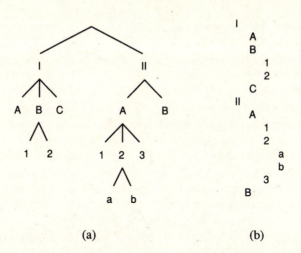

(a)   (b)

Figure 4.8 (a) Structure tree of a book; (b) its preorder traversal, an outline.

procedure *Inorder*(**pointer** *P*):
{*P* is a pointer to the root of a binary tree}
    if $P = \Lambda$ **then return**
    else
        Inorder(LeftChild(P))
        Visit(P)
        Inorder(RightChild(P))

Algorithm 4.4 Inorder traversal of a binary tree.

the names, $20 \div 2 + 3$. Notice that the inorder traversal of an expression tree yields an infix expression corresponding to that tree—but without the parentheses needed to make the expression unambiguous. Thus while the preorder and postorder traversals of an expression tree uniquely determine preorder and postorder arithmetic expressions, an inorder traversal of an expression tree does not in general correspond to a unique inorder expression—parentheses must be added to represent the structure of the tree. The two trees of Figure 4.7 correspond to two different ways of making the infix expression $20 \div 2 + 3$ unambiguous by adding parentheses, as $(20 \div 2) + 3$ and as $20 \div (2 + 3)$.

Now let us suppose that we wish to use a binary tree structure to represent some data, and we want to take advantage of some property of the data to help organize it. A commonly exploited property is *linear order*. A **linear order** is a relation $<$ such that for any x, y, and z,

- If x and y are different then either $x < y$ or $y < x$.
- If $x < y$ and $y < z$ then $x < z$.

For example, the universe of numbers is linearly ordered by ordinary comparison of numbers, and the universe of words is linearly ordered by the dictionary or **lexicographic** ordering (cat < catastrophe < category < cell < cellophane).

Consider a binary tree in which the nodes are labelled with elements of some linearly ordered set; for example, a tree with a word attached to each node. Such a tree is a **binary search tree** if the inorder traversal of the tree yields the labels in order. Equivalently, the search tree property can be stated recursively as follows: the label of each node comes after the labels of all the nodes in its left subtree and before the labels of all the nodes in its right subtree. Search trees are useful structures for implementing set abstract data types because a question of the form "$x \in S$?" can be answered by following a unique path from the root, moving from a node to its left child if the node's label is after x and to its right child if the node's label is before x. Search trees will be studied in detail in Chapters 6 and 7.

In addition to the preorder, inorder, and postorder traversals, a fourth traversal of ordered trees is the **level-order** or **breadth-first** traversal, which visits the nodes in order of increasing depth and, among nodes of the same depth, in left-to-right order. For example, a level-order traversal of the tree of Figure 4.7(a) would visit the nodes in the order A, B, E, C, D, while the tree of Figure 4.7(b) would yield the traversal order B, C, A, D, E.

4.4 TREE IMPLEMENTATIONS

We consider three basic memory representations of special kinds of trees: one for general binary trees, one for general ordered trees, and one for complete binary trees. In each case we assume that, in addition to whatever structure is needed to represent the tree structure itself, an Info field is to be part of each node to contain information about that node.

Representation of Binary Trees

The obvious representation of binary trees uses two fields for each node, say LC and RC, to point to the left and right child of the node (Figure 4.9). When one of these fields has value Λ, that child is missing; thus Λ itself acts as the representation of the empty tree. This representation, which we call the **natural representation of binary trees**, directly generalizes the singly linked representation of lists. Just as a node in a singly linked list acts as a "handle" to the portion of the list beginning at that node, under this representation a tree can be identified with its root node. The operation of *LeftChild* is implemented simply by selecting the LC field of a node; and similarly for *RightChild* and RC.

Parent cannot be implemented in $\Theta(1)$ time with only these fields; however, a third field can be added to point back to a node's parent, resulting in a sort of

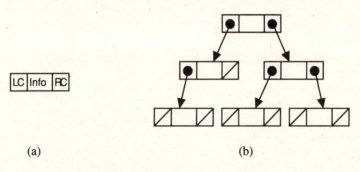

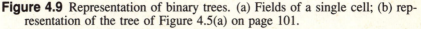

(a)   (b)

Figure 4.9 Representation of binary trees. (a) Fields of a single cell; (b) representation of the tree of Figure 4.5(a) on page 101.

"doubly linked tree" structure with **3p** bits per node. (Recall that **p** is the number of bits needed to represent a pointer.) The parsimoniously minded can devise a representation with only **2p** bits per node in which *LeftChild*, *RightChild*, and *Parent* all take $\Theta(1)$ time; the basic idea is to generalize the exclusive-or coding trick on page 89 by storing in the two fields of node X the quantities $Parent(X) \oplus LeftChild(X)$ and $Parent(X) \oplus RightChild(X)$ (Problem 16).

Representation of Ordered Trees

Binary trees are easy to represent because each node can have only two children, so the two fields to point to them can be allocated within each node. A similar idea would work for "ternary trees," that is, trees with at most three children at each node, and so on; a node with at most k children could be represented as a record with k pointer fields, and could be used to construct a k-**ary tree** (Problem 7). In essence, each node is then represented as a list of pointers to its children, and the list of child pointers is represented as a table in contiguous memory. A different strategy must be adopted for general ordered trees, since there is no *a priori* bound on the number of children a node can have. In this case a different representation must be used for the list of children, one that is more convenient when lists of different lengths need to be represented. These considerations lead to the **binary tree representation of ordered trees**.

A binary tree can be associated with each ordered tree as follows: instead of regarding the two children of a node as the "left" and "right" children, think of them as the *first child* and the *right sibling* of that node of the ordered tree. Figure 4.10 shows the ordered tree of Figure 4.4 on page 100, and its rendition as a binary tree; the "first child" of a node is drawn to its south or southwest, the "right sibling" of a node to its east. Since each node of the ordered tree has a child, a right sibling, both, or neither, each node of the corresponding binary tree has one, both, or neither of the two edges emanating from it. No information is lost in this correspondence; from a binary tree representing an ordered tree it is easy to reconstruct the ordered tree. Moreover, the correspondence is one-to-one; to be precise, each binary tree can be viewed as representing an ordered

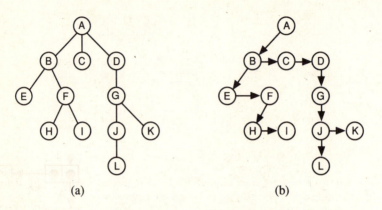

(a)   (b)

Figure 4.10 (a) An ordered tree; (b) its representation as a binary tree.

forest—if the root of the binary tree has a "right sibling," that sibling is the root of the second tree in the forest. Note that the height of the binary tree can be much greater than the height of the ordered trees in the forest it represents. For example, the ordered tree of Figure 4.10(a) has height 4, but the representing binary tree of Figure 4.10(b) has height 6; the difference arises from the fact that node B has two right siblings. They do not add height to the original tree, but they do add height to the binary tree.

When the binary trees representing ordered trees are themselves represented in memory by means records with two pointer fields, it is helpful to rename the two fields FirstChild and RightSibling instead of LC and RC (Figure 4.11(a)). Figure 4.11(b) shows the internal representation of the tree of Figure 4.10 by this method; in essence, the FirstChild field of a node points to a singly linked list of its children, linked through their RightSibling fields. Λ in one field or the other indicates that a node has no child or right sibling.

Of course, this representation of ordered trees supports $\Theta(1)$ implementation of *FirstChild* and *RightSibling* operations, and $\Theta(k)$ implementation of the abstract operation k^{th}-*Child*(k, v) that finds the kth child of node v; it also permits easy insertion and deletion of subtrees. Without additional fields, it does not support *Parent* operations in constant time.

Representation of Complete Binary Trees
Since there is only one complete binary tree with n nodes, in theory there should be a representation of the tree in n cells of contiguous memory—a table $T[0 .. n - 1]$—without any pointer information at all. Such a representation (called an **implicit representation**, since the edges between nodes are not part of the data structure, but are implied by relations between cell indices) amounts to a way of numbering the n nodes of the tree, so that node i is stored in $T[i]$. The trick is to do the numbering so that useful operations on the tree—for example, finding the root, the leaves, the parent or children of a node—can be done in $\Theta(1)$ time by arithmetic on the table indices.

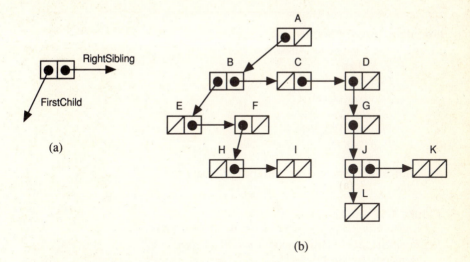

Figure 4.11 Binary tree representation of an ordered tree. (a) Fields of a node; (b) representation of the tree of Figure 4.10.

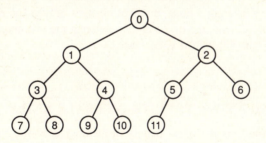

Figure 4.12 Implicit numbering of the nodes of a complete binary tree.

In fact there is such a representation: let the root be node 0 and let the left and right children of node i be nodes $2i + 1$ and $2i + 2$, respectively. This amounts to numbering the nodes in order by depth, and from left to right for nodes of a given depth; in other words, in level-order (Figure 4.12). The defining properties of a complete binary tree—that all nodes of depth k must be present if there are any of depth $k + 1$, and the nodes of maximal depth must be "at the left"—ensure that the n nodes are assigned the numbers $0, 1, 2, \ldots, n - 1$ in this way. Moreover, in this representation a great many useful tree operations can be implemented by purely arithmetical calculations. We use table indices as the names of nodes; the root has index 0.

IsLeaf(i): $2i + 1 \geq n$
LeftChild(i): $2i + 1$ (none if $2i + 1 \geq n$)
RightChild(i): $2i + 2$ (none if $2i + 2 \geq n$)
LeftSibling(i): $i - 1$ (none if $i = 0$ or i is odd)

---

procedure *Traverse*(**pointer** P):
{Traverse the binary tree whose root is P}
    if $P \neq \Lambda$ **then**
        PreVisit(P)
        Traverse(LC(P))
        InVisit(P)
        Traverse(RC(P))
        PostVisit(P)

Algorithm 4.5 Three-in-one traversal of binary tree.

   RightSibling(i): $i + 1$ (none if $i = n - 1$ or i is even)
   Parent(i): $\lfloor (i - 1)/2 \rfloor$ (none if $i = 0$)
   Depth(i): $\lfloor \lg(i + 1) \rfloor$
   Height(i): $\lceil \lg((n + 1)/(i + 1)) \rceil - 1$

Finally, note that extending a complete binary tree by adding a node, or contracting it by deleting a node, involves changes only at the *end* of the table that implicitly represents the tree. (In fact, deleting the last node happens automatically when the value of n is decreased.)

4.5 IMPLEMENTING TREE TRAVERSALS AND SCANS

This section considers the cost—mainly in memory used—of various methods for visiting the nodes of a tree. The emphasis is on traversals of binary trees.

Stack-Based Traversals

In order to study implementations of the preorder, inorder, and postorder traversals, we consider a single routine that carries out all three kinds of traversals. Let *PreVisit*, *InVisit*, and *PostVisit* be three arbitrary operations to be applied to the nodes of a binary tree when they are visited during preorder, inorder, and postorder traversals. The three traversals can be carried out in the single recursive routine of Algorithm 4.5. Or, to put it another way, deleting from Algorithm 4.5 the calls to any two of the three operations *PreVisit*, *InVisit*, and *PostVisit* yields an ordinary preorder, inorder, or postorder traversal algorithm.

This traversal algorithm takes $O(n)$ time to traverse a tree with n nodes (not counting the time taken by the calls to *PreVisit*, *InVisit*, and *PostVisit*). Since it calls itself recursively on both the left and right subtrees, *the height of the stack used by this recursive traversal algorithm is proportional to the height of the tree*. As the structure to be traversed may be extremely large, the size of the stack can limit the usefulness of this simple recursive method.

---

procedure *Traverse*(**pointer** *P*):
{Traverse the binary tree whose root is *P*}
    while $P \neq \Lambda$ **do**
        PreVisit(*P*)
        Traverse(LC(*P*))
        InVisit(*P*)
        $P \leftarrow$ RC(*P*)

Algorithm 4.6 Preorder and inorder traversal of binary tree, with recursion on left children only.

Notice that *in preorder and inorder traversals, one of the recursive calls is tail-recursive.* That is, if the call to *PostVisit* is eliminated from Algorithm 4.5, the last statement of *Traverse*(*P*) is the recursive call *Traverse*(RC(*P*)). This tail-recursion can be replaced by iteration, the result being an algorithm that carries out a recursion only on left children (Algorithm 4.6).

If we think of a binary tree as representing an ordered tree as in Figure 4.10, then the maximum size of the stack required by this algorithm when run on a binary tree *B* is proportional to the height of the ordered tree represented by *B*. To put it another way, define *OrdHt*(*P*) thus if *P* is a node of a binary tree:

$$OrdHt(P) = \begin{cases} 0, & \text{if } P = \Lambda; \\ OrdHt(\text{RC}(P)), & \text{if } \text{LC}(P) = \Lambda; \\ \max(1 + OrdHt(\text{LC}(P)), OrdHt(\text{RC}(P))), & \text{otherwise.} \end{cases}$$

That is, *OrdHt*(*P*), where *P* is the root of a binary tree, is the maximum number of left child pointers that must be followed from the root to reach any node of the tree. Then *OrdHt*(*P*) is the height of the ordered tree represented by the binary tree rooted at *P*, and is the maximum stack height needed to execute Algorithm 4.6 on this tree. This can be significantly less than the height of that binary tree. If the binary tree with root *P* represents the ordered tree *T*, then *OrdHt*(*P*) is at most the height of *T*, but the *height* of the binary tree rooted at *P* can be much greater—if *T* consists of a root with *k* children, then the height of *T*, and *OrdHt*(*P*), is 1, but the height of the binary tree rooted at *P* is *k*.

Link-Inversion Traversal

If the tree structure can be altered temporarily during the traversal, the link inversion method described on page 85 for singly linked lists can be adapted to provide a traversal technique for binary trees. As the algorithm descends through a node by following its LC or RC pointer field, this pointer is turned around to point back to the node's parent. Thus the contents of the stack used in the recursive algorithm (which consists of pointers to nodes along a path

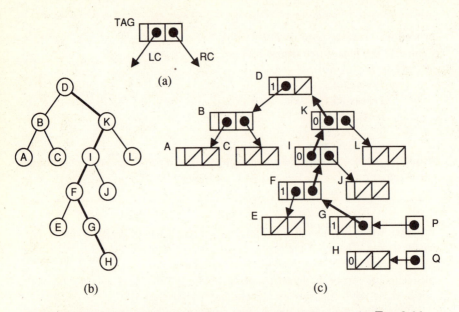

Figure 4.13 Link inversion traversal. (a) A node of the tree; the Tag field has value 0 or 1. (b) A binary tree, and a path showing a stage during its traversal. (c) The internal representation of the tree at this stage of the traversal; inverted pointers along the path are shown as heavy arrows.

from the root to a node in the tree) is stored in the tree itself as a list linked through LC and RC pointer fields. As the algorithm uses this list to ascend back towards the root, it again reverses these pointers to restore them to their original condition. A complication in the case of binary trees not present in the case of simple linked lists is that there are *two* pointer fields in a node, and a pointer in this chain points to a node, not a field of a node; therefore one additional bit per node on the implicit stack is needed to indicate whether the LC or RC field should be followed.* We call this the Tag bit, and add it as a new field of each node, along with LC and RC (Figure 4.13(a)).

This method, presented in detail as Algorithm 4.7, does not completely eliminate the memory used by the stack of the recursive algorithm, though it does reduce it to a single bit per cell. In essence, this bit encodes the same information as is needed in the recursive version (Algorithm 4.6) to indicate, when a recursive invocation finishes, which of the two recursive calls in the body of the program caused that invocation, and hence where in the body of the program execution should continue.

---

*Do not be deceived by the illustration into thinking that one can tell which pointer points "up" the tree; "up" and "down" are drawn this way only for illustrative purposes, and bear no relation to the relative values of machine addresses. In general, given two machine addresses and the knowledge that they are the addresses of tree nodes, and that one node is the parent of the other, there is no way to tell which is the parent and which the child.

procedure *LinkInversionTraversal*(**pointer** Q):
{Initially Q points to the root of the tree to be traversed}
 $P \leftarrow \Lambda$
 repeat forever
  {Descend as far as possible to the left (possibly not at all)}
  while $Q \neq \Lambda$ **do**
   PreVisit(Q)
   Tag(Q) $\leftarrow 0$
   descend to left
  {Ascend as far as possible from the right (possibly not at all)}
  while $P \neq \Lambda$ **and** Tag(P) $= 1$ **do**
   ascend from right
   PostVisit(Q)
  if $P = \Lambda$ **then return**   {If trailing pointer is Λ then done}
  else   {Ascend from left, descend to right, and repeat}
   ascend from left
   InVisit(Q)
   Tag(Q) $\leftarrow 1$
   descend to right

Algorithm 4.7 Binary tree traversal by link inversion.

Like the linked list version, Algorithm 4.7 uses two variables, P and Q, to keep track of its position in the structure. Q points to the next untraversed tree node, and everything that can be reached by following LC and RC pointers starting from Q is unchanged from its appearance in the original tree. P points to the node that is the parent of the one Q points to. This is the "top" node on the embedded stack; following the appropriate fields of nodes beginning with P (as indicated by their Tag bits) leads back to the root of the tree. Figure 4.13(b) shows a binary tree, and a path from its root to a leaf; Figure 4.13(c) shows the internal representation of the tree at the point the algorithm reaches node H. (The tag bits are shown only for the nodes along the path, since the others are irrelevant.)

To state this algorithm succinctly we have used code fragments to *descend* to the *left* and to the *right* and to *ascend* from the *left* and from the *right*. These cause the P–Q pair to move along one edge down or up the tree. On descent, the direction (*left* or *right*) indicates which child pointer to follow, and on ascent the direction indicates which field of the node to which P points contains the address of that node's parent. Descending to the left and then immediately ascending from the left leaves everything as it was; similarly, ascending from the right inverts the action of descending to the right.

$$\text{descend} \atop \text{to left:} \quad \begin{pmatrix} P \\ Q \\ \text{LC}(Q) \end{pmatrix} \leftarrow \begin{pmatrix} Q \\ \text{LC}(Q) \\ P \end{pmatrix} \qquad \text{descend} \atop \text{to right:} \quad \begin{pmatrix} P \\ Q \\ \text{RC}(Q) \end{pmatrix} \leftarrow \begin{pmatrix} Q \\ \text{RC}(Q) \\ P \end{pmatrix}$$

$$\text{ascend} \atop \text{from left:} \quad \begin{pmatrix} Q \\ P \\ \text{LC}(P) \end{pmatrix} \leftarrow \begin{pmatrix} P \\ \text{LC}(P) \\ Q \end{pmatrix} \qquad \text{ascend} \atop \text{from right:} \quad \begin{pmatrix} Q \\ P \\ \text{RC}(P) \end{pmatrix} \leftarrow \begin{pmatrix} P \\ \text{RC}(P) \\ Q \end{pmatrix}$$

The Tag bit of a node is 0 during the visit to the node's left subtree, and is 1 during the visit to the node's right subtree. This bit is used to distinguish, when $Q = \Lambda$, whether ascent should be through the LC or RC field of P.

A simple refinement of this algorithm is to note that the Tag bits are needed only for the nodes along the path being traversed. Therefore, instead of adding a one-bit field to each node of the tree, it suffices to create a stack of bits at the time the traversal takes place. The size this stack attains is exactly $Height(T)$ bits; in the worst case this is the same amount of memory as would be used by allocating a bit field in each node, but the memory is used only during the traversal. In any case, the link inversion method improves the memory utilization of the simple recursive method by a factor of exactly **p**.

Scanning a Tree in Constant Space

All the nodes of a binary tree can be visited without using any additional memory at all, save for a small fixed number of temporary variables, independent of the size of the tree. While this may seem remarkable, there is a catch: the algorithm chooses the order, so the method cannot be used to implement any of the "standard" traversals (preorder, inorder, postorder, or level-order). It is guaranteed that each node will be visited exactly three times. But there is no way to distinguish the first visit from the subsequent visits; that would require additional memory. For this reason, this algorithm is not considered to be a traversal at all, but rather a **scan** of the tree.

The scanning order provided by the algorithm gives a clue as to how it works. Consider once again the binary tree of Figure 4.13(b), but instead of regarding the edges as walkways that can be perambulated up and back, think of them as solid walls. The algorithm scans the tree by starting at the root, and *walking around it, keeping the tree nodes and edges always on its left*. Each node is visited three times, once going down from its parent, once going up from the left, and once going up from the right. The resulting order of visits is $D, B, A, A, A, B, C, C, C, B, D, K, I, F, E, E, E, F, G, G, H, H, H, G,$ $F, I, J, J, J, I, K, L, L, L, K, D$ (Figure 4.14). The first visits to each node form a preorder traversal of the tree, the second visits form an inorder traversal, and the third visits form a postorder traversal.

The method used can be pictured as a physical mechanism (Figure 4.15). Imagine each interior node of the tree to be a point where three sections of tubing are joined together. A ball is inserted in an opening at the root of the tree, and rolls through the tubing until it ultimately reemerges at the root. There

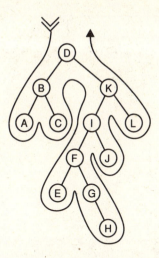

Figure 4.14 Order of visit to nodes during constant-space scanning of binary tree. The tree is followed as though it were a solid wall that the algorithm always keeps on its left.

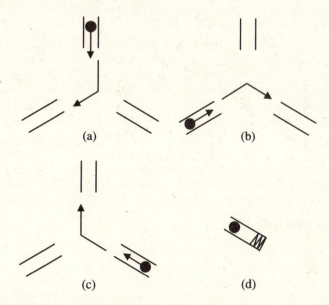

Figure 4.15 Physical metaphor for the constant-space tree scanning method. (a) Initially a ball enters from the top and is directed to the left; (b) this rotates the valve 120° so that on the return trip the ball is directed to the right; (c) this in turn rotates the valve so that on the return trip the ball is directed upwards. (d) The ends of the tubing contain springs so that the ball returns whence it came.

---

procedure *ConstantSpaceScan*(**pointer** Q):
{Γ is a distinguished value; initially Q points to the root of the tree.}

$\quad P \leftarrow \Gamma$
$\quad$**while** $Q \neq \Gamma$ **do**
$\quad\quad$**if** $Q \neq \Lambda$ **then**
$\quad\quad\quad Visit(Q)$
$$\begin{pmatrix} P \\ Q \\ LC(Q) \\ RC(Q) \end{pmatrix} \leftarrow \begin{pmatrix} Q \\ LC(Q) \\ RC(Q) \\ P \end{pmatrix}$$
$\quad\quad$**else**
$\quad\quad\quad P \leftrightarrow Q$

Algorithm 4.8 Binary tree scanning in constant space.

---

is a valve at each fork in the tubing that controls the direction in which the ball rolls when it reaches the fork. These valves have three possible orientations. As the ball passes through a fork it is redirected in the direction indicated by the valve, and at the same time the valve rotates counterclockwise by 120°. Thus on the first trip through a fork the ball rolls from the top down to the left (Figure 4.15(a)); on the second trip it returns from the left and is redirected down to the right (Figure 4.15(b)); and on the third trip it returns from the right and is redirected upwards (Figure 4.15(c)). The final trip through the junction restores the valve to its original orientation. The ball reverses direction when it reaches a leaf of the tree; we can think of the ends of the tubing as containing springs that cause the ball to reverse direction by bouncing (Figure 4.15(d)).

A "valve" is implemented by permuting a node's parent, LC, and RC fields; the LC field always indicates the node to be visited next. Thus initially the LC field points to the node's true left child, but after the first visit the LC field points to the node that was originally the right child, and after the second visit it points to the node's original parent.

The algorithm (Algorithm 4.8) uses two pointers, P and Q, to successive nodes in this sequence; thus while going down the tree, P and Q follow the same path as they would during the link-inversion traversal, but while going up the tree, Q is closer to the root than P. On entering a node, the values of P, Q, LC(Q), and RC(Q) are permuted in such a way that if the same permutation is applied three times, the node is restored to its original condition. Thus, like the link-inversion algorithm, this algorithm alters the tree during descent but repairs it during ascent. The algorithm starts with $Q = Root(T)$ and with P pointing to a distinguished node Γ. Node Γ need not have any particular values in its LC and RC fields; the algorithm terminates when the value of Q becomes Γ. In fact, Γ can be any value whatever, except for Λ or a node of the tree.

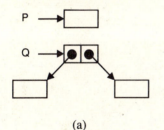

(a)

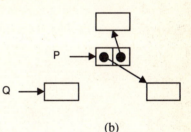

(b)

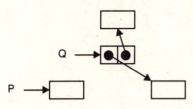

(c)

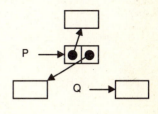

(d)

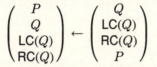

(e)

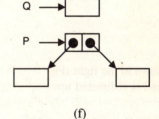

(f)

Figure 4.16 Pointer permutation during the three visits to a node with two children. (a) Prior to first visit (descent from above); (b) after first visit (descent to left); (c) prior to second visit (ascent from left); (d) after second visit (descent to right); (e) prior to third visit (ascent from right); (f) after third visit (ascent to above).

The crucial point to understand is the effect of the permutation

$$\begin{pmatrix} P \\ Q \\ LC(Q) \\ RC(Q) \end{pmatrix} \leftarrow \begin{pmatrix} Q \\ LC(Q) \\ RC(Q) \\ P \end{pmatrix}$$

on the three successive visits to a node. Figure 4.16 shows how the pointers change and are eventually restored to their original condition. This effect is achieved even if one or both of the LC and RC of Q are Λ.

Figure 4.17 shows the binary tree of Figure 4.13(b) at the time the constant-space scan reaches node H for the first time.

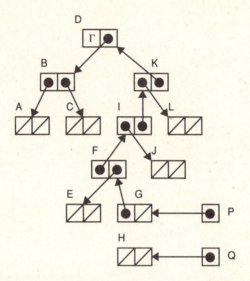

Figure 4.17 Internal representation of binary tree of Figure 4.13(b) at the time the constant-space scanning algorithm reaches node H.

Threaded Trees

Inorder traversal of part or all of a binary tree is a frequent operation in applications involving expression trees and search trees. The recursive methods of Algorithm 4.4 on page 107 and Algorithm 4.6 on page 113 have two principal disadvantages: they require extra memory to store a stack, and they require always starting at the root—it is impossible in general to start from an arbitrary node in the tree and to pass to the node's **inorder successor**, that is, the node that would be visited next during an inorder traversal. The following method stores additional structural information in the tree that makes it easy to find the inorder successor of any node. Since the tree is not altered during the traversal, the method is quite flexible and the tree can be stored in read-only memory. Moreover the method is entirely symmetric, and makes it equally easy to find the inorder *predecessor* of a node or to traverse the tree in "reverse inorder."

An observation that suggests how such a representation might be achieved is that in the natural representation of a binary tree, there are a great many Λ pointers. In a binary tree with n nodes there are $2n$ pointer fields, but $n + 1$ of these are Λ. (Each node except the root has a unique parent, so the number of pointers from parents to children is $n - 1$; the rest are Λ.) We make better use of these pointers by *storing as the* RC *of a node with no right child a pointer to the node's inorder successor, and storing as the* LC *of a node with no left child a pointer to a node's inorder predecessor.* These pointers must be distinguishable from ordinary pointers that point to left and right children, so one extra bit is required in each pointer field. Pointers of the new type are called **threads**. Figure 4.18 shows the tree of Figure 4.13(b) on page 114 with all the

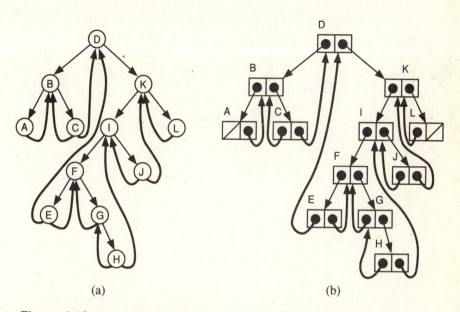

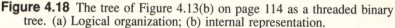

(a)   (b)

Figure 4.18 The tree of Figure 4.13(b) on page 114 as a threaded binary tree. (a) Logical organization; (b) internal representation.

threads added; rather than showing an extra one-bit field with each pointer, we draw the threads using heavier lines.*

Given a node N within a threaded tree T, Algorithm 4.9 finds the inorder successor of the node. It first follows one RC pointer; if this is a thread, it leads directly to the inorder successor. If it is not a thread, then it leads to the right child of N, and the inorder successor of N is found by passing through left children as long as possible (that is, until a thread or Λ is encountered as the value of an LC field). The same algorithm will find the first node in the inorder enumeration of the nodes of T, if it is passed as its argument a "header node" of which the root of T is the right child. Also, replacing "LC" by "RC" and *vice versa* in Algorithm 4.9 yields an algorithm for the inorder predecessor. (Indeed, if there is no need to be able to find predecessors, then there is no need to store left threads, and the representation can be simplified somewhat.)

Note that Algorithm 4.9 is *not* guaranteed to find the inorder successor of a node in $\Theta(1)$ time, since there is no bound, except for the height of the tree, on the number of times the loop which traces through LC pointers might be executed. On the other hand the *amortized* cost of visiting a node is a constant;

---

*In some cases it may be possible to get by without the extra bit entirely. For example, if the tree is prepared for storage in read-only memory, so that new cells will not be dynamically added to the tree, then it may be possible to arrange the location of cells in memory so that a parent always has smaller address than its children. If so, an LC or RC field that points to a cell that is lower in memory must be a thread.

function *InorderSuccessor*(**pointer** N): **pointer**
{Return the inorder successor of node N, or Λ if N has none}
      $P \leftarrow \mathrm{RC}(N)$ {P traces the path from N to its inorder successor}
      if $P = \Lambda$ **then return** Λ
      else if P is not a thread **then**
            while $\mathrm{LC}(P)$ is not a thread or Λ **do**
                $P \leftarrow \mathrm{LC}(P)$
      return P

Algorithm 4.9 Find the inorder successor of a node of a threaded binary tree.

---

procedure *ThreadedInsert*(**pointer** P, Q):
{Make node Q the inorder successor of node P}
$$\begin{pmatrix} \mathrm{RC}(P) \\ \mathrm{LC}(Q) \\ \mathrm{RC}(Q) \end{pmatrix} \leftarrow \begin{pmatrix} (\mathbf{child})Q \\ (\mathbf{thread})P \\ \mathrm{RC}(P) \end{pmatrix}$$
      if $\mathrm{RC}(Q)$ is not a thread
            then $\mathrm{LC}(\textit{InorderSuccessor}(Q)) \leftarrow (\mathbf{thread})Q$

Algorithm 4.10 Insertion of a node in a threaded binary tree.

---

that is, if the algorithm is executed n times to visit all the nodes in inorder, then the total time spent by the algorithm will be $\Theta(n)$, so an average of $\Theta(1)$ will be spent on each node. To see this, note that during those n calls the algorithm will traverse each pointer (be it a child pointer or a thread) at most once, and there are only $2n+2$ pointers if there are n nodes in the tree and a header node.

    Threaded trees are also not hard to construct and alter. To give just one example of what is involved, Algorithm 4.10 inserts a node in a threaded binary tree. Q points to the node to be inserted, and that node is to be inserted as the inorder successor of the node to which P points. (In presenting this algorithm, we explicitly refer to the creation of **child** and **thread** pointers; when a pointer is simply copied, its type should be preserved.) Figure 4.19 shows the four pointers that may be altered by this procedure; of these only the thread modified by the last step of Algorithm 4.10 is likely to be puzzling (Figure 4.19(a) and (b)). If P had a right child prior to calling the procedure, that is, if its RC field was not a thread, then the inorder successor of P was a descendant of P (called R in the figure) and now becomes a descendant of Q, and its LC field must be changed from a thread to P (its former inorder predecessor) to a thread to Q (its new inorder predecessor). Figure 4.19(c) and (d) illustrate the case in which the inorder successor of P is an ancestor of P; this node becomes the inorder successor of Q.

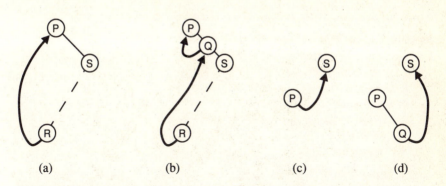

(a) (b) (c) (d)

Figure 4.19 Inserting a node Q as the inorder successor of node P in a threaded tree. (a) Situation prior to insertion, in case the inorder successor of P is a descendant of P, that is, in case RC(P) is not a thread. (b) Situation after insertion in this case. (c) Situation prior to insertion, in case RC(P) is a thread. (d) Situation after insertion in this case.

---

function *PreorderSuccessor*(**pointer** N): **pointer**
{Return the preorder successor of N, or Λ if N has none}
    if LC(N) is not a thread and is not Λ **then return** LC(N)
    else
        $P \leftarrow N$
        while RC(P) is a thread **do**
            $P \leftarrow$ RC(P)
        if RC(P) $= \Lambda$ **then return** Λ
        else return RC(P)

Algorithm 4.11 Find the preorder successor of a node of a threaded binary tree.

Surprisingly, the threaded representation can also be used to provide efficient implementation of *preorder* traversal. The preorder successor of a node N of a binary tree is

1. the left child of N, if N has one; otherwise
2. the right child of N, if N has one; otherwise
3. the right child of the lowest ancestor of N, call it A, such that A has a right child and N is in the left subtree of A. (If there is no such ancestor A, then N is the last node in preorder.)

If a node has a right thread, that thread points to its inorder successor, which is the lowest ancestor of the node such that the node is in its left subtree. Right threads can therefore be followed in search of the ancestor A satisfying condition (3). These considerations yield Algorithm 4.11 for preorder successor.

---

procedure *LevelOrder*(**pointer** R):
{R is a pointer to the root of the tree}
    $L \leftarrow MakeEmptyQueue(\;)$
    Enqueue(R, L)
    until *IsEmptyQueue*(L)
        $P \leftarrow Dequeue(L)$
        Visit(P)
        foreach child Q of P, in order, **do**
            Enqueue(Q, L)

Algorithm 4.12 Visit the nodes of a tree in level order. The tree is represented by a pointer to its root, and each node contains pointers to its children.

Like Algorithm 4.9, Algorithm 4.11 takes $\Theta(Height(T))$ time in the worst case to find the preorder successor of a node of tree T. However, if Algorithm 4.11 is called repeatedly to traverse a tree in inorder, each pointer will be traversed at most once, so the total time used is $\Theta(n)$ for a tree with n nodes; in the amortized sense, visiting each node takes constant time.

Implementing Level-Order Traversal

None of the recursive or link-following traversal methods are appropriate for implementing level-order traversal. However, a queue data structure provides exactly what is needed: after initializing the queue to contain just the root, the nodes are visited by dequeuing them, and a node's children are enqueued in left-to-right order as it is visited (Algorithm 4.12). For example, while traversing the tree of Figure 4.10 on page 110, on successive iterations of the main loop the queue would contain

    A
    B, C, D
    C, D, E, F
    D, E, F
    E, F, G
    F, G
    G, H, I
    H, I, J, K
    I, J, K
    J, K
    K, L
    L
    (empty)

The correctness of this method is easy to see by the following inductive conditions:

Algorithm (Alg. #)	Visit Order	Memory	Read Only
Recursive (4.5)	Pre, Post, In	$\mathbf{p} \cdot Height(T)$	Y
Left-Recursive (4.6)	Pre, In	$\mathbf{p} \cdot OrdHt(T)$	Y
Link Inversion (4.7)	Pre, Post, In	$Height(T)$	N
Constant Space (4.8)	Walk Around	$\Theta(1)$	N
Threaded (4.9, 4.11)	Pre, In	$2n$	Y
Level-Order (4.12)	Level	n	Y

Figure 4.20 Comparison of tree traversal and scanning methods. All the algorithms run in $\Theta(n)$ time in the worst case.

1. At any instant the queue contains nodes of at most two successive depths, say d and $d + 1$, with all nodes of depth d in the queue preceding all nodes of depth $d + 1$;
2. The nodes of depth d are all unvisited nodes of that depth in the tree, in left-to-right order;
3. The nodes of depth $d + 1$ are all children of the visited nodes of depth d, in left-to-right order.

Since these conditions are true at the beginning (when the queue contains only the root of the tree) and are maintained on each iteration of the main **while** loop of the algorithm, they are true throughout the algorithm. Moreover since the nodes are visited in the order in which they are dequeued, they are visited in order of increasing depth and left-to-right among nodes of the same depth, or in other words in level order.

Summary

Figure 4.20 provides a summary comparison of the traversal and scanning methods discussed in this section. The first column names the algorithm and gives the number by which it is referred to in the text. "*Memory*" is the number of bits required to completely visit a tree T with n nodes, beyond those used for the natural representation of T. Note that except in the case of the threaded representation, this memory is not needed when the algorithm is not running; only in the case of threaded trees is the required memory a permanent part of the tree structure. The "*Read Only*" column is "N" if the algorithm changes the fields of the tree nodes while it is running, so that the method cannot be used in read-only memory or in applications where several processes may want to access the tree simultaneously.

Problems

4.1   **1.** In Figure 4.1 on page 97, consider *Mammalia* (the mammals). What are the parent, children, siblings, descendants, ancestors, height, and depth of this node?

2. What is the length of the longest path on which node v lies, in terms of its height and depth?

3. Let $T_1, \ldots, T_k$ be trees with heights $h_1, \ldots, h_k$ and let T be a new tree formed from them in accordance with rule (2) on page 98. What is the height of tree T?

4. The **fan-out** of a tree node is the number of its children, and the **fan-out** of a tree is the maximum fan-out of its nodes. State an upper bound on the number of nodes in a tree, in terms of its fan-out and height. Conversely, state a lower bound on the height of a tree, in terms of its fan-out and the number of nodes it contains.

5. a. Formally define, using tree terminology: X and Y are k^{th} cousins, where k is a nonnegative integer.

   b. Repeat part (a) for the notion of "k^{th} cousins removed r" (for example, "second cousins twice removed").

   c. Write an algorithm that takes as arguments the root of a tree and two nodes of that tree, and determines numbers k and r such that the two nodes are k^{th} cousins removed r.

6. Prove that in a full binary tree the number of leaves is one more than the number of nonleaves.

4.2   **7.** A k-**ary tree**, where $k \geq 2$, is an ordered tree with at most k children per node, such that each child is distinguished as being the ith child of its parent for some i, $1 \leq i \leq k$. (Thus binary trees are 2-ary trees.)

   a. How many k-ary trees are there with two nodes?

   b. Explain, using natural generalizations of the ideas for binary trees, what **full**, **perfect**, and **complete** k-ary trees are.

   c. How many nodes does a perfect k-ary tree of height h have, and why?

   d. What are the bounds on the number of nodes of a complete k-ary tree of height h? Give examples of the two extremes.

   e. What is the relation between the number of leaves and the number of nonleaves in a full k-ary tree? Prove it.

8. Let $B(n)$ denote the number of different binary trees with n nodes.

   a. Determine $B(n)$ for $n = 1, 2, 3, 4$.

   b. Find a recurrence relation for $B(n)$.

9. Let $H(h)$ denote the number of different binary trees of height h.

   a. Determine $H(h)$ for $h = 1, 2, 3, 4$.

   b. Find a recurrence relation for $H(h)$.

10. (The terminology introduced in this problem is far from standard.)

    a. An **almost perfect** binary tree is a binary tree in which all leaves have the same depth. How many almost perfect binary trees of height h exist?

    b. A **not so perfect** binary tree is a full binary tree in which all leaves lie at one of only two distinct depths. How many not so perfect binary trees of height h exist?

4.3   11. a. Not every sequence of numbers and operators is a postfix expression; for example, "1, +, 1" is not. Show that a sequence of numbers and operators is a postfix expression if and only if it satisfies the following condition: if we examine the sequence from the end to the beginning and keep separate counts of numbers and of operators, the count of numbers exceeds the count of operators when the first element of the sequence is reached, and not before. (Thus a postfix expression always has exactly one more number than it has operators.)

    b. Rewrite Algorithm 4.3 on page 106 so that it checks for error conditions. For example, inputs such as "+, +, +," "1, 2, 3," and "1, +, 1" should be rejected.

12. Modify the general *Inorder* algorithm schema, Algorithm 4.4, so that it produces a fully parenthesized infix expression representing an arithmetic expression tree. For example, "((20÷2)+3)" and "(20÷(2+3))" should be produced from the trees in Figure 4.7 on page 104.

13. A **prefix expression** is the result of a preorder traversal of an expression tree. Give an alternative, recursive definition (like that given for postfix expressions on page 106), and give an algorithm for evaluating prefix expressions.

14. Let us say that one word is a **prefix** of another if letters can be appended to the first to produce the second; for example, cat is a prefix of catastrophe. (We also count cat as a prefix of cat.) Any finite set of words can be organized as a forest by the condition that u is an ancestor of v in the forest if and only if u is a prefix of v. Show the forest corresponding to the words need, needle, needless, needlepoint, negative, neglect, neigh, neighbor, neighborhood, neighborly.

4.4   15. Show that in the implicit representation of a complete binary tree of n nodes, $Height(i) = \lceil \lg((n+1)/(i+1)) \rceil - 1$.

16. Explain precisely how to implement tree-walking functions (*Parent*, *LeftChild*, and *RightChild*) starting from the root with only two pointer-sized fields per tree node, using the exclusive-or of pointers.

17. An alternative solution to the previous problem can be achieved without the need to take the exclusive-or of pointers. If each left child points to its left child and its right sibling, and each right child points to its left child and its parent, then the left or right child or parent of any node can be reached in at most two steps. Explain.

18. a. Write a function that takes a pointer to the root of an ordered tree represented as a binary tree and returns the number of nodes in the tree.

    b. Write a function that takes a pointer to the root of an ordered tree represented as a binary tree and returns the height of the tree.

    c. Write a function that takes a pointer to the root of an ordered tree represented as a binary tree and returns the largest fan-out (number of children) of any node in the tree.

    d. Write a function that takes both a pointer to the root of an ordered tree represented as a binary tree and a node in that tree, and returns the depth of the node in the tree.

19. Write a procedure *ShiftAllLeft* that takes a pointer to the root of an ordered tree represented as a binary tree, and restructures the tree so that the leftmost child of each node becomes its rightmost child, and the other children maintain their order.

20. Generalize the notation of a complete binary tree to a "complete k-ary tree," for any $k > 1$. What is the implicit representation of a complete k-ary tree, and how are the abstract tree operations implemented?

21. Suppose a link inversion traversal of a binary tree is interrupted and the values of P and Q are lost. Give an algorithm for reconstructing the original tree. You may assume that the tree has n nodes and that you have a table $T[0 .. n-1]$ storing a pointer to each node, with the root in $T[0]$. Can you solve the same problem in the case of constant-space traversal?

4.5   **22.** Give a nonrecursive version of Algorithm 4.6 on page 113 that manipulates the stack explicitly.

23. For this problem, you may use a routine *Output* that writes out the label of a node or a constant string; for example, *Output*(Label(n)) or *Output*("(") or *Output*("**newline**").

    a. Write a procedure that takes a binary tree and outputs a parenthesized expression for that tree, as in the caption of Figure 4.7 on page 104.

    b. Write a procedure that takes a binary tree and outputs the outline format of Figure 4.8(b) on page 107.

24. Show how to find the parent of a node N of a threaded tree. (Hint: This would not be hard if you knew that N was the left child of its parent. So make that assumption and then check that it was correct; if not, you know that N was the right child of its parent.)

25. Write an algorithm that substitutes one threaded tree for a given subtree of another. Specifically, $Replace(L, N)$ takes a locative L and a pointer N and replaces the entire subtree rooted at L in one threaded tree by the threaded tree rooted at N. Assume that neither L nor N is Λ.

26. Design a threaded version of binary trees that makes it possible to find the preorder successor of any node N in $\Theta(1)$ time in the worst case. Give algorithms for $PreorderSuccessor(N)$, for $RightInsert(N, P)$, which inserts N as the right child of P (between P and the previous right child of P, if it had one), and for $LeftInsert(N, P)$, which inserts N as the left child of P (between P and the previous left child of P, if it had one).

27. Consider trees with the property that no node has more than k children. Design a threaded representation of ordered trees that supports an $O(k)$ implementation of *Parent* operations.

28. Define a **reverse level order** traversal of a tree to be like a level order traversal, except that the nodes are visited from bottom to top rather than from top to bottom. For example, a reverse level order traversal of the tree of Figure 4.10(a) on page 110 would visit the nodes in the order L, H, I, J, K, E, F, G, B, C, D, A. Explain how to implement a reverse level order traversal, using only the stack and queue abstract operations.

References

The link-inversion algorithm (Algorithm 4.7 on page 115) and the constant-space algorithm (Algorithm 4.8 on page 118) for visiting the nodes of binary trees are special cases of more general algorithms for arbitrary list structures. In its general form, the link-inversion algorithm is called the Schorr-Deutsch-Waite algorithm, the version that stacks bits rather than using a reserved Tag *field is due to Ben Wegbreit, and the constant-space algorithm is due to Gary Lindstrom. See the end of Chapter 10 for citations of the original publications. Threaded trees were first described in*

A. J. Perlis and C. Thornton, "Symbol Manipulation by Threaded Lists," *Communications of the ACM* **3** (1960), pp. 195–204.

5

Arrays and Strings

5.1 ARRAYS AS ABSTRACT DATA TYPES

Arrays are the most familiar data structures that we shall study; almost every programming language provides at least one kind of array! The basic idea is simple and intuitive: an array is a data structure that stores a sequence of consecutively numbered objects, and each object can be accessed (a process sometimes called **selection**) using its number, which is known as its **index**. We now turn to a more formal analysis of the ubiquitous array and its most common special case: the string.

Given integers l and u with $u \geq l - 1$, the **interval** $l..u$ is defined to be the set of integers i such that $l \leq i \leq u$; when $u = l - 1$ the interval $l..u$ is empty. (In mathematics the term "interval" usually denotes a set of *real* numbers and has different notation; our intervals contain integers only.) An **array** is a function from any interval, called the **index set** (or simply the **indices**) of the array, to a set called the **value set** of the array. If X is an array and i is a member of its index set, we write $X[i]$ to denote the value of X at i. For example, let C be a function such that $C(1) = 10$, $C(2) = 20$, $C(3) = 15$, and $C(4) = 10$. Then C is an array with indices $1..4$, with $C[1] = C[4] = 10$, $C[3] = 15$, and so forth; the expression $C[5]$ is undefined, since 5 is not in the domain of C. We call the members of the range of X the **elements** of X. Note that the value set of an array need not be homogeneous in any way; arrays may contain any kinds of objects freely mixed. But only integers can be used to index arrays.*

Here are a few simple abstract operations on arrays. In the following definitions X is an array with index set $I = l..u$ and value set V, and i and v are respectively members of I and V:

Access(X, i): Return $X[i]$.

Length(X): Return $u - l + 1$, which is the number of elements in I.

---

*A few programming languages provide more general arrays. For example, the Unix utility awk permits arbitrary strings as array indices. On the other hand, many languages do not allow the index set to be an arbitrary interval; in C, for example, the lower bound must always be 0 while in FORTRAN it must be 1.

Assign(X, i, v): Replace array X with a function whose value on i is v (and whose value on all other arguments is unchanged). We also write this operation as $X[i] \leftarrow v$.

Initialize(X, v): Assign v to every element of array X.

Iterate(X, F): Apply F to each element of array X in order, from smallest index to largest index. (Here F is an action on a single array element.) This operation is often written in the form **for** i **from** l **to** u **do** $F(X[i])$.

One type of array is common enough to deserve special mention: if Σ is any finite set, then a **string over** Σ is an array whose value set is Σ and whose index set is $0 .. n - 1$ for some nonnegative n. If w is such a string, we have $Length(w) = n$; we frequently write $|w|$ for the length of a string w. The set Σ is called an **alphabet** and each element of Σ is called a **character**. Often Σ consists of the letters of the Roman alphabet plus digits, the space, and common punctuation marks; in this case we write a string over Σ by typesetting its elements in THIS FONT. For example, $w = $ CAT is a string of length 3 in which $w[0]$ is the character C, $w[1]$ is the character A, and $w[2]$ is the character T. The **null string** is the string whose domain is the empty interval; it has no elements and is written ϵ.

There are two abstract operations on strings that are not defined for arrays in general. Let w be a string and let i and m be integers. The operation *Substring*(w, i, m) returns the string of length m containing the portion of w that starts at position i. For example, if $w = $ STRING then *Substring*$(w, 2, 3) = $ RIN and *Substring*$(w, 5, 0) = \epsilon$. Formally, *Substring*(w, i, m) returns a string w' with indices $0 .. m - 1$ such that $w'[k] = w[i + k]$ for each k satisfying $0 \le k < m$. This definition is meaningful only if $0 \le i < |w|$ and $0 \le m \le |w| - i$; if not, then *Substring*$(w, i, m) = \epsilon$ by convention. Each string *Substring*$(w, 0, j)$ for $0 \le j \le |w|$ is a **prefix** of w; similarly, each string *Substring*$(w, j, |w| - j)$ is a **suffix** of w.

If w_1 and w_2 are two strings, then *Concat*(w_1, w_2) is a string of length $|w_1| + |w_2|$ whose characters are the characters of w_1 followed by those of w_2 (Problem 1 asks for a more formal definition). For example, if $w_1 = $ CONCAT and $w_2 = $ ENATE then *Concat*$(w_2, w_1) = $ ENATECONCAT. Notice that *Concat*$(w, \epsilon) = Concat(\epsilon, w) = w$ for any string w. This operation is analogous to the *Concat* operation on lists, defined on page 73.

At first it may seem that there is no difference between arrays and the tables that we have been using since Chapter 1. But there is an important distinction between these concepts. A table is a physical organization of memory into sequential cells. Arrays, on the other hand, constitute an abstract data type with specific operations such as accessing the ith element and finding the length. Arrays are frequently *implemented* using tables, as we shall study in the next section, but they may be implemented in other ways. For example, in §5.3 we discuss representations of arrays in which the *Access* operation is implemented with a search and requires non-constant time. But finding the ith element of a table always takes constant time, because (by assumption) the time required to access a physical memory cell is independent of its address.

Multidimensional Arrays

The arrays considered so far have been linear objects, but often it is important to model data with structure in two or more dimensions. A **multidimensional array** is a function whose range is any set V as before and whose domain is the Cartesian product of any number of intervals. (The **Cartesian product** of the intervals $I_1, I_2, \ldots, I_d$, written $I_1 \times I_2 \times \cdots \times I_d$, is the set of all d-tuples $\langle i_1, i_2, \ldots, i_d \rangle$ such that $i_k \in I_k$ for each k.) If C is a multidimensional array and if $\mathbf{i} = \langle i_1, i_2, \ldots, i_d \rangle$ is in its index set, then $C[i_1, i_2, \ldots, i_d]$ denotes the value of C at $\mathbf{i}$. The **dimension** of a multidimensional array is the number of intervals whose Cartesian product makes up the index set (d in this example). The **size** of the kth dimension of such an array is the number of elements in I_k; if we let s_k be the size of the kth dimension of C, then the total number of elements in C is the product $s_1 s_2 \ldots s_d$.

For example, suppose we wish to represent a standard three-by-three playing field for the game of tic-tac-toe, where each square either is empty or contains an X or an O. Let the characters B, X, and O respectively denote these three situations and let $V = \{B, X, O\}$. The playing field can then be represented as an array C with indices $(1 \ldots 3) \times (1 \ldots 3)$ and with value set V. Thus saying that $C[2, 2] = B$ means that the central square is empty, and $C[1, 1] \leftarrow X$ places an X in the lower left square. Each of the two dimensions of C has size 3. Arrays of three, four, and even more dimensions are frequently useful, although some languages place a limit on the number of dimensions in a multidimensional array.

You may have noticed that defining multidimensional arrays separately is not really necessary. From a formal standpoint it would suffice to make use of one-dimensional arrays whose elements are themselves arrays, as is actually done in several programming languages (such as C). The tic-tac-toe board, for example, would be modelled as an array with three elements each of which represents a row of the board as another array (also with three elements). But the structure of the board would be lost, or at least obscured, by taking that point of view. For example, there are many ways to *Iterate* over multidimensional arrays; we may wish to iterate over rows, columns, or even over diagonals. The necessity of translating algorithms into the language of one-dimensional arrays would just get in the way when we describe efficient implementations of these iterations. On the other hand, there are cases where arrays of arrays are appropriate. For example, a collection of short error messages that are to be selected by numbers can be represented naturally by an array of strings. In this case there is no logical connection between characters in the same position of different strings.

X	X+4	X+8	X+12	X+16	X+20
1	4	9	16	25	36
X[1]	X[2]	X[3]	X[4]	X[5]	X[6]

Figure 5.1 A one-dimensional array represented as a table in contiguous storage. The address of the beginning of the array is **X**; each element occupies four memory locations. The index set of this array is $1..6$ and $X[i] = i^2$ for each i.

5.2 CONTIGUOUS REPRESENTATION OF ARRAYS

The obvious way to represent an array in memory is to store its elements in a table, that is, in consecutive cells in memory. For example, consider an array X consisting of six elements $X[1]$ through $X[6]$, where $X[i] = i^2$ for each i. Figure 5.1 shows a contiguous representation of X starting at memory address **X**, where it is assumed that each integer occupies four memory locations. The ith element of X begins at address $X + 4(i - 1)$. In general, if **X** is the address of the first cell in memory of an array with indices $l..u$, and if each element has size L, then the ith element is stored starting at address $X + L \cdot (i - l)$ and can be retrieved in constant time.

What about iteration? It would be possible to iterate over the elements of X by accessing $X[l]$, then $X[l + 1]$, and so forth up to $X[u]$, thus performing the address calculation $Length(X)$ times. A better method is to start with **X** (which is the address of $X[l]$) and proceed from element to element by adding L on each iteration. Although this improvement reduces the amount of arithmetic that is performed, the overhead is still linear in the length of the array.

Of course, L, l, and u must be available somewhere in order to carry out these calculations. They can be stored in several places:

- The values L, l, and u can be stored starting at address **X**. The formula for the address of $X[i]$ must then be adjusted slightly to account for the extra space used.
- In strongly typed languages, some or all of L, l, and u may be part of the definition of X and may be stored elsewhere. Furthermore, if the language does not permit arbitrary lower bounds in indexing then the value l is fixed and need not be stored anywhere.
- A **sentinel value** can be stored just after the last element of the array. That is, memory address $X + L \cdot (u - l + 1)$ can contain some bit pattern that never occurs in the first word of the memory representation of any element of V. Now u need not be explicitly stored at all and iterations are terminated by detecting the sentinel value. A disadvantage of this method is that an iteration is required even to find the length of such an array. Nevertheless, this representation is often used when L and l are fixed. The programming language C, for example, represents character strings in this way.

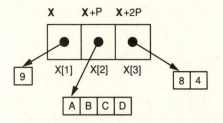

Figure 5.2 A three-element array implemented as a table of pointers.

Storage in contiguous memory is less attractive when the elements of the array have different lengths, because the ith element cannot be found in constant time by simple arithmetic. To handle this situation we can store the elements in memory anywhere and keep a table of pointers to the elements. Figure 5.2 shows an example of such an array whose elements in order are the integer 9, the string ABCD, and an array of two integers. (The latter two arrays are stored in contiguous memory, not as tables of pointers.) The address of the ith element is now stored in location $\mathbf{X} + P \cdot (i - l)$ where P is the size of a pointer in memory. The disadvantages of this implementation are two: an extra pointer must be followed to perform an *Access*, and an array of length n uses $\mathbf{p} \cdot n$ extra bits to store pointers in addition to the space needed to store the data. But a major advantage is that single pointer manipulations suffice to move elements within the array; for this reason, tables of pointers are often used when the elements are large (even if they are all of the same size).

A two-dimensional array whose elements all have the same size can also be represented efficiently in contiguous storage; the only problem is to determine the order in which the elements should be placed. The two most common schemes are **row major order**, in which the rows are placed one after another in memory, and **column major order**, in which the columns are placed one after another. For example, consider the following two arrays, each of which has indices $(1 . . 4) \times (1 . . 5)$:

$$R = \begin{pmatrix} 1 & 2 & 3 & 4 & 5 \\ 6 & 7 & 8 & 9 & 10 \\ 11 & 12 & 13 & 14 & 15 \\ 16 & 17 & 18 & 19 & 20 \end{pmatrix} \qquad C = \begin{pmatrix} 1 & 5 & 9 & 13 & 17 \\ 2 & 6 & 10 & 14 & 18 \\ 3 & 7 & 11 & 15 & 19 \\ 4 & 8 & 12 & 16 & 20 \end{pmatrix}$$

The entries in array R suggest the order in which the elements of R are stored in row major order. First comes $R[1, 1]$, then $R[1, 2]$, and so forth up to $R[1, 5]$ which is followed by $R[2, 1]$. In general, entry $R[i, j]$ is stored in memory at address $\mathbf{R} + L \cdot (5(i - 1) + (j - 1))$, where as usual each element requires space L and the first element begins at address $\mathbf{R}$. (The subtractions here reflect the fact that 1 is the first integer in each interval indexing R.) The entries in C suggest column major order. Again element $C[1, 1]$ is first in memory, but it is followed by $C[2, 1]$, $C[3, 1]$, $C[4, 1]$ and then $C[1, 2]$. If C is stored in column major order, entry $C[i, j]$ begins at address $\mathbf{C} + L \cdot (4(j - 1) + (i - 1))$. If particular iterations are anticipated—for example, if row-by-row iteration is more frequent than column-by-column iteration—then one of these layouts may be more advantageous than the other.

Row and column major order can be generalized to higher dimensions. Let X be a general d-dimensional array with indices $(l_1 \mathrel{..} u_1) \times \cdots \times (l_d \mathrel{..} u_d)$. When X is stored in row major order the first element is $X[l_1, \ldots, l_d]$, followed by $X[l_1, \ldots, l_d + 1]$, $X[l_1, \ldots, l_d + 2]$, and so forth up to $X[l_1, \ldots, l_{d-1}, u_d]$, after which the next element is $X[l_1, \ldots, l_{d-1} + 1, l_d]$. When arrays are represented in row major order we often say simply that "the last index varies fastest" as we examine successive elements in memory; each index is incremented only after all subsequent indices reach their upper bounds. Similarly, to store X in column major order we store $X[l_1, l_2, \ldots, l_d]$, $X[l_1 + 1, l_2, \ldots, l_d]$, and so forth up to $X[u_1, l_2, \ldots, l_d]$, and the next element is $X[l_1, l_2 + 1, l_3, \ldots, l_d]$, so that it is the first index that "varies fastest."

Now suppose X is an arbitrary d-dimensional array as in the previous paragraph, that X is stored in row major order starting at address $\mathbf{X}$, and that each element of X occupies space L. For arbitrary indices $j_1, \ldots, j_d$, where in memory is element $X[j_1, j_2, \ldots, j_d]$ located? (Of course, the answer is "nowhere" unless $l_k \leq j_k \leq u_k$ for each k. Verifying this condition is called **range checking**. Not all languages perform range checking; in some, it can be turned on for debugging and turned off when efficiency is important.)

For each $k = 0, \ldots, d$, define $M_k = L s_{k+1} \cdots s_d$ where $s_i = u_i - l_i + 1$ is the size of the ith dimension of X. M_k is the amount of memory required to store each $d - k$ dimensional "subarray" of X in which the first k indices are fixed; for example, M_k is the number of memory locations from the start of element $X[l_1, l_2, \ldots, l_d]$ to the end of element $X[l_1, l_2, \ldots, l_k, u_{k+1}, u_{k+2}, \ldots, u_d]$. In particular, $M_d = L$ and M_0 is the size of the entire array X. Therefore, there are $M_1 \cdot (j_1 - l_1)$ cells from $\mathbf{X}$ to the beginning of element $X[j_1, l_2, \ldots, l_d]$. From that point, there are $M_2 \cdot (j_2 - l_2)$ cells to the beginning of element $X[j_1, j_2, l_3, \ldots, l_d]$. Continuing in this way, we find that element $X[j_1, j_2, \ldots, j_d]$ is located at address

$$\mathbf{X} + M_1 \cdot (j_1 - l_1) + M_2 \cdot (j_2 - l_2) + \cdots + M_d \cdot (j_d - l_d). \qquad (1)$$

To make the *Access* operation as fast as possible, the values M_k should be computed in advance, once and for all. Moreover, we should compute and save the single constant value $X_0 = M_1 l_1 + \cdots + M_d l_d$, since then we can write expression (1) as

$$\mathbf{X} - X_0 + M_1 j_1 + M_2 j_2 + \cdots + M_d j_d$$

which is faster to evaluate, requiring only approximately $2d$ operations rather than $3d$ operations. Note that once we have the M_k and X_0, the l_k and u_k are unnecessary for *Access* unless we wish to perform range checking. Problem 6 explores another way that this computation can be arranged.

There is an independent context in which the M_k can be useful: as mentioned before, row major representation of X is especially appropriate when we desire to *Iterate* over the elements of X with the last index varying fastest. Suppose that we wish to have a version of the *Iterate* operation with the indices changing in some other order. Any such iteration can be implemented efficiently using the fact that the distance in memory between $X[j_1, \ldots, j_k, \ldots, j_d]$ and $X[j_1, \ldots, j_k + 1, \ldots, j_d]$ is exactly M_k.

When the elements of a multidimensional array are of different sizes in memory, we can extend the scheme of Figure 5.2 by storing pointers to the elements rather than the elements themselves. Then L is equal to the size of a pointer, and a pointer must be followed after the address calculation.

All of the methods so far considered for representing multidimensional arrays permit access to any element of the array in constant time. There is a subtle point here. You may feel that access to an element of a *multidimensional* array cannot be performed in constant time, since the number of arithmetic operations depends on the number of dimensions. But the "size" of an array is the total number of its elements; the cost of accessing any element of a d-dimensional array is independent of the number of elements in the array, although it does depend on d. This convention reflects the fact that the arrays used in computer programs typically have a fixed number of dimensions, although they may have more or fewer elements depending on the problem size. Indeed, few languages support arrays in which d is not fixed for each given array.

Constant-Time Initialization

One of the drawbacks of representing arrays in contiguous memory is the time required to initialize them; the obvious method of successively setting each element to its initial value uses time proportional to the number of elements. But occasionally we encounter an application where it is necessary to clear an array quickly, or where arrays are initialized extremely often. Some of the techniques we consider in the next section for handling sparse arrays yield constant-time initialization at a cost of non-constant access time. But if we are willing to use enough memory, we can represent arrays in contiguous storage and have both constant-time access and constant-time initialization.

Suppose M is a one-dimensional array with $n = Length(M)$ elements. We represent M as follows. First, maintain an integer *Count* that keeps track of the number of different elements of M that have been modified since the last time M was initialized. We also have a table *Which* with indices $0 .. n - 1$. As its name implies, *Which* remembers which elements of M have been modified; that is, for $0 \leq j \leq Count - 1$, we have $Which[j] = i$ if and only if $M[i]$ has been modified since the last initialization. The value of $M[i]$ is kept in $Data[i]$, where *Data* is another table with the same indices as M. The idea is that if index i is found among the first *Count* elements of *Which*, then $M[i]$ stores some

procedure *Initialize*(**pointer** M, **value** v):
{Initialize each element of M to v}
  Count(M) ← 0
  Default(M) ← v

function *Valid*(**integer** i, **pointer** M): **boolean**
{Return **true** if $M[i]$ has been modified since the last *Initialize*}
  return $0 \leq$ When(M)$[i] <$ Count(M) **and** Which(M)[When(M)$[i]] = i$

function *Access*(**integer** i, **pointer** M): **value**
{Return $M[i]$}
  if *Valid*(i, M) **then**
    return Data(M)$[i]$
  else
    return Default(M)

procedure *Assign*(**pointer** M, **integer** i, **value** v):
{Set $M[i] \leftarrow v$}
  if not *Valid*(i, M) **then**
    When(M)$[i] \leftarrow$ Count(M)
    Which(M)[Count(M)] $\leftarrow i$
    Count(M) ← Count(M) + 1
  Data(M)$[i] \leftarrow v$

Algorithm 5.1 Maintaining arrays with constant-time initialization and access.
Array M is represented as a record with five fields: a table of values Data(M),
tables of indices Which(M) and When(M), an integer Count(M), and an initial
value Default(M).

useful value. But if not, then the ith element of M has never been the target of
an assignment, *Data*[i] contains uninitialized garbage, and *Access*(M, i) should
return *Default*, which is the value to which all of M has been initialized. It is
now clear how to initialize M to a value v: simply set *Default* to v and set
Count to zero.

But we cannot afford to search the first *Count* elements of the *Which* table
each time an *Access* is to be performed, since we wish to retain the ability to
access any element in constant time. So we use a third table *When* that has the
same indices as M and, for each of these indices i, gives the location in *Which*
(if any) where i can be found. That is, if *When*[i] $= j$, we need only check
that $0 \leq j <$ *Count* and *Which*[j] $= i$ to determine that the ith element of M
has been modified. Note that both conditions must be checked: we could have
When[i] $= j$ and $0 \leq j <$ *Count*, but if *Which*[j] $\neq i$ then *When*[i] has its
value "by accident" and $M[i]$ has never been touched. The *When* table gets its

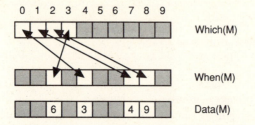

Figure 5.3 Array M, with indices $0..9$, after the operations $Initialize(M, 7)$, $M[4] \leftarrow 3$, $M[7] \leftarrow 4$, $M[8] \leftarrow 7$, $M[2] \leftarrow 6$, and $M[8] \leftarrow 9$. The fields Count(M) and Default(M) have values 4 and 7. The two-headed arrow between $Which[0]$ and $When[4]$ indicates that $Which[0] = 4$ and $When[4] = 0$. Shaded cells have undefined value.

name because it tells when each element of M was first modified; for example, if $Count > 0$ then $Which[0]$ is the index i of the first element of M to be modified, and $When[i] = 0$.

Algorithm 5.1 gives the details of the abstract operations on M using this method, assuming that the record structure for an array M has fields Which, When, and Count to store the tables $Which$ and $When$ and the number $Count$, plus a field Data containing the table where the values of M are maintained, and Default which stores the last value to which M was initialized. Figure 5.3 gives an example.

This method provides additional flexibility when we note that the default values of the elements of M need not be the same. For instance, it is easy to initialize each $M[j]$ to j in constant time by this method, by changing the last line of the function $Access$. Multidimensional arrays can also be accommodated (Problem 8). Unfortunately, this means of achieving constant time per array operation vastly increases the storage requirements—by a factor of 3 when array indices and elements of M are of comparable size.

5.3 SPARSE ARRAYS

The contiguous representation methods of the preceding section allocate storage for every element of an array. But in many applications the arrays under consideration are only partially filled. Sometimes only a scattering of the elements of an array have useful values. For example, consider an n by m array that represents the coefficients of n polynomials each with degree m or less; if each polynomial has at most a few terms, then such an array has mostly zero entries, although the nonzero entries may be located anywhere. In other cases the arrays have a special shape, in the sense that only elements occurring in certain cells can be nonzero; an example is given by the upper-triangular matrices below.

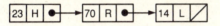

Figure 5.4 Sparse array represented as a linked list. Each list element contains Index, Value, and Next fields; each Value field stores a character.

A slightly different example is afforded by the Travelling Salesman Problem, first discussed in Chapter 2: the input to this problem is an n by n **distance matrix** M, which gives the distance between each pair of cities. Such a matrix is symmetric, that is, $M_{ij} = M_{ji}$ for every i and j. There is no need to store all n^2 entries of M in an array since nearly half of the elements are uniquely determined by the other half.

Arrays in which only a small fraction of the elements are significant in some way are known as **sparse** arrays. The "insignificant" elements of sparse arrays typically have a particular value (as in the polynomial example above in which most elements are zero), have no relevant value at all, or have value quickly computable from the other elements. The array elements that do not need to be stored in memory because their values are known or determined are called **null elements**. Depending on the application, accessing a null element might simply yield the **null value** (the value of all the null elements, frequently 0 or Λ), might fetch a different element as in the distance matrix example, or might be erroneous. We don't always know in advance which elements are null, and sometimes null elements can become nonnull via assignment of a significant value. The important point is that sparse arrays can frequently be implemented using space-efficient representations that do not use any memory for null elements. In this section we consider several representations for sparse arrays.

List Representations

Perhaps the most obvious way of dealing with sparse one-dimensional arrays is to store the nonnull elements in a list. Figure 5.4 shows a simple linked list representation of an array with indices $0 . . 1000$ but with only three nonnull elements. Each list element corresponds to a single array element and contains the index, the element value, and a pointer to the next list element. To access an element of such an array given an index, we simply search the list—if the element is not found, the null value is returned or an error signalled as appropriate. It is equally simple to add new elements if null elements are allowed to become nonnull. Of course, the disadvantage to this array representation is that *Access* can no longer be implemented in time $O(1)$; in the worst case, an access may take time proportional to the length of the array.

Many variations are possible: the list may be maintained in order by index, list elements may contain pointers to array elements rather than the elements themselves, the list may be doubly linked to facilitate deletions, and so forth. Actually, this approach merely treats sparse arrays as a special case of the more general problem of *set representation*, to be addressed in the next chapter. In

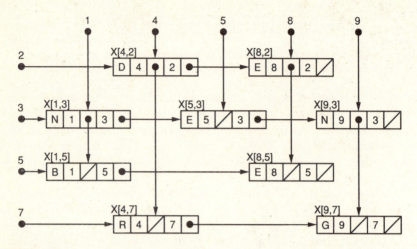

Figure 5.5 Sparse two-dimensional array X represented by lists of doubly threaded records. The data structure by which the lists themselves are accessed is not pictured. The first field of each record contains the value (a character) of the corresponding element of X.

other words, one way to represent a sparse array is to ignore the special structure of its domain and treat it as a set of ordered pairs that are accessed using the index values as keys.

Multidimensional arrays may also be stored as lists in much the same way: we simply store all the indices of each element in its list element. But here a more interesting method is possible. Suppose X is a two-dimensional array with indices $(l_1 .. u_1) \times (l_2 .. u_2)$. This array can be represented with a table of linked lists, using a separate list for each value of the first index, or $u_1 - l_1 + 1$ lists in all. So to access $X[5, 3]$, for example, we would search the list that contains those elements of X whose first index is 5. Each record on the list contains Value and Next fields as before, plus an Index field that contains the *second* index of this array element—the first index need not be stored, since its value is implied by membership in the list.

With the representation just discussed, we can easily *Iterate* over all array elements with a given first index. However, to iterate over all elements with a given second index it would be necessary to search all the lists, a process that might involve examining every element of the array. If iteration in both dimensions is important, the array elements can also be "threaded" in the second dimension as in Figure 5.5, which depicts a two-dimensional array with nine nonnull elements (the two tables of list heads are not pictured). Each record now contains a value plus two Next fields, one for each dimension. But now each record must record both indices of its element, since the record may have been reached by a search along either dimension. This technique easily generalizes to arrays of higher dimension.

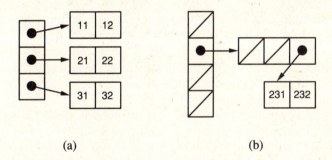

(a)   (b)

Figure 5.6 Array representation using hierarchical tables: (a) A two-dimensional array; (b) a sparse three-dimensional array with two nonnull elements. (Each value is simply the integer formed by concatenating the components of the index.)

Hierarchical Tables

In the preceding section we discussed the use of pointers to store arrays whose elements occupy varying amounts of memory: instead of storing the array elements contiguously, store a table of pointers to the elements. This scheme can be extended in a slightly different way to multidimensional arrays. For example, suppose that M is a two-dimensional array with indices $(1..3) \times (1..2)$. We can regard M as an array of three one-dimensional arrays, each of which has size 2. We then store M as a table of three pointers, each of which points to one of these arrays; Figure 5.6(a) illustrates this method. (Note that the one-dimensional arrays in this example are stored in contiguous memory without pointers.)

In general, a d-dimensional array with indices $(l_1..u_1) \times \cdots \times (l_d..u_d)$ is represented as a table of s_1 pointers, each of which points to a table of s_2 pointers, and so forth. (Recall that $s_i = u_i - l_i + 1$ is the size of the ith dimension.) The "bottommost" tables contain s_d entries, each of which is an element of the array. We can also describe the representation in a simple way by using recursion: a one-dimensional array is represented as a table, while a d-dimensional array with indices $(l_1..u_1) \times \cdots \times (l_d..u_d)$ is implemented as a table of pointers to $u_1 - l_1 + 1$ arrays, each with $(d-1)$ dimensions and indices $(l_2..u_2) \times \cdots \times (l_d..u_d)$. (If the array elements have different sizes, then the one-dimensional arrays at the base of the recursion can be stored as a table of pointers rather than a table of elements.) The extra memory in bits needed to store the pointer fields is

$$\mathbf{p} \cdot (s_1 + s_1 s_2 + s_1 s_2 s_3 + \cdots + s_1 s_2 \cdots s_d).$$

The *Access* operation is straightforward and can be accomplished in constant time.

Hierarchical tables of pointers are well-suited to representation of sparse arrays, because only those tables that are needed to access the nonnull elements need be allocated. Figure 5.6(b) shows how a three-dimensional array with indices $(1..3) \times (1..4) \times (1..2)$ might be represented when only a single element is nonnull. Notice that it is the task of the *Access* operation to handle Λ; whenever it encounters Λ before finding the element in the bottommost table, it should take the action appropriate to an attempt to access a null element (perhaps simply returning the null value).

When a d-dimensional array with a single nonnull element is represented in this way, the overhead for storing pointer tables is only $s_1 + s_2 + \cdots + s_d$ since only a single table need be stored at each level. When there are k nonnull elements the overhead is at most $s_1 + k(s_2 + \cdots + s_d)$ since only a single top-level table need be stored in any case. But the overhead may grow more slowly; for example, if there are two nonnull elements whose first indices are equal, then the overhead is only $s_1 + s_2 + 2(s_3 + \cdots + s_d)$ since only a single second-level table is required. Generally, this representation works well when the nonnull entries of a sparse array are "clumped" together, minimizing the number of pointer tables.

The method of hierarchical tables also lends itself well to an environment in which null elements become active dynamically. Suppose, for example, that all elements of an array M are 0, except for those explicitly changed. We can represent the initial state of M with a table of size s_1 containing Λ everywhere; the *Access* operation therefore returns 0 for every element. When we assign a nonzero value to an element of M the *Assign* operation creates any new tables that are necessary. In this way the overhead for M is allocated gradually. *Assign* might also detect when 0 is assigned to an element and deallocate tables if possible, replacing pointers to them by Λ; the deallocated tables might even be saved for reuse later. Problems 9 and 10 explore some of the possibilities. In Chapter 8 we shall encounter *tries*, an adaptation of hierarchical tables used for manipulating a small number of objects chosen from a much larger universe (a "sparse set").

Arrays with Special Shapes

An **upper-triangular matrix** of order n is a two-dimensional array with indices $(0..n-1) \times (0..n-1)$ in which every element below the "main diagonal" is null. That is, if M is an upper-triangular matrix then $M[i,j]$ is null whenever $i > j$. Here is an example with $n = 4$ and with 0 as the null element:

$$M = \begin{pmatrix} 103 & 42.2 & 0 & 9 \\ 0 & 1.0 & -9.3 & 4 \\ 0 & 0 & 6 & 18 \\ 0 & 0 & 0 & 1.1 \end{pmatrix}$$

It is obviously wasteful to store upper-triangular matrices in contiguous memory as in §5.2. An upper-triangle matrix of order n has (at most) $n(n+1)/2$ nonnull elements, but the contiguous representation uses space for n^2 elements. Thus storage for $n(n-1)/2$ elements—just about half—is wasted. One way to save space is to place nonnull elements consecutively in memory, omitting the null elements. Imitating row-major order, we allocate space for the n elements in row 0, followed by the $n - 1$ elements in row 1, the $n - 2$ elements in row 2, and so forth, thus wasting no memory at all. To find element $M[i, j]$ for $0 \le i, j \le n-1$, first check whether $i \le j$. If not, then $M[i, j] = 0$. Otherwise, the number of elements preceding $M[i, j]$ in rows 0 through $i - 1$ is

$$n + (n - 1) + (n - 2) + \cdots + (n - i + 1) = \sum_{k=1}^{n} k - \sum_{k=1}^{n-i} k$$

$$= \frac{n(n + 1)}{2} - \frac{(n - i)(n - i + 1)}{2}$$

$$= ni + \frac{i - i^2}{2},$$

and $j - i$ elements precede $M[i, j]$ in row i. So if M is stored at address $\mathbf{M}$ and each element has size L, the address of $M[i, j]$ is $\mathbf{M} + L \cdot (ni + (i - i^2)/2 + j - i)$.

This technique can be also used for distance matrices, which are symmetric (that is, $M[i, j] = M[j, i]$ for all i and j). Now to access $M[i, j]$ when $i > j$ we just return $M[j, i]$. Problems 13 through 15 discuss other special kinds of arrays that can be implemented by allocating contiguous space for the nonnull elements only; in each case, the problem is to choose the layout in memory and to determine the access function. When working in a programming language that provides multidimensional arrays, it is often simpler to arrange array elements so that the underlying access mechanism performs some of the necessary arithmetic; see Problem 14.

5.4 REPRESENTATIONS OF STRINGS

The type of array most commonly encountered in practice is the string. Virtually every interactive computer program uses strings of English characters for communication with humans. Strings also get much larger; every text file on a computer's disk system can be thought of as a single long string which is read into main memory in small chunks. Sometimes the "string" to be stored is so enormous—for example, the Encyclopædia Britannica or the complete works of Shakespeare—that even disk files can get unmanageably large, and the string must be broken up into multiple files or even onto separate disks. Since disk space is a finite resource it is important to find space-efficient ways to represent strings. Compact string representation yields another benefit as well: if a string is to be transmitted from one location to another, whether from the disk to main memory or from computer to computer, the time required for the transfer is shorter when the string is represented with fewer bits.

Throughout this section Σ denotes the alphabet used for all strings; recall that an element of Σ is called a character. When Σ is very small, compact string representations can sometimes be achieved using run-length encoding (discussed in Problem 2 of Chapter 3). But more often we are concerned with English (or other natural language) text, where Σ contains a hundred characters or so: the upper and lower case letters, the digits, a few dozen marks of punctuation, special characters such as space and tab, and so forth.

The most straightforward way to store strings is in contiguous memory as in §5.2. We simply assign a distinct bit sequence to each element of Σ and place the characters of the string consecutively in memory (or on the external storage medium). The bit sequence representing a character is called the **encoding** of that character.* Since there are only 2^n different bit sequences of length n, at least $\lceil \lg |\Sigma| \rceil$ bits are required to represent each character. The space required to store the string, in bits, is therefore equal to $\lceil \lg |\Sigma| \rceil$ times the length of the string. In common English-language applications Σ has 128 or 256 elements, so seven or eight bits per character are used.

When the strings to be stored are totally random (meaning that every character of Σ is equally likely to appear in any position of a string) very little improvement is possible; in fact, if $|\Sigma|$ is exactly a power of two then no representation at all is more space-efficient. However, we more frequently deal with strings whose elements are not at all random. For example, in long strings of English text the character e appears much more often than the character W, which in turn appears more often (in general) than a little-used character like @. This lack of randomness can be exploited to provide much more compact string representations.

In this section we shall study several such representations. The general statement of the problem is as follows: given a string w over Σ, store it using as few bits as possible in such a way that it can be recovered at will. (We shall consider only **lossless** techniques—those that allow w to be recovered exactly. **Noisy** or **lossy** techniques can be even more space-efficient, with the drawback that the original string can be reconstructed only approximately; such techniques could be appropriate when storing digitized representations of analog data, such as digitized voice transmission.) The string w is called the **text**; it may be "given" as a file on disk, as a string in memory, or as a stream of characters produced by a running program or an external communications line. The process of converting w to compact representation is called **encoding** or **compressing** w. Keep in mind that the length of w is typically tens of thousands or millions of characters; there is little to be gained by compressing strings that are already short. Finally, note that we are chiefly interested in the case in which w need not be modified or accessed randomly once it has been translated to compressed form; *Iterate* is the only abstract operation to be implemented in this section.

---

*By far the most common character encodings in use today are ASCII and EBCDIC, which use eight-bit sequences to represent all the standard characters plus a multitude of special-purpose control characters. But the assignments are not identical: uppercase A, for example, is represented by 01000001 in ASCII and by 11000001 in EBCDIC.

Huffman Encoding

One source of inefficiency in the straightforward representation of strings is the fact that just as many bits are used for characters that appear in the text as are used for characters that never appear. If only the characters in a subset S of Σ actually appear in a given string then we can simply choose shorter encodings, using only $\lceil \lg |S| \rceil$ bits for each character. For example, if the text consists only of digits and spaces then it can be represented with only four bits per element. The representation of w can begin with a table describing the bit sequence that encodes each character—the additional space used by the table is negligible when w is large.

One disadvantage of this method is immediate: the characters of Σ that actually appear in w must be known or determined in advance. If w is a disk file, we can read through the file once to build the table and then again to translate the characters. But reading w twice may be impossible if it is being received over a communication link or as program output. A stronger objection is that the method doesn't work very well in the general case. In fact, it saves nothing at all unless $\lceil \lg |S| \rceil < \lceil \lg |\Sigma| \rceil$, since each character that appears even once in w needs its own bit sequence.

We can improve upon this approach by using bit sequences of *different* lengths to encode members of Σ, with short sequences encoding common characters and longer sequences encoding rare characters. The idea is to represent most of w with a small number of bits per element, and only infrequently to pay the penalty of a longer bit sequence. If we can use only four or five bits for each of the most common characters of English text, we can afford to use ten or twelve bits to represent the rare characters and still come out ahead.

But the use of bit sequences of varying sizes to encode characters gives rise to another problem: if the bit sequences aren't carefully chosen, we will not be able to recover the original text. For example, if E is represented by 101, T by 110, and Q by 101110, then we cannot distinguish between an encoding of Q and an encoding of ET. One way to guarantee unambiguous "decodability" is to ensure that no bit sequence used to encode a character may be the beginning of the encoding of another character. In other words, if there do not exist distinct characters c_1 and c_2 such that the encoding of c_1 is a prefix of the encoding of c_2, then there do not exist strings w_1 and w_2 such that the encoding of w_1 is the same as the encoding of w_2 (Problem 16). The problem with the example in this paragraph is that the encoding of E is a prefix of the encoding of Q.

Binary trees can be used to provide an elegant description of these encodings. Consider a binary tree such as the one in Figure 5.7, in which each leaf has a field Char that contains a character of Σ. (In this example, Σ is a small alphabet containing only 9 letters plus the space character.) To find the bit sequence encoding character c we traverse the unique path from the root to the leaf containing c, writing a 0 every time an LC pointer is followed and a 1 every time an RC pointer is followed. For example, the encoding of H is 0110 and

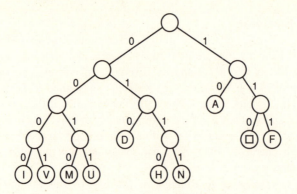

Figure 5.7 Encoding tree for a ten-character alphabet. A box is used to denote the space character, whose encoding is 110.

the encoding of A is 10. In general, each character is encoded by a bit string whose length is equal to the depth of the leaf in which that character appears. Since characters appear only in leaves of the tree, no character can be encoded by a bit string that is a prefix of some other character's encoding. A binary tree containing an element of Σ at each leaf, such that every element of Σ appears in exactly one leaf, is called an **encoding tree** for Σ. We shall assume that all encoding trees are full; that is, every nonleaf of an encoding tree is assumed to have two children (but see Problem 17).

It is easy to see how to represent a text w using an encoding tree: just output the bit sequence that encodes each character. For example, the encoding of the string AIDA FAN would be 10000001010110111100111. To recover the original text given the compressed representation w' and the encoding tree as pictured in Figure 5.7, we proceed as follows. Start at the root of T and walk down the tree using bits from w' as a guide. When the next bit of w' is a 0, proceed to the left child of the current node; when the next bit of w' is a 1, proceed to the right child. Each time we reach a leaf we have recovered a character of w; we then start again at the root of T reading further bits from w'. Algorithm 5.2 gives the details, using a routine *NextBit* that fetches the next bit of input from a source of bits called a **bitstream**, and a routine *OutputChar* that is called on each character as it is recovered. You may have noticed a drawback of this representation: it is impossible to retrieve substrings of w without starting at the beginning of the encoded bit string, since there is no way to tell where characters begin and end.

With these preliminaries out of the way, the most interesting problem is yet to be solved: how should the tree T be chosen to provide the best encodings? Suppose that for each character c_i we know f_i, the number of times that c_i appears in w (we shall explore later how to relax this assumption). We use the following method to construct T. Create one node for each character of Σ; each of these nodes will be a leaf of T. Let each node have a field containing a

procedure *TreeDecode*(**pointer** T, **bitstream** b):
{Call *OutputChar* on successive characters encoded in b}
{T is a pointer to the root of the encoding tree}
      $P \leftarrow T$ {P walks down the tree, guided by bits from b}
    until *Empty*(b) **do**
        if *NextBit*(b) = 0 **then** $P \leftarrow$ LC(P) **else** $P \leftarrow$ RC(P)
        if *IsLeaf*(P) **then**
            OutputChar(Char(P))
            $P \leftarrow T$

Algorithm 5.2 Decoding with encoding trees.

number called the **weight** of the node, and for each character c_i set the weight of the leaf containing c_i to f_i. Now repeatedly perform the following step: pick two nodes n_1 and n_2 that have the smallest weights (it doesn't matter how ties are broken; see Problem 21) and replace them with a new node whose children are n_1 and n_2 and whose weight is the sum of the weights of n_1 and n_2. Each such step replaces two nodes with one, so eventually there is only a single node left; this node is the root of the tree. The tree constructed by this algorithm is called a **Huffman encoding tree**.

Figure 5.8 gives a complete example of the construction of a Huffman tree for an unspecified text w. This time each character appears underneath its leaf and its frequency appears inside the circle; for example, the character U appears twice in w, A appears fifteen times, and the space character appears seven times. At the beginning only the leaves are present. In the first step the leaves containing V and I are selected and the internal node with weight three is created. (Node V was chosen because it has the smallest weight of any leaf, but M, U, or N could have been chosen in place of I since ties can be broken arbitrarily. Also notice that V could have been the left child instead of the right child; the order of the children is unimportant.) In the next step, M and U were combined to make an internal node with weight 4. Then H and N were combined to make an internal node with weight 5, two internal nodes were combined to make an internal node with weight 7, and so forth until the entire tree was constructed.

As we expect, the characters with higher frequency are placed nearer to the root of the tree and therefore have shorter codes. As an extreme example, consider what would happen if there were a sufficiently common character. Suppose in Figure 5.8 that the frequency of A were 20 instead of 15. Then at the end of the construction the leaf containing A would be a child of the root of the encoding tree, and each occurrence of A would be encoded by a single bit—which, of course, is exactly what we want. Problems 28 and 29 explore

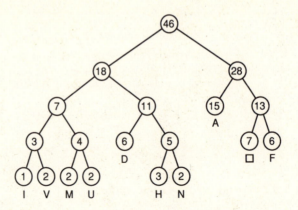

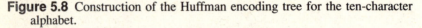

Figure 5.8 Construction of the Huffman encoding tree for the ten-character alphabet.

further the relationship between the frequency of a character and the length in bits of its representation.

The remarkable fact about the encoding tree produced by the Huffman algorithm is that no other encoding tree yields a smaller representation of w. In order to prove this we need a bit of notation. For any tree T and any node n in T let $Depth_T(n)$ denote the depth of n in T. Let $L(T)$ denote the set of leaves of T, and suppose that each leaf $n \in L(T)$ has been assigned a weight (or **cost**) denoted by $C(n)$. Then define $WPL(T)$, the **weighted path length** of T, as follows:

$$WPL(T) = \sum_{n \in L(T)} Depth_T(n) \cdot C(n).$$

For example, if T is the encoding tree of Figure 5.8, then

$$WPL(T) = 1 \cdot 4 + 2 \cdot 4 + 2 \cdot 4 + 2 \cdot 4 + 6 \cdot 3 + 3 \cdot 4 + 2 \cdot 4 + 15 \cdot 2 + 7 \cdot 3 + 6 \cdot 3 = 135.$$

If w is a string, T is an encoding tree for the alphabet of w, and the weight assigned to each leaf of T is the frequency of that character in w, then $WPL(T)$ is exactly the number of bits in the encoding of w using the encoding tree T.

We next need a lemma about trees and weighted path lengths in general:

■ **LEMMA** Let T be any full binary tree with weights assigned to its leaves. Suppose n_1 and n_2 are any two leaves of T with smallest weight. Then we can construct a new tree T' from T such that
1. the leaves of T' are the same as the leaves of T, except that n_1 and n_2 are not leaves of T' and T' has a new leaf n_3,
2. the weight of n_3 in T' is $C(n_3) = C(n_1) + C(n_2)$ and the weights of all other leaves are the same as their weights in T, and
3. $WPL(T') \leq WPL(T) - C(n_3)$, with equality if n_1 and n_2 are siblings in T.

PROOF First, assume that n_1 and n_2 are siblings in T. Then we can simply delete them; their parent becomes the new leaf n_3 to which we assign weight $C(n_1) + C(n_2)$. The resulting tree has the correct leaves and weights, but what is its weighted path length? Let d be the depth of n_1 and n_2; then the depth of n_3 is $d - 1$. Thus deleting n_1 and n_2 reduces $WPL(T)$ by $d \cdot (C(n_1) + C(n_2))$, and adding n_3 increases $WPL(T)$ by $(d - 1) \cdot C(n_3) = (d - 1) \cdot (C(n_1) + C(n_2))$. The net change to the weighted path length is exactly $-C(n_3)$ as required.

Now suppose n_1 and n_2 are not siblings and let s_1 be the sibling of n_1 in T. If the depth of n_1 is the same as the depth of n_2, first exchange nodes n_2 and s_1. That is, detach n_2 and the entire subtree whose root is s_1, move n_2 so it is the (new) sibling of n_1, and move s_1 to the place where n_2 used to be. This operation has no effect on $WPL(T)$ since we haven't changed the depth of any leaf. But since n_1 and n_2 are now siblings we can finish the construction as in the first case.

Finally, suppose that n_1 is deeper than n_2 in T. (The case where n_2 is deeper than n_1 is handled symmetrically.) Again, we exchange n_2 with s_1 and compute the change in $WPL(T)$. Moving n_2 down to the depth of n_1 increases $WPL(T)$ by $C(n_2)$ times $Depth_T(n_1) - Depth_T(n_2)$, the difference in depth. But all of the leaves in the subtree whose root is s_1 have moved up the same amount, and each one has weight at least as great as the weight of n_2 (since n_2 was a leaf of smallest weight). Therefore this operation decreases $WPL(T)$ or leaves it unchanged. After this exchange, n_1 and n_2 are siblings and we can continue as in the first case to produce a further reduction of $C(n_1) + C(n_2)$ in $WPL(T)$, thus the weight of the final tree is $WPL(T) - C(n_1) - C(n_2)$ or less. □

This Lemma does most of the work in proving that the Huffman algorithm does indeed yield the best encoding tree possible. The following Theorem is the formal statement of that fact.

■ **THEOREM** *(Huffman Optimality)* Let N be a set of nodes and let each node $n \in N$ be assigned a weight $C(n)$. Let T be the encoding tree constructed from the nodes in N by the Huffman algorithm. If X is any other encoding tree with the same leaves, then $WPL(T) \leq WPL(X)$.

PROOF By induction on the number of leaves of T. When T has two leaves the result is trivial. Otherwise, let n_1 and n_2 be the first two members of N that are selected by the Huffman algorithm, and apply the Lemma to T and to X producing T' and X'. Since T was constructed by the Huffman algorithm, n_1 and n_2 are necessarily siblings in T, therefore $WPL(T') = WPL(T) - C(n_1) - C(n_2)$. The Lemma also guarantees that

$WPL(X') \leq WPL(X) - C(n_1) - C(n_2)$. Finally, $WPL(T') \leq WPL(X')$ by the induction hypothesis, which applies since T' and X' have the same leaves and weights and have one less leaf than T, and since T' is equivalent to the tree that the Huffman algorithm constructs from the leaves of T'. These three inequalities combine to yield $WPL(T) \leq WPL(X)$, completing the proof.   □

Once the optimal encoding tree T has been constructed by the Huffman algorithm, the compressed representation of w consists of a description of T (Problem 25) followed by the bit sequence that encodes w according to T. The decoding process consists of building T from its description and then using it to decode the rest of w. The description of T takes up space in the output, of course, but this space is negligible if w is very long.

The chief difficulty with the Huffman algorithm is that all character frequencies must be known in advance; typically they must be counted with a preliminary pass through the text. But it may not be possible or feasible to read w twice, first to count its character frequencies and again to encode it. There are at least two simple ways to obviate the need for a second pass. The first is **static Huffman encoding**: fix a single encoding tree once and for all and use it for all texts. Static Huffman encoding works well when texts are of a similar makeup. For example, when large blocks of English text are to be compressed we can obtain near-optimal results by constructing a tree that reflects typical letter frequencies of English and then using that tree for every text. There is a side benefit: since T is fixed it need not be described in the encoded representations, saving a small amount of space and program complexity.

A more sophisticated method is **adaptive Huffman encoding**. Start with an empty encoding tree T constructed by assigning frequency 0 to each member of Σ. Now just after each character of w is processed, update T so that it is an optimum encoding tree for the portion of w encountered so far. The disadvantage of this method is that we must in principle perform the Huffman algorithm once for every character of the text. Fortunately there is a fast way to update an optimal encoding tree for a given string so that it is optimal for that string plus any given character; the update can be performed in time proportional to the length of the encoding of the character to be added. (The details are discussed in Problem 31 and on page 484.)

Interestingly, adaptive Huffman encoding is like static Huffman encoding in that the encoding tree T need never be described in the compressed string. The decoding algorithm simply starts with the same empty tree and updates the tree in the same way just after each character is recovered. So the two processes remain synchronized; at each point the decoding program reconstructs the same tree built by the encoding program.

Lempel-Ziv Encoding

In many texts certain sequences of characters occur with high frequency. In English, for example, the word "the" occurs more often than any other sequence of three letters, with "and", "ion", and "ing" close behind. If we include the space character, there are other very common sequences, including longer ones like "of the". Although it is impossible to improve on Huffman encoding with any method that assigns a fixed encoding to each character, we can do better by encoding entire *sequences* of characters with just a few bits. The method of this section takes advantage of frequently occurring character sequences of any length. It typically produces an even smaller representation than is possible with Huffman trees, and unlike basic Huffman encoding it reads through the text only once and requires no extra space for overhead in the compressed representation.

The algorithm makes use of a "dictionary" that stores character sequences chosen dynamically from w. With each character sequence the dictionary associates a number; if s is a character sequence, we use $\#(s)$ to denote the number assigned to s by the dictionary. The number $\#(s)$ is called the **code** or **code number** of s. All codes have the same length in bits; a typical code size is twelve bits, which permits a maximum dictionary size of $2^{12} = 4096$ character sequences. The dictionary is initialized with all possible one-character sequences, that is, the elements of Σ are assigned the code numbers 0 through $|\Sigma| - 1$ and all other code numbers are initially unassigned.

The text w is encoded using a greedy heuristic: at each step, determine the longest prefix p of w that is in the dictionary, output the code number of p, and remove p from the front of w; call p the **current match**. At each step we also modify the dictionary by adding a new string and assigning it the next unused code number. (We'll consider later the problem of what to do if the dictionary fills up, leaving no code numbers available.) The string to be added consists of the current match concatenated to the first character of the remainder of w. It turns out to be simpler to wait until the next step to add this string; that is, at each step we determine the current match, then add to the dictionary the match from the *previous* step concatenated to the first character of the current match. No string is added to the dictionary in the very first step.

Figure 5.9 demonstrates this process on the (admittedly contrived) example string **COCOA AND BANANAS**. In the first step $\#(C)$ is output and nothing is inserted in the dictionary. In the next step O is matched, so $\#(O)$ is output and CO is inserted in the dictionary. In step 3 the sequence CO is found in the dictionary, so its code is output and OC is inserted in the dictionary. Continuing in this way, fourteen codes are output to encode the example string. When very long strings are compressed by this method, longer and longer sequences are added to the dictionary; eventually, short code numbers can represent very long strings. Moreover, the dictionary becomes "tailored" to w because of the way strings are chosen for inclusion. When w consists of English text, for example, the words and even phrases that appear often in w eventually find their way into the dictionary and are subsequently encoded as single code numbers.

Step	Output	Add to Dictionary	Step	Output	Add to Dictionary
1	#(C)	—	8	#(D)	ND
2	#(O)	CO	9	#(□)	D□
3	#(CO)	OC	10	#(B)	□B
4	#(A)	COA	11	#(AN)	BA
5	#(□)	A□	12	#(AN)	ANA
6	#(A)	□A	13	#(A)	ANA
7	#(N)	AN	14	#(S)	AS

Figure 5.9 Lempel-Ziv encoding of COCOA AND BANANAS. The symbol □ denotes the space character, and #(s) is the code number associated with string s in the dictionary. Note that duplicate strings may be added to the dictionary.

Decoding is almost the same as encoding. First of all, the compressed representation consists simply of a sequence of code numbers; it is easy to retrieve them one by one since the length in bits of a single code number is fixed. The dictionary is *not* saved anywhere; as we shall see, the decoding process reconstructs at each step the same dictionary that the encoding process used (as in adaptive Huffman encoding). Consider the example of Figure 5.9 from the point of view of the decoder. It first sees the code for C, which is in the initial dictionary, so it knows that C is the first character of the text. In the next step, it reads the code for O; like the encoder, it now adds CO to the dictionary. The code number assigned to CO will be correct since both encoder and decoder assign the first unused number to new strings in the dictionary. The general decoding step is similar to the general encoding step: read a code, look it up in the dictionary and output the associated character sequence s, then add to the dictionary the sequence consisting of the *previous* sequence concatenated to the first character of s. (The *LookUp* will always succeed, but see Problem 34 for an interesting variation.) The complete decoder is shown in Algorithm 5.3.

Many implementation details remain to be discussed. For example, what should we do when the dictionary is full, that is, when all code numbers have been assigned? There are several possibilities:

- Stop placing new entries in the dictionary, encoding the rest of the text using the dictionary created so far.
- Clear the dictionary completely (except for the one-character sequences) and start afresh, allowing new sequences to accumulate.
- Discard infrequently used sequences from the dictionary and reuse their code numbers. (Of course, this requires keeping some statistical information during encoding and decoding.)
- Switch to larger code numbers. Adding even a single bit doubles the number of available codes. This scheme can be repeated until the dictionary grows too large to be stored in main memory.

procedure *LZDecode*(**bitstream** *b*):
{Recover the string encoded in *b*}
    {*D* is a dictionary associated code numbers with strings}
    $D \leftarrow MakeEmptySet(\ )$
    $nextcode \leftarrow 0$ {The next code number to be assigned}
    {Insert each single-character string into the dictionary}
    foreach $c \in \Sigma$ **do**
        Insert($nextcode, c, D$)
        $nextcode \leftarrow nextcode + 1$
    {Special first step with no dictionary updates}
    $current \leftarrow LookUp(ReadOneCodeNumber(b), D)$
    Output(*current*)
    {Main loop}
    until *Empty*(*b*) **do**
        $previous \leftarrow current$
        $current \leftarrow LookUp(ReadOneCodeNumber(b), D)$
        Insert($nextcode, Concat(previous, current[0]), D$)
        $nextcode \leftarrow nextcode + 1$
        Output(*current*)

Algorithm 5.3 Lempel-Ziv decoding. The functions *MakeEmptySet*, *Insert*, and *LookUp* are abstract operations on dictionaries, discussed more fully in Chapter 6. *Output* is an unspecified procedure that handles the encoded string as it is recovered.

(Yet another possibility is discussed on page 484.) The appropriateness of one method over another depends on the amount of storage and processor power available, but also on the characteristics of the data being compressed. For example, it is easy to stop putting new entries in the dictionary, but if the input is very long and of gradually changing character then clearing the dictionary is a better idea. Of course, no matter which method is used it is essential that the encoder and decoder agree on the method so that their dictionaries stay synchronized! A more interesting problem is how best to store the dictionary during encoding and decoding, to facilitate the special kinds of *LookUp*s performed by the encoder (Problem 33). The appropriate data structure is the *trie*, which we discuss in Chapter 8.

    To illustrate the potential savings that can be realized with the techniques of this section, we give here the results of an experiment using several methods of encoding. The text was a near-final version of this book (including commands used for formatting) comprising 1322028 eight-bit characters, for a total of 10576224 bits. A classical two-pass Huffman compression algorithm produced

---

function *SimpleStringSearch*(**string** p, t): **integer**
{Find p in t; return its location or -1 if p is not a substring of t}
　　for k **from** 0 **to** *Length*$(t) - $ *Length*(p) **do**
　　　　$i \leftarrow 0$
　　　　while $i <$ *Length*(p) **and** $p[i] = t[k + i]$ **do**
　　　　　　$i \leftarrow i + 1$
　　　　if $i = $ *Length*(p) **then return** k
　　return -1

Algorithm 5.4 Straightforward string searching.

---

an encoded text of 6469752 bits, about 61% of the size of the original. A one-pass adaptive Huffman algorithm produced 6470800 bits, saving an entire pass through the text at a cost of only about 1000 bits (although requiring nearly an order of magnitude more computation time). But a variant of the Lempel-Ziv method that begins with eight-bit codes and allows code size to grow yielded a compressed text of 4493168 bits, about 42.5% of the original size.

5.5 STRING SEARCHING

Retrieval of information from large text files is a very broad and important problem—numerous techniques have been developed and entire volumes written on the topic. One simple aspect of this problem is **string searching**: given two strings p and t over the same alphabet Σ, determine whether p occurs as a substring of t; that is, whether there exists k such that $p = $ *Substring*$(t, k, |p|)$. The strings p and t are called the **pattern** and **target** strings respectively.

The obvious method for string searching appears in Algorithm 5.4. Briefly, we set k to 0 and attempt to match p against the portion of t beginning at index k by comparing $p[0]$ to $t[j]$, then $p[1]$ to $t[j + 1]$, and so on until $p[|p| - 1]$ is compared to $t[k + |p| - 1]$. If each of these comparisons succeeds then the match is successful; otherwise, k is incremented and we start again. (All of our string searching algorithms return either the smallest k such that $p = $ *Substring*$(t, k, |p|)$, or -1 when the search is unsuccessful.)

There is a metaphor for string searching that helps to understand the algorithms of this section. Think of a string as a strip of boxes, each containing a character. The problem of string searching is then to place the pattern strip "beneath" the target strip in a location where characters in corresponding boxes match (Figure 5.10). In terms of this metaphor, Algorithm 5.4 can be restated as follows. Place the pattern strip at the leftmost edge of the target strip and try to match the characters in the two strips. If some character fails to match, move the

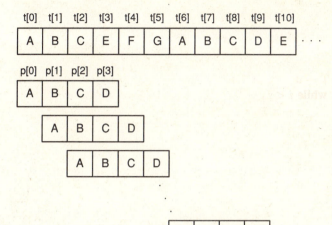

Figure 5.10 String searching metaphor, illustrating the naïve algorithm: the initial portion of the target t, three non-matching placements of the pattern string p, and the final matching placement.

pattern strip one box to the right and try again. Continue until a match is found or until the rightmost edge of the pattern strip passes the rightmost end of the target strip. (In Algorithm 5.4, and throughout this section, the variable k stores the index of the target character that lies "over" the first character of the pattern.)

How much time might be required by Algorithm 5.4? The worst possibility is an unsuccessful search in which the pattern string always matches completely except for the last character—for example, when pattern XXXXXY is matched against a long string of Xs. In this case the outer loop is executed once for each character of the target string and the inner loop is executed once for each character of the pattern string; that is, the search requires $\Theta(|p| \cdot |t|)$ time. In many applications this time is quite acceptable, especially where patterns are short and most of the time is spent retrieving chunks of the target from an external storage device. But there are much faster algorithms for string searching. Each of the next two algorithms that we shall study requires only $O(|p| + |t|)$ time for string searching, that is, they run in linear time. And the improvement is not just theoretical; implementations of these algorithms can be enormously faster than the naïve algorithm when the target is very long.

The Knuth-Morris-Pratt Algorithm

Although Algorithm 5.4 is very simple, it will sometimes do lots of superfluous work. For example, suppose again that the pattern p is ABCD and the target t begins ABCEFGABCD (Figure 5.10). Algorithm 5.4 aligns the left edge of the pattern with the left edge of the target and checks the characters of p against those of t. When $p[3]$ fails to match $t[3]$ the pattern is moved one box to the

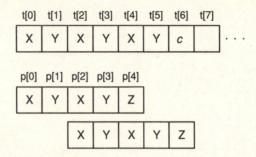

Figure 5.11 An example in which the pattern can be moved only two boxes to the right after the first mismatch.

right (to the second location pictured in Figure 5.10). The pattern in its new location is again checked against the target, and this check fails immediately since $p[0]$ doesn't equal $t[1]$.

But this last mismatch (and many to come) could have been foreseen. A better algorithm would realize after the first mismatch that the next three placements of the pattern are doomed to failure, since the pattern contains no character E. Therefore, the pattern may as well be moved four boxes to the right without delay, placing $p[0]$ beneath $t[4]$. This example illustrates the key idea of the Knuth-Morris-Pratt string search algorithm: when the pattern fails to match the current location in the target, slide the pattern rightwards not just one box, but as many boxes as possible consistent with the requirement that we must never miss a match.

The example of the previous paragraph is a special case where the pattern is moved to the right as far as possible, that is, over a distance equal to its own length. In general, it may not be possible to move the pattern that far. Consider a more complex example: suppose that p is XYXYZ and that t begins XYXYXY... (Figure 5.11). We start with p over the leftmost part of t as usual, and the first four characters match correctly. But when $p[4]$ fails to match $t[4]$ it would be incorrect to move the pattern five boxes to the right. The algorithm must recognize that the second XY in t also matches the *first* XY in p and therefore that the pattern can be moved only two boxes to the right.

Continuing this example, we see that correct motion of the pattern sometimes depends not only on the *location* of a mismatch, but also on the mismatching character itself. Consider the possibilities for $t[6]$ in Figure 5.11. After $p[3]$ matches $t[5]$, $p[4]$ is compared against $t[6]$. If $t[6]$ is X then the pattern should again be moved two boxes to the right, and the algorithm should continue by comparing $p[3]$ with $t[7]$ (since it already knows that $p[2]$ will match $t[6]$). But if $t[6]$ is (say) E, then the pattern can be moved five boxes to the right immediately, and the first character of the pattern should next be compared against $t[7]$. Of course, if $t[6]$ is Z then the pattern has been found in the target and the algorithm terminates.

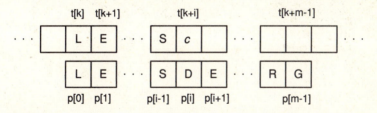

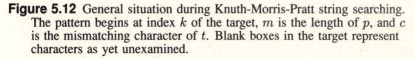

Figure 5.12 General situation during Knuth-Morris-Pratt string searching. The pattern begins at index k of the target, m is the length of p, and c is the mismatching character of t. Blank boxes in the target represent characters as yet unexamined.

The most general situation is depicted in Figure 5.12. Here the first box of the pattern lies under box k of the target, characters $p[0], p[1], \ldots, p[i-1]$ have matched characters $t[k], t[k+1], \ldots, t[k+i-1]$, but $p[i] \neq t[k+i]$. The problem is to determine d, the number of boxes that the pattern should be moved to the right so that as much of the pattern as possible still matches the already-encountered portion of the target. That is, we must find d such that $p[0] = t[k+d]$, $p[1] = t[k+d+1]$, and so forth up to $p[i-d] = t[k+i]$. We require the *smallest* d that satisfies these conditions, since otherwise we might miss a match. If no smaller d satisfies the conditions, $d = i+1$ always works; this corresponds to placing $p[0]$ under $t[k+i+1]$ and continuing from there.

Here is a crucial point: except for the reference to $t[k+i]$, each condition in the preceding paragraph can be stated in terms of the pattern alone. For example, the requirement $p[0] = t[k+d]$ is equivalent to requiring that $p[0] = p[d]$ since we know that $p[d] = t[k+d]$ for the current placement of the pattern. It follows that the desired value of d depends only on the pattern, on i, and on the mismatching character $t[k+i]$, which we call c. Thus we can define a function that yields the correct d in every case; let $KMPskip(p, i, c)$ be the smallest integer d, with $0 \leq d \leq i$, such that $p[i-d] = c$ and $p[j] = p[j+d]$ for each $0 \leq j \leq i-d-1$, and let $KMPskip(p, i, c) = i+1$ if no such d exists. This function encodes the heart of the algorithm: whenever a mismatch is detected between $p[i]$ and a character c in the target, we immediately move the pattern $d = KMPskip(p, i, c)$ boxes to the right.

Now, it is obviously too time-consuming to calculate $KMPskip(p, i, c)$ each time we have a mismatch! Instead, we calculate the values of $KMPskip$ for pattern p and all possible i and c once and for all, before we even look at the target—note again that $KMPskip$ depends only on the pattern, not on the target. These values are stored in an array $KMPskiparray$, where $KMPskiparray[i, c] = KMPskip(p, i, c)$ for each $0 \leq i < |p|$ and every character c in the alphabet.* As the algorithm runs, it can therefore find $KMPskip(p, i, c)$ quickly—in constant

---

*There is a side benefit here: since $KMPskiparray$ is constructed from the pattern alone, it can be reused if the same pattern is to be matched against several targets.

	A	B	C	D
A	0	1	2	3
B	1	0	3	4
C	1	2	0	4
D	1	2	3	0
other	1	2	3	4

(a)

	X	Y	X	Y	Z
X	0	1	0	3	2
Y	1	0	3	0	5
Z	1	2	3	4	0
other	1	2	3	4	5

(b)

Figure 5.13 *KMPskiparray* for patterns (a) ABCD and (b) XYXYZ. The value of $KMPskip(p, i, c)$ is in column i and the row labelled c, where each column has been labelled with $p[i]$ instead of with i. The row labelled "other" is used for all characters c that do not appear in the pattern. So, for example, we have $KMPskip(\text{ABCD}, 3, \text{B}) = 4$ and $KMPskip(\text{XYXYZ}, 2, \text{Q}) = 3$.

time—when a mismatch occurs. Figure 5.13 displays the *KMPskiparray* for the patterns of Figures 5.10 and 5.11.

Once the pattern has been moved to the right, where should comparisons continue? By the way *KMPskip* has been defined, we know that all of the characters up to and including $t[k+i]$ match correctly after the move. Therefore we continue by comparing $t[k+i+1]$ against the corresponding character in the new placement of the pattern, which is $p[i+1-d]$. Of course, these operations are carried out by manipulating the variables in the code: to move the pattern d boxes to the right we replace k with $k+d$, and to select the new position in the pattern we replace i with $i+1-d$. In terms of these new values of k and i the next comparison is between $t[k+i]$ and $p[i]$, just as before.

The algorithm becomes even more elegant if we use the same mechanism to handle the case of a *correct* match between the pattern and the target. Suppose in Figure 5.12 that $t[k+i]$ does match $p[i]$. Then the smallest d that satisfies the conditions of *KMPskip* is $d = 0$. That is, the definition of *KMPskip* implies that $KMPskip(p, i, c) = 0$ when $p[i] = c$, restating the fact that the pattern should not move at all when it matches the target. With this simplification, we find that there is no longer any reason to compare $t[k+i]$ with $p[i]$ since we take the same action whether they match or not: in either case we look up $d = KMPskiparray[i, t[k+i]]$, replace k with $k+d$, and replace i with $i+1-d$. The complete program appears in Algorithm 5.5. (We have not discussed the termination conditions, but it is easy to see that a match has occurred when i reaches the length of the pattern and that no match is possible when k gets close to the end of the target.) Notice how p has all but disappeared from the main loop of Algorithm 5.5; except for its length, all the necessary information about the pattern is encoded in *KMPskiparray*.

How fast is Algorithm 5.5? In the worst case, when no match is found, the main loop is executed at least $|t| - |p|$ times and at most $|t|$ times. (To see this, note that the value $k+i$ starts out 0 and increases by exactly 1 each time through

function *KMPSearch*(**string** p, t): **integer**
{Find p in t; return its location or -1 if p is not a substring of t}
    $KMPskiparray \leftarrow ComputeKMPskiparray(p)$
    $k \leftarrow 0$
    $i \leftarrow 0$
    while $k \leq Length(t) - Length(p)$ **do**
        if $i = Length(p)$ **then return** k
        $d \leftarrow KMPskiparray[i, t[k + i]]$
        $k \leftarrow k + d$
        $i \leftarrow i + 1 - d$
    return -1

Algorithm 5.5 Knuth-Morris-Pratt string searching. The function *Compute-KMPskiparray* is discussed in Problems 41 and 42.

the loop. The final value of k is $|t| - |p|$ and i ranges between 0 and $|p|$.) Every action in the main loop can be completed in constant time. So Algorithm 5.5 requires time at most $O(|t|)$ plus the time required to build the *KMPskiparray* for p. In fact, this array can be constructed in time $O(|p|)$ (Problems 41 and 42). Thus the Knuth-Morris-Pratt algorithm accomplishes string searching in linear time.

The Boyer-Moore Algorithm

The basic idea of the Boyer-Moore algorithm is the same as that of the Knuth-Morris-Pratt algorithm: the pattern is compared against the target, and on a mismatch the pattern is moved as far to the right as possible. The only difference is that the Boyer-Moore algorithm compares the pattern and the target from right-to-left, rather than from left-to-right. Although this change may seem unimportant, it results in a startling improvement in performance: in a typical Boyer-Moore string search, a large number of characters in the target string are never examined at all! This makes the Boyer-Moore algorithm much faster than the naïve algorithm on long targets even when the pattern is only a few characters long.

Figure 5.14 illustrates the idea, using the pattern and target of Figure 5.10. The first comparison tests $p[3]$ against $t[3]$. Of course these characters do not match, but more importantly we immediately see that since $t[3]$ is E, and since there is no occurrence of E in the pattern, the pattern cannot match if *any* of its characters lie under $t[3]$—the pattern can instantly be moved four boxes to the right, and the first three characters of the target can be ignored. Continuing the same example, after the pattern has been moved, $p[3]$ is compared against $t[7]$, a B. Again there is no match, but this time the pattern cannot be moved quite

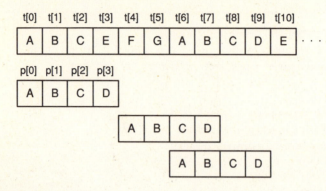

Figure 5.14 The target and pattern of Figure 5.10 revisited, showing pattern placements during a Boyer-Moore search. First, the fact that $t[3]$ does not occur in the pattern permits us to move the pattern four boxes to the right. Then $t[7]$ doesn't match B, but the pattern can be moved only until its rightmost B aligns with $t[7]$. Target characters $t[0]$, $t[1]$, $t[2]$, $t[4]$, and $t[5]$ are never examined.

so far. Since there *is* a B in the pattern, we might miss a match if we move $p[1]$ beyond $t[7]$. Therefore the pattern can be moved only two boxes to the right, but even so, characters $t[4]$ and $t[5]$ will never be examined. (If the pattern contained more than one B, it could be moved only until its *rightmost* B aligned with $t[7]$.)

In general the situation is a bit more complex because part of the pattern may correctly match the target before a mismatch is detected. Let us look at the general case, depicted in Figure 5.15. Here characters $p[m - 1]$, $p[m - 2]$, ..., $p[i+1]$ have matched characters $t[k+m-1]$, $t[k+m-2]$, ..., $t[k+i+1]$, but $p[i]$ does not match $t[k + i]$. (Figure 5.15 is the same as Figure 5.12, but now it is the characters to the *right* of $p[i]$ that are known to match the target.) Again the problem is to determine d, the number of boxes that the pattern can be moved to the right. Considering all the information now available about the target, we see that d should be the smallest integer such that $t[k+m-1] = p[m-1-d]$, $t[k+m-2] = p[m-2-d]$, ..., $t[k+i] = p[i-d]$. As in Knuth-Morris-Pratt searching, the *smallest* d must be chosen because otherwise a match might be missed.

But there is a difficulty here: this statement of the conditions for d is valid only for $d \leq i$. If no such d exists and we try to test $d = i + 1$ for compliance; we "fall off" the left edge of the pattern trying to ensure that $t[k + i] = p[-1]$. Put another way, if no such small d exists, the pattern will be moved so far that $t[k + i]$ is above empty space. When this happens we require only that the pattern match the target down to $p[0]$ (which lies under $t[k + d]$). Both of these situations are illustrated in Figure 5.16, where the final three characters match but $t[k + 5] \neq p[5]$. If $t[k + 5]$ is W then $d = 3$ is satisfactory and the pattern should be moved three boxes to the right. But if $t[k + 5]$ is R then the pattern

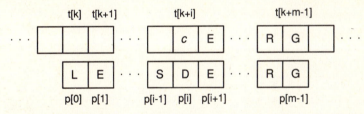

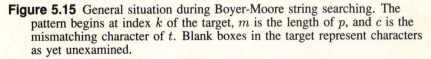

Figure 5.15 General situation during Boyer-Moore string searching. The pattern begins at index k of the target, m is the length of p, and c is the mismatching character of t. Blank boxes in the target represent characters as yet unexamined.

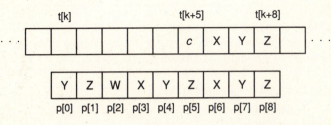

Figure 5.16 An illustration of Boyer-Moore string searching.

should be moved exactly $d = 7$ boxes to the right since $p[0] = t[k + 7]$ and $p[1] = t[k + 8]$. (Of course, if $t[k + 5]$ is Z then we continue by comparing $t[k + 4]$ to $p[4]$ without moving the pattern at all.)

As in Knuth-Morris-Pratt searching, the next step is to recast the conditions solely in terms of the pattern and the mismatching character c. Let $m = |p|$, and for any character c and any i such that $0 \le i < m$ define $BMskip(p, i, c)$ to be the amount that the pattern can move to the right when characters $i + 1$ through $m - 1$ of the pattern match corresponding characters in the target but $p[i]$ does not match a character c in the target. Translating the discussion of the previous paragraph into these terms, we find that $BMskip(p, i, c)$ must be the smallest d such that

- $p[j] = p[j - d]$ for all j such that $\max(i + 1, d) \le j \le m - 1$, and
- $p[i - d] = c$ if $d \le i$.

Since $i < m$, both conditions are vacuous for $d = m$; that is, $d = m$ satisfies the conditions for any i and c and can be used if no smaller d qualifies. Of course, $d = m$ corresponds to moving the pattern to the right over its entire length and is the most desirable value of $BMskip$ from the standpoint of speed (other than stopping with a successful match!). Figure 5.17 displays the $BMskiparray$ for the patterns of Figures 5.10 and 5.11. The superiority of the Boyer-Moore algorithm over the Knuth-Morris-Pratt algorithm is demonstrated by a comparison of Figure 5.17 with Figure 5.13; the entries in the Boyer-Moore

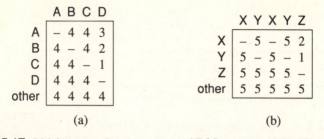

Figure 5.17 *BMskiparray* for patterns (a) ABCD and (b) XYXYZ, using the conventions of Figure 5.13.

---

function *BMSearch*(**string** p, t): **integer**
{Find p in t; return its location or -1 if p is not a substring of t}
    $BMskiparray \leftarrow ComputeBMskiparray(p)$
    $k \leftarrow 0$
    while $k \leq Length(t) - Length(p)$ **do**
        $i \leftarrow Length(p) - 1$
        while $i \geq 0$ **and** $p[i] = t[k + i]$ **do**
            $i \leftarrow i - 1$
        if $i = -1$ **then return** k
        $k \leftarrow k + BMskiparray[i, t[k + i]]$
    return -1

Algorithm 5.6 Boyer-Moore string searching.

---

arrays are generally larger and the pattern will therefore move faster. This is especially true for pattern ABCD which has the characteristics of patterns typically encountered, unlike the contrived pattern XYXYZ.

    The implementation of Boyer-Moore string searching (Algorithm 5.6) is quite similar to Knuth-Morris-Pratt string searching. Again we store all the values of *BMskip* in an array for rapid access in the main loop—and again, these values can be computed in time linear in the length of the pattern (Problem 43). The chief difference is the way that mismatches are handled. In Boyer-Moore searching comparisons must start afresh from the rightmost edge of p on *any* mismatch, since every time p is moved its rightmost edge goes into "unexplored territory" of t. As a consequence, the cases of matching and mismatching characters cannot be combined as they were in the Knuth-Morris-Pratt algorithm, and *BMskiparray* is not even consulted on a match. Thus the entries *BMskiparray*$[i, c]$ for $p[i] = c$ need not have any particular value; they show as blanks in Figure 5.17.

Fingerprinting and the Karp-Rabin Algorithm

A completely different string searching algorithm uses the following approach. Suppose χ is a function that produces from any string w a small number $\chi(w)$, called the **fingerprint** of w. Given a pattern p and target t, let $m = |p|$ and define $f_i = \chi(Substring(t, i, m))$; that is, f_i is the fingerprint of the m characters of t starting at index i. The algorithm first computes and compares $\chi(p)$ and f_0. If $\chi(p) = f_0$, there may be a match: compare p character by character with the first m characters of t to see if they agree. But if $\chi(p) \neq f_0$ then clearly p does not match the first m characters of t. In any case, if there is no match, continue by computing f_1 and comparing it to $\chi(p)$, and so forth. The idea is that the fingerprint function gives a quick preliminary test. If the fingerprint of the pattern is different from f_i then the pattern cannot match $Substring(t, i, m)$ and no further work is necessary for this placement of the pattern. If the fingerprints are equal, then a character by character comparison is needed because of the possibility of a correct match. But fingerprints are small numbers that can be compared in a single operation; the hope is to avoid most of the character comparisons entirely.*

There are two key ideas to the fingerprint method of string searching. First of all, the fingerprinting function χ should give "false matches" as rarely as possible. That is, if two strings s_1 and s_2 are different then $\chi(s_1)$ should be different from $\chi(s_2)$ with high probability. The reason is that a false match necessitates up to $|p| - 1$ character comparisons, which we wish to avoid. (Analogously, fingerprinting is useful as a method of identification only to the extent that different people are unlikely to have identical fingerprints!) Secondly, the method saves nothing if successive fingerprints f_i take a long time to compute. The trick is to choose a function χ with the property that the f_i need not be computed independently; f_{i+1} should be quickly computable from f_i and the "new" character $t[i + |p|]$.

Here is a complete but simple example. Let us assume that characters can be added and subtracted like numbers; formally, we identify each $c \in \Sigma$ with a unique integer (typically the integer that represents it in memory). Now let $\chi(w)$ be the sum of the characters of w. We then have that $f_i = \chi(Substring(t, i, m))$ is the sum $t[i] + t[i+1] + \cdots + t[i+m-1]$. To compute f_{i+1} from f_i it suffices to "add in" the new character $t[i+m]$ and "take away" the oldest character $t[i]$; that is, $f_{i+1} = f_i + t[i+m] - t[i]$. Algorithm 5.7 presents the complete string search procedure for this simple fingerprint function.

The Karp-Rabin algorithm for string searching uses precisely this framework with a more sophisticated fingerprinting function. For simplicity suppose that $\Sigma = \{0, 1, \ldots, N-1\}$. Then any string w can be interpreted directly as a

---

*The method of fingerprints is conceptually similar to *hashing*, which we shall encounter in Chapter 8.

function *FingerprintSearch*(**string** p, t): **integer**
{Find p in t; return its location or -1 if p is not a substring of t}
    $m \leftarrow Length(p)$

    {Compute the fingerprint of the pattern}
    fpattern $\leftarrow 0$
    for i **from** 0 **to** $m - 1$ **do**
        fpattern $\leftarrow$ *fpattern* $+ p[i]$

    {Compute the fingerprint of the first part of the target}
    ftarget $\leftarrow 0$
    for i **from** 0 **to** $m - 1$ **do**
        ftarget $\leftarrow$ *ftarget* $+ t[i]$

    {The main loop}
    for i **from** 0 **to** $Length(t) - m$ **do**
        if *fpattern* = *ftarget* **then**
            if $p = Substring(t, i, m)$ **then return** i
        if $i \neq Length(t) - m$ **then**
            ftarget $\leftarrow$ *ftarget* $+ t[i + m] - t[i]$
    return -1

Algorithm 5.7 Fingerprint string searching with a simple fingerprint function.

number in base N:

$$H(w) = \sum_{i=0}^{|w|-1} w[i] \cdot N^{|w|-1-i}.$$

For each positive integer b define a function $H_b(w) = H(w) \bmod b$. Each function H_b is easy to compute because of the identities

$$(x + y) \bmod b = ((x \bmod b) + (y \bmod b)) \bmod b, \qquad \text{and}$$
$$xy \bmod b = ((x \bmod b)(y \bmod b)) \bmod b. \tag{2}$$

That is, we can do all computation modulo b and need not worry about integers larger than we can conveniently handle. Moreover, it is easy to update fingerprints as the target string is scanned, since with $f_i = H_b(Substring(t, i, m))$ we have

$$f_{i+1} = (N \cdot f_i + t[i + m] - t[i] \cdot N^m) \bmod b$$

where $m = |p|$ as before.

    It is possible to show that the fingerprint function H_b performs very well when b is a prime number. Even so, for any given b there will be combinations of patterns and targets with many false matches; to guard against repeated bad performance (if, say, the same pattern is used several times on similar targets) the prime b should be chosen afresh each time the algorithm is run. An even better method is to switch to a different b whenever a false match occurs; with this procedure, it is not even necessary that b be prime. When the moduli b are chosen randomly, it can be shown that even an intelligent adversary cannot construct a pattern and target that will produce many false matches.

The method of fingerprints also applies to more general problems. For example, it can be used for two-dimensional pattern matching: given two rectangular blocks of zeroes and ones (a "pattern" and a "target") determine whether the pattern occurs within the target. The method generalizes to higher dimensions and even to patterns that are not rectangular.

In this section we have discussed several algorithms for string searching. But which of them is actually best in practice? Or, perhaps more urgently, which should be considered when a string searching problem is at hand? In practice, the fastest algorithm is that of Boyer and Moore, which is frequently implemented in general-purpose string searching tools that are used on targets of enormous size—usually with modifications as discussed in Problem 44 to limit the size of the *BMskiparray*. However, calculating that array requires some complex programming (especially if the linear time bound is to be preserved) which is often not worthwhile for simple, short-lived problems. In these cases, the Karp-Rabin algorithm can be coded easily, using a very simple fingerprint function, and will provide satisfactory performance.

Problems

5.1   **1.** Give a formal definition for the abstract operation *Concat* on strings.

     2. Let n be a fixed positive integer. Find all quadruples $\langle i_1, i_2, m_1, m_2 \rangle$ of integers such that, for all strings w of length n, it is true that $w = Concat(Substring(w, i_1, m_1), Substring(w, i_2, m_2))$.

5.2   **3.** Suppose M is a d-dimensional array stored in contiguous memory starting at address **M**. Element $M[l_1, l_2, \ldots, l_d]$ of M is located at address **M** whether M is stored in row-major or column-major order. Which other elements of M (if any) necessarily have this property, independent of the dimensions of M? Find all such elements in the case $d = 2$, as a function of l_1, l_2, u_1, and u_2.

     4. Suppose that a two-dimensional array with indices $(0 \mathinner{.\,.} n - 1) \times (0 \mathinner{.\,.} n - 1)$ is stored in row-major order in a table T. Write a program that transforms T so that the array is stored in column-major order. You may not copy T or use auxiliary storage that depends on n; all you may do is move elements within T.

     5. a. Solve Problem 4 for arrays with arbitrary dimension and indices.

b. Find a more practical solution to this problem that uses as little auxiliary storage as possible.

6. An efficient way of calculating expression (1) on page 135 is suggested by Horner's rule for evaluating polynomial expressions, which says that

$$a_n x^n + a_{n-1} x^{n-1} + \cdots + a_1 x + a_0 = a_0 + x(a_1 + x(a_2 + \cdots + x(a_n) \cdots)).$$

The same idea can be applied here, yielding

$$\mathbf{X} + L \cdot (j_d - l_d + s_d \cdot (j_{d-1} - l_{d-1} + s_{d-1} \cdot (j_{d-2} - l_{d-2} + \cdots + s_2 \cdot (j_1 - l_1) \cdots)))$$

as the address of element $X[j_1, j_2, \ldots, j_d]$. Show how to arrange this computation so that *Access* can be implemented in only about $2d$ operations.

7. Implement the abstract operation *Iterate* for arrays represented as shown in Figure 5.3 on page 138. What improvements are possible if we relax the requirement that *Iterate* process array elements in order?

8. Show how to represent multidimensional arrays with constant-time initialization and access.

9. Choose a record structure for 3-dimensional arrays represented by hierarchical tables as in Figure 5.6 on page 141, and write appropriate procedures *Initialize*, *Access*, *Assign*, and *Iterate* (with the last index varying fastest). You may use the function *NewTable(n)* which creates a table of n pointers. Unused tables should eventually be deallocated so that the storage can be reused (assume a function *FreeTable* that returns a table to the storage allocator). Since we require that *Access* and *Assign* use only constant time, and since we want to use a minimum of storage overhead, you should check for table deallocation only during *Iterate* and *Initialize*.

10. Solve Problem 9 with the additional requirement that tables are deallocated as soon as possible, still with constant-time *Access* and *Assign*. (You will have to use slightly more storage overhead.)

11. Let M be an upper-triangular matrix of order n represented as described on page 142. Show how to determine i and j given n and the address in memory of element $M[i, j]$. (As usual, each element occupies L physical memory cells and $M[0, 0]$ begins at address $\mathbf{M}$.)

12. Upper-triangular matrices may be generalized to higher dimensions. A d-dimensional upper-triangular matrix of order n is an array M with d indices each between 0 and $n - 1$, where $M[i_1, i_2, \ldots, i_d]$ is zero unless $i_1 \leq i_2 \leq \cdots \leq i_d$.

a. How many nonzero elements are contained in a d-dimensional upper-triangular matrix of order n?

b. Show how to represent d-dimensional upper-triangular matrices in contiguous memory so that no space is wasted.

13. Define a **tridiagonal matrix** of order n to be an array with index set $(0..n-1) \times (0..n-1)$ in which all nonzero entries are on either the main diagonal or one of the two adjacent, parallel diagonals. That is, for each i the only possible nonzero elements whose first index is i are $M[i, i-1]$, $M[i, i]$, and $M[i, i+1]$.

a. How many nonzero elements are contained in a tridiagonal matrix of order n?

b. Find a representation for tridiagonal matrices that wastes no storage and such that the address of $M[i, j]$ can be computed from i and j in as few arithmetic operations as possible. As usual, L is the length of a single element; operations involving only L, n, and the starting address of M can be "precomputed" and don't count.

14. Suppose we wish to implement upper-triangular matrices in a programming language that supports multidimensional arrays efficiently. Devise a space-efficient representation that requires no explicit multiplications. (In practice, such techniques are rarely better than using one-dimensional arrays since the arithmetic saved is performed anyway by the underlying implementation of multidimensional arrays.)

15. A **checkerboard** is a multidimensional array in which the sum of the indices of each nonnull element is even. Devise a space-efficient representation for checkerboards in contiguous memory.

5.4 **16.** Prove the assertion on page 145, that unique decodability is assured if no character's encoding is the prefix of another character's encoding. Is the converse true? That is, given an alphabet and a bit sequence encoding each character, with the property that the encoded version of any string can be unambiguously decoded, does it follow that no character's encoding is the prefix of another character's encoding?

17. By definition, every encoding tree is full; that is, each nonleaf has exactly two children. Show that nothing is lost by this requirement in the sense that if T is an "encoding tree" that is not full, then there is always a full encoding tree T' for the same alphabet such that, for any string w, the encoding of w using T' is no larger than the encoding of w using T.

18. By definition, the leaves of an encoding tree must contain distinct characters. Show that nothing is lost by this requirement in the sense that if T is an "encoding tree" with duplicate characters in its leaves, then there is always an encoding tree T' for the same alphabet without duplications such that, for any string w, the encoding of w using T' is no larger than the encoding of w using T.

19. Which was the second-to-last internal node created in the example of Figure 5.8 on page 148?

20. The following data are from Storer (see the references) and give the number of occurrences (in hundreds) of the lower-case letters in a set of large text files: e 933, t 675, a 571, o 570, i 556, n 537, s 524, r 483, h 349, l 295, c 268, d 255, u 211, m 192, p 183, f 170, g 144, b 120, y 108, w 96, v 71, k 37, x 24, q 11, j 10, z 9. Construct a Huffman tree for these twenty-six characters.

21. a. Show that tiebreaking is not significant in the Huffman algorithm in the sense that the total size of the encoded text is the same regardless of how the tree construction algorithm breaks ties when selecting nodes of minimum weight.

   b. Give a proof or counterexample of the following converse of the Huffman Optimality Theorem on page 149. Let T be any encoding tree for text w such that $WPL(T)$ is a minimum over all encoding trees for w. Then there is some way of breaking ties in the Huffman algorithm such that T is constructed.

22. Notwithstanding Problem 21(a), the trees produced by the Huffman algorithm may differ when different tiebreaking schemes are used. In particular, for a given text there may be Huffman trees of different heights. (For example, the string ABCCDD has Huffman trees of heights 2 and 3.) Find a tiebreaking scheme for the Huffman algorithm such that the resulting tree has minimum height among all possible Huffman trees for the given text.

23. a. Find a string of minimum length that could give rise to the Huffman encoding tree of Figure 5.7 on page 146.

   b. The string w actually used by the authors to construct Figure 5.7 has 15 characters. That fact does not uniquely determine w. Find w anyway.

24. The Lemma on page 148 applies only to *full* binary trees. Precisely where in the proof of the Lemma is this assumption used?

25. When using the Huffman algorithm, the compressed text must begin with a description of the encoding tree. Suppose that the alphabet Σ is fixed and consists of 256 characters, each encoded as a distinct sequence of eight bits (this is usually the case, as when ASCII or

EBCDIC is the understood alphabet). Devise a scheme for describing the encoding tree in the encoded text, and write the programs used by the encoder to describe the tree and by the decoder to recover the tree. Of course, your representation should be as space-efficient as possible!

26. Solve Problem 25 without the assumption of a universal alphabet. That is, the decoding algorithm must be assumed to know nothing at all about the size of Σ.

27. Our discussion of the Huffman algorithm has assumed that encoded text is represented by a sequence of bits. Generalize this assumption: suppose that the encoded text is represented by a sequence of characters from an arbitrary alphabet which has more than two characters. Describe the generalized version of the Huffman tree-construction, encoding, and decoding algorithms, and state and prove the generalized optimality theorem.

28. Suppose c_1 and c_2 are two characters of frequencies f_1 and f_2 in text w, and let d_1 and d_2 be the depths of c_1 and c_2 in a Huffman encoding tree for w.

   a. Show that $f_1 > f_2$ implies $d_1 \leq d_2$.

   b. Show that $f_1 = f_2$ implies $|d_1 - d_2| \leq 1$.

29. We have constructed Huffman trees based on the frequencies f_i of the members of Σ in the text w. For each character c_i of Σ, define the **probability** p_i of c_i as $p_i = c_i/|w|$. (Since frequencies and probabilities differ only by the constant factor $1/|w|$, the Huffman algorithm can use either when constructing the encoding tree.) Let T be a Huffman encoding tree for w. Recall that the Fibonacci sequence is defined by $F_0 = 0$, $F_1 = 1$, and $F_n = F_{n-1} + F_{n-2}$ for $n > 1$.

   a. Show that if n is positive and $p_i \geq 1/F_{n+1}$, then the depth of c_i in T must be less than n.

   b. Suppose conversely that p_i is known to be less than $1/F_{n+1}$. What can be concluded about the depth of c_i in T?

30. Determine exactly the worst-case performance of Huffman encoding; that is, find the maximum possible size in bits of the Huffman encoding of a string w over an alphabet Σ, in terms of $Length(w)$ and $|\Sigma|$.

31. Suppose that T is any binary encoding tree for a string w over an alphabet Σ and assume that each leaf of T represents a character that occurs at least once in w. As usual, for each node n of T let $C(n)$ be the weight of n: the weight of each leaf is the frequency of occurrence of its character in w, and the weight of each nonleaf is the sum of the weights of its children.

   a. Show that T is an *optimal* encoding tree for w if it satisfies the following condition: there is an ordering n_1, n_2, ..., $n_{2|\Sigma|-1}$ of the nodes of T such that $C(n_i) \leq C(n_{i+1})$ for each i, and moreover each adjacent pair of nodes n_{2k-1}, n_{2k} are siblings in T.

   b. Let T be an optimal encoding tree for w, let an ordering of the nodes of T be given as in part (a), and let n_i be any leaf of T. Suppose that $n_i < n_{i+1}$, and moreover suppose that $n_{i'} < n_{i'+1}$ for every ancestor $n_{i'}$ of n_i. Show that T is an optimal encoding tree for the string $Concat(w, c)$, where c is the character represented by n_i.

(These results are the crucial facts used in an efficient implementation of the adaptive Huffman encoding algorithm—see page 484.)

32. Show the operation of the Lempel-Ziv compression algorithm on the following tercet (from a poem by J. Holobom, as quoted by A. Bierce). Assume that lines are separated by a single space.

    abracadabra, abracadab,
    abracada, abracad,
    abraca, abrac, abra, ab!

33. Write the procedure *LZEncode*, the inverse of procedure *LZDecode* (Algorithm 5.3 on page 153). *LZEncode* takes two arguments: a **string** to be encoded and a **bitstream** to receive the encoding. You may use a subroutine *WriteOneCodeNumber*(c, b) that outputs an integer c to a **bitstream** b. *LZEncode* also uses the same abstract dictionary operations as the decoder. (For purposes of this exercise, don't worry about generating a large number of calls on *LookUp* nor about dictionary overflow. But see page 484.)

34. In Lempel-Ziv encoding the input string is considered one character at a time as we search for the longest match. This process ends when we encounter the first character such that the string-so-far is not in the dictionary. At that point, we have in our hands the string that will be added to the dictionary in the *next* step, and might as well add it immediately. For example, consider again the text **COCOA AND BANANAS**. In the first step, we would match C, fail to match CO, and thus output #(C) and add CO to the dictionary. In the second step, we match O, fail to match OC, and so output #(O) and add OC to the dictionary.

   a. Show how Figure 5.9 on page 152 would be constructed by this variation of the encoding algorithm. Warning: it is not sufficient to advance each entry in the "Add to Dictionary" column!

   b. With this variation of the algorithm, it is possible that *LookUps* by the decoder might fail! Show how this occurs in the example, and explain clearly how the decoder should proceed to resolve the problem correctly.

c. Compare this version of Lempel-Ziv encoding with that described in the text. Approximately how much difference can there be in the size of the encoding of a text of length n?

35. For each integer $n \geq 0$, let w_n be the string consisting of n character As, followed by a single character B, followed by n more As. For example, $w_3 = $ AAABAAA and $w_0 = $ B.

a. What is the length in bits of the Huffman encoding of w_n?

b. Find (to within a small constant) the length in bits of the Lempel-Ziv encoding of w_n, under the assumption that each code number has k bits and that the dictionary never overflows.

c. What is the largest value of n such that the assumption in part (b) (that the dictionary does not overflow) is valid?

36. Suppose that $\Sigma = \{A, B\}$ and that w is a string of length n over Σ containing at least one of each character.

a. If Huffman encoding is used, what are the smallest and largest possible sizes (in bits) of the compressed representation of w?

b. If Lempel-Ziv encoding is used, approximately what are the smallest and largest possible sizes (in code numbers) of the compressed representation of w? (Assume that the dictionary never overflows.)

37. Suppose you have several very large files to store. You may either concatenate the files into one large file and then compress that file, or you may compress the files individually. Assuming that you are using one of the compression algorithms described in this section, does it make a difference which method you use?

5.5 38. Suppose $t = $ ABCDE and $p = \epsilon$, the unique string of length zero. According to the definition on page 154, does p occur as a substring of t, and if so, what should the string searching algorithms of the section return given p and t? What if t also equals ϵ?

39. Let Σ be the alphabet consisting of the uppercase letters. Find both the *KMPskiparray* and the *BMskiparray* associated with the string ABCABACABCAB.

40. The captions of Figures 5.12 and 5.15 each contain the sentence "Blank boxes in the target represent characters as yet unexamined." Explain carefully why this statement is not strictly true in either case.

41. If w is any string, define *PrefSuf*(w) to be the largest $j < |w|$ such that *Substring*$(w, 0, j) = $ *Substring*$(w, |w| - j, j)$; that is, *PrefSuf*(w) is the

---

function *AllPrefSufs*(**string** p): **array**
{The result ps is an array of integers with the same indices as p}
$\quad ps[0] \leftarrow 0$
$\quad$ **for** j **from** 1 **to** *Length*$(p) - 1$ **do**
$\quad\quad ps[j] \leftarrow Extend(ps[j - 1], j)$
$\quad$ **return** ps

function *Extend*(**integer** i, j): **integer**
{Chain through ps looking for an extendible value}
$\quad$ **if** $p[j] = p[i]$ **then return** $i + 1$
$\quad$ **if** $i = 0$ **then return** 0
$\quad$ **return** *Extend*$(ps[i - 1], j)$

Algorithm 5.8 Compute *PrefSuf* of each prefix of the input string p.

---

length of the longest prefix of w (other than w itself) that is also a suffix of w. For example, *PrefSuf*(ABCAB) = 2, *PrefSuf*(AAAAA) = 4, and *PrefSuf*(ABC) = 0. Given any string p, the function *AllPrefSufs* described in Algorithm 5.8 computes an array ps such that $ps[i] = $ *PrefSuf*(*Substring*$(p, 0, i+1)$) for each $0 \leq i < |p|$; that is, ps contains the value of *PrefSuf*(p') for each non-empty prefix p' of p.

a. Prove that Algorithm 5.8 works as advertised.

b. Prove that Algorithm 5.8 works in linear time; that is, in time $O(|p|)$.

42. Use the results of Problem 41 to write a linear-time version of the function *ComputeKMPskiparray* used in Algorithm 5.5 on page 159, completing the demonstration that Knuth-Morris-Pratt string searching requires only linear time. (Hint: *KMPskiparray*$[i, c]$ can be quickly computed using $ps[i]$. Since the alphabet is fixed, a loop of the form '**foreach** c **in** Σ ...' introduces only a constant factor into the time analysis.)

43. Write a linear-time version of the function *ComputeBMskiparray* used in Algorithm 5.6 on page 162. (Proving that Boyer-Moore string searching requires only linear time is not a trivial matter; see the references.)

44. We have defined *BMskip*(p, i, c) as the smallest d that simultaneously satisfies both conditions displayed on page 161. Most implementations of the Boyer-Moore algorithm treat these conditions separately, modifying the second one slightly: let *BMskip1*(p, i) be the smallest d

that satisfies the first condition, and let $BMskip2(p, c)$ be the smallest d such that $p[m - d - 1] = c$, or m if no such d exists. When the pattern does not match the target we move the pattern rightwards by $\max(BMskip1(p, i), BMskip2(p, c) - (|p| - i - 1))$ boxes. The advantage of this approach is that, since $BMskip1$ does not depend on c and $BMskip2$ does not depend on i, two small one-dimensional arrays suffice to store the precomputed values rather than a two-dimensional array as pictured in Figure 5.17 on page 162.

   a. Write routines that compute $BMskip1array$ and $BMskip2array$ from a given pattern p in linear time.

   b. Find an example in which the pattern moves farther when both conditions must be satisfied simultaneously.

45. Prove the identities (2) on page 164.

46. Let alphabet Σ consist of the uppercase letters. Identify **A** with 1, **B** with 2, and so forth, so that characters can be added (e.g. **Z**+**C** = 29). With the simple fingerprint function of Algorithm 5.7 on page 164, what is the maximum possible number of false matches while searching a target of length n?

47. A **wildcard** in a search pattern is a character that matches any character from the text. Discuss string searching algorithms that permit wildcards in the pattern.

References

Huffman encoding was first described in

David A. Huffman, "A Method for the Construction of Minimum-Redundancy Codes," *Proceedings of the IRE* **40** (1952), pp. 1098–1101.

Adaptive Huffman encoding is the invention of

R. G. Gallager, "Variations on a Theme by Huffman," *IEEE Transactions on Information Theory* **IT-24** (1978), pp. 668–674

and was extended in

D. E. Knuth, "Dynamic Huffman Coding," *Journal of Algorithms* **6** (1985), pp. 163–180,

from which Problem 31 is taken (and which inspired Problem 32). Problem 22 is from

E. S. Schwartz, "An Optimum Encoding with Minimum Longest Code and Total Number of Digits," *Information and Control* **7** (1964), pp. 37–44.

Lempel-Ziv encoding was first presented in

J. Ziv and A. Lempel, "Compression of Individual Sequences via Variable-Rate Coding," *IEEE Transactions on Information Theory* **IT-24** (1978), pp. 530–536.

We have described a simplification of a version of this algorithm that appears in

T. A. Welch, "A Technique for High-Performance Data Compression," *Computer* **17** (1984), pp. 8–19

and in Problem 34. (A patent that is claimed to cover Welch's variation has been issued to Unisys.) A general reference for variants on these methods and many others, including parallel and lossy techniques, is

J. A. Storer, *Data Compression*, Computer Science Press, 1988.

The remarkable story of the discovery of the Knuth-Morris-Pratt string searching algorithm is recounted in

D. E. Knuth, J. H. Morris, Jr., and V. R. Pratt, "Fast Pattern Matching in Strings," *SIAM Journal on Computing* **6** (1977), pp. 323–350

In the same paper Knuth presents a proof of the linearity of the Boyer-Moore algorithm, which itself is from

R. S. Boyer and J. S. Moore, "A Fast String Searching Algorithm," *Communications of the ACM* **20** (1977), pp. 762–772.

Knuth's account of the Boyer-Moore algorithm contains an error, which is corrected in

W. Rytter, "A Correct Preprocessing Algorithm for Boyer-Moore String-Searching," *SIAM Journal on Computing* **9** (1980), pp. 509–512.

Knuth proves that the Boyer-Moore algorithm makes no more than about $7|t|$ comparisons in the worst case. A better bound (of $3|t|$ comparisons) and a matching lower bound are proved in

R. Cole, "Tight Bounds on the Complexity of the Boyer-Moore Pattern Matching Algorithm," *2nd ACM-SIAM Symposium on Discrete Algorithms*, 1991.

The Karp-Rabin algorithm is from

R. M. Karp and M. O. Rabin, "Efficient Randomized Pattern-Matching Algorithms," *IBM Journal of Research and Development* **31** (1987), pp. 249–260.

But every linear-time string searching algorithm that we have discussed requires either a source of random numbers or storage space linear in the size of the pattern string plus the size of the alphabet. A string searching algorithm that requires only constant space and works in linear time without using arithmetic at all is described in

Z. Galil and J. Seiferas, "Time-Space-Optimal String Matching," *Journal of Computer and System Sciences* **26** (1983), pp. 280–294.

A very useful and widely-implemented algorithm for string searching, permitting wildcards as in Problem 47 and even more general patterns called **regular expressions**, *is the work of*

K. Thompson, "Regular Expression Search Algorithm," *Communications of the ACM* **11** (1968), pp. 419–422.

6

List and Tree Implementations of Sets

6.1 SETS AND DICTIONARIES AS ABSTRACT DATA TYPES

The next four chapters deal with the computer representation of the objects known in mathematics as *sets*. In all cases of interest here, the members of a set are drawn from a single universe. For example, we might have a set of numbers, or a set of words, or a set of pairs each consisting of a word and a number. Once the universe of possible members is known, a set is determined by its members; that is, if S is a set and x is in the universe, either $x \in S$ (x is a member of S) or $x \notin S$ (x is not a member of S). For our purposes, sets are always finite, since computers can represent only finite objects; but the universe from which the set elements are drawn may be infinite, so there is no *a priori* bound on the size of a set. Also, sets cannot have duplicate members; if $x \in S$, then there is only one "copy" of x in S. Nonetheless, several of the set representations we discuss can also be used to represent **multisets**, in which the same element can occur two or more times.

The reason that sets deserve such extensive treatment in a book of this sort is that a great many computer algorithms employ steps that, abstractly, consist of answering questions of the form "is $x \in S$?" (For example, "is this identifier in the compiler's symbol table?" "Is this person in the employee data base?") As programmed, the subroutine that answers such a question is often a **search** procedure: a traversal of part or all of a data structure, comparing x to various things stored in the data structure. It is important to remember, however, that search is only a means to an end; sometimes a set representation can be found that avoids searching entirely, if the universe has a special structure and only a limited number of set operations need be implemented.

Here are some of the abstract operations that might be useful in applications involving sets:

Member(x, S): Return the boolean value **true** if x is a member of the set S, otherwise **false**.

Union(S, T): Return $S \cup T$, that is, the set consisting of every x that is a member of either set S or set T or both.

175

Intersection(S, T): Return $S \cap T$, that is, the set consisting of all x that are members of both sets S and T.

Difference(S, T): Return $S - T$, that is, the set of all x in set S that are not in set T.

MakeEmptySet( ): Return the empty set $\emptyset$.

IsEmptySet(S): Return **true** if S is the empty set, otherwise return **false**.

Size(S): Return $|S|$, the number of elements in the set S.

Insert(x, S): Add x to set S, that is, change S to $S \cup \{x\}$. (This has no effect if $x \in S$ already.)

Delete(x, S): Remove x from set S, that is, change S to $S - \{x\}$. (This has no effect if $x \notin S$ already.)

Equal(S, T): Return **true** if $S = T$, that is, if sets S and T have the same members.

Iterate(S, F): Perform operation F on each member of set S, in some unspecified order.

These operations make sense for any sets, regardless of the universe. Some other operations are appropriate in case the universe has special properties. For example, in the case of a linearly ordered universe, the *Min* operation may be useful, where

Min(S): Return the smallest member of set S, that is, that x in S such that $x < y$ for every other y in S.

Even when no linear order is used by the application that is manipulating sets, a linear order that is easily computed can be useful in *implementing* a representation of sets. For example, when storing sets of words it is useful to exploit the lexicographic order to reduce search times, even if relations of the type "is $x < y$?" are not needed at the abstract level.

An important practical variation on the general abstract model presented above recognizes that inserting, deleting, and testing membership of elements of a single universe is often somewhat less than is really desired. To take a simple example, a telephone book can be viewed abstractly as a set, where the elements are pairs consisting of a name and a telephone number. It makes sense to insert a pair such as ⟨Harry Lewis, 495–5840⟩, and perhaps even to delete such a pair; but instead of asking whether ⟨Harry Lewis, 495–5840⟩ is in the phone book, we are much more likely to want to know whether Harry Lewis is in the phone book, in the hope of getting back ⟨Harry Lewis, 495–5840⟩, or perhaps simply 495–5840, if so.

More generally, we can regard a member of the universe from which a set is constructed as a pair ⟨K, I⟩ consisting of a **key** K, which is an element of a **key space**, together with certain additional information I of data type **info**, which is not further analyzed. We assume that the key value is unique; that is, there cannot be two different elements of the set with the same key value. Typically a set will be implemented by storing its elements as records with fields for the key, the additional information, and perhaps pointers or other values used to implement a data structure. In place of the *Member* relation, we require a *LookUp* operation:

LookUp(K, S): Given a key value K, return an **info** I such that $\langle K, I \rangle \in S$; if there is no such member of set S, then return Λ.

A call *LookUp*(K, S) is said to be a **successful search** if it actually finds a pair in S with key value K; otherwise (if it returns Λ) it is said to be **unsuccessful**.

In this context the *Insert* operation takes three arguments K, I, and S, and is required to add the pair $\langle K, I \rangle$ to S. If there already is a pair with key K, *Insert* should replace it with the new pair. The *Delete* operation takes K and S as arguments and deletes from S the pair with key K, if there is one; otherwise it does nothing.

A set abstract data type with just the operations *MakeEmptySet*, *IsEmptySet*, *Insert*, *Delete*, and *LookUp* is called a **dictionary**. We begin by examining implementations of the dictionary abstract data type, noting occasionally when the implementation permits efficient implementation of other set operations. In Chapter 9 we return to the question of representations specifically designed to support other set operations.

6.2 UNORDERED LISTS

The simplest implementation of the dictionary abstract data type is to represent the set as a list of its elements, using any of the internal representations for lists discussed in Chapter 3—a table in contiguous memory, or a singly or doubly linked list structure, for example. These representations are also the most general, in the sense that they apply to sets drawn from any universe, whether the keys are ordered or not; the list is kept in whatever order results from the particular sequence of operations that constructed it. The only operation required on keys is the ability to tell whether or not two are identical. *LookUp* is implemented as a simple sequential search, starting from the beginning of the list and comparing the value being sought to the key of each successive item in the list. If the dictionary has n elements then the cost of a *LookUp* is $\Theta(n)$, since it takes linear time to find the last item in the list or to search for any key that is not in the list at all. If a linked representation is used then insertions can be done at any convenient position, but the implementation of the *Insert* operation must first check that the key value is not already in the list. Thus an *Insert* requires an implicit *LookUp* and is at least as costly as a *LookUp*. Similarly, a *Delete* requires an implicit *LookUp* to find the position of the item to be deleted, but the removal itself takes constant time if a linked representation is in use. Moving to a contiguous-memory representation saves space but does not make the operations any faster; the maximum size of the dictionary must be known in advance, and deletions become problematical if "holes" are not to be created. Thus with either a linked-memory or contiguous-memory representation of lists, each of the dictionary operations take time $\Theta(n)$ in the worst case if the lists are unordered.

To get a more precise picture of the time required by the *LookUp* operation when the dictionary is represented as a list, we measure the number of key comparisons "$K = K'$?" performed during the operation. (It is reasonable to focus on the situation in which *LookUp*s are much more common than *Insert*s or *Delete*s, so we concentrate on the cost of *LookUp*s.) If a linked representation is used, then n comparisons are needed to look up the last key in the list, or any key that is not in the list at all. It seems that this representation has little to recommend it, unless the size n of the dictionary is so small that even a linear algorithm is reasonably fast.

The list implementation of dictionaries is more promising when we consider the *expected* cost of operations rather than the *worst-case* cost, and contemplate strategies that reorganize the list to reduce the expected search time. If the *LookUp*s have uniform distribution across the keys in the dictionary, that is, if we are equally likely to do a *LookUp* on any one of the n keys of the dictionary, then the expected number of comparisons is $(\sum_{i=1}^{n} i)/n = (n + 1)/2$, so the expected time for a successful *LookUp* is $\Theta(n)$, like the worst-case time. In practice, however, the uniform distribution assumption is often violated dramatically; relatively few keys may account for most of the *LookUp*s. Consider, for example, the symbol table for a compiler, which is used to record information about the various identifiers that appear in a program being compiled. If the program is written in Pascal, there are probably many more occurrences of **begin** and **end** than of any of the variable names invented by the programmer.

To model this situation, let the keys in the dictionary be $K_1, \ldots, K_n$, in decreasing order of the frequency with which they are the subject of *LookUp*s. That is, we assume that when a *LookUp* occurs, its argument is K_1 with probability $p_1, \ldots$, and K_n with probability p_n, where $p_1 \geq p_2 \geq \cdots \geq p_n$ and $\sum_{i=1}^{n} p_i = 1$. (For the purposes of the present discussion, we ignore unsuccessful searches, which always take $\Theta(n)$ time.)

Under these circumstances, the expected search time is minimized if the list is in frequency order, that is, the keys are in the order $K_1, \ldots, K_n$. In this case the expected number of comparisons for a successful search is

$$C_{\text{OPT}} = \sum_{i=1}^{n} i p_i,$$

since K_i takes i comparisons to find. To prove formally that no other ordering of the keys can beat this one, suppose that the ordering with the minimum expected number of comparisons were $K_{m_1}, \ldots, K_{m_n}$, where $m_1, \ldots, m_n$ is a permutation of $1, \ldots, n$ and that $p_{m_i} < p_{m_j}$ for some $i < j$. Then reversing the positions of K_{m_i} and K_{m_j} in the list would reduce the expected number of comparisons by $ip_{m_i} + jp_{m_j} - ip_{m_j} - jp_{m_i} = (j - i)(p_{m_j} - p_{m_i}) > 0$. This is essentially the same argument as was used in establishing the correctness of the greedy algorithms on page 60.

If the probabilities of accessing the various keys are sufficiently different, C_{OPT} can be much less than the $(n+1)/2$ that we expect in the case of the uniform distribution. To see this, suppose that $p_i = 2^{-i}$ for $i < n$, and $p_n = 2^{-n+1}$. (For example, if $n = 4$, then the probabilities are $\frac{1}{2}$, $\frac{1}{4}$, $\frac{1}{8}$, and $\frac{1}{8}$.) Then the expected number of comparisons is $\sum_{i=1}^{n-1} i \cdot 2^{-i} + n2^{-n+1}$, which is less than 2, independent of n (compare this sum to the one on page 36).

Of course the actual probability distribution is unlikely to be known in advance, and the dictionary may grow or shrink as it is used. The frequency-ordered list is therefore useful mostly as a theoretical optimum against which other orderings can be compared. It is quite reasonable, however, to reorder the list as a result of searches that actually occur, in the hope of keeping higher-frequency items closer to the beginning. To this end we consider two **heuristics**—rules that result in behavior which may not be exactly predictable, but which there is reason to believe will be good in general. One intuitively appealing proposal is the

> **Move-to-Front Heuristic**: After each successful search, move the item that was sought to the front of the list.

If the list is represented in linked form, the Move-to-Front Heuristic is easy to implement since it requires only a small number of pointer operations once the search has been completed. Since high-frequency items are moved regularly to the front, we expect them rarely to be far from the front; low-frequency items will occasionally jump to the front, interfering for a while with searches for more common items, but then they will gradually drift far back in the list as they fail to be accessed for a long time.

It is not too hard to carry out a precise analysis of the expected number of comparisons in a list constantly reorganized by means of the Move-to-Front Heuristic. Let us assume that the process of looking up keys in the dictionary has continued for a long time, so that all keys have been looked up several times and the reorganization has reached a kind of steady state. (See Problem 11 for an assessment of the significance of this assumption.) Let $p(i, j)$ be the probability that K_i precedes K_j in the list; our first task is to find the value of $p(i, j)$ in terms of the values of $p_1, \ldots, p_n$. In order for K_i to be before K_j in the list, the last $LookUp(K_i, S)$ must have occurred more recently than the last $LookUp(K_j, S)$. If we consider the last $LookUp$ of a key that is either K_i or K_j and ignore all other $LookUps$, then $p(i, j)$ is the probability that of these two possibilities, that $LookUp$ is for K_i; therefore

$$p(i, j) = \frac{p_i}{p_i + p_j}.$$

The expected number of keys preceding K_j in the list is then $\sum_{i \neq j} p(i, j)$, so the number of comparisons needed to find K_j is one more than this number. Therefore the expected number of comparisons made in looking up a key is

$$C_{\text{MTF}} = \sum_{j=1}^{n} p_j \left(1 + \sum_{i \neq j} p(i, j) \right)$$

$$= \sum_{j=1}^{n} p_j + \sum_{j=1}^{n} p_j \sum_{i \neq j} p(i, j)$$

$$= 1 + \sum_{i \neq j} p_j p(i, j)$$

$$= 1 + \sum_{i \neq j} \frac{p_i p_j}{p_i + p_j}$$

$$= 1 + 2 \sum_{i < j} \frac{p_i p_j}{p_i + p_j}.$$

How does C_{MTF} compare with C_{OPT}? Let

$$\sigma = \sum_{i < j} \frac{p_i p_j}{p_i + p_j}$$

$$= \sum_{j=1}^{n} p_j \sum_{1 \leq i < j} \frac{p_i}{p_i + p_j}$$

$$\leq \sum_{j=1}^{n} p_j (j - 1) \qquad \text{since } \frac{p_i}{p_i + p_j} \leq 1 \text{ for each } i \text{ and } j$$

$$= C_{\text{OPT}} - 1 \qquad \text{since } \sum_{j=1}^{n} p_j = 1.$$

Therefore

$$\frac{C_{\text{MTF}}}{C_{\text{OPT}}} \leq \frac{1 + 2\sigma}{1 + \sigma} = 2 - \frac{1}{1 + \sigma} < 2.$$

That is, the expected number of comparisons when the Move-to-Front Heuristic is in use is no more than twice the optimum. If the list is stored in linked form (so that moving an element to the front is cheap) and there is a reasonable expectation that the probabilities for the various keys differ significantly from each other, this rule can be recommended for its performance and low overhead. Moreover, it reaches a "steady state" fairly quickly, and adapts fairly quickly if the probabilities change over time.

An alternative to the Move-to-Front Heuristic is the

Transpose Heuristic: If the item sought is not the first in the list, move it one position forward by exchanging it with the item just before it.

The expected performance of the Transpose Heuristic, once a steady state has been reached, is even better than that of the Move-to-Front Heuristic. We do not demonstrate the good performance of the Transpose Heuristic formally, but the reason is clear intuitively: once a list is in roughly the correct order, an occasional reference to a low-probability item does not derange the list very much if the Transpose Heuristic is used; but under the Move-to-Front Heuristic a low-probability item is moved all the way to the front of the list when it is accessed and it then gets in the way of searches for high-frequency items until it eventually settles back into its proper position towards the end of the list. Although the Transpose Heuristic has good performance in the long run, it tends to stabilize on a steady state more slowly than the Move-to-Front Heuristic since it reorders the list less drastically at each step, and is therefore less suitable in an environment where the probabilities change rapidly over time. For example, if an element that has had low frequency for a long time, and has therefore settled near the end of the list, suddenly becomes more frequently accessed, it will move only gradually towards the front of the list, one position at a time, and time required for it to reach the front of the list is bounded by the number of items in the list. Under the Move-to-Front Heuristic an item can leap to the front of the list in a single bound, no matter how long the list may be.

In Chapter 7 we shall encounter a tree version of the Move-to-Front Heuristic, called "splaying," which leads to efficient implementation of the dictionary operations.

6.3 ORDERED LISTS

If the key space has a linear order that can be tested easily and dictionary items are kept in a list ordered by key value, then strategies can be applied to reduce search times. At a bare minimum, the naïve sequential search algorithm can be "smartened" to recognize an unsuccessful outcome when a value greater than the key sought is encountered in the list. Provided that the ordering of the key space is unrelated to the frequency with which keys are sought, this strategy reduces the expected number of comparisons in an unsuccessful search by 50%, to $n/2$, but it has no effect on the time for successful searches.

Binary Search
A more effective approach is to use a tabular representation for the list and binary search. We assume that the records in the table are ordered by their Key field. The binary search algorithm has been seen several times before; we repeat it here in its nonrecursive form as an implementation of the *LookUp*

---

function *BinarySearchLookUp*(**key** K, **table** $T[0 .. n - 1]$): **info**
{Return information stored with key K in T, or Λ if K is not in T}
    Left $\leftarrow 0$
    Right $\leftarrow n - 1$
    repeat forever
        if *Right* < *Left* **then**
            return Λ (1)
        else
            Middle $\leftarrow \lfloor (Left + Right)/2 \rfloor$ (2)
            if $K = $ Key($T[Middle]$) **then return** Info($T[Middle]$)
            else if $K < $ Key($T[Middle]$) **then** *Right* $\leftarrow$ *Middle* $- 1$
            else *Left* $\leftarrow$ *Middle* $+ 1$

Algorithm 6.1 Binary search of an ordered table.

---

operation (Algorithm 6.1). The algorithm returns the Info field of a table entry with key K; if there is no such table entry, it returns Λ. Of course the loop does not repeat forever; it eventually ends with execution of one of the two **return** statements.

Figure 6.1 shows as a binary tree the sequence of values of *Left*, *Middle*, and *Right* during all possible executions of the algorithm in case $n = 10$. The round nodes show these three values as the algorithm finishes executing line (2); therefore *Middle* is always $\lfloor (Left + Right)/2 \rfloor$ in these triples. The rectangular nodes show the values of *Left* and *Right* when the algorithm ends unsuccessfully at line (1); the value of *Middle* is omitted. Each path in the tree, starting at the root, represents a possible execution. If the algorithm successfully finds K as Key($T[i]$), then the round node whose middle number is i represents its termination point, and if the algorithm ends unsuccessfully because K is between Key($T[i]$) and Key($T[i + 1]$), then the square node labelled "$i + 1, , i$" represents its termination point. (The "$0, , -1$" and "$10, , 9$" nodes represent cases in which K is smaller than Key($T[0]$) and larger than Key($T[9]$), respectively.)

The tree of Figure 6.1 is a full binary tree constructed from the binary tree consisting of just the round nodes by attaching a square child wherever a round node has no child. Call a tree of this type an **extended binary tree**, and refer to the round nodes as **internal nodes** and to the square nodes as **external nodes**. In any extended binary tree there is one more external node than internal, for the same reason that in any full binary tree there is one more leaf than there are nonleaves (page 101).

We can use the extended binary tree to analyze exactly the performance of binary search. Let us count one **comparison** for each distinct item $T[i]$ with whose key K is compared; this provides an accurate measure of the running

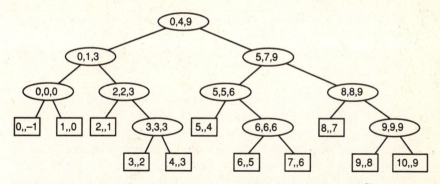

Figure 6.1 Tree of possible executions of binary search algorithm on a table of size 10. Each node shows the values of *Left*, *Middle*, and *Right*.

time of the algorithm.* If the algorithm terminates successfully, the number of comparisons it has made is one more than the depth of the internal node corresponding to its termination point; if it terminates unsuccessfully, the number of comparisons is equal to the depth of the corresponding external node.

If the number n of internal nodes is $2^k - 1$ for some k, then the internal nodes form a perfect binary tree of height $k - 1$; this can be proved by induction. It follows that the maximum depth of an internal node is $\lfloor \lg n \rfloor$, and the maximum depth of an external node is $\lfloor \lg n \rfloor + 1$; there are also external nodes at depth $\lfloor \lg n \rfloor$ unless n is one less than a power of two. Consequently,

> ■ **THEOREM** *(Binary Search)* The binary search algorithm uses between 1 and $\lfloor \lg n \rfloor + 1$ comparisons in a successful search of a table of size n, and either $\lfloor \lg n \rfloor$ or $\lfloor \lg n \rfloor + 1$ comparisons in an unsuccessful search ($\lfloor \lg n \rfloor + 1$ exactly, if n is one less than a power of two). □

What about the expected number of comparisons used by the binary search algorithm? In an unsuccessful search, the expected number must be more than $\lfloor \lg n \rfloor$ but at most $\lfloor \lg n \rfloor + 1$, so it is pinned down about as well as we could hope; but in the case of a successful search, it is not obvious where in the range from 1 to $\lfloor \lg n \rfloor + 1$ the expected number lies. Are there enough opportunities for the algorithm to terminate quickly (that is, at a node close to the root) to make the expected number of comparisons significantly less than $\lfloor \lg n \rfloor + 1$? Intuition suggests not, since the number of internal nodes at depth d drops off so rapidly as d decreases from $\lfloor \lg n \rfloor$ to 0. This intuition is correct.

---

*Thus in Algorithm 6.1 we do not count the *Right* < *Left* comparison, and we count only a single comparison in the lines following (2) even if both the equality and inequality comparisons are executed. Counting more than one comparison per execution of the **repeat** loop would change the total number of comparisons by a constant factor of three at most.

■ **THEOREM** *(Expected Binary Search)* In a successful binary search of a table of size n, the expected number of comparisons is between $\lfloor \lg n \rfloor - 1$ and $\lfloor \lg n \rfloor + 1$, provided that searches have uniform distribution across the n keys.

PROOF If T is an extended binary tree with n nodes having depths $d_1, \ldots, d_n$, then define the **internal path length** of T to be the sum of the depths of all its internal nodes, that is, $I = \sum_{i=1}^{n} d_i$. Similarly, define the **external path length** E to be the sum of the depths of all the external nodes. Then in any extended binary tree with n internal nodes, $E = I + 2n$. (This is easily proved by induction; see Problem 15.) Now let C_{EXP} denote the expected number of comparisons in a successful search of a table of size n, with all elements equally likely to be sought. Since the number of comparisons used in a successful search is 1 more than the depth of the corresponding internal node,

$$C_{\text{EXP}} = \frac{1}{n} \sum_{i=1}^{n} (d_i + 1) = \frac{I}{n} + 1 = \frac{E - 2n}{n} + 1 = \frac{E}{n} - 1.$$

Since each of the $n + 1$ external nodes has depth greater than or equal to $\lfloor \lg n \rfloor$, $E \geq (n + 1)\lfloor \lg n \rfloor$, and therefore

$$C_{\text{EXP}} \geq \frac{n + 1}{n} \lfloor \lg n \rfloor - 1 > \lfloor \lg n \rfloor - 1.$$

No successful search can take more comparisons than the costliest unsuccessful search; and since an unsuccessful search uses $\lfloor \lg n \rfloor + 1$ comparisons at most,

$$\lfloor \lg n \rfloor - 1 < C_{\text{EXP}} \leq \lfloor \lg n \rfloor + 1. \quad \square$$

The performance of binary search is therefore extremely stable; its expected running times and its worst-case running times, for both successful and unsuccessful searches, are all very close to each other.

Interpolation Search

When I look up a number in a telephone book, I use a strategy that resembles binary search but differs from it in an important respect. The first page I look on is not always the same, and not always in the middle of the book; if I am looking up "Boone," I look first close to the beginning of the book, and if am looking up "Wilson," I look near the end of the book. I use my knowledge of the rough percentage of names preceding a given one to estimate a position in the book where I expect the given one might appear. If I am wrong, I use the names on the page I do turn to in order to revise my estimate.

This strategy is the basis for the **interpolation search** algorithm. Note that it requires a somewhat different model for the possible operations than we have

function *InterpolationSearchLookUp*(**key** K, **table** $T[0..n-1]$): **info**
{Return information stored with K in ordered table T, or Λ if K is not present}
{Table positions $T[-1]$ and $T[n]$ are assumed to be available to the algorithm}
    $\mathsf{Key}(T[-1]) \leftarrow -1$
    $\mathsf{Key}(T[n]) \leftarrow N$
    Left $\leftarrow 0$
    Right $\leftarrow n-1$
    repeat forever
        if *Right* $<$ *Left* **then return** Λ
        else
$$p \leftarrow \frac{K - \mathsf{Key}(T[\textit{Left}-1])}{\mathsf{Key}(T[\textit{Right}+1]) - \mathsf{Key}(T[\textit{Left}-1])}$$
        Middle $\leftarrow \lfloor p \cdot (\textit{Right} - \textit{Left} + 1) \rfloor + \textit{Left}$
        if $K = \mathsf{Key}(T[\textit{Middle}])$ **then return** $\mathsf{Info}(T[\textit{Middle}])$
        else if $K < \mathsf{Key}(T[\textit{Middle}])$ **then** *Right* $\leftarrow$ *Middle* -1
        else *Left* $\leftarrow$ *Middle* $+1$

Algorithm 6.2 Interpolation search.

been using heretofore; we must not only be able to tell whether one key value precedes or follows another, we must have a measure of *how far apart* they are. The simplest situation in which interpolation search can be applied is when the keys are integers in the range from 0 to some large number $N-1$. We assume that we are to search a table $T[0..n-1]$, where $0 \leq \mathsf{Key}(T[0]) < \mathsf{Key}(T[1]) < \cdots < \mathsf{Key}(T[n-1]) \leq N-1$; moreover the probability distribution of the N possible keys is uniform. It simplifies the description of the algorithm if we assume that the table positions just before the first and just after the last can be used to store key values that are out of range. Algorithm 6.2 presents the Interpolation Search technique.

    The search is confined to the portion of the table between indices *Left* and *Right* inclusive; on each iteration of the main loop the key values residing just beyond these boundaries are used to calculate the next position to be probed. More precisely, at the beginning of each iteration of the **repeat** loop, no key in the range of indices from *Left* to *Right* inclusive has been examined, but the keys at positions *Left* -1 and *Right* $+1$ have been seen already. The variable p is a number, strictly greater than 0 and strictly less than 1, describing the fraction of the distance from position *Left* to position *Right* $+1$ where the next probe into the table should occur; this is calculated as the ratio of the difference between the key value sought and the value just beyond the left end of the interval, to the difference in key values just beyond the two ends of the interval. When this fraction is converted to an index *Middle*, the result is rounded down to make it an integer in the range from *Left* to *Right* inclusive. If the key is not found at this position, one of the two ends of the interval is adjusted, just as in the binary search algorithm, before the next iteration takes place.

For example, suppose that $n = 10$, $N = 1000$, and the table $T[-1 .. 10]$ contains

-1	0	1	2	3	4	5	6	7	8	9	10
-1	11	72	93	260	316	431	788	798	903	910	1000

Here the real data are in $T[0 .. 9]$; $T[-1]$ and $T[10]$ have been filled as they would be in the first two steps of the algorithm. Let us trace the steps to find 316 in this table. Initially $Left = 0$ and $Right = 9$, so the first calculation of p is

$$p \leftarrow \frac{316 - (-1)}{1000 - (-1)} = 0.31668,$$

whence $Middle \leftarrow \lfloor 0.31668(9 - 0 + 1) \rfloor + 0 = 3$. $T[3] = 260$, which is too small, so $Left \leftarrow 4$. On the next iteration

$$p \leftarrow \frac{316 - 260}{1000 - 260} = 0.07568,$$

which yields $Middle \leftarrow \lfloor 0.07568(9 - 4 + 1) \rfloor + 4 = 4$, and indeed $T[4]$ is the desired element.

The performance characteristics of this algorithm are quite interesting. The *worst-case* performance is much worse than for binary search; in fact, one can concoct sequences of n keys that will force this algorithm to iterate n times before finding the key or concluding failure. However, these sequences are so "skewed" that they are extremely unlikely to arise if the distribution of key choices is truly uniform (Problem 21). On the other hand, the *expected-case* performance of this algorithm is astonishingly good: *The expected number of iterations of the loop of the Interpolation Search algorithm is just* $\lg \lg n$ *plus a constant less than* 1. This means, for example, that the expected number of comparisons to pinpoint an element of a table of size 2^{32}—more than four billion—is less than 6. The very small number of loop iterations for tables of feasible size is counterbalanced by the greater complexity of the calculations that happen within the loop; Algorithm 6.2 uses real arithmetic, while Algorithm 6.1 can be implemented, on many computers, with only addition of small integer indices and "shift" operations to divide the sum by 2. Nonetheless the algorithm can sensibly be applied when the cost of testing an element of the table is relatively large. For example, if the table is stored externally, examining each element might mean reading a new disk block, so it might be worth calculating extensively with known data in order to reduce the number of requests for new data.

The analysis that establishes the $O(\lg \lg n)$ expected performance of this algorithm requires a bit of probability theory and statistics (see the references on page 217).

We mentioned that this algorithm relies on a uniform probability distribution for its fast operation. If the distribution is known but not uniform, it is (in theory) easy to fix the interpolation formula to be appropriate. For any key value K, let $F(K)$ be the probability that a *LookUp* is for a key value $\leq K$. Then change the interpolation formula in the algorithm so that it uses, instead of key values, F of those values (Problem 23). Finding a suitable formulation for F may well, however, be problematical.

Skip Lists

It is, of course, impossible to do binary search, much less interpolation search, on a linked list. There is simply no way to calculate, from the addresses of two records, the address of a record with an intermediate key value, since the records can be scattered in memory arbitrarily. Suppose, however, that an ordered list were structured so that the second, fourth, sixth, ... records were linked together by a separate pointer field, and the fourth, eighth, ... were linked together by a third pointer field, and so on (Figure 6.2(a)). About $\lg n$ pointers per element would be needed to fully link a list with n records, but most records would not need that many pointers; half the records would need just a single pointer field, and of the remainder, half would need only one extra pointer, and so on. Let us call the original pointers the **level**-0 pointers, and in general call the pointers that skip forward 2^i records the **level**-i pointers. A header node would have an unused key field but would have the initial pointers of all levels. With this representation the high-level pointers could be used during a search to skip rapidly through large segments of the list; only when a high-level pointer led to a record with a key greater than the search key would a lower-level pointer be followed instead. The search algorithm would be roughly:

> Starting with the pointers of the highest level, follow pointers until a record with key greater than or equal to the search key is encountered. If the key encountered is equal to the search key, stop—the search has succeeded; if it is greater than the search key, back up one pointer and continue following the pointers of the next lower level. If a level-0 pointer leads to a key greater than the search key, stop—the search has failed.

"Backing up" does not require truly reversing direction, but simply keeping track of the source of the last pointer followed. For this algorithm to be completely correct, the Λ record should have a key value exceeding any possible real key.

If the list were perfectly organized as shown in Figure 6.2(a), any record could be found (or discovered not to be present) in $O(\log n)$ steps, since there are only $\lg n$ levels and we could follow only two pointers per level before dropping down to a lower level. In fact the access pattern would be much the same as for binary search.

While lists with the structure of Figure 6.2(a) would have good performance characteristics for searching, they would be utterly impractical if the data might

Level

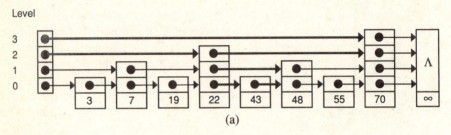

(a)

Level

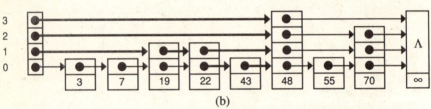

(b)

Figure 6.2 (a) A "perfect" skip list of 8 records. (The specific arrangement of fields and pointers within records was chosen for visual clarity, not physical accuracy; the key field would most naturally be the first field in a record, and all pointers would point to the beginnings of records, not to the corresponding pointer fields of those records.) The heavier pointers indicate those that are followed during a search for key value 46. Starting from the header, first follow the level 3 pointer; it leads to a record with key 70, so we have gone too far. Drop down to the level 2 pointer; it leads to 22, so we have not gone far enough. Following the level 2 pointer out of that record again leads to 70, so drop down to the level 1 pointer. It leads to 48, so we have gone too far. The level 0 pointer leads to 43, and its level 0 pointer leads to 48, so 46 is missing. (b) A "random" skip list. Records with various numbers of pointers exist in roughly the same proportions as in (a), but their succession is not predictable. Once again, however, the search can proceed by using the pointers in order of decreasing level, dropping down a level whenever a pointer leads to a record whose key is greater than that of the search key. The heavier pointers again show those followed during an unsuccessful search for the key value 46.

change, since inserting even a single item could force the data structure to be completely reorganized. Let us call a record with $i+1$ pointers, having levels 0, 1, ..., i, a **level-i** node in the structure. Then inserting a record at the front of the list—for example, inserting a record with key value 2 in Figure 6.2(a)—would cause every node already in the list to change levels.

However, the *expected* performance of the structure will be roughly the same if, instead of the perfect alternation of levels shown in Figure 6.2(a), the same general pattern were followed, with the nodes of various levels present in roughly the same proportions, but scattered randomly through the list (Figure 6.2(b)). Nodes of higher level are relatively infrequent, and therefore the pointer chains of higher levels enable a search to skip rapidly down the list. (We shall analyze the performance more precisely below.) Now if we do not need to maintain perfect structure, but need only ensure that nodes of the various levels exist in the right proportions and are likely to be scattered uniformly through the list, the insertion problem becomes much simpler. To insert a node, find its proper position in the list, and *generate its level randomly*, subject to the condition that for any i the level should be twice as likely to be i as to be $i+1$ or greater. Most programming environments have random-number generators that make this an easy calculation.

It is possible that through bad luck a long sequence of insertions might occur at level 0, in which case the structure would not resemble Figure 6.2 but would simply be an ordinary linked list with its poor search characteristics. But this circumstance is highly improbable; for example, the likelihood that a sequence of 20 insertions would all be at level 0 is only $(1/2)^{20}$, or less than one in a million. Moreover these odds do not depend on the key values in any way; there are no "bad" sequences of key values for this algorithm, only "bad" sequences of outputs from the random-number generator. If the same keys were inserted into a new structure using a new sequence of outputs from the random-number generator, the odds that all 40 insertions would be at level 0 would be only $(1/2)^{40}$.

To give the details of the algorithms for these **skip lists**, we need to fix a maximum level for the nodes, since there would be no use in having levels so high that the entire list would be skipped at once. The maximum useful level is about $\lg n - 1$, since only one node is expected to have a level greater than this (see Problem 31). For convenience we set $MaxLevel = \lfloor \lg N \rfloor - 1$, where N is the largest anticipated size of the data structure. For example, if $N = 16384$, then $MaxLevel$ is 13, corresponding to a structure in which the nodes have fourteen possible levels.

The skip list itself is a record structure of two fields: Header, which is dummy node to begin the lists, and Level, which is an integer giving the largest level of any node currently in the list. A node has, in addition to its Key and Info fields, a table Forward of pointers; the size of this table depends on the level of the node, but that number does not need to be stored in the node. Initially the Level of an empty skip list is 0 and all the pointers point to a Λ record whose key value exceeds any possible real key. The search algorithm is then as shown in Algorithm 6.3.

To insert in a skip list we need first of all a routine to generate appropriate random level numbers. If we assume that a function *Random*( ) is available that returns a random number x in the range $0 \le x < 1$, then *RandomLevel*( ) does the trick (Algorithm 6.4).

To insert a record with a new key in a skip list, begin by using the search algorithm to find its proper location (Algorithm 6.5). During the search process, a table *Update*[0 . . *MaxLevel*] is maintained; *Update*[i] will contain a pointer

---

function *SkipListLookUp*(**key** K, **pointer** L): **info**
{Return information stored with key K in skip list L, or Λ if K is missing}
    $P \leftarrow$ Header(L)
    for i **from** Level(L) **downto** 0 **do**
        while Key(Forward(P)[i]) $< K$ **do** $P \leftarrow$ Forward(P)[i]
    $P \leftarrow$ Forward(P)[0]
    if Key(P) $= K$ **then return** Info(P)
    else return Λ

Algorithm 6.3 Search in a skip list.

---

function *RandomLevel*( ): **integer**
{Produce a random level between 0 and *MaxLevel*}
    $v \leftarrow 0$
    while *Random*( ) $< \frac{1}{2}$ **and** $v < MaxLevel$ **do** $v \leftarrow v + 1$
    return v

Algorithm 6.4 Generate a random level in the range $0, \ldots, MaxLevel$ with exponentially declining probabilities, by repeated calls on a routine that generates reals in the range $0 \leq x < 1$.

---

to the rightmost node of level i or higher that is to the left of the position of the insertion. When that position has been located, a node of a randomly generated level *NewLevel* is created and is spliced into all the lists of levels up to *NewLevel*. The function *NewCell*(Node, i) returns a skip list cell of level i.

Deletion from a skip list is quite similar to insertion (Problem 28(c)).

We are now ready to demonstrate good performance of skip lists in the expected case.

■ **THEOREM** *(Skip List)* When skip lists are used, the dictionary operations of *LookUp*, *Insert*, and *Delete* all take expected time $O(\log n)$, where n is the size of the dictionary, and *MakeEmptySet* and *IsEmptySet* take constant time.

    PROOF The only hard part is to establish that searching for a node in a skip list is expected to take logarithmic time; the logarithmic cost of *LookUp*, *Insert*, and *Delete* all follow from this, and it is easy to see that *MakeEmptySet* and *IsEmptySet* take constant time (Problem 28). A search starts at the pointer of level Level(L) in the header node and proceeds by steps of two kinds: following pointers within a level, and dropping down within a node from a level to the next lower level. When we follow a

---

procedure *SkipListInsert*(**key** K, **info** I, **pointer** L): **pointer**
{Insert information I with key K in skip list L}
{If a new node is inserted, *Update*[i] will point to
    the existing node that will precede the new node in the level i list}
    $P \leftarrow$ Header(L)
    for i **from** Level(L) **downto** 0 **do**
        while Key(Forward(P)[i]) < K **do** $P \leftarrow$ Forward(P)[i]
        Update[i] $\leftarrow P$
    $P \leftarrow$ Forward(P)[0]
    if Key(P) = K **then** Info(P) $\leftarrow I$
    else
        NewLevel $\leftarrow$ *RandomLevel*( )
        if *NewLevel* > Level(L) **then**   {A new maximum level for this list}
            for i **from** Level(L) + 1 **to** *NewLevel* **do**
                Update[i] $\leftarrow$ Header(L)   {Link node directly to header}
            Level(L) $\leftarrow$ *NewLevel*
        $P \leftarrow$ *NewCell*(Node, *NewLevel*)   {Create node of level *NewLevel*}
        Key(P) $\leftarrow K$; Info(P) $\leftarrow I$
        for i **from** 0 **to** *NewLevel* **do**   {Splice it into *NewLevel* + 1 lists}
            Forward(P)[i] $\leftarrow$ Forward(*Update*[i])[i]
            Forward(*Update*[i])[i] $\leftarrow P$

Algorithm 6.5 Insertion of a new key in a skip list. If the key is already present, replace the associated information; otherwise create and insert a new record.

---

pointer, its level is always equal to the level of the node to which it points. We shall calculate the expected length of such a search path, counting either pointer-following or level-dropping as a step of cost 1.

To calculate the expected length of a path to reach a node of level 0 in the list, we trace the path backwards. More generally, we ask: Suppose we are tracing a path backwards from a pointer of level i in a node P; how long should we expect the path to continue before it rises k levels? If we focus just on node P at the end of the path, there are two possibilities; either

1. P is a node of level i and the path proceeds backwards one pointer to a node of level at least i, from which it still must rise k levels, or else
2. the path rises a level in node P and must yet rise $k - 1$ more levels as it proceeds backwards from P.

Each of these cases has probability $\frac{1}{2}$. Therefore, if we let $C(k)$ be the expected length of a path that rises k levels on its backward trajectory, we get the recurrence

$$C(k) = \frac{1}{2} \cdot ((\text{cost of going back one pointer at level } i) + C(k))$$
$$+ \frac{1}{2} \cdot ((\text{cost of going up from level } i \text{ to } i+1) + C(k-1))$$
$$= \frac{1}{2}(1 + C(k)) + \frac{1}{2}(1 + C(k-1))$$

and therefore

$$C(k) = 2 + C(k-1),$$

which leads to the solution $C(k) = 2k$ since $C(0)$, the path length needed to rise 0 levels, is 0. This analysis is actually a bit pessimistic, since it assumes that the path does not reach the header node in the course of rising k levels; once the header node is encountered the path can only rise, not proceed leftward.

Now we apply this analysis to determine the length of a path from a node of level 0 all the way back to the pointer of level $\text{Level}(L)$ in the header node. To get from a node of level 0 back to a node of level $\lg n - 1$ is expected to take $2(\lg n - 1)$ steps. If this path does not end at the header node, we need to follow a path through pointers of levels $\lg n - 1$ and higher back to the header node, but the expected number of leftward steps in this path is no more than the expected number of nodes of level $\lg n - 1$ or higher in the entire list. Since the probability that a node has level i or higher is $1/2^i$ (Problem 31), among the n nodes the expected number of level $\lg n - 1$ or higher is

$$n \cdot \left(\frac{1}{2}\right)^{\lg n - 1} = n \cdot \frac{1}{n} \cdot 2 = 2.$$

If $\text{Level}(L) > \lg n - 1$ the path must also rise $\text{Level}(L) - (\lg n - 1)$ steps, but the expected value of $\text{Level}(L)$ is at most $\lg n + 1$ (Problem 30), so the expected rise beyond level $\lg n - 1$ is at most 2. Therefore the expected total path length is

$$2(\lg n - 1) + 2 + 2 = 2 \lg n + 2 \in O(\log n),$$

and so the dictionary operations *LookUp*, *Insert*, and *Delete*, which take time linear in the length of the path traversed, have running time $O(\log n)$ in the expected case. □

On the other hand, there is no guarantee about the worst-case performance of the skip list algorithms, except that it is not much worse than the worst case for the corresponding linked list algorithms. But the worst case is exceedingly unlikely, and more importantly is out of the control of the agent supplying the data. The worst case depends only on the performance of the random-number generator within the skip list algorithms themselves; the algorithms would be immune even to attack by a malicious adversary who knew the program code and supplied specially chosen sequences of insertion and deletion requests in an attempt to force the worst-case behavior to occur.

Though skip lists are a relatively recent invention, experimental evidence suggests that they are competitive in performance with the more sophisticated balanced-tree dictionary structures discussed in Chapter 7, and are much easier to program. One useful generalization: there is no need to organize the lists so that nodes of each level are half as frequent as those of higher levels. The ratio can be any other fixed number, and because of the overhead of pointer manipulations it probably makes sense to use a somewhat lower ratio, such as one-fourth, that will make the pointers somewhat sparser. Problem 33 explores the impact of choosing a different ratio on the details of the proof of the Skip List Theorem, which remains true as stated.

6.4 BINARY SEARCH TREES

As described on page 108, a **binary search tree** is a binary tree having a value associated with each node, such that the values have a linear order, and at each node the value is greater than any value in the left subtree and less than any value in the right subtree. Binary search trees are a natural structure for implementing dictionaries, since a *LookUp* is done by following a single path starting at the root, thus avoiding all nodes not on that path.

Let us assume that the tree nodes have Key and Info fields for storing the key value and any associated information, as well as the customary LC and RC fields for the child pointers. Then Algorithm 6.6 presents the implementation of the *LookUp* operation; the algorithm simply echoes the recursive definition of the binary search tree property, following the LC or RC pointer at each node, depending on the relative order of the key sought and the value stored at the node.

Algorithm 6.6 is tail-recursive; it is a simple matter to make it iterative by changing the first **if** statement to a **while** and replacing the recursive calls by assignments to P (Algorithm 6.7).

The maximum height binary tree with n nodes has height $n-1$; this happens, for example, if all the LC pointers are Λ, so that the tree is really a linked list with an extra field in each record. The minimum height binary tree with n nodes has height $\lfloor \lg n \rfloor$; the tree corresponding to binary search of a table of size n is one such minimum height binary tree (see Figure 6.1 on page 183). Hence the worst-case search time, over all possible binary search trees with n nodes, is $\Theta(n)$; but in the best n-node binary search tree, the worst-case search time is $\Theta(\log n)$.

It is possible to regard binary search in an ordered table (Algorithm 6.1 on page 182) as search of a special kind of binary tree (Figure 6.1), whose structure is represented implicitly by arithmetic relations among the indices,

function *BinaryTreeLookUp*(**key** K, **pointer** P): **info**
{Find key K in tree P, by recursive search, and return its Info}
{Return Λ if there is no such record}
    if $P = \Lambda$ **then**
        return Λ
    else if $K = $ Key(P) **then**
        return Info(P)
    else if $K < $ Key(P) **then**
        return *BinaryTreeLookUp*$(K, LC(P))$
    else   {Now we know that $K > $ Key(P)}
        return *BinaryTreeLookUp*$(K, RC(P))$

Algorithm 6.6 Recursive implementation of *LookUp* for binary tree dictionary.

function *BinaryTreeLookUp*(**key** K, **pointer** P): **info**
{Find key K in tree P, by iterative search, and return its Info}
{Return Λ if there is no such record}
    while $P \neq \Lambda$ **do**
        if $K = $ Key(P) **then**
            return Info(P)
        else if $K < $ Key(P) **then**
            $P \leftarrow $ LC(P)
        else   {Now we know that $K > $ Key(P)}
            $P \leftarrow $ RC(P)
    return Λ

Algorithm 6.7 Iterative implementation of *LookUp* for binary tree dictionary.

rather than explicitly by pointers. In this view each subtree consists of the elements in a subtable $T[Left \,.\, . \, Right]$; its root is the element $T[Middle]$, where $Middle = \lfloor (Left + Right)/2 \rfloor$, and the left and right subtrees are those consisting of $T[Left \,.\,.\, Middle - 1]$ and $T[Middle + 1 \,.\,.\, Right]$.

Insertion
Up to this point explicitly represented binary search trees offer no advantages over ordered tables and binary search; but we have not considered the cost of insertions. Insertion in a table is expensive, since a "hole" has to be made to hold the new item; this costs $\Theta(n)$. In a binary search tree, however, insertion costs $\Theta(1)$ if we are willing always to insert at the leaves, and if the time to find the insertion point is not counted as part of the cost of the insertion. Let us scrutinize these provisos a bit more carefully.

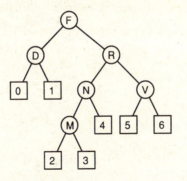

Figure 6.3 A binary search tree, with external nodes added to represent the ranges of keys on which a search may fail.

Figure 6.3 shows a binary search tree which has been augmented with external nodes; we might call this an **extended binary search tree**, by analogy with the extended binary trees introduced in the discussion of binary search (Figure 6.1 on page 183). The external nodes in essence represent ranges of keys between the keys stored in the tree, or less than the smallest key or greater than the largest. External node 2, for example, represents all keys greater than F and less than M. Note that the external nodes are not actually new nodes added to the data structure; instead, they are illustrations of the various occurrences of Λ as LC and RC pointers in the binary tree.

Suppose that we search the tree for H; the search fails, and we wish to insert H in the tree. The simplest insertion strategy is to add a new node in place of the external node that is reached when the search fails; for example, a node with key H would be added to this tree in place of external node 2. The modified tree has one new internal node, for H, which replaces a prior external node; this new internal node has two new external children. Adding nodes as leaves has the advantages of minimal work, since only one pointer needs adjustment, and convenience, since the search routine leads us directly to the insertion point. Algorithm 6.8 is a modification of Algorithm 6.7 with insertion code added. This routine should be called with an argument which is a locative that points to the root of the tree; this makes it possible for the routine to change the pointer field where the Λ is eventually discovered if the search is unsuccessful, even if the tree is initially empty so that the ordinary value of P is Λ initially.

However, a leaf may not be the best place to add a node. For example, if the data are sorted before insertion, Algorithm 6.8 will produce a tree that is nothing more than a linked list, with one child pointer of each node empty. More generally, data that are approximately in order, either increasing or decreasing, will produce trees that are "skinny" rather than "bushy," and will in general take longer to search. We shall study in detail in the next chapter several strategies for controlling the height of trees when doing insertions.

What is the *expected* time for a successful search in a binary search tree?

---

procedure *BinaryTreeInsert*(**key** K, **info** I, **locative** P):
{Initially P is a locative that points to the root of the tree}
   while $P \neq \Lambda$ **do**
      if Key(P) = K **then**
         Info(P) ← I
         return
      else if $K <$ Key(P) **then**
         $P \leftarrow$ LC(P)
      else   {Now we know that $K >$ Key(P)}
         $P \leftarrow$ RC(P)
   {Create new node and add it as a leaf}
   $Q \leftarrow$ *NewCell*(Node)
   Key(Q) ← K; Info(Q) ← I
   LC(Q) ← RC(Q) ← Λ
   $P \Leftarrow Q$

Algorithm 6.8 Insertion at leaves of binary search tree.

If the leaves all have the same depth, or the depths of the leaves differ by at most 1, then the tree has a shape similar to that of Figure 6.1 on page 183, and by the Expected Binary Search Theorem the expected number of comparisons is between $\lfloor \lg n \rfloor - 1$ and $\lfloor \lg n \rfloor + 1$. On the other hand, a tree that is essentially a linear list has a much larger expected number of comparisons—$(n+1)/2$. (As in the analysis of binary search, we count only a single comparison per iteration of the **while** loop of Algorithm 6.8.) If trees are constructed by "random" insertions at the leaves, is the expected search time logarithmic, or linear, or perhaps something in between? In other words, if a tree is constructed by random insertions, are we more likely to wind up with a reasonably well-balanced tree of logarithmic height, or a stringy tree of linear height?

It turns out that the expected number of comparisons in a successful search of a randomly constructed tree is only 39% more than the theoretical minimum; well-balanced trees predominate. This is a gratifyingly low figure, and implies that a procedure like Algorithm 6.8 may reasonably be used in applications such as compiler symbol tables where the order of insertions can be expected to be random.

As with all expected-case analyses, it is important to pin down the assumptions about the probability distribution of events. A fair definition of "random insertion" in this context is the following assumption: *Suppose that m keys $K_1 < K_2 < \cdots < K_m$ have already been inserted in the tree, in some unspecified sequence. Then the next key inserted, say K, is equally likely to belong in any of the $m + 1$ possible positions: $K < K_1$, or $K_1 < K < K_2$, ...,*

$K_{m-1} < K < K_m$, or $K_m < K$. Another way of stating the same assumption is that when a tree of size n is constructed, each of the $n!$ permutations of the key values is equally likely to be the order in which the keys are inserted (Problem 35).

■ **THEOREM** *(Expected Binary Search Tree)* Let S_n be the expected number of comparisons in a successful search of a randomly constructed n-node binary tree, and let U_n be the expected number of comparisons in an unsuccessful search. Then

$$S_n = 2\left(1 + \frac{1}{n}\right) H_n - 3 \approx 2 \ln n \approx 1.386 \lg n, \quad \text{and}$$

$$U_n = 2H_{n+1} - 2 \approx 1.386 \lg(n+1),$$

where H_n is the nth harmonic number.

PROOF The crux of the proof is to recognize that *it takes one more comparison to find a key in a successful search than it took to insert the key in the unsuccessful search that preceded its insertion.* Therefore $U_{i-1} + 1$ is the expected time to find the key that was inserted i^{th}. Now when an n-node tree is searched, the key sought is equally likely to be the one that was inserted first, second, ..., or n^{th}, so

$$S_n = \frac{(U_0 + 1) + (U_1 + 1) + \cdots + (U_{n-1} + 1)}{n} = 1 + \frac{1}{n}\sum_{i=0}^{n-1} U_i.$$

But we have another relation between S_n and U_n on the basis of internal and external path length. The expected number of comparisons in a successful search is 1 more than the average internal path length, and the expected number of comparisons in an unsuccessful search is the average external path length. Letting I_n and E_n denote the expected internal and external path length, respectively, we have $S_n = 1 + (I_n/n)$ and $U_n = E_n/(n+1)$ (since there are n internal nodes but $n + 1$ external nodes). Furthermore $E_n = I_n + 2n$ as was used in the proof of the Expected Binary Search Theorem. Together these imply that

$$S_n = 1 + \frac{E_n - 2n}{n} = \frac{n+1}{n}U_n - 1. \tag{1}$$

Substituting this value for S_n in the previous equation and simplifying yields

$$(n+1)U_n = 2n + \sum_{i=0}^{n-1} U_i.$$

Replacing n by $n - 1$ gives

$$nU_{n-1} = 2n - 2 + \sum_{i=0}^{n-2} U_i,$$

and subtracting the left sides and right sides of these two equations yields

$$(n + 1)U_n - nU_{n-1} = 2 + U_{n-1}$$

or in other words

$$U_n = \frac{2}{n+1} + U_{n-1}.$$

The value of U_{n-1} can be expressed in terms of U_{n-2} in the same way, and after repeated substitutions we have

$$U_n = \frac{2}{n+1} + \frac{2}{n} + \cdots + \frac{2}{2} + U_0,$$

and since $U_0 = 0$,

$$U_n = 2H_{n+1} - 2.$$

Then by Equation (1),

$$S_n = \frac{n+1}{n}U_n - 1 = \frac{n+1}{n}(2H_{n+1} - 2) - 1$$

$$= 2\frac{n+1}{n}\left(H_n + \frac{1}{n+1} - 1\right) - 1 = 2\left(1 + \frac{1}{n}\right)H_n - 3. \quad \square$$

Deletion

When a node is deleted from a binary search tree, the inorder traversal of the remaining nodes must yield the keys in the same order they had before the deletion. If the node to be deleted is a leaf, it is a simple matter to replace the appropriate pointer in the node's parent by Λ. (For example, in Figure 6.4(a) and (b), deleting node N simply changes the right child of M to Λ.) Also, if the node is not a leaf but has only one child, the correct effect is achieved if the appropriate pointer in the node's parent is replaced by a pointer to the child. (For example, in Figure 6.4(a) and (c), to delete M we can simply make N the left child of P.) Difficulties arise only in the case in which the node to be deleted has two nonempty children. The strategy to be adopted in this case is to replace the node by its inorder successor, and to delete the inorder successor. Since *the inorder successor of a node that has a right child has no left child*, the operation of deleting the inorder successor in this case is a simple one. For example, in Figure 6.4(a) and (d) we delete the root node F by replacing F by M and deleting M.

Algorithm 6.9 gives the precise details. This routine uses a locative P that points initially to the root of the tree, and ultimately to the node to be deleted,

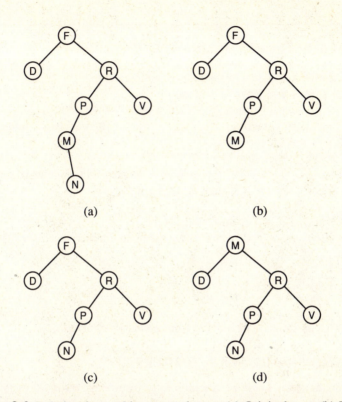

Figure 6.4 Deletion from a binary search tree. (a) Original tree. (b) Tree
of part (a) after deleting the leaf N. (c) Tree of part (a) after deleting
node M, which has one child N; that child replaces M. (d) Tree of
part (a) after deleting node F, which has two children; F is replaced by
its inorder successor in the tree, node M.

which is discovered by searching for the key value that has been passed as an
argument. If the node to be deleted has no right child, then the node is deleted
by replacing it by its left child (which may or may not be empty); otherwise, it
is replaced by its inorder successor.

This deletion algorithm has an asymmetry—the node deleted is either the
node containing the key or its inorder *successor*, but never its inorder *predecessor*. Over time, even a "random" sequence of deletions interspersed with
random insertions can cause the root to migrate towards the right and the tree to
become skewed to the left. Eventually the average search path will have length
$\Theta(\sqrt{n})$, rather than $O(\log n)$. This tendency towards increasingly unbalanced
trees when deletions are mixed in with insertions can be combatted by choosing
at random, when a deletion must be performed, between Algorithm 6.9 and
its symmetric counterpart in which inorder predecessors are deleted instead of
inorder successors.

---

procedure *BinaryTreeDelete*(**key** K, **locative** P):
{K is the key value of the item to be deleted}
{P is a locative that points to the root of the tree}
    while $P \neq \Lambda$ **and** Key(P) $\neq K$ **do**
        if $K <$ Key(P) **then** $P \leftarrow$ LC(P) **else** $P \leftarrow$ RC(P)
    if $P = \Lambda$ **then return**   {Key K is not in the tree}
    if RC(P) $= \Lambda$ **then** $P \Leftarrow$ LC(P)
    else if LC(P) $= \Lambda$ **then** $P \Leftarrow$ RC(P)
    else   {Locative P points to the node to be deleted}
        {Find the inorder successor. Q is a locative}
        $Q \leftarrow$ RC(P)
        while LC(Q) $\neq \Lambda$ **do** $Q \leftarrow$ LC(Q)
        {Replace the node P to be deleted by its inorder successor Q}

$$\begin{pmatrix} P \\ Q \\ \text{LC}(Q) \\ \text{RC}(Q) \end{pmatrix} \Leftarrow \begin{pmatrix} Q \\ \text{RC}(Q) \\ \text{LC}(P) \\ \text{RC}(P) \end{pmatrix}$$

Algorithm 6.9 Deletion of an item from a binary search tree.

6.5 STATIC BINARY SEARCH TREES

The assumption that *LookUps* are uniformly distributed across keys is likely to be inaccurate in many applications, so it is worth considering strategies that lessen the search time to find the more frequently accessed keys. On page 177 we considered such a strategy for organizing a list implementation of a dictionary, and concluded that the best possible ordering keeps the keys in order by frequency of access. The analogous line of thought in the case of binary trees suggests that *more frequently accessed keys ought to be kept closer to the root*. This is a plausible principle; it is the essential idea behind Huffman codes (§5.4). However, this idea cannot be put into effect naïvely, since the inorder traversal of the nodes must be maintained (unlike in the case of Huffman coding). Conflicting objectives can come into play, since the dictionary ordering of the keys can be at odds with their frequency ordering.

    Consider, for example, the keys A, B, and C, and assume that their frequencies are 0.35, 0.3, and 0.35, respectively. There are five possible binary search trees on these three nodes (Figure 6.5). The symmetric tree (Figure 6.5(c)), which would clearly minimize the expected search time if all keys were equiprobable, has the low-frequency key at the root. On the other hand, if a higher-frequency key is moved to the root then the height of the tree is increased. As it turns out in this particular case, the symmetric tree is the best; the expected number of comparisons is

$$2 \cdot 0.35 + 1 \cdot 0.3 + 2 \cdot 0.35 = 1.7.$$

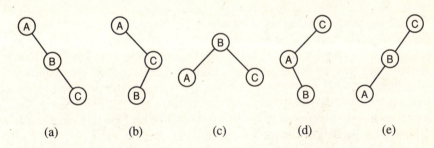

(a)   (b)   (c)   (d)   (e)

Figure 6.5 The five binary search trees on three keys.

But with other probability distributions the advantage of having a high-frequency key at the root outweighs the disadvantage of increasing the depth of some nodes of the tree. For example, if A, B, and C have frequencies 0.45, 0.1, and 0.45, respectively, then Figure 6.5(b) and (d) are superior to Figure 6.5(c).

Optimal Trees

An **optimal binary search tree** is one that minimizes the expected search time. How can we find an optimal tree, given the access frequency of each key? (There can be more than one optimal tree; for example, in the example just given, the trees of Figure 6.5(b) and (d) are both optimal.) A brute-force approach that checks each of the possible binary search trees is impractical, because there are far too many trees to check. (The number of binary trees on n nodes turns out to be $\binom{2n}{n}/(n+1)$, where $\binom{m}{n} = m!/n!(m-n)!$. The number of binary trees is therefore in $\Theta(4^n n^{-3/2})$.) A little planning cuts down the work considerably, however.

Let the keys be $K_1 < K_2 < \cdots < K_n$ in their dictionary order, and let p_i be the probability of accessing K_i. Thus $\sum_{i=1}^{n} p_i = 1$. (We omit consideration of unsuccessful searches; these techniques can be extended to optimize the tree when the external nodes also have known probabilities, that is, when the probability of searching for a key between K_i and K_{i+1} is known for each i.)

Now let $1 \leq j \leq k \leq n$, and let T be any tree constructed from the keys $K_j, \ldots, K_k$. As on page 148, we define $Depth_T(K_i)$, where $j \leq i \leq k$, to be the depth in T of the node where K_i is stored, and define the **cost** of T to be

$$C(T) = \sum_{i=j}^{k} p_i(Depth_T(K_i) + 1).$$

If $j = 1$ and $k = n$ then the cost is the expected number of comparisons to find a key in the tree; if T holds only a subset of the keys then $C(T)$ represents the cost of searching within the tree for only those keys, with searches for other keys regarded as free. We extend our previous terminology by saying that any tree T is **optimal** if its cost is as small as the cost of any other tree with the same keys.

The expression for the cost of a tree is very similar to that on page 148 for the cost of a Huffman tree. There are two significant differences. First, in the present case all nodes contribute to the sum since all nodes represent keys (in a Huffman tree only the leaves represent character codes). Second, the frequency is multiplied by the depth plus 1, not the depth itself, since even testing the root requires one comparison (in weighing Huffman trees path length from the root measures the number of bits, while here the number of nodes encountered measures the number of comparisons performed).

Thus our objective is to find that tree T on all n keys that minimizes $C(T)$. The crucial observation in reducing the number of trees to be considered is that *every subtree of an optimal tree is itself optimal.* That is, if T is an optimal tree for $K_j, \ldots, K_k$ and its root is K_l, then its left subtree must be an optimal tree for $K_j, \ldots, K_{l-1}$, and its right subtree must be an optimal tree for $K_{l+1}, \ldots, K_k$. For if the left and right subtrees of T are T_L and T_R, then the depth of each node of T_L or T_R increases by one when it is viewed as a node of T; for example,

$$Depth_T(K_i) = 1 + Depth_{T_L}(K_i)$$

for any i such that K_i is in T_L. So it follows that if K_l is at the root of T then

$$C(T) = p_l + \sum_{i=j}^{l-1} p_i(Depth_T(K_i) + 1) + \sum_{i=l+1}^{k} p_i(Depth_T(K_i) + 1)$$

$$= p_l + \sum_{i=j}^{l-1} p_i + C(T_L) + \sum_{i=l+1}^{k} p_i + C(T_R)$$

$$= \sum_{i=j}^{k} p_i + C(T_L) + C(T_R). \tag{2}$$

Therefore replacing T_L or T_R by any tree on the same nodes with lower cost would result in a tree of lower cost than T.

If $d \geq 0$ and we know an optimal tree for each set of nodes $K_{j'}, \ldots, K_{k'}$, where $k' - j' < d$, then for any $j \leq n - d$ we can find an optimal tree for $K_j, \ldots, K_{j+d}$ by evaluating the cost (2) for each l such that $j \leq l \leq j + d$ and choosing the trees T_L and T_R to be optimal for the keys $K_j, \ldots, K_{l-1}$ and $K_{l+1}, \ldots, K_k$, respectively. This approach suggests a recursive procedure for finding optimal subtrees, but implementing this approach directly would lead to a great deal of repeated computation. Instead the computation can be organized as a dynamic programming algorithm, so that each optimal subtree is determined only once.

Let $T(j, k)$ denote an optimal subtree for the keys $K_j, \ldots, K_k$, where $k \geq j - 1$. There are $\Theta(n^2)$ of these subtrees $T(j, k)$ in all, and they can be found by induction on $k - j$. When $k - j = -1$, the tree $T(j, j - 1)$ contains

procedure *OptimalBinarySearchTree*$(p_1, \ldots, p_n)$:
{Construct optimal search tree}
{Here $p(j, k) = p_j + \cdots + p_k$}
>   **for** i **from** 1 **to** n **do**
>> $r[i, i] \leftarrow i$
>> $C[i, i - 1] \leftarrow 0$
>   **for** d **from** 0 **to** $n - 1$ **do**
>>   **for** j **from** 1 **to** $n - d$ **do**
>>> $k \leftarrow j + d$
>>> $r[j, k] \leftarrow MinIndex(C, j, k)$
>>> $C[j, k] \leftarrow p(j, k) + C[j, r[j, k] - 1] + C[r[j, k] + 1, k]$

Algorithm 6.10 Computation of optimal binary search tree on $K_1, \ldots, K_n$. The input to the algorithm is the sequence of probabilities $p_1, \ldots, p_n$, with $0 \le p_i \le 1$ for each i and $\sum_{i=1}^{n} p_i = 1$; the arrays r and C are filled in by the algorithm as explained in the text. The function $MinIndex(C, j, k)$ returns an index l such that $j \le l \le k$ and $C[j, l - 1] + C[l + 1, k]$ is minimized; the order in which calls on *MinIndex* occur in this algorithm ensures that the necessary entries of C have already been calculated when they are needed.

---

no keys and therefore must be Λ; and when $k - j = 0$, the tree $T(j, j)$ consists of the single node with key K_j. For $k - j > 0$, $T(j, k)$ is, for some l such that $j \le l \le k$, a tree with K_l at the root, $T(j, l - 1)$ as the left subtree, and $T(l+1, k)$ as the right subtree; and these subtrees have been determined already, since $(l - 1) - j < k - j$ and $k - (l + 1) < k - j$. When $k - j = n - 1$ there is only one tree to be determined, namely, $T(1, n)$, the optimal tree for the entire set of keys.

To be specific, Algorithm 6.10 computes $C[j, k] = C(T(j, k))$, the cost of any optimal tree for $K_j, \ldots, K_k$, and $r[j, k]$, the root of $T(j, k)$. (There may be several choices for $r[j, k]$ since there may be several for $T(j, k)$; it does not matter which one the algorithm selects.) The tree can be recovered from the $r[j, k]$, since its root is $r[1, n]$, the root of its left subtree is $r[1, r[1, n] - 1]$, etc. In the algorithm, we let $p(j, k) = \sum_{i=j}^{k} p_i$; these values can be computed iteratively in the algorithm's doubly nested loop (Problem 42).

Algorithm 6.10 has much better performance than the brute-force method, but it is still not fast enough to be useful for large n. If function $MinIndex(j, k)$, which finds an index l between j and k minimizing $C[j, l - 1] + C[l + 1, k]$, is implemented simply by searching through all the possibilities $j, j + 1, \ldots, k$, then the total number of different triples j, k, l that are considered in the minimizing step is

$$\sum_{d=0}^{n-1}\sum_{j=1}^{n-d}(d+1) = \sum_{d=0}^{n-1}(n-d)(d+1)$$

$$= n \cdot 1 + (n-1) \cdot 2 + \cdots + 2 \cdot (n-1) + 1 \cdot n.$$

This sum can be rewritten as

$$
\begin{array}{ccccccc}
n & + & (n-1) & + & \cdots & + & 1 \\
  & + & (n-1) & + & \cdots & + & 1 \\
  &   &   & + & \cdots & + & 1 \\
  &   &   &   &   & \vdots & \\
  &   &   &   &   & + & 1
\end{array}
$$

$$= \sum_{j=1}^{n}\sum_{k=1}^{j} k = \sum_{j=1}^{n}\frac{j(j+1)}{2},$$

which involves the sum of the first n squares and is therefore in $\Theta(n^3)$ as follows from the Sum of Successive k^{th} Powers Theorem (page 24). Actually, the algorithm can be sped up by a factor of n quite easily; it can be shown (Problem 43) that an l that minimizes the cost falls in the range $r[j, k-1] \leq r[j, k] \leq r[j+1, k]$, and that restricting the search for $r[j, k]$ to this range reduces the running time to $\Theta(n^2)$.

Probability-Balanced Trees

For larger numbers of nodes, two alternatives can be suggested for the construction of static binary search trees. The first is a **balancing heuristic**: in the notation used earlier, it directs that the key at the root K_l be chosen so that

$$p(1, l-1) \approx p(l+1, n),$$

and that the roots of successive subtrees be chosen to equalize the probabilities of access to *their* subtrees in the same way. Let us call a tree constructed in this way **probability-balanced**. Probability-balanced trees are a natural generalization of optimal search trees for a uniform distribution; there the tree is constructed so as to have approximately equal numbers of keys in each subtree, and here, with the access probabilities known, we equalize instead the access probabilities to the subtrees. This heuristic works well in practice, and typically yields trees whose expected search times are within a few percent of the optimum; it yields even better trees if the keys one or two away from the one that balances the access probabilities are also tried as possible roots. (This refinement attempts to take advantage of placing a high-frequency key at the root, in case the next or previous key is a low-frequency key that happens to be the one around which the probabilities balance.)

The balancing heuristic can be implemented to run in linear time, though doing so requires some ingenuity. To find the "balancing point" in the interval (j, k), we need to find that l such that $j \leq l \leq k$ and

$$p(j, l-1) - p(l+1, k) \leq 0 < p(j, l) - p(l+2, k);$$

this will be the point where the probabilities nearly balance. (The same method will be used, recursively, to find the "balancing points" of the subintervals.) We will then take the root of the tree to be either K_l or K_{l+1}, depending on whether $|p(j, l-1) - p(l+1, k)|$ or $p(j, l) - p(l+2, k)$ is smaller.

To find that l, first let $w_i = \sum_{j=1}^{i} p_j$ for $i = 0, \ldots, n$; these can be calculated in linear time, and once they are known any desired probability $p(j, k)$ can be calculated quickly as $w_k - w_{j-1}$. (In particular, $p(j, j-1)$ is always 0.) One approach to finding l is binary search; we could first try $l = \lfloor (j+k)/2 \rfloor$, and then depending on the sign of $p(j, l-1) - p(l+1, k)$, search in the upper or lower half of the possible indices for the balancing point. Finding the balancing point of the interval $(1, n)$ takes time $\Theta(\log n)$, but that point might be very close to one end or the other of the interval, in which case the problem remaining to be solved might be almost as large; if the probabilities for $K_1, \ldots, K_n$ were $\frac{1}{2}, \frac{1}{4}, \frac{1}{8}$, etc., the running time of this method would be proportional to $\sum_{i=1}^{n} \lg i \in \Theta(n \log n)$. Instead we use an approach that will find the balancing point of an interval (j, k) more quickly if it is near one of the endpoints, but will still take $O(\log(k-j+1))$ time in the worst case. Using successive increments $d = 1, 2, 4, 8, \ldots, 2^{\lceil \lg(k-j+1) \rceil}$, we check the points d from each end of the interval, that is, $l = j+1, k-1, j+2, k-2, j+4, \ldots$, until we find a d such that $p(j, j+d-1) - p(j+d+1, k) > 0$ or $p(j, k-d-1) - p(k-d+1, k) \leq 0$. This takes $\lg d$ iterations. Once d has been found, the exact point l such that $p(j, l-1) - p(l+1, k) \leq 0 < p(j, l) - p(l+2, k)$ takes time $O(\log d)$ to locate exactly by binary search, since it must be sought in the interval $(j, j+d)$ or $(k-d, k)$.

Let $B(n)$ denote the time to construct the "probability-balanced" static search tree for an interval of length n. Then

$$B(n) \leq \max_{1 \leq l \leq n} \{c \cdot (1 + \lg \min(l, n-l+1)) + B(l-1) + B(n-l)\},$$

where c is a constant. The first term represents the time to find the root, the second and third terms the time needed to construct the left and right subtrees. It can be shown by induction that $B(n) \leq 2cn$ (Problem 45), so that this is a linear-time technique.

How good an approximation to the optimal binary search tree is the tree constructed by this method? A fairly straightforward argument shows that the expected search time in such a probability-balanced tree is within a factor of two of that in the optimal static binary search tree. We need one preliminary lemma; the cost $C(T)$ of a search tree T is defined as on page 201.

■ **LEMMA** Let T_{opt} be the optimal tree for a set of keys. Consider the tree T that is formed from the same keys by applying the balancing heuristic at the root, but finding the optimal search trees for the keys in the left and right subtrees. Then

$$C(T) \leq C(T_{\text{opt}}) + \frac{1}{2}.$$

PROOF   If the root of T is the same as the root of T_{opt} then $T = T_{\text{opt}}$ and there is nothing to prove. Otherwise one subtree of T, say the left, contains a subset of the keys on the same side of T_{opt}, and the right subtree of T contains a superset of the keys on the right side of T_{opt}. The expected cost of finding a key that is in the left subtree of T is certainly at less than the expected cost of finding it in T_{opt}, since both left subtrees are optimal and the left subtree of T has fewer keys. The expected cost of finding a key in the right subtree of T may be higher than the expected cost of finding it in T_{opt}, but it is certainly no more than the whole cost $C(T_{\text{opt}})$ plus the expected cost of descending the one link from the root of T to the root of its right subtree. Because of the balancing rule the probability that a key is actually in the right subtree of T is less than $\frac{1}{2}$, so $C(T) \leq C(T_{\text{opt}}) + \frac{1}{2}$.   □

■ **THEOREM** *(Probability-Balanced Trees)* The tree that is constructed by balancing probabilities has cost at most $2C(T_{\text{opt}})$, where T_{opt} is the optimal binary search tree with the same keys.

PROOF   The proof is by induction on the number of keys. There is only one possible tree with a single key so in this case the Theorem follows trivially. If we use the balancing heuristic to construct a tree T' with subtrees T'_L and T'_R, then by the induction hypothesis

$$C(T') = C(T'_L) + C(T'_R) + 1 \leq 2C(T''_L) + 2C(T''_R) + 1,$$

where T''_L and T''_R are the optimal trees with the same keys as T'_L and T'_R. But now the Lemma applies, with T being the tree with the same root as T' and with T''_L and T''_R as its subtrees, so it follows that

$$C(T') \leq 2C(T''_L) + 2C(T''_R) + 1 = 2C(T) - 1 \leq 2C(T_{\text{opt}}).   □$$

In fact the upper bound of 2 on the ratio of the search cost in a probability-balanced tree to the search cost in an optimal tree is conservative. A more careful analysis (cited at the end of the chapter) reveals that the tree constructed by balancing probabilities has cost that never exceeds that of the optimal tree by more than about 44%.

Median Split Trees

A second alternative approach to the construction of high-performance static search trees is the use of **median split trees**. In a median split tree each node contains *two* keys. One is called the **node value**; any additional information in the node (the Info field) is associated with this key. The node value is chosen to be the key with highest probability in the subtree, in an attempt to keep search times to a minimum. The other key, called the **split value**, is used to direct the search to the left or right subtree, in case the value sought is not equal to the node value. This key is chosen to equalize the numbers of nodes in the left and right subtrees, in order to keep the tree well balanced; in other words, the split value is the median of the keys in the subtree, in their dictionary order.

At first thought it might appear that the time to search a single node of a median split tree is greater than that for an ordinary binary search tree, since two keys must be checked; but in fact the search procedure is nearly identical. In an ordinary binary search tree one checks $K = \mathsf{Key}(P)$, then $K < \mathsf{Key}(P)$, and then concludes that $K > \mathsf{Key}(P)$; in a median split tree one checks $K = \mathsf{NodeValue}(P)$, then $K < \mathsf{SplitValue}(P)$, and then concludes that $K > \mathsf{SplitValue}(P)$. So the gain in search time by keeping the highest-frequency key of each subtree at its root is quite real. Moreover the *maximum* number of nodes to be searched for any key is bounded by $\lfloor \lg n \rfloor + 1$, since all leaves are at depth $\lfloor \lg n \rfloor$ or $\lfloor \lg n \rfloor - 1$. Therefore median split trees combine good expected-case performance and guaranteed logarithmic worst-case performance.

Median split trees require more memory than ordinary binary search trees since each node holds two keys. This overhead is, however, partly balanced by the possibility of using an implicit representation. In a subtree of size n, instead of choosing the exact median to be the split value, choose the key whose index is $2^{\lfloor \lg n \rfloor - 1}$ or $n - 2^{\lfloor \lg n \rfloor - 1}$, whichever is smaller. The result will be a complete binary tree, which can therefore be stored and searched without the aid of pointers.

The median split tree on n keys can be constructed in time $O(n \log n)$. The construction algorithm is in fact quite simple: to construct a tree for n keys, it is necessary to find the key with the greatest frequency, to find the median (or something close to the median, as suggested in the last paragraph) with respect to the lexicographic ordering, and to construct recursively two subtrees with about half as many nodes. To find the lexicographic median at each stage, it suffices to sort the keys on their lexicographic order once at the beginning of the algorithm, and then the median of any subrange (excluding keys that should be omitted because they have already been used as node values) can be found in linear time by a simple scan (Problem 48). The initial sort can be done in time $O(n \log n)$; all other operations except the recursion take linear time; and the recursive subdivision produces a binary tree that is complete, and hence has logarithmic depth.

Problems

6.2   1. Consider the following alternative implementation of the dictionary operations by means of unordered linked lists. Allow multiple nodes to exist with the same key value, and implement *Insert* simply by adding a new node to the front of the list.

    a. Give algorithms for the *Insert*, *LookUp*, and *Delete* operations and analyze their complexity. (Be sure to say what n is.)

    b. Under what circumstances (as measured by the relative frequency of the three kinds of operations) might this implementation make sense?

  2. **a.** In the notation of this section, what is the value of $p(i, i)$?

    b. Compute $p(i, j, k)$, the probability that key K_i precedes key K_j which in turn precedes key K_k. Can you generalize the result?

  3. Suppose that the keys in a list are of two kinds: those accessed frequently and those accessed rarely. For example, suppose that a list of $2n$ keys contains n keys each accessed with probability $0.99/n$ and n keys each accessed with probability $0.01/n$. (Of course, initially we don't know which keys are in each class!) What is the expected search time for an item if the Move-to-Front Heuristic is used for a long time?

  4. **Zipf's law** for the probability distribution of a set of items states that the ith most frequently occurring item occurs with probability proportional to $1/i$. That is, there is a constant c such that if $K_1, \ldots, K_n$ are the keys in order of decreasing frequency, then the frequency of K_i is c/i. (This law is a reasonably accurate model for the frequency of occurrence of words in the English language.) If the keys obey Zipf's law, what is the expected number of comparisons to find a key in a list of size n ordered by frequency?

  5. Which is more suitable if the list is implemented as a table in contiguous memory, the Move-to-Front Heuristic or the Transpose Heuristic? Why?

  6. This problem explores the use of the Move-to-Front Heuristic with tables.

    a. Suppose that the list is stored as a table $K[0 \ldots n - 1]$, that accessing (reading or storing) any element $K[i]$ takes time α, and that the number of such accesses is the main determiner of the speed of the heuristic when implemented for tables. Derive an expression for the expected time to perform a successful search if the Move-to-Front Heuristic is in use.

b. Suppose it is known that every search will be successful; what is the expected time for a search? (Hint: Some preparation for the movement to front can take place as the table is searched.)

7. A linked representation, rather than a tabular representation, saves time when rearranging items if the Move-to-Front Heuristic is used. But it costs memory; how might the extra memory be better utilized by a different heuristic?

8. The Move-To-Front and Transpose Heuristics can be blended; for example, we could devise a "Move-k-Forward" and a "Move-$k\%$-Forward" Heuristic. State exactly what these might be, and what advantages or disadvantages they might have by comparison with the simpler heuristics.

9. Suppose that a demon alters your Move-To-Front algorithm so that it moves a key to the *end* of the list each time it is accessed. Express the expected number of comparisons to find a key under this "Move-To-End" Heuristic in terms of the access probabilities of the keys in the list.

10. Suppose that a list of n keys $K_1, \ldots, K_n$ is to be searched, where the probability of key K_i being sought is p_i. Suppose moreover that key K_i costs c_i to read, so that the cost of searching for K_m is the sum $\sum_{i=1}^{m} c_i$. Show that the ordering $K_1, \ldots, K_n$ has the minimum expected search cost provided that the ratios p_i/c_i are monotone nonincreasing:

$$\frac{p_1}{c_1} \geq \frac{p_2}{c_2} \geq \cdots \geq \frac{p_n}{c_n}.$$

11. Our analysis of the Move-to-Front Heuristic assumed that the dictionary had been in use for a long time, so that the repeated accesses had left the list in a "steady state." In this problem we consider how long it takes for such a "steady state" to be reached. As in the text, assume there are n items $K_1, \ldots, K_n$ with access probabilities $p_1, \ldots, p_n$. Also assume that these items are initially in random order in the list; that is, all $n!$ orderings are equally likely.

a. Define $p_t(i, j)$ to be the probability that K_i precedes K_j at time t (that is, after t *LookUps* have occurred). Thus $p_0(i, j) = \frac{1}{2}$ for all i and j, and $p_t(i, j)$ should be approximately equal to $p(i, j)$ for large t. Give an exact formula for $p_t(i, j)$.

b. The sum $O_t = \sum_{i \neq j} p_j(p_t(i, j) - p(i, j))$ describes how much more the tth *LookUp* is expected to cost than the steady-state cost, due to the lingering effect of the start-up ordering of the items. Define the **overwork** of the heuristic to be $\sum_{t=0}^{\infty} O_t$; this is the total number of extra comparisons that are expected to be done over the long haul due to the ordering of the list at the beginning. Show that the overwork is at most $n(n-1)/4$. (It follows that once $n(n-1)$ *LookUps* have been done, the amortized cost per *LookUp* of having started with the list in a random order rather than in something close to the optimal order is less than $\frac{1}{4}$ of a comparison.)

 c. Consider the particular probability distribution in which $p_1 = 1$ and all the other p_i are 0. (Thus K_1 is the only item that is ever accessed.) Show that the overwork of the Move-to-Front Heuristic is $(n-1)/2$, but the overwork of the Transpose Heuristic is much larger, namely, $(n^2-1)/6$. (This supports the intuition that the Transpose Heuristic takes longer to reach "steady state" than the Move-to-Front Heuristic.)

6.3 **12. a.** Write the insertion algorithm for a dictionary represented as an ordered table, that is, the algorithm *Insert*$(K, I, T[0..n-1])$. Assume that the maximum length of the table is given by the constant N, and attempting to exceed this bound is an error condition. Also assume that the current size of the table can be changed simply by changing the value of n within the algorithm. What is the order of the time complexity of your algorithm?

 b. Under the same assumptions, write the algorithm for deleting an item from a dictionary represented as an ordered table.

13. Suppose we are given two key values K_1 and K_2, where $K_1 \leq K_2$, and an ordered table $T[0..n-1]$. We want to find the *range* within T corresponding to the lower and upper limits K_1 and K_2, that is, we want to find the minimum i and maximum j such that $K_1 \leq T[i]$ and $T[j] \leq K_2$. (It is possible that no such i or j might exist.) According to the Expected Binary Search Theorem this problem can be solved by doing binary searches for K_1 and K_2 at an expected cost of about $2\lfloor \lg n \rfloor$ comparisons. Devise and analyze a better method.

14. Prove that an extended binary tree can have n external nodes at depths $d_1, \ldots, d_n$ if and only if $\sum_{i=1}^{n} 2^{-d_i} = 1$.

15. Prove by induction on the number of internal nodes that $E = I + 2n$ for any extended binary tree with n nodes, where E is the external path length and I is the internal path length.

16. Using the table of ten numbers on page 186, use the interpolation search algorithm to find 93.

17. Consider the following sequence of twenty numbers: 71, 147, 175, 182, 270, 290, 303, 335, 356, 379, 508, 525, 559, 590, 591, 610,

684, 710, 789, 873. Use both binary search and interpolation search to find each of the numbers 175, 290, 356, 525, 591, and 710. In this small sample, does interpolation search use fewer comparisons than binary search?

18. Using the same numbers as in Problem 17, perform an *unsuccessful* search for the number 500 using both binary and interpolation search.

19. Suppose you would like to search a list of keys $K_1, \ldots, K_n$ whose probabilities of being sought decrease geometrically: $p_i = a \cdot p_{i-1}$ for each i such that $1 < i \leq n$, where a is a constant in the range $0 < a < 1$.

   a. Show that p_1 must be about $1 - a$.

   b. Under what circumstances, if any, would linear search be preferable to binary search? For example, if we regard a as fixed, is there a minimum n at which one method becomes preferable to the other?

20. This problem concerns the (rather fanciful) question of how quickly one can search an *infinite* sorted table. Imagine that the infinite table $A[1 .. \infty]$ is sorted, so that $A[i] < A[i+1]$ for every i, and we want to find the unknown position n of an item $K = A[n]$. The complexity measure will be the number of comparisons performed. The simplest imaginable method is the **order-0 algorithm**: Start at position 1 and then search positions 2, 3, ... sequentially until reaching $A[n] = K$. Clearly this method uses n comparisons.

   a. An alternative, called the **order-1 algorithm**, first tries to find the smallest integer k such that $2^k \geq n$, by probing positions 1, 2, 4, 8, ... When such a k has been determined, the exact value of n is found by binary search. Show that the order-1 algorithm takes about $2 \lg n$ comparisons at worst.

   b. Notice that the first stage of the order-1 algorithm is actually a search for an unknown value of k by trying $k = 0$ first, then $k = 1$, then $k = 2$, ...; in other words, k is located by the order-0 algorithm. Show that an **order-2 algorithm** can be defined by replacing the first stage of the order-1 algorithm by a search for k using the order-1 algorithm. How many comparisons does the order-2 algorithm use?

   c. Generalize the method of part (b) as much as possible to reduce the number of comparisons needed.

21. Describe a set of n key values and a value to be sought that will force *InterpolationSearchLookUp* to iterate almost n times.

22. If the worst-case performance of interpolation search is really a concern, it is possible to guarantee $O(\log n)$ worst-case performance

while maintaining $O(\log \log n)$ expected-case performance by alternating steps of binary and interpolation search. Present an algorithm that does this gracefully, and justify the time bound.

23. Give the exact formula that should replace the assignment to p in the interpolation search algorithm (Algorithm 6.2 on page 185) in case the *LookUps* are not uniformly distributed but the function $F(K)$ gives the probability that a *LookUp* is for a key value less than or equal to K.

24. Sam needs a data structure for searching 10,000 keys, but he knows that 80% of the searches for keys that are actually present involve only 20% of the keys. He decides to separate these 2000 keys into one ordered table, and keep the other 8000 keys in a separate table. To find a key he'll look in the small table first, using binary search, before looking in the big table using the same algorithm.

   a. How does Sam's algorithm compare to binary search of a single table of size 10,000 in the *worst* case?

   b. How does Sam's method compare to searching a single table in the *expected* case for *successful* searches?

   c. How do the methods compare in terms of expected performance on *unsuccessful* searches?

   d. What do you think of Sam's algorithm? Would any change to the 80%–20% division alter your opinion?

25. A **padded list** is an ordered list stored in a table in contiguous memory that is somewhat larger than the actual number of elements in the list. With padded lists, the dictionary operations can all be implemented in expected time $O(\log \log n)$. Let k be an integer greater than 0. Initially one out of every $k+1$ positions in the table is unused; if N is the length of the table, then an auxiliary table of N bits records which table positions are in use. (Thus n, the number of elements actually in the dictionary, is about $kN/(k + 1)$ initially. An "empty" table position is actually filled with a copy of the next lower list element to facilitate searching.) As insertions and deletions are performed, this regular pattern of empty slots is destroyed.

   a. Write the *LookUp* and *Delete* routines for padded lists.

   b. Explain how to insert an element in a padded list, on the assumption that there is an empty slot in the table.

   c. The insertion method of part (b) is likely to take a long time if the table grows through insertions until it is nearly full (that is, if $n \approx N$), since relatively few gaps will remain. Likewise, searching the table of length N will be too slow if n, the actual number of elements, shrinks through deletions to a value much smaller than N. For these reasons we reinitialize the table into a new block of memory if the ratio n/N drops below some fixed threshold α or exceeds some fixed threshold β (where $0 < \alpha < k/(k+1) < \beta < 1$). We assume that a new block of memory of size N' can be obtained in time $O(N')$. Show that under these circumstances, *LookUp*, *Insert*, and *Delete* can all be implemented to run in expected time $O(\log \log n)$, including time for all initializations and reinitializations. (Hint: The only tricky part is to assess the expected amount of time to find a gap in which to do an insertion. Without trying to calculate the expected number of positions that will need to be inspected, argue that this number depends on the constant parameters of the algorithm [such as k, α, and β], but not on the size of the data set on which the algorithm is run [that is, not on n].)

26. Insert the following keys into an initially empty skip list: 055, 032, 132, 200, 861, 823, 937, 916, 524. Assume that *MaxLevel* $= 3$ and that the following sequence of bits is returned by the random-number generator (that is, the test "*Random*( ) $< 1/2$" is false or true depending on whether the bit is 0 or 1): 01011100110000111110. ...

27. How much memory do skip lists take, beyond that needed to store the data? Find the expected case and the worst case for a dictionary of n items, in terms of n and the size of a pointer.

28. Write these skip list algorithms:

a. *MakeEmptySet*;

b. *IsEmptySet*;

c. *Delete*.

29. Write an algorithm that merges two skip lists into one.

30. Show that the expected maximum level in a skip list is at most

$$\log_{1/p} n - 1 + 1/(1 - p),$$

where $p < 1$ is the ratio with which nodes of successive levels are expected to occur.

31. Show that in a skip list the probability that a node has level at least i is p^i, where $i \leq$ *MaxLevel* and p is defined as in the previous problem.

32. Algorithm 6.3 on page 190 might actually do a bit more work than is really necessary in the case of a successful search. Where does the inefficiency arise, and how can it be repaired?

33. Prove the Skip List Theorem in the case of an arbitrary ratio $p < 1$. In particular, show that the expected total path length is

$$(\log_{1/p} n)/p + 1/(1 - p).$$

6.4   **34.** Show the result of inserting the following keys into an initially empty binary search tree: 232, 827, 782, 050, 887, 619, 703, 351, 662, 544.

35. This problem concerns the expected-case analysis of the construction of binary search trees.

    a. Show that if each key is equally likely to stand in any of the $m+1$ possible positions relative to the m keys inserted before it, then all $n!$ permutations of the keys are equally likely to be the order in which the keys are inserted.

    b. Show that the conditions of part (a) are *different* from saying that all the binary search trees are equally probable. This idea can be refuted by considering the permutations of just three keys.

36. Show that a binary search tree can be reconstructed from its postorder traversal. That is, show that if the key sequence $K_1, \ldots, K_n$ is the postorder traversal of a binary search tree, then the structure of the tree is uniquely determined from this sequence and in fact can be determined as the sequence is read from left to right. Does the same hold for the preorder traversal? What about the inorder traversal?

37. Given an ordered table $T[0 .. n - 1]$, suppose we search it by a "random binary search" strategy. If the range remaining to be searched is from index *Left* to *Right*, instead of probing at position $\lfloor (Left + Right)/2 \rfloor$, we probe at a position that is randomly chosen, according to a uniform distribution, from among *Left*, *Left* + 1, $\ldots$, *Right*. What are the best-case, worst-case, and expected-case performance of this method?

38. Consider the abstract operation *Equal* on sets and the abstract operation *Subset*, where *Subset*(S, T) returns **true** if set S is a subset of set T and **false** otherwise. Explain how to implement these two abstract operations for each of these data structures: unordered lists, ordered lists, and binary search trees. (Try to avoid using a sequence of *LookUp*s.)

39. Implement the following alternative to Algorithm 6.9 for deletion from a binary search tree dictionary: once the node to be deleted and its inorder successor have been located, copy the Key and Info fields from the latter to the former, and change a single pointer.

6.5   **40. a.** For each tree in Figure 6.5 on page 201, give a probability distribution on the three keys for which that tree is optimal.

b. Suppose the probabilities of A, B, and C are p, $1 - 2p$, and p, where $0 < p < \frac{1}{2}$. For what value of p, if any, are trees (b), (c), and (d) equally good?

41. Find the optimal binary search tree for the keys A, B, C, D, E, F with the access probabilities being .20, .16, .08, .22, .21, and .13, respectively.

42. In Algorithm 6.10 on page 203, where and how should the $p(j, k)$ be calculated?

43. As in Algorithm 6.10, let K_1, ..., K_n be keys to be sought with probabilities p_1, ..., p_n, where each $p_i \geq 0$ and $\sum p_i = 1$. Let $r[j, k]$, where $1 \leq j \leq k \leq n$, be the root of an optimal binary search tree for the keys K_j, ..., K_k.

a. Show that there are optimal trees such that $r[j, k-1] \leq r[j, k] \leq r[j+1, k]$ whenever $1 \leq j < k \leq n$. Intuitively, this says that adding a new key at the right end of a sequence cannot cause the root of the optimal search tree to move to the left in the sequence, and similarly if the key is added to the left end of the sequence. (Hint: Use induction on $k - j$.)

b. Show that if these bounds are used to limit the search for $r[j, k]$ in Algorithm 6.10, then for each value of d the time to execute the "**for** j ..." loop is $O(n)$, so that Algorithm 6.10 so modified runs in time $O(n^2)$. (Hint: It will not work to get a single bound for the body of the "**for** j ..." loop, and then multiply it by n. Instead, the lengths of the ranges that must be searched for all values of j must be added together.)

44. Give an example of a distribution for which the probability-balanced tree is not the optimal binary search tree.

45. Show that the inequality for $B(n)$ given on page 205 implies that the balancing heuristic runs in linear time.

46. A heuristic for the construction of static search trees that turns out *not* to work very well is the "heaviest-first" heuristic: put the node of highest probability at the root, and then follow the same strategy recursively for the subtrees of the root.

a. Find an assignment of probabilities to the keys A, B, C for which this strategy does not yield the optimal tree.

b. Let $h \geq 2$, let $n = 2^h - 1$, let $\epsilon_1 > \cdots > \epsilon_n > 0$ be any monotonically decreasing sequence of positive real numbers such that $\sum_{i=1}^{n} \epsilon_i = 2^{-h}$, and let $p_i = 2^{-h} + \epsilon_i$ for each $i = 1, \ldots, n$. Show that the cost of the search tree constructed by the heaviest-first heuristic is $\Omega(n)$, whereas the cost of the optimal search tree is $O(\log n)$, so that the heaviest-first heuristic can actually produce trees that are exponentially more costly than the optimum.

47. A **lopsided** binary tree is one in which the cost of an edge to a left child need not equal the cost of an edge to a right child. To be precise, let α and β be fixed numbers and let T be a binary tree. The **cost** of a node N is the sum of the costs of the edges from the root to N, where edges to left children cost α and edges to right children cost β. The cost of the tree as a whole is the maximum cost of any external node. Show that the minimal-cost lopsided tree on n (internal) leaves has cost $C(n)$ in the range

$$\log_\rho(n+1) - \beta \leq C(n) \leq \log_\rho(n+1),$$

where ρ is that number in the range $1 < \rho \leq 2$ such that

$$\rho^{-\alpha} + \rho^{-\beta} = 1.$$

48. Explain how to construct a median split tree in time $O(n \log n)$, with special attention to the problem of finding all the necessary lexicographic medians.

References

A very readable presentation of the Move-to-Front and Transpose Heuristics can be found in

R. L. Rivest, "On Self-Organizing Sequential Search Heuristics," *Communications of the ACM* **19** (1976), pp. 63–67.

The analysis on page 179 that shows that the Move-To-Front Heuristic produces a list that is within a factor of 2 of optimal for search efficiency is actually not the best possible. It turns out that through a mathematically more sophisticated analysis it can be shown that the number of comparisons needed to search the list produced by the Move-To-Front Heuristic is no more than $\pi/2 \approx 1.57$ times the number of comparisons required by the optimal ordering. See

G. H. Gonnet, J. I. Munro, and H. Suwanda, "Toward Self-Organizing Linear Search," *Proceedings, 20th Annual IEEE Symposium on Foundations of Computer Science,* 1979, pp. 169–174

and

F. R. K. Chung, D. J. Hajela, and P. D. Seymour, "Self-Organizing Sequential Search and Hilbert's Inequalities," *Proceedings, 17th Annual ACM Symposium on Theory of Computing,* 1985, pp. 217–223.

The notion of "overwork" (Problem 11) is from

J. R. Bitner, "Heuristics that Dynamically Organize Data Structures," *SIAM Journal on Computing* **8** (1979), pp. 82–110.

Problem 20 on searching an infinite sorted table is from

J. L. Bentley and A. C. Yao, "An Almost Optimal Algorithm for Unbounded Searching," *Information Processing Letters* **5** (1976), pp. 82–87,

and the results of that paper were extended in

R. Beigel, "Unbounded Searching Algorithms," *SIAM Journal on Computing* **19** (1990), pp. 522–537.

For the analysis of the interpolation search algorithm, see

A. C. Yao and F. F. Yao, "The Complexity of Searching an Ordered Random Table," *Proceedings, 17th Annual IEEE Symposium on Foundations of Computer Science,* 1976, pp. 173–176;

Y. Perl, A. Itai, and H. Avni, "Interpolation Search—A Log Log N Search," *Communications of the ACM* **21** (1978), pp. 550–553;

and

G. H. Gonnet, L. D. Rogers, and J. A. George, "An Algorithmic and Complexity Analysis of Interpolation Search," *Acta Informatica* **13** (1980), pp. 39–52.

Problem 22 is addressed in

N. Santoro and J. B. Sidney, "Interpolation-Binary Search," *Information Processing Letters* **20** (1985), pp. 179–181.

Skip lists were developed by William Pugh in 1987. They are described in

W. Pugh, "Skip Lists: A Probabilistic Alternative to Balanced Trees," *Communications of the ACM* **33** (1990), pp. 668–676.

Padded lists (Problem 25) are from

W. R. Franklin, "Padded Lists: Set Operations in Expected $\theta(\log \log N)$ Time," *Information Processing Letters* **9** (1979), pp. 161–166.

The binary tree deletion algorithm (Algorithm 6.9 on page 200) was originally suggested by

T. N. Hibbard, "Some Combinatorial Properties of Certain Trees with Applications to Searching and Sorting," *Journal of the ACM* **9** (1962), pp. 13–28,

but it defied analysis until it was shown to yield trees of nonlogarithmic depth by

J. Culberson, "The Effect of Updates in Binary Search Trees," *Proceedings, 15th Annual ACM Symposium on Theory of Computing,* 1985, pp. 205–212.

The number of binary trees on a given number of nodes is calculated on page 54 of the book by Standish cited on page 45. $O(n^2)$ algorithms for the construction of optimal binary search trees were discovered by

T. C. Hu and A. C. Tucker, "Optimal Computer Search Trees and Variable-Length Alphabetic Codes," *SIAM Journal on Applied Mathematics* **21** (1971), pp. 514–532 *and*

D. E. Knuth, "Optimum Binary Search Trees," *Acta Informatica* **1** (1971), pp. 14–25.

The improvement described in Problem 43 from $O(n^3)$ to $O(n^2)$ running time is actually not a special feature of the construction of search trees, but an instance of a more general fact about dynamic programming that is explained in

F. F. Yao, "Speed-Up in Dynamic Programming," *SIAM Journal on Algebraic and Discrete Methods* **3** (1982), pp. 532–540.

The algorithm for construction of optimal binary search trees can be improved still further, so that it runs in time $O(n \log n)$; see pp. 173–180 of the book

T. C. Hu, *Combinatorial Algorithms*, Addison-Wesley Publishing Company, 1982,

or the paper

A. M. Garsia and M. L. Wachs, "A New Algorithm for Minimum Cost Binary Trees," *SIAM Journal on Computing* **6** (1977), pp. 622–642.

The balancing heuristic for static binary search trees is analyzed in

K. Mehlhorn, "Nearly Optimal Binary Search Trees," *Acta Informatica* **5** (1975), pp. 287–295;

this paper is also the source of Problem 46. The behavior of the balancing heuristic is also treated in

K. Mehlhorn, *Data Structures and Algorithms I: Sorting and Searching*, Springer-Verlag, 1984.

Median split trees are an invention of

B. A. Shiel, "Median Split Trees," *Communications of the ACM* **21** (1978), pp. 947–958.

Problem 47 is from

S. Kapoor and E. M. Reingold, "Optimum Lopsided Binary Trees," *Journal of the ACM* **36** (1989), pp. 573–590.

7

Tree Structures
for Dynamic Dictionaries

7.1 AVL TREES

This chapter deals with further tree implementations of dynamic dictionaries—that is, dictionaries with insertions and deletions, as well as lookups. The binary tree implementation analyzed in §6.4 is simple and elegant, but has the serious disadvantage of a worst-case $\Omega(n)$ running time for a single operation, because the height of a tree can be as large as $n-1$ if the n keys are inserted in increasing lexicographic order.

Several tree structures have been devised that permit worst-case running time of $O(\log n)$ for insertions, deletions, and lookups. The simplest of these are the *AVL trees*, so called after the Russian scientists Adel'son-Vel'skii and Landis who first studied them.

To understand the special structure of AVL trees, let us define, for any nonempty binary tree T,

$$LeftHeight(T) = \begin{cases} 0, & \text{if } \mathsf{LC}(T) = \Lambda; \\ 1 + Height(\mathsf{LC}(T)), & \text{otherwise.} \end{cases}$$

RightHeight is defined similarly. Also, for any node v of T, define *LeftHeight*(v) to be the *LeftHeight* of the subtree rooted at v, and similarly for *RightHeight*(v). Thus a leaf has *LeftHeight* and *RightHeight* both equal to 0, and the height of any node is the maximum of its *LeftHeight* and its *RightHeight*.

The **balance** of node v is *RightHeight*(v) − *LeftHeight*(v). T is an **AVL tree** if every node of T has balance −1, 0, or +1. Figure 7.1 shows some binary trees with the balance at each node; (a), (b), and (c) are AVL trees, while (d) and (e) are not.

These trees have the following two characteristics that make them attractive as data structures for search operations:

- every AVL tree with n nodes has height $O(\log n)$; and
- a node can be added to or deleted from an AVL tree with n nodes in time $O(\log n)$, while preserving the AVL property.

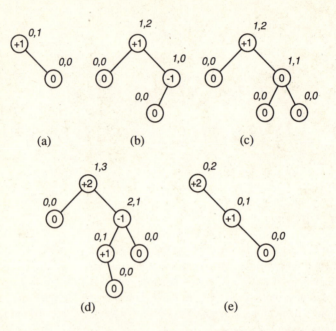

Figure 7.1 Binary trees with the *LeftHeight, RightHeight,* and balance of each node. The *LeftHeight* and *RightHeight* are the italic numerals above the node. The balance is the number inside the node. Trees (a), (b), and (c) are AVL trees; (d) and (e) are not.

The first characteristic implies that if a search tree is AVL, then any successful or unsuccessful search will take time $O(\log n)$. The second characteristic implies that items can be inserted into or removed from the tree in time $O(\log n)$. The first characteristic is stated more precisely as follows:

■ **THEOREM** *(AVL Tree Height)* Any AVL tree with n nodes has height less than $1.44 \lg n$.

PROOF We want to find an upper bound on the length h of the longest path in any n-node AVL tree. To turn the question around, fix h, and ask: what is the smallest n such that there is an AVL tree of height h with n nodes? Let W_h (for "worst") be the set of all AVL trees of height h that have as few nodes as possible, and let w_h be the number of nodes in any one of these trees. Thus $w_0 = 1$ and $w_1 = 2$. Let T be any tree in W_h, where $h \geq 2$, and let T_L and T_R be its left and right subtrees. Since T has height h, either T_L or T_R has height $h - 1$; without loss of generality, assume that T_R has height $h - 1$. Since T is AVL and both subtrees of an AVL tree are AVL trees, T_R is an AVL tree of height $h - 1$. Moreover, it must be a *worst* AVL tree of height $h - 1$, since otherwise it could be replaced by a smaller AVL tree of height $h - 1$ to yield an AVL tree of

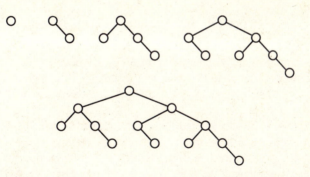

Figure 7.2 "Worst" AVL trees of heights 0 through 4. In these particular trees, the balance of each nonleaf is +1. The other members of W_h are obtained from these trees by swapping left and right subtrees of any nodes.

height h that is smaller than T. That is, $T_R \in W_{h-1}$. Similarly, since T is an AVL tree, T_L has height $h - 1$ or $h - 2$; but since T is supposed to be as small as possible, T_L must in fact be in W_{h-2}. Therefore

$$w_h = 1 + w_{h-2} + w_{h-1},$$

and since $w_0 = 1$ and $w_1 = 2$, the first few values of w_h are 1, 2, 4, 7, 12, 20, ... (Figure 7.2 shows a representative member of each W_h for $h = 0$, 1, 2, 3, 4.) In general, it can be shown by induction (Problem 7(a)) that

$$w_h = F_{h+3} - 1$$

where F_i is the ith Fibonacci number (see page 26). Since $F_i > \phi^i/\sqrt{5} - 1$, where $\phi = (1 + \sqrt{5})/2$ (Problem 7(b)), the number of nodes in an AVL tree of height h, say n, satisfies $n \geq w_h > \phi^{h+3}/\sqrt{5} - 2$, or

$$h < \log_\phi(\sqrt{5}(n + 2)/\phi^3).$$

Therefore $h < \log_\phi n = \lg n / \lg \phi < 1.44 \lg n$ if $\sqrt{5}(n + 2)/\phi^3 < n$, or in other words if $n > 2\sqrt{5}/(\phi^3 - \sqrt{5}) = \sqrt{5}$ (Problem 7(c)). This establishes the Theorem for all $n \geq 3$; the $n = 1$ and $n = 2$ cases can be checked individually. □

It remains to show that insertion or deletion of a node in an n-node AVL tree can be accomplished in $O(\log n)$ time.

Insertion

An AVL tree is represented internally as a standard binary tree, with each node having LC and RC fields; in addition, each node has a **Balance** field. Since the balance of an AVL tree node is either -1, 0, or $+1$, two bits are sufficient for the balance field.* Using this data structure, insertion can be accomplished as follows:

1. Following the standard binary tree insertion method, trace a path from the root and insert the node as a new leaf. Remember the path traversed.
2. Retrace the path from the new leaf back towards the root, updating the balances along the way.
3. Should a node be encountered for which the balance becomes ±2, readjust the subtrees of that node and its descendants—by a method described later. The result is an equivalent binary search tree (that is, one with the same keys and still obeying the binary search tree property) with balance -1, 0, or $+1$ at each node.

Figure 7.3(a,b) shows the simplest case; a node that was out of balance becomes perfectly balanced due to an increase in height in one of its subtrees. In this case there is no need to update the balance of the node's ancestors, since its height has not changed and only its height affects the balance of its ancestors. Figure 7.3(c,d) shows a slightly more complicated situation; a node that had been in balance becomes unbalanced due to an increase in the height of one of its children. In this case the node's height increases, so the node's parent (and possibly other ancestors) must be updated as well.

It turns out that there are only two ways that a node with balance out of range can arise. These two cases, and the transformations to correct them, are illustrated in Figure 7.4 and Figure 7.5. In Figure 7.4(a) node A of height $h+2$ has balance $+1$ because its left subtree has height h, and its right child C has two subtrees of height h. When a node is inserted into the right subtree of C in such a way as to increase the height of that subtree to $h+1$, the balance of A becomes $+2$ (Figure 7.4(b)). An attempt to restore the balances by (for example) exchanging the subtrees T_1 and T_3 will not work since it would rearrange the positions of the keys in a way that would destroy the search tree property. However, making A the left child of C and moving the left subtree of C to become the right subtree of A leaves the balance of both A and C at 0, while preserving the order in which the keys would be enumerated during an inorder traversal of the tree. Using a parenthetical notation for the structure of the tree (like that in Figure 4.7 on page 104), this operation changes the structure $(T_1A(T_2CT_3))$ to $((T_1AT_2)CT_3)$. This action is called a **single left rotation**; note that, once the nodes to be altered have been determined, only three pointer operations need to be carried out to effect the rotation (one on the appropriate child pointer of the parent of A). Of course, there is a completely symmetric case in which the balance of a node changes from -1 to -2 because the height of the left subtree of its left child increases by one; the operation to correct this is called a **single right rotation**.

---

*Actually, with cleverness all the balance information can be represented in just a single bit per node—see Problem 6.

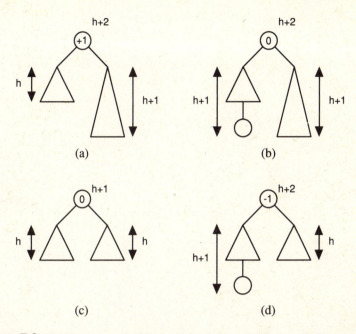

Figure 7.3 Simple cases of AVL insertion. (a) and (b) A node becomes balanced; no change to its height. (c) and (d) A balanced node becomes unbalanced, but only to −1; since its height increases, its parent's balance must also be updated.

In the only other case node A again has height $h+2$ and balance $+1$ because its left subtree has height h and its right child has two subtrees of height h (Figure 7.5(a)). However, in this case the balance of A becomes $+2$ because the *left* child, B, of C increases in height to $h+1$ (Figure 7.5(b)). There are two subcases. We illustrate only that in which the insertion happens in the right subtree of B; in the other case, in which the insertion happens in the left subtree of B, the same actions are taken, but the balances of the nodes wind up slightly different. Nodes are brought back to legal balance by a sequence of maneuvers that can be pictured as a single right rotation at C (Figure 7.5(c)) followed by a single left rotation at A (Figure 7.5(d)). Accordingly this rearrangement is called a **double rotation** (an RL rotation, in this case). The parenthetical version of this transformation is to change $(T_1A((T_2BT_3)CT_4))$ to $((T_1AT_2)B(T_3CT_4))$. Naturally there is a symmetric case in which a double LR rotation is called for.

Let us examine more closely step (2) in the algorithm sketched on page 222, the updating of balances along the path back from the leaf. Call the first node reached along this path that has—prior to any changes—balance ±1 the **critical node**. (There may not be any critical node.) Any node between the critical node (or the root, if there is no critical node) and the new leaf had balance 0, and acquires balance ±1: the balance becomes $+1$ if the path goes to the node's right

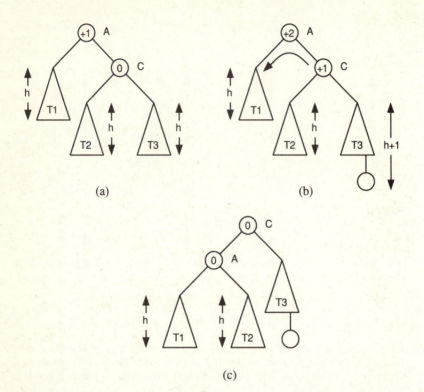

Figure 7.4 Single left rotation after insertion in an AVL tree. In actual
practice the middle stage, part (b) of the figure, is skipped, and the tree
is transformed directly from (a) to (c), so there is never a time when a
balance of +2 must be recorded in the tree.

child, and becomes −1 if the path goes to the node's left child. The balance
of the critical node becomes either 0 or ±2. If the balance of the critical node
was +1 and the path goes to the node's left child, or if the balance was −1 and
the path goes to the node's right child, then the balance becomes 0. On the
other hand, if the balance of the critical node was +1 and the path goes to the
node's right child, or the balance was −1 and the path goes to the left child,
then the balance becomes ±2 and the situation is one of those illustrated in
Figure 7.4 or 7.5 (or their mirror images, or the variant of the case of Figure 7.5
in which the insertion is in the left subtree of B). Notice that in each of these
cases the height of the critical node does not change, once the rotations have
been carried out, so no rebalancing needs to be done above the critical node.
Consequently, only the portion of the path from the critical node to the leaf
need have its balances readjusted after an insertion; and if a rotation maneuver
(single or double) is needed anywhere, it is needed only at one point, namely,
at the critical node.

It follows from all this that the algorithm implied in (1)–(3) can actually be

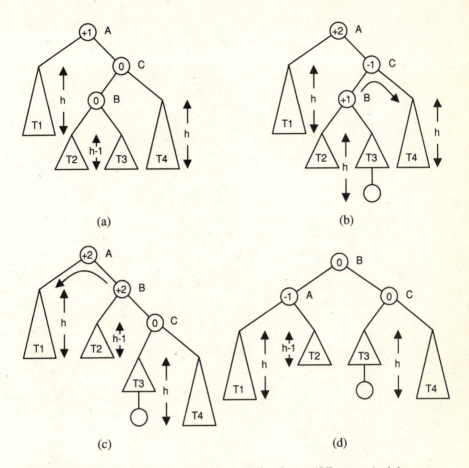

(a)   (b)

(c)   (d)

Figure 7.5 Double RL rotation after insertion in an AVL tree. A right
rotation around node C is followed by a left rotation around A.

implemented much more simply. As the path is traced from the root towards the
insertion point, instead of remembering the entire path, simply remember the
critical node; this is the most recently seen node with balance ± 1 (any higher
node with balance ± 1 can be forgotten when a new one is discovered). After
the insertion has been made at a new leaf, trace the path down from the critical
node (or from the root of the tree, if there is no critical node) a second time,
using the key inserted to direct the search as was done during the first search,
and using the rules just described to adjust balances, and perhaps carry out one
rotation maneuver. Since the path has length $O(\log n)$, the time required is
$O(\log n)$. Instead of remembering the whole path, we remember just one node,
so the memory used is a constant independent of n.

Algorithm 7.1 is the AVL tree insertion algorithm in full detail. Initially,
K is the key value and I is the associated information to be inserted into the

procedure *AVLTreeInsert*(**key** K, **info** I, **locative** T):
$\{T$ is a locative that points to the root of the tree$\}$
$\quad P \leftarrow T$ $\qquad\qquad\qquad\qquad\quad$ $\{P$ is a locative used for tracing the path$\}$
$\quad CritNodeFound \leftarrow$ **false** $\qquad\qquad$ $\{$No critical node found so far$\}$
$\quad$ **while** $P \neq \Lambda$ **and** Key$(P) \neq K$ **do**
$\qquad$ **if** Balance$(P) \neq 0$ **then**
$\qquad\qquad A \leftarrow P$ $\qquad\qquad\qquad$ $\{$Locative A points to critical node$\}$
$\qquad\qquad CritNodeFound \leftarrow$ **true** $\qquad\qquad$ $\{$A critical node exists$\}$
$\qquad$ **if** $K <$ Key(P) **then** $P \leftarrow$ LC(P) **else** $P \leftarrow$ RC(P)
$\quad$ **if** $P \neq \Lambda$ **then** $\qquad\qquad$ $\{K$ is already in tree, just update Info$\}$
$\qquad$ Info$(P) \leftarrow I$
$\qquad$ **return**
$\quad P \Leftarrow NewCell$(Node) $\qquad\qquad\qquad\qquad$ $\{$Insert new leaf$\}$
$\quad$ Key$(P) \leftarrow K$; Info$(P) \leftarrow I$; LC$(P) \leftarrow$ RC$(P) \leftarrow \Lambda$; Balance$(P) \leftarrow 0$
$\{$Rotate and adjust balances at critical node, if any$\}$
$\{C$ is a locative that points to a child of the critical node$\}$
$\quad$ **if not** *CritNodeFound* **then** $R \leftarrow T$ $\qquad\qquad$ $\{$No critical node$\}$
$\quad$ **else**
$\qquad (d_1, C) \leftarrow K :: A$
$\qquad$ **if** Balance$(A) \neq d_1$ **then** $\qquad\qquad$ $\{d_1 \neq 0$, no rotation necessary$\}$
$\qquad\qquad$ Balance$(A) \leftarrow 0$
$\qquad\qquad R \leftarrow P$
$\qquad$ **else** $\qquad\qquad\qquad$ $\{$Balance$(A) = d_1$, rotation necessary$\}$
$\qquad\qquad (d_2, B) \leftarrow K :: C$ $\qquad$ $\{B$ is child of C in search direction$\}$
$\qquad\qquad$ **if** $d_2 = d_1$ **then** $\qquad\qquad$ $\{d_2 \neq 0$, single rotation$\}$
$\qquad\qquad\qquad$ Balance$(A) \leftarrow 0$
$\qquad\qquad\qquad R \leftarrow B$
$\qquad\qquad\qquad Rotate(A, -d_1)$
$\qquad\qquad$ **else** $\qquad\qquad\qquad\qquad$ $\{d_2 = -d_1$, double rotation$\}$
$\qquad\qquad\qquad (d_3, R) \leftarrow K :: B$
$\qquad\qquad\qquad$ **if** $d_3 = d_2$ **then**
$\qquad\qquad\qquad\qquad$ Balance$(A) \leftarrow 0$
$\qquad\qquad\qquad\qquad$ Balance$(C) \leftarrow d_1$
$\qquad\qquad\qquad$ **else if** $d_3 = -d_2$ **then** Balance$(A) \leftarrow d_2$
$\qquad\qquad\qquad$ **else** Balance$(A) \leftarrow 0$ $\qquad$ $\{d_3 = 0, B = R$ is a leaf$\}$
$\qquad\qquad\qquad Rotate(C, -d_2)$
$\qquad\qquad\qquad Rotate(A, -d_1)$
$\quad$ $\{$Adjust balances of nodes of balance 0 along the rest of the path$\}$
$\quad$ **while** Key$(R) \neq K$ **do** (Balance$(R), R) \leftarrow K :: R$

Algorithm 7.1 Insertion in an AVL tree.

if $K = \text{Key}(P)$ **then**
    $d \leftarrow 0$
    $Q \leftarrow P$
else if $K < \text{Key}(P)$ **then**
    $d \leftarrow -1$
    $Q \leftarrow \text{LC}(P)$
else
    $d \leftarrow +1$
    $Q \leftarrow \text{RC}(P)$

Algorithm 7.2 Code to implement the operation $(d, Q) \leftarrow K :: P$, which compares key K to the key stored at node P of a binary tree, and sets Q to P or its left or right child, depending on whether K is at P or should be sought in one of P's subtrees. At the same time the number d is set to 0, -1, or $+1$. This operation is used in the AVL tree insertion algorithm (Algorithm 7.1).

procedure *Rotate*(**locative** P, **integer** d):
{Rotate around P in direction $d = \pm 1$}
    if $d = -1$ **then** {Rotate left}

$$\begin{pmatrix} P \\ \text{RC}(P) \\ \text{LC}(\text{RC}(P)) \end{pmatrix} \Leftarrow \begin{pmatrix} \text{RC}(P) \\ \text{LC}(\text{RC}(P)) \\ P \end{pmatrix}$$

    else {Rotate right}

$$\begin{pmatrix} P \\ \text{LC}(P) \\ \text{RC}(\text{LC}(P)) \end{pmatrix} \Leftarrow \begin{pmatrix} \text{LC}(P) \\ \text{RC}(\text{LC}(P)) \\ P \end{pmatrix}$$

Algorithm 7.3 Single rotation around a node in a binary tree.

AVL tree, and the locative T points to the root of the tree. In order to treat various cases uniformly, the numerical values -1 and $+1$ are used to represent the left and right directions, respectively. Algorithm 7.1 uses two auxiliaries $K :: P$ and *Rotate*. The construction $(d, Q) \leftarrow K :: P$ is an abbreviation for the code of Algorithm 7.2, which assigns to d a number indicating the direction of search for key K through node P, and assigns to Q the corresponding child of P. *Rotate*(P, d) carries out a single rotation in direction d at node P; here P is passed in as a locative. The details are given in Algorithm 7.3.

    In Algorithm 7.1 A is a locative that points to the critical node, if there is a critical node; the boolean flag *CritNodeFound* indicates whether a critical node was discovered, and the value of A is therefore meaningful. If there is a critical node, the number d_1 indicates the direction the search path follows through the critical node—to its right child if $d_1 = +1$, and to its left child if $d_1 = -1$. The pointer C points to that child. A rotation is needed if the balance of the critical node is the same as d_1. The direction of the search path through the child C is d_2, and the child of C in that direction is B. A single rotation is required if d_2 is the same as d_1, and a double rotation is needed if d_2 is the opposite direction from d_1. In the case of a double rotation, d_3 is the direction the search path follows through the grandchild of the critical node. During rotation, C and B refer to the child and grandchild of the critical node along the search path. Node R is the first node below the critical node not involved in the rotation; nodes along the search path from R down to (but not including) the node inserted have balance 0 before the insertion but wind up with balance ± 1 after the insertion.

Deletion

To delete a node from an AVL tree, first follow the standard binary tree deletion algorithm (Algorithm 6.9 on page 200), deleting the node itself if it is a leaf, replacing it by its child if it has only one child, and otherwise replacing it by its inorder successor and deleting the inorder successor. If the node itself is deleted, the balance of the node's parent changes; if the inorder successor is deleted, the balance of the parent of the inorder successor changes. For example, Figure 7.6(b) shows the result of deleting the node with key B from the AVL tree of Figure 7.6(a); the balance of its parent, F, changes from 0 to +1. Figure 7.6(c) shows the result of deleting the key at the root, F, from the tree of part (a); its inorder successor, M, becomes the root and the balance of M's former parent, P, is changed.

   If the balance of the parent changes from 0 to ± 1 then the algorithm terminates; this is the case in part (b) of Figure 7.6. On the other hand, if the balance of the parent changes from ± 1 to 0, as in parts (c) and (d), then the height of the parent decreases and the balance of the parent's parent is affected. Similarly, Figure 7.6(e) and (f) show a case in which the balance of the parent changes from ± 1 to ± 2, forcing a rotation; when the rotation has been completed, the height of the subtree has decreased and its parent's balance must be changed. In sum, if the balance of the parent was ± 1, it changes to 0 or ± 2 and it may be necessary to repeat the rebalancing process on the grandparent. Indeed, it may be necessary in the worst case to rebalance, and even rotate at, *every* node along the path back to the root; this will happen, for example, if the shallowest leaf in any one of the three largest trees of Figure 7.2 on page 221 is deleted. Thus the entire search path must be remembered in case of deletion, and must be retraced until a node of balance 0 is encountered; the balance of that node becomes ± 1, but its height does not change so no further rebalancing is necessary. Even though $\Omega(\log n)$ rotations may be necessary when deleting a node from an n-node AVL tree, the total time required is only $O(\log n)$ since each rotation takes constant time.

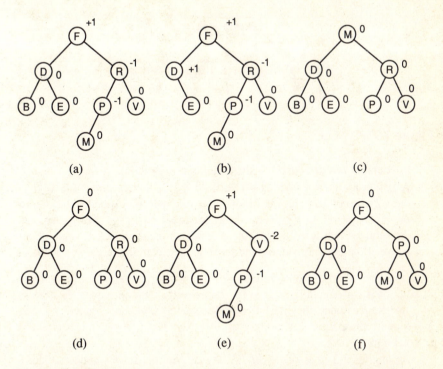

Figure 7.6 Deletion from an AVL tree. (a) An AVL tree; (b) the result of deleting B from the tree of part (a); (c) the result of deleting F from the tree of part (a); (d) the result of deleting M from the tree of part (a); (e) and (f) the result of deleting R from the tree of part (a). In the last case a rotation is needed to restore the AVL property.

7.2 2-3 TREES AND B-TREES

2-3 Trees

AVL tree algorithms try to keep a binary tree well-balanced by keeping the maximum distance from a node to external leaves in its left and right subtrees roughly the same—differing by at most 1. Of course, if these distances were identical at each node then the tree would be perfectly balanced, but then it would have to have exactly $2^h - 1$ nodes for some h. 2-3 tree algorithms achieve a similar effect by a different strategy. In a 2-3 tree a node that is not a leaf may have either 2 or 3 children. By suitably arranging nodes of both kinds, it is possible to construct a search tree that is "perfectly balanced"—that is, all leaves have the same depth—and contains any desired number of leaves.

In a **2-3 tree**,

1. All leaves are at the same depth and contain 1 or 2 keys.
2. An interior node (a node that is not a leaf) either
   a. contains one key and has two children (a **2-node**) or

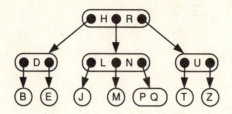

Figure 7.7 A 2-3 tree.

    b. contains two keys and has three children (a **3-node**).

3. A key in an interior node is between (in the dictionary order) the keys in
   the subtrees of its adjacent children. If the node is a 2-node, this is just
   the binary search tree property; in a 3-node the two keys split the keys in
   the subtrees into three ranges, those less than the smaller key value, those
   between the two key values, and those greater than the larger key value.

Note that the "2" in "2-node" refers to the number of children, not the number
of keys. It is convenient to refer to leaves, as well as interior nodes, as 2-nodes
or 3-nodes; in essence, they have two or three empty children. Figure 7.7 shows
a 2-3 tree representing a dictionary of 14 keys. The tree has 7 leaves and 4
internal nodes.

    Among all 2-3 trees of height h, the one with the fewest nodes is one in
which all interior nodes have one key and two children. Since all leaves must
have the same depth, the tree is perfect and $n = 2^{h+1} - 1$; so in this case the
height $h = \lfloor \lg n \rfloor$. (Here n is the number of nodes or the number of keys, which
are the same.) On the other hand the largest 2-3 tree of height h occurs when
all interior nodes have two keys and three children; in this case the number of
nodes is $\sum_{i=0}^{h} 3^i = (3^{h+1} - 1)/2$. Since there are two keys in each node, the
number of keys is then $n = 3^{h+1} - 1$, so that $h = \lfloor \log_3 n \rfloor$.

    2-3 trees are easy to draw on paper but are awkward to manipulate in
computer programs, because 2-nodes and 3-nodes have to be handled as separate
cases in many algorithms. Programmers in higher-level languages are inclined
to use "variant records" or "union types" to represent nodes, but these can waste
memory by requiring the same storage space for a 2-node as for a 3-node. In
this section we avoid such awkward programming constructs by giving only
outlines of the algorithms, not detailed pseudocode. In the next subsection we
shall outline an elegant but nonobvious concrete implementation of trees like
these.

    Since the height of a 2-3 tree with n nodes is at most $\lfloor \lg n \rfloor$, it follows
that 2-3 trees can be searched in time $O(\log n)$ by an algorithm that is a simple
generalization of search in a binary search tree. (Perhaps 3-nodes take a bit
longer to search through than 2-nodes, but the time to search a single node is
bounded by a constant.)

Insertion in a 2-3 tree tries to take advantage of the "extra room" that may exist in a leaf, if it has only one key. Only if this fails is a new node added to the tree. The following steps constitute a rough outline of the procedure.

1. Search for the leaf where the key belongs. Remember the path that has been followed.
2. If there is room (that is, if there is only one key in the leaf) add the key to the leaf and stop. (This is the applicable case if F is added to the tree of Figure 7.7.)
3. If there is no room in the node (that is, it is already a 3-node) split it into two 2-nodes—with the first and third keys—and pass the middle key up to the parent to separate the two keys left behind. That is, one child of the parent is replaced by two children and an additional key. (Refer to step (5) if there is no parent node.)
4. If the parent was a 2-node, it has now changed from a 2-node into a 3-node and the algorithm stops. Otherwise, we are trying to add a third key to a node that already has two; return to step (3) to split the parent node in the same way.
5. This process is repeated up the tree until there is room for a key or the root must be split. In the latter case a new root node is created (a 2-node) and the height of the tree increases by one.

To illustrate the creation of new nodes, consider the insertion of key O in the tree of Figure 7.7. The search directs us to the leaf containing P and Q (Figure 7.8(a)). This node is split; the middle key, P, is passed up to the parent (Figure 7.8(b)). This violates the 2-3 condition since the parent node now has three keys and four children. This node is split as well, into two 2-nodes, and the middle key, N, is passed on up to *its* parent (Figure 7.8(c)). Once again there is insufficient room for the additional key, so the root is split and a new root is created (Figure 7.8(d)).

Deletion presents the inverse problems of insertion: nodes can underflow, in other words be left with no keys. When this happens, we can correct the situation by moving a key (and possibly a child pointer) out of a sibling, if some sibling is a 3-node. If each sibling already has but one key, we try to consolidate two siblings with a key from the parent to reduce by one the number of children of the parent; however this may cause the parent to underflow and the process to be repeated. More precisely:

1. If the key to be deleted is in a leaf, then remove it from the leaf. If the key to be deleted is not in a leaf, then the key's inorder successor is in a leaf; replace the key by its inorder successor and remove the inorder successor from the leaf in which it occurs.
2. At this stage a key has been removed from a node N. If N still has one key, the algorithm ends. Otherwise, if N now has no keys:

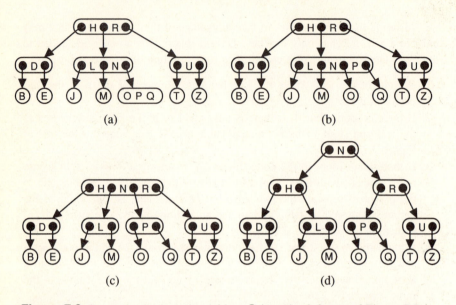

(a)   (b)

(c)   (d)

Figure 7.8 Stages in the insertion of key O into the 2-3 tree of Figure 7.7.
(a) Overflow of a leaf, which causes (b) splitting of the leaf, with key P
passing up to the parent. This key overflows the parent, causing (c) splitting of this node, with key N passing up to its parent, the root. The root
overflows as well, causing (d) the root to be split and a new root to be
created, and increasing the height of the tree as a whole. (The overflowing 4-nodes do not actually get created; they are shown only by way of
illustration.)

   a. If N is the root, delete it. In this case, if N had no child, the tree
      becomes empty; otherwise, if N had a child, the child becomes the root.
   b. (We now know that N has at least one sibling.) If N has a sibling N'
      that is immediately to its left or right and has two keys, then let S be
      the key in the parent of N and N' that separates them. Move S to N,
      and replace it in the parent by the key of N' that is adjacent to N. If N
      and N' are interior nodes, then also move one child of N' to be a child
      of N. N and N' wind up with one key each, instead of 0 and 2. This
      completes the algorithm in this case.
   c. (We now know that N has a sibling N' immediately to its left or right
      that has only one key.) Let P be the parent of N and N', and S the
      key in P that separates them. Consolidate S and the one key in N' into
      a new 3-node, which replaces both N and N'; this reduces by one both
      the number of keys in P and the number of children of P. (If N and N'
      are interior nodes, then they have 2 and 1 children, so the new node has
      3 children.) Let $N \leftarrow P$, and repeat step (2).

   For example, if M is deleted from the tree of Figure 7.7, case 2(b) applies;
key N is moved to the leaf, key P replaces N in the parent, and the tree of

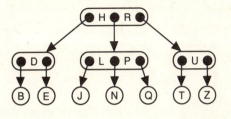

(a)

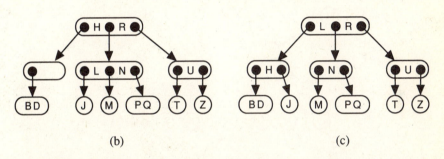

(b)   (c)

Figure 7.9 Deletion from a 2-3 tree. (a) Result of deleting M from the tree
of Figure 7.7. (b) and (c) Stages in the deletion of E from the tree of
Figure 7.7.

Figure 7.9(a) results. On the other hand, if key E is deleted from the tree
of Figure 7.7, then case 2(c) applies on the first iteration; keys B and D are
consolidated into a new node, causing the parent to underflow (Figure 7.9(b)).
On the second iteration case 2(b) applies; a key and a child are borrowed from
the parent's sibling (the node with keys L and N), and the tree of Figure 7.9(c)
results.

Since the work to be performed at each node requires only constant time,
the total time required for a deletion is at worst proportional to the length of the
longest path, and is therefore $O(\log n)$.

Red-Black Trees

We mentioned earlier that programs to manipulate 2-3 trees are rather awkward
because of the multiplicity of cases that must be handled. (Indeed, this is
the reason we resorted to a less formal notation for our account of 2-3 tree
algorithms.) In this section we present a binary tree structure that provides a
straightforward implementation of 2-3 trees.

We represent 2-3 trees by means of *red-black trees*. A **red-black tree**
is a binary search tree in which the nodes and edges are of two colors, Red
and Black. The color of the root is always black, and the color of any edge
connecting a parent to a child is the same as the color of the child node; in
deference to the difficulties of color printing we use heavy lines to represent

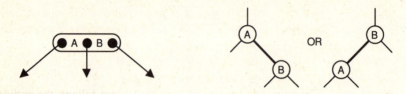

Figure 7.10 A 3-node, and the corresponding substructures of a red-black tree.

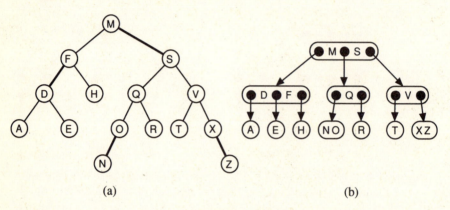

Figure 7.11 A red-black tree and the corresponding 2-3 tree.

red and lighter lines to represent black. The coloring of nodes and edges of a red-black tree obeys the following constraints:

1. On any path from the root to a leaf, the number of black edges is the same.
2. A red node that is not a leaf has two black children.
3. A black node that is not a leaf has either
   a. two black children; or
   b. one red child and one black child; or
   c. a single child, which is a red leaf.

If the pairs of nodes of a red-black tree that are connected by red edges are coalesced into single nodes, the result is a 2-3 tree. Constraints (2) and (3) ensure that no more than two nodes can be coalesced into one in this way, and that in the coalesced tree there are no nodes with only one child; and constraint (1) ensures that all leaves of the resulting tree have the same depth. Conversely, replacing the 3-nodes of a 2-3 tree by the configurations shown in Figure 7.10 turns it into a red-black tree. Figure 7.11 shows a red-black tree and the corresponding 2-3 tree; in the red-black tree all maximal paths contain two black edges, and the 2-3 tree has height 2.

The height of a red-black tree is at most twice the height of the corresponding 2-3 tree, by constraint (2). Therefore the logarithmic-time operations on 2-3 trees will be logarithmic-time on the red-black implementations of those trees, provided that we can develop constant-time implementations of the various operations on 2-3 tree nodes, such as splitting.

The 2-3 tree *LookUp* operation is implemented for a red-black tree by ordinary binary tree search, ignoring colors entirely.

Insertion into the red-black representation of a 2-3 tree follows the outline presented earlier for insertion into a 2-3 tree. First the tree is searched, starting from the root, for the Λ child where the insertion should occur; a stack is used to record the path. When the frontier of the tree is reached, a new binary node is created and inserted in the tree, and it is colored red in an effort to make it part of the same 2-3 tree node as its parent. Two cases then arise, depending on the color of the node's parent.

If the parent is black, then two subcases must be distinguished. If the parent's other child is black or empty, then the situation is as shown in Figure 7.12(a), or its mirror image. A 3-node has been successfully formed, and the insertion algorithm terminates. (The lowest pointers are shown as black; they will actually be empty if we are at the frontier of the tree, but as will be evident in a moment these configurations can also arise higher in the tree.) But if the parent's other child is red (Figure 7.12(b)), then constraint (3) has been violated. In this case we rectify matters simply by recoloring the edges as shown, without changing the structure of the tree at all: change both children from red to black, and change the parent from black to red. After changing the parent to red, we must check whether the implied coalescence of that node with *its* parent is legal. Note that the effect of the recoloring shown in Figure 7.12(b) is to change a node with three keys into two nodes with one key each, while increasing the size of the parent 2-3 tree node; in other words, it is a step in the splitting process of 2-3 tree insertion.

On the other hand, if the parent is red, then it cannot be the root, and the configuration looks like Figure 7.12(c) or 7.12(d), or their mirror images; the grandparent itself must be black, since otherwise the grandparent would have violated constraint (2) even before the insertion. These configurations can be transformed into that of Figure 7.12(b) by single or double rotations, respectively, exactly the maneuvers used to rebalance AVL tree nodes, and the process of splitting by recoloring can then continue as before.

Note that none of the transformations shown in Figure 7.12 changes the number of black edges on a path, so they preserve constraint (1) as well as (2) and (3). The "black-height" of the tree (the number of black edges on any path from the root to a leaf, which is the height of the corresponding 2-3 tree) increases only in the case that transformation of Figure 7.12(b) is applied at the root. The root remains black by fiat, but an additional black edge has been added to each path in the tree. This corresponds to splitting the root of the 2-3 tree and thus increasing the tree's height.

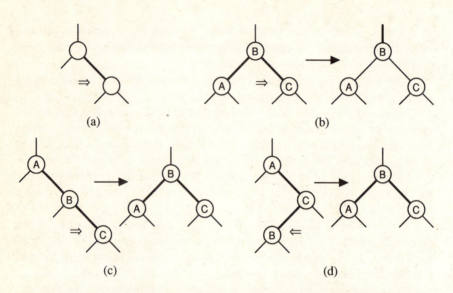

Figure 7.12 Possible situations when a node is reddened in a red-black tree. The node that has just been reddened is indicated by a double-shafted arrow ⇒. (a) The parent is black and does not have another red child; a legal configuration. (b) The parent is black and the sibling is also red; rectify by recoloring, then examine the effect of reddening the parent. (c) and (d) The parent is red (but the grandparent is black); transform into case (b) by a single or double rotation.

Algorithm 7.4 is the complete red-black tree insertion algorithm. Red-black trees are represented interally by means of records that have, in addition to the two child fields LC and RC, a one-bit field Color that has two possible values, Red and Black. While inserting a node, we remember on the stack locatives that point to the nodes that will have to be changed in case of a rotation. For convenience the direction of descent through each node is recorded on the stack as a number together with the node, −1 for left and +1 for right. This algorithm uses the *Rotate* procedure of Algorithm 7.3 on page 227, as well as the comparison operation $(d, P) \leftarrow K :: Q$ used in describing the AVL tree algorithms.

(a, b)-**Trees and B-Trees**

The basic idea in the design of the 2-3 trees discussed above is to introduce some flexibility in the size of individual nodes in order to achieve uniformity in the depth of the leaves. In an (a, b)-tree we introduce even more flexibility, so that the size of a node can approximate the size of some naturally determined storage unit, such as a disk block.

If $a \geq 2$ and $b \geq 2a - 1$, then an (a, b)-**tree** is a tree, each of whose nodes either is a leaf or has c children for some c such that $a \leq c \leq b$; moreover, all

procedure *RedBlackTreeInsert*(**key** K, **info** I, **locative** P):
{Initially P points to the root of the tree}
    $S \leftarrow MakeEmptyStack(\,)$ {S is a stack that remembers the search path}
    while $P \neq \Lambda$ **and** Key(P) $\neq K$ **do**
        $Push(P, S)$
        $(d, P) \leftarrow K :: P$
        $Push(d, S)$
    if $P \neq \Lambda$ **then**
        Info(P) $\leftarrow I$
        return
    $P \Leftarrow NewCell($Node$)$
    Key(P) $\leftarrow K$; Info(P) $\leftarrow I$
    LC(P) $\leftarrow$ RC(P) $\leftarrow \Lambda$; Color(P) $\leftarrow$ Red
    repeat forever
        if *IsEmptyStack*(S) **then**
            Color(P) $\leftarrow$ Black   {Root remains black}
            return
        {P is red. Q, R are locatives pointing to P's parent and grandparent}
        $d \leftarrow Pop(S)$; $Q \leftarrow Pop(S)$
        if Color(Q) $=$ Red **then**
            {Q is red, so it is not the root and stack is not empty}
            $d' \leftarrow Pop(S)$; $R \leftarrow Pop(S)$
            if $d = d'$ **then**   {Single rotation}
                Color(P) $\leftarrow$ Black
                $Rotate(R, -d)$
            else   {Double rotation}
                Color(Q) $\leftarrow$ Black
                $Rotate(Q, d)$
                $Rotate(R, -d)$
            $P \leftarrow R$
        else   {Q is black, $C \leftarrow$ the other child of Q}
            if $d = +1$ **then** $C \leftarrow$ LC(Q) **else** $C \leftarrow$ RC(Q)
            if $C = \Lambda$ **or** Color(C) $=$ Black **then return**
            Color(C) $\leftarrow$ Color(P) $\leftarrow$ Black
            Color(Q) $\leftarrow$ Red
            $P \leftarrow Q$

Algorithm 7.4 Insertion into a red-black tree representing a 2-3 tree.

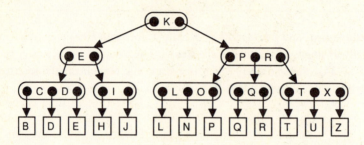

Figure 7.13 A (2,3)-tree, with all keys in external leaves.

leaves have the same depth. The constraint on the number of children of a node may be violated at the root, which may have anywhere from 2 to b children.*

When $a = 2$ and $b = 3$, a (2,3)-tree is very much like what we have heretofore called a 2-3 tree. However, we make one important change, for consistency with the way (a, b)-trees are generally used: we regard the keys and any associated data as stored exclusively in the leaves; the interior nodes simply provide an **index** to aid in locating the appropriate leaf. Thus each leaf contains but a single key (we draw them as squares, to emphasize that they are external to the tree structure), and the search tree property for internal nodes is

> If key value K is stored in an interior node between pointers to subtrees T and T', then every key in (a leaf of) T is less than or equal to K, and every key in (a leaf of) T' is greater than K.

Thus a key value in a leaf may occur in an interior node as well, but in the interior node it appears without any associated data and is used only to send the search in the right direction. Conversely, the key values appearing in the interior nodes need not be values that actually occur in the dictionary. For example, if the greatest dictionary item in one subtree is insect and the smallest in the adjacent subtree is insert, the separating key value might be insed since insect $\leq$ insed $<$ insert in the standard lexicographic order. Figure 7.13 shows a (2,3)-tree index for the keys in the 2-3 tree of Figure 7.9(a).

The height of an (a, b)-tree that stores n keys is at most $\lfloor \log_a n \rfloor + 1$, so the time to search an (a, b)-tree is logarithmic in its size provided that a and b are regarded as constants. One may ask, however, what purpose is served by considering large values of a and b, since the time to search *within* a node will be larger when the node itself is larger. The answer is that (a, b)-trees with large a and b (in the hundreds, say) are useful structures for external storage of data, on a disk, for example. On such devices it is fairly expensive to access the device to read or write data, but once an access is made, an entire block consisting of hundreds or thousands of bytes is read or written at once and can

---

*Two extreme cases must also be allowed: an empty tree, and a tree consisting of just a single leaf, are also (a, b)-trees.

be searched relatively quickly. Blocks are, moreover, of some fixed size, which is a parameter of the device hardware. In order to take advantage of the "block transfer" character of access to such an external device, b is chosen as large as possible so that a b-node will fit in a single block. (Fixed block size also argues for using the tree as an index, rather than storing the dictionary values themselves in the interior nodes, since the additional information stored along with them would take up space and lower the possible value of b.) And to keep the height of the tree as small as possible (that is, to minimize the number of accesses required to locate a key) a is chosen as large as possible. A **B-tree** of order b is an (a, b)-tree such that $b = 2a - 1$. To get a rough idea of the performance that can be achieved with trees of this kind, suppose that $a = 100$ and $b = 199$; since $\log_{100} 10^6 = 3$, any record in a dictionary of a million items can then be found with only four accesses to the external device (including one to read the leaf).

The algorithm to insert key K and its associated information in an (a, b)-tree is then as follows:

Search for the external node where the record with key K belongs. Let P be the parent node. Create a new leaf node containing K and its associated information, and add to P a pointer to this new leaf node, together with an appropriate key value to separate this leaf from its neighbor. If P still has at most b children, the algorithm terminates.

while P has $b + 1$ children **do**

> **if** P is the root **then**
>
>> Create a new root, Q, whose only child is P
>
> **else**
>
>> Let Q be the parent of P.
>
> Put the last $\lceil (b + 1)/2 \rceil$ children of P into a new node P', leaving the first $\lfloor (b + 1)/2 \rfloor$ children in P. Make P' the right sibling of P by adding it as a child of Q just to the right of P, using the key that separated the two groups of children in P as the separator in the parent. (Figure 7.14(a) illustrates this maneuver, with $a = 3$ and $b = 5$ in the example.)
>
> $P \leftarrow Q$

The analysis of this algorithm is the same as for the corresponding 2-3 tree algorithm. The path must be stacked as it is searched and popped in order to retrace it as splits are required. A node is split if it has $b + 1$ children, and

$$a \leq \lfloor (b + 1)/2 \rfloor \leq \lceil (b + 1)/2 \rceil < b$$

since $a \geq 2$ and $b \geq 2a - 1$, so the two nodes that are created are of legal size. (If a new root is created, it has only two children, but a special exception

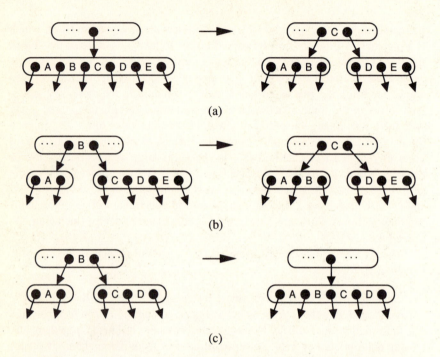

(a)

(b)

(c)

Figure 7.14 Critical maneuvers in $(3, 5)$-tree algorithms. (a) Splitting an illegal 6-node that arises during insertion into two 3-nodes. (b) Repairing an illegal 2-node that arises during deletion by borrowing a child from a sibling 4-node. (c) Eliminating a 2-node by combining it with a 3-node to form a 5-node.

covers this case.) Splitting a node takes time $O(b)$, but this is constant since b is constant.

As in the case of 2-3 trees, deletion is only slightly more complex. To delete the leaf with key K from an (a, b)-tree:

Find the leaf where K is located, and let P be its parent. Remove this child from P, and also remove an adjacent separating key. If P still has at least a children, or if P is the root, the algorithm terminates. Otherwise,

while P has $a - 1$ children **do**

(P is not the root and therefore has a sibling.) **If** P has a sibling, P', with more than a children **then**

(Assume that P' is the right sibling of P; the other case is symmetrical.) Move the leftmost child of P' to be the rightmost child of P; use the key that separates P and P' in their parent to separate this new rightmost child of P from its neighbor; and replace that key in the parent by the key that had separated that child from its neighbor in P'. Terminate the algorithm (Figure 7.14(b)).

> **else**
>
> > Let P' be a sibling of P with only a children, and let Q be the parent of P and P'. Move all the children of P' to P, and move the key in Q that separates P and P' to P to separate the two sets of children. This reduces the number of children of Q by one (Figure 7.14(c)).
> >
> > **if** Q is the root, **then**
> >
> > > **if** Q has but one child, then delete it and make that child the new root.
> > >
> > > Terminate the algorithm.
> >
> > **else**
> >
> > > $P \leftarrow Q$.

The collapsing of two nodes into one results in a legal node, since one has $a-1$ children, the other has a children, and $b \geq 2a - 1$.

We have not specified the exact nature of the data structures by which the internal nodes and the leaves are organized. The operations we must be able to perform on internal nodes are the following: insertion and deletion of key values, finding a key value, or the position between two key values or less than the smallest key value or greater than the largest key value. A binary search tree, or a balanced tree structure such as an AVL tree or red-black tree, is a suitable implementation. It may also be sensible to use an unlinked, contiguous-memory structure within a node; although changes within a node will then be slower, there will be more data items per node and hence fewer nodes, so the frequency of external storage accesses will be reduced on the average.

The leaves, which contain data records, must be grouped into blocks of the external storage device in some way. The best organization depends on details of the storage device and the file system, but the following is one reasonable approach in many cases. Store the data records in the internal nodes at the bottom level of the tree; but use different values of a and b for these nodes, say a' and b', depending on the size of the data records. That is, if r is the record size and k is the block size, then let $b' = \lfloor k/r \rfloor$, and $a' = \lfloor (b+1)/2 \rfloor$, so that b' records will fit in a single block. When such a node is split, the records are distributed between two blocks, but only a separating key is passed up to the parent; the previously described (a, b)-tree algorithms are used to manage the upper levels of the tree.

As successive dictionary elements generally belong to the same node and hence to the same disk block, the organization just described also facilitates sequential (inorder) traversal of the dictionary, which is important in many applications. The nodes at the lowest level of the tree can be linked together by a pointer in each block, so the entire dictionary can be processed in order without any reference to the index tree. Such a tree is sometimes called a **B*-tree** (Figure 7.15).

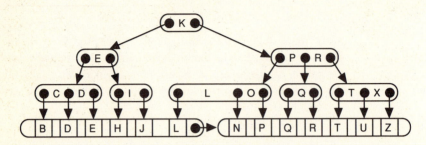

Figure 7.15 A B*-tree for the data for the (2,3)-tree of Figure 7.13, with leaves organized into blocks of maximum size $b' = 7$. The leaves are linked together so that the entire data file can be processed sequentially without using the index tree.

A significant disadvantage to (a, b)-trees is the possibility of low storage utilization. Even if the maximum value of a is used for a given value of b, it is possible for nearly 50% of the storage space to be unused if all nodes are minimally full. An alternative strategy keeps most nodes at least 66% full: if a node overflows because of an insertion, shift one child to a neighboring sibling, if one of them has less than b children. Then splitting is required only when an adjacent sibling is full. In this case create a new node and split up the $2b + 1$ children ($b + 1$ in the node that has overflowed, and b in the adjacent sibling) among them; each of the three nodes will then have at least $2b/3$ children. (The root, and the children of the root, may violate this condition.)

Another concern arises in environments where the dictionary is used by several processes concurrently. This is the usual situation in many database applications, where several client processes wish to read and change the database; insofar as possible, the database system should allow simultaneous access. Simply reading (that is, performing *LookUp*s) presents no difficulties, but our insertion algorithm stacks the entire search path. No other process could be allowed to change any node along that path until the insertion is complete, for then the stacked path might no longer reflect the actual condition of the tree. In database terminology, the nodes along the path must be **locked** during the insertion. However, locking during insertion can be avoided, at a cost of somewhat lower storage utilization. Let $b = 2a$ (this method does not work with $b = 2a - 1$). When a full node (a b-node) is encountered on the search down the tree, split it immediately into two a-nodes, even though it is not yet necessary to do so. Then the parent of every node reached during the search must be less than full; therefore if the node is split, the parent can absorb the extra child. Only two nodes need then be locked at any time, the node being searched and its parent; the search path need not be saved, and as soon as the search has passed a node's child another process can access or modify that node.

7.3 SELF-ADJUSTING BINARY SEARCH TREES

Our final tree implementation of the dictionary abstract data type is in many respects simpler than the balanced tree structures considered in the previous sections. The data structure is a pure binary search tree—the nodes have no balance, color, or other auxiliary fields, only left and right child pointers and fields for the key itself and any associated data. The structure is distinguished from a simple binary search tree by the algorithms that are used to implement the *LookUp*, *Insert*, and *Delete* operations. If the dictionary contains n items, these algorithms are *not* guaranteed to operate in $O(\log n)$ time in the worst case. But we do have a guarantee of *amortized* logarithmic cost: Any *sequence* of m of these operations, starting from an empty tree, is guaranteed to take a *total* amount of time that is $O(m \log n)$. Therefore the average time used by an operation in the sequence of length m is $O(\log n)$, and the amortized cost of an operation is $O(\log n)$. Though the amortized cost of an operation is $O(\log n)$, there may be single operations whose cost is much higher—$\Omega(n)$, for example— *but this can happen only if those operations have been preceded by many whose cost is so small that the cost of the entire sequence is $O(m \log n)$.* For many applications the guarantee of logarithmic amortized time is quite sufficient, and the algorithms are sufficiently simpler than AVL tree or red-black tree algorithms that they are preferable.

The algorithms operate by applying a tree version of the Move-to-Front Heuristic discussed on page 179; each time a key is the object of a successful search, its node is moved to the root of the binary tree. (However, the movement must happen in a very particular way, which is described below. And to reemphasize, unlike the results of the analysis in §6.2, the guarantees on the performance of these trees do *not* depend on any assumption about the probability distribution of the operations on keys.) The critical operation is called *Splay*. Given a binary search tree T and a key K, $Splay(K, T)$ modifies T so that it remains a binary search tree on the same keys. But the new tree has K at the root, if K is in the tree; if K is not in the tree, then the root contains a key that would be the inorder predecessor or successor of K, if K were in the tree (Figure 7.16). We call this "splaying the tree around K," and we refer to trees that are manipulated using the splay operation as **splay trees**. (To "splay" something is to spread it out or flatten it.)

Suppose that we are given an implementation of the *Splay* operation (we shall see just below how *Splay* can be implemented efficiently). Then the dictionary operations can be implemented as follows:

LookUp(K, T): Execute *Splay*(K, T), and then examine the root of the tree to see if it contains K (Figure 7.17).

Insert(K, I, T): Execute *Splay*(K, T). If K is in fact at the root, then simply install I in this node. Otherwise create a new node containing K and I and break one link to make this node the new root (Figure 7.18).

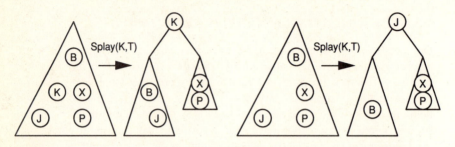

Figure 7.16 Effect of *Splay*(*K, T*). If key *K* is in tree *T*, it is brought to the root, otherwise a key in *T* that would neighbor *K* in the dictionary ordering is brought to the root.

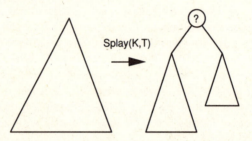

Figure 7.17 Implementation of *LookUp*(*K, T*) with the aid of *Splay*. Splay the tree around *K*, then see if *K* is at the root.

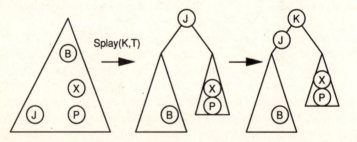

Figure 7.18 Implementation of *Insert*(*K, T*) with the aid of *Splay*. Splay the tree around *K*, then make *K* the root.

Delete(*K, T*) is implemented with the aid of an operation *Concat*(T_1, T_2). If T_1 and T_2 are binary search trees such that every key in T_1 is less than every key in T_2, then *Concat*(T_1, T_2) creates a binary search tree containing all keys in either T_1 or T_2. *Concat* is implemented with the aid of *Splay* as follows:

> *Concat*(T_1, T_2): First execute *Splay*($+\infty, T_1$), where $+\infty$ is a key value greater than any that can occur in a tree. After this has been done, T_1 has no right subtree; attach the root of T_2 as the right child of the root of T_1 (Figure 7.19).

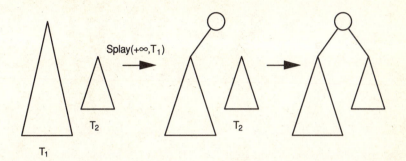

Figure 7.19 Implementation of *Concat*(T_1, T_2) with the aid of *Splay*. Splay the first tree around $+\infty$, then make the second tree the right subtree of the root.

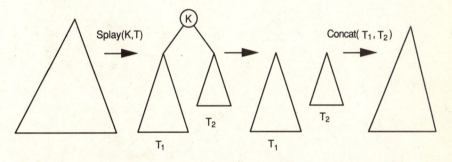

Figure 7.20 Implementation of *Delete*(K, T) with the aid of *Splay* and *Concat*. Splay the tree around K, then concatenate the two subtrees of the root.

Then *Delete* is implemented thus:

> *Delete*(K, T): Execute *Splay*(K, T). If the root does not contain K then there is nothing to do. Otherwise apply *Concat* to the two subtrees of the root (Figure 7.20).

Thus to complete the account of the dictionary operations, it remains only to describe the implementation of the splay operation. To splay T around K, first search for K in the usual way, remembering the search path by stacking it.* Let P be the last node inspected; if K is in the tree, then K is in node P, and otherwise P has an empty child where the search for K terminated. When the splay has been completed, P will be the new root. Return along the path from P back to the root, carrying out the following rotations, which move P up the tree.

---

*The size of the stack can be $\Omega(n)$, but link inversion can be used to reduce memory utilization.

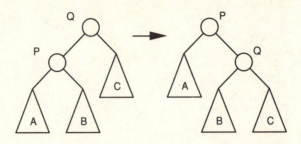

Figure 7.21 Rotation during splay, Case I: P has no grandparent.

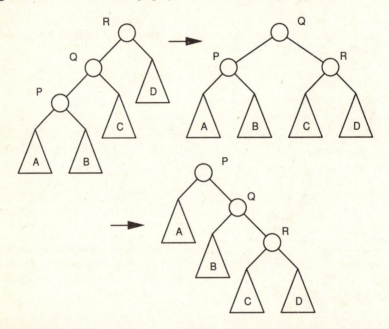

Figure 7.22 Rotation during splay, Case II: P and its parent are both left children.

Case I. P has no grandparent, that is, $Parent(P)$ is the root. Perform a single rotation around the parent of P, as illustrated in Figure 7.21 or its mirror image.

Case II. P and $Parent(P)$ are both left children, or both right children. Perform two single rotations in the same direction, first around the grandparent of P and then around the parent of P, as shown in Figure 7.22 or its mirror image.

Case III. One of P and $Parent(P)$ is a left child and the other is a right child. Perform single rotations in opposite directions, first around the parent of P and then around its grandparent, as illustrated in Figure 7.23 or its mirror image.

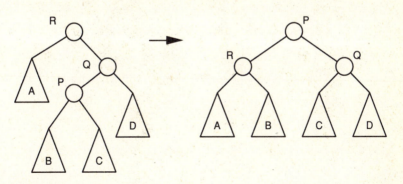

Figure 7.23 Rotation during splay, Case III: P is a left child and its parent is a right child.

Ultimately P becomes the root and the splay algorithm is complete.

Note that Cases I and III are AVL tree single and double rotations, but Case II is special to this algorithm. Figure 7.24 gives an example of splaying. The effects of the rotations are fairly mysterious; note that they do not necessarily decrease the height of the tree (in fact, they can increase it), nor do they necessarily make the tree more well-balanced in any evident way. The analysis of these algorithms is more subtle than those of previous sections, because it must take into account that the time "saved" while performing low-cost operations can be "used" later during a time-consuming operation. To capture this idea, we use a banking metaphor.

(The remainder of this section deals only with the *analysis* of the algorithms that have already been presented; the numerical quantities discussed below—"money," for example—play no role in the actual *implementation* of the algorithms.)

We regard each node of the tree as a bank account containing a certain amount of money. The amount of money at a node depends on how many descendants it has; nodes with more descendants have more money. Thus as nodes are added to the tree, more money must be added in order to keep enough money at each node. Also any fixed amount of work—performing a single rotation at a single node, for example—costs a fixed amount of money. The essence of the proof is to show that any sequence of m dictionary operations, starting from an empty tree and with the tree never having more than n nodes, can be carried out by a total investment of $O(m \log n)$ dollars. On any single operation some of these dollars may come out of the "bank accounts" already at the nodes of the tree, and some may be "new investment"; and on any single operation some of these dollars may go to keep the bank accounts up to their required minimums, and some may go to pay for the work done on the tree. But in aggregate $O(m \log n)$ dollars are enough, so that the amortized cost of any single operation is only $O(\log n)$.

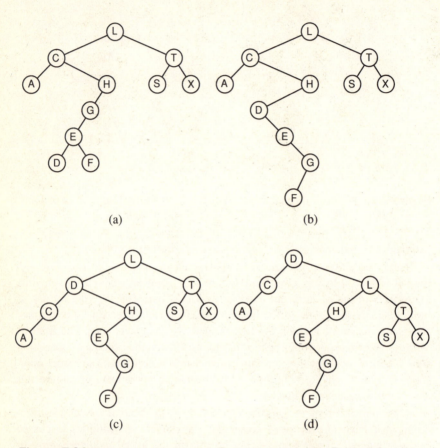

(a)

(b)

(c)

(d)

Figure 7.24 Splaying a tree around D. (a) Original tree; D is a left child of a left child, so Case II applies. (b) After applying the rotations of Figure 7.22 at D, E, and G. D is now a left child of a right child, so Case III applies. (c) After applying the rotation of Figure 7.23 at D, H, and C. D now has no grandparent, so Case I applies. (d) After applying the rotation of Figure 7.21 at D and L.

To be precise about the necessary minimum bank balance at each node, for any node N let $w(N)$ (the **weight** of N) be the number of descendants of N (including N itself), and let $r(N)$ (the **rank** of N) be $\lfloor \lg w(N) \rfloor$. Then we insist that the following condition be maintained:

The Money Invariant: Each node N has $r(N)$ dollars at all times.

Initially the tree is empty, and so there is no money in it. Money gets used in two ways while a splay is in progress.

1. We must pay for the time used. A fixed amount of time costs a fixed amount of money (say, $1 per operation).

2. Since the shape of the tree changes as the splay is carried out, we may have to add some money to the tree, or redistribute the money already in the tree, in order to maintain the Money Invariant everywhere.

Money that is spent, either to pay for time or to maintain the invariant, may be taken out of the tree or may be "new money." The critical fact is this:

■ **LEMMA** *(Investment)* It costs at most $3\lfloor \lg n \rfloor + 1$ new dollars to splay a tree with n nodes while maintaining the Money Invariant everywhere.

Let us defer the proof of the Investment Lemma for the time being, and suppose that it is true. The Investment Lemma provides all the information that is needed to complete the amortized analysis of splay trees.

■ **THEOREM** *(Splay Tree)* Any sequence of m dictionary operations on a self-adjusting tree that is initially empty and never has more than n nodes uses $O(m \log n)$ time.

PROOF Any single dictionary operation on a tree T with at most n nodes costs $O(\log n)$ new dollars:

- *LookUp*(K, T) costs only what it costs to do the splay, which is $O(\log n)$.
- *Insert*(K, I, T) costs what it costs to do the splay, plus what must be banked in the new root to maintain the invariant there; this is $\lfloor \lg(n+1) \rfloor$ additional dollars, for a total of $O(\log n)$. (The new root is the only node that gains descendants when the new root is inserted.)
- *Concat*(T_1, T_2), where T_1 and T_2 have at most n nodes, costs what it costs to splay T_1, which is $O(\log n)$, plus what must be banked in the root in order to make T_2 a subtree, which is at most $\lfloor \lg n \rfloor$, for a total of $O(\log n)$.
- *Delete*(K, T) costs what it costs to splay T, plus what it costs to concatenate the two resulting subtrees, which is again $O(\log n)$.

This is the amount of new money required in each case. Nonetheless an operation may take more than $\Omega(\log n)$ *time*, since the time can be paid for with money that had previously been banked in the tree. However, if we start with an empty tree and do m operations, then the amount of money in the tree is 0 initially and ≥ 0 at the end, and by the Investment Lemma at most $m(3\lfloor \lg n \rfloor + 1)$ dollars are invested in the interim. This must be enough to pay for all the time used as well as to maintain the invariant, so the amount of time used must be $O(m \log n)$. □

Now we turn to the proof of the Investment Lemma. For this we shall need two simple observations about the ranks of nodes. Clearly the rank of a node is greater than or equal to the rank of any of its descendants. Slightly less obvious is the

■ **LEMMA** *(Rank Rule)* If a node has two children of equal rank, then its rank is greater than that of each child.

PROOF Let N be the node and let U and V be its children. By the definition of rank, $w(U) \geq 2^{r(U)}$ and $w(V) \geq 2^{r(V)}$. If $r(U) = r(V)$, then $w(N) > w(U) + w(V) \geq 2^{r(U)+1}$. Therefore $r(N) = \lfloor \lg w(N) \rfloor \geq r(U) + 1$. □

Now consider a single step of a splay operation, that is, a rotation as described in Case I, II, or III. We write $r'(P)$ to denote the rank of P *after* the rotation has been done, and $r(P)$ to denote its value beforehand.

■ **LEMMA** *(Cost of Splay Steps)* A splay step involving node P, the parent of P, and (possibly) the grandparent of P can be done with an investment of at most $3(r'(P) - r(P))$ new dollars, plus one more dollar if this was the last step in the splay.

Deferring for the moment the proof of this Lemma, we show that it implies the Investment Lemma. Let us write $r^{(i)}(P)$ for the rank of P after i steps of the splay operation have been carried out. According to the Lemma, the total investment of new money needed to carry out the splay is at most

$$3(r'(P) - r(P))$$
$$+ 3(r^{(2)}(P) - r'(P))$$
$$+ \cdots$$
$$+ 3(r^{(k)}(P) - r^{(k-1)}(P)) + 1,$$

where k is the number of steps needed to bring P to the root. But $r^{(k)}(P)$ is the rank of the original root, since the tree has the same number of nodes after the splay as before, so $r^{(k)}(P) \leq \lfloor \lg n \rfloor$. The middle terms of the sum cancel out, and the total is $3(r^{(k)}(P) - r(P)) + 1 \leq 3\lfloor \lg n \rfloor + 1$.

PROOF (of the Cost of Splay Steps Lemma)   The three types of rotation must be treated separately. In each case, let Q be the parent of P, and R the parent of Q, if it has one.

- **Case I.** P has no grandparent. This must be the last step. The one extra dollar pays for the time used to do the rotation. Since $r'(P) = r(Q)$ (Figure 7.21), the number of new dollars that must be added to the tree is

$$r'(P) + r'(Q) - (r(P) + r(Q))$$
$$= r'(Q) - r(P)$$
$$\leq r'(P) - r(P) \quad \text{since } Q \text{ becomes a child of } P.$$

This is $1/3$ of the amount specified in the Lemma.

- **Case II.** Here $r'(P) = r(R)$ (see Figure 7.22; r' refers to the situation in the rightmost tree, after both rotations have been completed). So the total amount that needs to be added to the tree to maintain the invariant is

$$r'(P) + r'(Q) + r'(R) - (r(P) + r(Q) + r(R))$$
$$= r'(Q) + r'(R) - (r(P) + r(Q))$$
$$\leq 2(r'(P) - r(P)),$$

which is $2/3$ of the available money. If $r'(P) > r(P)$, then a dollar is left over to pay for the work. So assume for the duration that $r'(P) = r(P)$. Then also

$$r'(P) = r(R) \tag{IIa}$$

(since R is the root of the subtree before the rotations and P is the root afterwards). If $r'(R)$ were equal to $r(P)$, then by the Rank Rule on the middle tree of Figure 7.22, $r(P) < r'(P)$, contrary to assumption. Hence

$$r'(R) < r(P), \tag{IIb}$$

since $r'(R) \leq r'(P) = r(P)$. Finally

$$r'(Q) \leq r(Q), \tag{IIc}$$

since $r'(Q) \leq r'(P) = r(P) \leq r(Q)$. By (IIa), (IIb), and (IIc) we can move R's money to P, P's money to R, and leave Q's money where it is, maintain the invariant everywhere, and still have a dollar left over to pay for the work.

- **Case III.** In this case $r'(P) = r(R)$ and $r'(Q) \leq r(Q)$ (see Figure 7.23). So if we move R's money to P and leave some or all of Q's money on Q, the invariant will remain true at P and Q. To satisfy the invariant on R, use the money from P plus an additional $r'(R) - r(P) \leq r'(P) - r(P)$ dollars, one third of the new dollars available. If $r'(P) > r(P)$, then there is one dollar left over to pay for the work. Otherwise $r'(P) = r(P) = r(Q) = r(R)$ and hence either $r'(Q) < r'(P)$ or $r'(R) < r'(P)$ (since $r'(P) = r'(Q) = r'(R)$ is impossible by the Rank Rule applied to the right-hand tree in Figure 7.23). So either $r'(Q) < r(Q)$ or $r'(R) < r(P)$ and there is a dollar left over to pay for the work.   □

Problems

7.1   **1. a.** Show the AVL trees that result from inserting the keys 186, 039, 991, 336, 778, 066, 564, 154, 538, and 645 into an initially empty tree.

   b. Show the result of deleting the key 186 from the tree of part (a).

   2. a. Show the results of inserting the keys 1, 2, ..., 10 in ascending order into an AVL tree.

b. Show that if an AVL tree is constructed by inserting the keys 1, 2, ..., n in ascending order, then for some d all leaves in the resulting tree have depth d or $d+1$.

3. A "worst" AVL tree is one in which no nonleaf has zero balance (Figure 7.2 on page 221 shows some worst AVL trees). How many worst AVL trees of height h exist?

4. Say that a k-AVL tree, where k is a small number, is a binary search tree in which the balance is allowed to be any number in the range from $-k$ to $+k$, for some small number k. (Ordinary AVL trees are then 1-AVL trees.)

   a. Write a recurrence relation for $w_h^{(k)}$, the maximum number of nodes in a k-AVL tree of height h, and calculate $w_h^{(3)}$ for a few small values of h.

   b. Estimate, as accurately as you can, the maximum height of any k-AVL tree with n nodes.

   c. How would you do an insertion in a k-AVL tree?

5. Explain carefully why no sequence of single and double rotations of a binary tree changes the result of an inorder traversal of the tree.

6. There are three possibilities for the balance of an interior node of an AVL tree: 0, +1, or -1. But leaves always have balance 0. Show how this fact can be used to provide a representation for AVL trees in which the balance field of each node is only a single bit.

7. This problem establishes several relations used in the proof of the AVL Tree Height Theorem.

   a. Show that $w_h = F_{h+3} - 1$.

   b. Show that $F_i > \phi^i/\sqrt{5} - 1$ for every i.

   c. Show that $2\sqrt{5}/(\phi^3 - \sqrt{5}) = \sqrt{5}$.

8. In the proof of the AVL Tree Height Theorem it is implicitly assumed that w_h increases monotonically with h. Where is this assumption used, and what justifies it?

9. Write the complete procedure *AVLTreeDelete* according to the algorithm outlined in this section.

10. **a.** Describe an implementation of *Union*(S, T), where S and T are represented as AVL trees, that runs in time $O(|S| + |T|)$.

    b. Show that if every key in S is less than every key in T, then *Union* of AVL trees can be computed in time $O(\log |S| + \log |T|)$. Estimate the exact number of rotations required in the worst case.

11. Show that AVL trees can be used to provide an implementation of an abstract data type "list" with the following operations. Each operation should take time $O(\log |L|)$. (Hint: Store in each node the number of items in the left subtree of that node.)

 a. *Access(L, i)*: Return the ith element of L.

 b. *Insert(x, L, i)*: Return the result of inserting x after the ith element of L.

 c. *Length(L)*: Return $|L|$.

 d. *Delete(L, i)*: Return the result of deleting the ith element of L, thus shortening L by one element.

12. Show that any n-node binary tree can be converted into any other by means of at most $2n$ single rotations. (Hint: Show that it takes only n rotations to covert any binary tree into the tree in which all left children are empty.)

13. Suppose that S and T are sets of size m and n. Choose a representation that makes it possible to implement *Intersection(S, T)* (which returns $S \cap T$) in time $O((m + n) \log m)$.

7.2   14. Show the result of inserting the keys 1, 2, ..., 10 in ascending order into a 2-3 tree.

15. a. Suppose that S and T are disjoint sets, and every member of S is smaller than every member of T. Show that if these sets are represented by 2-3 trees, then the function *Union(S, T)* can be computed in $O(|(\log |S| - \log |T|)|)$ time (the absolute value of the difference of the logarithms of the sizes of the sets).

 b. Find and analyze a 2-3 tree algorithm for the operation *Prefix*, where $Prefix(S, x) = \{y \in S: \ y \leq x\}$.

16. a. Repeat Problem 11 for 2-3 trees.

 b. Show that the operations $Concat(L_1, L_2)$ and $Initial(L, i)$ (which returns a sublist consisting of the first i elements of L) can also be implemented in logarithmic time.

17. If the depth of a red-black tree increases as a result of an insertion, precisely where in Algorithm 7.4 on page 237 does it do so?

18. Present an algorithm to delete a node from the red-black representation of a 2-3 tree, following the style of Algorithm 7.4.

19. For any $n > 0$, let T_n be the B-tree of order $b = 2a - 1$ obtained by inserting the keys 1, 2, ..., n in ascending order. Find, as a function of p, the smallest value of n such that T_n has height p.

20. Suppose that a B-tree of order b grows only through addition of records (no deletions). What is the *expected* storage utilization (averaged over all values of n, the number of items in the tree)? What would be the expected storage utilization if storage is kept at least 66% full by the strategy described on page 242?

21. As in the previous problem, suppose that a B-tree of order b grows through addition of records only (no deletions). When the tree has n items, what is the average number of times, per item, that nodes have been split in two?

22. It was suggested that at least when data records are held in external storage, it is better to keep all the data records in the leaves of a B-tree, and to use the interior nodes of the tree strictly as an index to help find the appropriate leaf page. Donald Dumb favors using only one node format and keeping data in the interior nodes as well. He argues that by storing data records in the upper levels of the tree, some of them will be found quickly, and this effect will compensate for the fact that it might take more page accesses to reach those data that are stored lower in the tree. What do you think of Donald's argument? Analyze the situation on the assumption that an index entry takes 10 bytes and a data record takes 100 bytes, pages are 2000 bytes, nodes are organized internally as balanced binary trees and searching for an item within a node takes 100 ns per tree edge, and reading in a new page takes 100 ms. Does Donald's view of the world make sense for these or any other values of these parameters?

23. Why does the method of "anticipatory splitting" of B-tree nodes described on page 242 not work with $b = 2a - 1$?

24. Show how a version of red-black trees can be used to implement $(2, 4)$-trees in such a way that insertions can be done while rebalancing the tree "on the way down," thus not requiring the insertion path to be retraced.

7.3 25. Show the result of inserting the keys 1, 2, ..., 10 in ascending order into a splay tree.

26. **a.** Show the result of inserting the keys 312, 488, 682, 405, 170, 242, 230, 264, 890 into a splay tree.

   b. Show the result of deleting 488 and 170 from the resulting tree.

27. **a.** You are given a splay tree such that the path from the root to the key 90 passes through the following keys in order: 10, 20, 30, 40, 50, 60, 70, 80, 90. Show the result of splaying 90 to the top.

   b. You are given another tree such that the path to 90 passes through 50, 130, 60, 120, 70, 110, 80, 100. Show the result of splaying 90 to the top.

c. Assume that before the splaying operation, all the nodes of the tree of part (a) on the path to 90 had rank k. Show that after the splay operation of part (a) the ranks of these nodes do not increase, and the ranks of at least three of them decrease.

d. Under the same hypothesis as in part (c), show that the splay operation of part (b) causes no increase in ranks, and causes at least four nodes to decrease in rank.

28. Suppose that sets are represented by splay trees. Give an implementation of the following operation: $Range(S, K_1, K_2)$, which changes S to the set of all its members for which the key value K satisfies $K_1 \leq K \leq K_2$. Analyze this implementation.

29. Explain how to implement the operation *Prefix* defined in Problem 15 if sets are represented by splay trees. If this operation is added to the repertoire, is it still true that any sequence of m operations involving at most n items takes time $O(m \log n)$?

30. Here is the lazy man's approach to maintaining a balanced tree representation of a set. Use ordinary binary tree insertion and do no rebalancing at all until the tree gets too badly out of balance; then completely reconstruct the tree to be as balanced as possible. Various criteria can be used to determine when the tree is badly out of balance; one that works is to keep track of the actual internal path length in the tree I_T and the optimal internal path length O_T (which depends only on the number of nodes), and to restructure whenever $I_T > \delta O_T$, where $\delta > 1$ is a constant parameter of the algorithm governing how badly out of balance we are willing to allow the tree to get.

a. Write the restructuring algorithm.

b. How can the quantities I_T and O_T be determined?

c. Show that the lazy man's method takes linear worst-case time but logarithmic expected time for any insertion, deletion, or search.

31. Design an implementation for a set abstract data type with the following operations: $LookUp(K, S)$, which locates the record with key K in set S; and $InsertNext(K, I, S)$, which inserts into S the pair $\langle K, I \rangle$. The following special restrictions apply on the use of *InsertNext*: either S is empty, or K is the successor of the key value of the last operation performed (a *LookUp* or an *InsertNext*). For example, the following sequence of operations is valid: insert 1, 5, 10, 30; find 5; insert 6, 7; find 30, 1; insert 3; find 7; insert 8, 9. Your algorithm should perform any sequence of insertions and finds on an initially empty set in time $O(f \log n + n)$, where n is the number of insertions

and f is the number of finds. (Hint: Use a splay tree, but don't actually insert the records until a *Find* is performed; instead save the insertions in a list and convert the list into a complete binary tree at the appropriate time.)

References

AVL trees were the invention of

G. M. Adel'son-Vel'skii and E. M. Landis, "An Algorithm for the Organization of Information," *Soviet Math. Doklady* **3** (1962), pp. 1259–1262.

The generalization to k-AVL trees (Problem 4) is from

C. C. Foster, "A Generalization of AVL Trees," *Communications of the ACM* **16** (1973), pp. 513–517.

It appears that the reduction in the number of rebalances made possible by letting $k > 1$ does not compensate for the expected increase in search times. The first (unpublished) use of 2-3 trees was by John Hopcroft in 1970. Our presentation of the red-black tree representation of 2-3 trees derives from

L. J. Guibas and R. Sedgewick, "A Dichromatic Framework for Balanced Trees," *Proceedings, 19th Annual IEEE Symposium on Foundations of Computer Science*, 1978, pp. 8–21,

which also contains information about the red-black representation of other types of balanced trees. The "B" in "B-tree" is not a variable; it stands for either "Bayer," who was one of the inventors of the method, or "Boeing," where the work was done. B-trees were described in

R. Bayer and E. M. McCreight, "Organization and Maintenance of Large Ordered Indices," *Acta Informatica* **1** (1972), pp. 173–189.

For a more recent description of B-trees and some of their variations, see

D. Comer, "The Ubiquitous B-Tree," *Computing Surveys* **11** (1979), pp. 121–137.

Splay trees are the invention of

D. D. Sleator and R. E. Tarjan, "Self-Adjusting Binary Search Trees," *Journal of the ACM* **32** (1985), pp. 652–686.

Comparative discussions of some of the tree structures discussed in the last two chapters, and some other variations on these, may be found in

J. Nievergelt, "Binary Search Trees and File Organization," *Computing Surveys* **6** (1974), pp. 195–207;

J.-L. Baer and B. Schwab, "A Comparison of Tree-Balancing Algorithms," *Communications of the ACM* **20** (1977), pp. 322–330.

Problem 30 is from

W. A. Martin and D. N. Ness, "Optimizing Binary Trees Grown with a Sorting Algorithm," *Communications of the ACM* **15** (1972), pp. 88–93.

8

Sets of Digital Data

8.1 BIT VECTORS

This chapter deals with implementations of sets (both dictionaries and sets with other operations) that take advantage of the structure of keys. Unlike the set implementations of Chapters 6 and 7, which perform no operations on keys except comparisons for order or equality, these implementations treat the key as an index, or as a string that can be decomposed into characters, or as a numerical quantity on which arbitrary arithmetic operations can be performed. Each of these ways of handling keys is of broad but not universal applicability, so we shall point out the limitations as well as the advantages of each technique.

Let us assume that we are to construct and manipulate sets of elements that are drawn from a universe U of fixed size N, say $U = \{u_0, \ldots, u_{N-1}\}$. Suppose, moreover, that there is a relatively simple procedure to compute, given an element $u \in U$, the index i such that $u = u_i$. (One situation fitting this description is that in which U is exactly a set of integers $\{0, \ldots, N-1\}$. Another is when U is a set of characters, such as the printing characters in the ASCII character set, which have character codes in a contiguous interval C, $\ldots$, $C + N - 1$; the translation of a character into its code takes constant time.) Among the simplest ways of representing a subset $S \subseteq U$ is as a **bit vector**, that is, a table of N bits $Bits[0 .. N-1]$ with $Bits[i] = 1$ if $u_i \in S$ and $Bits[i] = 0$ if $u_i \notin S$. If determining the index of an element and accessing that position in the table both take constant time, such a representation permits implementations of *Insert*, *Delete*, and *Member* in constant time. Depending on the value of N and the operations available for testing and setting the individual bits of a machine word, accessing an individual bit may take several operations, but the number of operations does not vary with the size of the set represented.

When a bit vector representation is used, a subset of a set of size N takes N bits of memory to represent, independent of the size of the subset, so such a representation makes most sense when N is not too large and there is a need to represent sets of size comparable to N. Compare the storage efficiency of this scheme with that of binary trees, for example: a binary tree representation of a set of keys of size n takes $n(2\mathbf{p} + K)$ bits, where $K \geq \lg N$ is the size of the field needed to represent a key value and $\mathbf{p}$ is the number of bits in a pointer; whereas the bit vector representation takes N bits. Though the bit vector representation is much more compact when $n \approx N$, even if $\mathbf{p} = K = 32$ the tree representation becomes more storage-efficient when $n/N \approx 1\%$.

For this reason the bit vector representation is useful only when the universe is relatively small, or the sets are typically fairly large in relation to the size of the universe. However these conditions are not so uncommon; many algorithms, for example, manipulate sets of array indices or sets of characters. (Some implementations of Pascal require that the members of sets be drawn from a universe of size 128 or 256, evidently for the convenience of the author of the set package, who can then use a bit vector representation regardless of what the universe may be.)

Another significant advantage of the bit vector representation is that a number of other operations have straightforward implementations. In addition to *Insert*, *Delete*, and *Member*, which as was observed earlier have $O(1)$ time implementations independent of the size of the universe or the subset, *Union* and *Intersection* can be implemented almost trivially by means of boolean **and** and **or** operations. Not only do these operations take time linear in N, but they may take less than one machine operation per set element, since an instruction may operate on an entire word at once. If the word length is, say, 32, then it takes the same time to compute unions and intersections if the universe has size 30 as if it has size 10.

A disadvantage of the bit vector representation that may balance the benefits of operating in parallel on all the bits of a word is that on some computers access to the individual bits of a word may require relatively expensive shifting and masking operations. Therefore a *Member* operation may be significantly more expensive than a *Union*.

Unfortunately, one indispensable operation takes time $\Omega(N)$: initialization, that is, *MakeEmptySet*. This must be accomplished by zeroing all the bits of the bit vector. This is in practice a relatively rapid operation, since zeroing a byte or a word takes little time on most machines, but there is at least a theoretical interest in knowing whether a representation can be devised that supports $O(1)$ time implementation of *MakeEmptySet*, as well as *Insert*, *Delete*, and *Member*. In fact all these operations can be implemented in constant time if the method described in Algorithm 5.1 on page 137 is used to initialize the bit vector.

Algorithm 8.1 shows the full details. These routines manipulate a single set S, which is a subset of **U** represented as a record structure with four components:

function *BitVectMakeEmptySet*( ): **pointer**
{Return the empty set}
    $S \leftarrow NewCell(\text{Set})$
    $\text{Count}(S) \leftarrow 0$
    return S

function *Valid*(**integer** i, **pointer** S): **boolean**
{True if i has ever been inserted in S}
    return $0 \leq \text{When}(S)[i] \leq \text{Count}(S) - 1$ **and** $\text{Which}(S)[\text{When}(S)[i]] = i$

function *BitVectMember*(**integer** i, **pointer** S): **boolean**
{True if $i \in S$}
    return $Valid(i, S)$ **and** $\text{Bits}(S)[i] = 1$

procedure *BitVectInsert*(**integer** i, **pointer** S):
{Add i to S}
    if not $Valid(i, S)$ **then**
        $\text{Count}(S) \leftarrow \text{Count}(S) + 1$
        $\text{When}(S)[i] \leftarrow \text{Count}(S) - 1$
        $\text{Which}(S)[\text{Count}(S) - 1] \leftarrow i$
    $\text{Bits}(S)[i] \leftarrow 1$

procedure *BitVectDelete*(**integer** i, **pointer** S):
{Remove i from S}
    if $Valid(i, S)$ **then**
        $\text{Bits}(S)[i] \leftarrow 0$

Algorithm 8.1 Maintaining a set with constant time for each operation. The set S is represented as a structure with four components: a bit vector Bits(S), tables of indices Which(S) and When(S), and an integer Count(S).

Bits(S), the bit vector itself;
Count(S), the number m of items that have ever been inserted into the set;
When(S) and Which(S), the tables of indices of the same names in Algorithm 5.1 on page 137.

The universe **U** is assumed to consist of the N integers $0, \ldots, N - 1$. The routine *Valid* is an auxiliary routine that indicates whether an element has ever been inserted into the set; position i in the tables Bits(S) and When(S) are meaningful only when $Valid(i, S)$ is true.

Unfortunately, this means of achieving constant time per set operation increases the storage requirements from one bit per element of the universe to $2\mathbf{p} + 1$ bits per element of the universe, almost certainly too great a price to pay in practical situations.

8.2 TRIES AND DIGITAL SEARCH TREES

When a binary search tree is searched for a key value, each comparison of the search key to a key stored in the tree extracts a single bit of information about the search key (whether it is the same as or different from a stored key, or whether it is greater than or less than a stored key). But when the search key can be decomposed into characters, the character values can be used as indices, and a single indexing operation can extract far more information about the key since there are as many possible index values as characters.

The simplest structure based on this idea is the **trie**.* Suppose that there are k possible character values. A trie is a $(k + 1)$-ary tree with each node implemented as a table of $k + 1$ pointers—one for each possible character, and one for an "end-of-string" indicator $\triangle$. The root node serves as a "thumb index" of the keys in the dictionary according to their first characters; each key beginning with the ith character belongs in the ith subtree. At the second level of the tree, the indexing is similar, but according to the second character of the key; and so on. If a key has but m characters, then the search path for that key ends in a node of depth m, at the pointer position within that node corresponding to the $\triangle$ indicator (Figure 8.1). In this simple structure, there is no need to store the key itself at a leaf of the tree, since the key is completely determined by the path that has been followed; of course any information to be associated with the key can be stored at a leaf.

Let n be the number of keys stored in a trie, and let l be the length (in characters) of the longest key. Also, let s be the number of nodes in the trie. The principal advantage of the trie structure is access time; a key can be accessed in time $O(l)$, independent of n and k. The severe disadvantage of tries as just described is their storage requirements; a trie takes $(k + 1) \cdot s \cdot \mathbf{p}$ bits to represent, independent of n. For example, a trie containing the single word IMPOSSIBILITY in the Roman alphabet ($k = 26$) would occupy $13 \cdot 27 = 351$ pointers, all but 13 of which would be Λ. In general, the difficulty is that given the first few characters $c_1 c_2 \ldots c_i$ of a word, there are relatively few possibilities for c_{i+1}, even though the number of characters in the character set is relatively large. So except near the root of the tree, the actual branching at a node is closer to 1 or 2 than to k.

Just as hierarchical table representation can significantly reduce the storage required to store a sparse array (§5.3), there are a number of fairly simple ideas that can significantly reduce storage requirements of tries.

1. Because tries have relatively few nodes but the nodes may have many children, a k-ary trie with m nodes can be implemented space-efficiently as a two-dimensional, m by k table with each entry being a number between 1 and m. The table entry corresponding to the jth child of the ith node is

---

*$Trie$ is the middle syllable of *retrieval*, and is a pun on *tree*; but it is pronounced the same as *try*.

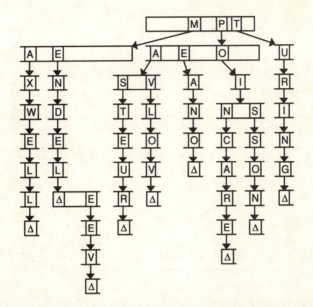

Figure 8.1 A trie on the names MAXWELL, MENDEL, MENDELEEV, PASTEUR, PAVLOV, PEANO, POINCARE, POISSON, and TURING. Only cells with nonempty pointers are shown. A cell labelled with △ points to the information record for the character string on the path from the root to the node.

the index, in the range from 1 to m, that has been assigned to that child node. Such numbers take only $\lceil \lg m \rceil$ bits to represent, typically much less than the number of bits to represent a full pointer.

2. Nodes with only one nonempty child can be eliminated by storing with each node the index of the character position on which that node discriminates. In essence this compresses the trie by deleting any node with one child, and labelling each remaining node with a character position, namely, the node's depth in the original uncompressed trie (Figure 8.2). If a node is labelled i and the ith character of the search key is character number j, the search continues by following the jth pointer in the node. (If the search key has fewer than i characters, it is not in the trie.) A key is no longer uniquely determined by a search path, so it is necessary to store the key itself in the leaf. Such a compressed trie is called a **Patricia* tree**. In a Patricia tree the branching at each node is at least binary, so the storage requirements for the interior nodes are at most $k \cdot \mathbf{p} \cdot n$ bits; but additional memory must be used to store the keys themselves. These trees are especially useful when the keys are very long.

---

*Practical Algorithm To Retrieve Information Coded In Alphanumeric.

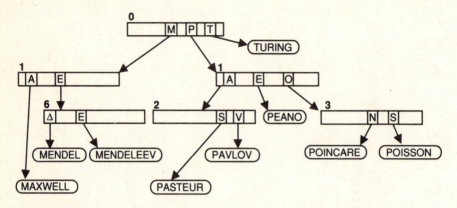

Figure 8.2 Patricia tree for the keys of Figure 8.1.

3. Instead of using a table to represent a node, a linked list can be used. Each pointer must be accompanied by an identifying character; a node is really a linked list of character-pointer pairs. The time to search a single node rises by comparison with the trie structure, and is no longer independent of the size of the character set; but for nodes with only a few pointers the savings in memory is significant. This type of compression can be implemented with or without also eliminating nodes with one child as described earlier; if all nodes are represented explicitly, so that the keys are implicit in the paths, these trees are called **de la Briandais trees** (Figure 8.3).

It is difficult to provide useful estimates of the expected storage requirements of de la Briandais trees, and the expected time needed to search them. The length of the linked list of a node's children is bounded above by the number of characters in the character set, and so the time to locate a key is proportional to its length. However, the actual number of children of a node will almost certainly be much less than the size of the character set; let us suppose that nodes at all depths have similar numbers of children on average, and let this average be α. Then the expected time to search a node's children is also proportional to α, since we expect to search through half the child pointers of a node before finding the appropriate one. Unfortunately, this assumption about the number of children of nodes is probably inaccurate; as noted above, nodes closer to the root tend to have more children, since the subtree rooted at a node of great depth contains only keys with a long common prefix. (Since the pointers are identified, there is no need to keep them in alphabetical order; they could be kept in an order that minimizes expected search time, if such an order can be determined, or reorganized dynamically using, for example, the Move-to-Front Heuristic.)

4. If nodes close to the root tend to be "dense" while those of greater depth tend to be "sparse," it may be possible to use a hybrid tree structure to gain

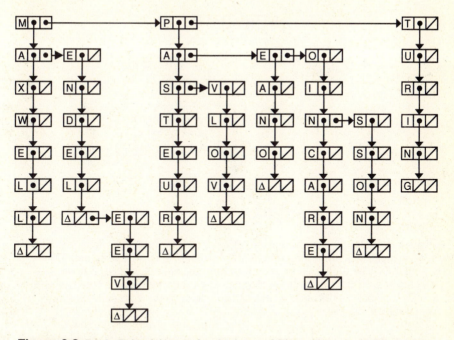

Figure 8.3 De la Briandais tree for the keys of Figure 8.1. As in Figure 8.1, we use an explicit "end-of-string" marker △ to identify the end of a key; for example, the L in MENDEL has two children, one for the end of that key and one for the second E in MENDELEEV.

the speed advantage of a trie structure without paying a heavy penalty in storage utilization. Trie nodes can be used for the first few levels of the tree, but a more space-economical structure is used at deeper levels. The structures used at deeper levels could be de la Briandais trees, or ordinary binary search trees; in the latter case the keys (or at least the suffixes of the keys not determined by the search path through the trie nodes) must be stored in binary search tree nodes.

5. Another approach to economizing in the use of memory while retaining the speed advantages of the trie structure is to treat keys as bit strings, that is, strings over an alphabet of size $k = 2$. Such a **digital search tree** is essentially a binary tree, but search is directed to the left or right depending on whether a particular bit of the search key is 0 or 1. In addition to the two pointers, however, each node contains one of the keys that begins with the bit string implicit in the search path. Before the search proceeds to the left or right child of a node, the search key is compared for equality with the key stored in the node. Figure 8.4 shows such a tree for the set of keys used in the previous examples; the character code is the last five bits of the ASCII code, so $A = 00001$, $B = 00010$, ..., $Z = 11010$.

The search procedure for digital search trees works correctly regardless of

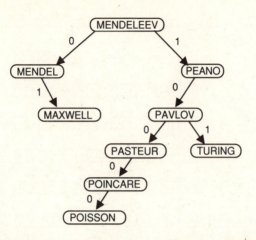

Figure 8.4 Digital search tree for the keys of Figures 8.1 through 8.3. Each character has a five-bit code, with M = 01101, P = 10000, and T = 10100. The digital codes for all keys in the subtree rooted at node u begin with the bit string on the path from the root of the entire tree to u. No special significance is attached to which of the keys in a subtree is stored at its root.

which of the keys that belong in the subtree is stored in the node. If the structure is static and the frequency distribution of the keys is known in advance, then it makes sense to store in each node the key of highest frequency that belongs in the subtree rooted at that node. That is, the root contains the key of highest frequency in the entire tree; the left child of the root contains the key of highest frequency that begins with a 0 bit (with the possible exception of the key at the root) and the right child of the root contains the key of highest frequency that begins with a 1 bit (with the possible exception of the key at the root); and so on. Then if n keys are to be represented, the tree has exactly n binary nodes, each of which has two pointer fields and a Key field.

A digital search tree can also be grown dynamically, with each new key inserted at the node where an unsuccessful search for it terminates. Deletions can be supported as well; when a key in an interior node is to be deleted, it is replaced by the key in any of its descendants that has two empty children, and that leaf is deleted from the tree.

Digital search trees have storage utilization and search time characteristics similar to those of random binary search trees. In particular, expected search time in a tree with n keys is $O(\log n)$, given natural assumptions about the distribution of keys. (Note the sort of circumstance that can make a digital search tree badly imbalanced: if 0 bits are more likely to occur than 1 bits, the tree will become imbalanced because left children are more common than right children.)

6. Let us return to the basic trie structure and its elementary variants, the

de la Briandais tree and the Patricia tree. If the keys are English words or sequences of English words, the lack of uniformity in the distribution of letter sequences can result in tries that are imbalanced, that is, discriminate poorly for several levels because certain letter combinations are so common and others so uncommon. In English there are a great many *th-* words, but no *tx-* or *td-* words. Instead of indexing on the first character of a word at the root, the second character at the second level of the tree, and so on, the indexing could proceed from the last letter of the key back towards the first, or alternately from the two ends (first letter, last letter, second, second to last, ...), or in any other way that improves the balance of the trie.

8.3 HASHING TECHNIQUES

Let **K** be a **key space**, that is, a large (possibly infinite) set from which keys are to be drawn. For example, **K** might be the set of all strings of characters constructible using the ASCII character set. Let $\{K_0, \ldots, K_{n-1}\}$ be a particular set of keys on which dictionary operations (*Insert* and *LookUp* at least, and possibly *Delete* as well) are to be performed. The basic idea of hashing is to store the members of this set in a **hash table** $T[0 \ldots m-1]$ with the aid of a **hash function** $h : \mathbf{K} \rightarrow \{0, \ldots, m-1\}$. For each j, key K_j is to be stored in the table at position $h(K_j)$. If h can be computed quickly, then to retrieve a key K one can compute $h(K)$ and retrieve the key (and any associated data) from that position in the table. The number $h(K)$ is called the **hash value** of key K.

The problem, of course, is that h probably cannot be a one-to-one mapping, since the size of **K** is in general much larger than m. Therefore **collisions** may occur: that is, there may be distinct keys in the set, say K_i and K_j where $i \neq j$, such that $h(K_i) = h(K_j)$. Since the two items cannot be stored in the same position, some strategy must be adopted for **resolving** the collision, that is, relocating one of the items in such a way that each can be found on subsequent *LookUp*s.

Besides being easy to compute, the basic property of a good hash function h is that it tends to spread keys out uniformly in the table. That is, if a key K is drawn at random from the key space **K** then the probability that $h(K) = i$ should be $1/m$, independent of i. This will tend to make collisions as infrequent as possible. A good simple method is to treat K as an integer and to let $h(K) = K \bmod m$, that is, to use as the hash value of a key the remainder when it is divided by the length of the hash table. If the keys are alphabetic and a binary code is in use, then m, the table size, should not be a power of 2, since $K \bmod m$ will then be just the $\lg m$ low-order bits of K, independent of the rest of K. For example, if K is in 8-bit ASCII and $m = 256$, then $K \bmod m$ is nothing but the ASCII code for the last character of K. As a rule of thumb,

Name	Date of Death	$h(K)$	$h_2(K)$
J. Adams	July 4, 1826	4	7
S. Adams	October 2, 1803	2	10
J. Bartlett	May 19, 1795	19	5
C. Braxton	October 10, 1797	10	10
C. Carroll	November 14, 1832	14	11
S. Chase	June 19, 1811	19	6
A. Clark	September 15, 1794	15	9
G. Clymer	January 23, 1813	23	1
W. Ellery	February 15, 1820	15	2
W. Floyd	August 4, 1821	4	8
B. Franklin	April 17, 1790	17	4
E. Gerry	November 23, 1814	23	11
B. Gwinnett	May 19, 1777	19	5
L. Hall	October 19, 1790	19	10
J. Hancock	October 8, 1793	8	10
B. Harrison	April 24, 1791	24	4
J. Hart	May 11, 1779	11	5
J. Hewes	November 10, 1779	10	11
T. Heyward	March 6, 1809	6	3
W. Hooper	October 14, 1790	14	10

Figure 8.5 Names of the first twenty (in alphabetical order) signers of the Declaration of Independence, and their death dates. (Source: *The World Almanac 1987*, p. 442.) To experiment with various hashing techniques, we use the hash function $h(K) =$ the day of the month on which K died. (Later in this chapter we use the secondary hash function $h_2(K) =$ the month in which K died.)

remainder modulo m provides a decent hash function if m is prime. We shall have more to say about hash functions in §8.5.

Whatever the hash function, there are two general types of strategy for organizing the hash table and resolving collisions: *chaining* and *open addressing*.

Chaining Strategies
Separate Chaining In the most straightforward strategy, $T[i]$ is used not to store a single datum, but as a pointer to a dynamic data structure containing data for all key values K such that $h(K) = i$. This data structure might be any that supports the dictionary operations, but since the number of collisions is expected to be small, elaborate structures can be avoided; ordinarily a simple linked list is used. In this case the entire data structure is on two levels; the hash table is an index that divides the dictionary into m linked lists, which are referred to as **buckets**.

To illustrate the notion of separate chaining, consider the data of Figure 8.5, the names of the first twenty (in alphabetical order) signers of the Declaration of Independence, together with their death dates.

Figure 8.6 shows a hash table of 31 buckets constructed by inserting these names in alphabetical order, using as the hash function *the day of the month on which the individual died*. (Of course, one could not in practice calculate

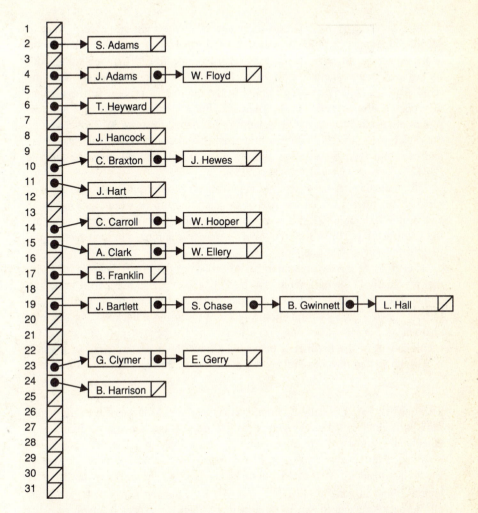

Figure 8.6 Hash table with separate chaining for the data of Figure 8.5, with the name of a man hashed to the day of the month on which he died.

that day from an individual's name; this "function" is being used for illustrative purposes only. Also, for the purpose of this illustration we have suspended our convention that table indexing is zero-based; the indices run from 1 to 31, like the days of the months, rather than from 0 to 30.) For example, since four of these men happened to have died on the nineteenth day of a month, bucket 19 has four members. We assume that insertions occur at the *ends* of chains, so that each chain is in alphabetical order.*

---

*This makes the diagrams easier to follow, since the chains show the keys in the order in which they are inserted. But it is, of course, quicker to insert at the *beginning* of a linked list.

Let us count as one **probe** each access to the data structure. Thus in separate chaining one probe is used to get a list header; if it is nonnull, a second probe is needed to retrieve the first record of the linked list, including both its key and pointer fields, and so on. For a given hashing structure the time required for a *LookUp* is proportional to the number of probes, so the number of probes is a good indicator of efficiency. For the example of Figure 8.6, two probes are needed to retrieve S. Adams or J. Adams; three for W. Floyd; and so on. Since there are 12 chains with at least one element, six with at least two, and one with four, the average number of probes to find a key in the table is $(2 \cdot 12 + 3 \cdot 6 + 1 \cdot 4 + 1 \cdot 5)/20 = 2.55$.

To understand more generally the performance of hashing strategies such as separate chaining, let n be the size of the dictionary to be stored and m be the size of the hash table. Then $\alpha = n/m$ is called the **load factor**; in our example the load factor is $20/31 \approx 0.65$. (With separate chaining, the load factor may be greater or less than one.)

Let $S(\alpha)$ be the expected number of probes to perform a *LookUp* on a key that is actually in the hash table, and $U(\alpha)$ be the expected number of probes in an unsuccessful *LookUp*, on the hypothesis that the key sought is equally likely to be mapped by the hash function to each of the m hash buckets. For separate chaining, a *LookUp* takes one probe to get the list header, plus one probe for each element of the list that is inspected. Since the average length of a list is $\alpha = n/m$ and an unsuccessful search always goes through an entire list,

$$U(\alpha) = 1 + \alpha.$$

The quantity $S(\alpha)$ is slightly trickier to analyze. A successful search goes through roughly half the elements of a list, on average, since a random key is equally likely to be the first, second, ..., or last key in a list. To be precise, the average number of probes in a successful search, not counting the one to get the list header, is 1 if the list is of length 1, $(1+2)/2 = 3/2$ if the list is of length 2, and in general $(1/k)\sum_{i=1}^{k} i = (k+1)/2$ if the list is of length k. If all the buckets were known to be nonempty, then the expected length of a list would again be $\alpha = n/m$, and the expected search time, including the probe to get the list header, would be $1 + (\alpha + 1)/2 = 3/2 + \alpha/2$. In fact, a successful search never inspects an empty bucket, and $S(\alpha)$ is 3/2 plus half the expected length of a *nonempty* list. Since some buckets might be empty, the expected length of a nonempty list is slightly larger than α, and the expected time for a successful search with separate chaining is

$$S(\alpha) \approx 2 + \frac{\alpha}{2}.$$

(See Problem 22.) Of course the worst-case number of probes is very much worse; if the keys all happened to have the same hash value, they would all be in the same bucket, and it would take $n+1$ probes, in the worst case, for either a successful or an unsuccessful search.

Ideally, if the expected size n of the dictionary is known in advance, the size m of the hash table can be chosen to be proportional to n, so that α is a constant. In this case expected access time is bounded by a constant and no elaborate data structure is needed for the buckets.

A major advantage of separate chaining strategies is that deletion is easy, or, to be precise, as easy as deletion from a bucket. If the buckets are linked lists, deletion is completely straightforward. The price paid for this ease in deletion, and for the opportunity to have a dictionary that is larger than the hash table, is the memory used by pointers, and the fact that a dynamic memory manager must be used to satisfy requests for allocation and deallocation of cells.

Coalesced Chaining   Looking up a key in the hash table of Figure 8.6 takes at least two probes; the head of a linked list must be found by indexing, then that pointer must be followed to get the first element of the linked list. An alternative organization stores the first cell of the linked lists in the hash table itself (Figure 8.7). This organization is plausible if the key field is not too large or the hash table is likely to be rather full, so that the space lost to empty key fields is not great.

From this modest variation on the separate chaining scheme another idea arises: to use the empty cells of the hash table itself to store the second and subsequent cells of the chains. In essence, the dynamic memory allocator is replaced by sequential allocation of empty cells, starting, say, from the top of the table and working down towards the bottom. Unfortunately, a slot that is occupied by such a "displaced" cell might be wanted later on to store an item that hashes to that slot. Such a collision is treated like any other; the key is stored in the next available position, as discovered by sequential search through the table.

The *LookUp* operation is implemented exactly as in the case of separate chaining, but the chains may contain elements with several different hash values. However, all elements with a given hash value are in the same chain, so only one chain need be searched for a key, namely, the chain that is entered at the key's hash value. In general the first probe does not go to the beginning of a chain, so even in case of an unsuccessful search only part of a chain is searched. The *Insert* operation is also essentially the same as for separate chaining, except that new cells are allocated from within the table, and the table can become full. The table is detected to be full when a search for an empty slot wraps around to its starting point.

Figure 8.8 shows the data of Figure 8.5 stored according to a coalesced chaining strategy, with collisions resolved by searching the table from top to bottom for a free slot. There are four chains of length 1, four of length 2, one of length 3, none of length 4, and one of length 5, so the expected number of probes to find an element in the table is

$$((4+4+1+0+1)\cdot 1+(4+1+0+1)\cdot 2+(1+0+1)\cdot 3+(0+1)\cdot 4+1\cdot 5)/20 = 1.85.$$

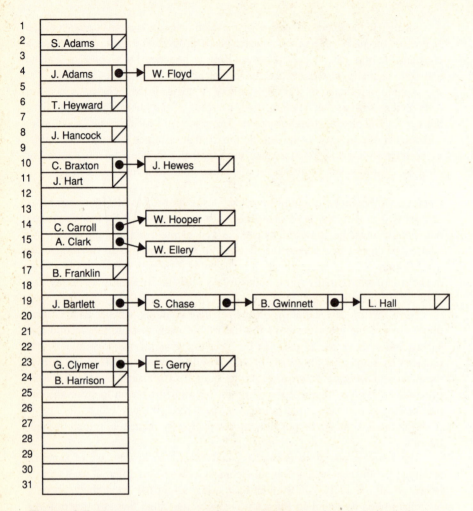

Figure 8.7 Hash table of Figure 8.6, with first entry of each chain (rather than a pointer to that entry) stored in the hash array proper.

For separate chaining the figure calculated earlier was 2.55 probes, but a fair comparison with the separate chaining method would have to discount the first probe used in that method, which simply accesses the first cell of the chain, so these data support the intuition that coalesced chaining is not much less efficient than separate chaining in expected access time.

Since some collisions are almost certain to occur, and these interfere first with the placement of records that hash to positions early in the hash table, a logical strategy to improve the performance of coalesced chaining is to leave the first few slots in the table strictly for resolving collisions. In other words, have the table indices extend from $-v$ to $m - 1$, but hash only to the indices

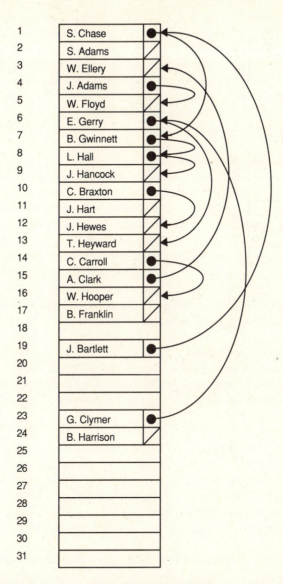

Figure 8.8 Hashing with coalesced chaining. The hash table of Figure 8.7 is organized with all hash table entries stored internally. If position $h(K)$ is occupied when key K is to be installed, the first free slot in the table is used to store K, and that cell is added to the list that contains slot $h(K)$. As a result keys with different hash values can fall in the same chain, so the chains "coalesce." For example, Hancock ($h(K) = 8$) is in the same chain with Hall ($h(K) = 19$) because Hall was put in the table before Hancock, and at that time slot 19 was occupied and slot 8 was the first free slot.

0 through $m-1$; this leaves v positions that can be used for resolving collisions, before starting to use the main part of the hash table for this purpose. The first v slots are sometimes called the **cellar**, and the strategy is referred to as *coalesced chaining with cellar*. Experimental and theoretical work suggests that making the cellar about 14% of the total space allocated (that is, $v/(m+v) = 0.14$) yields good performance for both successful and unsuccessful searches over a wide range of values of the load factor.

Open Addressing Strategies

In an open addressing strategy items are stored directly in the hash table, but no pointers are used to direct the search from one slot to another. Instead, if the intended position of a key is found to be occupied, some method, perhaps depending on properties of the key, is used to determine a sequence of positions to be searched.

The sequence of positions searched is called the **probe sequence** for the key. We let $H(K,p)$ denote the pth position tried for key K, where $p = 0$, 1, ... Thus $H(K,0) = h(K)$, the primary hash position for the key. To search for a key, look at the successive positions in its probe sequence, until either the key is found or an empty ("open") position is encountered; if an empty position is encountered, the key is known not to be in the table. If the key is to be inserted in the table, it may be inserted in the open position just discovered, or the table may first be reorganized somewhat to reduce search times in the future.

We first describe two methods for determining the probe sequence, *linear probing* and *double hashing*, and then discuss several insertion strategies that reduce search times.

Sequential or Linear Probing   If key K hashes to index i, but that position is occupied by another record, just try positions $i+1$, $i+2$, ... until an empty slot is found, and store the record with key K there. If the search must continue beyond the end of the table, that is, beyond position $m-1$, then continue from the top of the table (position 0). That is,

$$H(K,0) = h(K)$$

$$H(K,p+1) = H(K,p) + 1 \bmod m.$$

Of course, if the search reaches the initial probe position a second time, then the table is full and there is no hope of inserting the key.

For example, Figure 8.9 shows the result of inserting the data of Figure 8.5 and Figure 8.6 into a hash table, using the same hashing function as before (day of the month on which death occurred) and using linear probing to resolve collisions. The third column shows the number of probes needed to look up a key K in the hash table; this is 1 if the key is in its natural position $h(K)$, but is greater than 1 if the key collided with a previously inserted key when it was inserted.

1		
2	S. Adams	1
3		
4	J. Adams	1
5	W. Floyd	2
6	T. Heyward	1
7		
8	J. Hancock	1
9		
10	C. Braxton	1
11	J. Hart	1
12	J. Hewes	3
13		
14	C. Carroll	1
15	A. Clark	1
16	W. Ellery	2
17	B. Franklin	1
18	W. Hooper	5
19	J. Bartlett	1
20	S. Chase	2
21	B. Gwinnett	3
22	L. Hall	4
23	G. Clymer	1
24	E. Gerry	2
25	B. Harrison	2
26		
27		
28		
29		
30		
31		

Figure 8.9 Open-addressed hash table for the data of Figure 8.5, with linear probing used to resolve collisions. The names have been inserted in alphabetical order. The third column shows the number of probes required to find a key in the table; this is the same as the number of slots that were inspected when it was inserted.

The last name inserted in this table was that of T. Hooper, with hash value 14; but at the time his name was inserted, positions 14, 15, 16, and 17 in the table were all occupied, so his name wound up in position 18.

Linear probing is extremely easy to implement and has satisfactory behavior when the table is not too full. Unfortunately, it suffers from a phenomenon called **primary clustering**. Once a block of a few contiguous occupied positions emerges in the hash table, it becomes a "target" for subsequent collisions; a collision at any of the positions in the cluster makes the cluster grow larger, and the larger the cluster becomes, the bigger a target it is. As clusters grow, they also merge to form larger clusters; in our example this happened when Hooper filled up the last open space between clusters of size 4 and 7. In Figure 8.9, 20 of the 31 table entries are filled, but the filled entries form five clusters, one of them 12 entries long.

Large clusters tend to increase the expected search time. In the example of Figure 8.9, the expected number of probes to find a key in the table (provided that all keys are equally likely to be sought) is the average of the values in the third column, which turns out to be 1.8 (versus a minimum of 1.0 probes per *LookUp*). The time required for an *unsuccessful* search increases even more dramatically as a result of clustering. Consider the number of probes required to look up K, if K is not in the hash table. If K hashes to an empty slot, only one probe of the table is needed; but if K hashes to a slot that is not empty, the search must proceed to the end of the cluster before it can be abandoned. With clusters of size 1, 3, 1, 3, and 12 the expected number of probes in an unsuccessful search is $1/31$ of the sum

$$
\begin{aligned}
&11 \cdot 1 && (h(K) \text{ is an empty slot}) \\
+\ &5 \cdot 2 && (h(K) \text{ is the last slot of a cluster}) \\
+\ &3 \cdot 3 && (h(K) \text{ is the next to last in a cluster of size at least 2}) \\
+\ &3 \cdot 4 && (h(K) \text{ is the third to last in a cluster of size at least 3}) \\
+\ &1 \cdot 5 && (h(K) \text{ is the fourth to last in a cluster of size at least 4}) \\
+\ &1 \cdot 6 && \\
+\ &\cdots && \\
+\ &1 \cdot 13, && (h(K) \text{ is the first slot of the cluster of size 12})
\end{aligned}
$$

or about 3.97. But if the 20 entries happened to fall into ten clusters each of size 2, the expected number of probes for an unsuccessful search would be less than 2.

An attempt to improve this strategy by adding some constant k greater than one to the index would not help at all; the clusters would then become sequences of the form i, $i + k \bmod m$, $i + 2k \bmod m$, ...

Open Addressing with Double Hashing   Clusters can be broken up if the second and subsequent positions in the probe sequence for a key are chosen in a way that is independent of its primary position. One way to do this is to use a second hash function h_2, the values of which are independent of the values of the primary hash function h. When key K is sought, each probed position is $h_2(K)$ beyond the previous one, with the search wrapping around to the top of the table if it goes beyond the end of the table. In other words,

$$H(K, 0) = h(K)$$

$$H(K, p+1) = \bigl(H(K, p) + h_2(K)\bigr) \bmod m.$$

Linear probing is double hashing with $h_2(K) = 1$ for all K.

To ensure that the probe sequence visits all positions in the table, $h_2(K)$ must be greater than zero and relatively prime to m for any K. That is, $h_2(K)$ and m should have no common divisor. For if d divides both m and $h_2(K)$, then

$$\left(\frac{m}{d} \cdot h_2(K)\right) \bmod m = \left(m \cdot \frac{h_2(K)}{d}\right) \bmod m = 0,$$

1	J. Hewes	3
2	S. Adams	1
3	E. Gerry	2
4	J. Adams	1
5		
6	T. Heyward	1
7		
8	J. Hancock	1
9		
10	C. Braxton	1
11	J. Hart	1
12	W. Floyd	2
13	W. Hooper	4
14	C. Carroll	1
15	A. Clark	1
16		
17	W. Ellery	2
18		
19	J. Bartlett	1
20		
21	B. Franklin	2
22		
23	G. Clymer	1
24	B. Gwinnett	2
25	S. Chase	2
26		
27		
28	B. Harrison	2
29	L. Hall	2
30		
31		

Figure 8.10 Open-addressed hash table for the data of Figure 8.5 on page 266, inserted in alphabetical order, with double hashing used to resolve collisions; $h(K)$ = day of month on which death occurred, and $h_2(K)$ = month in which death occurred. The third column shows the number of probes used when the key was inserted, which is the number that would be used during a search for that key.

so that the m/d^{th} probe in the sequence will be the same as the first. Therefore the probe sequence will not reach all positions in the table. Of course, the simplest way to ensure that $h_2(K)$ is always relatively prime to m is to choose m to be a prime number in the first place. For example, in the hash tables of Figures 8.6 through 8.9 we have chosen $m = 31$, a prime number.

Figure 8.10 shows the data of Figure 8.5 on page 266 entered into a hash table by double hashing. The primary hash function is, as before, the day of the month on which death occurred; the secondary hash function is the month of death, with January = 1, February = 2, and so on.

The last name inserted, W. Hooper, has hash values $h(K) = 14$ and $h_2(K) = 10$. Position 14 in the table is found to be occupied (by Carroll); next position $14 + 10 = 24$ is checked, but this too is occupied (by Gwinnett);

then position $14 + 2 \cdot 10 \bmod 31 = 3$ is checked, but it is occupied (by Gerry); finally position $14 + 3 \cdot 10 \bmod 31 = 13$ is checked and found to be vacant.

In the example the secondary hashing breaks up the clusters and shortens the expected search time. For example, each of the four keys with primary hash value of 19 can be looked up with at most one extra probe. The expected number of probes to look up a key (the average of the values in the third column of Figure 8.10) is $33/20 = 1.65$.

The exact performance of open addressing with double hashing is difficult to determine analytically, but the behavior of double hashing can be approximated by the assumption that *each probe into the hash table is independent and has a probability of hitting an occupied position exactly equal to the load factor.* Of course this assumption is false; successive probes are to algorithmically related positions, and it is impossible to probe the same position twice. But the use of the second hashing function sufficiently disorganizes the probe sequences of different keys that the algorithm behaves empirically as though the italicized statement were true.

Suppose that the assumption is true, and we insert n items into an initially empty hash table of size m; what is the expected number of probes in a successful or unsuccessful search? Let $\alpha_i = i/m$ for each $i \leq n$; thus by the assumption the probability of a collision on any probe was α_i after i keys had been inserted. Then the expected number of probes in an unsuccessful search when $n - 1$ items have been inserted is

$$
\begin{aligned}
U_{n-1} &\approx 1 \cdot (1 - \alpha_{n-1}) + 2 \cdot \alpha_{n-1} \cdot (1 - \alpha_{n-1}) + 3 \cdot \alpha_{n-1}^2 \cdot (1 - \alpha_{n-1}) + \cdots \\
&= 1 + \alpha_{n-1} + \alpha_{n-1}^2 + \cdots \\
&= \frac{1}{1 - \alpha_{n-1}}.
\end{aligned}
$$

That is, with probability $1 - \alpha_{n-1}$ the first slot probed will be empty, so only one probe is needed to insert it; with probability $\alpha_{n-1} \cdot (1 - \alpha_{n-1})$ the first slot will be full but the second slot probed will be empty, so exactly two probes are needed for the insertion; and so on. (Of course the sum is not truly infinite, since it stops after m terms.) The number of probes in a successful search is the average of the number of probes it took to insert each of the n items; and the expected number of probes to insert the ith item is the expected number of probes in an unsuccessful search when $i - 1$ items have been inserted. Therefore

$$
\begin{aligned}
S_n &\approx \frac{1}{n} \sum_{i=1}^{n} U_{i-1} \\
&= \frac{1}{n} \sum_{i=1}^{n} \frac{1}{1 - \alpha_{i-1}}
\end{aligned}
$$

$$= \frac{m}{n} \sum_{i=1}^{n} \frac{1}{m-i+1} = \frac{m}{n}(H_m - H_{m-n}),$$

where $H_i = 1 + \frac{1}{2} + \frac{1}{3} + \cdots + \frac{1}{i} \approx \ln i$ is the ith harmonic number. Therefore

$$S_n \approx \frac{m}{n}\left(\ln m - \ln(m-n)\right) = \frac{m}{n} \ln \frac{m}{m-n} = \frac{1}{\alpha_n} \ln \frac{1}{1-\alpha_n}.$$

When $\alpha_n = 20/31$ as in the example, $S_n \approx 1.606$, in good agreement with our observed value of 1.65. Even when the table is 90% full, S_n is only 2.56, though $U_n \approx 1/(1 - .9) = 10.0$.

While double hashing can be modelled rather accurately in this way, sequential probing is much harder to analyze. Knuth shows that for sequential probing,

$$S_n \approx \frac{1}{2}\left(1 + \frac{1}{1-\alpha}\right)$$

$$U_n \approx \frac{1}{2}\left(1 + \frac{1}{(1-\alpha)^2}\right).$$

When $\alpha = .9$ the expected times for successful and unsuccessful searches are $S_n \approx 5.5$ and $U_n \approx 50.5$, in contrast to the figures of 2.56 and 10.0 for double hashing. The small extra effort required to implement double hashing certainly pays off!

Ordered Hashing   The time required for unsuccessful searches with double hashing can be reduced if some care is taken with the way insertions are done. In the hash tables of Figures 8.6, 8.7, and 8.8, the names have been inserted in alphabetical order; since insertions are performed at the ends of the lists, the chains are in alphabetical order. This ordering could be used to reduce search times during *unsuccessful* searches, since a search for key K can safely be abandoned once a key alphabetically greater than K has been found. The special nature of the ordering has no impact on the expected time for *successful* searches, however.

With separate chaining, even if the data are not inserted in the hash table in order, the chains can still be kept alphabetically ordered, simply by inserting keys at their alphabetic positions in the chains. This requires a search, unless the appropriate position is known as a result of a previous *LookUp*.

The same basic idea can be applied to hash tables with open addressing, though the manipulations required to keep the data organized are somewhat more complicated. The items must be inserted in such a way that if key K is in the table, then *during the probe sequence for key K, the keys encountered before reaching K are alphabetically smaller than K*. Clearly, if this is the case then when key K is sought, the search can be abandoned as soon as a key is encountered in K's probe sequence that is alphabetically greater than K. The question is how to perform the insertions so that this property is maintained regardless of the order in which the keys are inserted. The trick is this: *As the probe sequence for key K is followed, if a key K' is encountered such that K < K', replace K' by K, and proceed to insert K' as dictated by its probe sequence.*

To see how this works, imagine the keys to be students (male students, for grammatical simplicity) who are to be seated in a classroom. Each student has his own preferences of where to be seated (probe sequence), and students vary in size (the alphabetic ordering, with bigger students being the alphabetically earlier strings). When a student enters the classroom, he first tries his first-choice seat; if it is empty he occupies it. If it is not empty and the student sitting in it is bigger than he is, he tries his next-highest choice seat. But if the seat is occupied by a smaller student, he ejects the student from the seat, sits down himself, and sends the displaced student off to try *his* next-highest choice seat. Algorithm 8.2 shows the details.

It is not completely obvious that this algorithm creates a hash table with the critical property that if a record with key K is in the table then the keys preceding K in its probe sequence are necessarily smaller than K alphabetically. In fact this property follows by a simple induction. When the table is empty the property holds trivially. Thereafter, the only operations on the table are

1. to put a key, which is greater than any of its predecessors in its probe sequence, in a previously empty slot, and
2. to replace a key already in the table by a smaller key.

Neither of these operations can cause a greater key to come before a lesser key in the probe sequence of the latter.

Indeed, if Algorithm 8.2 is used, *the final state of the hash table for a given set of keys will be the same, regardless of the order in which the keys were inserted.* In fact, the hash table will have the same appearance as it would if the keys had been inserted in alphabetical order. For example, any of the 20! ways of inserting the 20 keys of Figure 8.5 on page 266 in an ordered hash table would result in the table of Figure 8.10. To see why this is so, let K_1, ..., K_n be the keys in alphabetical order, and suppose that there are different insertion sequences yielding distinct hash tables. Let i be the smallest number such that K_i can fall in different positions depending on the order in which the keys are inserted. Thus K_1, ..., K_{i-1} are in the same positions in all hash tables derived from these keys. But then K_i must also be in a unique position, namely, the earliest position in its probe sequence not occupied by one of K_1, ..., K_{i-1}; if it were located any later than this in its probe sequence, it would be preceded in its probe sequence by one of K_{i+1}, ..., K_n, and Algorithm 8.2 would not work.

Algorithm 8.2 uses double hashing to calculate the probe sequence, and assumes that $h_2(K)$ is relatively prime to the table size m for any key K,

procedure *OrderedHashInsert*(**key** K, **info** I, **pointer** P):
    if Size(P) $= m - 1$ **then error**   {Hash table is full}
    $T \leftarrow$ Table(P)
    $p \leftarrow h(K)$
    while $T[p] \neq \Lambda$ **do**   {Table position $T[p]$ is not empty}
        if Key($T[p]$) $> K$ **then**
            $K \leftrightarrow$ Key($T[p]$)
            $I \leftrightarrow$ Info($T[p]$)
        else if Key($T[p]$) $= K$ **then**
            Info($T[p]$) $\leftarrow I$
            return
        $p \leftarrow p + h_2(K)$ mod m {Next position in K's probe sequence}
    Key($T[p]$) $\leftarrow K$
    Info($T[p]$) $\leftarrow I$
    Size(P) $\leftarrow$ Size(P) $+ 1$

function *OrderedHashLookUp*(**key** K, **pointer** P): **info**
    $T \leftarrow$ Table(P)
    $p \leftarrow h(K)$
    while $T[p] \neq \Lambda$ **and** Key($T[p]$) $< K$ **do** $p \leftarrow p + h_2(K)$ mod m
    if $T[p] \neq \Lambda$ **and** Key($T[p]$) $= K$
        then return Info($T[p]$)
        else return Λ

Algorithm 8.2 Insertion and search in an ordered, open-addressed hash table. The hash table is passed as a pointer P to a record with two fields, $T =$ Table(P), which is the hash table itself, and $n =$ Size(P), which is the number of occupied positions in the hash table. The constant m is the length of table T.

so that any key's probe sequence would eventually visit all positions in the table. To make it possible to discover quickly whether the table is full, the dictionary is implemented as a record with two components, the hash table itself $T =$ Table(P) (a table of which each entry has Key and Info fields) and the number $n =$ Size(P) of items in the table. The length of the table is a constant m; thus the table indices are $0 .. m - 1$.

If we assume that all keys are equally likely to be sought, the ordering strategy does not change the expected time for a successful search; S_n is the same as for the double hashing strategy of the last section. However, the number of probes in an unsuccessful search is essentially the same, on average, as in a successful search, since in both cases about half of the occupied portion of a key's probe sequence will have to be inspected on average, either to find the key or to determine that it is not present. So for ordered hashing with double hashing,

$$S_n \approx U_n \approx \frac{1}{\alpha_n} \ln \frac{1}{1 - \alpha_n}.$$

Deletions

Deleting from a separately chained hash table is easy; indeed it is one of the principal advantages of separate chaining that deletion from the hash table is as easy as deletion from the chain, which typically is a linked list. Deletion from an open-addressed hash table is not so simple. A key to be deleted cannot simply be removed from the hash table, leaving its position empty, since the position of the key being deleted might be on a probe sequence for a key that remains in the hash table.

Suppose for simplicity that sequential probing is used, and consider what happens when two keys with the same primary hash value i are inserted into an otherwise empty hash table, and then one of them is deleted. The other will be left at position $i + 1 \bmod m$, but a subsequent *LookUp* would stop on finding position i empty. The usual way of avoiding this problem is to add a one-bit Deleted field to each table entry; when an entry is deleted, the Deleted bit is set to 1. Searches proceed over both the occupied slots and the empty slots that have Deleted bit 1; insertions occur at the first position that is empty or has a Deleted bit 1. With these algorithms the data structure correctly implements the dictionary operations, but searches, particularly unsuccessful searches, tend to be lengthy once a large number of insertions and deletions have occurred, since eventually nearly every unoccupied position will have its Deleted bit 1.

Other strategies for resolving collisions, such as coalesced chaining and double hashing, can make use of Deleted bits, but the side-effect—increased search times—occurs with these methods as well. As a last resort, if a hash table becomes too cluttered with deleted entries, it can be rebuilt from scratch by inserting all its members into a new hash table that is initially empty. Naturally this is a time-consuming process, but its cost may be worth while; the size of the hash table can be increased at the same time, if necessary, to respond to what may have been learned about the number of entries that must be accommodated.

8.4 EXTENDIBLE HASHING

Open-addressing hashing strategies have the advantages over separate chaining strategies that they do not use space for pointers and do not rely on dynamic memory management. But they have the significant disadvantages that deletions cause performance to be degraded and that the size of the table cannot be adjusted if the number of entries is larger than was anticipated when the table

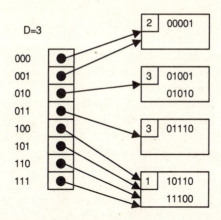

Figure 8.11 Extendible hash table, consisting of a directory and four leaf
pages. The four leaf pages contain all keys whose hash values begin with
00, 010, 011, and 1, respectively. The box in the upper left corner of a
leaf page shows the *depth* of the page, that is, the length of the prefix of
the hash value of all keys in that page.

was initialized. The only practicable course of action, in case an open-addressed
table becomes heavily contaminated by deleted entries or becomes full, is to
allocate an entirely new table of the appropriate size and to transfer the contents
of the old hash table, one entry at a time, into the new table.

Extendible hashing is a method that allows a hash table to grow and shrink
gracefully while keeping access times bounded. It is especially useful in organizing data in secondary storage, and can be used as an alternative to a B-tree
structure. The extendible hashing data structure has two levels: a top-level
directory, and a set of **leaf pages** (Figure 8.11). The directory is a table of
pointers to leaf pages; the data records themselves are kept in the leaf pages. It
is easiest to think of the directory as held in internal storage and the leaf pages
as held in external storage; then finding any item takes only a single reference
to external storage. The leaf pages are of fixed size, say b records; we assume
that a memory manager is available to allocate or release leaf pages on request.

Extendible hashing is based on a hash function h that maps keys to bit
strings of, say, L bits in length; it is important that the distribution of keys
across the 2^L hash values be uniform. If $d \leq L$, let $h_d(K)$ be the first d bits
of $h(K)$, that is, the prefix of $h(K)$ of length d. For example, if $L = 5$ and
$h(K_0) = 01010$, then $h_3(K_0) = 010$. A leaf page consists of all keys in the
hash table whose hash values have a particular prefix; the length of this prefix
is the **depth** of the page. Figure 8.11 shows an extendible hash table consisting
of a directory and four leaf pages; the depths of those pages are shown in their
upper left-hand corners. (The boxes denoting the leaf pages contain not the
keys themselves, but their hash values.) Since the page containing the key that
hashes to 01010 has depth 3, that page also contains any other key in the hash

table whose hash value begins with 010 (01001 is such a page in our example). However, not all pages need have the same depth. In Figure 8.11 there are four pages, which have depths 2, 3, 3, and 1; these pages contain records whose keys have hash values with prefixes 00, 010, 011, and 1, and every bit string begins with exactly one of these prefixes.

The maximum depth of any leaf page is called the depth of the hash table as a whole, and is denoted by D; in our example $D = 3$. The directory is a table T of length 2^D containing pointers to leaf pages; thus to locate the page containing key K, compute $h_D(K)$ and follow the pointer in $T[h_D(K)]$. If the depth of a leaf page is less than the depth of the table, several pointers will point to it; to be exact, a leaf page of depth d will be pointed to by 2^{D-d} consecutive entries of T. Thus the directory is essentially the top level of a trie structure, discriminating on the first D bits of the hash value of the key.

The choice of the internal structure of a leaf page is independent of the other considerations about the data structure; the pages could be open-addressed hash tables, or search trees, for example. But their capacity is limited to exactly b items; if a page overflows due to an attempted insertion, it must be split. Splitting is accomplished by increasing the depth of the page and creating a "buddy" page. For example, Figure 8.12(a) shows the effect of inserting a key with hash value 11101, on the assumption that $b = 2$. Since the page of depth 1 corresponding to the prefix string 1 is already full, the page is split into two pages of depth 2, one for prefix 10 and one for prefix 11; the records are distributed between these two pages as appropriate. Conceivably this process might have to be iterated, because all the records move to one of the pages, but unless b is very small such an occurrence probably indicates some nonuniformity in the hashing function.

If a page of less than maximal depth is split, one or more pointers in the directory need to be changed to point to the new leaf page. But if increasing the depth of a leaf page causes the depth of the whole table to increase (because the page being split was of maximal depth), then the size of the directory must be doubled. Figure 8.12(b) shows what happens when a key with hash value 01011 is inserted into the table of Figure 8.12(a). In general, entries $2i$ and $2i + 1$ of the new directory both point to the same leaf page as entry i of the old directory, except if entry i pointed to the page that was being split. Of course, increasing the size of the directory requires recourse to a memory manager, and if the directory becomes too large it will not be possible to hold it in internal memory.

Extendible hashing is capable of accommodating deletions. Suppose that directory entries $2i$ and $2i + 1$ point to distinct pages of maximal depth. If deleting an entry from one of them causes their collective size to be b entries or less, then the two pages can be collapsed into a single page; if they were the only leaf pages of maximal depth, then the directory can be halved in size. When and how to carry out such operations may require some judgment and tuning;

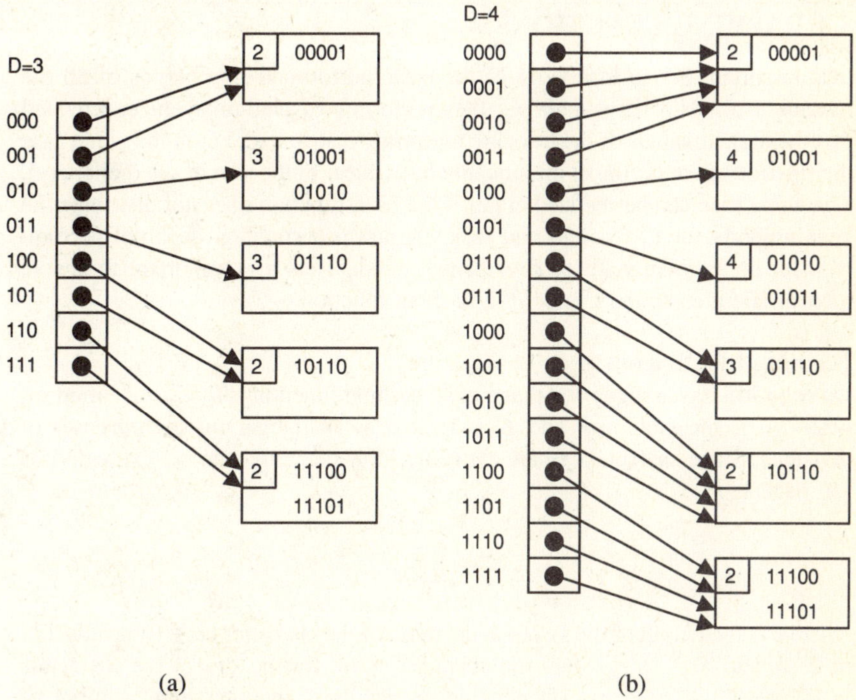

D=4

D=3

(a)

(b)

Figure 8.12 Insertion into the extendible hash table of Figure 8.11. The leaf pages can hold only two records; if a page overflows as a result of an insertion, it is split. (a) The result of inserting a record that hashes to 11101 into the table of Figure 8.11; the last leaf page splits. (b) The result of inserting a record that hashes to 01011 into the table of part (a); the page containing 01001 and 01010 splits.

collapsing two half-full pages into one full page is an expensive operation, especially if it happens to be followed by splitting the full page as a result of an insertion.

How efficient is extendible hashing? There is no question about time efficiency, since by definition any record can be found with a single probe of the directory and a single access to a leaf page. However, storage efficiency is an important issue, since leaf pages are generally underfull and since the directory usually has duplicate entries. A complex analysis (cited on page 297) shows that if pages can accommodate b items, then the expected number of pages needed to store n items is roughly $n/(b \cdot \ln 2)$; that is, the pages are about 69% full on average, and about 44% more pages are needed than the theoretical minimum. The expected size of the directory is about $(e/(b \cdot \ln 2)) \cdot n^{1+1/b}$; thus for large b, the directory is expected to have about 2.7 times as many slots as there are leaf pages.

8.5 HASHING FUNCTIONS

It is important not to lose sight of the basic performance properties of all the hashing methods discussed above: they perform very well on average, provided that the hashed values of the keys are uniformly distributed, but in the worst case their performance is almost unthinkably bad (linear in the size of the dictionary). The worst case can be realized either if the hash function does not distribute the keys properly, or if, through bad luck, the hashing function does not perform well for the particular set of keys being stored. Thus it is important to devote a bit of attention to the choice of a hashing function.

Hashing by Division

On page 265 it was suggested that a good hashing function is $h(K) = K \bmod m$, where m is the table size and K is treated as an integer for the purposes of division. Since in fact keys are typically alphabetic, K can be expressed as (cf. page 164)

$$K = \sum_{i=0}^{p-1} c_i r^i,$$

where p is the length of the key, r is the radix of the character code (typically 128 or 256), and $c_{p-1}, \ldots, c_0$ are the character codes for the successive characters in the key ($0 \leq c_i < r$). (Depending on details of the encoding, p might be fixed, and "blank" or "null" characters might be used to pad a short string out to length p at either the left or the right end.) Any hashing function causes many distinct keys to collide; the trick is to avoid *systematic* collisions in cases where the source from which the keys originate is likely to exhibit a systematic, nonrandom pattern in its selection of keys. For example, it is clearly a bad idea, as already noted, to choose m to be r or r^2, since the division then simply retains the last character or two in the string. If the keys are the identifiers in the source text of a computer program, the last character is likely to be very unevenly distributed, with a heavy concentration of a few printing characters. Similarly, choosing m to be even is a poor idea, since $h(K)$ would then be odd or even depending on whether the last character in K has an odd or even code.

It is safest, when using this method, to choose m to be prime, and moreover to have the property that m does not divide $r^k \pm a$ for any small value of k or a. For example, taking $m = r - 1$ is a poor choice, even if it happens to be a prime, since

$$\left(\sum_{i=0}^{p-1} c_i r^i\right) \bmod (r-1) = \left(\sum_{i=0}^{p-1} \left(c_i r^i \bmod (r-1)\right)\right) \bmod (r-1)$$

$$= \left(\sum_{i=1}^{p-1} c_i\right) \bmod (r-1),$$

since for any i,

$$r^i \bmod (r-1) = \left(1 + (r-1)\sum_{j=0}^{i-1} r^j\right) \bmod (r-1) = 1.$$

Therefore using $m = r-1$ results in all permutations of the same character string (ABC, BCA, etc.) having the same hash value. In practice these considerations rule out only a few values; for example, if $r = 256$ then values of m in the neighborhood of 256 and $256^2 = 65536$ should be avoided, but the latter figure is probably impractically large anyway in many applications.

One difficulty with the division method (as well as the multiplication method discussed below) is that the length of the key may well be much greater than the machine word size on which integer division can be performed. The usual way to work around this problem is to **fold** the key into a single machine word before carrying out the division. Folding is the act of breaking an alphabetic key into chunks of length, say, two or four characters, and combining them together by an operation such as integer addition or logical exclusive-or. The folding operation can be more complex; for example, cyclically shifting successive chunks by 1, 2, 3, ... bit positions prevents keys made up of the same chunks in different orders from having the same folded value.

Hashing by Multiplication

The division method is simple and fast, but it is not suitable in all situations. The method of the last section yields a hash function $h : \mathbf{K} \to \{0, \dots, m-1\}$, where m is prime; but sometimes we need m to be nonprime. For example, in the implementation of extendible hashing, the range of h should include all bit strings of a specified length; the number of such bit strings is a power of 2.

If x is a nonnegative real number, let $\{x\} = x - \lfloor x \rfloor$ be the fractional part of x. It is an interesting fact of mathematics that if θ is any irrational number, then for large enough n the n fractions $\{\theta\}, \{2\theta\}, \{3\theta\}, \dots, \{n\theta\}$ are distributed very uniformly across the interval from 0 to 1. It turns out that the $n+1$ segments formed by 0, 1, and the n fractions have only three lengths, and the next fraction in the sequence, $\{(n+1)\theta\}$, falls in one of the segments of greatest length. Choosing θ to be the reciprocal of the golden ratio

$$\theta = \phi^{-1} = -\hat{\phi} = \frac{\sqrt{5}-1}{2} \approx 0.61803399$$

causes the distribution of the fractions to be particularly even; each new point splits one of the largest existing intervals in the golden ratio (Figure 8.13).

Having chosen $\theta = \phi^{-1}$ and fixed the range size m, we define the multiplicative hash for key K as

$$h(K) = \lfloor m\{K\theta\} \rfloor. \tag{1}$$

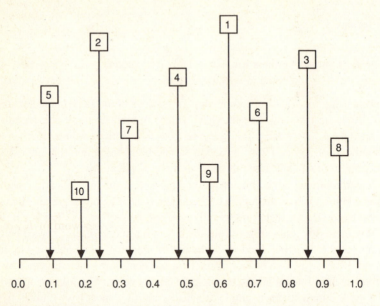

Figure 8.13 The values of $\{K\phi^{-1}\}$ for $K = 1, \ldots, 10$, where ϕ^{-1} is the reciprocal of the golden ratio, 0.61803.... Each new value divides one of the existing intervals of maximal size in the golden ratio, so the values are distributed evenly across the interval from 0 to 1.

That is, K is treated as an integer, as in the case of the division method, and the fractional part of $K\theta$, which is nonnegative and less than 1, is scaled to fit the range of the possible values $0, 1, \ldots, m - 1$.

Mathematically, this method has a number of attractive properties. If the key space consists of all character strings of up to a certain length, the method provably distributes the keys uniformly across hash values. The hash value depends on all the characters of the key and their positions (so permutations are no more likely to collide than other pairs of keys). Keys that are "close" to each other, like SUM1 and SUM2, differ in numerical value by a small constant, so their hash values are widely separated. However, it is not evident that the computation of (1) can be carried out easily, especially on machines lacking floating-point capabilities.

In fact, if m is a power of 2, the computation is quite easily programmed using only fixed-point arithmetic, if we think of machine words as representing fractions between 0 and 1 (with the "binary point" at the left end) rather than integers. Let $m = 2^k$, and let $s \geq k$ be the number of bits of precision with which a positive fixed-point number is represented. For example, if the machine has 16-bit words and all 16 bits can be used to represent "unsigned" fixed-point numbers, then $s = 16$. The largest integer representable is $2^s - 1$, but as a binary fraction this bit pattern (a string of s 1 bits) represents a number just slightly less than 1. We refer to an s-bit number as a **word**. On typical computers, two positive one-word fixed-point numbers can be multiplied to produce a two-word fixed-point product. If we think of both the numbers being multiplied as fractions, the result is a two-word fraction with the binary point at the left end; the product of two numbers in the range $[0, 1)$ is in the range* $[0, 1)$. But if we think of one as a fraction and the other as an integer, then the binary point of the result is between its two one-word halves—the product of an s-bit fraction in the range $[0, 1)$ and an integer in the range $[0, 2^s - 1]$ is in the range $[0, 2^s - 1)$ and has an s-bit integer part and an s-bit fractional part.

Let σ be a one-word binary fraction approximately equal to the irrational number θ. For reasons explained below, the low-order bit of σ should be 1; that is, if σ is regarded as an s-bit integer, then σ should be odd and $\sigma/2^s \approx \theta$. Then the quantity $\lfloor m\{K\theta\} \rfloor$ can be approximated by multiplying K by σ, and taking the k high-order bits of the low-order word of the result. That is, if K is regarded as an integer and σ as a fraction, the low-order word of $K \cdot \sigma$ is a binary fraction approximating $\{K\theta\}$; taking the high-order k bits of the result and treating them as an integer effectively multiplies $\{K\theta\}$ by $m = 2^k$ and discards the fractional part (Figure 8.14).

If σ is chosen so that, when regarded as an integer, it is odd, then different values of K produce different values of the low-order word of the product $K\sigma$. That is, no collisions will occur until the last step of the computation of the hash function, which is essentially to truncate the value to the precision determined by the size of the range. To see this, let σ be the bit string $\sigma_{s-1}\sigma_{s-2}\ldots\sigma_1\sigma_0$, so that when viewed as an integer, $\sigma = \sum_{i=0}^{s-1} \sigma_i 2^i$. We wish to show that if $\sigma_0 = 1$, then for any distinct K_1 and K_2,

$$\sigma K_1 \bmod 2^s \neq \sigma K_2 \bmod 2^s,$$

where all numbers are treated as integers. Suppose $K_1 < K_2$ and let $D = K_2 - K_1$; then we must show that $\sigma D \bmod 2^s \neq 0$ provided that $D \neq 0$. If the binary representation of D is $d_{s-1}d_{s-2}\ldots d_1 d_0$, so that $D = \sum_{i=0}^{s-1} d_i 2^i$, then

$$\sigma D = \sum_{i=0}^{2s-2} \left(\sum_{j=0}^{i} \sigma_j d_{i-j} \right) 2^i.$$

Let p be the position of the rightmost nonzero bit of D; that is, $0 \leq p \leq s - 1$, and $d_p = 1$, but $d_{p-1} = \cdots = d_0 = 0$. Then the term in parentheses in the

---

*For any numbers a and b,

$$[a, b] = \{x : a \leq x \leq b\};$$
$$(a, b) = \{x : a < x < b\}; \quad \text{and}$$
$$[a, b) = \{x : a \leq x < b\}.$$

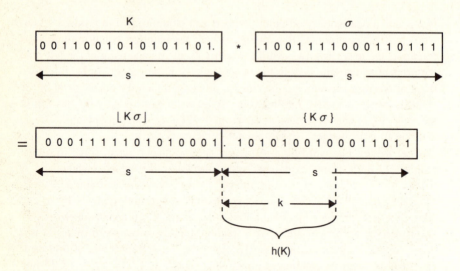

Figure 8.14 Computing a multiplicative hashing function. The key K and
the constant σ are both fixed-point unsigned numbers of $s = 16$ bits.
K is an s-bit integer, while σ is the fractional representation of the
golden ratio, with the low-order bit adjusted to be 1. Their product is a
$2s$-bit number, with the binary point between the two halves; the high-
order s bits represent $\lfloor K\sigma \rfloor$ and the low-order bits represent $\{K\sigma\}$. The
high-order k bits of the low-order s bits yield an integer in the range
$\{0, \ldots, 2^k - 1\}$ that is uniformly distributed in that range as K varies
over all s-bit keys.

above sum will be 0 for $i = 0, \ldots, p - 1$, but for $i = p$ it will be

$$\sum_{j=0}^{p} \sigma_j d_{p-j} = d_p \sigma_0 = 1,$$

so bit p of σD will be 1. It follows that multiplication by σ distributes the keys
uniformly across the range from 0 to $m - 1$.

Perfect Hashing of Static Data

If the data are known in advance, it may be possible to design a hash function
that completely avoids collisions. A hashing function for a fixed finite set
of keys that maps them one-to-one onto a set of values is called a **perfect
hashing function**. For example, Pascal has 36 reserved words; it is possible to
discover an easily computable function that maps these words one-to-one onto
the numbers $\{0, \ldots, 35\}$. Of course it is always possible to find *some* function
that achieves something like this; for example, use binary search to find the
keyword in an ordered table, and return the table position. The trick, however,
is to find a function that can be computed quickly, and without use of auxiliary
storage tables. Several techniques, some theoretically justified and some *ad*

hoc, have been developed for finding perfect hashing functions for given sets of keys. However, the applicability of perfect hashing is quite limited, since in most applications the data do not sit still, so no predetermination of the hash function is possible.

Universal Classes of Hash Functions

In the case of a dynamically changing dictionary, with the set elements not known in advance, any preselected hash function will have bad behavior on certain sets of inputs, and there is always the possibility that a particular set of data on which it is used will be one on which collisions cause its performance to be poor. Even worse, it is possible that someone using a system repeatedly will systematically choose inputs in a way that turns out to be biased, so that the hashing function performs poorly over and over again. (For example, I am using a compiler, and I always use the names of my relatives as variable names in my programs, and these happen to collide under the hashing function chosen by the compiler-writer.) Universal hashing is designed to defeat this kind of bias, by choosing the hash function at random from a large class of hash functions at run time. It is still possible that the particular hash function chosen will behave badly for the particular data supplied, but the odds are low; moreover the odds are equally low even if the program is run a second time on the same input data. In other words, our previous analyses were based on the assumption that the outside world provides the program with random input data; universal hashing works well even if the input data are highly nonrandom, because the program itself has a random element. (A similar argument justifies the fingerprinting method for string searching described on page 164.)

Let $\mathbf{K}$ be the key set, let m be the desired size of the range of the hash function, and let H be a set of functions from $\mathbf{K}$ to $\{0, \ldots, m-1\}$. Then H is said to be **universal** provided that for any distinct $x, y \in \mathbf{K}$,

$$\frac{|\{h \in H : h(x) = h(y)\}|}{|H|} \leq \frac{1}{m}.$$

In other words, H is a universal class if no pair of distinct keys collide under more than $1/m$ of the functions in the class. Thus there can be no "bad" pairs of keys; picking a function from the class at random leaves at worst a $1/m$ chance of any given pair colliding. It is easy to show by a counting argument (Problem 30) that if the key space is large relative to m, this $1/m$ chance of collision in the worst case is as small as can be achieved by any hashing scheme. Moreover, no matter what subset of the key space is in the dictionary during a particular execution run, if the hashing function is chosen at run time from a universal class then the expected number of collisions of any one key with others is no more than the ratio of the size of the set that is being represented to the total number of values of the hashing function (Problem 31). Thus universal hashing functions are expected to spread out any subset of the key space across the range of the hashing functions as evenly as can be conceived.

The following Theorem shows that a very simple division method provides a universal class of hashing functions. The method treats keys as integers and requires expanding the key space up to a prime larger than the largest actual key. However, the size m of the range of the hashing function can be chosen arbitrarily. In particular m could be a power of two, so this method can be used in conjunction with the extendible hashing scheme of §8.4.

■ **THEOREM** *(Universal Classes of Hash Functions)* Let $|\mathbf{K}| = N$ be a prime number, and regard the members of $\mathbf{K}$ as the integers $0, \ldots, N - 1$. For any numbers $a \in \{1, \ldots, N - 1\}$ and $b \in \{0, \ldots, N - 1\}$ let

$$h_{a,b}(x) = \big((ax + b) \bmod N\big) \bmod m.$$

Then

$$H = \{h_{a,b} : 1 \le a < N \text{ and } 0 \le b < N\}$$

is a universal class.

PROOF   We first show that $|\{h \in H : h(x) = h(y)\}|$ is the number of pairs of distinct numbers $\langle q, r \rangle$, where $0 \le q, r < N$, with the property that $q \equiv r \pmod{m}$.* First note that

$$h_{a,b}(x) = h_{a,b}(y) \qquad\qquad \text{if and only if}$$

$$\big((ax + b) \bmod N\big) \bmod m = \big((ay + b) \bmod N\big) \bmod m \qquad \text{if and only if}$$

$$(ax + b) \bmod N \equiv (ay + b) \bmod N \pmod{m}.$$

Then for any fixed x, $y < N$, there is a one-to-one correspondence between the pairs $\langle a, b \rangle$ such that $0 < a < N$ and $0 \le b < N$ and $h_{a,b}(x) = h_{a,b}(y)$, and the pairs of distinct numbers $\langle q, r \rangle$ with the property that $0 \le q, r < N$ and $q \equiv r \pmod{m}$. The correspondence is given in one direction by

$$q = ax + b \bmod N$$

$$r = ay + b \bmod N$$

($q \ne r$ since $\{az + b : z = 0, \ldots, N - 1\} = \{0, \ldots, N - 1\}$ when N is prime and $a \ne 0$). In the other direction the correspondence is given by the condition that a and b are the unique integers in $\{0, \ldots, N - 1\}$ such that

$$ax + b \equiv q \pmod{N}$$

$$ay + b \equiv r \pmod{N}.$$

These equations have a unique solution for a and b since N is prime, and $a \ne 0$ since $q \ne r$.

---

*This means that $q \bmod m = r \bmod m$.

Clearly $|H| = N(N-1)$. How many pairs of distinct numbers $\langle q, r \rangle$ are there such that $0 \le q, r < N$ and $q \equiv r \pmod{m}$? For any fixed $d < m$ there are at most $\lceil N/m \rceil$ numbers $q < N$ such that $q \equiv d \pmod{m}$. Since N and m are integers,

$$\left\lceil \frac{N}{m} \right\rceil \le \frac{N-1}{m} + 1$$

(see Problem 13 of Chapter 1). Therefore for each $q < N$ there are not more than $\lceil N/m \rceil - 1 \le (N-1)/m$ numbers $r < N$ distinct from q such that $q \equiv r \pmod{m}$, and the total number of such pairs $\langle q, r \rangle$ is at most $N(N-1)/m$. Hence for any fixed distinct x, y the fraction of H that cause x and y to collide is at most $1/m$, so H is universal.   □

This Theorem suggests the following strategy for choosing a hashing function at run time, once the set of keys to be hashed is known: let N be the next prime number larger than the size of the key set, let a and b be randomly chosen integers less than N such that $a > 0$, and use the function $h_{a,b}$ as defined in the statement of the Theorem.

Problems

8.1   **1.** Show the data structure that would result if Algorithm 8.1 on page 259 were used to implement the following sequence of set operations on an initially empty set S: *Insert*$(5, S)$, *Delete*$(5, S)$, *Insert*$(8, S)$, *Insert*$(6, S)$, *Insert*$(1, S)$, *Insert*$(9, S)$, *Insert*$(0, S)$, *Delete*$(1, S)$.

2. a. With the data structure of Algorithm 8.1, the operation *IsEmptySet* cannot be implemented in constant time. Describe the changes needed to make this possible, while preserving the performance of the other operations.

b. Can the function *Size*(S), which returns the number of elements in S, be implemented to run in constant time?

3. Modify the routines of Algorithm 8.1 so that attempts to insert an item that is already in the set, or to delete an item that is not already in the set, are error conditions rather than null operations.

4. Implement these operations using the data structure of Algorithm 8.1:

a. *Union*(S, T);

b. *Intersection*(S, T);

c. *Complement*(S), which replaces S by $\{u_0, \dots, u_{N-1}\} - S$.

8.2   **5.** Organize the words need, needle, needless, needlepoint, negative, neglect, neigh, neighbor, neighborhood, and neighborly into

a. a trie;

    b. a Patricia tree;

    c. a de la Briandais tree.

6. Construct from the titles of the chapters of this book:

    a. a trie;

    b. a Patricia tree.

7. Insert the following words in order into a digital search tree, where $a = 00001$, $b = 00010$, $\ldots$, $z = 11010$: four score and seven years ago.

8. Choose a representation for the nodes of a trie, and write the appropriate routines *LookUp*, *Insert*, and *Delete*.

9. Choose a representation for the nodes of a Patricia tree, and write the appropriate routines *LookUp*, *Insert*, and *Delete*.

10. Choose a representation for the nodes of a de la Briandais tree, and write the appropriate routines *LookUp*, *Insert*, and *Delete*.

11. Design a hybrid data structure of the type suggested in item (4) on page 262. Can you propose algorithms that cause the representation to shift from "sparse" to "dense" as keys are added?

12. A **binary trie** is a trie with binary branching at depth k based on the kth bit of the key. Instead of extending the tree to have height equal to the number of bits in the longest key, a branch is terminated when it corresponds to but a single key, and the key itself is stored in a leaf node.

    a. Construct a binary trie from the keys of Figure 8.4 on page 264.

    b. Show that the structure of a binary trie is independent of the order in which the keys are inserted.

    c. Write the algorithm for binary trie insertion.

8.3 **13.** Let **p** be the number of bits needed for a pointer and **r** the number of bits needed for a record, and let α be the load factor. Under what circumstances, in terms of these three parameters, is the hash table organization of Figure 8.7 more economical in its use of storage than that of Figure 8.6?

14. Consider a separately chained hash table in which the lists are reorganized on each *LookUp* using the Move-to-Front Heuristic. Under what circumstances might this make sense, and what can you say about the improvement in search time that might result?

15. In ordered hashing with open addressing, is it true that the keys encountered along the probe sequence of a key in the table are in alphabetical order?

16. Show that, in ordered hashing with open addressing, the contents of the hash table are uniquely determined by the set of keys that are inserted, independent of the order in which they are inserted.

17. Make a table of birthdays of your classmates, like Figure 8.5 on page 266, and insert their names in a hash table using

   a. separate chaining;

   b. coalesced chaining;

   c. linear probing;

   d. double hashing;

   e. ordered hashing.

18. The following idea leads to an open addressing strategy called **binary tree hashing** that is superior to ordered hashing for *LookUp* operations, though it is more costly for insertions. When a collision is discovered between a key K that is being inserted and a key K' that is already in the hash table, consider the next positions in the probe sequences of K and K'. If one of these is empty, move the corresponding item to that position, and put (or keep) the other in the position originally considered. On the other hand, if the next positions in the probe sequences of both K and K' are occupied, say by L and L', then consider the following four positions: the subsequent positions in the probe sequences for K and K', and the next positions in the probe sequences for L and L'. Once again, if one of these four positions is empty, put the appropriate key in that position, and rearrange the others. At each additional stage that needs to be considered, the number of probe positions under consideration doubles (though they do not all need to be distinct), so an empty position is likely to be located before many stages have been considered, and probe sequences are likely to be kept short.

   a. Insert the names of Figure 8.5 on page 266 into a hash table with binary tree hashing, using double hashing to calculate the probe sequence.

   b. Write the detailed algorithm for *Insert* and *LookUp* in a hash table of this kind.

19. The Quicksearch Center is hired to design a data structure for storing 10,000 names. The client informs the Center that one-quarter of the names will account for three-quarters of the successful searches, and the remaining three-quarters of the names will account for only one-quarter of the successful searches. (There will also be searches for names not in the data structure at all.) The Center first decides to store all 10,000 names in an open-addressed hash table of size 12,000 using double hashing. But then one of its employees, C. Wizard, suggests splitting the 12,000 locations into two tables, a small table of size 3000 to hold the high-frequency quarter of the names and a larger table of size 9000 to hold the low-frequency three-quarters.

a. Is Wizard's suggestion a good one? Analyze both proposals with respect to their performance in the case of both successful and unsuccessful searches.

b. Repeat the analysis, on the assumption that the Center always implements ordered hashing.

c. Suppose that the proportions in the statement of the problem are not $1/4$ and $3/4$ but p and $1 - p$, where $0 < p < 1$. For what values of p, if any, would it make sense to isolate the fraction p of the most frequently occurring keys in a subtable consisting of the fraction p of the available memory?

20. In Algorithm 8.2 on page 279, explain exactly why the test in the first line of the *Insert* algorithm tests $\text{Size}(P) = m - 1$, and what would go wrong if the test were $\text{Size}(P) = m$ instead.

21. One situation in which hashing with separate chaining may present problems is when the size of a record is comparable to the size of a pointer; then separate chaining may devote too large a percentage of memory to the pointers that hold the chains together. Assume that the total number of records is very large, so that it is impractical to use a single large hash table with open addressing. Devise and analyze a variation on the separate chaining algorithm that dynamically allocates blocks of memory larger than single linked list cells.

22. Let $S(n, m)$ represent the expected time for a successful search in a separately chained hash table of m buckets containing n keys, not counting the probe to get the list header. By considering separately the case in which the key is in the first bucket or in one of the other $m - 1$ buckets, show that $S(n, m)$ is equal to

$$\sum_{k=0}^{n} \binom{n}{k} \frac{(m-1)^{n-k}}{m^n} \left(\frac{k}{n} \cdot \frac{k+1}{2} + \frac{n-k}{n} \cdot S(n-k, m-1) \right).$$

Here k is the number of keys in the first bucket. Then prove by induction on m that

$$S(n, m) = 1 + \frac{n-1}{2m}.$$

You will want to use the identities

$$\sum_{k=0}^{n} \binom{n}{k} p^k = (1 + p)^n$$

$$\sum_{k=0}^{n} k \binom{n}{k} p^k = np(1+p)^{n-1}$$

$$\sum_{k=0}^{n} k^2 \binom{n}{k} p^k = np(1+np)(1+p)^{n-2}.$$

8.4   **23.** Illustrate the effect of inserting into the extended hash table of Figure 8.11 on page 281 a sequence of keys that hash to the following hash values: 01101, 01100, 01000.

24. Suppose that a deletion strategy is employed that attempts to keep the directory as small as possible. Show the effect of deleting the key with hash value 01110 from the extended hash table of Figure 8.11.

25. Show the structure of the extendible hash table that would result in the (unlikely) event that records with hash values 000, 001, 010, 011, 100, 101, 110, 111 were inserted into an initially empty hash table.

26. Assume that every effort is made to keep the directory as small as possible. What are the minimum and maximum number of leaf pages of an extended hash table of depth D?

27. It may be possible to collapse two adjacent leaf pages of an extendible hash table—say distinct pages pointed to by directory entries j and $j + 1$—even when these pages are not of maximal depth. Explain exactly the conditions under which this is possible, and what should be done.

8.5   **28.** When you buy a ticket in the State Lottery, you choose six different numbers between 1 and 36. The lottery officials keep a dictionary keyed on the set of six numbers chosen on each ticket. After the officials pick the winning numbers, they access this dictionary to identify the winning ticket or tickets, if any. Since millions of tickets are sold, the officials have decided to keep the dictionary in external storage with a directory in an internal hash table. Their computer consultant, S. L. Ow, has recommended that they use the hash function

$$h(x_1, x_2, x_3, x_4, x_5, x_6) = (x_1 + x_2 + x_3 + x_4 + x_5 + x_6) \bmod m,$$

where m is the number of external buckets in which the records will be stored. Give a critique of this recommendation, and suggest a better alternative.

29. a. In which of the intervals of Figure 8.13 does the next value of $\{K\phi^{-1}\}$ lie (the one for $K = 11$)?

   b. Using standard 8-bit ASCII character codes and the 16-bit value of σ shown in Figure 8.14, determine the 8-bit multiplicative hash values of the keys AA, AB, and BA.

30. Let H be any set of functions from $\mathbf{K}$ to $\{0, \ldots, m-1\}$. Show that there are distinct $x, y \in \mathbf{K}$ such that

$$\frac{|\{h \in H : h(x) = h(y)\}|}{|H|} > \frac{1}{m} - \frac{1}{|\mathbf{K}|}.$$

31. Let H be a universal class of hash functions from $\mathbf{K}$ to $\{0, \ldots, m-1\}$, let S be any subset of $\mathbf{K}$, let x be any member of S, and let h be a randomly chosen member of H. Show that the expected value of

$$|\{y \in S : x \neq y \text{ but } h(x) = h(y)\}|$$

is at most $|S|/m$.

32. Let $N = 31$ and $m = 5$ and consider the universal class of hash functions defined in the Theorem.

    a. *Exactly* how many pairs of distinct numbers $\langle q, r \rangle$ are there such that $0 \leq q, r < N$ and $q \equiv r \pmod{m}$?

    b. What is the *exact* maximum probability, over all pairs of distinct keys x, y, that a randomly chosen hash function $h_{a,b}$ will cause x and y to collide?

References

Tries were first described by

E. Fredkin, "Trie Memory," *Communications of the ACM* **3** (1960), pp. 490–499.

Patricia trees, as we have described them, are a variation on those presented in

D. R. Morrison, "PATRICIA—Practical Algorithm To Retrieve Information Coded in Alphanumeric," *Journal of the ACM* **15** (1968), pp. 514–534,

and digital search trees are from

E. G. Coffman and J. Eve, "File Structures Using Hashing Functions," *Communications of the ACM* **13** (1970), pp. 427–432, 436.

All these structures are presented and analyzed by Knuth, in Sorting and Searching *(cited on page 44). See also*

P. Flajolet and R. Sedgewick, "Digital Search Trees Revisited," *SIAM Journal on Computing* **15** (1986), pp. 748–767.

Ordered hashing is from

O. Amble and D. E. Knuth, "Ordered Hash Tables," *Computer Journal* **17** (1974), pp. 135–142.

Binary tree hashing (Problem 18) is described in

G. H. Gonnet and I. Munro, "The Analysis of an Improved Hashing Technique," *Proceedings, 9th ACM Symposium on Theory of Computing*, 1977, pp. 113–121.

These and many other hashing algorithms are described in Standish's book (cited on page 45). Coalesced chaining is analyzed in detail in

J. S. Vitter and W.-C. Chen, *Design and Analysis of Coalesced Hashing,* Oxford University Press, 1987.

Extendible hashing was presented in

R. Fagin, J. Nievergelt, N. Pippenger, and H. R. Strong, "Extendible Hashing—A Fast Access Method for Dynamic Files," *ACM Transactions on Database Systems* **4** (1979), pp. 315–344.

A detailed analysis of its efficiency appears in

P. Flajolet and J.-M. Steyaert, "A Branching Process Arising in Dynamic Hashing, Trie Searching, and Polynomial Factorization," in *Automata, Languages, and Programming, Lecture Notes in Computer Science* **140** (1982), Springer-Verlag, pp. 239–251.

The theory of the multiplication-based and division-based hashing functions was developed by Knuth, in Sorting and Searching; *see that book for references to the underlying mathematical results. A simple heuristic that often produces a perfect hash function for a small set of keys is presented in*

R. J. Cichelli, "Minimal Perfect Hash Functions Made Simple," *Communications of the ACM* **23** (1980), pp. 17–19.

Universal classes of hash functions were the invention of

J. L. Carter and M. N. Wegman, "Universal Classes of Hash Functions," *Journal of Computer and System Sciences* **18** (1979), pp. 143–154.

9

Sets with Special Operations

9.1 PRIORITY QUEUES

The data structures of Chapters 6, 7, and 8 are primarily designed to support the dictionary operations of *Insert*, *LookUp*, and *Delete*. However, other fairly common set operations admit efficient implementation by means of specialized data structures. This chapter deals with three of these set abstract data types: priority queues, whose elements are retrieved in order of their value, regardless of the order in which they were inserted; union-find structures, which manage a partition of a finite universe into disjoint subsets; and range query structures, which permit retrieval not only of a single key value, but of all keys with values falling between certain bounds, perhaps in several independent dimensions. Each of these abstract data types has important practical applications to a variety of kinds of problems.

Structures for the dictionary abstract data type solve the problem of storing and retrieving data according to a distinguishing key value: store key K together with certain associated information, look up the information associated with key value K. If the universe from which the keys are drawn has a natural linear order, such as the lexicographic order on alphabetic keys, then this order can be used (in binary search trees, for example) to structure the sets internally to speed up the insertion and retrieval times.

In this section we imagine that such an ordering is associated with the items to be stored, and that the items are to be retrieved *according to this order*, smallest first, for example. To be precise, consider a set of key values **key** that is linearly ordered by some ordering relation. The items to be stored are pairs $\langle K, I \rangle$, where $K \in$ **key** and I is some associated information of type **info**, about which no more will be said. A **priority queue** is a set abstract data type of such pairs $\langle K, I \rangle$ supporting the following operations:

MakeEmptySet( ): Return the empty set $\emptyset$.
IsEmptySet(S): Return **true** if $S = \emptyset$, otherwise **false**.
Insert(K, I, S): Add the pair $\langle K, I \rangle$ to the set S.

FindMin(S): Return an **info** I such that $\langle K, I \rangle \in S$ and K is minimal with respect to the ordering.

DeleteMin(S): Delete an element $\langle K, I \rangle$ from S such that K is minimal, and return I.

Note that in a priority queue the ordering plays an explicit role in the semantics of the abstract operations; in the dictionary structures of previous chapters, the key ordering did not appear in the definitions of the abstract data type operations, but was utilized in the *implementation* of those operations. Moreover, note that the **key** value need not be unique; there may be several pairs in S with the same value K. If there are, then *FindMin* and *DeleteMin* may return the information component of any one of those pairs (but they should find the *same* pair).

The term "priority queue" is now enshrined by tradition, but it may have an odd ring to those hearing it for the first time. When working with a *queue* structure we can insert items in any order, and then withdraw them in the sequence in which they were inserted. In a *priority queue* the items have a certain intrinsic "priority," or relative value; we can insert items, and withdraw them in order of their priority, independent of the time sequence in which they were inserted. To stress this interpretation, and the fact that these values need not be unique, we refer in this section to the **key** value of an item as its **priority value**.

As mentioned on page 17, any priority queue provides a basis for a sorting algorithm: make the priority queue empty, then insert the items to be sorted, then repeatedly remove the smallest remaining element (via *DeleteMin*s) until the structure is once again empty. Of course the efficiency of such an algorithm depends on the efficiency of the priority queue operations. Priority queues have many other applications; we shall touch on some of them in Chapter 12.

Balanced Tree Implementations

The dictionary organizations that utilize key value comparisons all provide implementations of priority queues, at no extra charge. In particular, the balanced tree structures of Chapter 7—AVL trees, 2-3 trees, red-black trees, B-trees—all provide implementations of priority queues supporting *FindMin* and *DeleteMin*, as well as the dictionary operations *LookUp* and *Delete*, in $O(\log n)$ time for sets of size n. With any of these structures, the minimal element is found by searching from the root, following the leftmost pointer out of each node, until that pointer is Λ; the value stored at the last node along that path is the smallest value in the tree. (This assumes that values are stored in the internal nodes; if all values are in the leaves and the tree simply provides an index, then the minimum value is in the leftmost leaf, which is also easy to find.) Since these tree structures have logarithmic height, *FindMin* takes logarithmic time. *DeleteMin* takes logarithmic time because deletion of *any* element takes logarithmic time.

As an added feature, in these structures the *maximal* element can be found by searching along the *rightmost* path from the root. So the operations of

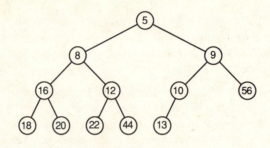

Figure 9.1 A partially ordered tree.

FindMax and *DeleteMax* are automatically supported in logarithmic time, and these operations can be interspersed with *FindMin*, *DeleteMin*, and the others in any combination. A structure supporting these operations is called a **double-ended priority queue** (Problems 5 and 6). In spite of their flexibility, the memory used to store child pointers make these balanced tree structures both larger to represent and slower to update than the heap structures to which we now turn.

Heaps

A **partially ordered tree*** is a binary tree of elements that have a priority ordering such that *the priority of each node is less than or equal to that of each of its children.* This property must hold at every node in the tree, so in particular it holds at the root, which must therefore contain the smallest element in the whole tree. On any path from the root, the elements encountered are in increasing order, but no conclusion can be drawn about the relative order of the items in the left and right subtrees of a node.

For the remainder of this section, all trees considered will be binary trees. For example, Figure 9.1 shows a partially ordered binary tree with twelve nodes. Note that although this tree happens to be well-balanced, there is no special relationship among the values on the branches of the tree, except for the partial ordering property; for example, there is a node of depth 2 with a larger value than any node of depth 3.

In any partially ordered tree, it is easy to find a minimal element, since one is located at the root. The difficulty in using partially ordered trees as priority queue structures is in reorganizing the tree when the minimal element is deleted, or when a new element is inserted into the tree. Since we want these operations to be efficient, that is, taking time at worst logarithmic in the size of the tree, it is natural to expect that the tree should be kept well balanced, that is, of height $O(\log n)$ if its size is n. But if the root node is deleted as the result of

---

*"Partially ordered trees" should not be confused with "ordered trees," as defined on page 100. An ordered tree is one in which the *children* of each node have a specified order; a partially ordered tree is one in which the *keys stored in parent and child* have a specified order.

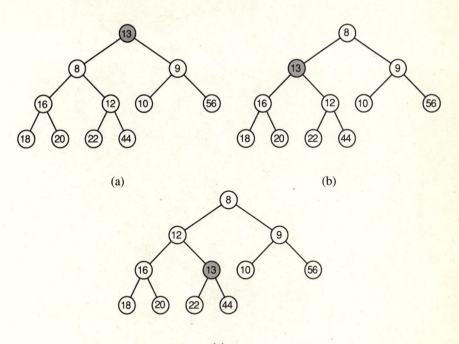

(a)   (b)

(c)

Figure 9.2 Deleting the minimal element from the partially ordered tree of
Figure 9.1. (a) The item in the root is removed, and is replaced by the
item in the bottommost, rightmost leaf, which has priority value 13. The
leaf itself is deleted. (b) The root is swapped with its left child (8), which
is the child of smaller priority value. (c) The node is swapped with its
right child (12), which is the child of smaller priority value. It is now
smaller in priority than both children, and the deletion procedure stops.

a *DeleteMin* operation, how can the two resulting partially ordered subtrees be
merged into a single partially ordered tree in logarithmic time?

The answer is not to delete the root *node*, but instead to transfer into it the
information from one of the leaves, and to delete the leaf instead.* If this is done
properly, only minimal alteration of the structure of the tree will be needed. The
resulting tree will, however, not be partially ordered any longer, since the item
at the root will probably not be of minimal priority. For example, Figure 9.2(a)
shows the result of replacing the value in the root of Figure 9.1 with that of the
rightmost leaf of maximum depth, and then deleting that leaf; the root node now
has priority 13, which is greater than that of its children. Except at the root,
however, the partial ordering property will be satisfied throughout the tree. The
partial ordering property can be restored at the root by swapping its value with

---

*Of course, if the data record associated with a node is large, the nodes should contain only pointers
to these records, and only the pointers are moved, not the records themselves.

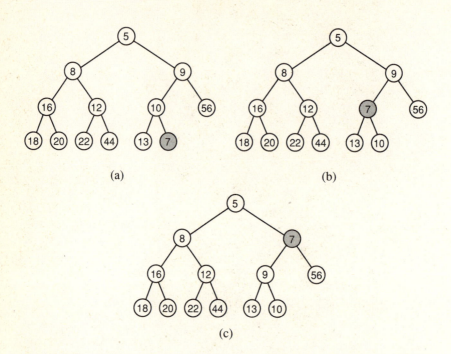

(a)

(b)

(c)

Figure 9.3 Inserting a node of priority 7 into the heap of Figure 9.1. (a) The node is appended as a leaf; (b) it is exchanged with its parent; (c) it is again exchanged with its parent, but then stops, since its priority value is now larger than that of its parent.

that of its smaller child. That is, if R is the root and it has children A and B, and the priority of A or B (or both) is smaller than R, then after swapping the contents of R with whichever of A and B has the smaller priority value, R will have the smallest priority value of the three nodes. In Figure 9.2(b), the root has been exchanged with its left child. Now the partial ordering property has been restored at the root, but possibly destroyed at one (but only one) of the root's children, so the same strategy must be applied to the new node (Figure 9.2(c)). Eventually the key value comes to rest at a node where its children have larger values, or it winds up at a leaf; the entire tree then enjoys the partial ordering property. If the tree was of logarithmic height to begin with, any such path is of logarithmic length and the operation requires logarithmic time at worst.

How can the leaf to be deleted be chosen and located? If the tree is a *complete* binary tree, then it can be stored using the implicit representation on page 110, and the position of the rightmost leaf of maximum depth can be determined arithmetically from the number of nodes and the address of the beginning of the table used to store the structure. Deleting this leaf results in a complete tree, so the balance property is maintained. Moreover all the memory that would be used in an explicit representation to store the linkage pointers is saved. An implicitly represented complete partially ordered tree

procedure *HeapInsert*(**key** K, **info** I, **heap** h):
{Insert the pair $\langle K, I \rangle$ into heap h}
    $H \leftarrow$ Table(h)
    $n \leftarrow$ Size(h)
    if $n = N$ **then error**   {Heap is full}
    $m \leftarrow n$ {m is a "pointer" that moves up a path in the tree}
    while $m > 0$ **and** $K <$ Key($H[\lfloor (m-1)/2 \rfloor]$) **do**
        $H[m] \leftarrow H[\lfloor (m-1)/2 \rfloor]$
        $m \leftarrow \lfloor (m-1)/2 \rfloor$ {That is, $m \leftarrow Parent(m)$}
    Key($H[m]$) $\leftarrow K$; Info($H[m]$) $\leftarrow I$ {Move item to its resting place}
    Size(h) $\leftarrow n + 1$ {One more record now in the heap}

function *HeapDeleteMin*(**heap** h): **info**
{Delete an item of smallest priority from heap h, and return it}
    $H \leftarrow$ Table(h)
    $n \leftarrow$ Size(h)
    if $n = 0$ **then error**   {Heap is empty}
    $I \leftarrow$ Info($H[0]$)   {The item to be returned}
    Size(h) $\leftarrow n - 1$ {The new size of the heap}
    if $n = 1$ **then return**   {Heap is now empty}
    $K \leftarrow$ Key($H[n-1]$)   {The priority value of the item to be moved}
    $m \leftarrow 0$ {m is a "pointer" that moves down the tree}
    while $2m + 1 < n$ **and** $K >$ Key($H[2m+1]$)
               or $2m + 2 < n$ **and** $K >$ Key($H[2m+2]$) **do**
        if $2m + 2 < n$ **then**   {Node m has two children}
             if Key($H[2m+1]$) $<$ Key($H[2m+2]$) **then**
                $p \leftarrow 2m + 1$
             else
                $p \leftarrow 2m + 2$
        else   {Node m has only one child, the last leaf in the tree}
          $p \leftarrow n - 1$
        $H[m] \leftarrow H[p]$ {Move the child up}
        $m \leftarrow p$ {Move the pointer down}
    $H[m] \leftarrow H[n-1]$ {Finally, move the item into its position}
    return I

Algorithm 9.1 Insertion and deletion in a heap. The heap h is a record with two fields, the table $H =$ Table(h) and its current size $n =$ Size(h). The partially ordered tree is stored implicitly in the table $H[0..N-1]$, that is, N is the maximum size of the heap.

is called a **heap**, and is a particularly efficient structure for the basic priority queue operations. (This use of the term "heap" is entirely distinct from another meaning: that portion of the memory of a computer software system—operating system, compiler, etc.—from which blocks of memory are allocated in response to specific requests. Heaps in this sense are discussed in Chapter 10. The coincidence is an unfortunate historical accident.)

To insert an item into a heap, append it as a new leaf in its natural position. (For example, Figure 9.3(a) shows the result of inserting a node of priority 7 into the heap of Figure 9.1.) The partial ordering property may be violated, but only at the parent of this leaf, which may now have larger priority value than its new child. If it does, exchange it with that child, and repeat the same process at *its* parent. Eventually the value either rises to a level where it is smaller than its parent, or reaches the root; in either case the partial ordering property has been restored throughout, at the expense of $O(\log n)$ exchanges. (See Figure 9.3(b,c). Recall that in an implicitly represented tree it is easy to locate the parent of a node, by dividing by 2 the node's index in the table.)

Algorithm 9.1 presents the details for the deletion and insertion routines. The heap h is a record with two fields, the table $H = \text{Table}(h)$ and its current size $n = \text{Size}(h)$. Note that in practice there is no "exchanging" of values as the proper position of an item is located by searching up the tree (during insertion) or down the tree (during deletion); instead, a "hole" is moved up or down the tree, by shifting the items along a path down or up single edges of the tree. The item is moved only once, at the last step.

Leftist Trees

The heap data structure is extremely compact and the algorithms for insertion and deletion are very efficient, but heaps are not perfect in all situations. Because an implicit, tabular representation is used for the partially ordered tree, the maximum size of the priority queue must be known ahead of time; if the structure becomes full there is no way to utilize dynamic memory except to reallocate the structure completely in a larger table and to copy the old values into the new heap. Also, because the representation is so compact, it is not easy to implement additional operations, such as the dictionary operations of *LookUp* and *Delete* (by key value). Another operation that is needed for some applications is

Union(S_1, S_2): Return the set consisting of the members of the disjoint sets S_1 and S_2,

but heaps cannot be so merged in less than linear time.

Leftist trees are an ingenious variety of explicitly represented partially or- dered binary trees that provide logarithmic time implementations of the priority queue operations of *Insert* and *DeleteMin*, and *Union* as well. With a bit more work, the full set of dictionary operations can be provided.

Recall (pages 182 and 195) that an *external node* of a binary tree is a node attached anywhere a node of the tree has no child; in terms of the natural

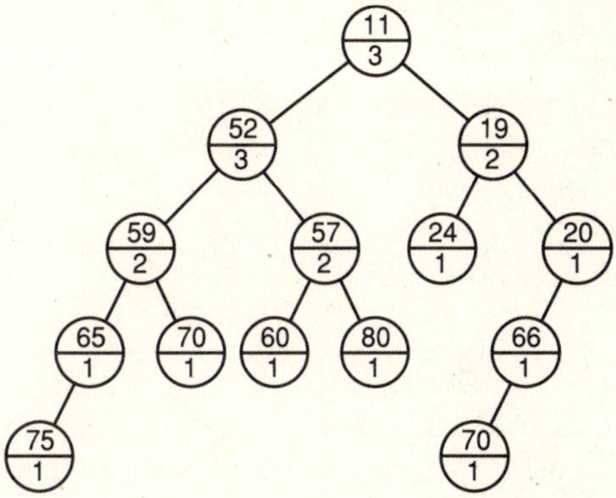

Figure 9.4 A leftist tree. The number in the lower half of a node is the distance to the nearest external node; the external nodes themselves are not illustrated. The number in the upper half is a key value, since the tree is to be used to represent a priority queue.

representation of binary trees, external nodes correspond to LC or RC fields that have the value Λ. The defining property of a leftist tree is that from any node, the external node reached by descending through right children is at least as near as any other external node. To be specific, in any binary tree, let $Dist(N)$ denote the distance from node N to the nearest external node. That is,

$$Dist(N) = \begin{cases} 0, & \text{if } N = \Lambda; \\ 1 + \min(Dist(\text{LC}(N)), Dist(\text{RC}(N))), & \text{otherwise.} \end{cases}$$

Note that if the root of the tree has distance d, then the tree has at least $2^d - 1$ nodes, since the nodes of depths $0, 1, \ldots, d - 1$ form a perfect binary tree. A **leftist tree** is a binary tree such that *the distance of each node's left child is at least as great as that of its right child:*

$$Dist(LeftChild(N)) \geq Dist(RightChild(N)), \quad \text{for every node } N.$$

By applying the definition repeatedly it is clear that no path from the root to an external node is shorter than the path that always goes through right children; hence if the tree has n nodes then this shortest path can contain at most $\lfloor \log_2(n+1) \rfloor$ nodes. Because of this property the trees tend to "lean" to the left (Figure 9.4). To implement leftist trees as data structures, the distance of each node is stored as a field Dist within the node itself, and, as operations are performed on the tree, the subtrees of nodes are occasionally swapped so that this leftist inclination is maintained. In general, therefore, the values stored in the left and right children of a node will not be in any particular order relative to each other.

A leftist tree can be used to represent a priority queue if the tree is partially ordered. The crucial operation is the formation of the union of two leftist

function *LeftistUnion*(**pointer** A, B): **pointer**
{Return the union of the leftist trees A and B}
    if $A = \Lambda$ **then return** B
    else if $B = \Lambda$ **then return** A
    else if Key$(A) <$ Key(B) **then**
        return *MergeRight*(A, B)
    else
        return *MergeRight*(B, A)

procedure *MergeRight*(**pointer** A, B):
{Replace right child of A by its union with B, and preserve leftist property}
{Both A and B are assumed to be nonempty}
    RC$(A) \leftarrow$ *LeftistUnion*(RC$(A), B$)   {Now RC(A) is nonempty}
    if LC$(A) = \Lambda$ **or** Dist(LC(A)) $<$ Dist(RC(A)) **then**
        LC$(A) \leftrightarrow$ RC(A) {Restructure to preserve leftist property}
    Fixdist(A) {Recalculate Dist field of A}

procedure *LeftistInsert*(**key** K, **info** I, **locative** T):
{Create and insert a new node into leftist tree T}
    $P \leftarrow$ *NewCell*(Node)
    Key$(P) \leftarrow K$; Info$(P) \leftarrow I$
    LC$(P) \leftarrow$ RC$(P) \leftarrow \Lambda$
    Dist$(P) \leftarrow 1$
    $T \Leftarrow$ *LeftistUnion*(T, P)

function *LeftistDeleteMin*(**locative** T): **info**
{Delete root element of leftist tree T, and return the associated information}
    $R \leftarrow T$
    $T \Leftarrow$ *LeftistUnion*(LC(T), RC(T))
    return Info(R)

procedure *Fixdist*(**pointer** A):
{Recalculate distances of a node whose children have changed}
{Assume that the tree already has the leftist structure,
    and that the Dist fields of its children are correct}
    if RC$(A) = \Lambda$ **then** Dist$(A) \leftarrow 1$
    else Dist$(A) \leftarrow 1 +$ min(Dist(LC(A)), Dist(RC(A)))

Algorithm 9.2 Union of leftist trees, insertion into a leftist tree, and deletion of the root. Union is achieved by merging the rightmost paths, exchanging subtrees if necessary to maintain the leftist property. Insertion of a new value is the union of the old tree with a new tree consisting of a single node. Deletion of the root is accomplished by forming the union of its subtrees.

trees with roots A and B, which is accomplished recursively by the function $Union(A, B)$ (Algorithm 9.2). The union of a nonempty tree and an empty tree is the nonempty tree. The union of two nonempty trees is the result of retaining the smaller root as the root of the new tree and replacing its right subtree by the (recursively formed) union of that right subtree with the other tree. After forming this union, it may be necessary to exchange the left and (new) right subtree of the root so that the leftist property is preserved. The routine *MergeRight* carries out this restructuring, as well as calling on *Fixdist* to update the Dist fields as necessary.

With the aid of the *Union* operation the other priority queue operations are easy to implement. The *DeleteMin* operation on leftist trees is a special case of the *Union* operation: to delete the minimal element, form the union of the left and right subtrees of the root, since the root must contain a smallest item (function *LeftistDeleteMin* in Algorithm 9.2). And to insert a new item into a leftist tree, simply form the union of the tree with a new tree consisting of a single node that contains the item (function *LeftistInsert* in Algorithm 9.2).

With a little more work leftist trees can handle the full range of dictionary operations. This seems impossible at first since the internal structure of the leftist tree is dictated by considerations other than the lexicographic order of the keys stored in the tree; the same tree cannot simultaneously be partially ordered by key values and be a search tree on those key values. The trick is to construct, in addition to the leftist tree, an *entirely separate balanced tree structure organized by key value*, a 2-3 tree, for example. The data records (or pointers to them) are stored in the leftist tree; the dictionary tree is simply an index to help locate those primary data records by key value. When a record is inserted, it is inserted first in the leftist tree, and then a reference by key value is inserted into the dictionary tree. When a record is deleted via a *DeleteMin* from the leftist tree, the key value is used to locate and delete the record from the dictionary tree. And if a record is deleted via a *Delete* from the dictionary tree, it must be removed from the leftist tree as well by forming the union of its left and right subtrees (but see Problem 7).

9.2 DISJOINT SETS WITH UNION

Most of the data structures discussed in Chapters 6, 7, and 8 pertain to the problem of maintaining a single set S through incremental changes (inserting and deleting single elements) in such a way as to support queries (is $X \in S$?). Here we deal with the problem of maintaining information about a fixed set $\mathbf{U}$ that is divided into a number of disjoint subsets $S_1, \ldots, S_k$; that is, $S_i \cap S_j$ is empty if $i \neq j$, and $S_1 \cup \cdots \cup S_k = \mathbf{U}$. The relevant operations include the following:

MakeSet(*X*): Return a new set consisting of the single item *X*.

Union(*S*, *T*): Return the set $S \cup T$, which replaces *S* and *T* in the data base.

Find(*X*): Return that set *S* such that $X \in S$.

For example, imagine the elements of **U** to be people, each of whom belongs to a family; *Find*(*X*) identifies the unique family to which *X* belongs. Occasionally a marriage occurs, which unites two families into one; *Union*(*S*, *T*) returns the new family, and a subsequent *Find* of a person that was in either *S* or *T* would return that new family. In particular these operations make it possible to tell whether two individuals are related; *X* and *Y* are related just in case *Find*(*X*) = *Find*(*Y*).

Up-Trees

If each element can belong to only one set, a simple data structure for maintaining disjoint sets is an **up-tree**: a tree structure with the pointers pointing up the tree, from children to parents (Figure 9.5). Each node needs only a single pointer field, to point to its parent; at the root of the tree, this pointer field is empty. A node can have any number of children, since there is no limit on the number of pointers that can be pointing at a node. The sets are identified by their root nodes, so to *Find* which set an element belongs to, just follow pointers up the tree until reaching the root, and to check whether element *X* is a member of set *S*, do *Find*(*X*) and see if the result is *S*. To form the *Union* of sets *S* and *T*, just make one set point to the other, that is, make the root of one tree point to the root of the other. If we make the root of *S* point to the root of *T*, we shall say that we are **merging** *S* **into** *T*.

How efficient is the up-tree structure for implementing *Union*s and *Find*s? If we assume that the roots of the two trees are in hand, forming their *Union* takes constant time, since it simply involves changing one pointer field. A *Find* operation, however, takes time proportional to the length of the path from a node to the root, that is, in the worst case, time proportional to the height of the tree. So once again, there is good reason to keep trees well-balanced. The height of a tree representing a set can be drastically affected by the way it is constructed while doing *Union*s; for example, in Figure 9.5(b) the height of the tree increases as a result of the *Union* operation, while in Figure 9.5(c) it does not. In the worst case, if we start with *n* singleton sets $\{a_1\}$, ..., $\{a_n\}$ and form the set $\{a_1, \ldots, a_n\}$ by repeatedly merging the set $\{a_1, \ldots, a_i\}$ into $\{a_{i+1}\}$ for $i = 1, \ldots, n - 1$, we will wind up with a tree of height $n - 1$ consisting of a single path of length $n - 1$.

However, this linear growth in the height of the tree can be avoided if we adopt the strategy of *always merging the smaller tree into the larger* (that is, merging the tree with fewer nodes into the one with more nodes). To be specific about how this is done, let us call Parent the field of a node that points to the node's parent (except when it is the root), and let every node have an additional

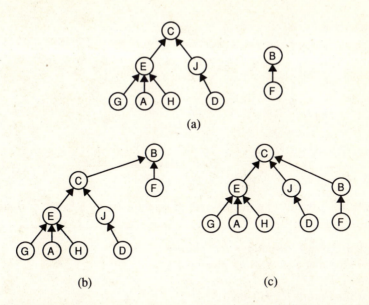

Figure 9.5 The basic up-tree structure for representing disjoint sets. (a) Two disjoint sets, $\{A, C, D, E, G, H, J\}$ and $\{B, F\}$. (b) and (c) Two ways of forming the union of these sets, by making the root of one point to the root of the other.

field Count that is used, if the node is the root of a tree, to hold a count of the number of nodes in the tree.* Thus $MakeSet(R)$ would initialize a node R to represent a singleton set by setting $Parent(R) \leftarrow \Lambda$ and $Count(R) \leftarrow 1$. The basic algorithms for *Union* and *Find* are shown in Algorithm 9.3.

■ **LEMMA** *(Height of Balanced Up-Trees)* Let T be an up-tree representing a set of size n constructed from singleton sets by repeatedly forming unions by the method of Algorithm 9.3. Then the height of T is at most $\lg n$.

PROOF Let us write $|T|$ for the number of nodes in the tree. We prove the Lemma by showing that for any h, if T is a tree of height h created by a sequence of *Unions*, then T has at least 2^h nodes, that is, $|T| \geq 2^h$. The lemma as stated follows immediately.

The proof is by induction on h. If $h = 0$, that is, $Height(T) = 0$, then T consists of a single node, that is, $|T| = 1 \geq 2^0$. Now assume that for any S, if $Height(S) \leq h$, then $|S| \geq 2^{Height(S)}$. Suppose that T is the first tree created of height $h + 1$ (Figure 9.6). Then T must have been created

---

*In any node, only one of these fields is used; Parent for a node that is not a root and Count for a root. Thus the two fields can actually be the same, if there is some way to distinguish between a number and a pointer, and the test "is $Parent(X) = \Lambda$?" is changed to "is $Parent(X)$ a number?"

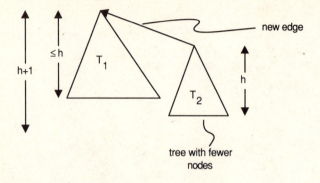

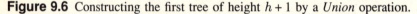

Figure 9.6 Constructing the first tree of height $h + 1$ by a *Union* operation.

---

function *UpTreeFind*(**pointer** P): **pointer**
{Return the root of the tree containing P}
    $R \leftarrow P$
    while Parent(R) $\neq \Lambda$ **do**
        $R \leftarrow$ Parent(R)
    return R

function *UpTreeUnion*(**pointer** S, T): **pointer**
{S and T are roots of up-trees}
{Return result of merging smaller into larger}
    if Count(S) $\geq$ Count(T) **then**
        Count(S) $\leftarrow$ Count(S) + Count(T)
        Parent(T) $\leftarrow S$
        return S
    else
        Count(T) $\leftarrow$ Count(S) + Count(T)
        Parent(S) $\leftarrow T$
        return T

Algorithm 9.3 Union and Find algorithms, using balanced up-trees.

---

by merging T_2 into T_1, where T_2 has height h and T_1 has height at most h (otherwise T would not have been the *first* such tree), and $|T_1| \geq |T_2|$ (otherwise T_1 would have been merged into T_2). But then $|T_2| \geq 2^h$ by the induction hypothesis, so

$$|T| = |T_1| + |T_2| \geq 2 \cdot |T_2| \geq 2^{h+1}. \quad \square$$

It follows from the Lemma that *Find* can be implemented in logarithmic time. However, our explanation contains a small cheat. It is easy to implement

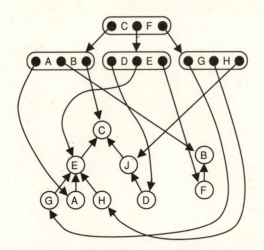

Figure 9.7 The up-trees of Figure 9.5(a), together with an auxiliary 2-3 tree to serve as an index for the keys.

Find(X) by following **Parent** pointers from X up to the root of the tree, if we know the location of the node representing X; but if X is actually a key value of some kind, how are we to locate the node where X is represented? In other words, how do we do a *LookUp*? If the key space from which X is drawn is small and can be indexed, for example, if it is a numerical interval such as $\{1, \ldots, 100\}$, then the records can be allocated in an array and the *LookUp* can be implemented in constant time by an array reference based on the key value. Otherwise, an auxiliary tree structure of some kind can be used as a dictionary (Figure 9.7). To do a *Find* might then take logarithmic time to locate the node via the dictionary, and then logarithmic time to search the up-tree, but the total would still be logarithmic.

Path Compression

If *LookUp*s take logarithmic time, the time bounds achieved by Algorithm 9.3 for *Union* and *Find* are the best possible; if a *LookUp* takes logarithmic time, no improvement to *Find* can make the combination of the two sublogarithmic. Nonetheless there is a simple modification to the algorithm for *Find* that restructures the tree in such a way that subsequent *Find*s will execute somewhat more quickly. Although in general the speedup will not change the order of the complexity of the algorithm, in the special case in which *LookUp*s can be done in constant time, this modification actually makes the algorithm's behavior sublogarithmic. Thus the technique is practically useful in any case, and is theoretically significant when the items being stored are array elements accessed by their indices.

A *Find* would take less time in a shallow, bushy tree than it would in a tall, skinny tree. Use of the balanced merging strategy guarantees, by the Height

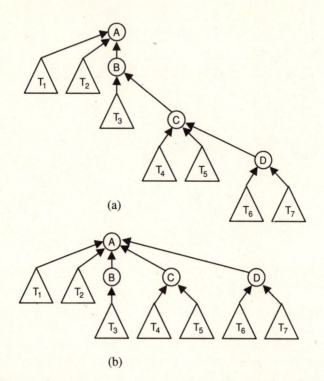

(a)

(b)

Figure 9.8 Path compression. (a) An up-tree; (b) the same tree restructured
   after executing *Find(D)*. Nodes *C* and *D*, which were encountered
   while traversing the path starting from *D*, are made children of the root.
   Thereafter, a *Find* on *C*, *D*, or a node in any of the trees T_4, T_5, T_6,
   or T_7 will be faster.

of Balanced Up-Trees Lemma, that trees will not be too skinny; the height of
a tree can be at worst logarithmic in its size. However, since any number of
nodes of an up-tree can have the same parent, we may be able to restructure our
up-trees to be even bushier. It may be hard to justify taking the time to perform
such restructuring for its own sake, but there is one built-in opportunity to do
it: during a *Find* operation. During such an operation several nodes are visited;
it is a simple matter to redirect their Parent pointers to point to the root, once
the root has been found. This restructuring increases the work done by the *Find*
by only a constant factor, but it may reduce the work required of subsequent
*Find*s by a significant amount.

   The resulting **path compression rule** is very simple: after doing a *Find*,
make any node along the path to the root point directly to the root, rather than to
its previous parent along that path (Algorithm 9.4, Figure 9.8). Any subsequent
Find on one of these nodes, or on any descendant of one of these nodes, will
take less time since the node is now closer to the root.

   When path compression is used, *MakeSet* and *Union* still take constant time,

---

function *PathCompressFind*(**pointer** P): **pointer**
{Return the root of the tree to which P belongs}
    $R \leftarrow P$
    while Parent(R) $\neq \Lambda$ **do** $R \leftarrow$ Parent(R)
    $Q \leftarrow P$ {Now retrace the path}
    while $Q \neq R$ **do**
$$\begin{pmatrix} Q \\ \text{Parent}(Q) \end{pmatrix} \leftarrow \begin{pmatrix} \text{Parent}(Q) \\ R \end{pmatrix}$$
    return R

Algorithm 9.4 Find algorithm, using path compression.

---

of course. How quickly does *Find* execute after a series of path compression steps? The answer is that each *Find* operation takes time that is almost—but not quite—constant. To make that idea more precise, we need to introduce some new notation.

For any $i \geq 0$, let

$$F(i) = 2^{2^{2^{\cdot^{\cdot^{\cdot^2}}}}} \Big\} i.$$

That is, $F(i)$ is defined inductively by

$$F(0) = 1$$

$$F(i + 1) = 2^{F(i)} \qquad \text{for any } i \geq 0.$$

The values of $F(i)$ grow very rapidly with i; for $i = 5$ already

$$F(5) = 2^{2^{2^{2^2}}} = 2^{2^{2^4}} = 2^{2^{16}} = 2^{65536} \approx 10^{19728}.$$

It is hard to get a sense of how big this number is—by way of comparison, the diameter of the universe is less than 10^{40}, even when measured in angstroms, and the number of particles in the universe is less than 10^{120}.

To describe the running time of the *Find* algorithm, we need the inverse of the function F, which is called $\log^*$:

$$\log^* n = \text{ the least } i \text{ such that } F(i) \geq n$$

$$= \text{ the least } i \text{ such that } \underbrace{\lg \lg \ldots \lg}_{i} n \leq 1.$$

Thus $\log^* n \leq 5$ for all $n \leq 2^{65536}$. Although $\log^* n$ grows inexorably towards infinity as n increases without bound, as a practical matter $\log^* n$ is less than 5 for any n of useful size!

■ **THEOREM** *(Path Compression)* If balanced up-trees and path compression are used, then any sequence of $m \geq n$ of the operations *MakeSet*, *Union*, and *Find* on the universe $\{1, \ldots, n\}$ takes total time $O(m \log^* n)$.

Thus in the amortized sense each operation takes time $c \log^* n$ for some constant c, an amount that is independent of n for all practical purposes. The proof of this Theorem follows from three Lemmas.

Let $O_1, \ldots, O_m$ be any sequence of the operations *MakeSet*, *Union*, and *Find*. Imagine executing only the *MakeSets* and *Unions* (not the *Finds*, so no path compression is done). Let T^* be the set of trees that would result; in other words, T^* is the forest that would result if $O_1, \ldots, O_m$ were carried out using Algorithm 9.3 for the *Finds* instead of Algorithm 9.4. For each node v, let *level(v)*, the **level** of node v, be the height of v in T^*.

■ **LEMMA** *(Level Census)* There are at most $n/2^l$ nodes at level l in T^*.

PROOF   By the Height of Balanced Up-Trees Lemma, each node at level l is the root of a subtree of T^* with at least 2^l nodes. These subtrees are disjoint (since no tree of height l can be a subtree of another tree of height l). So there are at most $n/2^l$ of them.   □

■ **LEMMA** *(Levels of Descendants)* If node w is a descendant of v during the execution of $O_1, \ldots, O_m$ using Algorithm 9.4 then w is a descendant of v in T^*, and hence $level(w) < level(v)$.

PROOF   The *Finds* eliminate, but do not create, descendancy relationships; and the height of a proper subtree is strictly less than the height of the tree itself (Figure 9.9).   □

Now define $G(v)$, the **group** of node v, to be $\log^* level(v)$.

■ **LEMMA** *(Group Numbers)* $G(v) \leq \log^* n$ for each node v.

PROOF   Since there are only n nodes, the level of each is at most $\lg n$ by the Height of Balanced Up-Trees Lemma. Therefore

$$G(v) = \log^* level(v) \leq \log^* \lg n \leq \log^* n.   □$$

PROOF *(of the Path Compression Theorem)*   Now we are ready to show that the time used for the m operations $O_1, \ldots, O_m$ is $O(m \log^* n)$. First of all, the *MakeSets* and *Unions* take $O(1)$ time each, for a total of $O(m)$. So we need only determine the time required for the *Finds*. Let

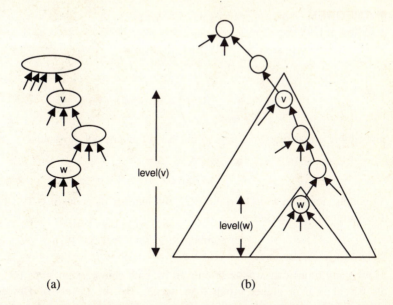

Figure 9.9 Tree constructed (a) with and (b) without doing path compression during *Find*s. If w is a descendant of v in a tree constructed using path compression, it is also a descendant of v if path compression is not used. In this case the level of w must be less than that of v.

O_i be a *Find* operation, and let X_i be the set of all nodes on the path traversed while executing O_i. The cost of a *Find* is proportional to the length of the path traversed while executing it, so the cost of all *Find*s is proportional to

$$\mathbf{F} = \sum_{\text{all } Finds \, O_i} |X_i|.$$

If v is a node in X_i such that v is not a root during O_i, then let $p_i(v)$ be the parent of v during the execution of O_i. Then X_i can be divided into three subsets:

$$Y_i = \{v \in X_i : v \text{ is a root or a child of a root during } O_i,$$
$$\text{and hence is not moved during } O_i\}$$

$$Z_i = \{v \in X_i : v \text{ is moved during } O_i, \text{ and } G(v) < G(p_i(v))\}$$

$$W_i = \{v \in X_i : v \text{ is moved during } O_i, \text{ and } G(v) = G(p_i(v))\}.$$

(The case $G(v) > G(p_i(v))$ is impossible by the Levels of Descendants Lemma.) Clearly $|Y_i| \le 2$, and $|Z_i| \le \log^* n$ by the Group Numbers

Lemma. Therefore

$$\mathbf{F} = \sum_{\text{all } Finds\ O_i} (|Y_i| + |Z_i| + |W_i|)$$

$$\leq \left(\sum_{\text{all } Finds\ O_i} |W_i| \right) + m \cdot (2 + \log^* n),$$

since there are at most m *Finds* in all. So it remains only to bound

$$\mathbf{F'} = \sum_{\text{all } Finds\ O_i} |W_i|.$$

$\mathbf{F'}$ counts, for each *Find* operation O_i, the number of nodes $v \in W_i$; but this sum can be reversed:

$$\mathbf{F'} = \sum_{\text{all nodes } v} (\text{the number of } O_i \text{ such that } v \in W_i).$$

How many times can a node be moved by path compression steps before its parent is in a higher group than itself? By the Levels of Descendants Lemma, each time a node is moved during path compression its new parent is at a higher level than its old parent. Therefore the maximum number of times that a node v at level l can be moved before acquiring a parent in a higher group is the maximum number of different numbers l' such that $\log^* l' = \log^* l$. If $G(v) = \log^* l = g$, this number is at most $F(g)$. Therefore, breaking the nodes down by groups, we find that

$$\mathbf{F'} \leq \sum_{g=0}^{\log^* n} (\text{the number of nodes in group } g) \cdot F(g).$$

But by the Level Census Lemma the number of nodes in group $g > 0$ is at most

$$\sum_{l=F(g-1)+1}^{F(g)} \frac{n}{2^l} \leq \frac{n}{2^{F(g-1)+1}} (1 + \tfrac{1}{2} + \tfrac{1}{4} + \cdots) = \frac{n}{F(g)},$$

which is clearly a bound for group $g = 0$ as well. Hence

$$\mathbf{F'} \leq \sum_{g=0}^{\log^* n} \frac{n}{F(g)} \cdot F(g) \in O(n \log^* n) \subseteq O(m \log^* n). \quad \square$$

It is remarkable that such a simple algorithm has such an exotic analysis. Even more strangely, the $O(\log^* n)$ amortized cost per operation is not the end of the story about the efficiency of *Find* when path compression is used. It is possible to establish *identical* lower and upper bounds on the efficiency of the algorithm. This bound is not constant, but a function that grows even more slowly than $\log^* n$ (see the references at the end of this chapter).

procedure *BSTRangeSearch*(**key** L, U; **pointer** P; **procedure** Op):
{Perform Op on each $\mathsf{Info}(X)$ such that $L \leq \mathsf{Key}(X) \leq U$}
    if $P = \Lambda$ **then return**
    $K \leftarrow \mathsf{Key}(P)$
    if $L \leq K \leq U$ **then** $Op(\mathsf{Info}(P))$
    if $L \leq K$ **then** *BSTRangeSearch*$(L, U, \mathsf{LC}(P), Op)$
    if $K \leq U$ **then** *BSTRangeSearch*$(L, U, \mathsf{RC}(P), Op)$

Algorithm 9.5 Range searching in a binary search tree.

9.3 RANGE SEARCHING

The search problem, as we have considered it so far, is to find the record corresponding to a given key value, or to determine that no such record exists in the data structure. If the data have a natural linear order (for example, the lexicographic order of words), it makes sense to study a related problem, called **range searching**. This is the problem of locating, not the *single* record for a *particular* key value, but *all* records for key values that fall *between* two specified limiting values. For example, if the data structure is used to represent a dictionary of English words, and I asked for the words between chili and chin (inclusive), I might get back chili, chill, chilly, chime, chimera, chimney, chimpanzee, and chin. Perhaps I would like these returned in their own data structure, or perhaps I want them printed or otherwise operated upon; for the sake of formulating the problem abstractly, let us assume that we wish to represent a set of pairs $\langle K, I \rangle$ consisting of **key** and **info** values, and for an arbitrary operation Op on **info** values we wish to implement

> *RangeSearch*(L, U, S, Op): Perform operation Op on each **info** I such that $\langle K, I \rangle \in S$ and $L \leq K \leq U$.

It is easy to search a range in ordinary binary search trees. The basic plan, starting from a node of the tree, is to perform the appropriate operation on the information stored at that node, if its key K is in the range; to search recursively in the left subtree if $L \leq K$ (since there might be additional elements of the range in that subtree), and to search recursively in the right subtree if $K \leq U$. The method (Algorithm 9.5) is a combination of the recursive algorithms for ordinary searching (Algorithm 6.6 on page 194) and for preorder traversal (Algorithm 4.2(b) on page 105).

For example, consider the binary search tree of Figure 9.10, and suppose we search for the range from E to P inclusive. Starting at the root, we find that F is in the range (E $\leq$ F $\leq$ P) and process it. Since E $\leq$ F we descend to the left subtree, whose root is B. B is not in the range, so it is not processed; moreover it is less than the lower limit of the range (E) so we do not descend to the left subtree; but it is less than the upper limit of the range, so we must descend to

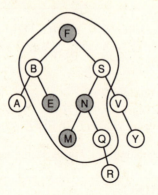

Figure 9.10 Searching a binary search tree for the range from E to P.
Only the nodes within the curve are visited; the rest of the tree is never
searched. The four shaded nodes are discovered to be in the range.

the right subtree. Here E is discovered to be in the range; both children of E
are explored, but both are Λ. Returning to the root, the right subtree is searched
since F ≤ P. Its root, S, is not in the range, so it is not processed, but is greater
than the lower limit of the range, so the left subtree is searched. Both N and its
left child M are discovered to be in the range; but its right child Q is discovered
to be outside the range. The left child of Q is explored and discovered to be Λ,
but the right child of Q need not be explored. On returning to node S, the right
subtree is not searched since P < S. In sum, then, nodes E, F, N, and M are
discovered to be in the range.

Note that there is nothing magic about mimicking the *preorder* traversal
algorithm; if the postorder or inorder traversal were used instead, the only effect
would be to process the nodes in the range in a different order. For example,
if it were desired to print the items in lexicographic order of their keys, then
inorder traversal should be used, and the next-to-last and third-from-last lines
of Algorithm 9.5 should be exchanged. Also, note that the use of less-than-or-
equal (rather than strict inequality) in the last two lines permits the algorithm to
operate correctly even if there are multiple occurrences of the same key value
in the tree (for example, in a real dictionary the word cleave appears twice).

Essentially the same range searching algorithm works in any tree data structure in which the sets of records in the subtrees of a node are determined by
comparing their keys to the key or keys stored in that node. Thus range searching works in AVL trees, 2-3 trees, B-trees, and splay trees.

What is the complexity of Algorithm 9.5, and its relatives for the other
types of search trees? For plain, unbalanced binary search trees it can take
$\Omega(n)$ time to find a single key, and it cannot take less than this, in the worst
case, to do a range query, since an ordinary *LookUp* can be viewed as a special
case of *RangeSearch* in which the lower and upper limits are the same. Using
a balanced tree structure should help, but a range search can still take $\Omega(n)$

time—if the range includes all the keys in the tree! To get at more meaningful analysis we have to use two measures of the "size of the problem": the size of the question and the size of the answer. If we let n be the number of nodes in the tree and m the number of keys in the tree that actually fall in the range, then a reasonable analysis must take both n and m into account. We cannot hope for an algorithm that is better than $O(m)$, since it takes that much time just to present the answer. In fact a range search in a balanced tree structure takes time that is linear in the sum of m and $\log n$.

■ **THEOREM** *(Range Search in Search Trees)* A range search in a search tree takes time $O(m+p)$, where m is the number of elements of the tree that are in the range and p is the height of the tree. In particular, in a balanced tree with n nodes, a range search takes time $O(m+\log n)$.

We shall prove this Theorem just for binary search trees; the generalization to other kinds of search trees is straightforward. Before proceeding to the proof, let us introduce the important notion of a *bounding path* of a range in a binary search tree. Let T be a binary search tree and let L and U be the limits of a search range. The **left bounding path** is the sequence of nodes $L_0, \ldots, L_l$ defined as follows. L_0 is the root of T; and for any $i \geq 0$,

1. if $L \leq \mathsf{Key}(L_i)$, then
   a. if $\mathsf{LC}(L_i) \neq \Lambda$, then $L_{i+1} = \mathsf{LC}(L_i)$;
   b. if $\mathsf{LC}(L_i) = \Lambda$ but $\mathsf{RC}(L_i) \neq \Lambda$ and $\mathsf{Key}(L_i) \leq U$, then $L_{i+1} = \mathsf{RC}(L_i)$;
   c. if $\mathsf{LC}(L_i) = \Lambda$ and either $\mathsf{RC}(L_i) = \Lambda$ or $U < \mathsf{Key}(L_i)$, then $l = i$ (that is, L_i is the last node on the path).
2. if $\mathsf{Key}(L_i) < L$, then
   a. if $\mathsf{RC}(L_i) \neq \Lambda$, then $L_{i+1} = \mathsf{RC}(L_i)$;
   b. if $\mathsf{RC}(L_i) = \Lambda$, then $l = i$.

Thus the left bounding path delimits the left edge of the part of the tree in which it makes sense to search for an element of the range. For example, the left bounding path in the tree of Figure 9.10 goes from F to B to E. The **right bounding path** $R_0, \ldots, R_r$ is defined similarly (Problem 20(a)); in Figure 9.10 the right bounding path goes from F to S to N to Q. Note that the ith node on either bounding path is a node of depth i. The two bounding paths begin at the same node (the root) and may coincide through some additional nodes; in fact if the lower and upper limits of the search range are the same then both bounding paths are identical to the search path for that key value.

PROOF   As in the definitions above, let T be a binary search tree and let L and U be the limits of a search range. Assume that T is nonempty and moreover contains an element of the range; otherwise the Theorem follows easily. Let $L_0, \ldots, L_l$ and $R_0, \ldots, R_r$ be the left and right bounding paths for the search, respectively.

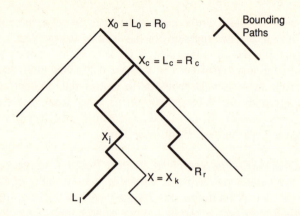

Figure 9.11 Schematic illustration of a range search in a binary search tree. The tree is encompassed by the diagonal lines running down from the root to the left and right; the heavy lines represent the bounding paths. The portion of the path from X_0 to X_c belongs to both bounding paths. $X = X_k$ denotes a typical node that is visited but is not on either bounding path; its key must be in the range, since it is a right descendant of X_j and a left descendant of X_c, both of whose keys are in the range.

Let c be the largest index such that $L_c = R_c$; that is, $L_c = R_c$ is the last node that is common to both bounding paths. (See Figure 9.11; in Figure 9.10, $c = 0$.) If $L_c = R_c$ is the last node on both bounding paths then the Theorem follows immediately. It is impossible for one of the bounding paths to end and the other to continue; for example, it is impossible to have $l = c < r$ (Problem 20(b)). Therefore $\mathsf{Key}(L_c)$ is in the range, since the search from $L_c = R_c$ extends to both its left child and its right child.

Now let X be any node visited during the range search of T, and let $X_0, \ldots, X_k = X$ be the path from the root to X. We claim that if X is on neither bounding path then $\mathsf{Key}(X)$ is in the range. The Theorem will follow, since then the only visited nodes that are not in the range are on the bounding paths, and there cannot be more than $2p$ of them, where p is the height of T.

So suppose that X is on neither bounding path and let j be the largest index such that X_j is on a bounding path; thus $c < j < k$ and none of $X_{j+1}, \ldots, X_k$ is on either bounding path. Without loss of generality, assume that X_j is on the left bounding path; the case in which X_j is on the right bounding path can be treated symmetrically. X_j cannot be the last node on the left bounding path (Problem 20(c)), and since X_j is on the left bounding path but X_{j+1} is not, X_{j+1} is the right child of X_j and $L \leq \mathsf{Key}(X_j)$. Then node X_k is in the subtree rooted at the right child of X_j, and so $\mathsf{Key}(X_k) \geq \mathsf{Key}(X_j) \geq L$. On the other hand, $\mathsf{Key}(X_k) \leq \mathsf{Key}(X_c)$, since

X_k is in the left subtree of X_c, and $\mathsf{Key}(X_c) \leq U$, since the right bounding path goes to the right from X_c. Therefore $L \leq \mathsf{Key}(X_k) \leq U$. $\quad \square$

It is not hard to see that this Theorem gives the best result possible, since any unsuccessful range search (one that finds no records) in a tree with minimum path length $\Omega(\log n)$ will take time $\Omega(\log n)$.

k-d-Trees for Multidimensional Searching

An interesting generalization of the range searching problem is to consider the keys to be coordinates in a space of dimension two or higher. An application in computer graphics is to find all the objects being displayed in a given rectangular region of the screen. For another example, suppose we had a data base of cities, together with their latitudes and longitudes, and we wished to be able to answer queries of the form "find each city with latitude between 41° and 42° N, and longitude between 90° and 91° W." (We would want to get back Clinton, IA, and Rock Island, IL.) It is not at all obvious how such queries could be processed efficiently using any of the data structures presented so far. We could store the cities in a search tree by latitude, say, but the cost of searching through all the cities between 41° and 42° N latitude to find the few having the appropriate longitudes would seem to be prohibitive. Even hashing, generally a robust and flexible data storage and retrieval technique, is wholly inapplicable here, since our searches will not be for exact key values that are known in advance, but for key ranges instead.

In its general form, the **multidimensional range searching** problem can be described as follows. Suppose that $k \geq 1$ and there are k key components. The data structure is to contain $(k + 1)$-tuples $\langle K_0, \ldots, K_{k-1}, I \rangle$, where I is information to be associated with the sequence of key values. Since these structures are used to represent items that may not be uniquely determined by the sequence of key values, the data structure should accommodate multiple items with the same key sequence. The values of each key are drawn from a domain **key** which is linearly ordered (for simplicity, we assume that all field values are drawn from the same domain). Also, let **L** and **U** be k-tuples of values; L_d and U_d are members of **key** bounding the range to be searched in dimension d.

RangeSearch(**L**, **U**, S, *Op*): Perform operation *Op* on each I such that

$$\langle K_0, \ldots, K_{k-1}, I \rangle \in S$$

for some K_0, ..., K_{k-1} such that $L_d \leq K_d \leq U_d$ for $d = 0, \ldots, k - 1$.

A variety of methods have been proposed for this problem, including some involving very complex data structures and some that are analytically very difficult. The simplest data structure that performs satisfactorily in practice is the k-dimensional binary search tree, or k-**d tree**.

City	N Latitude	W Longitude
Appleton, WI	44.17	88.24
Beloit, IL	42.31	89.04
Clinton, IA	41.51	90.12
Dubuque, IA	42.31	90.41
Elgin, IL	42.03	88.19
Fond du Lac, WI	43.48	88.27
Freeport, IL	42.17	89.38
Iowa City, IA	41.39	91.31
Joliet, IL	41.32	88.05
La Crosse, WI	43.48	91.04
Madison, WI	43.04	89.22
Rockford, IL	42.16	89.06
Rock Island, IL	41.30	90.34
Winona, MN	44.02	91.37

Figure 9.12 Some U.S. cities located between 92° and 88° west longitude and between 41° and 45° north latitude, listed in alphabetical order. (Source: *The Times Atlas of the World.*)

A k-d tree is a binary tree with k key fields and an information field at each node. Each item in the left subtree of the root has a Key_0 value less than or equal to that of the root, and each item in the right subtree of the root has a Key_0 value greater than that of the root. At the nodes of depth 1, the keys are split according to the value of the Key_1 field, and so on. Nodes at depth k are again split according to Key_0, and in general nodes at depth d are split according to dimension $d \bmod k$.

For example, consider the geographic data of Figure 9.12. Figure 9.13 shows a 2-d search tree (one of many possibilities, constructed to be well-balanced) based on these data. At the root the keys in the subtrees are divided by longitude, with the more eastern cities (the ones with smaller longitude) in the left subtree and the more western cities in the right subtree. The longitude of the city at the root is the dividing line. At the nodes of depth 1 the division is by latitude, at depth 2 by longitude, and so on. The geometrical effect is to split the rectangle in which all the cities lie into a sequence of subrectangles by alternating vertical and horizontal divisions running through cities on the map (Figure 9.14).

The search procedure for this data structure is a straightforward generalization of that for the one-dimensional case. Starting with longitude, see if the key at the root lies inside or outside the range in that dimension. If it is outside the longitudinal range then search is restricted to one of the two subtrees, depending on whether the longitude at the root is too large or too small. If the key at the root is inside the longitudinal range then its latitude is checked as well; if the latitude is also in range the record is processed as appropriate. Then both subtrees must be searched. At the next level the search begins by checking the latitudinal dimension.

Algorithm 9.6 is the range search algorithm for arbitrary k-d trees. The

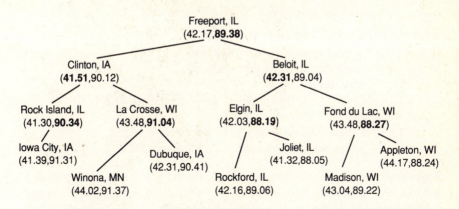

Freeport, IL
(42.17,**89.38**)

Clinton, IA
(**41.51**,90.12)

Beloit, IL
(**42.31**,89.04)

Rock Island, IL
(41.30,**90.34**)

La Crosse, WI
(43.48,**91.04**)

Elgin, IL
(42.03,**88.19**)

Fond du Lac, WI
(43.48,**88.27**)

Iowa City, IA
(41.39,91.31)

Dubuque, IA
(42.31,90.41)

Joliet, IL
(41.32,88.05)

Appleton, WI
(44.17,88.24)

Winona, MN
(44.02,91.37)

Rockford, IL
(42.16,89.06)

Madison, WI
(43.04,89.22)

Figure 9.13 Cities of Figure 9.12 arranged into a 2-d tree. At each nonleaf
node the records in the subtrees are partitioned around the dimension
shown in boldface; for example, all cities in the left subtree of the root
have longitude greater than that of Freeport, IL, namely, 89.38, while all
cities in the right subtree of the root have longitude less than 89.38. (A
split according to longitude has the *larger* values in the *left* subtree so as
to correspond to the orientation of maps of the western hemisphere.) At
the first and third levels the split is according to longitude, while at the
second and fourth levels the split is according to latitude.

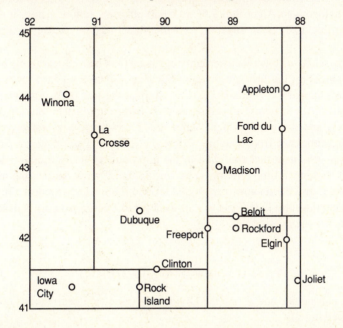

Figure 9.14 Partition of two-dimensional space implicit in 2-d search tree of
Figure 9.13.

---

procedure *kdRangeSearch*(**key** **L**, **U**; **integer** *d*; **pointer** *P*; **procedure** *Op*):
{Perform *Op* on each element in the range from **L** to **U**}
{*P* points to a node that splits on dimension *d*}
    if $P = \Lambda$ **then return**
    if $L_i \leq \mathsf{Key}_i(P) \leq U_i$ **for** $i = 0, \ldots, k - 1$ **then** $Op(\mathsf{Info}(P))$
    $K \leftarrow \mathsf{Key}_d(P)$
    if $L_d \leq K$ **then** *kdRangeSearch*(**L**, **U**, $d + 1$ mod k, $\mathsf{LC}(P), Op$)
    if $K \leq U_d$ **then** *kdRangeSearch*(**L**, **U**, $d + 1$ mod k, $\mathsf{RC}(P), Op$)

Algorithm 9.6 Range searching a k-d tree. On entry P points to the root of a k-d tree (that is, k is the dimensionality of the data set) and L_d and U_d bound the dth dimension of the range to be searched ($d = 0, \ldots, k - 1$). Parameter d is the tree depth currently being searched, modulo k; when the procedure is called nonrecursively from the outside, d should be 0. Procedure Op is to be performed on the Info field of each item whose Key fields are in the range.

---

parameter d cycles through $0, 1, \ldots, k - 1, 0, 1, \ldots$ as the procedure calls itself recursively, so the original call should have $d = 0$. This procedure is closely analogous to Algorithm 9.5, with one other exception: before it can be concluded that a key is in range, all its dimensions must be checked against the bounds.

It is possible to construct a perfectly balanced (and hence logarithmic height) k-d tree quickly if the data are given in advance. Given a set of n items and a "dimension number" d (initially 0), if $n = 0$ then the tree is Λ; otherwise, find the median of the n items, according to their Key_d coordinates; that item goes at the root, and the left and right subtrees are constructed recursively on the next dimension, each from roughly half of the remaining $n - 1$ items. Finding the median—the item that would be in the middle if the data were sorted—can of course be done in time $O(n \log n)$ by sorting, but it turns out that the median can be found and the data set partitioned around the median in linear time (see §11.8). Therefore the time $T(n)$ to construct a k-d tree on n items is described by the recurrence relation

$$T(0) = c$$

$$T(n + 1) = dn + T(\lfloor n/2 \rfloor) + T(\lceil n/2 \rceil),$$

for some constants c and d. By the Divide-and-Conquer Recurrences Theorem, $T(n) \in O(n \log n)$.

Unfortunately there is no simple variation, analogous to AVL trees and 2-3 trees, that makes it possible to keep the tree balanced as insertions are performed. A simple insertion algorithm that does not preserve good balance is, however,

---

procedure *kdInsert*(**key** $K_0, \ldots, K_{k-1}$, **info** I, **locative** P):
{Insert $\langle K_0, \ldots, K_{k-1}, I \rangle$ into the k-d tree with root P}
    $R \leftarrow NewCell(\mathsf{Node})$
    for d **from** 0 **to** $k-1$ **do** $\mathsf{Key}_d(R) \leftarrow K_d$
    $\mathsf{Info}(R) \leftarrow I$
    $\mathsf{LC}(R) \leftarrow \mathsf{RC}(R) \leftarrow \Lambda$
    $d \leftarrow 0$
    while $P \neq \Lambda$ **do**
        if $K_d \leq \mathsf{Key}_d(P)$ **then** $P \leftarrow \mathsf{LC}(P)$ **else** $P \leftarrow \mathsf{RC}(P)$
        $d \leftarrow d+1 \bmod k$
    $P \Leftarrow R$

Algorithm 9.7 Insertion into a k-d tree. The tree is searched until an appropriate leaf position is found, where a new node is implanted. This algorithm permits more than one item to exist in the tree with the same key values.

---

not hard to devise; Algorithm 9.7 is a generalization of recursive binary tree insertion.

Even if a k-d tree is well-balanced, a range search may take more than logarithmic time to report even a single item in response to the query. Thus the situation summarized in the Range Search in Search Trees Theorem does not apply to k-d trees when $k > 1$. In fact, it can be shown that in the worst case a range search in a k-d tree with n nodes takes time $\Theta(m + kn^{1-1/k})$ to find m elements in the range. For example, when $k = 2$ this is $\Theta(m + \sqrt{n})$, a very poor response time if n is large but m is small.

Quad Trees

A **quad tree** is another data structure that can be used to organize data with two independent key coordinates, such as spatial coordinates. In a quad tree each node that is not a leaf has four children. Such a node represents a square region; its four children represent its northwest, northeast, southeast, and southwest quarters. If a particular region contains more than one data point, it must be recursively subdivided until it contains only one data point. A leaf of a quad tree represents either a single data point, in which case the leaf record contains the point's key coordinates and any associated data, or an empty square region, in which case the leaf pointer is Λ.

For example, Figure 9.15 is a quad tree representing the data of Figure 9.12. The four children of a node represent the northwest, northeast, southeast, and southwest quarters in that order; a square represents a child which is Λ because the corresponding quadrant contains no data point. The spatial partition that gives rise to this quad tree is shown in Figure 9.16.

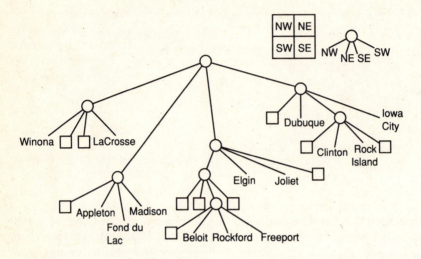

Figure 9.15 Quad tree representation of the data of Figure 9.12. Square nodes represent children which are Λ.

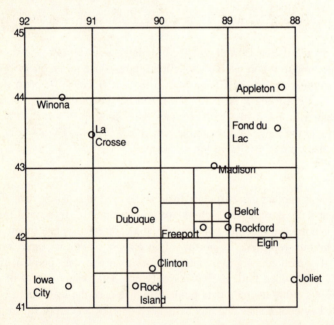

Figure 9.16 Spatial subdivision corresponding to the quad tree of Figure 9.15. The initial square is divided into quarters, and each quarter is recursively subdivided, until each region either is empty or contains a single data point.

A quad tree is really more like a trie than like a search tree because the structure of the tree depends on the numerical values of the coordinates, not on the relative coordinate values of the items being stored. If two data points have coordinates that are numerically close, a quad tree of great height may result, even if these are the only data items in the tree. For example, in Figure 9.15 an extra layer of subdivision is needed to discriminate Beloit, Rockford, and Freeport; all three cities fall in the same squares of size 1° and 0.5°, aligned on multiples of these dimensions, and so space must be partitioned to the level of 0.25° before the cities fall in different squares.

The precise correlation between quad trees and tries may be expressed as follows. Suppose that the data to be represented are of the form $\langle x, y \rangle$, where $0 \leq x < 1$ and $0 \leq y < 1$. Number the four children of a node 00, 01, 10, and 11. Then the node that is reached from the root via the children x_0y_0, x_1y_1, ..., $x_{p-1}y_{p-1}$, where each x_i and y_i is 0 or 1, represents the set of all keys whose x-coordinates, in binary notation, begin with $.x_0x_1 \ldots x_{p-1}$ and whose y-coordinates begin with $.y_0y_1 \ldots y_{p-1}$. For example, the root represents all the points, and its 10 child represents all points whose x-coordinates begin with 1 and whose y-coordinates begin with 0, that is, the points that look like $\langle .1 \ldots , .0 \ldots \rangle$ in binary, or in other words the points with $\frac{1}{2} \leq x < 1$ and $0 \leq y < \frac{1}{2}$. If there is more than one such point in the data set, this node is not a leaf, but has four children representing squares of side $\frac{1}{4}$.

As is the case for tries, it is relatively easy to search a quad tree for a data point, or to insert or delete a data point. Range search queries are also straightforward; to search a tree T representing a square region R for all points lying in a rectangular region S, recursively search each of the four children of T representing a quadrant of R that overlaps with S. Determining "overlap" entails simple comparison of coordinate values that are passed as arguments to the search procedure (see Problem 28).

However, because the height of a quad tree is related to the key values, not just to the number of data items to be stored, quad trees can be inefficient in their use of memory. A second source of storage inefficiency is the fact that each node has four children; in a large tree many Λ children will have to be stored. Quad trees can be generalized to more than two dimensions, but the storage inefficiencies become even more severe in higher-dimensional spaces. In a three-dimensional space, for example, each node would have eight children; such a structure is called an **octtree**.

Storage compaction techniques like those discussed for tries in §8.2 can be applied to quad trees, but another difficulty with quad trees renders them impractical for really large data sets, namely, their very poor storage locality. That is to say, since the data structure will have to be stored on disk or in some other secondary storage medium if it is really large, it is important to ensure that as the data structure is searched successive probes are usually not to different blocks of secondary storage. Quad trees do not enjoy good storage locality; however, the next structure we discuss is designed to address the locality problem.

Grid Files

A **grid file** is a two-level data structure consisting of a **grid directory** and a set of **buckets**. The buckets are disk blocks of fixed size, which can therefore hold only a bounded number of data records. As we will see, the directory is split between main and secondary memory in such a way that the bucket in which a record is stored can be identified with at most one disk access; thus any record access should take only two disk accesses, one within the directory and one to access the bucket itself.

It will be helpful to explain in advance a few of the structures and operations on which grid files are based. By a **scale** we mean a monotone increasing array $A[0 \,.. \, m]$ for some $m > 0$; we may as well think of the elements as numbers, but they can actually be drawn from any linearly ordered set. Thus $A[0] < A[1] < \cdots < A[m]$. Given any value a such that $A[0] \le a < A[m]$, we can find a particular index i such that $A[i] \le a < A[i + 1]$. We call i the result of **locating** a on the scale A.

A two-dimensional grid file is used to represent data that can be located on two scales, $X[0 \,.. \, m_x]$ and $Y[0 \,.. \, m_y]$. (Grid files in higher dimensions can be defined similarly.) Thus the keys are really ordered pairs $\langle x, y \rangle$, where $X[0] \le x < X[m_x]$ and $Y[0] \le y < Y[m_y]$. The location of the record with this key (if it is in the file at all) is then determined as follows. The values x and y are located on the scales X and Y, yielding indices i and j. A two-dimensional array reference $G[i, j]$ then gives the location of the bucket containing the record with key $\langle x, y \rangle$. In general several grid coordinates $G[i, j]$ may point to the same bucket; thus the grid file can efficiently represent data that may be distributed quite nonuniformly in two-dimensional space.

More precisely, a grid directory consists of

1. two positive integers m_x and m_y, which are the sizes of the scales in the x and y dimensions;
2. two scales X and Y, of sizes m_x and m_y;
3. a two-dimensional array $G[0 \,.. \, m_x - 1, 0 \,.. \, m_y - 1]$, which gives, for each pair of indices $\langle i, j \rangle$ of locations on the scales, the bucket $G[i, j]$ in which items belonging to that part are stored.

The scales X and Y need not be regular; for example, if the data set happens to be denser in the smaller values of x then the values of $X[i]$ might increase rather slowly for small i and then more rapidly for larger i. Also, although several $G[i, j]$ may well point to the same bucket, in general buckets will be organized to correspond to consecutive values of the index coordinates. The scales X and Y can be kept entirely in main memory, but the array G may well be too large to fit in main memory; however, since finding a record requires accessing only a single array position, the limit of two disk accesses for looking up a single key pair is satisfied. The internal organization of a bucket might be according to a 2-d tree or some other data structure that supports efficient *LookUp*s or range searches.

For example, Figure 9.17 illustrates the construction of a grid file for the cities of Figure 9.12 on page 322, inserted in alphabetical order, on the assumption that a bucket can hold only two cities and that the dimension of splitting alternates between x and y. (Of course, the figure of two records per bucket is rather small, and is used only for illustrative purposes.) The rectangles with rounded corners show all of the grid squares that point to the same bucket. Figure 9.17(a): Until there are three cities the region does not need to be subdivided; when Clinton is inserted, the first division occurs, into two vertical regions. Figure 9.17(b): Dubuque can be accommodated in an existing bucket, but adding Elgin forces the right-hand region to be subdivided, this time by a horizontal subdivision. Still, only a single bucket represents the entire left-hand region. Figure 9.17(c): Fond du Lac fits into an existing bucket, but Freeport forces a new vertical subdivision. Figure 9.17(d): Iowa City fits into an existing bucket, but Joliet forces a new horizontal subdivision. At this point the directory is a 3×3 array dividing space into nine regions, but there are only five buckets; several directory entries point to the same bucket. Figure 9.17(e): Adding La Crosse causes a bucket to overflow, but no addition need be made to the grid scales; it suffices to split an existing bucket horizontally and change the grid directory. Figure 9.17(f): Inserting the remaining cities requires one more vertical partition; in the end the fourteen cities in twelve regions fit into nine buckets, so disk storage is utilized with an efficiency of $14/18 = 78\%$.

Within the general framework sketched here, there are many possible strategies for splitting buckets. Figure 9.17 was obtained by splitting first in the vertical direction, and then alternately in the horizontal and vertical dimensions; when a scale must be expanded, because a bucket overflows but no suitable scale division partitions the bucket, a single new value is inserted into the scale so as to divide the records in the bucket roughly in half. Notice that expanding the grid directory in this way may entail significant disk access to rewrite the directory; it may be worthwhile, since the directory has to be rewritten anyway, to subdivide it more finely if other buckets are also near to overflowing.

Note that it is possible to delete records from a grid file; if a bucket becomes too empty it may be possible to merge it with one of its neighbors. Another set of strategic decisions revolve around how such mergers might occur. The most restrictive strategy would allow a bucket to be merged only with the "buddy" bucket from which it was split when it was created. But other pairs might be merged with equal ease; for example, in Figure 9.17(f), if Appleton were deleted it might make sense to merge the buckets containing Fond du Lac and Madison together, even though they had not been formed by splitting apart a single bucket earlier.

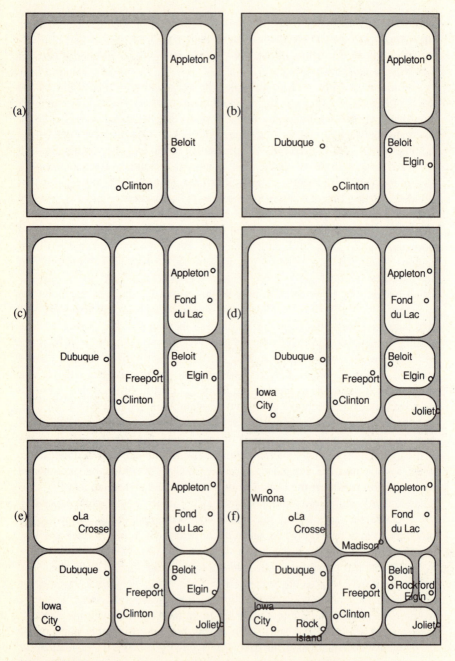

Figure 9.17 Construction of a grid file for the data of Figure 9.12 on page 322.

Grid files bear many similarities to extendible hash tables (page 280), which also have a two-level structure of a directory and a set of buckets; in each structure the directory is refined and grows as data are added, and several directory entries may point to the same bucket. The most important difference between an extendible hash table and a grid file (aside, of course, from the multidimensional organization of a grid file) is that the values located in the directory of an extendible hash table are guaranteed by the hash function to be uniformly distributed across the range; that is why it makes sense to double the size of the directory if it needs to be expanded at all. The key values in a grid file cannot be assumed to be at all uniformly distributed, and they cannot be transformed by hashing into a uniform distribution since this would make it impossible to search ranges by probing only a subset of the buckets. Instead the linear scales X and Y can adapt gradually to any nonuniformity in the data.

Problems

9.1 **1. a.** Show the heaps that result from inserting 6, 5, 2, 4, 7, 1, and 3 into an initially empty heap. (Draw the partially ordered trees, not the actual tables.)

    b. Show the heaps that result from three successive *DeleteMin*s on the heap resulting from part (a).

2. Show that deletion of an *arbitrary* element (not just the *minimal* element) of a heap can be done in $O(\log n)$ time, if its index in the heap is known. That is, give an $O(\log n)$ implementation of a routine *HeapDelete(i, h)* that deletes the item with index i in the heap h.

3. Algorithm 9.1 on page 303 gives an implementation of *HeapInsert* that takes time $O(\log n)$ in the worst case.

    a. Show that the *exact* number of comparisons between data items is about $\lg n$ in the worst case, and that the exact number of movements of data items is also about $\lg n$.

    b. Show that the number of comparisons can be reduced to about $\lg \lg n$ by performing binary search, without changing the number of movements of data items.

4. a. Suppose that H_1 and H_2 are two heaps of size n_1 and n_2, that $n_1 \geq n_2$, and that every element of H_2 is greater than every element of H_1. Explain how to merge H_1 and H_2 into a single heap in time $O(n_1)$.

    b. Why is the condition $n_1 \geq n_2$ needed, and how quickly can the heaps be merged if this condition is violated?

5. Heaps permit one to find the minimum element in constant time and to insert or delete an element in $O(\log n)$ time. Explain how to modify the heap data structure and algorithms to provide an implementation of a double-ended priority queue with the following characteristics: the data structure can be constructed in $O(n)$ time, a record can be inserted or deleted in $O(\log n)$ time, and either the minimum *or the maximum* can be found in constant time. (Hint: Arrange the records so that each node at *even* depth has key value *greater* than that of any of its descendants, and each node at *odd* depth has key value *less* than that of any of its descendants. This data structure is called a **min-max heap**.)

6. Another variant of the heap data structure that solves Problem 5 is called a **deap** ("double-ended heap"). A deap is like a heap except that (1) no record is at the root; (2) the left subtree of the root is a heap arranged so that the minimal element is at the top and each node has key less than or equal to those of its children; (3) the right subtree of the root is a heap arranged so that the maximal element is at the top and each node has key greater than or equal to those of its children; and (4) each leaf of the "min" heap is less than the corresponding leaf of the "max" heap, where the node "corresponding" to a leaf N of the left subtree is the leaf in the same position as N in the right subtree, if it exists, and is otherwise the node in the same position as the parent of N. Show that there are algorithms for this data structure that implement the same operations as those of Problem 5 in the same time bounds.

7. Suppose that a balanced dictionary tree is used in conjunction with a leftist tree to implement dictionary operations as well as priority queue operations. There is a problem with the suggested implementation of *Delete*, since deleting a node in the leftist tree seems to require knowing the location, not of the node, but of its parent. Suggest how this difficulty might be overcome (there is more than one acceptable method).

8. Devise a priority queue representation that permits each *FindMin* and *DeleteMin* operation to run in constant time, while *Insert* takes time $O(\log n)$. (Hint: Keep the records both in a list and in an AVL tree. When deleting an item, remove it completely from the list, but leave it in the AVL tree, with its priority changed to -1. Remove nodes from the AVL tree only when the root acquires priority -1.)

9. A priority queue is said to be **stable** if deletions of items with equal priority value occur in the order in which they were inserted. Which of the priority queue structures discussed in this section are stable? Explain why, or give counterexamples.

10. A **p-tree** is a binary tree structure used to implement priority queues. These trees satisfy the following constraints:

1. Any node lacking a left child also lacks a right child.

2. The priority value of any node is greater than or equal to that of its left child (if it has a left child).

3. All priority values in the right subtree of a node P are less than the priority value of P itself, and are greater than or equal to the priority value of P's left child.

a. Where are the maximum and minimum items in the entire tree?

b. Show that priority trees can be used to implement priority queues by giving implementations of *Insert* and *DeleteMin*. It may be helpful to augment the trees with pointer fields in addition to the left and right child pointers.

c. Show that the algorithms of part (b) can be implemented so that the priority queue is stable, in the sense of Problem 9.

d. Show that p-trees can also support *DeleteMax*, thus providing an implementation of double-ended priority queues.

e. Show that after a sequence of n insertions in a p-tree (with no deletions), the length of the path from the root through left children to a leaf is about $2 \ln n$.

11. A **binomial tree** of **order** n is an ordered tree consisting of a root B with n children, such that the ith child of B is a binomial tree of order i for each $0 \le i \le n - 1$ (Figure 9.18 depicts several binomial trees). It is easy to see that any binomial tree of order n has exactly 2^n nodes. A **binomial forest** is a forest of binomial trees with no two trees of the same order. There is only one way to construct a binomial forest with k nodes for any given k: the forest will have one tree for each 1 in the binary representation of k. A **binomial queue** is a binomial forest in which each node stores a key value (and possibly other information associated with the key) such that each tree is partially ordered; that is, the key of each node is less than the keys of its children.

a. Devise a representation for binomial queues that allows two trees of order n to be combined into a single tree of order $n + 1$ in constant time, preserving the tree partial ordering, and that allows two binomial queues having n_1 and n_2 nodes respectively to be combined into a queue with $n = n_1 + n_2$ nodes in time $O(\log n)$, thus implementing the abstract operation *Union*. (Hint: Consider the usual addition algorithm for binary numbers.)

b. Show how to implement the *Insert* and *DeleteMin* abstract operations on a binomial queue in time $O(\log n)$, where n is the number of elements in the queue.

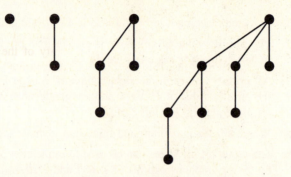

Figure 9.18 Four binomial trees, of orders 0, 1, 2, and 3. As a whole, these four trees make up the (unique) binomial forest with 15 nodes.

    c. Show how to implement $Delete(X, B)$, which deletes from a binomial queue B an arbitrary node X (whose location is given) in time logarithmic in the number of nodes. You may need to change your representation.

    d. Analyze the space requirements of your representation.

9.2   **12.** Starting with a singleton set S_i for each item i, where $1 \le i \le 10$, show the forest of up-trees that results after each of the following operations, if balanced union and path compression are used: $A \leftarrow Union(S_1, S_2)$; $B \leftarrow Union(A, S_3)$; $C \leftarrow Union(S_4, B)$; $D \leftarrow Union(S_5, S_6)$; $E \leftarrow Union(D, S_7)$; $F \leftarrow Union(C, E)$; $Find(7)$.

  13. Consider a sequence of operations that starts with n singleton sets and consists of a sequence of $m \le n$ Union operations followed by a sequence of $n - m$ Find operations (with path compression). Show that the time for the whole sequence is $O(n)$.

  14. The numbers $1, 2, \ldots, 2^k - 1$ are merged into a single perfect binary up-tree by a sequence of *unbalanced* Union operations, in such a way that the leaves are numbered $1, 2, \ldots, 2^{k-1}$ from left to right.

    a. The operations $Find(1), Find(2), \ldots, Find(2^{k-1})$ are then carried out using path compression. What is the order of the time required for this sequence of Find operations? (That is, the answer should be of the form "$\Theta(f(k))$" for some function f.)

    b. Prove that no sequence of balanced Union operations can produce this tree.

  15. Show that $\Omega(m \log n)$ is a lower bound on the time to perform m operations on n elements if up-trees are used with balancing but *without* path compression. That is, exhibit a sequence of m operations that will require $\Omega(m \log n)$ time.

16. Precisely where in the proof of the Path Compression Theorem (including its Lemmas) do we use any property of the function $\log^*$ other than the fact that it is monotone nondecreasing?

17. **a.** Where in the proof of the Path Compression Theorem do we use the assumption that $m \geq n$?

   b. Suppose that assumption is violated; what is the time needed to carry out m operations on a universe of size n if $m < n$?

18. Suppose that the balancing heuristic is implemented by always merging a tree of lesser *height* into a tree of greater height. Show that the Lemma on Page 309 remains true.

9.3   **19.** Carry out a range search of the tree in Figure 9.10 on page 318 for the range from O to W. What are the left and right bounding paths for this search?

20. **a.** Define the *right bounding path*, by analogy with the given definition of *left bounding path*.

   b. Show that it is impossible for the left and right bounding paths to coincide up to a node, and for one bounding path to continue while the other ends at that node.

   c. Let X be a node whose key is in the range but which is not on either bounding path, and let Y be the last node on the path from the root to X that is on a bounding path. Show that Y is not the last node on the bounding path.

21. Show how to do range searching in one dimension using threaded trees, and analyze the method you propose.

22. Where in the proof of the Theorem on Range Search in Search Trees is the assumption used that the tree contains at least one element of the range? What can be done if we do not wish to make this assumption?

23. Suppose that the specification of the range searching operation is redefined so that, instead of performing Op on all items in the range, it returns as a value the set of all items in the range. Show that by using a search tree representation, range searching in this sense can be performed in one dimension in time $O(\log n)$, where n is the number of items in the set being searched, independent of the number of items in the range. Show that this worst-case logarithmic time bound can be maintained even if points are dynamically inserted into and deleted from the data structure.

24. The problem of retrieving sets of cities from a geographical data base according to minimum and maximum latitude and longitude does not, in fact, quite fit the model for multidimensional range searching

presented on page 321. While latitudes have natural minimum and maximum values (90° S and 90° N), longitudes vary in cyclical fashion, from 0° E (= 0° W) to 90° E to 180° E = 180° W to 90° W back to 0°. Thus we might want to do a range search for the range from 10° W to 10° E longitude, or from 170° E to 170° W, or, for that matter, from 10° E to 10° W (that is, most of the way around the globe). Explain how to do range searching in a domain of this type, and present pseudocode for your algorithm.

25. Insert the cities of Figure 9.12 into a 2-d tree by starting with a split on *latitude*, rather than longitude as in Figure 9.13. Illustrate the corresponding spatial partition.

26. Show that range searching in a 2-d tree of size n can take time $\Omega(\sqrt{n})$, independent of the number of items in the range.

27. Consider the following data structure for range searching in two dimensions. Items are organized into a binary search tree on their key values in the first dimension; but attached to each node X of this binary search tree is a separate binary search tree containing all items in the subtree rooted at X, organized according to their key values in the second dimension.

   a. Give an algorithm for inserting an item into such a "tree of trees."

   b. Give an algorithm for range searching such a structure.

   c. Show that under reasonable assumptions about the distribution of key values, inserting n items into an initially empty structure takes expected time $O(n(\log n)^2)$, and range searching a structure with n items when there are m items in the range takes expected time $O(m + (\log n)^2)$.

   d. Show that the expected time to search a range in this structure is $O((\log n)^2)$ if the objective is not to perform an operation on every item in the range but to return a representation of the set of all items in the range.

   e. What are the memory requirements for this data structure?

   f. Generalize this structure to more than two dimensions, and give the corresponding results about expected time complexity for insertions and range searches.

28. Write an algorithm that performs a range search in a quad tree.

29. Explain why the structure of a quad tree does not depend on the order in which items are inserted into it.

30. Quad trees are used in computer graphics for representing digitized images. An image is divided into $2^k \times 2^k$ picture elements, or **pixels**, each of which is either black or white. (The value of k is typically 10 or 11.) Each leaf of the representing quad tree has a binary **Shade** field, indicating that the pixels in the entire square corresponding to that leaf are either all black or all white.

a. What are the maximum and minimum sizes of quad trees that represent images in this way, and what are the worst-case and best-case images? What is the maximum size of the quad tree representation of a $2^{k-1} \times 2^{k-1}$ square with its sides parallel to the sides of the image?

b. Explain how to transform a quad tree representing an image into a quad tree representing the same image rotated 90°.

c. Write an algorithm for computing the black area of an image, that is, for counting the number of black pixels of an image represented by a quad tree.

d. Write an algorithm that converts a square array of binary values (0s and 1s representing pixels) into a quad tree. Naturally, the quad tree should be as small as possible. Assess the complexity of your method.

e. Write an algorithm that converts a quad tree representation of an image into a square array of binary values.

f. In practice the problem of part (e) is not really what is wanted in computer graphics, since the array would be huge and the pixels are wanted in **scan-line order**: first all the pixels in the first row, from left to right, then all the pixels in the second row, and so on. Devise an algorithm that produces the pixels from a quad tree in this order without precomputing the entire image.

31. Show the stages in the construction of a grid file from the data of Figure 9.12 on page 322 when the cities are inserted in *reverse alphabetical order*, rather than in alphabetical order as in Figure 9.17 on page 330.

32. Design a data structure that can be used to answer questions of the following kind about a fixed set of n points in the plane with integer coordinates: Given a rectangle, how many points does it contain? The data structure can be as big as you want and you may take as much time as you want to prepare the data structure from the points, but once the data structure is ready the questions must be answered in constant time. How big is the data structure, and how much time does it take to prepare?

33. a. Suppose we are given n points on the x-axis by the values of their x-coordinates. Suppose further that we are given constants

c and d such that the following "sparseness" condition holds: no interval on the line of length $2d$ contains more than c of the points. Find an $O(n \log n)$ algorithm for discovering all pairs of points that are within distance d of each other. Why is the sparseness condition necessary?

b. Now consider a collection of n points in the plane governed by the sparseness condition that no circle of radius d contains more than c of the points. Find an $O(n \log n)$ algorithm for discovering all pairs of points that are within distance d of each other. (Hint: Use divide and conquer, and the result of part (a).)

c. Generalize the method of part (b) to obtain a $O(n(\log n)^{k-1})$ algorithm in k dimensions.

34. a. Suppose we are given n points on the x-axis by the values of their x-coordinates. Give an algorithm that finds the closest pair of points in $O(n \log n)$ time.

b. Repeat part (a) for a collection of n points in two dimensions. (Hint: Divide and conquer.)

References

Heaps were first used as part of the sorting algorithm known as Heap Sort (see page 386) by

J. W. J. Williams, "Algorithm 232: Heapsort," *Communications of the ACM* **7** (1964), pp. 347–348,

and

R. W. Floyd, "Algorithm 245: Treesort 2," *Communications of the ACM* **7** (1964), p. 701.

The data structure for Problem 5 is described in

M. D. Atkinson, J.-R. Sack, N. Santoro, and T. Strothotte, "Min-Max Heaps and Generalized Priority Queues," *Communications of the ACM* **29** (1986), pp. 996–1000.

Deaps (Problem 6) are from

S. Carlsson, "The Deap—A Double-Ended Heap to Implement Double-Ended Priority Queues," *Information Processing Letters* **26** (1987), pp. 33–36.

Problem 3 is from

G. H. Gonnet and J. I. Munro, "Heaps on Heaps," *SIAM Journal on Computing* **15** (1986), pp. 964–971.

If the priority values are arbitrary, then any priority queue structure must use $\Omega(\log n)$ time for insertions and deletions. But if the universe of priority values is small, for example, if it is $\{1, \ldots, n\}$ where n is the size of the priority queue itself, then sublogarithmic cost can be achieved. (The situation resembles that for the disjoint sets problem *discussed in §9.2.) Priority queue implementations with $O(\log \log n)$ cost per insertion or deletion under these circumstances are described in*

P. van Emde Boas, R. Kaas, and E. Zijlstra, "Design and Implementation of an Efficient Priority Queue," *Mathematical Systems Theory* **10** (1977), pp. 99–127

and

P. van Emde Boas, "Preserving Order in a Forest in Less than Logarithmic Time and Linear Space," *Information Processing Letters* **6** (1977), pp. 80–82.

The p-tree structure (Problem 10) is explored in

A. Jonassen and O.-J. Dahl, "Analysis of an Algorithm for Priority Queue Administration," *BIT* **15** (1975), pp. 409–422.

Leftist trees were discovered by

C. A. Crane, *Linear Lists and Priority Queues as Balanced Binary Trees*, PhD Thesis, Stanford University, 1972.

They are described in detail in Knuth's book Sorting and Searching *cited on page 44. Binomial queues (Problem 11) are from*

J. Vuillemin, "A Data Structure for Manipulating Priority Queues," *Communications of the ACM* **21** (1978), pp. 309–314.

Balanced up-trees are from

R. Bayer, "Oriented Balanced Trees and Equivalence Relations," *Information Processing Letters* **1** (1972), pp. 226–228.

The full union-find algorithm, using path compression, was analyzed by

R. E. Tarjan, "Efficiency of a Good but Not Linear Set Union Algorithm," *Journal of the ACM* **22** (1975), pp. 215–225.

The data structures known as k-d trees were invented by Jon Bentley; see

J. L. Bentley, "Multidimensional Binary Search Trees Used for Associative Searching," *Communications of the ACM* **19** (1975), pp. 509–517;

J. L. Bentley, "Multidimensional Binary Search Trees in Database Applications," *IEEE Transactions on Software Engineering* **SE-5** (1979), pp. 333–340.

Problem 26 is from

D. T. Lee and C. K. Wong, "Worst-Case Analysis for Region and Partial Region Searches in Multidimensional Binary Search Trees and Balanced Quad Trees," *Acta Informatica* **9** (1977), pp. 23–29.

Problem 27 is from

G. Lueker, "A Data Structure for Orthogonal Range Queries," *Proceedings, 19th Annual IEEE Symposium on Foundations of Computer Science*, 1978, pp. 28–34.

Data structures with guaranteed worst-case behavior for range searching in higher dimensions are discussed in

D. E. Willard, "New Data Structures for Orthogonal Range Queries," *SIAM Journal on Computing* **14** (1985), pp. 232–253;

B. Chazelle, "Filtering Search: A New Approach to Query-Answering," *SIAM Journal on Computing* **15** (1986), pp. 703–724.

These papers contain references to many papers on related problems. An extensive explanation of quad trees and their variants is in

H. Samet, "The Quadtree and Related Hierarchical Data Structures," *Computing Surveys* **16** (1984), pp. 187–260.

Grid files are discussed in

J. Nievergelt, H. Hinterberger, K. C. Sevcik, "The Grid File: An Adaptable, Symmetric, Multikey File Structure," *ACM Transactions on Database Systems* **9** (1984), pp. 38–71.

Some interesting and useful generalizations of binary search to higher dimensions are discussed in

J. L. Bentley, "Multidimensional Divide-and-Conquer," *Communications of the ACM* **23** (1980), pp. 214–229.

This paper is the origin of Problems 33 and 34. (Problem 33(c) can actually be solved in time $O(n \log n)$, independent of k.) Problem 32 is from

J. L. Bentley and M. I. Shamos, "A Problem in Multivariate Statistics," *15th Allerton Conference on Communication, Control, and Computing*, 1977, pp. 193–201,

and also appears in the following book, a good source of algorithms for related problems:

F. P. Preparata and M. I. Shamos, *Computational Geometry: An Introduction*, Springer-Verlag, 1985.

For an introduction to computational geometry, including a discussion of range searching, see

R. Graham and F. Yao, "A Whirlwind Tour of Computational Geometry," *American Mathematical Monthly* **97** (1990), pp. 687–702.

10

Memory Management

10.1 THE PROBLEM OF MEMORY MANAGEMENT

In our model the memory of a computer consists of a single large table of cells of small fixed size (typically 8 bits). The only basic operations directly supported by the memory are storage into and retrieval out of a memory cell, as functions of its address. Programming language systems, operating systems, and other "service" programs provide more abstract interfaces for dealing with memory. For example, programming languages provide a mechanism for referring to an integer quantity by a variable name such as "X," rather than by its true position and extent in memory. The label "X" is an abstraction of an address. Indeed, the quantity referred to as X in a subroutine may be located in different places in memory on different occasions that the subroutine is called; it may even move within memory while the subroutine is active. As another example, we have used in our descriptions of several algorithms a general routine *NewCell* that provides a chunk of memory of a specific requested size, but whose location we consider irrelevant. Similarly, an operating system may locate a 50 kilobyte program in a particular chunk of a much larger memory, and then relocate it elsewhere in memory when other programs start to run. As long as the behavior of the program does not depend in any relevant way on its position in memory, we are happy to let the operating system move it around.

The semantic advantages of an abstract, high-level interface to memory are obvious: the size of fields can be determined by considerations external to the program, such as the characteristics of the machine on which the program is to be run, and the program's view of the structure of memory can be much less rigid than reality would otherwise dictate. Equally important, however, is the finiteness of memory. An abstract interface supports the view that memory is unlimited: if you need to create an object that takes up memory, just ask for the amount of memory you need. Reality is quite different in this respect as well: if all the memory cells have been allocated to one use or another, no more are available. **Memory management** is the prudent utilization of this scarce resource, whether by conservation, recycling, or other strategies. It is carried out in a way that tries to interfere as little as possible with the high-level view of memory as a resource that can be consumed on request in specified amounts.

Let us agree on the following terminology. The portion of memory to be managed is a table $M[0 .. N - 1]$ of N cells, called the **heap**,* from which smaller blocks are from time to time to be **allocated**. When a block has been allocated, it is said to be **reserved** or **in use**; it may later be **freed** or **deallocated**, and it is then available to satisfy further allocation requests.

What makes a good heap scheme depends critically on many characteristics of the system in which it is being used. There are few absolute rules; techniques that are effective in one context may be suboptimal in another, where the number or size of the memory requests may be different. Here are some of the characteristics of the memory management environment that affect the choice of scheme to be employed:

Blocks of fixed size vs. blocks of various sizes: In some contexts all memory requests are for records of the same size, or at least one size is requested in such quantity that it makes sense to set aside a heap to be managed for just those requests. An example is the allocation of list cells in a system like Lisp that manipulates list structures extensively. In other contexts the size of memory requests is unpredictable within a certain broad range; an example is the allocation of large chunks of memory within an operating system for programs to run in, or the allocation of memory for array storage in a programming language system. Fixed-size blocks are much easier to manage than diverse-sized blocks, because any one can occupy the position of any other.

Linked blocks vs. unlinked blocks: Suppose A and B are records in memory, and somewhere within A is a pointer to B (for example, A and B might be logically adjacent cells in a linked list). Although the specific location of B in memory is unimportant, B cannot be moved without updating the reference to B that occurs in A. To do so would leave in A a "dangling pointer" that now points not to B but perhaps to some other structure that was created when B was moved. The memory blocks used by the independent programs managed by an operating system, on the other hand, generally have no linkage between them. Linked structures present management difficulties that unlinked structures do not.

---

*The term "heap" is also used in an entirely different sense, to mean an implicitly represented tree structure in which the datum at each parent node stands in a particular ordering relation to the data stored in its children (page 300). Heaps in this sense are the basis for a useful sorting algorithm called "Heap Sort" (page 386). The coincidence of terminology is a historical accident.

Small blocks vs. large blocks: Memory management routines may be called on to handle blocks as small as a few bytes or as large as a few megabytes. To handle a request it may be reasonable to move a small block, or to zero it, or to do something else that takes time proportional to the size of the block, since if the block is small the time spent in this way is only a small fraction of the total time spent by the memory management routine. To handle a request for a large block it is probably undesirable to carry out an operation that takes time proportional to the size of the new block.

Time vs. memory: In some environments the heap may be much larger than the part used at any one time (though smaller than the sum of all requests over a long period of time). Some underutilization of the memory may then be perfectly acceptable, if it permits use of a much faster memory management algorithm. In other environments every bit may be precious, and complex algorithms operating in limited amounts of memory may be required.

Explicit vs. implicit release: When a block of memory ceases to be needed, will the user of the memory notify the memory management system, or must the system determine by itself that the block is no longer in use? The answer to this question is in part a matter of protocol between the "service" that provides memory and the "clients" that use it, and as such affects the abstract interface between them. In extreme cases, however, the choice is fairly clear. An operating system that requests of its memory management subsystem huge blocks in which to run programs is in a good position to inform the memory management system when the programs stop running. Deallocation of small blocks in a programming language context can be extremely tricky, however. Assignment is a form of implicit release. If explicit release were required, one could not even say

$$P \leftarrow NewCell(\text{Node})$$
$$P \leftarrow Q$$

without remembering to release, before the second assignment, the memory to which P points. Otherwise that memory would become **garbage**, that is, considered allocated by the memory manager but not referenced by any variable or data structure that still exists and is significant to the client. In this context counting on explicit release is not only delicate, it is dangerous, since it relies on cooperation by a user who may be hostile or ignorant. On the other hand, implicit release is a subtle matter as well, since a block cannot be considered free until *all* use of it has ceased; the flip side of the problem of failing to release a block when appropriate is reclaiming a block before it is really free, since one cannot tell by looking at a block how many pointers may be pointing to it.

Scheduled vs. unscheduled release: Anything that is known about the order in which allocated blocks of memory will be released can be helpful to the memory manager. As an extreme example, if the manager knows that certain requests are released in last-in-first-out fashion, it can simply allocate them on a stack—no more efficient or economical scheme is possible. (This is exactly what happens when memory is allocated for local variables and procedural parameters in recursive program calls, see page 79.) But in general nothing can be known about the release schedule, and the memory manager must plan for the worst.

Initialized vs. uninitialized blocks: The memory manager may be given the responsibility of initializing allocated blocks by setting bits to 0 or to some other pattern. For example, the runtime system for a higher-level programming language may expect this because the semantics of the programming language defines the value of newly allocated variables. As another example, an operating system may want to initialize blocks that are supplied in response to memory requests by user programs as a security measure, to ensure that data in memory released by one user program do not become visible to another user program. On the other hand, initialization takes time proportional to the size of the block, and may not be worth doing if the clients of the memory manager do not require it.

This chapter considers various combinations of these situational characteristics and describes some of the techniques that have proved useful repeatedly.

10.2 RECORDS OF A SINGLE SIZE

If all records are the same size k, the heap $M[0..N-1]$ can be partitioned once and for all into a table of cells of size k, say $T[0..m-1]$, where $m = \lfloor N/k \rfloor$. Any request for a cell is satisfied by allocating one of the $T[i]$; there is no need to consider allocating a record across the boundaries separating the $T[i]$ from each other. At any point in time certain of the $T[i]$, scattered through the table, are **in use** and the rest are **free**; in general no pattern describes which of the cells are in use.

To satisfy requests for cells a **free list** is maintained; this is a singly linked list of the cells that are not in use. No additional memory is required to maintain this list, since the Next fields can be part of the cells themselves. (We assume that k, the size of a cell, is at least **p** bits, the size of a pointer. Using part of a cell as a pointer may be inconsistent with the fields of a cell as viewed by the client; but since the cell is linked into the free list only when it is free, no conflict can arise.) The list is accessed as a stack; retrieving a cell from the list is a *Pop*, and adding a cell to the list is a *Push*. Therefore allocating a cell takes $\Theta(1)$ time.

The difficulties come in returning used cells to the free list once they are no longer needed by the client; this process is called **garbage collection**. To define "no longer needed" a little better, we need to make some assumptions about how the client is using the cells. In the worst case, there are links to a cell from other cells and also from variables or data structures outside T. In this case "use" can be indirect; there may be no pointer directly from a known object to a cell, but a long chain of anonymous links might still connect a cell to one that is in use, and cause it to be "in use" as well. (However, we assume the client performs no pointer operations except assigning one pointer to another, moving from a pointer to the thing to which it points, and comparing two pointers for equality. For example, the client never has occasion to utilize the arithmetic order of two different pointers, to calculate the numerical difference between two pointers, or the like. Bugs of an entirely different order can be created in programming languages like C, in which such operations are possible!)

Reference Counts

Explicit deallocation may be possible in principle, though it is likely to be awkward even under the best of circumstances. Each time the address of a cell is copied, another "use" is created; the cell cannot reliably be deallocated until all the copies of its address have been destroyed. One method for keeping track of the use of cells is to maintain a **reference count** for each cell, that is, a count of the number of pointers that point to a cell. When a new copy of the address of a cell X is created, the cell's reference count must be incremented; when a copy is destroyed (because a pointer that used to point to X is assigned some other value) the reference count is decremented. When the reference count becomes 0, then X can safely be deallocated; at the same time, the reference count of any cell pointed to from within X must be decremented. The disadvantages of the reference count method are at least three:

1. It requires careful handling of pointers at all times. For example, even a simple assignment $P \leftarrow Q$ of one pointer to another must be preceded by the following sequence of actions: decrement the count of the cell P now points to (since that reference is about to be destroyed) and release that cell if the count is now 0; then increment the count of the cell Q points to (since a new reference to it is about to be created).*

2. It requires a new field in each cell to contain the count. Moreover, unless there is some externally supplied bound on the number of pointers that can point to a cell, there will be no bound on the size of this field; for example, a one-byte reference count field would be sufficient only if it is known that no more than 255 pointers could ever point to a cell.

---

*Even this cautious procedure has a subtle bug (see Problem 1).

3. Most important, it doesn't work at all if "circular" list structures can be created. For example, if cell X has a pointer to cell Y and Y has a pointer to X, then both X and Y will have nonzero reference counts even if there are no other references to either cell. In this case both X and Y will appear to be in use, when in fact neither is in use. The problems of such "islands of garbage" are the most crippling of all, and limit the use of the reference count method to specialized applications in which circular structures cannot be created.

Mark and Sweep Garbage Collection

A commonly used alternative to the reference count method is to wait until the free list becomes empty, and then to scavenge memory for unused cells from which a new free list can be created. This process proceeds in two stages. First, the cells that are in use are **marked**, that is, a bit called the Mark bit is turned on for each cell that is accessible by some chain of pointers that begins outside the block T. Anything unmarked must then be garbage, and can be put on the free list.

The Mark bits may occupy a new field in each cell, or may be kept in a bit table in the same order as the cells they are intended to mark. If they are kept in a table, access to them may take a little longer, but the space they occupy can be used for something else when garbage collection is not going on.* In order to avoid these implementation details, we assume the existence of two routines, $Mark(P)$, which turns on the mark bit of the cell to which P points, and $Marked(P)$, which returns **true** if that bit is already on. All the mark bits can be turned off during an address-order scan (that is, a scan of the form **for** i **from** 0 **to** $n - 1$ **do** $\ldots T[i] \ldots$). Another address-order scan of the cells will collect the unmarked cells into the free list. (The mark bits can be turned off as the cells are collected, so that subsequent calls to the garbage collector need not be preceded by a pass to turn the mark bits off.) Thus the only part of the procedure that remains to be specified is the marking algorithm itself.

The marking algorithms we consider are generalizations of the tree traversal and scanning algorithms of §4.5. Of course cells may be linked together in quite complex patterns, not just as trees; nonetheless the tree visiting algorithms serve as marking algorithms almost without modification. If a cell can be reached via more than one sequence of links, it is marked the first time it is encountered; the subsequent times it is reached the Mark bit is found to be on, so it is not explored further.

For the purpose of discussion we assume that all cells are instances of the same record type, and that they have k pointer fields, which we call C0, C1, C2, $\ldots$, C($k - 1$). Binary tree nodes correspond to the $k = 2$ case, with LC = C0

---

*In many cases an unused bit can be found within the record structure. For example, if all records are located at even addresses, the low-order bit of any pointer field will be 0; this bit can be "temporarily borrowed" for another purpose as long as it is returned to its original condition later.

FullyRecursiveMark(**pointer** P):
  if not *Atom*(P)
    and not *Marked*(P) **then**
  Mark(P)
  for j **from** 0 **to** $k - 1$ **do**
    FullyRecursiveMark($Cj(P)$)

Algorithm 10.1(a)

PartlyRecursiveMark(**pointer** P):
  while not *Atom*(P)
    and not *Marked*(P) **do**
  Mark(P)
  for j **from** 0 **to** $k - 2$ **do**
    PartlyRecursiveMark($Cj(P)$)
  $P \leftarrow C(k - 1)(P)$

Algorithm 10.1(b)

and $RC = C1$. The references in the tree algorithms to the empty tree Λ serve only the purpose of stopping a traversal or scan once it has reached the frontier of the tree, or worked its way back to the root; therefore in the new context a test of the form "$P = \Lambda$?" should sometimes be replaced by a question "Does P point to a cell of the type that is to be marked, or does P point outside the table T?" As shorthand, we say that $Atom(P)$ is true (and that P points to an **atom**) if P points outside the table T; exactly what P does point to in such a case is a matter of interest only to the application.

Recursive, Depth-First Marking   The most straightforward methods are those that are based on preorder versions of the recursive traversals, Algorithms 4.5 and 4.6; these are shown as Algorithm 10.1(a) and (b) generalized to the case of k pointers and incorporating a test that avoids retraversal of structure that has already been marked.

Algorithm 10.1(a) checks that P points to an unmarked list cell, and if so marks it and recursively follows all its pointer fields. Algorithm 10.1(b) does the same, except that the tail-recursive call to follow the last pointer is replaced by an iteration. (If $k = 2$, there is just one recursive call, to follow C0.) Note the importance of the *pre*order traversal, that is, marking a node *before* marking its children; in this way a circular structure will not be reentered.

The difficulty with both algorithms is the amount of memory they may require for a stack; Algorithm 10.1(a) needs a stack of pointers as large as the maximum number of links that may be traversed before an atomic value is found, and Algorithm 10.1(b) needs a stack of pointers as large as the maximum number of C0, ..., C($k - 2$) links that may be so traversed. Neither requirement is at all satisfactory, especially since garbage collection is called into action exactly when memory is in shortest supply.*

---

*In many environments the stack space is entirely separate from the heap space where garbage is produced and collected. In this situation there is no interference between the stack and heap, but it is still important to keep the stack size as small as possible, since a failure of the garbage collection algorithm is likely to be fatal to the entire system.

---

procedure *LinkInversionMark*(**pointer** Q):
{Mark all cells reachable from the cell Q}
    $P \leftarrow \Lambda$
    $S \leftarrow MakeEmptyStack(\,)$
    repeat forever
        if $Q \neq \Lambda$ **and not** *Atom*(Q) **and not** *Marked*(Q) **then**
            Mark(Q)
            Push(0, S)
            descend via C0
        else if $P = \Lambda$ **then return**
        else
            $j \leftarrow Pop(S)$
            ascend via Cj
            $j \leftarrow j + 1$
            if $j < k$ **then**
                Push(j, S)
                descend via Cj

Algorithm 10.2 Link inversion (or "Schorr-Deutsch-Waite") marking algorithm for cells with k pointers.

Link-Inversion, Schorr-Deutsch-Waite Marking The adaptation of the link-inversion traversal algorithm for binary trees (Algorithm 4.7 on page 115) to the marking problem is called the **Schorr-Deutsch-Waite** method and is shown as Algorithm 10.2. It stores the stack of Algorithm 10.1(a) as a pointer chain in the structure itself. Two general comments are in order. Instead of using a Tag bit in each cell as in Algorithm 4.7 to record whether descent through that cell has been to the left or right, Algorithm 10.2 pushes a number in the range $0, \ldots, k - 1$ onto a stack to indicate which of the pointers has been descended through. (If $k = 2$, this number carries the same information as the Tag bit.) If it is more convenient to keep this number as a statically allocated field in each record, it is easy to modify the algorithm so that it does (Problem 3). The *ascend* and *descend* code used by the algorithm is similar to the code shown on page 115 to ascend or descend to the left or right, but it is now used to ascend or descend through any of the k fields C0, $\ldots$, C($k - 1$):

$$\text{descend} \atop \text{via C}j: \begin{pmatrix} P \\ Q \\ Cj(Q) \end{pmatrix} \leftarrow \begin{pmatrix} Q \\ Cj(Q) \\ P \end{pmatrix} \qquad \text{ascend} \atop \text{via C}j: \begin{pmatrix} Q \\ P \\ Cj(P) \end{pmatrix} \leftarrow \begin{pmatrix} P \\ Cj(P) \\ Q \end{pmatrix}$$

Since this algorithm never follows the same pointer twice and marks each cell only once, it uses $\Theta(n)$ time to mark n cells. It is likely to be a bit slower than the naïve recursive algorithm, since the code to *descend* and *ascend* does more work than a simple *Push* and *Pop*; but it uses only $\lceil \lg k \rceil \cdot h$ bits, where h is the length of the longest pointer chain from the root to any cell (in the worst case, h can be as large as n).

Link-Inversion, Constant-Space Marking If even this much memory cannot be given over to the marking task, the constant-space scanning algorithm (Algorithm 4.8 on page 118) can be adapted to the marking task as well—in the case of binary cells. Recall that when used on binary trees, this algorithm visits each node with two children three times, rotating the pointers on each visit so that they are restored to their original condition after the third visit. When the algorithm encounters a node, it does not "know" whether the encounter is the first, second, or third; all three are handled identically. This feature of the algorithm raises problems when it is used to mark structures that are not trees, but may have more than one sequence of pointers that lead to the same cell.

The recursive and link inversion algorithms refuse to visit a cell that is found to have been marked already, and in this way avoid repetitive searches of structures that can be reached along more than one sequence of links. If the constant-space algorithm is to be used, a similar refusal to revisit a marked cell would cause the algorithm to quit before making its crucial second and third visits. If we simply dispense with this test, and follow all pointers blindly, even if they lead to marked cells, then the algorithm will loop endlessly if it encounters a cycle of pointers (say A contains a pointer to B which contains a pointer to A). It will work slowly but correctly if there are multiple paths to certain cells, but no cycles (Problem 4). We might be tempted to include a count field to tell how many times a cell has been visited, but then we might as well use the link inversion method.

Instead there is a clever way to use the Mark bit itself to indicate not only that a cell has been visited but in what direction it was last departed. Unfortunately both pieces of information cannot be represented perfectly in a single bit, but we can come close enough that a cell's status can be determined exactly by some retracing of the path from the root to the cell.

The basic idea is to complement the Mark bit of a cell each time we go through it. Thus the Mark bit is

0 initially;
1 after the first visit, that is, while descent is through the LC;
0 after the second visit, that is, while descent is through the RC;
1 after the third and last visit, that is, after ascending from the cell.

So it winds up marked, as it should. Algorithm 10.3 gives the details of the pointer and Mark bit manipulations (the pointer rotations are the same as in Algorithm 4.8 on page 118).

Algorithm 4.8 does "know" when it has reached the frontier of the tree: when $Q = \Lambda$. When this happens Algorithm 4.8 "turns around" and starts to

procedure *Rotate*(**locative** P, Q):
{Rotate P, Q, and the children of Q, and complement the mark bit of Q}

$$\begin{pmatrix} P \\ Q \\ LC(Q) \\ RC(Q) \\ \text{Mark}(Q) \end{pmatrix} \Leftarrow \begin{pmatrix} Q \\ LC(Q) \\ RC(Q) \\ P \\ 1 - \text{Mark}(Q) \end{pmatrix}$$

Algorithm 10.3 Pointer rotation and Mark bit manipulation for use in constant-space marking algorithm.

___

ascend the tree. On return to the previous node, the information that the algorithm is "ascending" rather than "descending" is lost, because in Algorithm 4.8 there is no way to tell whether the node has been reached from the left child (so that it will continue by descending to the right) or from the right child (so that it will continue by ascending to its parent). With the Mark bit as just described, however, these two cases can be distinguished: during an ascent, if a node with Mark bit 1 is encountered, ascent has been from the left (and so descent to the right is about to take place); if a node with Mark bit 0 is encountered, ascent has been from the right (and so ascent is to be continued). So the algorithm can tell when it is descending, and when it is ascending.

Now for the question of how to avoid repenetrating into portions of the data structure that have already been visited. This is a concern only during the descent phase of the algorithm. If, during descent, a marked cell is encountered, that cell should not be entered, since it must have been visited previously. But if an unmarked cell is encountered, it could be either a brand new cell or a cell along the path back to the root from which descent has been to the right. To tell which, we can retrace the path back to the root; P points to the first cell on that path, and if R is any cell on the path, then the next cell on the path is

$LC(R)$ if R is unmarked, that is, descent from R was to the right;
$RC(R)$ if R is marked, that is, descent from R was to the left.

The *OnPath* routine retraces the path in this way to determine whether its argument points to a new node. The full details are in Algorithm 10.4.

A significant price in performance is paid by Algorithm 10.4 in exchange for its savings in memory. Each time a new cell is encountered, the full path from that cell back to the root must be traversed in order to verify that it is indeed a new cell, and not a cell along that path through which descent has been to the right. The time needed to retrace the path grows at least in proportion to the length of the shortest sequence of links that connect the root to the cell in the original structure. If the structure is a binary tree of height $n - 1$ with

procedure *ConstantSpaceMark*(**pointer** Q):
{Γ is a distinguished value; initially Q points to the root of the tree}
   $P \leftarrow \Gamma$
  while $Q \neq \Gamma$ **do**
     if $Q \neq \Lambda$ **and not** *Atom*(Q)
             and not *Marked*(Q) **and not** *OnPath*(Q, P) **then**
       Rotate(P, Q)
     else
       $P \leftrightarrow Q$

function *OnPath*(**pointer** Q, P): **boolean**
{Return **true** if unmarked cell Q is on path from P back to root}
{R traces the path from P back to Q or to the root}
   $R \leftarrow P$
  while $R \neq \Gamma$ **do**
     if *Marked*(R) **then**
       $R \leftarrow \text{RC}(R)$ {Ascend from left}
     else
       if $R = Q$ **then return true**
       else $R \leftarrow \text{LC}(R)$ {Ascend from right}
  return false

Algorithm 10.4 Marking binary cells with the aid of Mark bits only.

---

n nodes, each having an empty child, then the time used to check all the cells is $\Omega(\sum_{i=1}^{n} i) = \Omega(n^2)$. So Algorithm 10.4 takes time $\Theta(n^2)$ in the worst case to mark n cells, significantly more than Algorithm 10.1 and Algorithm 10.2, which take time $\Theta(n)$.

Collecting by Copying

If memory is relatively abundant, an alternative strategy to marking and sweeping is to divide memory into two spaces of equal size, and to allocate cells from only one space until it is exhausted. (Thus at least half the memory is always "dormant," that is, unoccupied by active cells.) When no free cells are available in the space currently being used, the active cells are copied to the other space, and the pointers to them and between them are adjusted to point to the new copies. The cells are compacted as they are copied; when the copying is complete, the copies of the active cells are all at one end of the new space, and the rest of that space is free and can be used for allocation of new cells in serial address order. Since the free cells are contiguous, there is no need to keep them in a free list; it suffices to use a single pointer *free* that advances after each cell allocation. When the *free* pointer reaches the end of the new space,

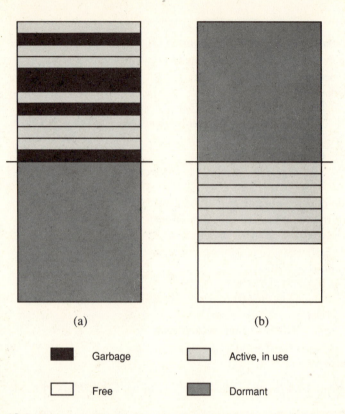

(a)   (b)

■ Garbage   □ Active, in use

□ Free   ■ Dormant

Figure 10.1 Garbage collection by copying. (a) Memory is divided into two equal spaces. The lower space is dormant; the upper space is a mixture of active cells and garbage. There are no free cells, so garbage collection is triggered by the next allocation request. (b) The active cells are copied to the lower space, and the remainder of the lower space is free. The upper space is now regarded as dormant.

that space is exhausted, the roles of the two spaces are reversed and the active cells are copied back (Figure 10.1).

This method has the advantage that *the garbage is never touched*; only the active cells are explored. Since pointers are adjusted when they are copied, the cells can be moved in any order. A simple recursive exploration would work, as would depth-first, link-inversion strategies. But the availability of the space into which the cells are being copied also makes possible an ingenious breadth-first strategy that avoids using the extra memory required by the linear-time recursive and link-inversion marking algorithms. Let us call the space initially containing the active cells and the garbage the **from-space**, and the initially dormant space into which the active cells are to be copied the **to-space**. We shall use a contiguous portion of the to-space to represent the queue needed to implement breadth-first search; this portion of to-space is bounded by two pointers, *head* and *tail*. Initially both pointers point to the beginning of to-space.

Once again we assume that each cell consists of k pointer fields; the algorithm can easily be adapted to the case in which other types of fixed-sized fields are located at fixed locations within the cells. We assume that memory addresses are pointers, so that if a cell begins at $M[p]$ then $Cj(p)$ is at $M[p + j]$. Algorithm 10.5 gives the details; the "roots" referred to in procedure *CopyCollect* are the locations, typically machine registers or global variables, from which the search for active cells must proceed.

When a cell is moved from from-space to to-space, the first field of its former location is left containing a **forwarding address**, that is, the address in to-space to which it has been moved, so that pointers to it that are subsequently discovered can be redirected correctly. (There is no need to reserve a special field of the record to contain the forwarding address. The forwarding address simply replaces in memory whatever used to be stored at the beginning of the record, so it results in no overhead in the size of a record.*) In Algorithm 10.5, procedure *Forward* updates a single pointer as follows. If the pointer does not point into from-space, it is unchanged; if it does point into from-space but the memory location to which it points points into to-space, then the cell must already have been moved and this location must contain the forwarding address; otherwise, the cell must be copied into to-space, to locations which are simultaneously the first free locations in to-space and the tail of the breadth-first search queue, which advances in memory by k pointers.

When the size of memory is large, collection by copying is much more efficient than marking and sweeping. This fact, though not obvious, can be derived quite easily. Recall that N is the size of the heap, and let A be the amount of active data in the heap. We analyze the efficiency of the alternative algorithms by measuring the time required by the algorithms *per cell that is actually made available*. The number of active cells A is a property of the program being run and its input, not of the memory management algorithm; increasing N or changing the memory manager may change the frequency with which the garbage collection algorithm is invoked, but it will not change the value of A. Thus it is reasonable to regard A as fixed and see what happens to the cost per cell as N increases.

Consider first the cost per cell of a mark-and-sweep algorithm. If a linear-time mark-and-sweep algorithm is used, the marking phase takes time proportional to A and the sweep phase takes time proportional to N, for a total time of $c_1 A + c_2 N$ for some constants c_1 and c_2. Therefore the amortized cost per collected cell is

$$C_{\text{mark-and-sweep}} = \frac{c_1 A + c_2 N}{N - A}.$$

---

*We have assumed for simplicity that all fields of a record are pointers. If the first field of a record was in fact of some other data type, then a strongly typed programming language would consider it a type violation to replace a something that is not an address by an address in this way.

procedure *CopyCollect*:
{Garbage collect by copying cells from from-space to to-space}
    head ← *tail* ← beginning of to-space
    foreach root pointer p **do** *Forward*(p)
    while *head* < *tail* **do**   {Update next pointer in pointer queue}
        Forward($M[head]$)
        head ← *head* + 1
    free ← *head*   {Set free space pointer to *head* (= *tail*)}
    Exchange roles of from-space and to-space

procedure *Forward*(**locative** p):
{Copy an uncopied record from from-space into to-space}
{Adjust pointer that is passed as argument to point to new location of cell}
{Records are assumed to consist of k pointer fields}
    if p does not point into from-space **then return**
    else if $M[p]$ points into to-space **then**
        $p \Leftarrow M[p]$ {Record already copied, this is the forwarding address}
    else   {Copy the record}
        for i **from** 0 **to** $k - 1$ **do** $M[tail + i] \leftarrow M[p + i]$
        $M[p] \leftarrow tail$ {Install forwarding address}
        $p \Leftarrow tail$ {Adjust the pointer}
        tail ← *tail* + k

Algorithm 10.5 Garbage collection by copying.

On the other hand copying collection takes time proportional to the number of active cells, but the amount of memory available after copying is only $N/2 - A$. Therefore the amortized cost per cell made available is

$$C_{\text{copying}} = \frac{c_3 A}{N/2 - A}.$$

As N becomes large, we find that $C_{\text{mark-and-sweep}}$ approaches the constant c_2, but C_{copying} approaches 0! Thus there is no lower limit on the cost per reclaimed cell of copying collection, and for this reason copying collection is frequently used in systems that expect to have large amounts of heap memory available.

Though we have assumed throughout this section that all cells are the same size, note that since copying collection compacts the active cells, it would be easy to allocate cells of different sizes, provided that the copying algorithm can determine the size of a record as it scans through the pointer queue in to-space.

Final Cautions on Garbage Collection

As a practical matter it should be noted that the performance of a system that relies on garbage collection is dramatically degraded as memory becomes heavily utilized, whichever algorithm is used. As the system demands more and more cells, the garbage collector is called more and more frequently, and fewer and fewer cells are released between those calls. The time to do the marking or copying increases, but the return achieved diminishes each time, and the next call on the garbage collector comes even sooner. Ultimately the garbage collector cannot recover any memory at all.

Even if a system does not attempt to use more memory than is available, the intermittent and unpredictable timing of calls on the garbage collector can make garbage collection an unsuitable strategy in some applications, for example those requiring real-time response. However, the unpredictability of garbage collection can be combatted by invoking the garbage collector pre-emptively at points that are known to be convenient, rather than always waiting until free space is completely exhausted. There are also several so-called **incremental garbage collection** algorithms, which collect garbage a little bit at a time rather than all at once (Problem 6).

10.3 COMPACTION OF RECORDS OF VARIOUS SIZES

If cells can be of different sizes, the general strategy used with fixed-sized records—to maintain a free list of available cells and to remove one from the front of the list any time a request is made—will not work, since small cells are not interchangeable with large cells. A number of alternative approaches to memory management suggest themselves:

1. Keep a single set of all the cells, regardless of size. When a request is made for a cell of size k, find a cell of size at least k on the list; if its size is greater than k, put the leftover back in the set as a smaller cell. The set of cells will be called the **pool**; the pool might be implemented as a linked list, like the free lists of the previous sections, or it might be implemented by some other set data structure, such as a binary tree. Maintaining such a pool of available cells is an important technique, which is studied in detail in the next section. However, it suffers from the possibility that the "leftovers" may be too small to use for anything. Also, if a cell that is being deallocated is adjacent in memory to a cell that is already free, the two ought to be combined into a single larger free cell to maintain maximum flexibility for later allocations.

2. Keep several pools of free cells according to the size of the cells. Allocate a cell of size k by selecting a cell from the appropriate pool. This avoids the decision problem of how to select a larger cell and subdivide it, but

unless some subdivision strategy is incorporated the algorithm may fail to satisfy a request even though there is a block of memory available that is sufficiently large. Certain approaches of this type, called *buddy systems*, are discussed starting on page 367.

3. Allocate in address order from a single large block of memory. When the heap has been exhausted, some of the cells that had been allocated have presumably been freed; squeeze them out by compressing together the cells that are still in use. The result is a partition of the original heap into a block that is completely in use, followed by a block that is completely free; the allocation strategy continues as before, using the new free block.

Approach (3), a so-called **compaction** scheme, fully utilizes the available memory, but at a cost: it takes time to move cells within memory, and any pointers to those cells, either from other cells or from elsewhere in the system that is using the cells, must be readjusted to point to their new locations. Nonetheless this approach may be the only practical one, especially if the allocated cells are many in number but relatively small in size. In such cases approach (1) will tend to leave many unusably small "slivers" of memory, and the overhead required to move cells will not grossly exceed the time required to perform any other contemplated operation on the cells. (That is, suppose that the average number of memory bytes per cell is μ. If μ is small, say 5 or 10, then an algorithm that moves every byte of memory does not take significantly longer than an algorithm that does something to a pointer to each cell. If μ is in the thousands, however, we would be willing to do a lot of work with the pointers to memory cells to avoid moving the memory cells themselves.)

The "Collection by Copying" method of the previous section compacts memory and can be adapted to work with blocks of different sizes, but it never utilizes more than half the available memory. We consider here another approach that "shuffles" cells into lower addresses after first readjusting pointers between cells to maintain the integrity of the structure. We make the following specific assumptions about the cells to be compacted (clearly the algorithm presented can be modified to work in other circumstances):

- The heap $M[0 .. N-1]$ is completely partitioned into cells, some of which are "in use" and some of which are "free." They can be distinguished because *Marked*(P) is **true** if P points to a cell that is in use, and **false** if P points to a free cell. (Whether *Marked* is implemented by means of a Mark bit stored in the cell, or in some other way, is unimportant, as is whether a marking algorithm, explicit deallocation, or some other method is used to determine which cells are in use.)

- *First* is the address of memory location $M[0]$; *Last* is the address of memory location $M[N-1]$.

- Each cell (in use or free) has a Size field, such that the next cell after the one beginning at address P begins at address $P + \text{Size}(P)$.

- The pointer fields of a cell that is in use are known in advance, because the cell represents a structure in a strongly typed language, or can be recognized by inspecting the cell.
- Each cell that is in use contains a pointer field ForwardingAddress that is reserved for use by the compaction algorithm. This field will contain the so-called **forwarding address** of the cell, that is, the address to which the cell will be moved. The forwarding addresses of all cells are calculated and stored in the cells before any cell is actually moved.

The compaction algorithm first calculates the forwarding address of each cell by scanning through M in address order; the forwarding address of cell C is one more than the aggregate size of all allocated cells having addresses smaller than C. A second scan through memory adjusts all internal links to point to cells' destined locations, rather than their present locations. (References to the cells from outside M can be adjusted at this time, but how these references can be traced is a matter external to the compaction algorithm.) Finally, a third scan through memory actually moves the cells.

Algorithm 10.6 presents the details. In it, we use the abbreviation

> **for** each cell P, in address order, **do**
>   * * *

for the following loop:

> $P \leftarrow First$
> **while** $P \le Last$ **do**
>   * * *
> $P \leftarrow P + \text{Size}(P)$

Note that the memory manager performs the kind of pointer arithmetic we have assumed the client program may not do.

Algorithm 10.6 takes time linear in the amount of memory that is actually compacted; aside from the multiplicative constant, this is of course as fast as can be hoped for. Nonetheless the algorithm does make three passes over the memory to be compacted (four, if there is an initial marking scan). The requirement that a special field ForwardingAddress be set aside strictly for the use of the memory manager can be alleviated somewhat; see Problem 9.

10.4 MANAGING A POOL OF BLOCKS OF VARIOUS SIZES

We now consider the situation in which the size of blocks is substantial, so that compaction methods should be considered only as a last resort. The memory manager starts with a heap that is entirely free space, and handles calls of two kinds:

---

procedure *Compact*:
{Compact cells into low memory addresses, adjusting pointers between cells}
{Assumes that marking of cells in use has already been done}
{*First* and *Last* are the memory addresses at the ends of the heap}
    {Compute forwarding addresses of cells}
    Destination ← *First*
    for each cell P, in address order, **do**
        if *Marked*(P) **then**
            ForwardingAddress(P) ← *Destination*
            Destination ← *Destination* + Size(P)
    {Adjust internal links}
    for each cell P, in address order, **do**
        if *Marked*(P) **then**
            for each pointer field Link **do**
                Link(P) ← ForwardingAddress(Link(P))
    {Move the cells}
    for each cell P, in address order, **do**
        if *Marked*(P) **then**
            Copy Size(P) bytes beginning at P
              to ForwardingAddress(P)

Algorithm 10.6 Compaction of cells of various sizes.

Allocate(n): Return the starting address of a block of size n, if one exists.
Free(B): Put the block with starting address B back in the available storage.

Thus deallocation is here assumed to be explicit, as is reasonable in the case of large blocks. What strategy should be used for maintaining a pool of free blocks, selecting from among them, subdividing them, and recombining them? The criteria on which a strategy should be judged are

- *memory utilization:* the memory manager should not fail to satisfy a request if the aggregate amount of memory that is reserved is a small percentage of the total memory available;
- *memory overhead:* the amount of memory occupied by data structures needed only by the memory manager should be minimal; and
- *time efficiency:* allocation and deallocation requests should be handled quickly.

The first thing to understand is that perfection should not be hoped for. Suppose that the memory is a block of size 100, and the following requests are received (Figure 10.2):

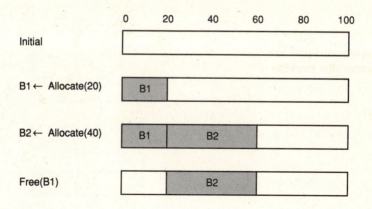

Figure 10.2 A sequence of requests that defeats a simple strategy of allocating in address order.

$$B1 \leftarrow Allocate(20)$$
$$B2 \leftarrow Allocate(40)$$
$$Free(B1)$$
$$B3 \leftarrow Allocate(50)$$

If the first two requests are allocated sequentially starting from the beginning of the heap, then after $Free(B1)$ the heap has 40 in use in the middle, preceded by a free block of size 20 and followed by a free block of size 40, so the request for 50 cannot be satisfied, even though more than 50 units of storage are actually free. This problem could have been avoided if the request for 40 had been allocated from the end of the heap, but a slightly more complex example involving four allocation requests defeats the strategy of allocating "from the ends in" (Figure 10.3). It is hard to imagine how the proper allocation pattern can be predicted, unless the memory manager has the clairvoyance to know in advance the sequence of requests it will receive. Indeed, in a certain sense even clairvoyance does not help: even if the whole sequence of requests is given in advance, the problem of determining whether the requests can all be satisfied is NP-complete, and is therefore believed to be computationally intractable. So we should not worry about designing a perfect memory manager; we should strive for reasonable performance for a reasonable amount of effort.

One thing is clear: two blocks of size s_1 and s_2 are never more useful than one block of size $s_1 + s_2$, but the opposite is frequently true. Therefore it should be a goal of any allocation strategy to reduce the number of free blocks and to increase their size. **External fragmentation** is the splitting of free storage into a relatively large number of relatively small free blocks, thus decreasing its usefulness. External fragmentation can be combatted by refusing to subdivide

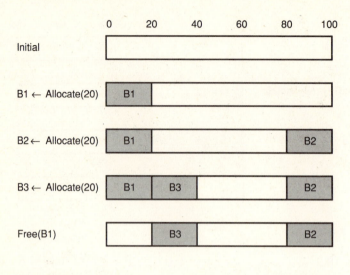

Figure 10.3 A sequence of requests that defeats a strategy of allocating from the ends of the heap inward. If *B*3 were allocated from the right end, then freeing *B*2 instead of *B*1 would cause the same problem. Yet if the whole sequence of requests were known in advance, it could be satisfied.

a free block if the leftover would be too small to be useful, instead allocating a block somewhat larger than was actually requested. The result, however, can be **internal fragmentation**, that is, the distribution of a significant amount of free storage within allocated blocks, where it cannot be used. Some degree of internal fragmentation is inevitable, since no free block can be smaller than the space required to hold the block's size, one or more pointers to link the block to others in the pool, and perhaps some additional fields used by the memory system to manage free blocks. We refer to the amount of this overhead as δ: if subdividing a block would leave over less than δ bytes, the entire block is allocated.

So the general situation is this: we wish to maintain a pool of free blocks, to adopt some strategy for selecting a block from the pool when an allocation request is made (returning the leftover, if any, to the pool), and to develop a method for returning a freed block to the pool and fusing it with a free block, if there is one, that comes just before or after it in memory. If the selection of a free block is made, in one way or another, on the basis of the size of the request and the sizes of the available blocks, there seems to be an incentive for keeping the pool organized by block size; on the other hand, we might also consider keeping the pool organized by address, or letting it have no particular structure at all. Let us examine the consequences of various choices in greater detail.

Allocation Strategies

Two general approaches seem reasonable. The **best fit** strategy allocates a request of size n out of the smallest free block in the pool that has size greater than or equal to n. The **first fit** strategy allocates out of the first block found in the pool that is large enough to satisfy the request.*

Let us consider the best fit strategy first. If the pool is implemented as a linked list ordered by increasing size, and the free blocks are comparable in size to the requested blocks, then on the average half the free list must be scanned to locate the block from which the allocation should be made. A further scan must occur to put the leftover part of the block in its proper position on the free list. If the free list is kept in any other order (for example, by address or randomly) then the entire list must be searched to find the best fit.

A more efficient implementation of best fit organizes the pool as a binary search tree, with the search key being the block size. However, such a search tree would not quite result in a solution to the problem at hand, since the best fit for a request of size k is *the smallest block of size greater than or equal to k*. If we simply searched a binary tree for k, the node we would find would be either the best fit node or its inorder predecessor. We can find the best fit node by a single scan from the root to a leaf either by using a threaded tree structure, which makes it easy to find inorder successors, or by storing in each node the size of the largest block in the left subtree of that node (see Problem 17).

Whether the pool is implemented as a list or as a tree, the search time becomes unpleasantly long when the number of free blocks becomes large; we would prefer a method that uses an amount of time independent of the number of blocks being managed. What is worse, the best fit strategy tends to leave a large number of small "splinters" that are almost useless for allocation purposes but slow down the searches that must occur when allocation requests are made. Moreover, simulation experiments suggest that any advantage best fit may have over first fit in memory utilization is likely to be negligible.

The first fit strategy is most naturally used with a linked list implementation of the pool. First fit has its own disadvantage: blocks that are near the beginning of the list tend to get subdivided more often than blocks that are later, so small fragments tend to accumulate near the beginning of the list; this increases the search time since all searches start there. (This happens whether or not the list is in order by memory address.) To *this* problem there is an easy fix, however: begin each search where the last one left off, starting over at the beginning of memory when the search extends beyond the end. Maintaining such a **roving pointer** makes the algorithm behave similarly in all parts of the free list; small blocks do not accumulate near the beginning or anywhere else. Moreover a

---

*These are not the only alternatives. The **worst fit** strategy always allocates out of the *largest* free block. This makes it easy to decide which block to use, but squanders the precious large blocks unnecessarily on medium-sized requests. Worst fit rarely works well in practice.

block that has just been subdivided or passed over as too small will not be considered again until all the other free blocks have been examined, so it has as much time as possible to be coalesced with its neighbors into a larger block.

Data Structures for Freeing

It is time to be more specific about the format of blocks and the structure of the pool of free blocks. So far we have implicitly assumed that each block B, whether free or in use, has a Size field and a Mark bit that indicates whether it is free (Mark(B) = 0) or in use (Mark(B) = 1). To simplify the later discussion, let us assume that the pool is implemented as a doubly linked list; nothing fundamental depends on this assumption, but the doubly linked representation has the advantage that a block can be deleted easily given just the address of the block, rather than the address of a block that points to it. To hold the free list together, a free block must have Next and Prev fields that point to block's successor and predecessor on the free list; however, these fields are needed only when the block is free, so they do not consume any space in blocks that are in use. These fields alone are sufficient to support the search required by the first fit with roving pointer algorithm; as a convenience we make the list circular, with the Next field of the last free block pointing to the first free block, and the Prev field of the first free block pointing to the last free block. Subdivision of a block is also easy: if a request of size n is allocated out of a free block of size $m > n$ (but $m - n > \delta$), the simplest procedure is to allocate the *last* n bytes of the block, since the "leftover" can then replace the block from which the allocation took place simply by changing its Size from m to $m - n$. Allocation of an entire block requires deleting the block entirely from the free list; this is where the doubly linked representation is handy.

We must now face the questions of how to implement the *Free* operation, and whether there is good reason to keep the free list in address order. While it might seem at first that keeping the list in address order would facilitate the fusion of free blocks, there is a fundamental reason to avoid it: placing a block on the free list would then require an expensive search to locate its proper position. So we make no assumption about the order of blocks on the free list, and use other methods to determine if a block has a free neighbor.

There is no difficulty in determining if the next *higher* block in memory after block B is free; that block begins at address $B + \text{Size}(B)$, and is therefore free if Mark($B+\text{Size}(B)$) = 0. To help determine the character of the next *lower* block, we replicate the Mark bit of each block at its end; then by examining a bit at a fixed displacement from B, it can be determined whether B's lower neighbor is free. We call this field LowMark(B); it can even be implemented as a field of B, rather than of B's lower neighbor, if it is inconvenient to use a bit from the end of blocks that are in use. If B's lower neighbor is free (LowMark(B) = 0), then we also replicate its size near its end, in a field we refer to as LowSize(B); this also could be allocated out of B, though it logically

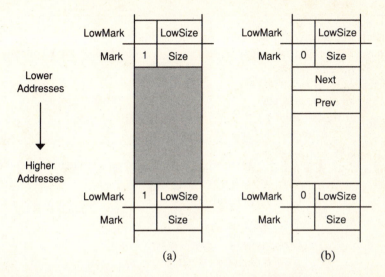

Figure 10.4 Fields of a block in the boundary-tag data structure. One block
is shown in its entirety, together with the end of the previous block and
the beginning of the subsequent block. (a) Reserved block; (b) Free
block. The LowMark and LowSize fields at the end of the block are
copies of the Mark and Size fields, but are properly considered fields of
the *subsequent* block.

is part of B's lower neighbor. Because LowMark(B) and LowSize(B) describe
properties not of B but of B's lower neighbor, these fields must be permanently
allocated, whether or not block B is free. The freeing algorithm can then locate
B's lower neighbor thus: check LowMark(B) to discover that the neighbor is
free; if it is, $B -$ LowSize(B) is its address. The algorithm that frees a block
may therefore add a block to the free list, while removing one or two others; it
is because we may need to replace two blocks on the free list by one that the
doubly linked representation of the free list is helpful.

Figure 10.4 illustrates the reserved fields of blocks, both free and in use.
The replication of the Mark bit at both ends of each block gives this technique
its name, the **boundary-tag** method.

Algorithm 10.7 is the allocation algorithm. *Rover* is the roving pointer.
Before the search for a suitable block begins, the value of *Rover* is preserved as
SaveRover; if *Rover* gets this value again, then the free list has been searched
completely without successfully finding a large enough block, so the allocation
algorithm fails. The algorithm uses a subroutine *DoublyLinkedDelete(P)*, which
deletes the cell with address P from a doubly linked list (Algorithm 3.11 on
page 88).

The freeing algorithm (Algorithm 10.8) takes as argument a pointer P to
the block to be freed, and assumes that *Free* is the address of a header cell
for the doubly linked free list. That is, Next(*Free*) is the first block on the

---

function *BoundaryTagAllocate*(**integer** n): **pointer**
{Return address of a free block of size n, or Λ if no block is large enough}
    SaveRover ← *Rover*
    repeat
        m ← Size(*Rover*)
        if $m < n$ **then**
            Rover ← Next(*Rover*)
        else
            if $m - n < \delta$ **then**   {Almost exact match, no leftover}
                P ← *Rover*
                DoublyLinkedDelete(*P*)
            else   {Inexact match, subdivide the block}
                P ← *Rover* + $m - n$
                Size(*Rover*) ← LowSize(*P*) ← $m - n$
                Size(*P*) ← LowSize(*P* + n) ← n
                LowMark(*P*) ← 0
            Mark(*P*) ← 1
            LowMark(*P* + Size(*P*)) ← 1
            Rover ← Next(*Rover*)
            return P
    until *Rover* = *SaveRover*
    return Λ {No large enough block is available}

Algorithm 10.7 Allocate a block of size n using first fit with roving pointer and boundary tags.

---

free list, and Prev(*Free*) is the last block on the free list. (Also, Size(*Free*) should be 0, so that the allocation algorithm will not try to allocate any cells from this "block.") To make certain that the freeing algorithm does not try to fuse a block with memory that lies outside the heap, it is also important that LowMark(*First*) = Mark(*Last*) = 1, where *First* is the first location in the entire heap and *Last* is the first location after the end of the heap. *BoundaryTagFree* adopts a straightforward strategy for coalescing the block to be freed with the block before or after, should one or both be free: it removes the neighbor from the free list and adds its size to the size of P (possibly readjusting P so that it points to the beginning of the combined block). When any such fusion has been carried out, block P is placed on the beginning of the free list. One detail to be noted is that the roving pointer must be left pointing to the beginning of a block that is still on the free list; this requires a special check in one place. In addition to the *DoublyLinkedDelete* routine, Algorithm 10.8 uses *DoublyLinkedInsert*(*P*, *Q*) (Algorithm 3.10 on page 88), which inserts cell P

procedure *BoundaryTagFree*(**pointer** P):
{Deallocate the block pointed to by P}
    if LowMark(P) = 0 **then**
        {Preceding block is free, merge them together}
        $Q \leftarrow P$
        $P \leftarrow P - $ LowSize(P)
        Size(P) $\leftarrow$ Size(P) + Size(Q)
        DoublyLinkedDelete(P)
    else   {Preceding block is in use, mark this block as free}
        Mark(P) $\leftarrow$ 0
    $Q \leftarrow P + $ Size(P)   {$Q \leftarrow$ address of subsequent block}
    if Mark(Q) = 0 **then**
        {Subsequent block is free, merge them together}
        Size(P) $\leftarrow$ Size(P) + Size(Q)
        if *Rover* = Q **then** *Rover* $\leftarrow P$
        DoublyLinkedDelete(Q)
        $Q \leftarrow P + $ Size(P)
    {P now points to the block to be put on the free list}
    {Q points just after the end of that block}
    LowSize(Q) $\leftarrow$ Size(P)
    LowMark(Q) $\leftarrow$ 0
    DoublyLinkedInsert(P, *Free*)

Algorithm 10.8 Freeing a block using boundary tags.

just after Q in a doubly linked list.

The performance of algorithms like these is notoriously difficult to pin down analytically, and most knowledge we have of their behavior is based on the results of simulation experiments. Nonetheless a few interesting analytic results are easy to derive. First of all, we can claim success in deriving a method with low memory overhead; if σ is the number of bits needed to store the size of a block and **p** is the number of bits needed to store a pointer, then $2 + \sigma$ bits are used in reserved blocks, and $2 + 2\sigma + 2\mathbf{p}$ in free blocks (which have unused space anyway). Of course, these numbers may have to be rounded up in practice to the next larger number of bytes or words.

The time to free a block is bounded by a constant, independent of the number of blocks or the size of the memory. However, allocation of a block requires a search, which in the worst case traverses the entire free list. How long can the free list be, and how long is it likely to be? To answer such questions we must make some assumptions about the behavior of the system that is calling upon the memory manager. A reasonable scenario to consider is one in which memory utilization has reached a *steady state*; that is, blocks are being freed at the same rate at which they are being reserved, and the sizes of these requests are such that the memory manager is able to accommodate them. (These are only statistical assumptions, however; it is not assumed that from instant to instant the number of free or reserved blocks remains exactly constant.) We also assume that a request is unlikely to be satisfied by allocating one of the free blocks in its entirety; that is, nearly every allocation entails subdivision of a block. This is a reasonable assumption if the requests are relatively large and variable in size, and it implies that allocations do not change the number of free blocks. Given this scenario, let

F = the expected number of free blocks, and

R = the expected number of reserved blocks.

Knuth (see the references at the end of the chapter) observed the following rule:

Fifty-Percent Rule: $F = \frac{1}{2}R$, that is, there are about half as many free blocks as reserved blocks.

Thus the length of the free list increases as the number of reserved blocks increases, but only about half as quickly. Of course, the blocks on the free list may be of widely differing sizes, and how much of the free list must actually be searched depends on the distribution of requests and the allocation strategy.

To derive the Fifty-Percent Rule, classify the reserved blocks into three types:

Type A: a block whose lower and upper neighbors are both free;
Type B: a block that has exactly one free neighbor;
Type C: a block whose lower and upper neighbors are both reserved.

Now let A, B, and C denote the expected number of blocks of each type. Clearly

$$R = A + B + C, \tag{1}$$

and since each free block (except, possibly, for a free block at the beginning or end of the heap) has two neighbors that are reserved, it is also true that

$$2F \approx 2A + B, \tag{2}$$

where the equality is approximate to accommodate an error of 1 or 2 due to conditions at the ends of the heap. When a type A block is freed, the number of free blocks decreases by one; when a type B block is freed, the number remains the same; and when a type C block is freed, the number of free blocks increases by one. Finally, because the system is assumed to be in steady state and allocations do not change the number of free blocks, when a block is freed it must be equally likely to be one that increases the number of free blocks as one that decreases the number of free blocks; that is,

$$A = C. \tag{3}$$

The Fifty-Percent Rule follows immediately from (1), (2), and (3). (It is evident from the argument used to derive this rule that it is at best a rule of thumb, which may be violated if the behavior of the system deviates from the assumed steady state for a period of time.)

The maximum length of the free list is $R + 1$; the fifty-percent rule implies that its expected length is $R/2$. These quantities govern the performance of the best fit strategy, since it searches the entire free list on each allocation call. It can be shown (Problem 19) that without a roving pointer the first fit strategy searches half the free list, or $R/4$ blocks, on average. With a roving pointer, however, its performance improves dramatically; in a simulation carried out by Knuth, the expected number of blocks searched, out of a free list of length 250, dropped from 125 to 2.18 when the roving pointer was introduced.

The third criterion to be considered is memory utilization. The fifty-percent rule has an implication for this criterion as well, namely, the

> *Two-Thirds Rule:* No more than two-thirds of the heap can be in use, in steady state.

To derive the Two-Thirds Rule from the Fifty-Percent Rule, let

$$f = \text{the expected size of a free block, and}$$

$$r = \text{the expected size of a reserved block.}$$

Thus $fF + rR = N$, the total size of the heap. If the system is in steady state, then $f \geq r$, since otherwise it is likely that a request will be received that cannot be satisfied. Therefore $N = fF + rR \geq rF + rR = \frac{3}{2}rR$, and $rR \leq \frac{2}{3}N$.

The Two-Thirds Rule has implications for the size of the *maximum* request that the memory manager should be called on to satisfy. For if we hope for the most efficient utilization of memory, then requests bigger than $\frac{1}{3}N$ will, with high probability, be unsatisfiable. In practice requests should be kept a good deal smaller than this; Knuth suggests a maximum size of $\frac{1}{10}N$.

10.5 BUDDY SYSTEMS

Buddy systems trade external fragmentation for internal fragmentation, and utilize a block-freeing algorithm that is simple and fast but does not necessarily coalesce all neighboring free blocks into larger free blocks. Blocks can be allocated only in certain predetermined sizes and at certain positions in the heap. For each such allocatable block there is a unique neighboring block, called its **buddy**, which is the only block with which it can be coalesced to form a larger block; that larger block has a buddy of its own, and so on. The number of possible block sizes is small enough that separate free lists can be maintained

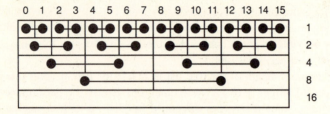

Figure 10.5 Legal blocks under a binary buddy system in a heap of size 16. Buddies of each size are joined by a line.

for each possible block size. When a request is made for an allocation of size n, n is rounded up to the next legal block size n', and a block of that size is allocated. If there are no free blocks of exactly size n', a larger block is subdivided into buddies until a block of the appropriate size is obtained.

The simplest buddy system is the so-called **binary buddy** system. In this system all allocatable blocks are a power of two in size. The heap itself is of size $N = 2^m$ for some m; the possible block sizes are then 2^m, 2^{m-1}, ..., 2^1, and $2^0 = 1$.* Therefore there are $m + 1$ free lists, whose headers we call *Free*[m], *Free*[m − 1], ..., *Free*[0]. Moreover, each block of size 2^k ($0 \le k \le m$) begins at an address which is a multiple of 2^k. That is, a block of size 2^k begins at address $p \cdot 2^k$ and ends at address $(p+1) \cdot 2^k - 1$ for some p with $0 \le p < 2^{m-k}$ (Figure 10.5). The buddy of a block of size 2^k is then uniquely determined by the rule that it is the *other* block of size 2^k within the *same* block of size 2^{k+1}. (The largest block has no buddy.)

If a block B of size 2^k begins at address P, then B's buddy begins at either $P - 2^k$ or $P + 2^k$. In fact it is easy to determine which, by inspection of the bits of the binary representation of P. Let this binary representation be $\beta_{m-1} \ldots \beta_1 \beta_0$. If $\beta_k = 0$ then the buddy begins at $P + 2^k$; if $\beta_k = 1$ the buddy begins at $P - 2^k$. In other words, the position of B's buddy is obtained by complementing bit k in the binary representation of B's address (with the rightmost bit being bit 0, and the numbering increasing to the left).† But this is just the exclusive-or of the block's position and size: *the buddy of the block of size 2^k beginning at P is the block of size 2^k beginning at $P \oplus 2^k$.*

For example, consider the blocks beginning at 24 in a heap of size $64 = 2^6$. Since 8 is the largest power of two that divides 24 evenly, there are blocks beginning at this position of sizes 1, 2, 4, and 8, but not of any larger size.

---

*Of course, these units need not be single bytes or words; for example, the blocks could be in these multiples of 128, or any other fixed number, of bytes. It is convenient in this section to refer to "addresses" in the heap which start at 0. These are really displacements from the beginning of the heap, and should be added to the true address at which the heap begins.

† This operation is easy to do in assembly language or C, but it may be impossible in a higher-level language. Of course, it can be done if the "addresses" are really array indices.

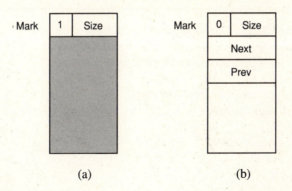

Figure 10.6 Fields of a block in binary buddy system. (a) Reserved block; (b) free block.

Since the six-bit binary notation for 24 is 011000, the buddies of these four blocks are those

of size $1 = 000001$ beginning at $011001 = 25$,
of size $2 = 000010$ beginning at $011010 = 26$,
of size $4 = 000100$ beginning at $011100 = 28$, and
of size $8 = 001000$ beginning at $010000 = 16$.

The free lists are kept in doubly linked form to facilitate deletions. Free blocks have a structure similar to that used in the boundary-tag algorithms, except that the "second copies" of the **Mark** and **Size** fields are not needed (Figure 10.6). (Also, the **Size** field can be smaller, since only the value of k need be stored if the block is actually of size 2^k.)

The allocation algorithm (Algorithm 10.9) tries to satisfy a request of size* n. It first finds the smallest free block of size greater than or equal to that requested. (*IsEmptyList* determines whether a doubly linked list is empty.) The block is removed from its free list, and if it is larger than the minimum suitable size ($2^{\lceil \lg n \rceil}$), its second half, second quarter, and so on are placed on the appropriate free lists. Finally the block is marked as in use and returned.

Freeing a block (Algorithm 10.10) may reverse the splits that occurred during allocation. If the block's buddy is free, it is removed from its free list and merged to form a larger block; this process is repeated until the buddy is in use or the block has become the entire heap. The free block, now of maximal size, is then placed on the appropriate free list.

With the buddy system both allocation and freeing a block involve an iteration and therefore take a nonconstant amount of time; but the iteration is over block sizes, so these algorithms take time $\Theta(\log N)$ in the worst case, where N

---

*Note that n must already include the overhead for the **Mark** and **Size** fields; that is, n is the size as the system sees it, not as the user sees it.

---

function *BinaryBuddyAllocate*(**integer** n): **pointer**
{Return pointer to a block whose size is the next power of $2 \geq n$}
{Return Λ if no sufficiently large block is available}
$\quad j \leftarrow k \leftarrow \lceil \lg n \rceil$
$\quad$ **while** $j \leq m$ **and** *IsEmptyList*(*Free*[j]) **do** $j \leftarrow j + 1$
$\quad$ **if** $j > m$ **then return** Λ
$\quad P \leftarrow$ *Free*[j]
$\quad$ *DoublyLinkedDelete*(*P*)
$\quad$ **while** $j > k$ **do**
$\quad\quad j \leftarrow j - 1$
$\quad\quad Q \leftarrow P + 2^j$
$\quad\quad$ Mark(Q) $\leftarrow 0$
$\quad\quad$ Size(Q) $\leftarrow j$
$\quad\quad$ *DoublyLinkedInsert*(Q, *Free*[j])
$\quad\quad$ {This actually inserts Q onto an *empty* list *Free*[j]}
$\quad$ Mark(P) $\leftarrow 1$
$\quad$ Size(P) $\leftarrow k$
$\quad$ **return** P

Algorithm 10.9 Allocation of a block, using binary buddies.

---

procedure *BinaryBuddyFree*(**pointer** P):
{Free the block of size 2^k beginning at location P}
$\quad k \leftarrow$ Size(P)
$\quad$ **while** $k < m$ **and** Mark($P \oplus 2^k$) $= 0$ **and** Size($P \oplus 2^k$) $= k$ **do**
$\quad\quad$ {P's buddy is free, so merge it to create a free block twice as big}
$\quad\quad Q \leftarrow P \oplus 2^k$
$\quad\quad$ *DoublyLinkedDelete*(Q)
$\quad\quad$ **if** $Q < P$ **then** $P \leftarrow Q$
$\quad\quad k \leftarrow k + 1$
$\quad$ Mark(P) $\leftarrow 0$
$\quad$ Size(P) $\leftarrow k$
$\quad$ *DoublyLinkedInsert*(P, *Free*[k])

Algorithm 10.10 Freeing a block, using binary buddies.

---

is the size of the heap. (Most requests take less than the worst case amount of time.) In fact, if it is unnecessary to provide for requests of size comparable to the size of the heap, it is a simple matter to restrict the maximum block size to some fraction of N, thereby eliminating a certain amount of pointless splitting and merging of large blocks. Then the maximum number of iterations of either the allocation or freeing algorithm is $\lg \rho$, where ρ is the ratio of the size of the largest allocatable block to the smallest—independent of the total number of blocks, or the number of free blocks. For example, if it is reasonable to accommodate requests that range in size over at most three (decimal) orders of magnitude, then the loops can iterate ten $(= \lceil \lg 1000 \rceil)$ times at most.

In practice, the time efficiency of buddy system algorithms is comparable to that of boundary-tag algorithms, and therefore quite acceptable. When the system reaches steady state, most of the free lists are nonempty most of the time, so allocation rarely requires several splits. Also, external fragmentation is not a problem for buddy systems. It is possible for two adjacent blocks of size 2^k to be free but unmergeable, because they are not buddies (consider, for example, the two blocks of size 4 beginning at 4 and 8 in Figure 10.5). And it is theoretically possible for this to happen just when a block of size 2^{k+1} is needed but none is available. But such problems seem not to be significant, either in the simulations that have been carried out or in actual systems that have been constructed.

The more serious problem is internal fragmentation, which can be significant. Since a request of size i is automatically rounded up to $2^{\lceil \lg i \rceil}$, almost half the allocated memory can be wasted, if each request is for just more than a power of 2. While this worst case is unlikely to occur, we can also analyze the expected case. For this purpose we assume that a request is equally likely to be for any size in the range from 1 to n; then after n requests the amount requested has expected value $R_n = \sum_{i=1}^{n} i = n(n+1)/2$. The total amount allocated, however, has expected value

$$A_n = \sum_{i=1}^{n} 2^{\lceil \lg i \rceil} = 1 + 2 + 4 + 4 + 8 + 8 + 8 + 8 + 16 + \cdots + 2^{\lceil \lg n \rceil}.$$

Let $k = \lfloor \lg n \rfloor$ and $\alpha = n/2^k$, so that $1 \le \alpha < 2$; then the sum of the first 2^k terms in the expression for A_n is $1 + 2\sum_{i=0}^{k-1} 4^i = 1 + \frac{2}{3}(4^k - 1)$, while the sum of the last $(\alpha - 1)2^k$ terms is $(\alpha - 1) \cdot 2^k \cdot 2^{k+1}$, for a total of $2^{2k+1}(\alpha - \frac{2}{3}) + \frac{1}{3}$. With $n = 2^k \cdot \alpha$, the value of R_n is $2^{2k-1}\alpha^2 + 2^{k-1}\alpha$, so the ratio

$$\frac{A_n}{R_n} = \frac{2^{2k+1}(\alpha - \frac{2}{3}) + \frac{1}{3}}{2^{2k-1}\alpha^2 + 2^{k-1}\alpha} \approx 4\frac{\alpha - \frac{2}{3}}{\alpha^2}.$$

Differentiating this expression reveals that when $1 \le \alpha < 2$ it ranges in value between $\frac{4}{3}$ and $\frac{3}{2}$, so *the binary buddy system should be expected to waste between a quarter and a third of the memory it allocates due to internal fragmentation* (Problem 25).

The problem of internal fragmentation suggests that another set of block sizes be used, which will provide better fits for a variety of requests and still permit a strategy of splitting and merging buddies like that of the binary buddy system. The most successful proposal has been to use the Fibonacci numbers F_k as the block sizes. These numbers were defined on page 26; they are defined by the property that $F_0 = F_1 = 1$ and $F_{k+2} = F_{k+1} + F_k$ for all $k \geq 0$. For all but small n, there are more Fibonacci numbers than powers of 2 less than n, so there is likely to be less wastage if blocks of these sizes are used instead. When allocating, the basic idea is to split a block of size F_{k+2}, if it is too big, into a left buddy of size F_k and a right buddy of size F_{k+1}, and to keep a separate free list, for each k, of the blocks of size F_k. There is, however, a bit more work to do when freeing a block than in the case of binary buddies, since there is no way to tell from a block's size and position alone whether it is the left or right buddy of a pair—that is, whether the buddy of a block of size F_k is a block of size F_{k+1} (because they arose from splitting a block of size F_{k+2}) or a block of size F_{k-1} (because they arose from splitting a block of size F_{k+1}). (Recall that in the case of binary buddies, the bits of the block's address and size can be used to determine whether it is a left or right buddy.) It is not sufficient to record this information as a single bit with each block, since the same problem will recur when the block is recombined with its buddy; is the larger block the left or right member of *its* buddy pair?

The following scheme records in one additional small field of each block the information necessary to maintain a so-called **Fibonacci buddy** system. Define the SplitCount of the largest block to be 0; and whenever a block is split, the SplitCount of the right buddy is 0, and the SplitCount of the left buddy is 1 more than the SplitCount of the block from which it was obtained. (Except for the largest block, the SplitCount of a block is the number of times it must be merged with right buddies to form larger blocks, before it becomes a right buddy.) If this information is maintained as blocks are split, it can be used to merge them; a block is a left buddy just in case its SplitCount is nonzero, and in that case the SplitCount of the block that results from merging it with its buddy is 1 less than its SplitCount. In other respects the allocation and freeing algorithms are straightforward generalizations of the algorithms for binary buddies.

Problems

10.2   **1.** As explained on page 345, the reference count method requires that the assignment $P \leftarrow Q$ be preceded by (i) decrementing the count of the cell P points to, (ii) releasing that cell if the count is zero, and (iii) incrementing the count of the cell that Q points to.

   a. Suppose that P and Q are the same variable, that is, the assignment is $P \leftarrow P$. What can go wrong with the procedure (i)–(iii), and how can it be repaired?

   b. Suppose that P and Q are different variables but that, before the assignment, P and Q point to the same cell. Could the sequence (i)–(iii) fail in that case? If so, how should it be recoded?

   2. Simplify Algorithm 10.2 on page 348 under the assumption that $k = 1$; that is, that each cell has only a single pointer.

3. Recode Algorithm 10.2 without using an auxiliary stack, under the assumption that each cell has a field Direction that can hold a value in the range $0 .. k - 1$. All Direction fields are initially 0, and should be 0 when the marking is complete.

4. Suppose that, as suggested on page 349, we use the constant-space scanning algorithm (Algorithm 4.8 on page 118) to mark list structure that has no cycles but may have multiple paths to some cells. How much time might it take to scan a structure composed of n cells, each containing two pointer fields?

5. Write the memory allocation algorithm that goes with Algorithm 10.5. Assume that every request is for a cell of k pointer fields.

6. The "collection by copying" method can be modified to provide one scheme for incremental garbage collection. Assume that there is a fixed set of locations, not part of the heap, such that a value must be explicitly fetched into one of these locations before it can be used for any operation. We can imagine these locations to be machine registers, and we refer to them as "registers" for convenience. Now when *CopyCollect* (Algorithm 10.5) is invoked, let it return immediately after all the registers have been treated as "root pointers" and have been forwarded. In general we wish to ensure that the registers *never* point into from-space, but in fact unforwarded locations in to-space might point back into from-space. Thus the client program is required to call *Forward* on *every* pointer that it fetches from memory into a register. Once most of the pointers have been redirected out of from-space, these calls to *Forward* will be relatively inexpensive.

   a. Explain how the computations carried out by the remainder of *CopyCollect* (the forwarding of the other root pointers and of pointers referenced indirectly through cells that have already been moved) can be spread out across the calls to the memory allocation routine.

   b. In Algorithm 10.5 the *free* pointer is set once the copying process has been completed and the amount of free space is known. If the copying is carried out incrementally this method will not work, since allocation requests must be serviced before the copying has been completed. How can allocation be done under this scheme?

   c. Compare the efficiency of this method to that of Algorithm 10.5.

10.3   7. Design a compaction algorithm for fixed-sized blocks that makes only a single pass over the memory being compacted and uses only a constant amount of additional memory.

8. Suppose that memory is allocated in blocks of varying size and that blocks are not linked (so that it is unnecessary to worry about pointers

to blocks). Suppose further that blocks are allocated and explicitly freed in strict first-in-first-out fashion, that is, no block is freed until after all previously allocated blocks have been freed. Design and code routines *FIFOAllocate* and *FIFOFree* in such a way that all requests can be satisfied, provided only that at any time the total size of the allocated blocks is less than or equal to the size of the heap.

9. Design a compaction algorithm for blocks of various sizes that does not use a dedicated ForwardingAddress field, but dedicates to the compaction algorithm one bit per cell and per pointer field, and makes use of an additional pointer-sized field per cell that does not contain pointer data while compaction is not in progress. (Hint: The pointer fields that point to a cell C are linked together into a linked list whose head is in C. The information that used to be where the head of the list is now can be stored at the end of the list.)

10. Consider a heap $M[0..N-1]$ containing diverse-sized blocks each of which has a Size field, with no free space intervening between the blocks (so, for example, the second block begins at $M[\text{Size}(0)]$). The heap may be full, or there may be free space at its end. Suppose now that each block also has a NewSize field, and that we wish to *change the size* of each block (by either expansion or contraction) under the assumption that all useful information within a block is at its beginning. That is, if $\text{Size}(B) = j$ and $\text{NewSize}(B) = k < j$, then the first k words of block B are important and must be preserved, while the final $j - k$ words can be forgotten; and if $k > j$ then we don't care about the contents of the final $k - j$ words of the expanded block. Devise an algorithm that restructures the heap, resizing each block as required, without using any additional storage. You may assume that there are no pointers to blocks (so that blocks can be moved without worrying about dangling pointers) and that the sum of the NewSize fields is at most N. When your algorithm finishes, the heap should once again consist of contiguous blocks with all free space (if any) at the end of the heap. Of course, the Size fields should be updated to their new values!

10.4 11. Show how the best fit, first fit with roving pointer, and worst fit strategies would handle the following sequence of requests, if the total memory size is 10:

$A \leftarrow Allocate(3)$
$B \leftarrow Allocate(2)$
$C \leftarrow Allocate(1)$
$Free(A)$
$D \leftarrow Allocate(3)$

> *Free(B)*
> *E ← Allocate(5)*

12. Using first fit with roving pointer, and starting with an empty block of size 100, can the following sequence of requests be satisfied? Show the state of memory at the end of the sequence, or when a failure occurs.

    A ← Allocate(40)
    B ← Allocate(10)
    Free(A)
    C ← Allocate(20)
    D ← Allocate(40)
    Free(B)
    E ← Allocate(25)

13. Show that there are sequences of allocation and deallocation requests that are successfully handled by the first fit strategy but not by the best fit strategy.

14. In each of the following cases, find a sequence of allocation and deallocation requests that defeats the strategy and has as few requests as possible.

    a. Construct a sequence of requests that defeats the best fit allocation strategy.

    b. Construct a sequence of requests that defeats the first fit allocation strategy.

    c. Construct a sequence of requests that defeats the worst fit allocation strategy.

15. Assume that allocation and deallocation requests cannot be predicted in advance and that blocks cannot be moved within the heap once they have been allocated. Show that any memory allocation algorithm is inferior to clairvoyance; that is, show that any algorithm that dynamically allocates blocks by responding to requests as they occur will fail to satisfy some sequence of requests that could be satisfied if the whole sequence were known in advance. (An algorithm must always respond to the same sequence of requests in the same way.)

16. Devise a sequence of requests that cannot be satisfied even if the memory manager knows the entire sequence in advance, even though at no time does the total size of the allocated and requested blocks exceed the size of the heap. (Blocks cannot be moved once they have been allocated.)

17. Explain carefully how to implement the best fit strategy using a binary tree implementation of the pool.

18. It appears that Algorithm 10.8 on page 365 does a little more work than is really needed when deallocating a block with exactly one free neighbor; in that case it removes a block from the free list and then inserts a block onto the free list, when it would suffice to change the description of that block. Explore whether this idea is really feasible, and worth the trouble.

19. Show that without a roving pointer the first fit strategy searches half the free list on average. What assumptions lead to this conclusion?

20. Derive the Fifty-Percent Rule from Equations (1)–(3) on page 366.

10.5 **21.** Show how the binary buddy strategy would handle the following sequence of requests, if the total memory size is 16:

$$A \leftarrow Allocate(3)$$
$$B \leftarrow Allocate(2)$$
$$C \leftarrow Allocate(3)$$
$$Free(B)$$
$$D \leftarrow Allocate(4)$$
$$Free(A)$$
$$Free(D)$$
$$E \leftarrow Allocate(5)$$
$$F \leftarrow Allocate(3)$$

22. In Algorithm 10.10 on page 370, what is the purpose of the clause

$$\ldots \mathsf{Size}(P \oplus 2^k) = k \ldots ?$$

23. Suppose that we use a binary buddy system with a memory size of 16. There are some sequences of allocation requests for a total of less than 16 cells that cannot be satisfied. What is the largest number n such that *any* sequence of requests for a total of n or fewer cells can be satisfied? Justify your answer, and give an example of a sequence of requests totalling $n + 1$ that cannot be satisfied.

24. Suppose the binary buddy system is to be used in a system where N, the total size of the heap, is not known in advance and is not necessarily a power of 2. Moreover, suppose the maximum block size should be 2^K, where K is known in advance. Write the routine

$$BinaryBuddyHeapInitialize(H[0 .. N - 1])$$

that initializes the heap and free lists for this situation, and rewrite Algorithm 10.9 and Algorithm 10.10 as necessary to take the new restrictions into account.

25. Complete the calculations needed to confirm the claim on page 371 about memory wasted by the binary buddy system due to internal fragmentation.

26. Write *Allocate* and *Free* routines for a Fibonacci buddy system, using the SplitCount field as described at the end of the chapter. Analyze the timing of these algorithms.

References

The Schorr-Deutsch-Waite marking algorithm (Algorithm 10.2 on page 348) was published in

H. Schorr and W. M. Waite, "An Efficient Machine-Independent Procedure for Garbage Collection in Various List Structures," *Communications of the ACM* **10** (1967), pp. 501–506,

and was discovered independently by L. P. Deutsch. The version presented here, which uses a stack rather than a reserved field in each node, is essentially that described for the k = 2 case in

B. Wegbreit, "A Space-Efficient List Structure Tracing Algorithm," *IEEE Transactions on Computers* **C21** (1972), pp. 1009–1010.

The constant-space algorithm (Algorithm 10.4 on page 351) is from

G. Lindstrom, "Scanning List Structures without Stacks or Tag Bits," *Information Processing Letters* **2** (1973), pp. 47–51.

Copying collection was described in

C. J. Cheney, "A Nonrecursive List Compacting Algorithm," *Communications of the ACM* **13** (1970), pp. 677–678,

and was analyzed in

A. W. Appel, "Garbage Collection Can Be Faster than Stack Allocation," *Information Processing Letters* **25** (1987), pp 275–279.

Our presentation of the copying algorithm follows

A. W. Appel, "Garbage Collection," in P. Lee, *Topics in Advanced Language Implementation*, MIT Press, 1990.

This paper also discusses the incremental garbage collection method of Problem 6, which was originally described in

H. G. Baker, "List Processing in Real Time on a Serial Computer," *Communications of the ACM* **21** (1978), pp. 280–294.

For an extensive survey of garbage collection see

J. Cohen, "Garbage Collection of Linked Data Structures," *Computing Surveys* **13** (1981), pp. 341–367.

The various dynamic storage allocation strategies (for example, first fit, best fit, worst fit) have been studied extensively. Knuth's Fundamental Algorithms *(cited on page 44) is a good general source; the derivations of the Fifty-Percent Rule and the Two-Thirds Rule are from Knuth. Standish (in the book cited on page 45) presents and cites a good deal of experimental evidence about the relative effectiveness of these strategies. The strategies have been analyzed in the context of the following* **bin-packing** *problem: Given a sequence of bins of identical size and a sequence of requests to put things of different sizes into the bins, what strategy should be followed to minimize the number of bins used? "First fit" and "best fit" are natural approaches, and have been shown to use at worst 70% more bins than would be used by an optimal strategy that could foresee future requests and exhaustively search through an exponential number of possibilities. For a summary, see*

D. S. Johnson, A. Demers, J. D. Ullman, M. R. Garey, and R. L. Graham, "Worst-Case Performance Bounds for Simple One-Dimensional Packing Problems," *SIAM Journal on Computing* **3** (1974), pp. 299–325;

a discussion of more recent results appears in

D. S. Johnson and M. R. Garey, "A 71/60 Theorem for Bin Packing," *Journal of Complexity* **1** (1985), pp. 65–106.

That dynamic storage allocation is NP-complete even in the presence of perfect information about the schedule of allocation and deallocation requests is noted on page 226 of the book by Garey and Johnson (cited on page 71). The binary buddy system was first published by

K. C. Knowlton, "A Fast Storage Allocator," *Communications of the ACM* **8** (1965), pp. 623–625.

The Fibonacci buddy system is described in

J. A. Hinds, "An Algorithm for Locating Adjacent Storage Blocks in the Buddy System," *Communications of the ACM* **18** (1975), pp. 221–222.

11

Sorting

11.1 KINDS OF SORTING ALGORITHMS

Sorting is among the most basic and universal of computational problems. Where data exist, there is often a need to put the data in order. Hundreds of algorithms, and variations on algorithms, have been proposed and implemented for sorting data. Entire books have been devoted to the study of sorting algorithms. A significant industry flourishes around the production of more efficient sorting software for mainframe computer systems. That such investment has been made in the engineering of sorting programs is testimony to the great amount of time that some computers spend sorting: in some commercial data processing applications, the processing consists of little else.

In spite of its omnipresence, one caution should be injected about sorting before we proceed further: naïve programmers sometimes do it more than is necessary. If the only reason to sort the data is to be sure you know where everything is, it may be cheaper to use a dictionary structure instead. For example, rather than sorting data into a table and then using linear or binary search to find individual items, insert the data into a balanced search tree instead. It will be just as easy to locate data items, and in addition it will be possible to modify the data set dynamically.

Sorting methods are in great variety, in part because of the variety of circumstances under which they can be used. Here are a few crucial distinctions to be borne in mind:

Internal vs. external sorting: If all the data to be sorted can be kept in main memory, then random-access addressing can be used without any cost overhead. Several independent pointers can move through memory with different patterns of movement, and it may be possible to calculate addresses from the values of key fields or to use dynamic data structures to organize the data. On the other hand, if the data to be sorted do not fit all at once in main memory, then access patterns are more restricted; once a block of data is retrieved it is important to make as much use of it as possible before abandoning it to probe another block. Consequently, many techniques that can be used for internal sorting are completely inappropriate for external sorting.

Sorting in place vs. sorting with auxiliary data structures: Some internal sorting methods use no memory beyond that in which the data are initially given; the data items are simply rearranged in their existing positions. (Use of a constant amount of memory, independent of the size of the data set, does not violate this paradigm; for example, a program may use a few local variables to hold single data items.) On the other hand some algorithms build data structures that require extra memory. For example, the *MergeSort* algorithm on page 29 requires that the lists to be merged be located separately from the space into which the result is to be placed. As another example, an algorithm called Tree Sort builds a binary search tree from the data and then does an inorder traversal of that tree to enumerate the data in sorted order.

Worst-case vs. expected-case performance: Some algorithms come with good worst-case performance guarantees; other algorithms, more efficient in practice, may come only with good expected-case guarantees.

What is the "expected case"? It is common practice, when assessing the expected-case performance of sorting algorithms, to consider all $n!$ permutations of a data set of size n to be equally likely. In fact this may be grossly inaccurate: in some applications a list may be sorted repeatedly, each time after adding a few new items to the end. In such a case the data are "nearly" in order, and it pays to use an algorithm that is efficient on such data sets, even if it is very slow on data sets that are very "far" from being in order.

Sorting by comparison vs. sorting digitally: This echoes a distinction we have already used in analyzing searching methods; Chapters 6 and 7 discuss comparison-based searching, while Chapter 8 is on digital searching. Many sorting algorithms use only comparison between key values to determine what to do next; that is, there is some linear order $<$, such as arithmetic comparison of numbers or lexicographic comparison of strings, that governs the control of flow in the algorithm. Any data set that is permuted in the same way would cause an essentially identical execution, just as the structure of a binary search tree depends only on the order in which the data are inserted, not on the values themselves. Other sorting methods use the actual bit values or character values in the keys to direct the algorithm, just as the shape of a trie structure depends on the bits and characters of the keys.

Stable vs. unstable sorting: This has to do with the possibility that multiple data items in the data set may have the same key value on which items are compared. A sorting algorithm is **stable** if such items retain their order relative to each other during the sort, and otherwise the algorithm is said to be **unstable**. Depending on the application, it may be essential that a stable sort be used. For example, suppose that a contest is held, the winner being the person who comes closest to guessing the number of pennies in a jar without going over. A tie will be resolved by the order in which the entries were submitted; if several entrants guess the exact number, or if no one guesses the exact number but several entrants come equally close, the winner will be the one of those entries that was submitted earliest. The contest data can be modelled as a file of records, each consisting of a person's name and a numerical guess, with the records appearing in the file in the same order in which they were submitted. The winning entry can then be found by sorting the file and finding the largest guess not exceeding the actual number of pennies; if there are several consecutive records in the sorted file with the winning guess, the first of these is the winning entry, provided that the algorithm used to sort the file was stable.

The "quick and dirty" vs. the efficient but hard to remember: There sometimes is an almost irresistible temptation to use the sorting algorithm I remember the best without looking it up, rather than a more efficient algorithm I remember studying but of which I have forgotten the details. This laziness is often justified by the allegation that (a) n is small, so it really doesn't matter much what algorithm I use; or (b) this is only temporary—I'll rip out this code and replace it when I have my reference work at hand; or (c) how much difference in running speed is there *really*—a factor of two is not worth my trouble to recapture. For many of us, the best-remembered algorithm is Bubble Sort. In fact, there are *enormous* differences in running times—a $\Theta(n^2)$ sorting algorithm like Bubble Sort is vastly slower than most $\Theta(n \log n)$ or $\Theta(n^{1.5})$ methods; and even among $\Theta(n^2)$ methods, Bubble Sort is the worst! Do it right the first time—the better methods are hardly more work to program.

11.2 INSERTION AND SHELL SORT

The first set of methods apply to data stored in a table. To fix our assumptions once and for all, assume that the table is $A[0 .. n-1]$, and that the table elements can be compared directly: for any elements x and y that might appear in the table, either $x < y$, or $x = y$, or $x > y$. We wish to rearrange A to be monotone nondecreasing; that is, we want to permute the elements of A so that at the end $A[0] \leq A[1] \leq \cdots \leq A[n-1]$.

---

procedure *InsertionSort*(**table** $A[0 .. n - 1]$):
{Sort by inserting each item in position in the table of elements to its left}
    for i **from** 1 **to** $n - 1$ **do**
        $j \leftarrow i$ {j scans to the left to find where $A[i]$ belongs}
        $x \leftarrow A[i]$
        while $j \geq 1$ **and** $A[j - 1] > x$ **do**
            $A[j] \leftarrow A[j - 1]$
            $j \leftarrow j - 1$
        $A[j] \leftarrow x$

Algorithm 11.1 Insertion Sort.

In practice this is a simplification of reality; often the table elements are records, which are to be compared according to key values. Of course, all the algorithms considered below continue to work, except that where an algorithm compares x and y (for example) the comparison should really be between Key(x) and Key(y). However, this introduces another problem: if the records are large, it may not make sense to move entire records around in the table. It makes more sense to create a table of pointers to the records, and to sort the pointer table by comparing the Key fields of the records to which the pointers point. (Of course, the table of pointers can be replaced by a table of indices, which may take less memory or be more easily implemented in some programming languages.)

The **Insertion Sort** algorithm (Algorithm 11.1) repeatedly expands a sorted subtable $A[0 .. i - 1]$ by comparing $A[i]$ with each item $A[i - 1]$, $A[i - 2]$, ... until its proper position is located. As each of these items is passed over, it is moved one position to the right in the table, thus opening up a "hole" into which $A[i]$ (now called x since another value may have been moved into position i of the table) can be dropped at the appropriate moment. The index i starts at 1, since the table consisting of the single element $A[0]$ is already sorted. On each successive iteration of the outer loop i moves one position to the right; in the inner loop, the index j moves from i to the left in search of the appropriate insertion point.

This algorithm is easy to remember, but has little else to recommend it in its present form. In the worst case it takes $\Theta(n^2)$ steps to sort a table of size n. To see this, note that two table elements that are initially out of order cannot wind up in the correct order without being directly compared to each other (via the comparison $A[j - 1] > x$). If the table is in reverse order initially, there are

$$1 + 2 + \cdots + (n - 1) = \frac{(n - 1) \cdot n}{2} \in \Theta(n^2)$$

such "out-of-order" pairs or **inversions** in the table. Therefore this is a lower bound on the running time of the algorithm. It is an upper bound as well, since each loop iterates fewer than n times, and the other statements take constant time independent of n. To describe the situation more loosely, in this algorithm the values move within the table in small steps, and so to reorganize a table that is initially far out of order will take many steps.

Even if we look at the expected-case running time of the algorithm we still get $\Theta(n^2)$. For if all permutations are equally likely, then the expected number of inversions in a randomly selected permutation is half the number in the worst case, or $(n-1) \cdot n/4$, since for every permutation with k inversions its reversal has $(n-1) \cdot n/2 - k$ inversions.

There is only one situation in which Insertion Sort can be relied on to work effectively: if the table is nearly in order to begin with, that is, no element is far from its proper position, then no single iteration of the main loop can take too long. For example, if no element is more than 5 away from its proper position, then the inner **while** loop cannot iterate more than 5 times, and the whole algorithm will run in linear time. Note that Merge Sort, while superior to Insertion Sort in the worst case, is inferior if the data to be sorted are known to be almost in order.

The Insertion Sort algorithm does have one remarkable property, however: it can be made into a very useful, efficient, and general-purpose algorithm by wrapping it in a third outer loop! The revised algorithm is called **Shell Sort**, after its inventor, Donald Shell, who discovered its good properties empirically.

Recall that the inefficiency in the Insertion Sort algorithm derives from its inability to move data quickly over long distances. To address this problem, suppose we pick some "increment" bigger than 1; for illustrative purposes let us choose an increment of 5. We can then imagine the table A subdivided into five interlaced subtables: one consisting of elements $A[0]$, $A[5]$, $A[10]$, ...; another consisting of elements $A[1]$, $A[6]$, $A[11]$, ...; and so on (Figure 11.1(a, b)). If we sort each of these five interlaced subtables independently, say by Insertion Sort, then we can hope that small elements that are far to the right and hence badly out of order will move to the left in a few large hops, skipping positions by increments of 5 rather than by increments of 1. It takes no more time to move an element five positions than one position, if it is moved by a statement of the form $A[j] \leftarrow A[j-5]$.

Of course, this is only a beginning; if the five interlaced tables are not compared with each other, the data will certainly not wind up sorted. We can finish up, however, by doing an Insertion Sort, with an increment of 1. If the table is nearly in order, then Insertion Sort will run quickly since there are relatively few inversions to repair (Figure 11.1(c, d, e)).

In general, Shell Sort uses not just two sorting increments, such as 5 and 1, but a sequence of increments h_t, ..., h_1, with the last, h_1, being 1. Thus the general outline of the algorithm is

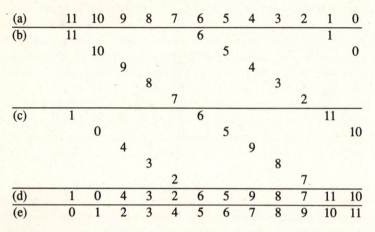

(a)	11	10	9	8	7	6	5	4	3	2	1	0
(b)	11					6					1	
		10					5					0
			9					4				
				8					3			
					7					2		
(c)	1					6					11	
		0					5					10
			4					9				
				3					8			
					2					7		
(d)	1	0	4	3	2	6	5	9	8	7	11	10
(e)	0	1	2	3	4	5	6	7	8	9	10	11

Figure 11.1 Example of Shell Sort running on a table of size 12 that is initially in reverse order. (a) The initial appearance of the table; (b) the five interlaced subtables; (c) the results of sorting the five interlaced subtables separately; (d) the appearance of the table after it has been sorted with increment 5; (e) the final sorted table, after it has been sorted with increment 1.

for k **from** t **downto** 1 **do**
    for d **from** 0 **to** $h_k - 1$ **do**
        Insertion Sort the sequence $A[d]$, $A[d + h_k]$, $A[d + 2h_k]$, ...

The last line would expand into a doubly nested loop like that for Algorithm 11.1, except that the loop indices i and j run only through values that leave a remainder of d when divided by h_k. However, there is no real reason to complete the Insertion Sort on one of these interlaced sequences before beginning to sort the next; since the sequences do not have any members in common, we can equally well consider each member of the table A in order from left to right, moving it to the left by jumps of h_k until it comes to rest in its appropriate position within its own subsequence of the table. The result is Algorithm 11.2.

As long as the last increment h_1 is 1, Shell Sort is a true sorting algorithm, regardless of what the other increments h_t, ..., h_2 may be. However, to achieve the desired efficiency the sequence of increments should have certain properties. The sequence should be decreasing, so that elements tend to move large distances in the early iterations of the outer loop and then move over shorter distances in the later iterations. The early increments should not be multiples of the later increments, since some of the comparisons made with the smaller increment will have been rendered redundant by comparisons made earlier. There should not be too many increments; for example, if there were $\lfloor n/2 \rfloor$ increments then the outer two loops would combine to cause the algorithm to be of complexity $\Omega(n^2)$, even if the innermost loop takes constant

procedure *ShellSort*(**table** $A[0 .. n-1]$):
{Sort by "diminishing increments"}
    $inc \leftarrow InitialInc(n)$
    while $inc \geq 1$ **do**
        for i **from** inc **to** $n-1$ **do**
            $j \leftarrow i$
            $x \leftarrow A[i]$
            while $j \geq inc$ **and** $A[j-inc] > x$ **do**
                $A[j] \leftarrow A[j-inc]$
                $j \leftarrow j - inc$
            $A[j] \leftarrow x$
        $inc \leftarrow NextInc(inc, n)$

Algorithm 11.2 Shell Sort. The increment sequence is determined iteratively using the two functions *InitialInc(n)*, which returns the largest increment to be used when sorting a table of length n, and *NextInc(inc, n)*, which returns the next increment smaller than inc to be used when sorting a table of length n. These two functions generate the monotone decreasing increment sequence h_t, $h_{t-1}, \ldots, h_1 = 1$. It is assumed that $NextInc(1, n) = 0$, so that the main loop terminates after the iteration with $inc = 1$.

time. Also there should not be too few; if there are only two increments then the analysis resembles that for Insertion Sort, and the complexity is quadratic (Problem 6).

Beyond such rules of thumb the exact analysis of various sequences of increments is extremely difficult. A good practical sequence is obtained by taking $h_1 = 1$ and $h_{i+1} = 3h_i + 1$ for each successive i, until the increment would be greater than or equal to n. This sequence begins 1, 4, 13, 40, 121, ..., and in general $h_i = (3^i - 1)/2$; therefore the sequence has $t = \lfloor \log_3(2n+1) \rfloor$ increments in all. Once the largest increment h_t has been determined, the successive increments to be used can be calculated iteratively by the formula $h_i = (h_{i+1} - 1)/3$; in the notation of Algorithm 11.2, $NextInc(inc, n) = (inc - 1)/3$. The exact computational complexity of Shell Sort with this sequence of increments is not known; however, empirical evidence shows that it is competitive with $O(n \log n)$ sorts for n in the range commonly encountered for internal sorting problems. Some other increment sequences yield algorithms that are known to have time complexity $O(n(\log n)^2)$, although in practice these variations are inferior to the $(3^i - 1)/2$ sequence. Remarkably, the best increment sequence to use with Shell Sort is still not known.

---

procedure *SelectionSort*(**table** $A[0..n-1]$):
{Sort A by repeatedly selecting the smallest element from the unsorted part}
    for i **from** 0 **to** $n-2$ **do**
        $j \leftarrow i$ {j will be the index of the smallest element in $A[i..n-1]$}
        for k **from** $i+1$ **to** $n-1$ **do**
            if $A[k] < A[j]$ **then** $j \leftarrow k$
        $A[i] \leftrightarrow A[j]$

Algorithm 11.3 Selection Sort.

11.3 SELECTION AND HEAP SORT

Insertion Sort, and its relative Shell Sort, work by repeatedly taking an element of an unsorted set and putting it in its proper position within a sorted table. No work is done to find the element; all the work is in locating its position and inserting it. By contrast, Selection Sort works by repeatedly finding in the unsorted set the element that should be next in the sorted table, and moving it to the end of the sorted portion. All the work is in selecting the right element; no work is required to put it where it belongs.

As with Insertion Sort, the simplest implementation of Selection Sort divides the table being sorted into a sorted part at the left and an unsorted part at the right (Algorithm 11.3). As the algorithm progresses the line dividing the sorted and unsorted parts of the table moves from the left end of the table (completely unsorted) to the right end of the table (completely sorted).

Selection Sort has time complexity $\Theta(n^2)$ since the outer loop iterates from 0 to $n-2$ and the inner loop iterates from the outer index to $n-1$. However, it is easy to see how to make it more efficient, since the repeated selection of the smallest remaining element is really a repeated appeal to a priority queue structure. In Algorithm 11.3 the priority queue is simply a table that is searched linearly, but there are other structures that yield more efficient implementations of priority queue operations. For example, we could start out by inserting all the table elements into a balanced tree structure, such as a 2-3 tree, and then repeatedly withdraw the smallest element and move it into the next position in the table. But building a 2-3 tree would require extra memory.

A better idea is to implement the priority queue as a heap; since the heap can be represented implicitly, the resulting sorting algorithm, called **Heap Sort**, does not require any memory beyond that occupied by the table being sorted (Algorithm 11.4). The index i is again the borderline between the sorted and unsorted parts of the table; the heap is represented in $A[i..n-1]$, with the root of the heap (which contains the smallest element) at the right end, in $A[n-1]$. This permits the sorted part of the table to grow at the left end as in Algorithm 11.3; every time the size of the sorted table increases by one element, the size of the heap de-

procedure *HeapSort*(**table** $A[0 .. n - 1]$):
{Sort by turning A into a heap and repeatedly selecting its smallest element}
    InitializeHeap($A[0 .. n - 1]$)
    for i **from** 0 **to** $n - 2$ **do**
        $A[i] \leftrightarrow A[n - 1]$
        Heapify($A[i + 1 .. n - 1]$)

procedure *InitializeHeap*(**table** $A[0 .. n - 1]$):
{Turn A into a heap}
    for i **from** 1 **to** $n - 1$ **do** *Heapify*($A[0 .. i]$)

Algorithm 11.4 Heap Sort algorithm. Once the table has been initially turned into a heap, the algorithm repeatedly exchanges the first element beyond the end of the sorted part of the table with the heap minimum, then calls *Heapify* (Algorithm 11.5) to let the element that has just been put at the root of the heap settle to its proper position and thus restore the heap's partial ordering property.

creases by one, with the left edge of the heap (index i) moving from left to right.*

To extend the sorted part of the table by one element, the heap root element (which is $A[n - 1]$) is exchanged with the leftmost "unsorted" element (which is $A[i]$). This destroys the partial order property of the heap, but only at the root; Algorithm 11.4 restores the partial order property of the heap by calling *Heapify*($A[i + 1 .. n - 1]$), which takes the rightmost element of $A[i + 1 .. n - 1]$ and lets it settle down (to the left) into the heap until it reaches its proper position.

It turns out that a small variation on this call to *Heapify* is exactly what is needed to set up the heap in the first place. In general, *Heapify*($A[i .. j]$) assumes that $A[i .. j - 1]$ is already partially ordered, and pushes $A[j]$ down as far as is necessary so that $A[i .. j]$ becomes partially ordered. Then to initialize the heap successively larger subtables $A[0 .. i]$ are passed to *Heapify*, thus turning the unsorted table into a heap from the leaves up to the root.

Thus it remains only to detail *Heapify* (Algorithm 11.5). The computation is very similar to that of Algorithm 9.1 on page 303, but the indexing is different because the root of the heap is at the right end. We use $\mathsf{LC}(j)$ and $\mathsf{RC}(j)$ to denote the indices of the left and right children of the heap element $A[j]$. Since the root of the heap is at $A[n - 1]$ and the leaves are the nodes with smaller indices in the table, $\mathsf{LC}(j) = 2j - n$ and $\mathsf{RC}(j) = 2j - n - 1$. Of course, if $\mathsf{RC}(j)$ is less than the index of the left end of the heap, then node j does not actually have a right child; and if $\mathsf{LC}(j)$ is less than the index of the left end of

---

*As a result of reversing the direction in which the heap is stored in the table, the right child of a node is stored in the table to the left of the left child (that is, the right child has a smaller table index than the left child).

---

procedure *Heapify*(**table** $A[i..j]$):
{Initially $A[i..j-1]$ is partially ordered}
{Afterwards $A[i..j]$ is partially ordered}
 if $RC(j) \geq i$ **and** $A[RC(j)] \leq A[LC(j)]$ **and** $A[RC(j)] < A[j]$ **then**
  $A[j] \leftrightarrow A[RC(j)]$
  Heapify($A[i..RC(j)]$)
 else if $LC(j) \geq i$ **and** $A[LC(j)] < A[j]$ **then**
  $A[j] \leftrightarrow A[LC(j)]$
  Heapify($A[i..LC(j)]$)

Algorithm 11.5 Push the element $A[j]$ down into a heap until it finds its resting place. The heap is organized so that the root is at the right end of the table, namely, $A[n-1]$; the elements to the left of $A[j]$ are assumed already to form a partially ordered tree. $LC(j) = 2j - n$ and $RC(j) = 2j - n - 1$ are the positions of the left and right children, if any, of $A[j]$. The algorithm is presented as recursive for clarity, but since it is tail-recursive it can be recoded so that it uses no extra memory (Problem 13).

---

the heap, then node j has neither child. (Strictly speaking, the value of n should be passed in to *Heapify* so that the LC and RC functions can be calculated; we omit this parameter to avoid clutter.)

 What is the complexity of *HeapSort*? A single call to *Heapify* takes time that is $O(\log n)$, since the **while** loop in Algorithm 11.5 essentially traces a path in a heap whose maximum height is $\lfloor \lg n \rfloor$. Since *HeapSort* creates and then repeatedly deletes from a priority queue for which the cost of a single deletion is $O(\log n)$, the time required for everything except the initialization of the heap is $O(n \log n)$. Also, the $n-1$ calls to *Heapify* from within *InitializeHeap* take $O(\log n)$ time each, so the initialization also takes time that is $O(n \log n)$. Therefore the worst-case running time of *HeapSort* is $O(n \log n)$.

 Actually, the time used to initialize the heap is linear in n; this does not change the end result of the analysis of *HeapSort*, but it is an interesting fact in its own right. For each $h = 0, \ldots, \lfloor \lg n \rfloor$, there are at most $n/2^h$ nodes of height h in the heap $A[0..n-1]$, and to *Heapify* a node of height h takes time proportional to h. The calls on *Heapify* for the nodes of height 0 take constant time each and hence $O(n)$ time in all. The rest of the calls on *Heapify* to initialize the heap take time proportional to

$$\sum_{h=1}^{\lfloor \lg n \rfloor} h \cdot \frac{n}{2^h} \leq n \cdot \left(\tfrac{1}{2} + \tfrac{2}{4} + \tfrac{3}{8} + \cdots \right).$$

The sum on the right was analyzed on page 36, and has the value 2, so the total cost of *InitializeHeap* is $O(n)$.

11.4 QUICK SORT

In Chapter 1 we analyzed the Merge Sort algorithm (Algorithm 1.7 on page 29), which sorts a table by recursively sorting the first and second halves of the table, and then merges the two sorted halves into a single sorted table. If the table is of size n, then everything except the recursive sorts takes time proportional to n; thus at each level of recursion the total time spent is $O(n)$, and since there are $\lfloor \lg n \rfloor$ levels of recursion, the total time for Merge Sort is $O(n \log n)$.

Merge Sort is simple, elegant, and much more efficient than quadratic-cost sorting algorithms like Insertion Sort for n small enough to be of practical interest. Nonetheless as an internal sorting algorithm Merge Sort has a significant disadvantage: it is very difficult to carry out the merge step in place. That is, the only practical way to merge the sorted halves $T[a .. middle]$ and $T[middle + 1 .. b]$ into a single sorted table $T[a .. b]$ is to copy the first half into some temporarily allocated memory block and then to merge this copy with the second half back to the table $T[a .. b]$. The data copying seems to be nonproductive effort, and using a general-purpose memory manager to allocate and deallocate these temporary blocks would entail significant overhead, especially since many of the blocks requested will be only a few cells long. We can avoid using a general-purpose memory manager by noting that only $\lfloor n/2 \rfloor$ cells are ever needed, so they can be allocated once and for all at the beginning of the algorithm and deallocated after the sorting is complete. Still, the extra memory required and the amount of data movement limit the usefulness of Merge Sort as an internal sorting method.

Quick Sort is a recursive sorting algorithm that resembles Merge Sort, but avoids the need for additional memory beyond that in which the data are presented. Before making the recursive calls, Quick Sort rearranges the data in the table so that every element in the first part of the table is less than or equal to every element in the second part of the table. Then when the two parts have been recursively sorted, no merge step is necessary; the whole table is in order automatically.

The rearrangement of the data before the recursive calls is called the **partitioning** step. To make Quick Sort efficient, partitioning must be done in linear time and without recourse to extra memory. Ideally we would like the two parts to be always exactly the same size. However, this is too much to hope for, since achieving such an exact partition would entail finding the median of the table. (While the median can be found in linear time (page 412), the linear-time algorithm uses extra memory, and the cruder methods employed in Quick Sort yield satisfactory performance in practice. But see Problem 24.)

For practical purposes, however, it is sufficient to partition the table somewhat sloppily. The basic approach is to choose some element from the table called the **pivot**, and then to rearrange the data so that elements less than the pivot are to its left and elements that are greater are to its right. In Algorithm 11.6 the pivot is simply the leftmost element in the table; of course by

---

procedure *QuickSort*(**table** $A[l..r]$):
{Sort $A[l..r]$. The outermost call should be *QuickSort*($A[0..n-1]$)}
    if $l < r$ **then**
        $i \leftarrow l$ {i scans from the left to find elements $\geq$ the pivot}
        $j \leftarrow r + 1$ {j scans from the right to find elements $\leq$ the pivot}
        $v \leftarrow A[l]$ {v is the pivot element}
        while $i < j$ **do**
            $i \leftarrow i + 1$
            while $i \leq r$ **and** $A[i] < v$ **do** $i \leftarrow i + 1$
            $j \leftarrow j - 1$
            while $j \geq l$ **and** $A[j] > v$ **do** $j \leftarrow j - 1$
            if $i \leq r$ **then** $A[i] \leftrightarrow A[j]$
        if $i \leq r$ **then** $A[i] \leftrightarrow A[j]$ {Undo extra swap}
        $A[j] \leftrightarrow A[l]$ {Move the pivot element into its proper position}
        QuickSort($A[l..j-1]$)
        QuickSort($A[j+1..r]$)

Algorithm 11.6 Quick Sort.

---

bad luck, or because the table was in order already, that element might turn out to be the smallest table element, and then the two parts would wind up very disproportionate in size. A couple of methods for avoiding this kind of imbalance are discussed below.

In Algorithm 11.6 the partitioning around the pivot element is carried out by running two scans, one from left to right in search of an element greater than or equal to the pivot, and one from right to left in search of an element less than or equal to the pivot. When two such elements are located, they are exchanged and the scan continues. The partitioning phase stops when the two scans meet each other (Figure 11.2).

Quick Sort has time complexity $O(n^2)$ in the worst case, and as implemented in Algorithm 11.6 this worst case occurs when the table is initially in order. We could try to avoid this worst case by exchanging the first and the middle element in the table before beginning the partitioning, by inserting a new step

$$A[l] \leftrightarrow A[\lfloor (l+r)/2 \rfloor]$$

at the beginning of Algorithm 11.6. Unfortunately this merely changes the permutation that leads to the worst-case performance; it does not eliminate such permutations (Problem 17).

A better variation on Algorithm 11.6 takes the first, middle, and last elements of the table, rearranges them in order, and then uses the median of the three as the partition element. This method is illustrated in Algorithm 11.7.

	0	1	2	3	4	5	6	7	8	9
(a)	9	1	11	17	13	18	4	12	14	5
		>	>							<
(b)	9	1	5	17	13	18	4	12	14	11
				>			<	<	<	
(c)	9	1	5	4	13	18	17	12	14	11
				<	$\gtrless$	<				
(d)	9	1	5	13	4	18	17	12	14	11
(e)	4	1	5	9	13	18	17	12	14	11
(f)	1	4	5	9	11	12	13	14	17	18

Figure 11.2 Example of partitioning a table $A[0..9]$. The pivot element v is $A[0] = 9$. The main **while** loop of Algorithm 11.6 iterates three times: (a)–(c) show the appearance of the table just before each iteration; (d) shows the table after the last iteration. The alternate rows show the movement of the i and j indices, which are represented by > and <, respectively. At the end of the partitioning $i = 4$ and $j = 3$. (e) Two swaps undo the extra exchange performed between (c) and (d), and leave the array with the pivot in its proper position; all numbers to the left of $A[3] = 9$ are less than 9, and all numbers to the right of $A[3] = 9$ are greater than 9. Then (f) sorting $A[0..2]$ and $A[4..9]$ sorts the entire table.

Since the median of three elements of the array is less likely than any one element to be nearly the smallest or largest element of the array, Algorithm 11.7 is more likely than Algorithm 11.6 to partition the array evenly. Moreover, positioning an element no larger than the pivot at the left end of the array and an element no smaller than the pivot at the right end of the array makes it possible to eliminate the tests in the inner loops which in Algorithm 11.6 ensure that the search indices i and j do not go out of range. The elements $A[l]$ and $A[r]$ become sentinels; the tests $A[i] < v$ and $A[j] > v$ must eventually fail since $A[r] \geq v$ and $A[l] \leq v$.

We can hope that permutations that force uneven splitting at every iteration will be rather rare. In fact the expected running time of Quick Sort, if all $n!$ permutations are assumed to be equally likely, is $O(n \log n)$. To derive this fact, let $T(n)$ represent the expected running time of Quick Sort on a table of length n. During the partitioning step, elements within the two subarrays are not compared to each other, but only to the pivot; this implies that all permutations of the subarrays are also equally likely. Therefore, if the pivot is the ith largest element in the table, where $1 \leq i \leq n$, then the expected running time of the two recursive calls is $T(i - 1) + T(n - i)$. Since all permutations are equally likely, it follows that the pivot element is equally likely to be the smallest, next-to-smallest, ..., or largest of the n table elements, and the expected time to complete the recursive calls is the average value of $T(i - 1) + T(n - i)$ over

---

procedure *QuickSort*(**table** $A[l..r]$):
{Sort $A[l..r]$. The outermost call should be *QuickSort*($A[0..n-1]$)}
    Put $A[l]$, $A[\lfloor(l+r)/2\rfloor]$, and $A[r]$ in order in the same positions
    if $r-l>2$ **then**   {Any shorter array is sorted by the previous step}
        $A[l+1] \leftrightarrow A[\lfloor(l+r)/2\rfloor]$
        $i \leftarrow l+1$ {i scans from the left to find elements $\geq$ the pivot}
        $j \leftarrow r$ {j scans from the right to find elements $\leq$ the pivot}
        $v \leftarrow A[l+1]$ {v is the pivot element}
        while $i < j$ **do**
            $i \leftarrow i+1$
            while $A[i] < v$ **do** $i \leftarrow i+1$
            $j \leftarrow j-1$
            while $A[j] > v$ **do** $j \leftarrow j-1$
            $A[i] \leftrightarrow A[j]$
        $A[i] \leftrightarrow A[j]$ {Undo extra swap at the end of the preceding loop}
        $A[j] \leftrightarrow A[l+1]$ {Move the pivot element into its proper position}
        QuickSort($A[l..j-1]$)
        QuickSort($A[j+1..r]$)

Algorithm 11.7 Quick Sort, modified to use median-of-three partitioning.

---

all n values of i. The nonrecursive part of Quick Sort takes time linear in n, so there is a constant c such that

$$T(n) = cn + \frac{1}{n}\sum_{i=1}^{n}\bigl(T(i-1)+T(n-i)\bigr).$$

Therefore

$$nT(n) = cn^2 + 2\bigl(T(0)+\cdots+T(n-1)\bigr).$$

Substituting $n-1$ for n and subtracting,

$$(n-1)T(n-1) = c(n-1)^2 + 2\bigl(T(0)+\cdots+T(n-2)\bigr)$$

$$nT(n) - (n-1)T(n-1) = c(2n-1) + 2T(n-1)$$

$$\frac{T(n)}{n+1} \leq \frac{T(n-1)}{n} + \frac{2c}{n+1}$$

$$\leq \frac{T(n-2)}{n-1} + \frac{2c}{n} + \frac{2c}{n+1}$$

$$\leq \cdots$$

$$\leq \frac{T(1)}{2} + 2c\sum_{i=3}^{n+1}\frac{1}{i}.$$

The first term in this sum is a constant; the second term is $2c$ times the sum of a harmonic series and is therefore bounded by $2c \ln(n + 1)$ plus a constant. Therefore $T(n) \in O(n \log n)$, as was to be shown.

The "improved" version of Quick Sort, Algorithm 11.7, uses recursive calls on itself to sort even small arrays. As discussed on page 33, it makes sense, because of the overhead for recursion, to use a simpler sorting algorithm when only a few elements need to be sorted. This could be effected by replacing the line "**if** $r - l > 2$ **then** ..." by "**if** $r - l < n_0$ **then** *NonRecursiveSort*$(A[l .. r])$ **else** ...," where n_0 is an appropriately chosen cutoff for recursive subdivision and *NonRecursiveSort* is some simple sorting algorithm. Even this approach can be simplified, however. If the subtables are not sorted at all when their size becomes smaller than n_0, then after the algorithm terminates the table will consist of small unsorted blocks of length less than n_0, but the blocks as wholes will be in the right order. A single call on Insertion Sort, outside and after the recursive code for Quick Sort, will then sort the entire table. Moreover, since Insertion Sort works well on input that is almost in order, this call on Insertion Sort will not be expensive.

One further observation about Quick Sort concerns its use of memory. We motivated the derivation of Quick Sort by the desire to eliminate Merge Sort's use of auxiliary memory; but Quick Sort uses an auxiliary data structure as well, namely, the stack that is used to implement recursion! What is worse, the depth of recursion on a table of size n could be as much as n, in case the table was permuted in one of those unfortunate ways that causes the worst-case running time. Thus it appears that a good deal of extra memory will be used by Quick Sort, in the worst case.

This is indeed true for Quick Sort as implemented in Algorithm 11.6 or Algorithm 11.7; but these implementations can be improved. Note that these algorithms are tail-recursive; thus the recursive call *QuickSort*$(A[j + 1 .. r])$ can be replaced by an iteration. Still it is possible that the remaining recursive call could result in recursion to depth n. However, the two recursive calls can actually be done in either order, and do not have to be done in the same order on each invocation of the procedure. If the smaller of $A[l .. j]$ and $A[i .. r]$ is sorted recursively, and the larger is sorted iteratively, then the maximum depth of recursion will be only $\lceil \lg n \rceil$, since the recursive call will always be on a table that is at most half the size of the original. In this way Quick Sort can be implemented to require a stack of depth that is only $O(\log n)$.

11.5 THE INFORMATION-THEORETIC LOWER BOUND

We have developed two sorting algorithms that take $O(n \log n)$ time in the worst case to sort a table of length n (Heap Sort and Merge Sort), and one that takes $O(n \log n)$ in the expected case (Quick Sort). And we have extolled the virtues of these algorithms by comparison with those that use $\Omega(n^2)$ time, in both the worst and the expected cases (Insertion, Selection, and Bubble Sorts). But why are we content with $\Theta(n \log n)$ algorithms—shouldn't we be trying to develop algorithms that take even less time, perhaps time that is $O(n\sqrt{\log n})$ or $O(n \log \log n)$ or even $O(n)$?

The answer is that there can be no such algorithms, at least no such algorithms of the general variety we have been discussing up till now. To be specific, we call a sorting algorithm **comparison-based** if the only operations it performs on keys are comparing them (that is, determining which of the three relations $a < b$, $a = b$, or $a > b$ holds between two keys) and moving them from place to place. Comparison-based methods exclude such operations as using the first character of a key as a table index or comparing the individual bits of two keys. In other words, the keys cannot be taken apart—in a comparison-based algorithm they must be treated as wholes.

All of the sorting algorithms discussed so far are comparison-based. Comparison-based algorithms have the attractive property that they can be used on data of many different types just by changing the comparison function and the way records are stored and moved from place to place; regardless of the underlying structure of the data, a comparison-based method will use exactly the same number of steps on two tables that are similarly permuted. Nonetheless, there are important and useful sorting algorithms that are not comparison-based; we shall see some in the next section. One of the reasons for seeking such methods is given by the following lower bound on the efficiency of comparison-based methods.

■ **THEOREM** *(Information-Theoretic Lower Bound)* Any comparison-based algorithm for sorting takes time that is $\Omega(n \log n)$ to sort tables of length n.

PROOF Consider any comparison-based sorting algorithm **P** applied to a table A of fixed size n. For simplicity we will assume that all elements of A are distinct; this assumption does not change the conclusions we draw. Since only comparisons can be used by **P** in its decision-making process, we may as well imagine A to contain a permutation of the integers $0, 1, \ldots, n - 1$; when the sorting is done, we should have $A[i] = i$ for each i. We shall show that sorting A must take $\Omega(n \log n)$ *comparisons* in the worst or expected case, even ignoring the cost of any other operations the algorithm might be performing (data movement, for example). The total time must be at least proportional to the number of comparisons, and is therefore $\Omega(n \log n)$.

The basic idea of the proof is intuitively very simple: A might be any one of $n!$ possible different permutations of the integers between 0 and $n-1$, and in the end enough information must have been extracted by the algorithm to determine which of these permutations A represents. For if **P** treated two different permutations identically, it could not sort them both; one or the other would wind up unsorted when the algorithm finished. But each comparison extracts only one bit of information about which permutation is being sorted, so the number of comparisons in the worst case, $c(n)$, must be at least large enough so that $2^{c(n)} \geq n!$; this turns out to mean that $c(n) \in \Omega(n \log n)$.

However, this appeal to an intuitive notion of "information" is rather shaky, so let us detail the argument more carefully. Imagine tracing the operation of $\mathbf{P}$ on a particular table A, and let us write $i :: j$ to mean that $\mathbf{P}$ compares the data element that was originally at $A[i]$ with the data element that was originally at $A[j]$. (Of course, the algorithm can move data around within the table and to and from temporary variables and auxiliary data structures, so a comparison $i :: j$ might well result when those data are no longer located at positions i and j in the table.) Once the original permutation A has been fixed, the sequence of comparisons $i_1 :: j_1, \ldots,$ $i_c :: j_c$ made by $\mathbf{P}$ is completely determined. Moreover the first comparison $i_1 :: j_1$ must be the same for all permutations A, since the decision about which two elements of A to compare first is coded into the algorithm. This first comparison has two possible outcomes, $<$ or $>$. Now if A and B are two different permutations of $0, \ldots, n-1$ such that $A[i_1]$ stands in the same relationship to $A[j_1]$ as $B[i_1]$ stands to $B[j_1]$, then the *second* comparison made by $\mathbf{P}$ must be between the same table positions whether the input is A or B; for $\mathbf{P}$ has no other basis for making a decision about which two data elements to compare except the result of the first comparison, which is the same whether A or B is being sorted. Extending this principle to subsequent comparisons, we see that the comparisons made by $\mathbf{P}$ when sorting a table of length n can be represented by a tree. Each node that is not a leaf is labelled by a comparison $i :: j$ and has at most two children, corresponding to the two possible outcomes of the comparison (Figure 11.3). Such a tree is called a **decision tree**.

The leaves in a decision tree (the square nodes in Figure 11.3) represent terminations of the algorithm; every possible permutation corresponds to a path from the root to one of the leaves. For example, in Figure 11.3 the permutation in which $A[0] < A[1] < A[2]$ initially corresponds to the path through left children only, and the permutation in which $A[0] > A[1] > A[2]$ corresponds to the path through right children only. Conversely every path corresponds to some permutation. The length of a path is the number of comparisons made while sorting that permutation. Moreover, *two different permutations must correspond to different paths;* otherwise the algorithm would carry out exactly the same data movements and one of the two permutations would not wind up sorted. Therefore the decision tree must have exactly $n!$ leaves.

If a tree has at most binary branching at each internal node and its height is h, then the tree can have at most 2^h leaves. Consequently the

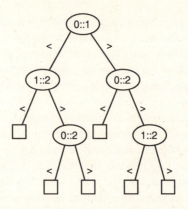

Figure 11.3 Decision tree for Insertion Sort (Algorithm 11.1 on page 382) on tables of length $n = 3$. The only comparison in the algorithm is "$A[j - 1] > x$" in the inner loop. The first level of the tree corresponds to the $i = 1$ case of the outer loop, the lower levels to the $i = 2$ case.

height of the tree is $\lg(n!)$ or greater. By Stirling's approximation, $n! \in \Omega(e^{(n+\frac{1}{2})\ln n - n})$, so $\lg n! \in \Omega(n \log n)$. Therefore the worst-case number of comparisons by algorithm **P** is in $\Omega(n \log n)$. $\square$

We might still hope to achieve an average-case performance that is better than $\Omega(n \log n)$, but this too is impossible if we are sorting permutations and all permutations are assumed to be equally likely. In this case the expected number of comparisons is the average length of the paths from the root to the leaves of the decision tree. The calculation of this value is almost exactly the same as that in the Expected Binary Search Theorem (page 184), and is therefore at least logarithmic in the number of leaves, that is, $\Omega(n \log n)$.

11.6 DIGITAL SORTING

The way to attempt escape from the Information-Theoretic Lower Bound is to treat the keys themselves as data on which calculations can be based. If the keys are numbers they might be used as addresses or table indices; if the keys are strings they can be broken down into their component characters which can be used as indices; and on any digital computer it is possible (at least in theory) to treat the keys as binary numerals whose component bits can be used in the sorting process. Thus the methods suggested in this section are akin to those used in Chapter 8 for implementing dictionaries of digital data.

Bucket Sort

The simplest digital sorting method is **Bucket Sort**, and it applies if the keys are small nonnegative integers which can be used as table indices. In other words, the size of the universe from which the keys are drawn must be fixed in advance, so that it is possible to represent a set of keys by a bit vector. To sort a table $A[0..n-1]$ of distinct numbers drawn from a universe $\mathbf{U} = \{0, \ldots, N-1\}$, we can then create a bit vector $B[0..N-1]$ representing the set of numbers appearing in A, by initializing B to be all 0s and then setting $B[A[0]]$, $B[A[1]]$, $\ldots$, $B[A[n-1]]$ to 1. The numbers in A have now served their purpose; the rest of the procedure reconstructs those numbers from left to right in A in their sorted order. This is done by traversing the bit vector B from left to right; each time we encounter a position in which a 1 occurs, we insert its index into the next position in A.

If this simple bit vector representation is used, then Bucket Sort takes $O(N)$ time to initialize B, $O(n)$ time to insert the elements of A, and $O(N)$ time to traverse B, for a total of $O(N)$. The initialization step can be sped up by the device shown on page 258, at a cost of much greater memory usage; but traversing the bit vector still takes $\Omega(N)$ time, so this refinement is not worth the trouble. Nonetheless there are many algorithms in which N is known in advance and there is a regular need to maintain and sort subsets of $\{0, \ldots, N-1\}$, and in these cases Bucket Sort is the algorithm of choice.

It should be noted that while Bucket Sort is indeed a linear-time algorithm in practice, in a theoretical sense it really is not. That is, if we consider N and n to be arbitrarily large, then the keys must have at least $\lg N$ bits for them to be distinct. If $\lg N$ were sufficiently large, then table indexing using indices of this size could not be considered a constant-time operation, but would cost $\Omega(\log N)$ time. If table references are regarded as costing $\Omega(\log N)$ rather than $O(1)$, then bucket sort becomes an $O(N \log N)$ algorithm. It is only because table indexing takes constant time for tables of practical size that Bucket Sort takes linear time.

If the numbers in A need not be distinct, then a very similar method can be used, but the bit vector must be replaced by a table representing the number of times each key appears in A. That is, in place of the table $B[0..N-1]$ of bits which can be 0 or 1, we need a table $C[0..N-1]$ whose elements are counts—values between 0 and n, inclusive. Reconstructing the table A from these counts simply requires replicating in A each index i a number of times equal to $C[i]$.

A further generalization extends Bucket Sort to the case in which A contains records, or pointers to records, which may themselves be large though the keys are small numbers. In this case simply keeping counts of the number of occurrences of a key is not sufficient, since the table A cannot be reconstructed from an enumeration of the keys. In place of the bit vector B or count table C we must use a table of sets $S[0..N-1]$, where $S[i]$ contains pointers to the records with key i. For example, S might be a table of linked lists. The set $S[i]$ is called the **bucket** of data with key i, and we think of the distribution part of the algorithm as picking up the members of A and dropping each into its appropriate bucket (Algorithm 11.8). The second phase of the algorithm goes

---

procedure *BucketSort*(**table** $A[0 .. n - 1]$):
{A is a table of pointers to records to be sorted on their Key fields}
{$S[0 .. N - 1]$ is a table of sets}
    for i **from** 0 **to** $N - 1$ **do** $S[i] \leftarrow MakeEmptySet(\,)$
    for j **from** 0 **to** $n - 1$ **do** $Insert(A[j], S[Key(A[j])])$
    $j \leftarrow 0$
    for i **from** 0 **to** $N - 1$ **do**
        until *IsEmptySet*($S[i]$) **do**
            $x \leftarrow$ any member of $S[i]$
            $Delete(x, S[i])$
            $A[j] \leftarrow x$
            $j \leftarrow j + 1$

Algorithm 11.8 Bucket Sort. The table passed as an argument contains pointers to the actual records; only this table of pointers is to be sorted.

---

through the bucket table in index order to construct a sorted version of A. If A contains pointers to records as in Algorithm 11.8, this construction can be done in place and in one pass, but otherwise it may be necessary to allocate separate memory in which to construct the final sorted table.

Whether or not Bucket Sort is stable depends on the implementation of the set data structure. If elements are withdrawn from the $S[i]$ in the same order in which they were inserted—that is, if the sets behave like queues—then bucket sort is stable. This effect can be achieved by using a linked queue representation, rather than a simple linked list representation; in this case, both insertion and deletion take constant time.

Radix Sort

If the keys are not small enough to use as table indices, bucket sort cannot be used in the form presented, but it may be possible to sort the data by doing several phases of bucket sorting on successive fragments of the keys. To take a simple example, suppose that the keys consist of two-character strings, and that a character is 8 bits. Thus there are 256 characters, which is a good length for a table, but there are $N = 65536$ possible keys, which is a bit large for a table. Let us assume that the sorting order for the keys is like the dictionary ordering, so that, for example, AA < AB < BA < BB. Then the keys can be sorted by

1. first, doing a bucket sort of all the records using only the *second* character as the key value; and
2. then, doing a bucket sort of the resulting table using only the *first* character as the key value. It is important that the algorithm used be stable, so that the relative order of two keys with the same first character but different second characters is preserved.

For example, consider the table of keys

$$\text{CX AX BZ BY AZ BX AY.}$$

When this table is sorted using only the second character as the key value, three buckets are used:

$$\overbrace{\text{CX AX BX}}^{\text{X}} \quad \overbrace{\text{BY AY}}^{\text{Y}} \quad \overbrace{\text{BZ AZ}}^{\text{Z}}.$$

When this list is bucket sorted on the first character of the keys, again three buckets result:

$$\overbrace{\text{AX AY AZ}}^{\text{A}} \quad \overbrace{\text{BX BY BZ}}^{\text{B}} \quad \overbrace{\text{CZ}}^{\text{C}}.$$

The concatenation of these three buckets is the sorted table. Each pair of keys is in the right order; for if the two keys have different first characters they are in the right order because they were put in separate buckets in Step 2, and if the two keys have the same first character then by stability Step 2 does not change their relative order, which was correct just before Step 2 since they were put in different buckets in Step 1.

Exactly the same method works if the keys are broken into more than two chunks; the resulting algorithm is called **Radix Sort**. To be specific, let us assume that the Key field is broken into K components, $\text{Key}_0, \ldots, \text{Key}_{K-1}$, each of which has value in the range from 0 to $N - 1$. For example, if the keys are character strings then K is their length and $N = 256$, or if the keys are identification numbers with nine decimal digits then $K = 9$ and $N = 10$. Moreover, let us assume that Key_{K-1} is the most significant position in the key and Key_0 is the least significant position; for example, if the keys are decimal numerals then Key_{K-1} is the leftmost digit and Key_0 is the rightmost digit. With these conventions, Algorithm 11.9 gives the details. This algorithm is quite similar to Algorithm 11.8, except that there is an outer loop that iterates over the components of the key, since the key component being sorted on depends on the loop iteration. Also, the general set operations of Algorithm 11.8 have been replaced by queue operations to ensure that the later phases of the algorithm are stable.

Radix Sort works best when maximum advantage is taken of the parallelism in the computer hardware, by using as large a key fragment as possible for the bucket sorting. For example, to sort a large number of 32-bit keys we could do four passes, sorting on 8-bit key components, or eight passes, sorting on 4-bit key components. The second method takes almost exactly twice as long as the first, since each pass of either version takes the same amount of time. The reason we seem to have gotten "something for nothing" is that the addressing hardware can as easily index on an 8-bit index as on a 4-bit index, and if we elect to use only 4-bit indices we do not gain anything in return. This reasoning

---

procedure *RadixSort*(**table** $A[0 .. n - 1]$):
{A is a table of pointers to records to be sorted}
{$S[0 .. N - 1]$ is a table of queues}
    for i **from** 0 **to** $N - 1$ **do** $S[i] \leftarrow MakeEmptyQueue(\ )$
    for k **from** 0 **to** $K - 1$ **do**
        for j **from** 0 **to** $n - 1$ **do** $Enqueue(A[j], S[\text{Key}_k(A[j])])$
        $j \leftarrow 0$
        for i **from** 0 **to** $N - 1$ **do**
            until *IsEmptyQueue*($S[i]$) **do**
                $A[j] \leftarrow Dequeue(S[i])$
                $j \leftarrow j + 1$

Algorithm 11.9 Radix Sort. The table A contains pointers to the records, which have K key components; record R is to be sorted on the K-tuple $\langle \text{Key}_{K-1}(R), \ldots, \text{Key}_0(R) \rangle$, with the leftmost component being the most significant. The table S of queues is used within the algorithm; there is one queue for each possible value of a key component.

---

breaks down when the key components become too big to use as table indices; for example, we could theoretically radix-sort the 32-bit keys in a single pass by bucket-sorting on the entire 32-bit key. But this would require a table of 2^{32} or over four billion entries and a computer that can index on a full 32-bit index into that table. Moreover if there are so many buckets that many of them are likely to be empty, then the time to initialize the queues and to concatenate empty queues becomes significant and degrades the performance of the algorithm; so the number N of queues should not be much greater than the number n of keys.

At the other extreme, we could sort 32-bit keys by doing thirty-two passes, each on a one-bit key. Note, however, that the linear time complexity has now been completely lost; 32 is really $\lg N$, and the result is effectively a $\Theta(n \lg N)$ sorting algorithm.

Radix Exchange Sort

Even though Radix Sort is not particularly effective when the keys are broken down into single bits, there is a digital sorting algorithm that works well when keys are viewed in this way. This algorithm, called **Radix Exchange Sort**, has the advantage that, like Quick Sort, it uses no auxiliary storage except for a stack used to implement recursion, which can be kept relatively small.

Imagine the keys themselves to be in the table $A[0 .. n - 1]$ (the same method works if A contains pointers). Starting with the *most* significant bit,

procedure *RadixExchangeSort*(**table** $A[l . . r]$, **integer** k):
$\{$Sort $A[l . . r]$ on bits $k, \ldots, 0\}$
$\{$The outermost call should be *RadixExchangeSort*$(A[0 . . n - 1], K - 1)\}$
　　if $k \geq 0$ **and** $l < r$ **then**
　　　　$i \leftarrow l$　　　　$\{i$ scans from the left to find elements with 1 in bit $k\}$
　　　　$j \leftarrow r$　　　　$\{j$ scans from the right to find elements with 0 in bit $k\}$
　　　　while $i < j$ **do**
　　　　　　while $i < j$ **and** bit k of $A[i]$ is 0 **do** $i \leftarrow i + 1$
　　　　　　while $i < j$ **and** bit k of $A[j]$ is 1 **do** $j \leftarrow j - 1$
　　　　　　if $i < j$ **then**
　　　　　　　　$A[i] \leftrightarrow A[j]$
　　　　　　　　$i \leftarrow i + 1$
　　　　　　　　$j \leftarrow j - 1$
　　　　RadixExchangeSort$(A[l . . i - 1], k - 1)$
　　　　RadixExchangeSort$(A[i . . r], k - 1)$

Algorithm 11.10 Radix Exchange Sort. The table contains K-bit values; the most significant bit is bit $K - 1$, and the least significant bit is bit 0.

search from the left for an entry that has a 1 and from the right for an entry that has a 0. If two such keys are found and the first is to the left of the second, exchange them and continue. Stop when the two searches meet. When this pass is done all keys with most significant bit 0 are to the left of all keys with most significant bit 1; something very like a partition step of Quick Sort has been effected, with the pivot value being $100 \ldots 0$. When this step has been completed the keys with most significant bit 0, which are at the left end of the table, are sorted recursively on the remaining bits, and the keys with most significant bit 1 are also sorted recursively (Algorithm 11.10).

The stack used implicitly by Algorithm 11.10 grows to height K, which in general does not place a limitation on the algorithm's usefulness. Probably the main inefficiency actually arises because the later sorting passes are likely to accomplish less than the first. For example, if the keys are alphabetic strings, they may be well-distinguished by their first few characters, so the table may be almost in order after sorting on the first few bits; but Algorithm 11.10 calls for many recursive invocations of itself, each of which sorts a subtable that probably is quite short. A strategy to increase the speed of the algorithm is to abandon the radix exchange method after a few bits and to switch to a method that works well on data that are almost in order, such as Insertion Sort.

11.7 EXTERNAL SORTING

All the sorting algorithms discussed in the previous sections depend in essential ways on the ability to move data to arbitrary locations in memory. If the data are on tape or in a disk file, then access may be restricted to a sequential scan, which must begin at the beginning of the file and cannot reach a later position without traversing all the intermediate records. Thus the constraints on *external* sorting methods are inherently more severe than those on *internal* sorting methods. For simplicity we shall refer to the external storage medium on which the data are stored as a **tape**, although similar restrictions may apply to disks either for physical reasons or because of conditions imposed by the operating system. (Even though it may be possible to access blocks of a disk file randomly, the cost of accessing a new block is so high by comparison with the cost of accessing another record in the same block that algorithms for sorting disk blocks must try to make good use of all the data in a block when any datum is accessed.)

Merge Sorts

Merge Sort was described in Chapter 1 as a recursive algorithm that sorts a table by recursively sorting its first and second halves and then merging the sorted halves. The computation preceding the innermost recursive calls consists of subdividing the table into smaller and smaller blocks; the computation following the innermost recursive calls consists of merging sorted blocks into larger sorted blocks until the whole table is sorted. If we ignore the recursive control structure and simply implement the repeated merging of blocks from the bottom up, we get a version of Merge Sort suitable for sequential-access media.

The Merge Sort algorithm for sequential files first organizes the file into a sequence of **runs**, which are sorted subfiles. In principle the runs could be of length 1 initially; this corresponds to Algorithm 1.7 on page 29, which carries out the recursion all the way to the level of single data items. In practice, however, it is more efficient to use whatever internal random-access memory is available to break the initial file into runs that are as long as possible. One way to do this is to transform the original completely unsorted file into runs by reading in a bufferfull of data, sorting it internally, and writing it out as a run to a new file. The larger the buffer that is available, the longer the runs. We shall see at the end of this section an interesting variation on this simple method of run generation.

Suppose that the original file has been transformed into a sequence of r runs, each of length roughly b, which are stored on a tape (Tape 1 in Figure 11.4). The simplest version of Merge Sort for sequential files, called **Straight Binary Merge Sort**, distributes these runs alternately onto two other tapes (Tapes 2 and 3), each of which winds up with roughly $r/2$ runs of length b. Pairs of runs, one from each file, are then merged together and stored back on Tape 1. The result of the merger is a file consisting of $r/2$ runs, each having length $2b$.

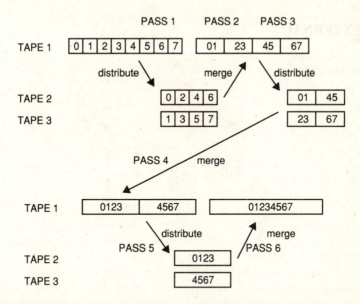

Figure 11.4 Merge Sort algorithm for sequential files. Originally the file is stored on Tape 1 and is broken into 8 runs, indicated by the numbers 0 through 7. These runs are distributed alternately on Tape 2 and Tape 3. Then Tape 2 and Tape 3 are merged back to Tape 1; for example, runs 0 and 1 are merged to form a new run, twice as long, which is called 01. The net effect is to halve the number of runs and to double their length. Repeating this process twice more results in a single run that is eight times as long as the original runs. Each scan through the data counts as a pass; thus the first, third, and fifth passes are distribution passes, and the second, fourth, and sixth passes are merge passes.

The splitting and merging process can be repeated in exactly the same way on the new sequence of runs, continuing until the file has been reduced to a single run of length n.

If the number of runs to be distributed is not even, one tape winds up with an extra run. During the merge phase of the algorithm the extra run is simply copied back; we can picture it as being merged with an **empty run** on the other tape. During the entire course of the algorithm, the net effect of introducing these empty runs is as though the number of initial runs had been rounded up to the next power of 2 greater than or equal to r. Therefore the total number of cycles of distribution and merging needed to sort the initial r runs is $\lceil \lg r \rceil$.

The crucial cost measure for an algorithm operating under these circumstances is the *total number of times that a record is handled*, that is, the total number of **passes** over the data. If the data are stored on tape, the number of passes is proportional to the total amount of tape movement, so reducing the number of passes is the most significant way of reducing the time used to sort the data. In Merge Sort as we have described it, every other pass, starting with

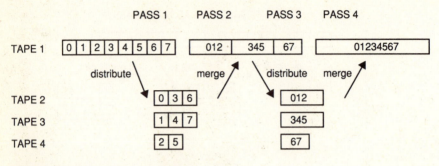

Figure 11.5 Straight Ternary Merge Sort.

the first, distributes the data from Tape 1 to Tapes 2 and 3, and the alternate passes merge Tapes 2 and 3 back to Tape 1. Since it takes $\lceil \lg r \rceil$ merges to transform the original sequence of r runs into a single run, the total number of passes required by Straight Binary Merge Sort is $2\lceil \lg r \rceil$.

If more than three tapes are available, the Straight Binary Merge Sort algorithm can be generalized to take advantage of the extra tapes. If there are $T = t + 1$ tapes available, where $t \geq 2$, then the **Straight Multiway Merge Sort** algorithm alternates between distributing runs from Tape 1 onto the other t tapes, and merging the t tapes back to Tape 1 (Figure 11.5). If there are originally r runs, one distribution and one merge pass produce a tape with about r/t runs, each of length about bt. Hence the total number of passes needed to sort the original r runs is $2\lceil \log_t r \rceil = 2\lceil \lg r / \lg t \rceil$. This is a decreasing function of t, but it flattens out rather dramatically as t increases; most of the advantage of a Multiway Merge is gained by increasing t to 3 or 4, and thereafter the percentage gain in using more tapes is relatively small.

The reason why adding more tapes to the Straight Multiway Merge Sort algorithm gains so little is that most of the tapes are quiet most of the time, especially during the distribution passes. A simple way to increase the activity level per tape is by a **Balanced Multiway Merge**. Suppose that the total number T of tapes is even. Then the merge and distribution passes can be united by dividing the tapes into two subsets of $T/2$ tapes each. Initially the runs are distributed among the first $T/2$ tapes with about $2r/T$ runs per tape, the other $T/2$ tapes being empty. In the first pass the $T/2$ runs are merged, and are redistributed among the other $T/2$ tapes (Figure 11.6). After this phase there are $T/2$ empty tapes, and $T/2$ tapes each containing $4r/T^2$ runs that are each about $T/2$ as long as the original runs. The same merge and redistribution pattern is then repeated in the opposite direction, and this process is repeated until there is only a single sorted run.

Balanced Multiway Merge reduces the number of runs by a factor of about $T/2$ on each pass, so the total number of passes is about

$$\lceil \log_{T/2} r \rceil = \left\lceil \frac{\lg r}{\lg T - 1} \right\rceil.$$

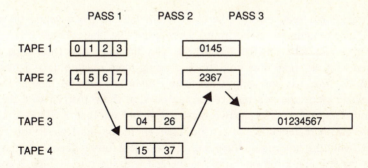

Figure 11.6 Balanced merge with $T = 4$ tapes.

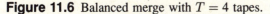
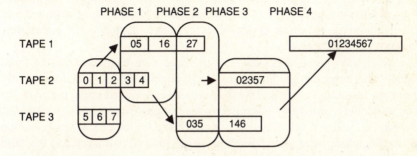

Figure 11.7 Polyphase Merge Sort. Each rounded rectangle encloses the runs that are processed during a particular phase of the algorithm; the arrow points to the tape that is created by merging these runs.

Perhaps it would be fair to add one additional pass to distribute the runs from a single tape among the initial set of $T/2$ tapes. For example, when $T = 4$, Balanced Multiway Merge uses about $1 + \lceil \lg r \rceil$ passes, whereas Straight Multiway Merge uses about $\lceil 2 \lg r / \lg 3 \rceil = \lceil 1.26 \lg r \rceil$ passes.

Polyphase Merge Sort

In Balanced Multiway Merge Sort the activity level per tape is increased because every pass is both a distribution pass and a merge pass. However, among the $T/2$ tapes being distributed to, only one is active at a time; the rest are simply waiting their turn to receive a run. It would be better if a $(T - 1)$-way merge could take place at every step. This effect can actually be achieved, by using runs of different lengths with different numbers of runs on each tape.

Polyphase Merge Sort proceeds in a sequence of **phases**, each of which may be only a partial pass over the data. A phase is defined as the time during which a particular set of $T-1$ tapes is being used as the source of a merge and the remaining tape is being used as the destination. To take a concrete illustration, suppose there are $T = 3$ tapes and $r = 8$ runs initially (Figure 11.7). Initially the runs are distributed on Tapes 2 and 3, but not evenly; Tape 2 has five runs and Tape 3 has only three. (We shall return later to the question of where these "magic numbers" come from.) During the first phase Tapes 2 and 3 are the source and Tape 1 is the destination. The first three runs from Tape 2 are merged with the three runs on Tape 3, creating three runs on Tape 1, each of length $2b$. Tape 3 is now empty, but there remain two runs on Tape 2. During the second phase the two runs remaining on Tape 2 are merged with the first two runs on Tape 1, creating two runs of length 3 on Tape 3. Tape 2 is now empty, but there remains one run on Tape 1. In the third phase this run is merged with the first run on Tape 3 to create a new run on Tape 2. In the final phase the remaining run on Tape 3 is merged with the run on Tape 2 and the result, which is a single run of length 8, is put on Tape 1. The total amount of data processed by this procedure, measured in units of the size of the original runs, is 6 in the first phase, 6 in the second phase, 5 in the third phase, and 8 in the fourth phase, for a total of 25; this works out to $25/8 = 3.125$ passes over the data using three tapes.

What was special about the way the runs were distributed on the tapes initially that permitted the Polyphase Merge algorithm to flow so conveniently from one phase to the next and wind up with a single sorted run in the end? We can work out the pattern by starting from the last phase and working backwards. To wind up with a single run after a binary merge in the end, at the beginning of the last phase there must have been single runs on two tapes and the third tape must have been empty. One of these single runs must have been created in the next-to-last phase, and the other must have been "left over"; this means that at the beginning of the next-to-last phase one tape must have had two runs, one must have had one run, and the remaining tape must have been empty. In the phase prior to that, the tape with two runs was created, out of a tape with three runs and a tape with two runs, leaving one run behind.

In general, if at the beginning of a phase the three tapes contain x, y, and 0 runs, where $x \geq y$, then at the beginning of the previous phase the three tapes must have contained 0, $x + y$, and x runs, respectively. At the beginning of the last phase the two nonempty tapes each contain 1 run. Therefore at the beginning of the kth from last phase the nonempty tapes contain F_{k+1} and F_{k+2} runs, where F_i is the ith Fibonacci number (and the last phase is viewed as the "0th from last"). In this way at the beginning of the $k + 1^{\text{st}}$ from last phase the nonempty tapes contain F_{k+2} and $F_{k+1} + F_{k+2} = F_{k+3}$ runs.

So to make the Polyphase Merge procedure "come out even" at the end, the number of initial runs r must be a Fibonacci number. If it is not, empty runs can be introduced, as many as are needed to bring r up to a Fibonacci number; merging a nonempty run with an empty run entails simply copying the nonempty run. Unfortunately, the device of empty runs reduces the efficiency of the method somewhat, since simply copying a run is relatively unproductive labor; and it is not even clear how the empty runs should be distributed initially in order to make the algorithm most efficient.

The number of passes required by Polyphase Merge Sort is a bit complicated to analyze, especially given the variety of options for distributing the empty runs. If the empty runs are distributed evenly between the two tapes initially, the number of passes turns out to be roughly $1 + 1.04 \lg r$, a little more than half as many as needed for Straight Binary Merge Sort with three tapes.

The Polyphase Merge Sort algorithm can be generalized to work for more than three tapes. For example, if there are four tapes, we would like every step to be a three-way merge. The initial distribution of runs must then follow a generalized Fibonacci pattern. If we start a sequence of numbers with 0, 0, 1, and then continue it in such a way that each subsequent number is the sum of the previous *three* numbers in the sequence, we get

$$0, 0, 1, 1, 2, 4, 7, 13, 24, 44, \ldots.$$

This sequence is called the **Fibonacci sequence of order 3**, F_0^3, F_1^3, ... (the ordinary Fibonacci sequence is then the sequence of order 2). The generalized Polyphase Merge Algorithm with four tapes ends with a single run on one tape if initially the four tapes contain

$$F_{n+2}^3, \quad F_{n+2}^3 + F_{n+1}^3, \quad F_{n+2}^3 + F_{n+1}^3 + F_n^3, \quad \text{and} \quad 0$$

runs, for some $n \geq 0$. Then after one pass the tapes will contain

$$0, \quad F_{n+1}^3, \quad F_{n+1}^3 + F_n^3, \quad \text{and} \quad F_{n+2}^3 = F_{n+1}^3 + F_n^3 + F_{n-1}^3$$

runs, respectively. As is the case with Straight and Balanced Merge, increasing the number of tapes decreases the number of passes, but the advantages of additional tapes diminish rapidly. With four tapes the number of passes is about $1 + 0.7 \lg r$—a 30% improvement over Balanced Multiway Merge with the same number of tapes—and with five tapes it is about $1 + 0.6 \lg r$, but to reduce the number of passes to $0.5 \lg r$, plus a constant, twenty tapes must be used!

Generating the Initial Runs

Of course, all these algorithms work faster if there are fewer runs to begin with, so it is worth spending some time finding ways to generate the initial runs so that they are as long as possible. Our original suggestion, made back at the beginning of this section, was to cut up the original data file into chunks of the size that could be accommodated in internal memory, use an internal sorting algorithm to sort each chunk, and write the sorted chunks out to tape as runs. If we can afford to allocate an internal buffer that can hold b records, then our original file of n records will be divided up into $r = \lceil n/b \rceil$ runs, each of which is of size b except for the last, which may be smaller.

At first it might appear that this is about as well as we can do, but a look at an extreme case shows how stupid this method actually is: if the file was sorted in the first place, the run generation process breaks it up into a sequence of many runs, which will be elaborately sorted by merging to restore their original order! Somehow we should try to take advantage of any preexisting order in the data.

The **replacement selection** procedure uses whatever internal buffer space is available to hold records which are classified into two types: records that will eventually be output into the *current* run, and records that will have to belong to the *next* run. Initially the buffer is filled up from the input file, and all the data items are designated as destined for the current run, which will be the first run. A run is produced by repeatedly selecting from the buffer and outputting the smallest item that should go into the current run; then another item is read from the input data file. If the new item is larger than the item that was just output, it will eventually become part of the current run. However, if the new item is smaller than the item just output, it will have to be part of the *next* run. Thus the total number of items in the buffer remains constant, but as a run is produced the balance between current-run items and next-run items tends to shift. When there are no more items for the current run, a new run begins on the output tape; the next-run items in the buffer are redesignated as the current-run items and the set of items designated for the next run once again becomes empty.

The replacement selection algorithm can be implemented elegantly and with no overhead for data structures by dividing a single block of buffer space into two priority queues implemented as back-to-back heaps, one whose root is at the left end and grows to the right and one whose root is at the right end and grows to the left (Figure 11.8). The point where the two heaps meet is the dividing line between the current-run items and the next-run items. Each item brought in from the input file goes into one of the two heaps, depending on a comparison of its key to the key of the last item that was output. When the current-run heap becomes empty the next-run heap becomes full, and their roles are reversed.

When replacement selection is applied to a file that is already sorted, the file flows through the buffer without interruption and emerges as a single sorted run. In fact only a single run will be produced provided that no item is preceded anywhere in the input file by more than $b - 1$ items that ought to follow it (Problem 43). On the other hand replacement selection works worst on a file that is initially in reverse order. In this case the priority queue is initially filled with the largest b items in the file; the smallest of these is output to begin the first run; it is replaced by an item that is smaller than any seen so far, including the one that was just output, so it must be marked to be part of the second run; and all subsequent selections of items to be output are made from the first bufferful of data, until it has been completely replaced by the second bufferful of data from the input file. So if the file is originally in reverse order replacement selection behaves exactly like the naïve method and produces $\lceil n/b \rceil$ runs of size b or less.

What is the expected behavior of replacement selection, between the extremes of a single run of size n and $\lceil n/b \rceil$ runs mostly of size b? In other

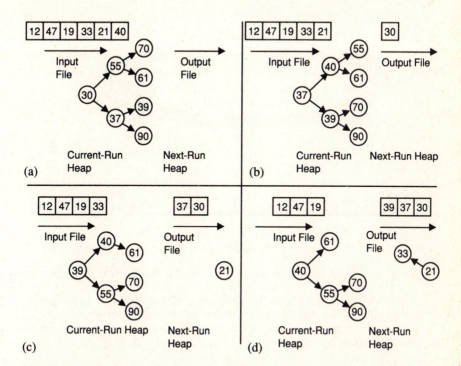

Figure 11.8 Replacement selection algorithm, implemented by means of
two heaps whose total size is 7. (a) Initially the output file is empty, the
current-run heap is filled with items from the input file, and the next-run
heap is empty. (b) The smallest datum in the current-run heap is 30;
this item is output. It is replaced by the next item from the input file,
namely, 40. Since 40 > 30 this item goes into the current-run heap.
(c) The smallest item in the current-run heap, namely, 37, is output. The
next item from the input file is 21, and since 21 < 37 this item goes
into the next-run heap. (d) The smallest item in the current-run heap, 39,
is output. The next item from the input file is 33, which goes into the
next-run heap since 33 < 39.

words, what is the expected length of a run, if all permutations of the input file
are assumed to be equally likely? This quantity can be analyzed quite readily
by appeal to a physical analogy.

For simplicity let us assume that the key values are in the range $0 \leq K < 1$.
Imagine the priority queue to be a circular track that is exactly 1 kilometer in
circumference; there is a fixed position that is marked as 0, and each position on
the track corresponds to a particular key value between 0 and 1 (Figure 11.9(a)).
The data items are snowflakes; when the priority queue is full there are exactly b
snowflakes piled up on the track, and a snowflake representing a datum with key
value K would rest on the track at position K. Just as the data coming in from
the input file are in random order, the snowflakes are falling at random places
along the track. Meanwhile a snowplow is plowing snow off the track, just as

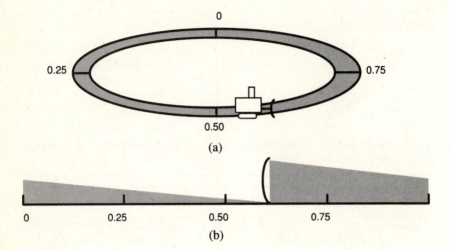

Figure 11.9 (a) The snowplow plowing its circular track. (b) If it snows steadily on the track at a rate that exactly matches the rate at which the snowplow is removing snow from the track, then the amount of snow plowed during a complete cycle is twice the amount of snow on the track at any point in time, since the snowplow always sees the pile at its maximum height.

data are being removed from the internal buffer for output to tape. When the snowplow passes the 0 point on the track, a new run on the tape is begun, since the key value of the snowflake being plowed changes from a number just less than 1 to a number that is 0 or just greater. It is snowing at just the same rate that the snowplow is plowing (every datum removed is immediately replaced), so the total amount of snow on the track (the total number of items in the buffer) remains constant.

Under this analogy, the question, "What is the expected length of a run?" becomes: "How much snow does the snowplow plow during one circuit of the track?" Since everything is assumed to be in steady state—the speed of the snowplow matches the intensity of the snowstorm, and the amount of snow on the track remains the same at all times—the height of the snow on the track is greatest just in front of the snowplow and decreases linearly around the track; just behind the snowplow the height of the snow is 0. But the height of the snow right in front of the plow remains constant during the plow's complete circuit of the track. Consequently during a complete circuit of the track the snowplow plows the area of a rectangle of constant height and of base equal to the circumference of the track, while the amount of snow on the track at any instant is the area of a triangle of the same height and base. Therefore the total amount of snow plowed is twice the amount that is on the track at any one time (Figure 11.9(b)). Thus the expected run length when replacement selection is used is $2b$.

11.8 FINDING THE MEDIAN

Let us return from the world of external data storage to consider a problem apparently related to internal sorting, the problem of finding the median of a table, or more generally, finding the jth smallest element in a table. The **median** of a table of n numbers is that number k in the table that would be in position $\lceil n/2 \rceil - 1$ (counting from 0) if the table were sorted into increasing order. For example, the median of the table 5, 7, 6, 3, 1, 2 is 3, and the median of the table 3, 1, 1, 3, 3 is 3. (We talk about the median of a table rather than the median of a set so that the same number can occur several times.) There are always at least $\lceil n/2 \rceil$ numbers in the table less than or equal to the median and at least $\lceil n/2 \rceil$ numbers in the table greater than or equal to the median. How can we find the median?

Of course, if the table is already in order from smallest to largest, we can simply look in position $\lceil n/2 \rceil - 1$; this takes constant time. If the table is not in order, we can sort it and then look in the middle; if we use a good sorting algorithm the whole process can be done in time $O(n \log n)$. Any approach that relies on sorting will take time $\Omega(n \log n)$ in the worst case; but sorting, of course, gives back much more information than we wanted to find. All the effort required to get the other $n - 1$ numbers in their correct positions in the table produces a result that really does not interest us. Is there some way to find the median in linear time, by avoiding some of the computation involved in a full sort of the data?

To most people the problem of finding the median does not "look" like a problem for which a divide-and-conquer strategy could be helpful; for example, the median of a table might bear no relation to the medians of its first and second halves. Indeed, at first it is hard to imagine that any divide-and-conquer strategy will be effective in attacking the median problem. The first case of the Divide-and-Conquer Recurrences Theorem suggests that to achieve a linear-time recursive algorithm, we need to do two things on each call, when the argument is of size n: first, ensure that the amount of time spent, except for the recursive calls, is linear in n; and second, ensure that the total amount of data passed to recursive calls is less than n by a fixed percentage. The algorithm we now design achieves the first goal, and approximately achieves the second goal as well, though it does not exactly fit the divide-and-conquer paradigm as presented on page 32.

The problem of finding the median by a recursive algorithm becomes more tractable if we recast it as a special case of the more general problem of finding the kth largest. That is, we wish to design an algorithm $Select(T, n, k)$ that returns, for any table T of $n > 0$ integers, the one that would be in position k if the table were sorted, where $0 \le k \le n-1$. Finding the median then amounts to calling $Select(T, n, \lceil n/2 \rceil - 1)$. Note that if k were always some small number such as 0 or 1 then it would be easy to find a linear-time method; the difficulty arises only because k might be somewhere "in the middle."

Consider a table T of length n, and call the numbers in the table $T[0]$, ..., $T[n-1]$. For the time being think of n as relatively large; we shall take care of the case in which n is small later (as well as defining exactly what "large" and "small" mean).

Imagine dividing the table into blocks of 5 numbers each (depending on the value of n, the last block might have anywhere between 1 and 5 numbers). We say "imagine," because we do not need to move the data; we simply think of the first block as consisting of $T[0]$, ..., $T[4]$, the second block as consisting of $T[5]$, ..., $T[9]$, and so on. (5 is not the only possible choice for the length of the blocks; actually any odd number greater than or equal to 5 will do. But the number has to be chosen once and for all before the value of n is known.) There are $\lfloor n/5 \rfloor$ blocks in all; let us call this number b. Any single block of 5 numbers can be sorted in constant time using any convenient sorting method, including one that is optimized for the special case of exactly 5 numbers. Therefore all the blocks can be sorted in $O(b) = O(\lfloor n/5 \rfloor) = O(n)$ time, with the proportionality constant depending on the speed with which we can sort a single block of 5 numbers. When this has been done we can assume that, if u, v, x, y, z is one of these blocks, then $u \leq v \leq x \leq y \leq z$. Thus we can compile (elsewhere in memory) a table of the medians of the blocks:

$$M[0..b-1] = T[2], T[7], T[12], ..., T[5b-3].$$

Now find (recursively!) the median of the table M, whose length is b, by calling

$$m \leftarrow Select(M, b, \lceil b/2 \rceil - 1).$$

Thus m is the "median of the medians" of the blocks.

At first it might seem that nothing has been accomplished, since the median of the medians might well not be near the median of the original table. But in fact we do know *something*; in the block u, v, x, y, z, if $x \leq m$ then we definitely know that $u \leq m$ and $v \leq m$, even though we know nothing about y or z. Likewise if $x \geq m$ then we definitely know that $y \geq m$ and $z \geq m$, even though we know nothing about u or v. That is, we can be certain about three out of the five members of each block, by comparing m with the "block median" x. Moreover we also know that about half the block medians are less than or equal to m, and about half are greater than or equal to m; this is because m is the median of M. To be precise, we know that at least $\lceil b/2 \rceil$ of the block medians are less than or equal to m and at least $\lceil b/2 \rceil$ of the block medians are greater than or equal to m. Now let $n_<$ be the number of elements of the original table T that are less than m, let $n_=$ be the number of elements of T that are equal to m, and let $n_>$ be the number of elements of T that are greater than m; thus $n_< + n_= + n_> = n$. Then because, in each block whose median is less than or equal to m, three out of the five elements are less than or equal to m,

$$n_< + n_= \geq 3\lceil b/2 \rceil, \tag{1a}$$

and similarly

$$n_= + n_> \geq 3\lceil b/2 \rceil. \tag{1b}$$

Now let us form two new tables: $T_<$, which is a table of all the members of T that are less than m; and $T_>$, which is a table of all the members of T that are greater than m. Then we can complete the call $Select(T, n, k)$ by returning m or recursively calling $Select$ on table $T_<$ or $T_>$, depending on the relation between the value of k and the values of $n_<$, $n_=$, and $n_>$:

> **if** $n_< > k$ **then return** $Select(T_<, n_<, k)$
> **else if** $n_< + n_= > k$ **then return** m
> **else return** $Select(T_>, n_>, k - n_< - n_=)$

It remains to specify the base case of this recursion. Let n_0 be some number such that, for all $k \geq n_0$,

$$3\lceil \lfloor k/5 \rfloor /2 \rceil \geq \lceil k/4 \rceil. \tag{2}$$

For example, the number 40 has this property (Problem 47).* Then if $n < n_0$ the recursive method is abandoned; instead the table is sorted directly and element $\lceil n/2 \rceil - 1$ is selected by indexing.

To show that this recursive method runs to completion in linear time, we must establish that $n_<$ and $n_>$—the size of the tables on which $Select$ might be recursively called—are not too large by comparison with n. But it follows immediately from (1) and (2) that

$$n_< \leq n - \lceil n/4 \rceil = \lfloor 3n/4 \rfloor,$$

and similarly $n_> \leq \lfloor 3n/4 \rfloor$. Therefore the running time of the algorithm can be characterized by the recurrence

$$T(n) \leq \begin{cases} c, & \text{if } n < n_0 \\ T(\lfloor n/5 \rfloor) + T(\lfloor 3n/4 \rfloor) + c'n, & \text{if } n \geq n_0. \end{cases} \tag{3}$$

This recurrence does not fit the format of the Divide-and-Conquer Recurrences Theorem because the two recursive terms have different arguments; however, the sum of the arguments is $\lfloor n/5 \rfloor + \lfloor 3n/4 \rfloor < n$ for $n \geq n_0$. This suggests that the solution will be linear, but we must check to be sure. (See Problem 43 of Chapter 1 for a general version of this argument.) First, assume that $20c' \geq c$; if this is not the case then the value of c' can be increased without affecting the validity of (3). Then it is easy to show by induction that $T(n) \leq 20c'n$ for all $n > 0$. For if $0 < n < n_0$ then $T(n) \leq c \leq 20c' \leq 20c'n$. And if $n \geq n_0$ and $T(m) \leq 20c'm$ for all $m \leq n$, then

$$T(n+1) \leq T(\lfloor (n+1)/5 \rfloor) + T(\lfloor (3n+3)/4 \rfloor) + c'(n+1)$$

---

*The value of n_0 is chosen once and for all at the time the algorithm is written; it does not depend on n.

$$\leq 20c' \lfloor (n+1)/5 \rfloor + 20c' \lfloor (3n+3)/4 \rfloor + c'(n+1)$$
$$\leq 4c'(n+1) + 5c'(3n+3) + c'(n+1)$$
$$= 20c'(n+1).$$

So this algorithm can be used to find the median value of a table, or the item in any other ordinal position, in time linear in the size of the table.

Problems

11.1   **1.** (This problem is one of psychology, not mathematics.) Suppose you are given two dozen numbers on a piece of paper, and are asked to produce—by hand—another piece of paper with the same numbers in order. What sorting method would you use? Does your answer change if there are five hundred numbers? What if there are five thousand numbers, with five hundred on each of ten pieces of paper?

2. You are given n intervals $l_i = [a_i, b_i]$ on the real line, where $a_i \leq b_i$ and $1 \leq i \leq n$. Give an algorithm that computes the measure of this set of intervals, that is, the total length of $\cup_{i=1}^{n} l_i$, in $O(n \log n)$ time.

11.2   **3.** Suppose that $A[0 .. n-1]$ has the property that no element is more than k away from its proper position; that is, there is a sorted version of A, say $A[p(0)] \leq A[p(1)] \leq \cdots \leq A[p(n-1)]$, where p is a permutation of $\{0, \ldots, n-1\}$, such that $|i - p(i)| \leq k$ for each i. Give an *exact* upper bound on the number of comparisons $A[j-1] > x$ performed by Insertion Sort (Algorithm 11.1 on page 382), and exhibit a table A for which that is the number of comparisons performed.

4. Show that if the increments for Shell Sort are defined by the recursion

$$h_1 = 1$$
$$h_{i+1} = 3h_i + 1,$$

then $h_i = (3^i - 1)/2$ and the index of the last increment that is less than n is $t = \lfloor \log_3(2n+1) \rfloor$.

5. In Figure 11.1 on page 384, how many element-to-element comparisons does Shell Sort make during the sorting passes with the two increments? Insertion Sort would make $11 \cdot 12/2 = 66$ comparisons.

6. Suppose that Shell Sort is run with only two increments, independent of n. (The increment h_2 might depend on n, but only two increments are used, whether n is 10 or 10 billion.) Show that under these circumstances Shell Sort has quadratic time complexity.

7. Sort the sequence 237, 563, 003, 876, 393, 323, 266, 591, 139, 041, 980, 769 using Shell Sort with the increments 4 and 1.

11.3 **8.** What arrangement of the table causes Selection Sort to have its worst-case behavior?

9. How does Heap Sort behave if the table is in order already? in reverse order?

10. a. Show that Heap Sort is unstable.

b. Find a table $A[0..3]$ such that $\text{Key}(A[0]) = \text{Key}(A[1])$ but the relative order of these two elements in the sorted output produced by Heap Sort depends on the value of one of the other elements of the table.

11. Algorithm 11.4 and Algorithm 11.5 provide an $O(n \log n)$ worst-case sorting algorithm. This problem concerns constant-factor improvements in the running time of Heap Sort that can be achieved by reducing the number of comparisons of data items. The key to these improvements is in the implementation of *Heapify*, which inserts a single item into a heap.

a. Show that a careful recoding of Algorithm 11.5 can reduce the number of data item comparisons to about $2n \lg n$ in the worst case.

b. Show that this number can be further reduced to about $n \lg n$ by first identifying the path on which the insertion should take place, then finding, by binary search, the point on the path where the insertion should occur, and only then moving the data items that need to be moved to open up the slot for the item being inserted.

12. In Algorithm 11.4, the procedure *InitializeHeap* does somewhat more work than is really necessary. What simple change will make this procedure more efficient?

13. Rewrite Algorithm 11.5 as an iterative algorithm by eliminating the tail-recursion.

14. Show how to find the k smallest elements of a table of size n in time $O(n \log k)$.

11.4 **15.** This problem deals with efficient implementation of the Merge Sort algorithm (Algorithm 1.7 on page 29).

a. Write an algorithm $Merge(A[l..m], A[m+1..r])$ that merges the sorted subtables $A[l..m]$ and $A[m+1..r]$ into $A[l..r]$ by using an auxiliary table of size $\lfloor (r-l)/2 \rfloor$ at most.

b. Design an "in-place" version of *Merge* that uses no extra memory. What is its time complexity, and what inputs cause its worst-case behavior? (For a linear-time algorithm, see the references.)

16. In Algorithm 11.6 on page 390 one of the two tests in the inner loops, "$i \leq r$" and "$j \geq l$", is unnecessary. Which one, and why?

17. What is the worst-case arrangement of the numbers 0, 1, ..., 9 for Algorithm 11.6?

18. Write the code for the first line of Algorithm 11.7 on page 392, which orders the three elements $A[l]$, $A[\lfloor(l+r)/2\rfloor]$, and $A[r]$. Try to be as efficient as possible.

19. Find a table of the numbers 0, 1, ..., 9 that causes Algorithm 11.7 to behave as badly as possible.

20. Is any of the versions of Quick Sort stable? Explain, or give counterexamples.

21. Suppose that we had a linear-time procedure that was guaranteed to find a pivot element for Quick Sort such that at least 1% of the array was less than or equal to the pivot and at least 1% was greater than or equal to the pivot. Show that Quick Sort would then have worst-case complexity $O(n \log n)$.

22. This problem concerns Quick Sort, Algorithms 11.6 and 11.7.

   a. How many comparisons does Algorithm 11.6 make if the table is of length n and is in order to begin with?

   b. How many comparisons does Algorithm 11.7 make if the table is of length n and is in order to begin with?

   c. How many comparisons does Algorithm 11.7 make if the table is of length n and is in *reverse* order to begin with?

23. Give a version of the Quick Sort algorithm that is not tail-recursive and that requires a stack that is only of height $O(\log n)$ to sort tables of length n.

24. The following sorting algorithm, called **distributive partitioning**, might be viewed as a cross between Quick Sort and Bucket Sort. It employs a partitioning step somewhat like that of Quick Sort, but with the pivot element chosen as the exact median. Since the linear-time median algorithm can be used (§11.8), this guarantees $O(n \log n)$ time complexity in the worst case. It also avoids deep recursion in the expected case by distributing the items to be sorted into buckets according to their key values, using a calculation like that in Interpolation Search; in fact the expected performance is linear if the data are uniformly distributed. Assume that the keys are numerical values, and that the table to be sorted contains n items. Then the algorithm proceeds as follows.

1. Find the minimum, median, and maximum items in the table; call these key values a, b, and c.

2. Divide each of the ranges from a to b, and from b to c, into $\lfloor n/2 \rfloor$ intervals of equal length, and distribute the items to be sorted into buckets corresponding to these intervals. The item with key K goes in bucket number

$$\left\lfloor \frac{K-a}{b-a} \cdot \frac{n}{2} \right\rfloor, \qquad \text{if } K < b;$$

$$\left\lfloor \frac{K-b}{c-b} \cdot \frac{n}{2} \right\rfloor + \left\lfloor \frac{n}{2} \right\rfloor, \qquad \text{if } b \le K < c;$$

$$2 \left\lfloor \frac{n}{2} \right\rfloor - 1, \qquad \text{if } K = c.$$

3. The buckets are scanned in order of increasing bucket number. If a bucket contains no element, it is passed over; if it contains one element, that element is appended to the sorted table; and if it contains more than one element, the algorithm is called recursively to sort the bucket.

   a. Give examples of tables of 16 numbers that result in the best- and worst-case performance of this algorithm.

   b. Show that this algorithm takes time $O(n \log n)$ in the worst case.

   c. Explain what data structures are needed to implement this algorithm efficiently. How much extra space is needed in addition to the input table?

   d. How can the assertion that this algorithm has expected linear-time performance be consistent with the Information-Theoretic Lower Bound?

25. Given $n < 2^m$ numbers of m bits each, show how to find a number different from all of them in time $O(n)$, on the hypothesis that comparing two m-bit numbers can be done in constant time.

26. a. Given a table of length n in which the first $n - \lceil \sqrt{n} \rceil$ items are sorted but nothing is known about the last $\lceil \sqrt{n} \rceil$ items, how would you sort the entire table in $O(n)$ time in the worst case?

   b. Find a larger function $f(n)$ such that $\sqrt{n} \in o(f)$ and such that a table of length n can be sorted in linear time in the worst case when the first $n - f(n)$ entries are known to be in order. How big can f be?

11.5 27. The proof of the Information-Theoretic Lower Bound assumes that a comparison can have only two outcomes, $<$ or $>$. But it is also possible for the items being compared to be equal; why does this not make any difference to the proof?

28. Show the decision tree that results from sorting a table of four unequal elements using

a. Selection Sort (Algorithm 11.3);

b. Heap Sort (Algorithm 11.4);

c. Quick Sort (Algorithm 11.6).

29. Find a way to sort five items using only seven comparisons.

30. a. It takes $n-1$ comparisons to find the largest of n numbers. Why?

b. But it takes only $\lceil 3n/2 \rceil - 2$ comparisons to find both the largest and smallest of n numbers. How can this be done?

c. Show that any comparison-based algorithm for finding both the largest and the smallest of n items must make at least $\lceil 3n/2 \rceil - 2$ comparisons in the worst case.

31. Show how to find the largest and next-to-largest elements of a table of length n by using only about $n + \lg n$ comparisons.

32. Suppose you are given a list of n integers with many duplications, so that there are only $O(\log n)$ distinct numbers in the list.

a. Show how to sort the numbers in time $O(n \log \log n)$.

b. Why is this result not a violation of the Information-Theoretic Lower Bound?

33. Suppose that a table of length n contains k distinct elements $x_1, \ldots, x_k$, where x_i occurs c_i times. (Therefore $n = \sum_{i=1}^{k} c_i$.) Prove that any comparison-based sorting algorithm must use

$$\Omega \left(\log \frac{n!}{c_1! c_2! \ldots c_k!} \right)$$

comparisons in the worst case to sort the list. (The algorithm does not know ahead of time the number and distribution of the duplicates.)

34. Show that $2n - 1$ comparisons are both sufficient and necessary to merge two sorted lists $A_0, \ldots, A_{n-1}$ and $B_0, \ldots, B_{n-1}$. (Hint for the lower bound: Show that if $B_i < A_i$ for each i and $A_i < B_{i+1}$ for each $i < n - 1$, then each of the comparisons $B_i :: A_i$ and $A_i :: B_{i+1}$ must actually be made.)

35. You are given a sequence of n elements to sort. The input is a sequence of $\lceil n/m \rceil$ subsequences each of length at most m, with all the elements in each subsequence less than all the elements in the next.

a. Show that the input can be sorted in time $O(n \log m)$.

b. Show that any algorithm for solving this problem takes time $\Omega(n \log m)$. (It is *not* sufficient simply to combine the lower bounds for the subsequences.)

11.6 **36.** Show how Radix Sort would be used to sort the numbers 217, 045, 232, 311, 565, 927, 361, 252, 087, 143, 409, 275, 511, 806, 695 by breaking them into their decimal digits.

37. Use Radix Exchange Sort to sort the numbers whose decimal representations are 160, 228, 756, 475, 170, 082, 616, 729, 570, 749, 643, 360, 158.

11.7 **38.** Joe's Sorting Shoppe uses Balanced Multiway Merge with 4 tape drives. Joe has a little capital to invest in making his Shoppe more efficient. For $500 each he can buy more tape drives of the same model as the ones he already has, and for $250 each he can upgrade his existing tape drives to run 50% faster. If he has $1000 to spend, should he buy or upgrade?

39. Consider Polyphase Merge Sort with three tapes and with $r = 9$ runs. Four empty runs must be introduced to bring the number of runs up to the next Fibonacci number. Investigate the consequences of

a. putting two empty runs on each of the initially nonempty tapes;

b. putting all four empty runs on one of those tapes.

40. Illustrate the number of runs on the various tapes as Polyphase Merge Sort is run on four tapes with 24, 20, 13, and 0 runs initially. Show the length of the runs on each tape, on the hypothesis that the runs were all of equal length initially. Calculate the average number of times a datum is moved in this process, and compare the result to the number of times a datum would be moved if the four tapes were used to sort the 57 runs by Balanced Multiway Merge instead, starting with 29, 28, 0, and 0 runs on the four tapes.

41. In general, if T tapes are used to implement Polyphase Merge Sort, how many runs should be on the tapes initially to leave a single nonempty tape containing one run at the end? Explain your answer.

42. Show the runs that replacement selection would generate, assuming that the available buffer space can hold only 3 numbers and the input is the sequence 583, 918, 946, 701, 528, 457, 195, 158, 785, 103, 014, 733, 864, 007, 203, 052, 602, 120, 771, 632, 660, 642, 541, 319.

43. Prove that replacement selection produces a single sorted run if and only if no item in the input is preceded by more than $b - 1$ items that ought to follow it, where b is the size of the buffer.

44. Explain how to make the replacement selection algorithm somewhat more efficient by refraining from organizing the next-run items into a heap until the current-run heap is completely exhausted.

45. This problem concerns the length of the *first* run that is produced when replacement selection is used with an initially empty buffer of size b and the input is random.

    a. Explain on an intuitive level why the expected length of the first run is less than the expected length of subsequent runs.

    b. Let α be the expected length of the first run if the buffer were of size one. That is, α is the expected length of the initial monotonically increasing sequence of items in a random permutation of a very large collection of items. Show that the expected length of the first run when a buffer of size b is used is αb.

    c. Show that $\alpha = e - 1$. (Hint: This can be done by counting permutations of various kinds and using the infinite series $e = \sum_{i=0}^{\infty} 1/i!$, or by using the snowplow metaphor and a bit of differential calculus.)

11.8 **46.** Let k be a fixed positive integer. Describe a simple nonrecursive algorithm that finds the kth smallest of a set of n numbers.

47. In the analysis of the linear-time median algorithm, show that the inequality (2) is satisfied whenever $k \geq 40$. Is 40 the smallest number with this property?

48. As described in the text, the linear-time algorithm for finding the median requires $\Theta(n)$ additional memory. Show how to find the median of n numbers in $O(n)$ time using only $O(\log n)$ memory.

49. It is not hard to develop a version of the linear-time algorithm for finding the median that works by segmenting the table into blocks of length 7 or 9. How might a version of the algorithm work that uses blocks of an even length, such as 6 or 8? Can the blocks be of length 3 or 4?

50. Design an algorithm for finding the median that is based on the partitioning step of Quick Sort. What are the worst-case and expected time complexity of your algorithm? Can it be generalized to find the kth largest, where k is a parameter that is an input to the algorithm?

51. Let $T[0 .. n - 1]$ be a table of n data items that can be compared for equality but not for relative order; likewise the data elements cannot be used as indices into another table. (Therefore it would be inherently impossible to sort the table, for example, since there is no notion of one element being "smaller" than another.) Find a linear-time algorithm for determining whether the table has a **majority** element, that is, an element that occurs in more than $n/2$ of the table positions. (You may allocate additional tables or other structures to contain elements of T, numbers, or other data, and you may do ordinary arithmetic on numbers, but the only thing you can do with elements of the table T is to move them around and to tell whether two are the same.)

52. The **mode** of a table is the item that occurs most frequently; for example, the mode of 4, 5, 5, 3, 5, 1, 2, 4 is 5.

    a. Show how to find the mode of a sorted table in linear time.

    b. Show how to find the mode of a table in time $O(n \log(n/m))$, where n is the size of the table and m is the number of times the mode occurs. (Hint: Maintain two collections, S and T. S contains items together with exact counts of their frequency in the input. T contains "disjoint multisets" of items; that is, each member of T is a collection of input items, possibly containing duplicates; but no member of a collection in T belongs either to S or to any other of the collections in T. Initially S is empty and T contains just one collection, namely, the entire input table. Repeatedly subdivide the largest collection in T and move its median to S.)

References

Knuth's Sorting and Searching, *cited on page 44, is a good general reference on most of the classical sorting algorithms. Shell Sort was first described in*

D. L. Shell, "A High-Speed Sorting Procedure," *Communications of the ACM* **2** (1959), pp. 30–32.

The analysis of Shell Sort remains mysterious, although progress in understanding it has been made in recent years. It has long been known that there are sequences of $O(\log n)$ increments for which Shell Sort runs in time $O(n^{3/2})$ in the worst case. On the other hand there are sequences of $O((\log n)^2)$ increments for which the running time is $O(n(\log n)^2)$; see

V. R. Pratt, *Shellsort and Sorting Networks*, Garland Publishing Company, 1979.

Improvements of the $O(n^{3/2})$ behavior for sequences of only $O(\log n)$ increments were obtained first to $O(n^{4/3})$, in

R. Sedgewick, "A New Upper Bound for Shellsort," *Journal of Algorithms* **7** (1986), pp. 159–173,

and then to $O(n^{1+\epsilon/\sqrt{\log n}})$, for any fixed $\epsilon > 0$, by

J. Incerpi and R. Sedgewick, "Improved Upper Bounds on Shellsort," *Journal of Computer and System Sciences* **31** (1985), pp. 210–224.

However, it is still unknown whether any version of Shell Sort runs in time $O(n \log n)$, how fast Shell Sort might run with only $O(\log n)$ increments, and what is the exact complexity of Shell Sort with simple sequences of increments such as the $3k+1$ sequence that seems to work so well in practice. Heap Sort was developed by J. W. Williams and R. W. Floyd; see the citations on page 338. The improvements discussed in Problem 11 are from

R. W. Floyd, "Algorithm 245—Treesort3," *Communications of the ACM* **7** (1964), p. 701,

and

S. Carlsson, "A Variant of Heapsort with an Almost Optimal Number of Comparisons," *Information Processing Letters* **24** (1987), pp. 247–250.

There is an in-place Merge algorithm (see Problem 15) that runs in linear time and uses no extra memory. It is described in

M. A. Kronrod, "An Optimal Ordering Algorithm without a Field of Operation," *Doklady Akademii Nauk SSSR* **186** (1969), pp. 1256–1258,

and in the solution to Problem 5.2.4-18 on page 623 of Knuth's Sorting and Searching. *A stable version of this merging algorithm is presented in*

L. T. Pardo, "Stable Sorting and Merging with Optimal Space and Time Bounds," *SIAM Journal on Computing* **6** (1977), pp. 351–372.

Quick Sort was discovered by C. A. R. Hoare in about 1959; the first published versions are

C. A. R. Hoare, "Algorithm 63: Partition, and Algorithm 64: Quicksort," *Communications of the ACM* **4** (1961), p. 321;

C. A. R. Hoare, "Quicksort," *Computer Journal* **5** (1962), pp. 10–15.

It is an interesting algorithm from both a theoretical and a practical standpoint. The versions presented here are due to Robert Sedgewick. For details, see

R. Sedgewick, *Quicksort,* Garland Publishing Company, 1980;

R. Sedgewick, "The Analysis of Quicksort Programs," *Acta Informat.* **7** (1977), pp. 327–355;

R. Sedgewick, "Implementing Quicksort Programs," *Communications of the ACM* **21** (1978), pp. 847–857.

Distributive Partitioning Sort (Problem 24) is from

W. Dobosiewicz, "Sorting by Distributive Partitioning," *Information Processing Letters* **7** (1978), pp. 1–6.

By taking advantage of the fixed-precision arithmetic and logical operations that are available on digital computers, as well as the comparison instructions, it is theoretically possible to "beat" the Information-Theoretic Lower Bound and to sort n numbers in $O(n \log n / \log \log n)$ time. See

M. L. Fredman and D. E. Willard, "BLASTING through the Information Theoretic Barrier with FUSION TREES," *Proceedings, 22nd Annual ACM Symposium on Theory of Computing,* 1990, pp. 1–7.

The analysis of the expected length of the runs produced by replacement selection was initially achieved by Betty Jane Gassner in 1958; the published version is

B. J. Gassner, "Sorting by Replacement Selection," *Communications of the ACM* **10** (1967), pp. 89–93.

The results of Problem 45 are established in this article. Knuth also obtained these results in

D. E. Knuth, "Length of Strings for a Merge Sort," *Communications of the ACM* **6** (1963), pp. 685–688.

The "snowplow" analysis of replacement selection is from Knuth's Sorting and Searching; *Knuth attributes it to E. F. Moore. The linear-time algorithm for finding the median (or any other ordinal value in a set of numbers) was discovered by*

M. Blum, R. W. Floyd, V. R. Pratt, R. L. Rivest, and R. E. Tarjan, "Time Bounds for Selection," *Journal of Computer and Systems Sciences* **7**, 4 (1972), pp. 448–461.

A more complicated but significantly faster version is described in

A. Schönhage, M. Paterson, and N. Pippenger, "Finding the Median," *Journal of Computer and Systems Sciences* **13** (1976), pp. 184–199.

Problem 52 on finding the mode is from

I. Munro and P. M. Spira, "Sorting and Searching in Multisets," *SIAM Journal on Computing* **5** (1976), pp. 1–8.

12

Graphs

12.1 GRAPHS AND THEIR REPRESENTATIONS

Graphs are among the most important mathematical tools of computer science. A graph consists of a set of points and a set of lines connecting pairs of points (Figure 12.1 gives a few examples). But this simple idea is an abstraction that models a wealth of problems. For example:

1. An airline company offers flights between certain cities. But not every pair of cities is served by a nonstop flights; sometimes you must make a connection. This situation can be modelled as a graph in which the cities are the points and there are lines connecting pairs of cities with nonstop service.

2. One of the traditions of mapmaking is that adjacent regions of a map (countries, states, or whatever) should always have different colors. This problem can be modelled using graphs; each region is a point and there is a line between each pair of adjacent regions. The problem is then to assign a color to each point such that no line connects two points of the same color. Figure 12.2 gives an example of a map and the associated graph.

3. Many games can be modelled as graphs. Each possible "situation" or "configuration" of the game is a point and each line represents a legal move. (Of course, the graph of a given game may be extremely large; the graph of chess, for example, has over one hundred million points just for the first six moves!) There is a complication here: for most games, there must be an asymmetry in the lines of the graph, because moves can be made in only one direction—one example is tic-tac-toe, in which the reverse of any legal move would be an illegal erasure. Thus when modelling games (and many similar problems) we typically use *directed* graphs, in which each line has a direction indicated by an arrowhead.

4. A classical use of graphs is in modelling the Travelling Salesman Problem discussed on page 59: given a set of cities and the distance between each pair of cities, find a route that visits every city and minimizes the total travel

424

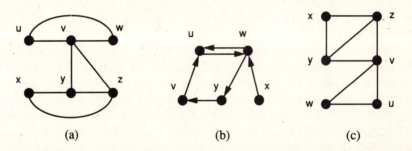

Figure 12.1 Three graphs. (a) and (c) are undirected graphs, (b) is a directed graph. The placement of the vertices on the paper is immaterial when we draw graphs; for example, (a) and (c) are in fact depictions of the same graph.

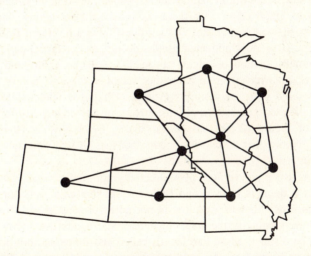

Figure 12.2 A map and its associated undirected graph. Each region is represented by a vertex, and an edge joins each pair of vertices that correspond to bordering regions.

distance. Here we may use an undirected graph, but each line contains a cost as an auxiliary piece of data.

Before considering how to represent graphs within the computer we need some definitions and terminology. An **undirected graph** is an ordered pair consisting of two sets: a finite, nonempty set whose elements are called the **vertices** of the graph, and a set of **edges** each of which is a set consisting of two distinct vertices. For example, let V be the set $\{u, v, w, x, y, z\}$ and let

$$E = \{\{u, v\}, \{w, u\}, \{y, x\}, \{y, v\}, \{w, v\}, \{y, z\}, \{v, z\}, \{x, z\}\}.$$

Then $G = \langle V, E \rangle$ is the graph depicted in Figure 12.1(a). If $\{v_1, v_2\}$ is an edge of graph G then v_1 and v_2 are said to be **adjacent** vertices; we also say that

v_1 and v_2 are **neighbors** of each other and that they are the **endpoints** of the edge $\{v_1, v_2\}$.

This simple definition merits a few additional comments. First, we have not placed any restriction at all on the nature of the vertices of a graph. In the examples just given the vertices are cities, game configurations, and regions of a map. In general, vertices may represent arbitrary entities, or may be simply places where auxiliary information is stored. The only requirement is that a graph must have at least one vertex. On the other hand, it is quite possible for E to be empty—that is, a graph need not have any edges at all. Consider, for example, the flight schedule of the airline during a work stoppage, or a world consisting entirely of island states, or any graph with only a single vertex.

As we saw in the third example above, sometimes it is important to assign a direction to graph edges. Or reconsider the airline example, and suppose that there exist two cities A and B such that flights are offered from A to B, but not from B to A. Undirected graphs do not model this situation because of the symmetric nature of edges. Instead, we define a **directed graph** as a pair $\langle V, E \rangle$ in which V is a nonempty set of vertices as before, and E is a set of *ordered pairs* of distinct vertices. On paper, directed graphs look just like undirected graphs except with arrows on the edges. So, for example, the graph of Figure 12.1(b) has edges $\langle v, u \rangle$, $\langle u, w \rangle$, $\langle w, u \rangle$, $\langle x, w \rangle$, $\langle w, y \rangle$, and $\langle y, v \rangle$. Notice that a "two-way" edge consists of two separate edges in a directed graph.

When u and v are vertices of a directed graph and $e = \langle u, v \rangle$ is an edge, we say that e **departs** from u and **enters** v. In this case, v is adjacent to u (and is thus a neighbor of u) but u is not adjacent to v unless $\langle v, u \rangle$ is also an edge of the graph. By the way, our definitions require that the two vertices of an edge be distinct; edges like $\langle u, u \rangle$, called **self-loops**, are not permitted in our version of directed graphs, although they are sometimes used in other contexts.

There are a large number of abstract operations that we might want to perform on a graph $G = \langle V, E \rangle$:

MakeGraph(V): Return a graph containing vertices V (and no edges).

Vertices(G): Return V, the set of vertices of G.

Edges(G): Return E, the set of edges of G.

Neighbors(v, G): Return the set of neighbors in G of vertex v.

AddVertex(v, G): Add a new vertex v to G.

AddDirectedEdge(u, v, G): Add a new edge $\langle u, v \rangle$ to G.

AddUndirectedEdge(u, v, G): Add a new edge $\{u, v\}$ to G.

DeleteVertex(v, G): Delete a vertex v from G, along with all edges that have v as an endpoint.

DeleteEdge(u, v, G): Delete an edge from G.

By convention, these operations are undefined in error situations such as deleting a nonexistent vertex from a graph. The graph algorithms of this chapter frequently make implicit rather than explicit use of the abstract operations; for example, a code fragment of the form '**foreach neighbor** w **of** v **do** ...' would actually be implemented using the *Neighbors* operation.

Now let G be a (directed or undirected) graph with vertices $v_1, v_2, \ldots, v_n$. Let M_G be a two-dimensional array where $M_G[i, j] = 1$ if v_j is a neighbor of v_i, and $M_G[i, j] = 0$ otherwise. For example, if G is the graph of Figure 12.1(b) then M_G is

$$
\begin{array}{c@{\quad}ccccc}
 & u & v & w & x & y \\
\begin{array}{c} u \\ v \\ w \\ x \\ y \end{array}
&
\left(\begin{array}{ccccc}
0 & 0 & 1 & 0 & 0 \\
1 & 0 & 0 & 0 & 0 \\
1 & 0 & 0 & 0 & 1 \\
0 & 0 & 1 & 0 & 0 \\
0 & 1 & 0 & 0 & 0
\end{array}\right)
\end{array}
$$

where we have added labels to make the indexing clear. Notice that when G is an undirected graph, M_G is necessarily symmetric; that is, $M_G[i, j] = M_G[j, i]$ for every i and j. Furthermore, $M_G[i, i] = 0$ for every i whether G is directed or undirected.

The array M_G is called the **adjacency matrix** of G, and is the simplest way to represent G within computer memory. It is particularly attractive when no additional information needs to be stored with vertices, so that the vertices can be integers and can be used directly as indices. (If the vertices have other information they can still be stored as records, each with a field containing the integer index of the vertex into the adjacency matrix; an auxiliary array can be used, if necessary, to find the record of the vertex associated with a given index.) The abstract operations can be implemented in a straightforward manner. The only difficulty comes when trying to add or delete a vertex, for then the size of the matrix must be changed. Of course, this problem is not important for algorithms that operate on static graphs, in which vertices and edges are neither added nor deleted.

Although it is simple, the adjacency matrix representation is not always as efficient as we would like. For example, to find the neighbors of a given vertex v we must examine $n - 1$ entries of M_G regardless of the number of neighbors v actually has—even if v has no neighbors at all! For this reason, graphs are frequently represented by **adjacency lists**: with each vertex keep a list of its neighbors. The whole graph is then represented by the set of its vertices, which may themselves be stored in a list. (Here there is no question of auxiliary indices; each vertex is represented as a record with a field called Neighbors and as many other fields as desired.) This representation has the advantage that vertices can be added and deleted as easily as edges. On the other hand, it takes more time to determine whether two given vertices are adjacent, since a list must be searched; also, adjacency lists typically require more memory than adjacency matrices.

Sometimes the edges of a graph as well as the vertices must store auxiliary information, as in the Travelling Salesman Problem. If so, edges can also be represented as records with as many fields as necessary. If adjacency lists are used then each vertex can store a list of pointers to edge records rather than to vertex records. A similar variation on the adjacency matrix representation is possible: let $M_G[i, j]$ be a pointer to the appropriate edge record when v_i is adjacent to v_j, and $M_G[i, j] = \Lambda$ otherwise.

A few words are in order about the "size" of a graph. In particular, what does it mean to say that an algorithm on graphs runs in linear time, or quadratic time, or polynomial time? The most obvious measure of the size of a graph G is the number of its vertices, which we denote by $|G|$ or simply by n. But the number of edges of the graph, which we denote by e, must be taken into account as well. A graph with n vertices may have as many as $n^2 - n$ edges or as few as 0 edges; thus, for example, an algorithm that runs in time $\Theta(e)$ would be preferable to one that runs in time $\Theta(n^2)$, since the former would be faster for graphs with relatively few edges. But such algorithms are rarely possible, since such an algorithm would not even be able to examine each vertex of a graph with very few edges. (We frequently speak of **sparse** graphs as those that contain relatively few edges, and **dense** graphs as those that contain relatively many edges.)

In light of this discussion, the time bound of a graph algorithm is often expressed using a function of both n and e. If the time of algorithm T is (say) $O(n + e)$, then T has enough time to examine each vertex and each edge regardless of how sparse or dense the graph is. Moreover, for very sparse graphs T will be linear in the number of vertices, whereas for very dense graphs it will be linear in the number of edges. Thus we would have no qualms calling T a fast algorithm.

Still another consideration is the choice of representation. For instance, the code fragment '**foreach edge** E **in** G ...' can be implemented in time $O(n+e)$ using adjacency lists, but requires time $\Omega(n^2)$ if only an adjacency matrix is available. Thus any discussion of the time bounds of a graph algorithm must include some consideration of the representation to be used. Certain algorithms may benefit from special representations: for example, when implementing an algorithm that requires frequent loops over all edges of a graph, it might be advantageous to represent the graph with a list of its edges and nothing more. The space required to represent a graph can also be measured in these terms; representation with an adjacency matrix typically uses space $\Theta(n^2)$, while representation with adjacency lists uses space $\Theta(n+e)$. But we must be careful of the multiplicative constants here, since the adjacency matrix uses n^2 *bits*, while the adjacency list method uses e *records* each of which contains at least one pointer plus other information.

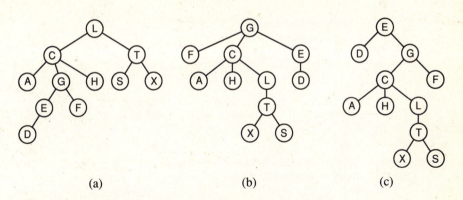

(a)   (b)   (c)

Figure 12.3 Three pictures of the same tree: (a) rooted at L, (b) rooted at G, (c) rooted at E. The height of the tree, the depth of each vertex, and the parent of each vertex all depend on which vertex is drawn at the root, but in each case the tree has the same vertices and edges.

Trees

Trees were defined in Chapter 4 as a special kind of directed graph.* Trees are such an important class of graphs that they deserve particular study. In this section we shall develop characterizations of trees that will be useful later; doing so also provides an opportunity to set forth more useful terminology and concepts about graphs in general. (Although we are mainly concerned with undirected graphs in this section, for completeness we shall extend new terminology to directed graphs where appropriate.)

The first thing to point out is that the concept of a "root" is in certain ways immaterial to the property of "tree-ness." Think of trees for a moment as *undirected* graphs—that is, erase the downward-pointing arrowhead on each edge. It may not be obvious, but now *any* vertex can serve as the root of the tree. That is, we can pick up the graph by any vertex and shake it out, and the resulting object is still a tree (although for some vertices a child becomes the parent and the former parent becomes a child; see Figures 12.3 and 12.4). Therefore we avoid defining trees in terms of roots, parents, and children, and use instead a definition that captures a property crucial to the important role of trees in computer science.

We first give some supporting terminology. A **path** in an undirected graph G is a sequence of vertices $\langle v_0, v_1, \ldots, v_n \rangle$ where $\{v_i, v_{i+1}\}$ is an edge of G for each $0 \leq i < n$; such a path is called a path from v_0 to v_n, or a path between v_0 and v_n. (Informally, a path is said to **contain** the n edges $\{v_i, v_{i+1}\}$ as well as the vertices v_i, even though only vertices appear in the formal definition.) The **length** of the path is n. For example, in Figure 12.1 $\langle u, v, y, z, v, w \rangle$ is

---

*In Chapter 4 we used the alternative terminology *node* instead of *vertex*, and the definition of a *path* in a tree was also slightly different from the one in this chapter.

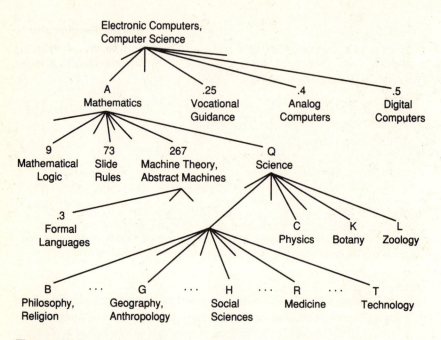

Figure 12.4 The tree of Figure 4.2 on page 98, redrawn from a more parochial point of view.

a path of length 5 from u to w. A path is **simple** if $v_1, \ldots, v_n$ are distinct vertices; that is, a simple path never encounters any vertex more than once (except that the first vertex might also be the last vertex). If a graph has a path between two vertices, it necessarily has a simple path between the same two vertices (Problem 5). These definitions also apply to directed graphs, replacing undirected edges with directed edges.

A **tree** is an undirected graph T that satisfies the following property: given any two vertices u and v of T, there is a unique simple path from u to v. It is straightforward to show that the definition in Chapter 4 agrees with this new definition once we have converted from directed to undirected graphs (Problem 6). We use the term **rooted tree** when it is important to pick a particular root and consider parents and children with respect to that root. Trees have a number of nice properties, but to study them we need some further definitions. An undirected graph is **connected** if there is at least one path between any two vertices; informally, this means that the graph is in one "piece." A path in a directed or undirected graph is a **cycle** if its first and last vertices are identical and if no two successive edges are the same. (Consequently, a cycle in an undirected graph must have length at least 3, while a cycle in a directed graph may have length 2.) A **simple cycle** is a cycle that is also a simple path; if a graph has a cycle starting and ending at v then it must have a simple cycle that starts and ends at v (a consequence of Problem 5). We make no distinction among cycles that differ only in starting from different vertices or in reversing the direction; that is, if $\langle v_0, v_1, \ldots, v_{n-1}, v_0 \rangle$ is a cycle, then $\langle v_j, v_{j+1}, \ldots, v_{n-1}, v_0, v_1, \ldots, v_{j-1}, v_j \rangle$ is the same cycle for any $0 \le j < n$. A graph is **disconnected** if it is not connected and is **acyclic** if it has no cycles at all.

■ **THEOREM** *(Tree Characterization, Part I)* Let $T = \langle V, E \rangle$ be a tree. Then T has the following properties:
1. T is connected;
2. T is acyclic;
3. deleting any edge of T yields a disconnected graph;
4. if $u, v \in V$ and $e = \{u, v\}$ is not an edge of T, then adding e to T yields a graph with exactly one simple cycle, and that cycle contains e;
5. T has exactly $n - 1$ edges, where n is the number of vertices of T.

PROOF Since these properties are fairly obvious from our mental picture of trees, we sketch the proof of (3) and leave the rest to Problem 7. Let $e = \{u, v\}$ be any edge of T. Then $\langle u, v \rangle$ is the unique simple path from u to v, and if e is deleted the resulting graph is disconnected since there is no path from u to v. □

Clearly, not every connected undirected graph is a tree. In fact, for each part of the Theorem we can find an undirected graph that satisfies that property but is not a tree (Problem 8). However, certain combinations of these properties do imply that an undirected graph is a tree; the next Theorem gives the details. We need one definition: an undirected or directed graph G is **complete** if u is a neighbor of v for every pair of distinct vertices u and v, that is, if G contains every possible edge.

■ **THEOREM** *(Tree Characterization, Part II)* Let G be an undirected graph with n vertices. If G satisfies any of the following conditions, then G is a tree:
1. G is connected and acyclic;
2. G is connected, but deleting any edge yields a disconnected graph;
3. G is not complete, and adding any edge to G yields a graph with exactly one simple cycle, which contains the added edge;
4. G is connected and has exactly $n - 1$ edges;
5. G is acyclic and has exactly $n - 1$ edges.

We leave the proofs of (1) through (3) to the exercises. Parts (4) and (5) are proved using the following Lemma, which is interesting in its own right:

■ **LEMMA**
a. A connected graph with n vertices has at least $n - 1$ edges.
b. An acyclic graph with n vertices has at most $n - 1$ edges.

PROOF To prove this Lemma we introduce the final terminology of this section. A **subgraph** of a (directed or undirected) graph $G = \langle V, E \rangle$ is a graph $G' = \langle V', E' \rangle$ such that $V' \subseteq V$ and $E' \subseteq E$. A **connected component** of an undirected graph G is a maximal connected subgraph of G; that is, if G' is a connected component of G then G' is *not* a subgraph of any larger connected subgraph of G. Informally, the connected components of a graph G are simply its disjoint pieces. Two extreme cases are these: any connected graph has a single connected component (consisting of the entire graph), and if a graph has no edges at all, each of its vertices lies in a separate edgeless connected component.

To prove part (a) of the Lemma, consider a graph G with n vertices and no edges; such a graph has n connected components. Now add edges to G; each edge either joins two vertices that are in the same connected component (leaving the number of components unchanged) or it joins two vertices that are in different components (reducing the number of components by 1). Therefore, at least $n - 1$ edges must be added before there is only a single component. To prove part (b), let G be any acyclic graph with n vertices. Suppose G has $k \geq 1$ connected components whose sizes are $n_1, n_2, \ldots, n_k$. Each component is acyclic and connected, hence each component is a tree and has one more vertex than it has edges. So the total number of edges in G is $(n_1-1)+(n_2-1)+\cdots+(n_k-1) = n-k \leq n-1$. $\square$

Now we can show parts (4) and (5) of the second part of the Tree Characterization Theorem. In (4), G must be acyclic, for if it had a cycle then deleting any edge from that cycle would produce a connected graph with $n - 2$ edges, contrary to the Lemma. In (5), G must be connected, for otherwise adding an edge between two vertices in different components of G would yield an acyclic graph with n edges, contrary to the Lemma. In either case G is connected and acyclic, and is therefore a tree by part (1) of the Theorem.

12.2 GRAPH SEARCHING

Suppose we are given a directed or undirected graph G and vertices v and w of G; how can we determine whether there exists a path from v to w in G? Intuitively, we would like to start at v and examine all vertices that can be reached from v by traversing edges of G, stopping when w is reached or when all vertices reachable from v have been examined. More generally, we may want to perform an arbitrary operation—called *Visit*, as in Chapter 4—on each vertex. This process is called a **search** of G starting at v. There are two differences between searching G and simply iterating over the vertices of G. First of all, an iteration visits every vertex of G by definition, while searching may reach only a subset of the vertices. In fact, a search starting at v visits exactly those vertices w such that there is a path in G from v to w. (In the case of an undirected graph a search starting at v will reach exactly those vertices in the same connected component as v.) Secondly, an iteration visits the vertices of G in some order unrelated to vertex adjacencies, whereas (as we shall see) searching is most often used precisely because of the order in which vertices are visited.

Breadth-First Search

If v and w are vertices of a directed or undirected graph, the **distance** between v and w is the length of a shortest path from v to w; more informally, the distance between v and w is the minimum number of edges that must be traversed to get from v to w. The definitions imply that the distance from a vertex v to itself is zero, since the sequence $\langle v \rangle$ is a path of length zero from v to v. If there is no path from v to w, the distance from v to w is undefined (although sometimes in this case we say that the distance is infinite). In the graph of Figure 12.1(b) on page 425, for example, the distance from u to y is 2, while the distance from u to v is 3 and the distance from u to x is undefined.

In a **breadth-first search**, the order in which vertices are visited is as follows: vertex v is visited first, then the vertices adjacent to v, then the vertices adjacent to those vertices (omitting any already visited), and so forth. In other words, we first visit v (which is at distance 0 from v), then all vertices at distance 1 from v, then all vertices at distance 2, and so on. Speaking metaphorically we might say that the search proceeds in an expanding circle centered at v. Figure 12.5(a) gives an example of breadth-first search. When the graph is a tree with root v, a breadth-first search visits the vertices in the same order as a level-order traversal of the tree (page 108).

An implementation of breadth-first search is sketched in Algorithm 12.1. It requires a one-bit field called Encountered in each vertex; this field is cleared at the start of the search and is set when the vertex is reached for the first time, at which point the vertex is placed in a queue of vertices to be visited. When a vertex is dequeued and visited each of its neighbors is added to the end of the queue, except that vertices already reached (as determined by the Encountered bit) are not reprocessed. The use of a queue to store encountered but unvisited vertices insures that all vertices at distance d from v are visited before any vertices at distance greater than d. (See Problem 15. Compare this algorithm with the level-order traversal in Algorithm 4.12 on page 124; the only difference is that no Encountered field is necessary when the graph is known to be a tree, since each vertex is encountered exactly once.) If the procedure *Visit* requires constant time per vertex and adjacency lists are used to represent G, a breadth-first search can be carried out in time $O(v + e)$: clearing all the Encountered fields at the beginning of the algorithm requires time $\Theta(v)$, but thereafter each edge of G is processed at most twice (once as each of its endpoints is *Visit*ed) and each vertex is enqueued, dequeued, and visited at most once.

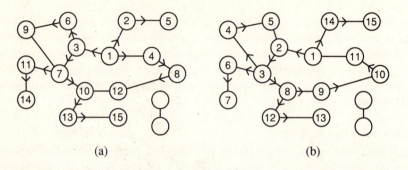

(a)   (b)

Figure 12.5 An undirected graph searched by (a) breadth-first and (b) depth-first search. In each case the search starts at the vertex labelled 1; the labels in the vertices show the order in which they are first encountered. (For breadth-first search this is also the order in which they are *Visited*. For depth-first search it is the order in which they are *PreVisited*; the *PostVisit* order is 5, 4, 7, 6, 11, 10, 9, 13, 12, 8, 3, 2, 15, 14, 1.) The arrows, which are not part of the graph, illustrate edges that were followed to previously unencountered vertices. Only the connected component containing the starting vertex is searched.

---

procedure *BreadthFirstSearch*(**graph** G, **vertex** v):
{Breadth-first search of G starting at v}
    foreach vertex w **in** G **do** Encountered(w) ← **false**
    {Q is a queue storing encountered but unvisited vertices}
    Q ← *MakeEmptyQueue*( )
    Encountered(v) ← **true**
    Enqueue(v, Q)
    until *IsEmptyQueue*(Q) **do**
        {Process the next vertex}
        w ← *Dequeue*(Q)
        Visit(w)
        foreach neighbor w' **of** w **do**
            if not Encountered(w') **then**
                Encountered(w') ← **true**
                Enqueue(w', Q)

Algorithm 12.1 Breadth-first search. The procedure *Visit* is to be executed on each vertex reachable from v.

Here is a small but important point: Algorithm 12.1 doesn't completely determine the order in which vertices of G are visited. The reason is that the neighbors of each vertex may be processed in any order, and changing that order changes the overall order of the search, although all vertices at any given distance from v will be visited before vertices at any greater distance. The order in which the neighbors of w are processed depends on the way G is stored in memory and the way the abstract operation *Neighbors* is implemented.

The original problem was to determine whether there is a path between two given vertices of G. Breadth-first search can be used to solve this problem, but so can any other search procedure. However, since breadth-first search processes vertices in order of distance from the source vertex, it finds not only whether a path exists but also the length of a shortest path between the given vertices—that is, the distance between them. With only a little extra work we can obtain the entire path (Problem 16).

Depth-First Search

A second important graph search technique is **depth-first search**. The defining characteristic of depth-first search is that each vertex is completely explored as soon as it is first encountered; that is, the vertex is visited and all as-yet-unencountered neighbors of the vertex are immediately processed. But "processing" each neighbor entails applying this same procedure recursively. To understand the pattern of the resulting search, suppose that we start the search from v. First v is visited, then its first neighbor, say v_1, is encountered and visited. Now the neighbors of v_1 are considered; each in turn is visited and explored as far as possible before the next is examined. Only after all neighbors of v_1 (except for v) have been completely explored do we continue with the second neighbor of v. (Of course, the second neighbor of v may have been visited at some point during the exploration of v_1, in which case it is not processed further.) The name "depth-first" reflects the idea that the search proceeds ever deeper—farther from its starting point—moving from each vertex to a neighbor of that vertex, to a neighbor of the neighbor, and so forth, retreating to check other neighbors only when a vertex with no unencountered neighbors is reached and thus no further "forward" progress is possible. Figure 12.5(b) gives an example of depth-first search.

In a depth-first search there are actually two points at which we might apply the *Visit* operation to the vertices: a vertex might be visited as soon as it is encountered for the first time, just before its neighbors are processed (as in the description in the preceding paragraph), or the vertex might be visited after all of its neighbors are completely explored. To distinguish these possibilities we define separate operations *PreVisit* and *PostVisit* in connection with depth-first search. When G is a tree and the source vertex is the root, a depth-first search with *PreVisit* is exactly a preorder traversal of the tree, and a depth-first search with *PostVisit* is exactly a postorder traversal of the tree. And like tree traversal, depth-first search is most naturally implemented by a recursive algorithm (Algorithm 12.2).

Topological Sorting Suppose we are given a set $T = \{T_1, T_2, \ldots, T_n\}$ consisting of n tasks that must be carried out. Only one task can be performed at

---

procedure *DepthFirstSearch*(**graph** G, **vertex** v):
{Depth-first search in G starting at v}
    foreach vertex w **in** G **do** Encountered(w) $\leftarrow$ **false**
    RecursiveDFS(v)

procedure *RecursiveDFS*(**vertex** v):
    Encountered(v) $\leftarrow$ **true**
    PreVisit(v)
    foreach neighbor w **of** v **do**
        if not Encountered(w) **then** *RecursiveDFS*(w)
    PostVisit(v)

Algorithm 12.2 Outline of depth-first search. The procedure *PreVisit* is to be called on each vertex before processing its neighbors and *PostVisit* is to be called afterwards.

---

a time and each task must be completed before the next task is begun. Assume further that we are given a set of constraints on the order in which tasks can be performed. Each constraint is an ordered pair of tasks; if the pair $\langle T_i, T_j \rangle$ is a constraint, then task T_i must precede task T_j. The problem is to find an order (or **schedule**) in which we can carry out the tasks such that all of the constraints are obeyed.

For example, suppose there are five tasks $\{A, B, C, D, E\}$ and constraints $\langle C, E \rangle$, $\langle E, D \rangle$, $\langle D, A \rangle$, and $\langle E, A \rangle$. Then we could perform the tasks in order C, E, B, D, A, satisfying every constraint. On the other hand, the order C, D, A, B, E is not satisfactory since E must be performed before A. (Notice that B is completely unconstrained in this example—it may be performed first, last, or anywhere in between.) Not every set of constraints is satisfiable: if another constraint $\langle A, C \rangle$ is added to this example, then E must be performed before A, and A before C, but also C before E.

There is an obvious relationship between directed graphs and the constrained task problem: each task corresponds to a vertex, and each constraint corresponds to a (directed) edge between two vertices. Figure 12.6(a) depicts the graph corresponding to the example of the previous paragraph. Informally, the problem can be stated as follows: find a linear order for the vertices of G such that every edge of G points "forwards." More precisely, given a directed graph G with n vertices, determine an order v_1, v_2, $\ldots$, v_n for the vertices of G such that there is no edge $\langle v_i, v_j \rangle$ of G with $j < i$. Such an ordering is called a **topological sort** of G.

A directed graph that contains no cycles is called a **directed acyclic graph**, or **dag**. Clearly, if a directed graph G has a cycle, then it cannot be topologically sorted—note in Figure 12.6(b) how a cycle is formed when the final impossible

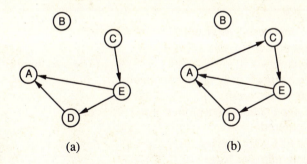

Figure 12.6 (a) Directed graph corresponding to the example of topological sorting in the text. (b) The same graph with an additional edge; this graph is not a dag and cannot be sorted.

constraint $\langle A, C \rangle$ is added to G. On the other hand, as we shall see, any dag can be topologically sorted.

A simple way to sort G is as follows. Find any vertex that has no entering edge, for example, either B or C in Figure 12.6(a). (Every dag has at least one such vertex; see Problem 20.) Call this vertex v_1; it clearly can be first in the sort since all of its departing edges will point forward and there are no entering edges that might point back. Now remove v_1 and all of its edges from G. The remaining graph is still a dag, so we can repeat the procedure to obtain v_2, the next vertex in the sort. Continue the process until G consists of a single vertex, which becomes v_n, the last vertex of the sort. The problem with this algorithm is its time complexity. With a straightforward approach it may require time proportional to the number of vertices remaining to find each vertex in the sort, yielding a time bound no better than $O(n^2)$.

We can use depth-first search to build a faster algorithm for topological sorting. In fact, the topological sort described in Algorithm 12.3 differs from the general depth-first search procedure only in that the entire graph must be explored, not just those vertices reachable from a given starting vertex. This is accomplished by modifying the main procedure to perform a depth-first search starting from *every* vertex of G. Of course, for many vertices there will be nothing to do, since they will have been visited during searches from other starting points.

Algorithm 12.3 has no *PreVisit*, but the *PostVisit* operation consists of assigning a number to each vertex, storing it in a field called Number; this number is the location of the vertex in the topological sort order. Recall that *PostVisit(v)* takes place just *after* v is completely explored, that is, just before the call of *WalkForSort* on v returns. (*WalkForSort* is called on each vertex exactly once.) Sort numbers are assigned in decreasing order: the first vertex that is completely explored receives number n, and so forth down to number 1.

It is not obvious that the ordering of the vertices produced by Algorithm 12.3

---

procedure *TopologicalSort*(**graph** *G*):
{*G* is the graph to be sorted}
    nextnumber ← |*G*| {The next number to assign}
    foreach vertex *v* **in** *G* **do** Encountered(*v*) ← **false**
    foreach vertex *v* **in** *G* **do**
        if not Encountered(*v*) **then** *WalkForSort*(*v*)

procedure *WalkForSort*(**vertex** *v*):
    Encountered(*v*) ← **true**
    foreach neighbor *w* **of** *v* **do**
        if not Encountered(*w*) **then** *WalkForSort*(*w*)
    Number(*v*) ← *nextnumber*
    nextnumber ← *nextnumber* − 1

Algorithm 12.3 Topological sort of a directed acyclic graph. The Number field of each vertex is set to its location in the sort order. Recall that |*G*| is the number of vertices of *G*.

---

does in fact constitute a topological sort.* To prove the correctness of the algorithm, let *v* and *w* be any two vertices of the dag *G* such that Number(*v*) < Number(*w*). We prove that ⟨*w*, *v*⟩ cannot be an edge of *G*.

Since vertices are numbered in decreasing order, *w* received its number before *v* did. At the moment that *w* received its number—that is, just after *w* was completely explored—Encountered(*v*) was either **true** or **false**. If Encountered(*v*) was **false** then ⟨*w*, *v*⟩ cannot be an edge of *G*, because the search of *w* would have followed that edge and encountered *v*, exploring and numbering it before returning. On the other hand, if Encountered(*v*) was **true** at this instant then *v* was encountered but not yet numbered, and an exploration of *v* was therefore in progress at that point. Since an exploration of *v* led to *w*, there must be a path in *G* from *v* to *w*. But then if ⟨*w*, *v*⟩ were an edge of *G* we could add it to that path to form a cycle in *G*, and this is impossible since *G* is a dag and has no cycles.

Notice that Algorithm 12.3 works only when the graph *G* is known to be a dag. But suppose *G* is an arbitrary directed graph; how can we tell whether *G* contains cycles, that is, whether *G* is a dag? One way is to assign a number to each vertex of *G* as in Algorithm 12.3, then check whether all edges do in fact point forward. But there are more clever algorithms for cycle detection; see Problem 23.

---

* In fact, the ordering is not even uniquely determined. As with depth-first search, the order produced by Algorithm 12.3 can depend on the order in which the neighbors of each vertex are processed, and moreover on the order in which vertices are processed in the second loop of the main procedure.

Biconnectivity Given an undirected graph G, it is easy to determine whether or not G is connected using either depth-first or breadth-first search: G is connected if and only if every vertex has been encountered upon completion of a single search (which can start anywhere).

Now let p_1 and p_2 be two simple paths in G, both from u to v. Two such paths are **vertex-disjoint** if no vertex (except for u and v) appears in both paths. An undirected graph is **biconnected** if, given any two distinct vertices u and v, there exist two vertex-disjoint paths from u to v. There is another way to formulate this definition. If G is a graph and v is a vertex of G, the graph $G - v$ is the graph obtained by deleting v from G, and also deleting all edges adjacent to v. A vertex v of G is a **cutvertex** of G (or an **articulation point** of G) if $G - v$ is not connected. We then say that a graph is **biconnected** if it has no cutvertices. (These two definitions of biconnectivity are equivalent for any graph that has more than two vertices; see Problem 24.) For example, the graph of Figure 12.1(a) on page 425 is not biconnected because vertex v is a cutvertex, but if the edge $\{u, x\}$ is added then the resulting graph is biconnected.

A graph can be tested for biconnectivity by deleting each vertex in turn and testing to see whether the remaining graph is connected, but this straightforward approach yields a time bound no better than $O(n^2)$. Depth-first search can be used to provide a much faster test for biconnectivity. Since every biconnected graph is connected, assume that G is a connected, undirected graph which is to be tested for biconnectivity.

To understand the approach, start with another look at the general depth-first search procedure, Algorithm 12.2. The recursive subroutine *RecursiveDFS* processes each vertex v by marking it encountered and considering its neighbors in turn. If a neighbor w has already been encountered the subroutine simply ignores it; we then say that the edge leading from v to w is **skipped**. When a neighbor w of v has not been encountered, *RecursiveDFS* is called recursively to process it. In this case, we say that the edge from v to w is **followed**. Now fix some starting vertex r for the search. Let T be the subgraph of G consisting of the vertices of G plus the followed edges; that is, T is just G with all skipped edges deleted. The following argument proves that T is in fact a tree. T contains all vertices of G by definition, and is connected since any depth-first search of G—which is assumed to be connected—reaches every vertex of G. Furthermore, if G contains n vertices then T contains $n - 1$ edges, since each vertex except for r is first encountered when some edge is followed (and no edge can be followed twice). Thus T is a tree by the second part of the Tree Characterization Theorem. It is natural to consider T as a rooted tree with root r; then v is the parent of w if and only if w is first encountered when the edge $\{v, w\}$ is followed from v.

The original graph G consists of T plus the skipped edges. The next crucial point to notice is that each skipped edge joins two vertices that are **ancestrally related** in T; that is, if $\{v, w\}$ is a skipped edge of G then either v is an ancestor

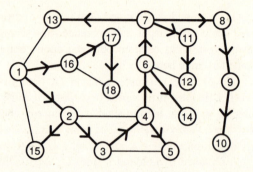

Figure 12.7 Depth-first search in an undirected graph. The search begins at the vertex labelled 1, and the vertices are labelled in the order they are encountered during the search. Followed edges are drawn with heavy lines and skipped edges with light lines; the arrows on the followed edges indicate the direction in which the edge was followed. When the skipped edges are deleted, the result is a tree; if vertex 1 is taken as the root of the tree then skipped edges join only ancestrally related vertices.

of w or w is an ancestor of v. To see this, let $\{v, w\}$ be any skipped edge of G, and suppose that the exploration of v was finished before the exploration of w was finished; we shall show that w must be an ancestor of v. (The other case is handled symmetrically.) Consider the instant at which exploration of v was completed. Clearly w must have been encountered already, for otherwise the edge $\{v, w\}$ would not have been skipped during the exploration of v. But then an exploration of w must be in progress at this instant, since we assumed that exploration of v completed before exploration of w. This exploration of w has progressed along a sequence of followed edges from w to v—that is, w is an ancestor of v. Since every edge of G is either part of T or is a skipped edge, it follows that *every* edge of G joins two vertices that are ancestrally related in T. Figure 12.7 shows an example of an undirected graph and the embedded tree of followed edges produced by a depth-first search.

This picture of the depth-first search process leads us to a precise characterization of the cutvertices of G. We must distinguish the root of T as a special case.

■ **LEMMA** Vertex r, the root of T, is a cutvertex of G if and only if it has more than one child in T.

PROOF Suppose u and v are distinct children of r. Then every path from u to v must contain r since there are no edges of G between different subtrees of T; thus r is a cutvertex. Conversely, if r has only one child v, then deleting r and all edges adjacent to it leaves G connected since the remainder of T is still connected; therefore in this case r is not a cutvertex. □

For example, in Figure 12.7, the root (vertex 1) is a cutvertex since it has two children 2 and 16. If the edge $\{1, 16\}$ were deleted and a new edge $\{2, 16\}$ added, the numbering of the graph would be unchanged but now 1 would no longer be a cutvertex since 2 would be its only child.

■ **LEMMA** Let v be any vertex of G other than r. Then v is a cutvertex of G if and only if it has a child w in T such that no skipped edge of G joins a descendant of w to a proper ancestor of v.

PROOF   (Recall that a *proper ancestor* of v is any ancestor of v other than v itself.) First, suppose that such a child w exists. Then any edge of G adjacent to a descendant of w either joins two descendants of w or is adjacent to v. (The reason is that edges of G join only ancestrally related vertices, and there are no edges between descendants of w and any proper ancestor of v by assumption.) Therefore, every path between w and the parent of v must contain v, so v is a cutvertex.

Now assume that no such children of v exist. We claim that for any vertex $u \neq v$ there is a path P_u not containing v between u and r. Once we prove this claim it follows that v is not a cutvertex, since any two vertices other than v can then be joined by a path (via r) not containing v. Obviously P_u exists if u is not a descendant of v. If u is a descendant of v, let w be that child of v that is an ancestor of u (w might be u itself). By assumption there is an edge of G between some descendant of w and some proper ancestor of v; we can use such an edge to "bypass" v in making the desired path P_u from u to r.   □

Again using Figure 12.7 as an example, vertex 7 is a cutvertex since one of its children, 8, has no descendant with a skipped edge leading back to a proper ancestor of 8. On the other hand, 4 is *not* a cutvertex, since the edge $\{3, 5\}$ joins a descendant of 5 (namely, 5 itself) to a proper ancestor of 4, and the edge $\{1, 13\}$ joins a descendant of 6 to a proper ancestor of 4. Notice that vertex 16 is a cutvertex even though the edge $\{18, 16\}$ joins a descendant of 17 to an ancestor of 16 (namely, to 16 itself)—the Lemma states that the ancestor must be a proper ancestor.

These ideas are exploited by Algorithm 12.4, which finds the cutvertices of a connected, undirected graph. Rather than numbering vertices in the order they are encountered we give each vertex a Depth field that stores its depth in the tree of followed edges rooted at *root*. The recursive function *WalkForCutVertices* sets this field with a standard depth-first search. The function *WalkForCutVertices* returns the minimum of the depths of the vertices encountered during the entire exploration of its argument v; as each neighbor of v is examined (and possibly explored recursively) we remember the smallest of all depths encountered, including those returned by recursive calls on *WalkForCutVertices*. As each descendant w of v is explored we can tell whether there is

---

procedure *FindCutVertices*(**undirected graph** *G*):
{Determine the cutvertices of graph *G*}
    foreach vertex *v* **in** *G* **do**
        CutVertex(*v*) ← **false**
        Depth(*v*) ← −1
    root ← any vertex of *G*
    Depth(*root*) ← 0
    WalkForCutVertices(*root*)
    if more than one neighbor of *root* has depth 1 **then**
        CutVertex(*root*) ← **true**

function *WalkForCutVertices*(**vertex** *v*): **integer**
{Walk *v* recursively; return the smallest depth encountered}
    mindepth ← Depth(*v*)
    foreach neighbor *w* **of** *v* **do**
        if Depth(*w*) = −1 **then**
            Depth(*w*) ← Depth(*v*) + 1
            m ← *WalkForCutVertices*(*w*)
            if *m* ≥ Depth(*v*) **and** *v* ≠ *root* **then**
                CutVertex(*v*) ← **true**
            mindepth ← min(*mindepth*, *m*)
        else
            mindepth ← min(*mindepth*, Depth(*w*))
    return *mindepth*

Algorithm 12.4 Find the cutvertices of a connected, undirected graph. Each vertex's CutVertex field is set to **true** if and only if the vertex is a cutvertex.

---

a descendant of *w* that is adjacent to a proper ancestor of *v*—such an ancestor would have depth less than Depth(*v*). (As in the Lemmas above, the root of the search is an exception and is handled specially in the main routine.) Notice that the test is applied only to descendants of *v* in the tree, not to all neighbors of *v*.

12.3 GREEDY ALGORITHMS ON GRAPHS

Minimum Spanning Trees

A communications network is to consist of a number of widely spaced relay stations called switches. Each switch will accept messages from nearby users of the network or from other switches, and will pass each message on towards its destination. The switches will communicate with each other using communications lines that must be purchased; the cost of each such line depends on the location of the two switches that it will connect—in general, longer lines are more expensive. There are $n(n-1)/2$ possible lines between n switches, but clearly it is not necessary to purchase every such line; it suffices to purchase enough lines so that there is at least one path between each pair of switches. How can we decide which communications lines to purchase to minimize the total cost?

More generally, let $G = \langle V, E \rangle$ be a connected undirected graph and let c be a function that assigns a positive **cost** to each edge of G. If $E' \subseteq E$ is any set of edges of G, we also write $c(E')$ to denote the total cost of the edges in E'. The problem is then to find a subset E' of the edges of G such that the undirected graph $G' = \langle V, E' \rangle$ is connected and such that $c(E')$ is minimal. (The assumption that G is connected ensures that such a set E' exists.)

The first point to note is that G' will surely be a tree, and therefore there are $|V| - 1$ edges in E'. For if G' is connected and is not a tree, then by the Tree Characterization Theorem it must have a cycle. But deleting any edge along this cycle yields a connected graph with smaller cost. The tree we are looking for is called a **minimum spanning tree** on the graph G with respect to the cost function c. There may be more than one minimum spanning tree for a given cost function and set of vertices, but all have the same total cost. There are two standard algorithms for finding minimum spanning trees:

- (Prim's Algorithm) Maintain two sets: a set E' of edges that is initially empty and a set N of vertices that initially contains a single vertex (any vertex at all). Repeat the following step $|V| - 1$ times: find an edge $e \in E$ of least cost that joins a vertex $u \in N$ to a vertex $v \notin N$, and add e to E' and v to N.
- (Kruskal's Algorithm) Maintain a set E' of edges, initially empty. Repeat the following step $|V| - 1$ times: find an edge $e \in E$ of least cost such that adding e to E' creates no cycles in $\langle V, E' \rangle$, and add e to E'.

Each of these algorithms is a greedy algorithm; at each step we take the cheapest possible action with no *a priori* certainty that doing so yields the cheapest possible overall result. The only difference between the algorithms is that Prim's algorithm builds the minimum spanning tree starting from an arbitrary vertex, using low-cost edges to connect new vertices into a single growing tree, whereas Kruskal's algorithm may "grow" large disconnected pieces of the tree before connecting them together. (By the way, ties may be broken arbitrarily in either algorithm.) The remarkable fact is that each of these algorithms always produces a minimum spanning tree. We will not consider Prim's algorithm further (except in Problem 30) but we will discuss an efficient implementation for Kruskal's algorithm after proving it correct.

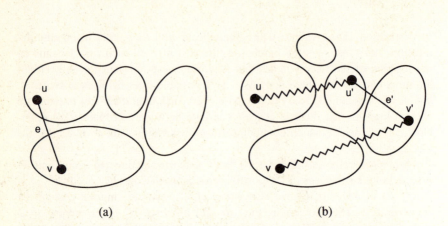

Figure 12.8 Illustration for the correctness proof of Kruskal's algorithm. (a) The graph $\langle V, E' \rangle$ and the new edge e. Each oval represents a connected component of $\langle V, E' \rangle$. (b) The path in F from u to v, which must contain an edge e' between distinct connected components of $\langle V, E' \rangle$. The set F' contains all of F except for e', and since it also contains e there is a path P' in F' from u' to v'.

Since adding an edge to a connected graph always creates a new cycle and since a connected component of a graph is a connected graph by definition, Kruskal's algorithm may be restated as follows: start with a graph consisting of vertices V and no edges, then at each step add a least-cost edge of G joining two distinct connected components of the graph constructed so far. If $\langle V, E \rangle$ is a graph and $E' \subseteq E$, a **connected extension** of E' with respect to E is any set of edges $F \subseteq E$ that contains E' and such that $\langle V, F \rangle$ is a connected graph. In this section the set E of available edges is always implicit; thus we refer more simply to connected extensions of E'. The proof of Kruskal's algorithm rests on the following Lemma, which states that taking the cheapest edge at each point leads to the cheapest solution overall:

■ **LEMMA** Let $\langle V, E \rangle$ be a connected graph and let $E' \subseteq E$ be such that the graph $\langle V, E' \rangle$ is not connected. Let $e \notin E'$ be a minimal-cost edge in E joining distinct connected components of $\langle V, E' \rangle$. Then there is a minimal-cost connected extension of E' that includes e.

PROOF Let the endpoints of e be u and v (Figure 12.8(a)). Let F be any minimal-cost connected extension of E'. If F contains e then there is nothing further to prove, so assume otherwise. Since $\langle V, F \rangle$ is connected, there is a path in $\langle V, F \rangle$ from u to v; this path must contain at least one edge $e' = \{u', v'\}$ that joins distinct connected components of $\langle V, E' \rangle$ since there is no path from u to v in $\langle V, E' \rangle$ (Figure 12.8(b)). Furthermore, $c(e) \leq c(e')$, since otherwise $c(e)$ is not minimal in $E - E'$.

Now let $F' = F \cup \{e\} - \{e'\}$; we claim that F' is a minimal-cost connected extension of E' that includes e. Obviously F' includes e, and it contains E' since $e' \notin E'$. Furthermore, $c(F') = c(F) + c(e) - c(e') \leq c(F)$. It remains only to prove that $G' = \langle V, F' \rangle$ is connected. To see this, first construct a path P' between u' and v' by taking the path in $\langle V, F \rangle$ from u to v and adjoining edge e, creating a cycle. Each edge of this cycle except for e' is in F'; thus deleting e' yields a path from u' to v' all of whose edges are in F' (Figure 12.8(b)). To show G' connected, let two arbitrary vertices be given and let P be the path between them in $\langle V, F \rangle$ (which is known to be connected). If P does not contain e' then it is also a path in $\langle V, F' \rangle$ and we are done. Otherwise, modify P by inserting the path P' in place of the edge e', producing a path in $\langle V, F' \rangle$.   □

Using this Lemma we can prove the correctness of Kruskal's algorithm with a simple induction on the number of edges in E'. Let K be the cost of a minimum spanning tree on G. Thus when E' is equal to the empty set it has a connected extension with cost K. At each step of the algorithm, the Lemma ensures that adding the edge chosen by Kruskal's algorithm yields a new set of edges that also has a connected extension with total cost K. Finally, when $\langle V, E' \rangle$ is connected, the total cost of E' must itself be K.

In fact, the Lemma proves something more. When E' starts as an empty set of edges, Kruskal's algorithm constructs a minimum spanning tree on G. But nowhere does the Lemma assume that E' is contained in a tree; E' is an arbitrary set of edges, possibly containing cycles. Therefore, Kruskal's algorithm solves the more general problem of finding a least-cost connected extension for an *arbitrary* graph. That is, if some of the communications lines in our network already exist (or are provided for free), even if they redundantly connect large portions of the network, we can still use Kruskal's algorithm to determine the cheapest set of lines that will ensure connectivity of the entire network.

Implementing Kruskal's Algorithm   Recall that the basic step in Kruskal's algorithm is to find and add an edge of least cost that joins two connected components of the graph. Let us break this operation into three subproblems: find an edge of least cost, determine whether a given edge joins two connected components of the graph-so-far, and add an edge to the graph-so-far (thus combining two connected components into one).

The key to the first subproblem is that when an edge cannot be added to the graph (because both of its endpoints lie in the same connected component) it will never be useful again, since the connected component in which it lies will never be broken apart. Therefore, it suffices to consider the edges of G in order from cheapest to most expensive. The simplest solution would be to sort all the potential edges by cost, which takes time $\Theta(e \log e)$. But this method will often incur extra work; in a lucky case, the $n - 1$ cheapest edges will suffice to

---

function *KruskalMST*(**undirected graph** G): **set**
{Find the edges of a minimum spanning tree on G}
    $E' \leftarrow MakeEmptySet(\,)$ {The set of edges in the tree}
    components $\leftarrow |G|$ {The number of components of $\langle G, E' \rangle$}
    edges $\leftarrow$ make a priority queue containing the edges of G
    foreach vertex u **of** G **do** *MakeSet*(u)
    while *components* > 1 **do**
        {Process the next edge in order}
        $\{u, w\} \leftarrow DeleteMin(edges)$
        $U \leftarrow Find(u)$
        $W \leftarrow Find(w)$
        if $U \neq W$ **then**
            Union(U, W)
            Insert$(\{u, w\}, E')$
            components $\leftarrow$ *components* $- 1$
    return E'

Algorithm 12.5 Kruskal's algorithm for finding a minimum spanning tree on a graph, where $c(e)$ gives the cost of adding edge e. This function returns E', the set of edges in the tree. The priority queue *edges* is ordered by the cost function c. As explained in the text, *edges* is typically implemented as a heap.

---

construct the minimum spanning tree. Therefore, a better method is to place all the potential edges in a priority queue, removing them one at a time as necessary until the tree is finished. If the priority queue is implemented as a heap it can be built in time $\Theta(e)$ as explained on page 387, and the cost of removing the edges is $\Theta(f \log f)$ where f is the number of edges examined before the tree is complete.

    The second and third problems admit an elegant solution using the Union-Find data structures of §9.2. At the beginning of the algorithm, each vertex lies in a connected component all by itself. An edge can be added if and only if its endpoints lie in different connected components, and adding an edge creates a new connected component that is the union of two extant connected components. Thus, the connected components are a partition of the vertices V into disjoint sets, which must be managed with the operations *Union* and *Find*. Kruskal's algorithm executes $2f$ *Find* operations (finding the connected component of each endpoint of each link considered) and $n - 1$ *Union* operations (joining n connected components into 1). The time for these $2f + n - 1$ operations is $O((2f + n) \log^*(2f + n))$, or $O(f \log^* f)$ since $f \geq n - 1$. The total time for the algorithm is thus $O(f \log f)$ which is $O(e \log e)$ in the worst case. The method is shown in full in Algorithm 12.5.

Single-Source Least-Cost Paths

In §12.2 we solved the problem of finding the shortest path between two given vertices of a graph, where the length of a path is defined as the number of edges it contains. We now generalize this problem a little. Let G be a directed graph* and suppose that each edge $\langle u, v \rangle$ of G has a nonnegative cost $c(u, v)$. Let the **cost** of a path be defined as the total cost of the edges contained in the path. Now consider the problem of finding the *least-cost* path between two given vertices. Of course, if each edge has cost 1 the problem is the same as before. But when the costs may differ it is not necessarily true that the shortest path is also the least-cost path. For example, in Figure 12.9(a) the *shortest* path from S to D is $\langle S, A, D \rangle$, but the *least-cost* path is $\langle S, B, E, A, D \rangle$. (The requirement that each edge cost is nonnegative guarantees that a least-cost path always exists and is well-defined; see Problem 35.) We redefine the **distance** between two vertices u and v as the minimum cost of a path between them, thus generalizing the previous definition to permit arbitrary edge costs.

The algorithm that we use to solve this problem, known as Dijkstra's algorithm, actually does more: given a source vertex S, the algorithm computes the distances between S and every other vertex of G. The idea is as follows. For each vertex v maintain a "tentative" distance from v to S; the tentative distance of a vertex may be too large, but it will never be less than the true distance. Initially, the tentative distance of S itself is zero, and all other vertices have infinite tentative distance. We store the tentative distance of each vertex v in a field **Distance** of the record associated with v. Also maintain a set of vertices U (for "unknown") whose actual distance to S is not yet known—when a vertex v is *not* a member of U, the tentative distance of v is the true distance from S to v. Initially, U contains every vertex of G; the algorithm will terminate when U is empty.

Now execute the following procedure repeatedly (Figure 12.9). Find a vertex $v \in U$ whose tentative distance is minimum and remove v from U. Consider each neighbor w of v and compare **Distance**(w) to $d = $ **Distance**$(v) + c(v, w)$. If **Distance**$(w) > d$ then reduce **Distance**(w) to d, reflecting the fact that a new, cheaper path from S (via v) to w has been encountered. In fact, this comparison need be performed only on neighbors w such that $w \in U$, for otherwise **Distance**(w) is the actual distance from w to S and will never exceed d. Each time this procedure is executed a single vertex is removed from U; therefore, we must perform the procedure exactly $|G|$ times and the algorithm terminates. The method is illustrated in Figure 12.9 and coded in Algorithm 12.6.

Dijkstra's is clearly a greedy algorithm; each time through the loop we select the vertex with smallest tentative distance and, by removing it from U, declare that its distance is not tentative at all. We must prove that these local optimal choices really do lead to the overall best result. We start with a Lemma:

---

*The algorithm in this section can be used on undirected graphs as well, with very little change.

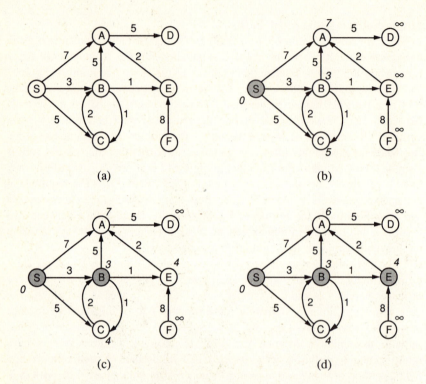

Figure 12.9 An example of Dijkstra's algorithm. (a) A directed graph, with a cost on each edge. We wish to find the least-cost path from S to each other vertex. (b) The distance to each vertex (except S) is tentatively set to ∞. (Tentative distances are shown in italics.) The vertex with least tentative distance is S, so it is removed from U, here depicted by shading the vertex. The tentative distance to each neighbor of S is updated. (c) Now vertex B has least tentative distance, and is removed from U. The tentative distance to C is updated from 5 to 4 and the tentative distance to E is updated from ∞ to 4. The distance via B to A is 8 which is greater than the tentative distance of A, so no update is necessary. (d) E is now removed from U (C could have been selected as well) and the distance to A is updated. The next vertex to be removed from U will be C (Problem 32).

■ **LEMMA** During the operation of Dijkstra's algorithm, vertices are deleted from U in nondecreasing order of their final tentative distances.

PROOF It suffices to show that the final value of Distance(v) is less than or equal to the final value of Distance(w), where w is the vertex that was removed from U immediately after v was removed from U. Now Distance(v) must have been less than or equal to Distance(w) at the instant that v was deleted from U, since otherwise w and not v would

procedure *DijkstraLeastCostPaths*(**directed graph** G, **vertex** S):
$\{S$ is the source vertex of graph $G\}$
    $U \leftarrow MakeEmptySet(\,)$
    foreach vertex v **in** G **do**
        Distance$(v) \leftarrow \infty$
        $Insert(v, U)$
    Distance$(S) \leftarrow 0$
    repeat $|G|$ **times**
        $v \leftarrow$ any member of U with minimum Distance
        $Delete(v, U)$
        foreach neighbor w **of** v **do**
            if $Member(w, U)$ **then**
                Distance$(w) \leftarrow \min($Distance(w), Distance$(v) + c(v, w))$

Algorithm 12.6 Dijkstra's algorithm for finding the distance between a given source vertex and all other vertices of a directed graph G. The cost function $c(u, v)$ gives the cost of the edge $\langle u, v \rangle$, with the convention that $c(u, v) = \infty$ when $\langle u, v \rangle$ is not an edge of G.

---

have been selected for deletion. From that point to the termination of the algorithm, the only possible change to either tentative value is reduction of Distance(w) to Distance$(v) + c(v, w)$, but then we still would have Distance$(v) \le$ Distance(w) since $c(v, w) \ge 0$. $\quad\square$

■ **THEOREM** *(Correctness of Dijkstra's Algorithm)* At the termination of Algorithm 12.6, Distance(v) is the distance from S to v for each vertex v of G.

    PROOF Clearly Distance(v) is the cost of some path from S to v, so the only thing to prove is that for each vertex v there is no path from S to v with cost less than Distance(v). Suppose to the contrary that v is such a vertex and that $\langle S, w_1, w_2, \ldots, w_k, v \rangle$ is such a path, and let $d <$ Distance(v) be the sum of the edge costs along this path. We may also assume that Distance(w_i) is the least-cost distance from S to w_i for each $1 \le i \le k$, since if not we can use the first offending w_i in place of v. At the instant that v was removed from U, none of the w_i was in U (since vertices are removed from U in nondecreasing order of tentative cost). Let $K =$ Distance$(w_k) + c(w_k, v)$. Then $K \ge$ Distance(v) since when w_k was removed from U the field Distance(v) was either set to K or was already smaller than K (and Distance values can never increase). But also $d \ge$ Distance$(w_k) + c(w_k, v) = K$ since Distance(w_k) is the minimum cost of a path from S to w_k. Combining these two inequalities yields $d \geq$ Distance(v), a contradiction.   □

One way to implement Dijkstra's algorithm is to represent the set U as a heap, thinking of it as a priority queue ordered by Distance fields. Initializing U can then be performed as a separate step in time $\Theta(n)$. Searching U for the vertex with minimum tentative distance and deleting it is then simply a *DeleteMin* operation; there are exactly n such operations in the second loop, which therefore takes time $O(n \log n)$. The *Member* operation in the final **if** statement can be implemented in constant time, say by using an additional field in each vertex. But changing the priority value of a heap element, as required by the last line of the algorithm, may require a number of operations that is logarithmic in the size of the heap. (Priority queues as abstract data types do not support the operation of altering priority values; it is just this added requirement of Dijkstra's algorithm that makes things interesting.) The total time used by the final loop is therefore $O(e \log n)$ since it executes once for each edge of the graph. Thus this implementation of Dijkstra's algorithm runs in time $O((n + e) \log n)$, which is quite acceptable when there are few edges in the graph.

On the other hand, a simpler implementation is superior for dense graphs. Suppose that we use a one-bit field in each vertex to denote whether that vertex is a member of U, and search for the minimum-distance vertex by examining every vertex of the graph. The search now requires time $\Theta(n)$ but insertion, deletion, and modifying Distance values are accomplished in constant time. Each iteration of the main loop consists of one search and at most $n - 1$ updates of Distance fields, so the total time of the algorithm is now $\Theta(n^2)$, which is better than the heap implementation when the number of edges is close to n^2. It is easy to see that no solution to the single-source least-cost path problem can run in time $o(n^2)$ in general: any such algorithm must examine each edge of G at least once and G may have $\Theta(n^2)$ edges. Problem 34 discusses another approach to the least-cost path problem.

12.4 ALL PAIRS LEAST-COST PATHS

Let $G = \langle V, E \rangle$ be a directed graph, and let c be a cost function assigning a non-negative cost to each edge of G. In the previous section we considered how to find the least-cost path between a given vertex of G and all other vertices of G. But suppose now that we wish to find the least-cost path between *every* pair of vertices of G. Clearly, it suffices to perform the algorithm of the previous section $n = |V|$ times, successively letting each vertex be the source vertex; this approach yields an algorithm whose time bound is $\Theta(n^3)$. In this section we present the Floyd-Warshall algorithm, a dynamic programming solution of

procedure *FloydWarshallAllShortestPaths*(**directed graph** *G*):
{Find the distance between each pair of vertices of *G*}
    {Set up $Cost_U$ for $U = \emptyset$}
    foreach vertex *u* **in** *G* **do**
        foreach vertex *v* **in** *G* **do**
            $Cost[u, v] \leftarrow c(u, v)$
    {Add each vertex *w* to *U*}
    foreach vertex *w* **in** *G* **do**
        foreach vertex *u* **in** *G* **do**
            foreach vertex *v* **in** *G* **do**
                $Cost[u, v] \leftarrow \min(Cost[u, v], Cost[u, w] + Cost[w, v])$

Algorithm 12.7 Floyd-Warshall dynamic programming algorithm for finding the cost of the cheapest path between every pair of vertices of directed graph *G*. The function $c(u, v)$ gives the cost of the edge from *u* to *v*, with $c(u, v) = \infty$ if there is no such edge and $c(u, u) = 0$ for all *u*. The results are stored in the array *Cost*.

the same problem that gives the same time bound using a different technique that is much easier to program.

We begin by extending the cost function *c* so that it produces a cost for every pair of vertices in *G*: if *u* and *v* are distinct vertices of *G* such that $\langle u, v \rangle$ is *not* an edge of *G* we let $c(u, v) = \infty$, and let $c(u, u) = 0$ for each $u \in V$. Now let *U* be a set of vertices, initially empty. (In this section, all vertices are integers so that we can use them directly as array indices.) For each *u* and *v* let $Cost_U[u, v]$ be the cost of the cheapest path from *u* to *v* whose intermediate vertices are all drawn from *U*. Of course, when *U* is empty this implies that $Cost_U[u, v] = c(u, v)$, which is the cost of the unique path with no intermediate vertices at all. As we add vertices to *U*, more and more of the graph is available to construct paths of lower cost. Finally, when $U = V$, there is no constraint on which vertices can be used in forming paths, so $Cost_V[u, v]$ is the cost of the cheapest path overall.

Now suppose that *U* is an arbitrary set of vertices and that $Cost_U$ is the array defined in the previous paragraph. How can we compute the array $Cost_{U \cup \{w\}}$? That is, how can we add a vertex *w* to *U*? Given any two vertices *u* and *v*, let us compute the cost of the cheapest path from *u* to *v* whose intermediate vertices consist only of vertices in $U \cup \{w\}$. There are two possibilities for the least-cost path: the least-cost path P_1 from *u* to *v* that does *not* contain *w*, and the least-cost path P_2 that *does* contain *w*. The cost of P_1 is known to be $Cost_U[u, v]$. To compute the cost of P_2, note that it has the form $\langle u, \ldots, w, \ldots, v \rangle$; that is, *w* occurs exactly once (otherwise we could excise a cycle from *w* to *w* and create a cheaper path). The first portion of this path, from u to w, uses only vertices in U as intermediate vertices and must be the least-cost path from u to w that does so (since otherwise we could construct a cheaper path from u to v). Therefore the cost of this portion of the path is $Cost_U[u, w]$. Similarly, the cost of the portion of P_2 from w to v is $Cost_U[w, v]$, and the cost of P_2 is thus $Cost_U[u, w] + Cost_U[w, v]$. The cheapest path from u to v that uses arbitrary vertices in $U \cup \{w\}$ is the cheaper of P_1 and P_2; that is, we have proved that

$$Cost_{U \cup \{w\}}[u, v] = \min(Cost_U[u, v], Cost_U[u, w] + Cost_U[w, v]).$$

Algorithm 12.7 incorporates this discussion, initially setting up $Cost_U$ for U equal to the empty set and adding vertices to U one by one. The only subtlety in the code lies in the fact that a single array $Cost$ suffices for the entire computation; that is, as the "new" costs $Cost_{U \cup \{w\}}$ are computed in the final line of the algorithm, they are stored in the same array from which the "old" costs $Cost_U$ are drawn in the same calculation! But there is no difficulty, because the only "old" costs that are used are those of paths that start or end at w, and none of these costs change while w is added to U. Assuming an implementation in which arrays can be accessed and modified in constant time, the total time used by Algorithm 12.7 is easily seen to be $\Theta(n^3)$, a bound that could also be attained using n separate invocations of Algorithm 12.6. (Indeed, in the case of sparse graphs, a heap implementation of Dijkstra's algorithm can be used to find all least-cost path lengths in time $O(n^2 \log n)$.) However, the simplicity of the Floyd-Warshall algorithm makes it quite appealing for practical use. Another important advantage of this approach is its behavior on graphs with negative edge weights (Problem 40).

12.5 NETWORK FLOW

A **network** is a directed graph $G = \langle V, E \rangle$ with a distinguished **source** vertex s that has no incoming edges, a **sink** vertex t that has no outgoing edges, and a function C that assigns to each edge $e \in E$ a positive real **capacity** $C(e)$. A **flow** on a network G is a function f that assigns a number to each edge under the following constraints:

- $0 \le f(e) \le C(e)$ for each $e \in E$; that is, each edge is assigned a nonnegative value that is no more than its capacity.
- For each vertex $v \in V$ other than s and t, the flow into v is equal to the flow out of v; that is, for each such v the sum of $f(e)$ over all edges e entering v is equal to the sum of $f(e')$ over all edges e' departing v. In other words, the **net flow** into v is zero.

When $f(e) = C(e)$, edge e is said to be **saturated**. The **value** of a flow f, written $f(G)$, is the total flow departing s; this is necessarily the same as the

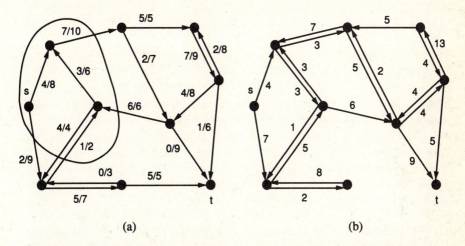

Figure 12.10 (a) A network G and a flow f on G. The notation a/b on edge e means $f(e) = a$ and $C(e) = b$; that is, flow a is assigned out of a maximum of b. The value of the flow is $f(G) = 6$. A cut $\langle N, \overline{N} \rangle$ with capacity $C(N, \overline{N}) = 23$ is indicated by a line around the vertices of N. (b) The augmenting network $A(G, f)$ corresponding to the network of part (a).

total flow entering t (Problem 43). By convention, we let $C(u, v) = 0$ when $\langle u, v \rangle$ is not an edge of G, and also let $f(u, v) = 0$ when $\langle u, v \rangle \notin E$.

Figure 12.10(a) gives an example of a network G and a flow on G. Think of each edge of G as a pipe with capacity specified by C (in liters per second, say). Each vertex of G is a complex valve, able to shunt fluid between the entering and departing pipes in any manner, but unable to produce or to absorb any fluid; the source and sink vertices are able respectively to produce and to absorb arbitrary amounts of fluid. The value of a flow is the rate at which fluid is transferred from the source to the sink. We wish to solve the **Max Flow** problem: given a network G, find a flow of maximum value. This problem has many important applications in situations where the notions of "flow" and "capacity" are more than metaphorical; the vertices may represent transfer locations, and the capacities of the edges represent the capacities of transportation media between them. We shall examine other applications at the end of this section and in Problems 55 through 58.

A **cut** in a network is a partition of its vertices into two sets N and $\overline{N}$ such that $s \in N$ and $t \in \overline{N}$. We write a cut as an ordered pair $\langle N, \overline{N} \rangle$. If f is a flow on G, then the **value** of the cut $\langle N, \overline{N} \rangle$ with respect to f is the net flow from N to $\overline{N}$, which is the total flow from N to $\overline{N}$ minus the total flow from $\overline{N}$ to N:

$$f(N, \overline{N}) = \sum_{u \in N, v \in \overline{N}} f(u, v) - \sum_{v \in \overline{N}, u \in N} f(v, u).$$

Define the **capacity** of a cut with respect to f as the sum of the capacities of the edges from vertices in N to vertices in $\overline{N}$; that is,

$$C(N, \overline{N}) = \sum_{u \in N, v \in \overline{N}} C(u, v).$$

The capacity of a cut is just the maximum imaginable value of the cut, where all "forward" edges are saturated and all "backward" edges have zero flow.

An example of a cut $\langle N, \overline{N} \rangle$ is drawn in Figure 12.10(a) as a line surrounding N. It should be obvious that if $\langle N, \overline{N} \rangle$ is any cut in G, then for any flow f the total flow $f(G)$ cannot exceed $C(N, \overline{N})$, since no greater flow can be pushed from N as a whole to $\overline{N}$ as a whole. This observation follows directly from the following stronger fact:

■ **LEMMA** If G is a network, f is a flow on G, and $\langle N, \overline{N} \rangle$ is any cut in G, then $f(G) = f(N, \overline{N})$.

> **PROOF** By induction on the size of N. If N contains one vertex, then $N = \{s\}$; since s has no incoming edges, $f(N, \overline{N})$ is the sum of $f(e)$ over all edges e leaving s, which is $f(G)$ by definition. Now suppose that $|N| > 1$ and let $N' = N - \{w\}$ where w is some element of N other than s. Then $f(N', \overline{N'}) = f(G)$ by the induction hypothesis. We can now compute $f(N, \overline{N})$ from $f(N', \overline{N'})$ by subtracting the flow on the edges entering w (each of which either no longer contributes to $f(N, \overline{N})$ or now contributes negatively) and adding the flow on the edges departing w (each of which either now contributes to $f(N, \overline{N})$ or used to contribute negatively and no longer contributes). The net change is zero since the net flow into w is always zero, thus $f(N, \overline{N}) = f(N', \overline{N'})$. □

Thus the flow on G cannot exceed the capacity of any cut. In particular, the maximum flow on G cannot exceed the capacity of a **minimum cut**, that is, a cut with least capacity. Remarkably, the converse is also true, as captured by the following Theorem:

■ **THEOREM** (*Max-Flow Min-Cut*) If G is a network, f is a flow on G with maximum value, and $\langle N, \overline{N} \rangle$ is a cut of G with minimum capacity, then $f(G) = C(N, \overline{N})$.

Before proving this Theorem we need a bit more machinery. If G is a network, f is a flow on G, and u and v are distinct vertices of G, define the **augmenting capacity** from u to v (with respect to f) as the amount of additional net flow that can be sent from u to v by increasing the flow on the edge $\langle u, v \rangle$ up to its capacity and decreasing the flow on the "reverse" edge $\langle v, u \rangle$ to zero. The augmenting capacity from u to v is thus $C(u, v) - f(u, v) + f(v, u)$. (One or both of these edges may not exist; we are using here the conventions about the values of C and f on nonexistent edges.) Now define the **augmenting network** $A(G, f)$ as follows. The vertices, source, and sink of $A(G, f)$ are the vertices, source, and sink of G. For each pair of distinct vertices u and v, $\langle u, v \rangle$ is an edge of $A(G, f)$ if and only if the augmenting capacity from u to v is positive, and in that case the capacity of the edge $\langle u, v \rangle$ is just the augmenting capacity from u to v with respect to f. As in any network, the source has no incoming edges and the sink has no outgoing edges, even if there is some "augmenting capacity" toward the source or away from the sink. When G and f are understood, we denote by C_A the capacity function of the augmenting network $A(G, f)$.

Figure 12.10(b) shows the augmenting network $A(G, f)$ corresponding to the network and flow of Figure 12.10(a). Notice that both $\langle u, v \rangle$ and $\langle v, u \rangle$ may be edges of $A(G, f)$ even when only one such edge exists in G, since that edge may have "unused capacity" in both directions. Given a network G and a flow f, the augmenting network describes the possibilities for adding flow to G.

An **augmenting path** for a network G (with respect to a flow f) is a path from s to t in the augmenting network $A(G, f)$. For example, the augmenting graph in Figure 12.10(b) has three augmenting paths of length 4; it has no shorter augmenting paths and several longer ones. Augmenting paths are central to the problem of finding maximum flows because given an augmenting path there is a simple way to increase the flow: let a be the minimum of the augmenting capacities of the edges along the path, and increase the flow on each edge of the augmenting path by a. Since each edge has augmenting capacity at least a, the forward flow along each edge can be increased by a (although sometimes this increase is brought about by decreasing the reverse flow as well). The net flow into any vertex on the path (other than s and t) remains zero as required, since as much additional flow leaves as enters. Finally, the overall value of the flow increases by a since the first edge of the path must depart from s.

■ **LEMMA** If a network G has no augmenting paths with respect to a flow f, then there is a cut in G whose capacity is exactly $f(G)$.

PROOF Let G and f be given and let N be the set of all vertices v such that there is a path from s to v in the augmenting network $A(G, f)$. Obviously $s \in N$, and $t \notin N$ since there is no path from s to t in $A(G, f)$ (any such path would be an augmenting path). Therefore $\langle N, \overline{N} \rangle$ is a cut in G. Now $f(N, \overline{N}) = f(G)$ by the previous Lemma, so it suffices to show that $f(N, \overline{N})$ is in fact equal to $C(N, \overline{N})$. Assume to the contrary that $C(N, \overline{N}) > f(N, \overline{N})$; this means that either there is an unsaturated edge from a vertex in N to a vertex in $\overline{N}$, or there is an edge with positive flow from a vertex in $\overline{N}$ to a vertex in N. Either way, there is an edge in $A(G, f)$ from a vertex $u \in N$ to a vertex $v \notin N$, but then there is a path from s to v in $A(G, f)$, contrary to the definition of N.   □

We have already seen that if a flow is maximum, it can have no augmenting paths. One consequence of this Lemma is the converse: if a flow f allows no augmenting paths then it is a maximum flow. For by the Lemma there is a cut in G whose capacity is exactly $f(G)$ and therefore no flow can have greater value. Another consequence of the Lemma is the proof of the Max-Flow Min-Cut Theorem: We know already that the maximum flow is no bigger than the mininum cut; it remains to prove that there is a cut whose capacity is equal to the maximum flow. But if f is a maximum flow then it has no augmenting paths; thus by the Lemma there is a cut whose value is $f(G)$, and the proof is complete.

Finding Maximum Flows

Given a network G, how can we find a maximum flow on G? A simple algorithm might work like this. Start with a flow f that assigns 0 to every edge of G. Construct the augmenting network, find an augmenting path and increase f accordingly, then repeat. Although this algorithm works, it can be very slow in some cases (Problem 45). The algorithm we describe uses a similar but more efficient strategy whose total time is $O(n^3)$ where, as usual, n is the number of vertices of G.

The key idea is to find and use augmenting paths in order of increasing length. Starting with an everywhere-zero flow f, the algorithm operates in a series of *phases*. In each phase, we first construct the augmenting network $A(G, f)$ and use it to find the length (say k) of the shortest augmenting path—if no augmenting path exists, the algorithm terminates. Then f is increased by adding flow along paths of length k until no further such paths exist, at which point the phase is over. As we shall show later, no new augmenting paths of length less than k are created during this process. Thus after at most $n - 1$ phases (the length of the longest possible path in G) there are no augmenting paths at all and f is a maximum flow.

The part of the algorithm that is tricky to implement efficiently is adding flow to f along the shortest augmenting paths. We give an overview of the process first, deferring implementation details until later. Suppose the augmenting graph $A(G, f)$ has been constructed and k, the length of the shortest augmenting path, has been determined. The next step is to delete from $A(G, f)$ any vertices and edges that lie on no path of length k from s to t; this process, in which only "useful" vertices and edges are retained, is called **pruning** $A(G, f)$. The pruned network has a very interesting structure: it is always a dag, and moreover each edge leads from a vertex at some distance d from s to a vertex at distance $d+1$ from s. We say that a vertex at distance d from s is in **layer** d. Figure 12.11 shows the pruned network constructed from the augmenting graph of Figure 12.10(b).

The simplest way to increase flow f using the pruned network would be to select an augmenting path P, find the edge of P with the smallest augmenting

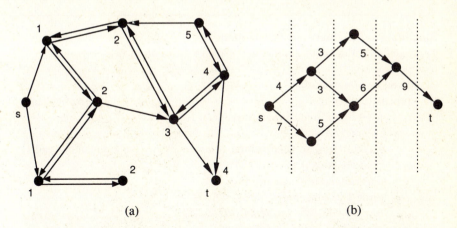

Figure 12.11 Construction of the pruned network corresponding to the augmenting graph of Figure 12.10(b). (a) Each vertex has been labelled with its distance from s, showing that k, the length of the shortest augmenting path, is 4. (For clarity, edge capacities are omitted.) (b) Edges and vertices that lie on no path of length 4 from s to t have been removed. (Edge capacities have been restored and the vertices have been rearranged slightly to emphasize the layers, which are separated by dotted lines.)

capacity, and increase the flow along P by that amount. Instead we must use a more efficient strategy that permits augmenting along many paths at once. For any vertex v other than s or t, define the **input capacity** of v to be the sum of the capacities of the edges entering v in the pruned network. Similarly, the **output capacity** of v is the sum of the capacities of the edges departing from v. The **capacity** of v is the minimum of its input and output capacities; the capacity of v is the largest flow that can possibly be added to augmenting paths of length k containing v. (Special case: s and t have infinite capacity.) For example, in Figure 12.11(b) the sole vertex in layer 3 has input capacity 11 and output capacity 9, and hence capacity 9.

Let v be a vertex in the pruned network with minimum capacity, let c be its capacity, and suppose v is in layer d. Because the capacity of a vertex is an aggregate of the capacities of its edges, it is not necessarily true that there is a single augmenting path through v along which we can increase the total flow by c. But we can increase the flow by c if we use many paths through v. We do so in two steps, called "pushing" and "pulling." In the first step flow is "pushed" forward from v toward t by increasing the flow on edges leaving v—as many edges as necessary—until the total net flow out of v has been increased by c. As flow is added to edges leaving v the new flow enters vertices in layer $d+1$; in each such vertex, we record the new amount of flow that must be pushed forward toward t. When flow c has been pushed out of v we visit these vertices in layer $d+1$; in each, we use the same procedure to push flow onward to vertices in layer $d+2$. Eventually, a total flow of c has been pushed to t. The process

---

function *MaxFlow*(**network** G): **number**
$\{s, t, \text{ and } C \text{ are the source, sink, and capacity function of } G\}$
    value $\leftarrow$ 0
    InitializeFlowsToZero(G)
    repeat forever   {New phase}
        $A \leftarrow$ *BuildAugmentingNetwork*(G)
        ComputeLayers(A)
        if Layer(t) $= \infty$ **then return** *value*   {No augmenting paths}
        PruneAugmentingNetwork(A)
        CalculateVertexCapacities(A)
        while t has incoming edges in A **do**
            $v \leftarrow$ *FindLeastCapacityVertex*(A)
            value $\leftarrow$ *value* + *Capacity*(v)
            AddFlow(A, v)

Algorithm 12.8 Find the maximum flow for a network G: main routine. The flow on each edge of G is determined and $f(G)$, the total flow from s to t, is returned. A is a "scratch" network that is set to $A(G, f)$ at the start of each phase and is then pruned and otherwise modified. Each vertex has a Layer field that is set to its distance from s in $A(G, f)$.

---

of "pulling" flow is the reverse: we first consider v and pull total flow c along edges entering v from vertices in layer $d - 1$, then we consider vertices in layer $d - 1$ and pull flow from layer $d - 2$, and so forth, until flow c has been pulled from s to v. The fact that v is a vertex of minimum capacity is critical to the success of this procedure; it guarantees that the pushing and pulling processes never fail because of inadequate edge capacities whether the flow from v moves along a single path or splits and is recombined at a subsequent layer.

Once flow c has been pushed to t and pulled from s we update the pruned network to reflect the new situation, deleting saturated edges and vertices whose capacity is now zero—in particular, v will be deleted. After all updates have been performed we again find the vertex of minimum capacity and repeat the entire process. No vertices or edges are ever added to the pruned network; eventually, only s and t remain, and the phase is over.

Implementing the Max Flow Algorithm

The top-level structure of the Max Flow algorithm is shown in Algorithm 12.8. Its input is a network, including a source s, sink t, and capacity function C; it returns the value $f(G)$ of the maximum flow. It also computes and stores the flow on each edge in an unspecified data structure accessed by *InitializeFlows-ToZero* and later *IncrementFlowOnEdge*. Although to prove that the algorithm attains the promised time bound we shall eventually have to worry about the details of the implementation, we shall defer doing so for as long as possible; for now we assume only that each vertex is represented by a record in which we specify fields as needed. Keep in mind that there are two graphs under consideration: the input graph G and an auxiliary graph A. The latter is set to the current augmenting network $A(G, f)$ at the start of each phase and is later pruned, modified, and so forth, while G always remains fixed except for the flow assigned to its edges. Each vertex of A is necessarily a vertex of G (and we assume that the same record is used in both graphs), but A may have edges that are not in G, as a comparison of Figures 12.10(a) and 12.10(b) shows. Furthermore, the capacity $C_A(e)$ of an edge e in A is quite different from the capacity of an edge between the same two vertices in G.

We now turn to a discussion of the subroutines of *MaxFlow*. Constructing the augmenting network is straightforward (Problem 46), and a breadth-first search can be used as in §12.2 to find the distance from the source to each other vertex; this distance is stored in a Layer field in each vertex (Problem 47). If t is not encountered during the search, there is no augmenting path at all in $A(G, f)$ and the algorithm terminates. Otherwise, let k be Layer(t), which is the length of the shortest augmenting path.

Pruning the network is also relatively easy (Algorithm 12.9). Recall that the objective is to retain exactly those vertices and edges that lie on some path of length k from s to t. Now any such path must start at s, proceed to a vertex in layer 1, then to a vertex in layer 2, and so forth until reaching t. Hence no edge of $A(G, f)$ is useful unless it goes from a vertex v to a vertex in the very next layer; all other edges can be deleted. Furthermore, the augmenting network may contain vertices that are farther from s than t is, and vertices that are closer than t but are on "dead end" paths (there is an example of such a vertex in Figure 12.11(a)). To find and eliminate these vertices and their associated edges we next perform a search *backwards* from t, that is, traversing the edges that enter each vertex rather than those that depart. Since only useful edges remain, the vertices that are encountered during this search are exactly those vertices that lie on some path of length k from s to t; all other vertices can now be deleted. Algorithm 12.9 gives the details.

The function *FindLeastCapacityVertex* finds and returns the vertex in A with minimum capacity, and *Capacity*(v) returns the capacity of any vertex v. As we shall see shortly, these function must not recalculate vertex capacities on every call because doing so would use too much time. Therefore we use a routine *CalculateVertexCapacities* that is called on the pruned augmenting network once at the beginning of each phase to set fields InputCapacity and OutputCapacity in each vertex; the routine *Capacity* then simply takes the minimum of these two fields (Problem 48). (Again, note carefully that the edges and capacities considered here are those in the auxiliary graph A, not the original graph G.)

---

procedure *PruneAugmentingNetwork*(**network** A):
$\{A$ is an augmenting network to be pruned$\}$
    foreach edge $\langle u, v \rangle$ **of** A **do**
        if Layer(v) $\neq$ Layer(u) $+ 1$ **then** *DeleteEdge*(u, v, A)
    foreach vertex v **of** A **do** Encountered(v) $\leftarrow$ **false**
    $Q \leftarrow$ *MakeEmptyQueue*( )
    Encountered(t) $\leftarrow$ **true**
    Enqueue(t, Q)
    until *IsEmptyQueue*(Q) **do**
        $w \leftarrow$ *Dequeue*(Q)
        foreach edge $\langle v, w \rangle$ **of** A **do**
            if not Encountered(v) **then**
                Encountered(v) $\leftarrow$ **true**
                Enqueue(v, Q)
    foreach vertex v **of** A **do**
        if not Encountered(v) **then** *DeleteVertex*(v, A)

Algorithm 12.9 Prune an augmenting network, leaving only those vertices and edges that lie on a path of length $k =$ Layer(t) from s to t. The Layer field of each vertex v already contains the length of the shortest path from s to v.

    The only remaining subroutine is *AddFlow*, which is detailed in Algorithm 12.10. The pushing and pulling subroutines use breadth-first search so that all vertices of one layer are considered before any vertices of the next layer. Each time the flow on an edge e is changed, there is a lot of bookkeeping to be performed. We update the scratch network A by reducing the capacity of e as appropriate, and if the edge is now saturated it is removed entirely. We also update the input and output capacities of the endpoints of e. After the pushing and pulling operations are complete, vertex v can be removed from the network. But we must also remove any other now-useless vertices of zero capacity; this operation is a bit tricky since deleting a single vertex can cause many other vertices to become "dead ends" (Problem 50).

    This completes the discussion of the code for the Max Flow algorithm. Since the *AddFlow* routine is the only place where the flow is modified, it is easy to see that we always have a legitimate flow between calls on *AddFlow*. Thus all that remains is to show that within total time $O(n^3)$ the algorithm terminates with no remaining augmenting paths (which implies that f is a maximum flow as implied by the Lemma on page 456). As already mentioned, we do so by showing that there are $O(n)$ phases and that each phase can be carried out in time $O(n^2)$. The first fact rests on the following rather technical Lemma whose proof we leave to Problem 51:

procedure *AddFlow*(**vertex** v, **network** A):
{Increment the flow on G by the capacity of vertex v}
    $c \leftarrow Capacity(v)$
    $PushFlow(v, A, c)$
    $PullFlow(v, A, c)$
    foreach vertex w **of** A **do** *DeleteUnusableVertex*(w, A)

procedure *PushFlow*(**vertex** v, **network** A, **number** c):
{Push flow c from v to the sink vertex t, using breadth-first search}
    foreach vertex w **of** A **do** FlowToPush(w) $\leftarrow 0$
    $Q \leftarrow MakeEmptyQueue(\ )$
    $Enqueue(v, Q)$
    FlowToPush(v) $\leftarrow c$
    until *IsEmptyQueue*(Q) **do**
        $u \leftarrow Dequeue(Q)$
        {Push flow over as many edges leaving u as necessary}
        while FlowToPush(u) > 0 **do**
            $e \leftarrow$ any edge $\langle u, w \rangle$ in A
            $newflow \leftarrow \min(C_A(e), \text{FlowToPush}(u))$
            {Add flow *newflow* to e, updating all data structures}
            IncrementFlowOnEdge(u, w, *newflow*)
            if $C_A(e) = 0$ **then** *DeleteEdge*(e, A)
            FlowToPush(u) $\leftarrow$ FlowToPush(u) $-$ *newflow*
            if FlowToPush(w) $= 0$ **and** $w \neq t$ **then** *Enqueue*(w, Q)
            FlowToPush(w) $\leftarrow$ FlowToPush(w) $+$ *newflow*
            OutputCapacity(u) $\leftarrow$ OutputCapacity(u) $-$ *newflow*
            InputCapacity(w) $\leftarrow$ InputCapacity(w) $-$ *newflow*

procedure *DeleteUnusableVertex*(**vertex** w, **network** A):
{If w is useless, delete it and all useless vertices reachable from it}
    if $Capacity(w) = 0$ **then**
        foreach edge $e = \langle w, u \rangle$ **of** A **do**
            InputCapacity(u) $\leftarrow$ InputCapacity(u) $- C_A(e)$
            DeleteUnusableVertex(u, A)
        foreach edge $e = \langle u, w \rangle$ **of** A **do**
            OutputCapacity(u) $\leftarrow$ OutputCapacity(u) $- C_A(e)$
            DeleteUnusableVertex(u, A)
        DeleteVertex(w, A)

Algorithm 12.10 Add flow to G starting at v, updating A as necessary. The routine *PullFlow* is analogous to *PushFlow* and is omitted.

■ **LEMMA** *(Termination of Max Flow)* Let G be a network and f a flow on G, and let k be the length of the shortest augmenting path in $A(G, f)$. Let E be the set of all edges of $A(G, f)$ that lie on at least one augmenting path of length k. Suppose f is increased on some or all edges of E in such a way that f is still a flow. Then no augmenting path with length less than k is created, and if any augmenting paths with length k remain, every edge of every such path is a member of E.   □

From this Lemma, it follows that the pushing and pulling operations create neither shorter augmenting paths nor new paths of the same length that are not already in the "scratch" network A. Therefore, each phase adds flow along paths strictly longer than those of the preceding phase, and thus there are at most $n - 1$ phases in all.

The next part of the analysis depends on the details of the implementation. We require a representation of graphs such that constructing the augmenting network, finding the layer of each vertex, pruning the scratch network, and calculating vertex capacities can all be carried out in time $O(n^2)$. We must also represent the (fixed) capacity $C(e)$ of each edge of G and the (changing) capacity $C_A(e)$ of each edge of A. Finally, we must keep track of the current value of the flow f on each edge of G—these values constitute the output of the algorithm. One twist is that from each vertex we must be able to find quickly its incoming as well as its outgoing vertices, because of the reverse search in *PruneAugmentingNetwork*. None of these requirements is difficult to fulfill (Problem 49).

The only remaining task is to prove that the innermost loop of the main procedure (Algorithm 12.8) also has time bound $O(n^2)$. A naïve argument does not work, since the loop may iterate $n - 2$ times (but no more, since at least one vertex is deleted from A each phase) and each call on *AddFlow* may require time $\Theta(n^2)$. So we have to take a more careful look at *AddFlow* and its subroutines.

We first show that there are $O(n^2)$ occasions per phase on which flow is added to an edge of G. When flow is added to an edge one of two things must happen: either the corresponding edge e of A becomes saturated and is deleted, or the edge does *not* become saturated because the remaining flow to be pulled or pushed is less than $C_A(e)$. The first of these possibilities occurs $O(n^2)$ times since A starts with $O(n^2)$ edges and no edges are added during a phase. In a single call to *AddFlow* there can be at most $n - 2$ edges that acquire new flow but do not become saturated, because at most one edge per vertex can fail to saturate. Thus, since there are at most $n - 2$ calls per phase on *AddFlow*, there are $O(n^2)$ occasions on which an edge fails to saturate after flow is added. In total, the number of times that flow is added to an edge of G is $O(n^2)$.

Finally, we must consider the recursive procedure *DeleteUnusableVertex* that deletes dead-end vertices and edges from A. Although any particular call on this routine can delete many vertices and edges, the routine never performs more than constant work without deleting an edge from A (recall that deleting a vertex from a graph entails deleting all edges adjacent to it). Thus the total time spent in this routine is also $O(n^2)$.

Applications of Max Flow

The **edge connectivity** of an undirected graph G is the minimum number of edges that must be deleted from G in order to produce a disconnected graph. The **vertex connectivity** of an undirected graph G is the minimum number of vertices that must be deleted from G in order to produce a disconnected graph (recall that deleting a vertex implies deleting every edge adjacent to that vertex).* Determining edge and vertex connectivity is important in communications networks, where the connectivity of the network must be preserved even though communications lines or switches may fail: if a communications network has (say) edge connectivity k, then it can maintain its function even if any $k - 1$ links fail. In this section, we show how to determine edge and vertex connectivity using the Max Flow algorithm.

Let G be an undirected graph, and let s and t be distinct vertices of G. Construct a directed graph G' from G as follows: G' has the same vertices as G, and for each edge $\{u, v\}$ of G there are two edges $\langle u, v \rangle$ and $\langle v, u \rangle$ in G'. Let C be the capacity function that assigns 1 as the capacity of every edge of G'. Apply the Max Flow algorithm to the network consisting of G', s, t, and C, and let k be the result. By the Max-Flow Min-Cut Theorem, any cut in the network has capacity at least k. But since the capacity of each edge is 1, this means that in any cut $\langle N, \overline{N} \rangle$ there are at least k edges between N and $\overline{N}$; that is, at least k edges of G must be deleted to disconnect s from t. If we repeat this process using every pair of vertices as the source and sink, the minimum of the resulting flows is exactly the edge connectivity of the graph G.

A slightly more complex procedure can be used to find the vertex connectivity of G. Again, let s and t be arbitrary vertices. Form a directed graph G' from G as follows. For each vertex v of G, there are two vertices v_{in} and v_{out} in G'. To each edge $\{u, v\}$ in G there correspond edges $\langle u_{out}, v_{in} \rangle$ and $\langle v_{out}, u_{in} \rangle$ in G'; in addition, there is an edge $\langle u_{in}, u_{out} \rangle$ for each vertex u of G (Figure 12.12). Finally, let k be the maximum flow across the network G' with source s_{in}, sink t_{out}, and a capacity function that assigns 1 to each edge of G'.

We claim that if any $k - 1$ vertices are deleted from G, then there still remains a path from s to t. For assume otherwise: let W be a set of $k - 1$ vertices such that every path from s to t contains at least one vertex in W. Let A be the set of vertices v of G such that there exists a path from s to v that contains no vertex in W; that is, A is the set of vertices in the connected component of $G - W$ that contains s. Let N consist of the vertices v_{in} and v_{out} for each $v \in A$, plus the vertices w_{in} for each $w \in W$. Then the cut $\langle N, \overline{N} \rangle$

---

*If G is complete, it is impossible to produce a disconnected graph by deleting vertices; in this case we arbitrarily say that the vertex connectivity of G is one less than the number of its vertices.

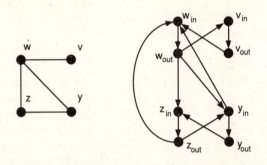

Figure 12.12 An undirected graph and the graph constructed from it by the vertex connectivity algorithm.

of G' has capacity $k-1$, since only the edges $\langle w_{in}, w_{out} \rangle$ can cross the cut, and this is impossible by the Max-Flow Min-Cut Theorem. So, as before, we need only repeat this procedure with every pair of vertices of G as s and t and take the minimum of the results obtained to find the vertex connectivity of G.

The problem with this approach is the time required. Determining either edge or vertex connectivity in this manner requires $\Theta(n^2)$ applications of the Max Flow algorithm, so the time bound of the algorithm is no better than $O(n^5)$. Frequently it suffices to verify that the vertex connectivity of a graph exceeds some fixed k; the Max Flow algorithm can be used to solve this problem, for arbitrary k, in time $O(n^4)$ (Problem 58). But for small k the time bounds are much better: as we have already seen verifying that the vertex connectivity of a graph is at least 2—which simply means checking that the graph is biconnected—can be done in time $O(n+e)$, and in fact the same time suffices to verify that the vertex connectivity of a given graph is at least 3.

Problems

12.1   **1.** Find a set of six U.S. states whose associated undirected graph is that of Figure 12.1(a) on page 425.

2. How many directed graphs are there on a given set of n vertices? How many undirected graphs are there on those vertices?

3. Two graphs with the same number of vertices are **isomorphic** if their vertices can be labelled in such a way that they have the same edges. More formally, undirected graphs $G_1 = \langle V_1, E_1 \rangle$ and $G_2 = \langle V_2, E_2 \rangle$ are isomorphic if there is a bijective function f from V_1 to V_2 such that $\{v_1, v_2\}$ is an edge of G_1 if and only if $\{f(v_1), f(v_2)\}$ is an edge of G_2. (The definition for directed graphs is similar.) Call two graphs **different** if they are not isomorphic.

a. How many different undirected graphs with four vertices exist?

b. How many different directed graphs with three vertices exist?

4. How many edges are in a complete undirected graph with n vertices? How many edges are in a complete directed graph with n vertices?

5. Prove that if a graph has a path between two vertices, it necessarily has a simple path between the same two vertices.

6. Suppose the recursive procedure for constructing trees described on page 98 is modified to construct *undirected* graphs; that is, instead of adding edges $\langle r, r_1 \rangle$, $\langle r, r_2 \rangle$, and so forth, we add edges $\{r, r_1\}$, $\{r, r_2\}$ and so forth. Show that the object constructed by the recursive procedure is a tree according to the definition on page 430. Conversely, show that any tree can be constructed by the recursive procedure, with any vertex at the root.

7. Complete the proof of the Tree Characterization Theorem (both parts).

8. For each of the five properties of the first part of the Tree Characterization Theorem, find a graph that has that property but is not a tree. For each of the ten possible pairs of properties, either show that any graph with those two properties is a tree or find a counterexample.

9. Explain why it is necessary to insist that G not be complete in the third clause of the second part of the Tree Characterization Theorem.

10. The **degree** of a vertex of a graph is the number of its neighbors. A **leaf** of a tree is a vertex with degree one. Find all trees with no leaves, with exactly one leaf, with exactly two leaves, and with exactly three leaves.

11. If $G = \langle V, E \rangle$ is an undirected graph, the **complement** of G is the graph $\langle V, E' \rangle$ such that $\{a, b\} \in E'$ if and only if $\{a, b\} \notin E$. Informally, the complement of G is constructed by adding all possible edges to G and then deleting the original edges of G.

   a. Proof or counterexample: if G is connected, then the complement of G is disconnected.

   b. Proof or counterexample: if G is disconnected, then the complement of G is connected.

12. Prove that any vertex of a graph G belongs to exactly one connected component of G.

13. Generalize the Lemma on page 431 by showing that a graph with n vertices and k connected components must have at least $n - k$ edges, and that a graph with n vertices and e edges must have at least $n - e$ connected components.

14. Suppose that graphs are represented by adjacency matrices. Show that any algorithm that determines whether a graph is connected must

examine $\Omega(n^2)$ entries of the adjacency matrix. (Hint: Find a class of graphs for which this is so.)

12.2 **15.** Prove formally the assertion on page 433, that if Algorithm 12.1 visits vertex w_1 before vertex w_2 then the distance from v to w_1 is less than or equal to the distance from v to w_2.

16. Show how to modify Algorithm 12.1 so that it yields a shortest path from v to each vertex. (One approach is simply to save, with each vertex, a list of the vertices in a path from v to that vertex. Try to find a better way.)

17. Improve Algorithm 12.1 so that it carries out a breadth-first search in time proportional to the number of vertices encountered plus the number of edges between those vertices.

18. Write an iterative version of depth-first search in which both *PreVisit* and *PostVisit* are carried out on each vertex.

19. Write a function *GraphFromDFS* that reconstructs a graph given the *PreVisit* and *PostVisit* orderings of the vertices. It should accept a table of vertices each of which has integer fields PreVisitOrder and PostVisitOrder, and should return a graph that yields these orders when searched depth-first starting at the vertex whose PreVisitOrder field contains 1. Is the resulting graph uniquely determined?

20. Prove that every dag has at least one vertex with no entering edge.

21. As pointed out in the text, the particular topological sort produced by Algorithm 12.3 on page 438 may depend on the order in which the vertices of G are processed in the main procedure and the order in which the neighbors of each vertex are processed. Is it true that *any* topological sort of a dag can be produced by some depth-first search?

22. Find a necessary and sufficient set of conditions for a dag to have a unique topological sort order.

23. a. Write a function that determines in linear time whether a directed graph has a cycle, using only 2 bits per vertex plus space for a stack.

  b. Explain how to detect cycles with only 1 bit per vertex plus constant space, using more time.

24. Show that the two definitions of biconnectivity on page 439 are equivalent for graphs with more than two vertices; that is, show that such a graph has no cutvertices if and only if, given any two vertices of the graph, there are two vertex-disjoint paths between those vertices.

25. A common error of nonspecialists is the belief that a biconnected graph is one in which every vertex has degree at least 2. Demonstrate the falsehood of this notion by exhibiting a graph that is not biconnected, but in which each vertex has degree at least 2.

26. In the Lemma on page 431 we proved that no connected graph with n vertices has fewer than $n - 1$ edges. What is the smallest number of edges in a biconnected graph with n vertices? What is the largest number of edges in a graph with n vertices that is not biconnected?

27. Consider the second Lemma used to characterize the cutvertices of an undirected graph (page 441). Where does the proof of this Lemma break down if v is the root of T?

28. Write a function that, given a graph, computes the length of its longest simple path. Do not worry about the time complexity of your algorithm!

29. A directed graph is called **strongly connected** if there is a path between any two of its vertices. Write a function that, given a directed graph, determines if it is strongly connected.

12.3 **30.** Implement Prim's algorithm for finding minimum spanning trees (described on page 443) and prove that it is correct.

31. Find the minimum and maximum number of edges that may be considered by Kruskal's algorithm (Algorithm 12.5 on page 446) when given a connected graph with n vertices.

32. Draw Figures 12.9(e), (f), (g), and (h), completing the example of Dijkstra's algorithm on page 448.

33. In the graph of Figure 12.10(a) on page 453, let the cost of each edge be the "numerator" of its label (so that, for example, the two edges departing vertex s have cost 2 and 4). Show the operation of Dijkstra's algorithm on this graph and find the distance from s to every other vertex.

34. Consider the least-cost paths problem in the special case where all edge costs are nonnegative *integers*. To solve this problem we can use Dijkstra's algorithm with a fast method of finding the members of U with least tentative cost. The crucial fact is that at each point in the execution of the algorithm, each vertex has tentative cost of either d, $d+1, d+2, \ldots, d+C$, or ∞, where d is the smallest tentative cost of any vertex in U and C is the maximum cost of any edge in the graph. We may therefore keep C sets, each containing vertices all with the same tentative cost, and such that every vertex is either in exactly one set or has tentative cost ∞. It is then a trivial matter to find a vertex of least tentative cost. Expand these ideas into a procedure that runs in time $O(e + nC)$, where as usual e is the number of edges and n is the number of vertices of the graph.

35. In our discussion of the least-cost paths problem we assumed that all edge costs are nonnegative. If edge costs can be negative, the graph may have **negative cycles**—those with total cost less than zero. If two vertices lie on a negative cycle there is no least-cost path between them, because paths of arbitrarily low cost can be constructed by traversing the cycle many times.

    a. Write a function that determines in linear time whether a given directed graph has a negative cycle.

    b. Modify Algorithm 12.6 on page 449 so that it works correctly on graphs with negative edge costs but no negative cycles. (Hint: The behavior of U will not be as simple in the modified algorithm, and the time bound will not be preserved.) What is the best time bound you can find for the modified algorithm?

36. Let an undirected graph with nonnegative edge costs be given, along with a source vertex s and a destination vertex t. Devise an algorithm that, in addition to finding the length of the least-cost path between s and t, finds *all* least cost paths between s and t. Try to make your algorithm as efficient as possible in time *and* space.

37. Let k be fixed. Show how to find the k shortest paths (not necessarily disjoint) between two vertices in a given graph.

12.4   38. Consider the effect of the last line of the Floyd-Warshall algorithm, Algorithm 12.7 on page 451, when u, v, and w are not all distinct. Recode the triple loop to avoid this inefficiency.

39. Trace the operation of Algorithm 12.7 on the graph of Figure 12.9 on page 448 by showing the contents of the *Cost* matrix just before each entry to the triple loop (that is, seven times) and after the algorithm terminates. (Assume that each loop processes the vertices in alphabetical order.)

40. Show that the Floyd-Warshall algorithm correctly finds the distance between all pairs of vertices even when edge costs may be zero or negative, as long as the graph has no negative cycles. What happens if the graph does have negative cycles?

41. Suppose that *LeastCostSimplePaths* is a routine that finds the cost of all cheapest *simple* paths in an undirected graph with possibly negative edge weights and negative cycles. Show how to construct a program that solves the Travelling Salesman Problem using *LeastCostSimplePaths* as a subroutine and only a small amount of additional time.

(You need not write any code; just describe the method.) This process is called a **reduction** of the Travelling Salesman Problem to the least-cost simple paths problem; it follows that finding least-cost simple paths in a graph with arbitrary edge costs is at least as hard as solving the Travelling Salesman Problem.

2.5 **42. a.** Compute the maximum flow of the network of Figure 12.10(a) on page 453.

b. Noting that an augmenting network is itself a network, compute the maximum flow of the network of Figure 12.10(b).

c. Proof or counterexample: If G is a network and f is any flow on G, then the maximum flow on G is equal to $f(G)$ plus the maximum flow on $A(G, f)$.

43. Suppose f is a flow on network G. We defined $f(G)$ as the total flow leaving s and required that the net flow into each vertex (except s and t) must be zero, but said nothing about the flow into t.

a. Show that the flow entering t is equal to $f(G)$.

b. Let a function on the edges of G be "almost a flow" if it satisfies all the requirements of a flow except that there is a single vertex v (distinct from s and t) whose net flow is allowed to be nonzero. Let g be almost a flow, and suppose that the total flow leaving s is equal to the total flow entering t. Show that g is a flow.

44. If $\langle N, \overline{N} \rangle$ is a cut in $G = \langle V, E \rangle$, define $E(N, \overline{N})$ to be the set of edges leading from vertices in N to vertices in $\overline{N}$. Suppose E' is a minimal subset of E such that there is no path from s to t in $\langle V, E - E' \rangle$. Is there necessarily a cut $\langle N, \overline{N} \rangle$ such that $E' = E(N, \overline{N})$? (Proof or counterexample.)

45. Reconsider the naïve algorithm on page 456 for finding maximum flow: build the augmenting network, find an augmenting path and increase the flow along it, and repeat until there are no augmenting paths. Find a network with integral edge capacities in which this procedure may iterate a number of times proportional to the maximum flow itself, that is, not bounded by any function of the number of vertices. (If edge capacities may be irrational, it is possible to construct a network in which the naïve algorithm does not terminate, and moreover converges to a flow whose value is strictly less than the maximum!)

46. Write the routine *BuildAugmentingNetwork* used in the Max Flow algorithm.

47. Write the routine *ComputeLayers* used in the Max Flow algorithm.

48. Write the routines *CalculateVertexCapacities*, *Capacity*, and *Find-LeastCapacityVertex* used in the Max Flow algorithm.

49. Design data structures for the Max Flow algorithm. You must implement routines *InitializeFlowsToZero*, *IncrementFlowOnEdge*, C, C_A, and the graph abstract operations used by the routines that create and manipulate the scratch network—including those in the three problems just preceding! Your solution must meet the time bounds discussed on page 462 but is otherwise unconstrained. Don't forget that graphs G and A must share vertices; that is, if a vertex v appears in both graphs then the same record is used for each. (On the other hand, there are many ways that edges might be represented. In particular, keep in mind that just because the algorithm carefully distinguishes between edges of G and edges of A, and between C and C_A, it doesn't follow that separate data structures must be maintained for each.)

50. Consider the last line of procedure *AddFlow* in Algorithm 12.10 on page 461. Explain clearly why it is necessary to call *DeleteUnusableVertex* on each vertex of A; in particular, what goes wrong if we replace this line with *DeleteUnusableVertex*(v, A)?

51. Prove the Max Flow Termination Lemma on page 462.

52. Our Max Flow algorithm yields the value of the maximum flow and a flow on each edge that realizes the maximum flow. Modify the algorithm so that it also produces a minimum cut of the network.

53. Show that the edge connectivity of a graph always equals or exceeds the vertex connectivity.

54. Show that the vertex connectivity of a graph is k if and only if the minimum number of vertex-disjoint paths between any pair of distinct vertices is k. (Hint: use the Max-Flow Min-Cut Theorem. This result is called Menger's Theorem; it generalizes Problem 24.)

55. An undirected graph is called **bipartite** if its vertices can be partitioned into disjoint sets V_1 and V_2 such that every edge of the graph connects a vertex in V_1 with a vertex in V_2. A **matching** of a graph (not necessarily bipartite) is a set of edges no two of which are adjacent to the same vertex. A **maximum matching** of a graph is a matching with maximum size. Show how to find the size of a maximum matching of a bipartite graph using the Max Flow algorithm. (The sets V_1 and V_2 are given.)

56. Show how to find the maximum flow through a network in which the vertices, as well as the edges, have assigned capacities. That is, the flow through each vertex must not exceed the capacity of the vertex;

of course, the net flow into each vertex must still be zero. (Hint: Consider how such an algorithm could be used to solve the vertex connectivity problem.)

57. Show how to find the maximum flow through a network that has multiple sources and sinks.

58. Given an undirected graph G, show how to determine whether its vertex connectivity exceeds a given number k with only $O(n)$ invocations of the Max Flow algorithm. (The constant implicit in "$O(n)$" depends on k.)

References

Graph theory is a wonderfully rich subject; for more information, consult any of the excellent texts on the subject. Two introductory texts are

F. Harary, *Graph Theory,* Addison-Wesley, 1969;

and

C. Berge, *Graphs and Hypergraphs*, North-Holland, 1973.

The interplay between data structures and graph algorithms is explored in greater detail in the monograph

R. E. Tarjan, *Data Structures and Network Algorithms,* Society for Industrial and Applied Mathematics (CBMS 44), 1983,

which discusses the topics treated in this chapter and a number of others, and which has an extensive bibliography of further references. More applications of depth-first search can be found in

R. E. Tarjan, "Depth-First Search and Linear Graph Algorithms," *SIAM Journal on Computing* **1** (1972), pp. 146–160.

Prim's algorithm is from

R. C. Prim, "Shortest Connection Networks And Some Generalizations," *Bell System Technical Journal* **36** (1957), pp. 1389–1401

and Kruskal's algorithm was published in

J. B. Kruskal, "On the Shortest Spanning Subtree of a Graph and the Traveling Salesman Problem," *Proceedings of the American Mathematical Society* **7** (1956), pp. 48–50.

A very interesting use of leftist trees (described in Chapter 9) as the basis of a faster algorithm with running time in $O(e \log \log n)$ is given in

D. Cheriton and R. E. Tarjan, "Finding Minimum Spanning Trees," *SIAM Journal on Computing* **5** (1976), pp. 724–742

which contains an excellent overview of the problem and survey of results. The shortest path problem is a fundamental technique that has been studied extensively. A good general discussion of the problem and overview of basic techniques (with particular application to sparse graphs) is found in

D. B. Johnson, "Efficient Algorithms for Shortest Paths in Sparse Networks," *Journal of the ACM* **24** (1977), pp. 1–13

and a survey of more recent work, including use of more sophisticated data structures, is in

R. K. Ahuja, K. Mehlhorn, J. B. Orlin, and R. E. Tarjan, "Faster Algorithms for the Shortest Path Problem," *Journal of the ACM* **37** (1990), pp. 213–223.

Dijkstra's algorithm appears in

E. W. Dijkstra, "A Note on Two Problems in Connexion with Graphs," *Numerische Mathematik* **1** (1959), pp. 269–271,

and the approach in Problem 34 first appeared in

R. B. Dial, "Shortest-Path Forest with Topological Ordering," *Communications of the ACM* **12** (1969), pp. 632–633.

An approach to the shortest-paths algorithm that works well in practice even on graphs with negative edges (as in Problem 35) is presented in

U. Pape, "Algorithm 562: Shortest Path Lengths," *ACM Transactions on Mathematical Software* **6** (1980), pp. 450–455.

The Floyd-Warshall algorithm for finding the least-cost path between all pairs of graph vertices was published independently in

R. W. Floyd, "Algorithm 97: Shortest Path," *Communications of the ACM* **5** (1962), p. 345

and

S. Warshall, "A Theorem on Boolean Matrices," *Journal of the ACM* **9** (1962), pp. 11–12.

Problem 37 is from

S. Dreyfus, "An Appraisal of Some Shortest-Path Algorithms," *Operations Research* **17** (1969), pp. 395–412

and Problem 41 is from

G. B. Dantzig, "All Shortest Routes in a Graph," in *Theory of Graphs*, Gordon and Breach, 1967.

The extremely important Max Flow problem first arose in connection with minimizing costs in transportation networks. A classic reference is

L. R. Ford, Jr. and D. R. Fulkerson, *Flows in Networks*, Princeton University Press, 1962,

which describes early solutions for the problem and many variations and applications. The Max-Flow Min-Cut Theorem was proved in

L. R. Ford, Jr. and D. R. Fulkerson, "Maximal Flow Through a Network," *Canadian Journal of Mathematics* **8** (1956), pp. 399–404.

The use of acyclic layered networks to solve the Max Flow problem quickly is the work of

E. A. Dinic, "Algorithm for Solution of a Problem of Maximum Flow in a Network with Power Estimation," *Soviet Math. Doklady* **11** (1970), pp. 1277–1280.

(Papadimitriou and Steiglitz, in their book cited below, point out that the last two words of this title are probably a bad translation for "complexity analysis.") Dinic's method has been the basis for several algorithms; the one we present is due to

V. M. Malhotra, M. P. Kumar, and S. N. Maheshwari, "An $O(|V|^3)$ Algorithm for Finding Maximum Flows in Networks," *Information Processing Letters* **7** (1978), pp. 277–278.

Increasingly sophisticated data structures have led to ever-faster algorithms for special kinds of graphs (especially sparse graphs) and on multiprocessor systems. For a brief survey with many references, see

R. K. Ahuja and J. B. Orlin, "A Fast and Simple Algorithm for the Maximum Flow Problem," *Operations Research* **37** (1989), pp. 748–759.

The connection between the Max Flow problem and other optimization problems is thoroughly explored in

C. H. Papadimitriou and K. Steiglitz, *Combinatorial Optimization,* Prentice-Hall, 1982.

Many applications of the Max Flow algorithm, including several discussed here and used in the problems, are presented in

S. Even and R. E. Tarjan, "Network Flow and Testing Graph Connectivity," *SIAM Journal on Computing* **4** (1975), pp. 507–518.

The linear-time test for triconnectivity mentioned at the very end of the chapter is from

J. E. Hopcroft and R. E. Tarjan, "Dividing a Graph into Triconnected Components," *SIAM Journal on Computing* **2** (1973), pp. 135–158.

13

Engineering with Data Structures

We study data structures so that when confronted with a computational problem we can choose intelligently among the alternatives for its solution. Up until now we have studied each data structure by itself, learning its properties and analyzing its performance. But a real problem arrives without a data structure attached—not even a hint inferred from the title of the chapter in which the problem appears! In this chapter we offer more involved and open-ended problems; solving each is an exercise in software design requiring one or more of the data structures studied in this book.

But this is not the end of the story. Selecting a data structure is usually a matter of balancing tradeoffs: space versus time, efficiency versus simplicity, and so forth. As we have seen in previous chapters, the distinctions may be very fine; one data structure may permit rapid search but slower insertion, another may have the opposite characteristics, and still another may allow fast insertion at the cost of slow deletion. Naturally, the specifics of the problem at hand dictate the final decision—and for many of the problems in this chapter, we have not provided detailed enough specifications to determine the "best" solution. It is part of the solver's task to determine the questions that must be answered, just as the software designer must often begin by resolving underspecified problems. (Another characteristic of some software designers is a tendency to justify the use of unsophisticated techniques on the grounds that the blinding speed of the computer will overcome any defects of the solution. The problems here should not be approached in this spirit; elegance and efficiency are paramount.)

So the problems presented here can be solved in different ways. You might want to do no more than to sketch a possible solution, or you might write some pseudo-code, or implement a solution in full on a machine. When criteria that determine a best solution are not apparent, so that you must identify the significant issues, you might discuss various alternatives and the approach to be taken in each case. Frequently the first task is to define precisely the arguments and functionality of the abstract operations that are required. Although some of the problems have clear-cut answers, some lie within open research areas and are not well understood. As you tackle some of these issues, a significant difference between real-world problems and textbook exercises will become apparent: real problems lack not only guidelines for their solution, but unambiguous notification that the best possible solution has been found.

1. Display Screen Window Management A computer display is addressed using a two-dimensional coordinate system that can be used to locate any point on the screen. Typically the point $(0, 0)$ represents the upper-left-hand corner, with x coordinates increasing to the right and y coordinates increasing downward. The screen displays a number of windows of various sizes. Each window occupies a rectangular region of the screen, which can be fully specified by giving the coordinates of the upper-left and lower-right corners of the window. Since windows may overlap, each window also has a z coordinate used to determine which window is "on top" and therefore visible; if several windows include the same point, that point on the screen "belongs" to the window with the largest z coordinate. Windows may be added, deleted, and resized, and may also change z coordinate. For example, we might have an abstract operation

$$AddWindow(S, \langle x_1, y_1 \rangle, \langle x_2, y_2 \rangle, z)$$

that adds a window named S with upper-left corner $\langle x_1, y_1 \rangle$, lower-right corner $\langle x_2, y_2 \rangle$, and "height" z. Devise data structures and algorithms for the use of the display manager, which must keep track of the windows and must at any time be able to determine the window that owns any given point. (In some systems this determination must be performed frequently and rapidly. For example, many workstations have a pointing device with which the user can indicate a location on the screen, and the window owning the pointer might have to be found each time the pointer moves.)

2. Display Screen Icon Management The display screen of the previous problem may also display **icons**, images of small objects with arbitrary shape. We require data structures and algorithms for handling icons as well. Icon handling differs from window handling in several ways. (a) As already mentioned, icons may be of arbitrary shape: circles, ellipses, irregular blobs, long lines, and so forth, possibly containing holes. (b) Generally, there are many more icons than there are windows. Consider, for example, a map of the world on which an airline draws its flight routes; each city and flight path may be represented by a separate icon. (c) Icons typically appear, disappear, and move much more frequently than windows. (d) Icons are typically much smaller than windows. Therefore we may require the ability to tell not only which icon is located at a given point but also which icons are nearby; this capability might be used to help the user select small icons in crowded regions. (e) In some systems, the process of determining which icon corresponds to a screen location need not be extremely fast, because icons are selected only by slow user actions (such as clicking a mouse). But it is also possible that the current icon, like the current window, might need to be determined each time the pointer moves.

Discussion: One way to approach the problem of icons with arbitrary shapes is to equip each icon with a **bounding rectangle** that completely contains the icon. For example, let each icon I have fields BoundingHeight(I) and BoundingWidth(I) that specify the size of a bounding rectangle for I. The details of the shape of I can be handled by a function *InternalPoint*, where *InternalPoint*$(I, \langle x, y \rangle)$ returns **true** if $\langle x, y \rangle$ is part of I when the upper-left corner of the bounding rectangle of I is placed at point $\langle 0, 0 \rangle$. This representation frees us from worrying about icon shapes (which are not part of this problem anyway) and permits us to manipulate bounding rectangles instead. Calls on *InternalPoint* might be expensive, but the bounding rectangle can be used to determine quickly whether a given point can possibly be part of an icon. (Bounding rectangles are not always too useful for this purpose; consider, for example, a long diagonal line.)

3. *Digitized Pictures* The use of quad trees for representing digitized images was introduced in Problem 30 of Chapter 9. Many other aspects of this representation do not have clear-cut answers. For example, one of the principal advantages of the quad tree representation over a complete array of bits is that the quad tree representation takes less space, since large monochromatic areas are represented by single tree nodes. But if we really want to save space, then the quad tree should not be represented using explicit pointers, but by some kind of implicit representation or two-dimensional run-length encoding. Devise such a representation, and try to assess its efficiency, and the difficulty of converting between it and a representation that uses explicit pointers or an array representation.

What if a quad tree is used to represent an image that consists simply of straight line segments? How easily can the quad tree be constructed from the endpoints of the line segments? Can the exact endpoints of the line segments be recovered from the quad tree, given reasonable assumptions about the lengths of the segments?

Many important geometrical properties can be computed from the quad tree representation of a digitized image. For example, a set of pixels forms a **connected component** of the image if they are connected by a sequence of horizontally or vertically contiguous pixels of the same color. Devise an algorithm that enumerates the connected components of an image and labels each quad tree node with the number of its connected component. A related problem is to find the area of the connected component containing a given pixel (specified by its coordinates). You might also try to calculate the perimeter of a connected component.

Sometimes it is necessary to produce a lower-resolution version of an image, that is, to scale an entire $n \times n$ image to fit into $m \times m$ pixels, where

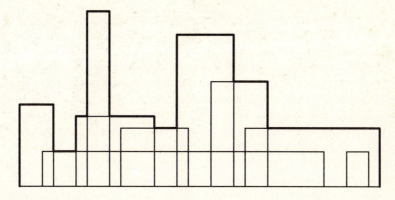

Figure 13.1 A number of rectangles, with their skyline indicated by the heavy line.

$m < n$. Obviously some of the sharpness of the original image will be lost, but some scaling methods produce significantly poorer results than others. Explore this problem. Do the methods you propose work well with a quad tree representation?

Finally, many problems can be generalized to higher dimensions—finding the area becomes, in three dimensions, finding the volume; finding the perimeter becomes finding the surface area; and so on. In three dimensions the octtree representation is also useful in computer graphics, and introduces a further set of problems, such as calculating the projection of a solid body onto a two-dimensional surface from an arbitrary projection point, or finding the digitized representation (as a quad tree, perhaps) of a slice through a solid object represented as an octtree.

4. Intersection of Rectangles   We wish to manipulate a large number of rectangles with edges parallel to the coordinate axes. Each rectangle is specified by name and by its upper-left-hand and lower-right-hand points; rectangles may be added and deleted dynamically. At any time, we must be able to determine the intersection of all the rectangles, that is, the set of points that belong to every rectangle. Find a representation of rectangles and a data structure that solves this problem.

5. Skyline of Rectangles   As in the previous problem, we have a dynamic set of rectangles with edges parallel to the coordinate axes. Assume further that the y coordinate of the lower corners of each rectangle is 0; that is, all rectangles sit on the x-axis. The problem is to determine (at any time) the **skyline** of the current set of rectangles. The skyline of a set of rectangles is most clearly defined by picture, as in Figure 13.1; part of your task is to find a definition of skyline more appropriate to computer representation.

6. Spelling Checker   The English language is notorious for its spelling anomalies; the mechanical spelling checker is a relatively recent development that has
been a boon to many writers. (Spelling checkers are not yet perfect; the semantic capability needed to detect the error in this sentence, for example, is beyond
there powers at this writing.) A spelling checker requires a dictionary of English
words, which of course should include common place names, personal names,
abbreviations, and so forth. Even using automated methods for dealing with
plurals, prefixes, suffixes, and other derived forms, such a dictionary must contain at least tens of thousands of words. Given a word *not* in the dictionary, we
might also wish to find "nearby" words that are in the dictionary—for example,
when confronted with "accomodate" we might suggest "accommodate" as an
alternative, and given "suick" we might suggest "sick," "stick," "slick," "quick,"
and perhaps others. Devise a dictionary representation for the use of a spelling
checker.

Discussion: The difficulty lies with the size of the dictionary, which may
well have hundreds of thousands of words of varying length, making it undesirable to store the entire dictionary in fast memory in order to perform a *LookUp*
on each word of the document. Many of these words are simply variations on
a standard pattern, such as plurals of nouns and the principal parts of regular
verbs. Another consideration is that no data are stored with the words—only
the presence of words in the dictionary is important. So one possibility is to
use a static hash table (built once and for all from the dictionary) whose entries
are single bits. A character string that hashes to an unoccupied table entry is
certainly not a word in the dictionary; unfortunately, if it hashes to an occupied
table entry it may or may not be a word. Can you improve this scheme to make
a useful and usably fast spelling checker?

7. Diff   The Unix utility program *diff* compares two text files A and B and
lists their differences. This is useful, for example, when you have two versions
of the same source file of a computer program and you wish to determine what
changes were made in producing one from the other. To be precise, *diff* matches
as many lines as possible from file A to identical lines, appearing in the same
order, in file B. These lines are then presumed to be of common origin, and
lines appearing in one file but not matched in this way in the other file are
presumed to be the result of insertions in the one file or deletions from the
other, and are listed as discrepancies.

Develop algorithms and data structures for implementing *diff*. To be specific, *diff* finds the **longest common subsequence** of the two sequences of lines;
that is, if we regard the lines in the two files as the lists $a_0, \ldots, a_{m-1}$ and $b_0, \ldots,$
b_{n-1}, then *diff* finds sequences of indices $0 \leq p_0 < p_1 < \cdots < p_{k-1} \leq m - 1$
and $0 \leq q_0 < q_1 < \cdots < q_{k-1} \leq n - 1$ of maximal length k such that $a_{p_i} = b_{q_i}$
for each $i = 0, \ldots, k - 1$. Is this in fact a reasonable notion of "finding the
differences"?

There is a fairly straightforward $O(mn)$ algorithm for the longest common subsequence problem that works essentially by comparing every line of each file with every line of the other, but if most of the lines of the files are unique (as will generally be the case in practice!) this seems an unreasonably slow method. Instead, try breaking this problem down into two steps. First, identify each line of file B by its line number, and build a data structure that will enable you to find quickly all the places in file A where each line of file B appears. Thereafter the length of the lines can be regarded as a small constant. Second, consider each line b_j of file B in turn and partition the lines of file A into consecutive blocks, such that if line i is in one block but line $i + 1$ is in the next, then the longest common subsequence of $a_0, \ldots, a_i$ and $b_0, \ldots, b_j$ is shorter than the longest common subsequence of $a_0, \ldots, a_{i+1}$ and $b_0, \ldots, b_j$. By judicious use of balanced tree structures this method can be implemented to run in time $O((m+n+p)\log(m+n))$ where p is the number of pairs $\langle i, j \rangle$ such that $a_i = b_j$. Explore this approach, and the various data structures that might be used in the implementation. This is an excellent problem for experimentation, since such parameters as the length of the lines, the relation between processor and disk speeds, and the number of duplicated lines may be as important as the theoretical analysis in determining the running speed.

What would be a useful format in which to present the output of this program? Are additional data structures needed to produce it? The actual *diff* program can be instructed (with "-h") to make a "fast, half-hearted" effort at matching the lines of the files. Speculate about what algorithm might be used when this option is requested.

8. Go   The game of Go is played by two players on a square board with 19 horizontal and 19 vertical lines producing 361 intersections called **points**. The players alternately place markers called **stones** on the points; one player uses black stones and moves first, the other player uses white stones. Stones are never moved once played but may be captured and removed from the board as described below. Two stones of the same color are **connected** if they are adjacent horizontally or vertically. A set of stones all of the same color is connected if there is a path of connected stones between each pair of stones in the set. A maximal set of connected stones is called a **group**.

A **liberty** of a group of stones is a vacant point adjacent to some stone in the group. A group of stones is captured when its last liberty is occupied; such a group is immediately removed from the board. An **eye** is (for the purposes of this problem) a maximal nonempty set of connected, vacant points that is completely surrounded by a single group, possibly with the help of the edges of the board. The object of the game is to control (by surrounding) more open territory than your opponent, under fairly simple rules which are nevertheless not detailed here.

Construct a data structure that keeps track of the Go board on behalf of a Go-playing computer program. It is important to determine rapidly the group of stones to which a given stone belongs, and the eyes and liberties of every group. For a bigger challenge, learn the complete rules of Go and extend your solution accordingly.

9. Gomoku   A game much simpler than Go that is played on the same board is Gomoku, or "five-in-a-row." The players alternately place stones as usual, but there is no capture, and the winner is simply the first player to construct a vertical, horizontal, or diagonal line containing five (but not six!) adjacent stones. The strategy for playing Gomoku is to attain winning configurations, those from which the opponent cannot prevent a victory. For example, four adjacent stones in a line is a winning configuration if there is sufficient open space at each end of the line. Two lines of three adjacent stones each, with sufficient open space on each end of each line, is also a winning configuration. (Of course, it does no good to have a winning configuration if your opponent has a better one, that is, one from which a victory can be achieved in fewer moves.)

Design a "configuration manager" for the use of an automated Gomoku player. Your manager should maintain a representation of the board as pieces are played. It must also store a dictionary of configurations and it must be able to search the board rapidly, finding any instances of the configurations in its dictionary. (A better manager would also be able to find configurations that are within a single move of configurations in the dictionary, either to block an opponent's incipient victory or to suggest a winning move. An even better manager could add configurations to its dictionary on the fly; the rest of the program could then analyze games that it loses in order to learn new winning configurations.)

10. Rubik's Cube   We assume familiarity with Rubik's Cube, the delights of which cannot be presented adequately in a textual description! The theory of groups gives a mathematical basis for a sophisticated representation of Rubik's Cube that is appropriate for many analyses and manipulations. Suppose, on the other hand, that our only interest is in drawing the cube; that is, we must be able to determine rapidly which colors are visible on any face of the cube, and must be able to apply rotations to the cube, where each rotation consists of a twist of one of the six faces. Define operations and devise a data structure that handles this more limited set of requirements.

11. Tetris   The video game called Tetris is played by a single player in a rectangular area n units wide by m units high that is initially empty. Randomly selected tetrominoes are dropped one by one into this area. (A **tetromino** is a planar shape consisting of four unit squares attached along their sides; two tetrominoes are considered identical if one can be rotated into the other.

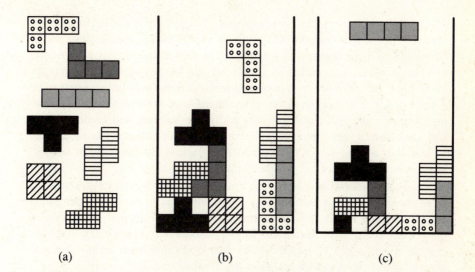

Figure 13.2 The game of Tetris. (a) The seven tetrominoes. (b) A game situation. The player has already selected a good position for the falling tetromino. (c) Two lines have been completed and removed, and the next tetromino has begun to fall.

Figure 13.2(a) shows all possible tetrominoes.) The tetrominoes fall with their sides parallel to the sides of the playing field and with vertical sides at integral distances from the side walls of the playing field. As each tetromino falls, the player can move it left and right by integral distances and rotate it in increments of 90°; the tetromino stops moving when it can descend no farther without overlapping the "ground" or a lower tetromino.

A **completed line** is a horizontal strip one unit high and n units wide consisting of n squares each of which is occupied by a portion of some tetromino. Each time a tetromino stops moving, any completed lines are removed from the playing field, and the portion of the playing field above the completed bands "slides down" to fill up the space (Figure 13.2(b,c)). The player's score is the number of lines that have been completed. The game ends when a stopped tetromino extends above the playing field. Completing lines therefore not only increases the player's score but also creates more vertical space and thus prolongs the game.

Devise data structures and algorithms to be used by the computer to implement the game of Tetris. Your implementation should be very fast, as though for a Tetris server that might be playing thousands of games at a time with playing fields of various sizes. Try to solve the problem in a way that would generalize to other shapes (such as pentominoes) or even to a three-dimensional version of the game.

12. Mazes   Build a system for representing, manipulating, and solving mazes. Formally, define a **lattice point** as a point $\langle x, y \rangle$ with integer coordinates x and y. Now define a **maze segment** as a horizontal or vertical line segment connecting two lattice points, and a **maze** as a finite set of maze segments. To keep paths through the maze distinct from maze segments, define a **half-lattice point** to be a point $\langle x + \frac{1}{2}, y + \frac{1}{2} \rangle$ where x and y are integers. A **maze problem** is a maze together with two half-lattice points s and t, the **starting** and **ending** points, and a **solution** to such a problem is a sequence of half-lattice points $p_0, p_1, \ldots, p_n$ such that $s = p_0$, $t = p_n$, and for each $0 \le i < n$ the line segment from p_i to p_{i+1} does not intersect any of the segments of the maze.

A user of your system may wish to create a maze from scratch, or to add or delete segments dynamically. It is most important to be able to determine quickly whether or not the line segment between a given pair of half-lattice points intersects a given maze. You should also develop an algorithm that finds a solution to a given maze problem or determines that none exists. Can you generalize this problem to three (or more) dimensions?

13. Fuzzy Sets   The sets typically used in mathematics (whose representations are discussed in Chapters 6 through 9) are all-or-nothing entities; given an object a and a set A, either $a \in A$ or $a \notin A$ obtains, and not both. **Fuzzy sets** give a more general formalism: an object a can be contained in a set A to any extent between 0 and 1, so we use phrases like "a is x in A" where $0 \le x \le 1$. Suppose, for example, that we have the fuzzy set T of tall people. Then Abraham Lincoln, say, might be 93% in T, whereas Napoleon might be only 6% in T. The union and intersection operations apply to fuzzy sets: if a is x in A and y in B, then a is $\min(x, y)$ in $A \cap B$ and is $\max(x, y)$ in $A \cup B$. By analogy with normal sets, fuzzy sets might be sparse (few elements of positive containment) and they support generalized versions of the dictionary operations, such as "increase the amount that a is contained in A." Define abstract operations and devise data structures for representing fuzzy sets and fuzzy containment.

14. Dynamic Partial Order   The members of a tennis club compete in an ongoing singles competition. After each match, a ranking of the players is computed as follows. Starting with the most recent match and working backward, the match results are used to construct a directed acyclic graph, where an edge $\langle A, B \rangle$ is added to the graph if player A beats player B. Any matches that are inconsistent with more recent results are ignored; that is, if incorporating a match into the growing graph would introduce a cycle then that match is skipped. The resulting graph is sorted topologically (as in Algorithm 12.3 on page 438) to determine the overall rankings.

For example, suppose that the following matches are played in the order given, where XY means that player X beats player Y:

$$GB, \ EA, \ CF, \ GD, \ FG, \ EF, \ EB, \ CD, \ DA, \ BD, \ BC, \ AC$$

After these twelve matches, player E is the champion and the rankings proceed F, G, B, D, A, C. The match in which player C beat player D was ignored since it is inconsistent with the later matches in which D beats A and A beats C. If now A beats B, the new ranking is $\langle E, A, B, C, F, G, D \rangle$ and the CD match is no longer ignored. (Note an anomaly here: by losing to player A, player B has risen in the rankings—given the situation after the first twelve matches, player B should intentionally lose if matched against A!)

Devise a program that accepts match results as they happen and after each one computes the ranking of the players. Your program should make no assumptions about the number of players and should not produce a ranking unless only one possible ranking exists. For example, after the first match above your program should produce the ranking $\langle G, B \rangle$ since it has no way of knowing that there are any other players, but after the second match the program should simply state that no unique ranking exists. (In fact, once a unique ranking exists, there will always be a unique ranking until a new player enters the tournament; can you prove this?) What would you do if matches were played so quickly that it was undesirable to reconsider all the data after each match?

15. Text Editor Design data structures and algorithms to support a simple text editor. Such a system must be able to handle standard editing operations such as insertion and deletion, which apply not only to single characters but also to words, lines, and perhaps sentences and paragraphs. It should also support simple motion commands (e.g., "Move the cursor down one line, remaining in the current column") and string searching. Furthermore, it should be possible to "cut and paste" easily, removing any selected portion of the text and moving it to another location.

16. Literature Search In Chapter 5 we considered the string searching problem. With large databases it is often important to be able to find data according to more general criteria. To be specific, consider an on-line index for a library containing a very large number of books. There are several restrictions that a library user may wish to apply in searching for a particular book: possibilities include author, title, year of publication, classification number, and subject. Furthermore, the user may not have complete information, remembering, say, only a word or two from the title. It may also be important to find all books whose bibliographies reference a given book, so that with each book must be stored a list of other books related to it. Finally, it is important to be able to combine these criteria in a search, finding, for example, all books published since 1991 on the topic of "Computers" and either "Data Structures" or "Algorithms."

Design data structures to be used in such a literature search system. Notice that books will be added to the library frequently, but will only rarely be deleted. As a more ambitious project you may wish to include the question of availability: the library possesses a certain number of copies of each book, some or all of which may be borrowed and due back on different days.

17. *Adaptive Huffman Encoding*   The results of Problem 31 of Chapter 5 can be used to implement adaptive Huffman encoding efficiently. The basic idea is as sketched on page 150: at all times maintain an encoding tree that is optimal for the text encountered so far. To process a character, first encode it using the current tree, then update the tree so that it is optimal when the new character is taken into account. The decoder works in step with the encoder, at each point reconstructing the same tree and therefore retrieving characters correctly.

The nodes of the encoding tree must contain weights as they would during the Huffman tree-construction algorithm: the weight of each leaf is the number of times its character has occurred in the text so far, and the weight of each nonleaf is the sum of the weights of its children. To update the tree after a character c is encoded, we increase by 1 the weight of the leaf corresponding to c and the weights of all ancestors of that leaf. The weights in the resulting tree correctly reflect the text encountered so far, but the tree is not necessarily optimal for that text unless the tree satisfied the conditions stated in part (b) of the problem. Therefore, before incrementing the leaf weights, we must adjust the tree so that condition (b) holds—it suffices to swap a few pairs of nodes of the tree. (Hint: two nodes that are to be swapped will have the same weight.)

Implement adaptive Huffman encoding and decoding routines. As we mentioned in Chapter 5, the advantage of adaptive Huffman encoding is that only a single pass through the input is required, but the disadvantage is that much more processing time is used. Therefore, your implementation should be as efficient as you can make it. In particular, each character should be processed in time proportional to its compressed length (as with non-adaptive Huffman encoding). There are several subproblems to solve and a good implementation may make use of a variety of data structures. There is a small problem getting started, which you will have to overcome; beware that Problem 31 requires that each node weight is at least 1, which is not so at the start of the encoding. However, note that the results of the problem are still valid if *at most one* node of the tree has zero weight.

18. *Lempel-Ziv Compression*   The algorithms used in Chapter 5 for Lempel-Ziv encoding and decoding (Algorithm 5.3 on page 153 and Problem 33 on page 170) are high-level, abstract descriptions of the technique. Production versions must incorporate solutions to at least two further problems. First of all, how should the dictionary *LookUp* and *Insert* operations be implemented, especially considering the special pattern of *LookUp*s performed by the encoding process? We mentioned in Chapter 5 that tries may be especially useful for implementing the dictionary, because of the property that every prefix of a string in the dictionary is also contained in the dictionary. However, the details were not considered in that chapter.

The second problem is to determine what action should be taken when the dictionary overflows, that is, when all available code numbers have been used up. Suppose we want to deal with this problem by discarding the *least-recently-used* entries when the dictionary is full. That is, if the string p is to be inserted and no further code numbers are available, we find the string q whose code hasn't been output in the largest number of steps, delete q from the dictionary, and insert p in its place.

Write the encoding and decoding procedures for this variant of Lempel-Ziv compression, choosing data structures that permit efficient implementation. Note that if the least-recently-used criterion is followed rigidly, then the prefix property described above is lost; strings of which q is a prefix may still be in the dictionary. You may therefore want to modify the criterion slightly, or change the circumstances under which a dictionary entry is marked "used."

19. *Squaring the Sets* Western Square Dancing takes place on a four by four grid of locations, each of which is called a **spot**. A **setup** is an assignment of eight (indistinguishable) dancers to the spots, along with a **facing direction** for each dancer, either North, South, East, or West. For example, Figure 13.3(a) is an illustration of the setup from which a dance begins. The dancers move in response to **calls**, each of which specifies a new spot and a new facing direction for every possible position in the grid. That is, a call is a function that accepts a spot and facing direction, and produces a new spot and a new facing direction. A call need not be a total function, that is, it may be undefined for some inputs. A call can be applied to a given setup only if (a) the call is defined for each dancer in the setup, and (b) the eight spots produced by applying the call to each dancer in the setup are distinct—in other words, no collisions ensue!

As an example, we give the complete definition of the call All Four Couples Square Chain Thru (Figure 13.3(b)). The call is undefined for the four central spots of the grid and for the four corners. Call the other eight spots the **O spots**. From the O spots, the call is undefined if the dancer is facing outside the set or towards a corner. If facing toward the center, the dancer moves to the O spot 90° counterclockwise around the grid that does *not* correspond to a 90° rotation, and faces outside the grid. If facing another O spot, the dancer moves to the similarly noncorresponding O spot in the *clockwise* direction, and faces the nearest corner spot. Notice that this call is rotationally symmetric: from any setup, the result of applying the call is identical to the result obtained by rotating the setup 180°, applying the call, and rotating back. All calls must be symmetric in this way; most have 90° and 270° symmetry as well.

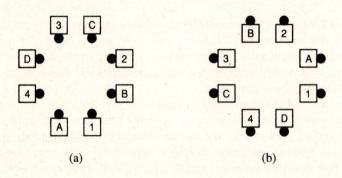

(a)   (b)

Figure 13.3 Bow to your partner! (a) Initial setup. Each dancer is drawn as a square with a dot indicating facing direction. (b) Result of executing All Four Couples Square Chain Thru from the initial setup. If a single couple began facing each other (rather than facing center) then the call would not be applicable because of collisions, even though it is defined for each dancer.

Devise data structures and algorithms for use in square dance analysis. The primary task is to determine which of the thousands of established calls is applicable to a given setup. More ambitiously, we would like to find a sequence of calls that will **resolve** a given setup, that is, transform it back into the initial setup. And often we want to experiment with new calls added on the fly. (The real-life problem is much more complicated, involving a larger grid with half-spots, invisible and faceless dancers called **phantoms**, and calls that depend on the gender of the dancer, the location of other dancers, and the preceding call. There are also **concepts** which transform calls into other calls—in fact, the call illustrated above results from applying the All Four Couples concept to the Square Chain Thru call.)

20. Air Traffic Control   Consider a simplified version of the air traffic control problem. We must manage a set of airplanes, each of which has a three-dimensional position and velocity specified as latitude, longitude, altitude, track (the direction along the ground, which is the airplane's heading corrected for wind velocity), groundspeed, and rate of climb or descent. Moreover, each airplane has a type that determines the radius of a sphere around it that must not be broached—two Grumman trainers can fly much closer together than two 747s! Our system must provide warnings whenever two planes are on a collision course, if the collision will occur in time less than some given threshold. Changes of course, speed, altitude and so forth arrive frequently, as do new flights. Flights that pass beyond some distance from our location become another controller's responsibility and leave the database, as do flights that land (or crash!). We must also handle hypothetical queries consisting of *proposed* changes of flight plan. Design a system to solve this problem, recalling that lives depend on its accuracy and rapidity.

21. Bounded-Degree Minimum Spanning Tree   As in the minimum spanning tree problem of §12.3, let $G = \langle V, E \rangle$ be an undirected graph and let c be a function that assigns a nonnegative cost to each edge of G. Also let $d \geq 2$ be a positive integer. The **bounded-degree minimum spanning tree** problem is to find a minimal-cost subset E' of E such that the graph $\langle V, E' \rangle$ is a tree in which each vertex has at most d neighbors. (The **degree** of a vertex of a graph is the number of its neighbors; the degree of a graph is the maximum of the degrees of its vertices. Thus the problem is to find a minimal-cost spanning tree of degree at most d.) Even when the original graph G is connected there may be no solution to the problem; this happens, for example, when $d = 2$ and G consists of a central vertex connected to each of many peripheral vertices of degree 1. To avoid this difficulty we assign infinite cost to edges not in G, thus ensuring that a solution exists even though it may have infinite cost.

The bounded-degree minimum spanning tree problem is NP-complete; as we have discussed, this means that no efficient algorithm that solves it is known. We describe here an algorithm that may run for an extremely long time but will always find the solution eventually. Essentially, the algorithm is an intelligent way of organizing a brute-force search over all possible trees on the set V of vertices of G.

Call a tree on V **feasible** if it has degree d or less; thus we are searching for the least-cost feasible tree. The algorithm maintains a partition of the trees on V, that is, a collection of disjoint sets whose union contains all the trees. Initially the partition consists of a single set S_0 containing all the trees on V. Now let T be a least-cost tree in S. If T is feasible, then it must be the solution to the problem (since no lesser-cost tree can exist) and we are done. Otherwise, select any edge, say e_1, and split S_0 into the set S_1 of all trees containing e_1 and the set S_2 of all trees not containing e_1; there are now two sets in the partition. Let T_1 and T_2 be minimal-cost trees in S_1 and S_2 respectively. Suppose that the cost of T_1 is less than that of T_2. If T_1 is feasible then it must be the solution to the problem. Otherwise, pick any edge other than e_1, call it e_2, and split S_1 into the sets S_3 and S_4 of trees containing and not containing e_2 respectively, and let T_3 and T_4 be least-cost trees in each set. The partition now consists of three sets: trees containing e_1 and e_2 are in S_3, trees containing e_1 but not e_2 are in S_4, and trees not containing e_1 are in S_2.

We continue in the same way. At each point the partition consists of a collection of sets of trees, where each set is defined by specifying which edges are required and which are forbidden in its member trees. (For example, the initial set S_0 has no restrictions. When we split S_0 using e_1 the set S_1 requires e_1 among all of its trees and forbids no edges, while S_2 forbids e_1 and requires no edges.) At each point we also know the least-cost tree T_i in each set S_i. If the cheapest tree among the T_i, say T_k, is feasible, then it is the solution to the original problem. Otherwise we select an edge e that is not among the edges defining S_k, split S_k into two subsets (one requiring e and one forbidding e), and find the least-cost tree in each subset. If S_k contains only a single infeasible tree then S_k is simply discarded. (After the first time this happens the sets S_i no longer partition all trees on V, but only infeasible trees are discarded.) The first feasible tree found by this procedure is in fact the minimal-cost feasible tree.

Implement this algorithm. Discussion: The problem hinges on finding a good representation for the sets of trees that make up the partition. It is a simple matter to take a specification of such a set (in terms of required and forbidden edges) and find its least-cost tree using (say) Kruskal's algorithm. But a naïve implementation with lists of edges representing the S_i entails much extra work, because the same minimum spanning trees will be computed repeatedly. (For example, notice that until there are $|V|$ sets in the partition, the set that splits is always the one containing the minimum unconstrained spanning tree of G, and that same tree will always be selected and found to be infeasible.) Try to avoid this extra recomputation as much as possible. Consider selecting edges e in the same way that Kruskal's algorithm does, that is, cheapest possible edge next.

22. *Crossword Puzzle Construction*   Design a tool, complete with data structures, to be used as an aid in the construction of crossword puzzles. Assume you are given a large, fixed dictionary D containing all of the legal words. There are several functions that you might provide. First of all, the user should be able to find quickly all words with any given restriction on their characters, such as all seven-letter words beginning with A and ending with TE, or all words of five or more letters whose second letter is S. You should also be able to find sets of words satisfying more complex requirements, such as the words that can be placed just under a given word without making it impossible to complete the puzzle. (For example, ODOR can be placed under HEMP since there exist words beginning with HO, ED, MO, and PR. But CHIP cannot be so placed.) More ambitiously, you might consider how to create small diagrams automatically.

23. *Hypergraphs*   Recall that an undirected graph is an ordered pair $\langle V, E \rangle$ consisting of a set V of vertices and a set E of edges, where each edge is a set containing two distinct vertices. A **hypergraph** is an ordered pair $\langle V, E \rangle$ consisting of a set V of vertices and a set E of edges, where each edge is a set containing *any number* of vertices. Most of the definitions and graph properties from Chapter 12 can be extended in a natural way to hypergraphs. For example, two vertices of a hypergraph are **adjacent** if there is an edge that contains both, and a **path** in a hypergraph is a sequence of adjacent vertices. Explore representation methods for hypergraphs, evaluating the advantages and disadvantages of each.

24. *Multidimensional Storage Allocation* Reconsider the problem of memory management, discussed in Chapter 10, in a context where the "memory" being managed is a two-dimensional structure. (This problem arises, for example, in a computer that consists of a large number of independent processors communicating along a two-dimensional rectangular grid; the system may wish to assign various subtasks to connected groups of processors and must keep track of which processors are free and which are available.) Let us assume that each allocation request is for a rectangular block of specified dimensions and that blocks are explicitly freed when no longer in use. Explore allocation and freeing strategies, and the data structures to support them. There are several different settings that might be examined. For example, you might assume that (a) all requests are of the same dimensions, (b) requests are of various dimensions, but allocated blocks may not be moved, or (c) requests are of various dimensions and blocks may be moved.

25. *Logical Inference* Aristotelian logic recognizes four kinds of **premises**, statements used to build logical arguments. A premise states a relationship between two **terms**, each of which can be thought of as a set. The forms of the premises are:

- (Universal Affirmative) All A are B.
- (Universal Negative) No A are B.
- (Particular Affirmative) Some A are B.
- (Particular Negative) Some A are not B.

For example, the statement "All humans are mortal" is a universal affirmative in which A is the term "humans" (that is, the set of all humans) and B is the term "mortals." A universal affirmative states that any element of A is an element of B, or equivalently that $A \subseteq A \cap B$. Similarly, the particular affirmative states that the set $A \cap B$ is nonempty.

We wish to build a system that can accept logical premises dynamically and can then decide on the validity of other premises. For example, after accepting premises "All A are B," "All B are C," and "No C is D," the system should respond with **true** when asked if all A are C, with **false** when asked whether some A is D, and with **maybe** when asked if all C are B. And of course, if "Some A are not B" is then asserted, an error condition should be reported.

Design such a logical engine. Assume that each term is represented by an integer; you must then implement the procedure $AssertUA(1, 2)$ (meaning that the premise "All S_1 is S_2" should be added to your data structure) and similarly $AssertUN$, $AssertPA$, $AssertPN$. The data structure is probed with function $QueryUA$ and three others like it. Additional capabilities might also be added. You may wish to extend the form of statements handled by your system, encompassing such possibilities as "All A are not-B" or "Some A exist." Another possibility is to permit the *deletion* of information, along the lines of "It is no longer known that all A are B." Finally, you may wish to have the data structure itself deduce premises that follow from the current information.

26. Music   Design data structures for computer representation of music. We wish to support tools that manipulate musical pieces, such as an engraver that prints a piece in standard notation, a music editor, or a sound synthesizer. You must determine the objects and relationships to be represented as well as the abstract operators required for your tools.

27. Genealogies   Suppose we wish to keep track of family trees for a very large number of people. With each person there is associated some identifying information (name, social security number, and so forth) and some auxiliary information. We would like to be able to trace family histories, finding the exact relationship or relationships between any two people in the database. Of course, new information comes in all the time: marriages, births, deaths, and so forth. We may also learn of previously unknown relationships, or even discover that two badly-identified persons were actually one and the same. Design data structures that might be used for this problem.

Problems

1. Discuss whether it makes sense to have problems in a chapter like this one.

References

Two excellent articles about spelling checkers are

J. L. Peterson, "Computer Programs for Detecting and Correcting Spelling Errors," *Communications of the ACM* **23** (1980), pp. 676–687

and

M. D. McIlroy, "Development of a Spelling List," *IEEE Transactions on Communications* **COM-30** (1982), pp. 91–99.

The longest common subsequence algorithm described in connection with diff is from

J. W. Hunt and T. G. Szymanski, "A Fast Algorithm for Computing Longest Common Subsequences," *Communications of the ACM* **20** (1977), pp. 350–353.

Much more about Rubik's Cube can be found in

E. Rubik, T. Varga, G. Keri, G. Marx, and T. Vekerdy, *Rubik's Cubic Compendium* (translated by D. Singmaster), Oxford University Press, 1987.

Fuzzy sets are the invention of

L. A. Zadeh, "Fuzzy Sets," *Information and Control* **8** (1965), pp. 338–353;

a good introductory text, including an extremely extensive bibliography, is

A. Kandel, *Fuzzy Mathematical Techniques with Applications*, Addison-Wesley, 1986.

The dynamic partial order problem (and the anomalous example) appeared in

C. L. Mallows, "Producing a Ranking from Recent Results" (problem E3240), *American Mathematical Monthly* **96** (1989), pp. 529–530.

Dynamic Huffman encoding is further discussed in

J. S. Vitter, "Design and Analysis of Dynamic Huffman Codes," *Journal of the ACM* **34** (1987), pp. 825–845.

The algorithm for the bounded-degree minimum spanning tree problem is similar to one for a problem with slightly different constraints; see

K. M. Chandy and R. A. Russell, "The Design of Multipoint Linkages in a Teleprocessing Tree Network," *IEEE Transactions on Computers* **C-21** (1972), pp. 1062–1066.

Some early work on automated crossword puzzle construction is due to

L. J. Mazlack, "Machine Selection of Elements in Crossword Puzzles," *SIAM Journal on Computing* **5** (1976), pp. 51–72.

Elementary logic, including Aristotelian premises and syllogisms, is beautifully laid out in

W. V. Quine, *Methods of Logic*, Harvard University Press, 1982 (Fourth Edition).

One piece of the genealogy problem is discussed in

A. V. Aho, J. E. Hopcroft, and J. D. Ullman, "On Finding Lowest Common Ancestors in Trees," *SIAM Journal on Computing* **5** (1976), pp. 115–132.

Berge's book Graphs and Hypergraphs, *cited in the references to Chapter 12, is a classic exposition of hypergraphs. References for adaptive Huffman encoding and Lempel-Ziv compression are given in Chapter 5.*

A

Locatives

Locatives were introduced in Chapter 1 as a programming convenience. Here is a quick review of their semantics. A locative is like any other variable, except that when assigned a value with the assignment operator "←" a locative both takes on the new value and "remembers" the place from which the new value came. When assigned a value with the *locative assignment* operator "⇐" a locative takes on the new value and also assigns the new value to the location it is remembering. For example, if P is a locative, then after the assignments

$$P \leftarrow Q; \quad P \Leftarrow R$$

all three variables have the same value, just as though the assignment $Q \leftarrow R$ had been carried out as well. In this book only pointers are assigned to locatives, but locatives may be used more generally; in this example, Q and R might just as well be integers.

We use locatives in order to focus on the important aspects of our algorithms, avoiding distracting details of pointer manipulation. But although elegant and handy, locatives are not featured in typical programming languages. Therefore, in this Appendix we describe carefully the behavior of locatives so that algorithms that use them are fully specified and unambiguous. Our discussion yields a concrete method for implementing locatives, one that could be realized fairly easily in any programming language. (In fact, for sufficiently powerful languages the implementation could be carried out in the language itself; that is, we could present a purely syntactic, mechanical procedure for transforming any program with locatives into an equivalent program without locatives.)

We begin by taking a closer look at ordinary variables. Every variable is associated with a memory cell in which the value of the variable is stored. The process of obtaining the address of the memory cell associated with a variable is called **L-evaluating** that variable. (Typically variables are "associated with" memory cells via a symbol table in which the variable can be looked up to find the address of the cell. Not all variables are associated with the same cell throughout the execution of a program.) When a variable is **evaluated**, that is, when its value is needed in an expression, it is not the address of the memory cell that is used but rather the contents of the cell. For example, when the expression $P + 3$ is evaluated the value that is added to 3 is the contents of the cell associated with P. The operation of taking the contents of a memory cell, given its address, is called **dereferencing**. Thus evaluating a variable is a two-step process: first the variable is L-evaluated to obtain the address of the cell with which it is associated, and then that address is dereferenced to obtain its contents.*

Now consider a simple assignment $P \leftarrow \alpha$ where P is a variable and α is an arbitrary expression. The first thing to notice is that the left-hand side of this assignment is *not* evaluated. It would serve no purpose to evaluate P, since to perform the assignment we need the associated cell itself and not its contents. The assignment is carried out by evaluating α and storing the resulting value in the memory cell whose address is obtained by L-evaluating P. (In so-called **strongly typed** languages it is also necessary to check that the value of α is a legitimate one for the memory cell; if not, it may be possible to convert it to an appropriate value, or an error condition may result.) L-evaluation is so named because of its use on the left-hand side of assignment statements.

The left side of an assignment statement need not be a variable, but it must in some way name a memory cell in which a value can be stored. In the pseudo-programming language used in this book the only legitimate targets for assignment (other than variables and array references) are field references, as in the statement $\mathsf{Next}(P) \leftarrow \Lambda$. Like variables, field references yield memory cells. But finding the memory cell may require some computation since a field reference may contain an arbitrarily complex subexpression, for example, $\mathsf{LC}(Pop(S))$. Again, we denote by L-evaluation the process of finding the address of a memory cell given a field reference. To L-evaluate a field reference $\mathsf{Field}(\alpha)$ we first evaluate α. The result should be a pointer to a record that contains a field called Field; the address of the cell within the record in which that field is stored is the result of the L-evaluation. (Keep in mind that the "address" of a memory cell need not be simply an integer, since memory cells are independent of addressable, physical memory. For example, L-evaluating a field reference like $\mathsf{Mark}(N)$ might yield the "address" of a one-bit cell.) Normal evaluation of a field reference, like evaluation of a variable, consists of L-evaluation followed by dereferencing the address obtained. Notice that the rule for performing an assignment is the same whether a field reference or a variable is on the left-hand side.

We now have all the machinery we need to implement locatives. Consider the assignment statement $P \leftarrow Q$ where P is a locative, and recall that we want P to store not only the value of Q but also the "place that value came from." That is, we want P somehow to remember the address of the memory

---

* We should note that our point of view regarding the semantics of variables and assignment is not universal; other authors explain the meaning of these constructs in a different manner.

cell associated with Q, so that a later locative assignment to P can change the value of Q as well. To accomplish this, we implement locatives as *pointers to memory cells*; that is, each locative stores the address of a cell. In the example, P will store the address associated with Q; we can later retrieve this address from P in order to modify Q. A simple rule is used to obtain this behavior: when a locative appears on the left-hand side of an ordinary assignment we perform L-evaluation (rather than ordinary evaluation) of the right-hand side, and the resulting address is stored into the locative. For example, to execute $P \leftarrow Q$ we note that P is a locative and thus we L-evaluate Q, obtaining the address of the associated cell, which is then stored into P. After an assignment like $P \leftarrow \mathsf{Mark}(Q)$ the locative P will store the address of the cell containing the Mark field of Q.

But now we must consider ordinary evaluation of locatives. The problem is that we wish to use locatives in expressions as though they were ordinary variables, even though they contain addresses of cells. For example, suppose P is a locative and Q is an integer. After the assignments $Q \leftarrow 3$ and $P \leftarrow Q$ the value of $P + 1$ should be 4, even though the cell associated with P contains not 3 but the address associated with Q. What is required is a special rule for evaluating locatives: a locative P is evaluated by L-evaluating P as usual and then dereferencing the resulting address twice instead of only once. In the example, the first dereference yields the address of the cell associated with Q, and dereferencing that address then yields 3. With this rule in place we can use locatives just like any other variables.

There is one case of ordinary assignment that needs special consideration: assignments like $P \leftarrow R$ in which *both* P and R are locatives. The desired behavior is that P and R should point to the same memory cell. For example, after the sequence

$$Q \leftarrow 3; \quad R \leftarrow Q; \quad P \leftarrow R; \quad P \Leftarrow 4$$

the expressions $P + 1$, $Q + 1$ and $R + 1$ should all evaluate to 5. To obtain this effect, we need to evaluate R normally—that is, with only a single dereference—and store the resulting value (the address of Q) in the locative P. This differs from the rule for ordinary assignment to a locative, which would dictate that we L-evaluate R. Put another way, ordinary assignment between two locatives is carried out just like ordinary assignment between any two variables; the special rule for assignment to a locative is not invoked.

It is now a simple matter to implement the locative assignment operator. To perform $P \Leftarrow \alpha$, where P is a locative and α is an arbitrary expression, just evaluate α as usual and store the result in the memory cell to which P points. More precisely, evaluate P normally (that is, L-evaluate P and dereference it only once) to obtain the address of a memory cell, and store into that cell the value obtained by evaluating α. To perform a locative assignment where the left-hand side is any expression *other* than a locative, we act as though an

	LHS action	RHS action
non-locative ← *any*	L-evaluate	evaluate
locative ← *non-locative*	L-evaluate	L-evaluate
locative ← *locative*	L-evaluate	1-evaluate
locative ⇐ *any*	1-evaluate	evaluate
non-locative ⇐ *any*	L-evaluate	evaluate

Figure A.1 Summary of the rules for ordinary and locative assignment. (To evaluate a locative we L-evaluate it and dereference the result twice; to 1-evaluate a locative we L-evaluate it and dereference the result only once.)

ordinary assignment was intended. (This typically occurs only during a parallel locative assignment where some of the left-hand elements are not locatives, as in Algorithm 7.3 on page 227.) Figure A.1 summarizes the rules that we have presented up to this point.

The next topic to discuss is the use of locatives in function and procedure calls. It may seem as though there are very tricky interactions involved; indeed, it is important to get the correct behavior, since our code sometimes depends on passing values to functions and procedures with locatives as formal arguments. However, the rules are simple if we take the right point of view, which is that *passing arguments to functions and procedures is an implicit use of ordinary assignment*. For example, suppose that *Proc* is a procedure with formal parameters A, B, and C. Then a call $Proc(\alpha, \beta, \gamma)$ is equivalent to the sequence

$$A \leftarrow \alpha; \quad B \leftarrow \beta; \quad C \leftarrow \gamma$$

followed by the code in the body of *Proc*. In other words, each argument in a procedure or function call is properly seen as the right-hand side of an implied ordinary assignment to the corresponding formal parameter. The appropriate dereferencing rules for function and procedure invocation follow immediately. The expression **return** α simply evaluates α and returns the resulting value; thus **return** P works as expected even when P is a locative (see also Problem 3).

Finally, there is one somewhat anomalous situation that deserves mention even though it never arises in this book. Our rules call for the use of L-evaluation in certain contexts. But not every expression can be L-evaluated! In fact, we have given L-evaluation rules only for variables and for field references; if some other construct must be L-evaluated we might have difficulty. For example, consider ordinary assignments like $3 \leftarrow x$ or $Q + 1 \leftarrow \min(y, z)$. The left-hand sides cannot be L-evaluated as required and it is not clear what action to take. This situation is erroneous in most programming languages; a few just evaluate the right-hand side (for its possible side effects) without storing the resulting value anywhere.

But when the left-hand side of an ordinary assignment is a locative and the right-hand side cannot be L-evaluated, the situation is more serious. To see the problem, let P be a locative and consider assignments like $P \leftarrow 3$ or $P \leftarrow \min(y, z)$. There is no cell whose address we can use as the result of L-evaluating the right-hand side, and yet we cannot simply ignore these assignments since we might later encounter the expression $P + 1$ where we expect to dereference the address associated with P twice and find the value most recently assigned to P. One solution is to extend the definition of L-evaluation to arbitrary expressions: if an expression is not a variable or field reference, then to L-evaluate it we evaluate it normally, store the result in a freshly allocated memory cell, and return the address of that cell as the result of the L-evaluation. In this way even subsequent statements like $P \Leftarrow 4$ will work as we would wish (see also Problem 1). Alternatively, we could simply declare assignments like $P \leftarrow 3$ to be erroneous when P is a locative, since they violate an implicit typing restriction that permits only locations to be assigned to locatives. (Either solution suffices for our purposes, since no such assignment appears in this text.)

Problems

1. **a.** Let P be a locative. If statements like $P \leftarrow 3$ are handled as suggested in the last paragraph of this appendix, is there any difference between the later statements $P \leftarrow Q$ and $P \Leftarrow Q$?

   b. Suppose that, although we forbid assignments like $P \leftarrow \alpha$ where P is a locative and α cannot be L-evaluated, we wish to permit as a special case the initialization $P \leftarrow \Lambda$. To conserve memory we allocate once and for all a cell containing Λ and use the address of that cell as the result of any L-evaluation of Λ. Are there any disadvantages to this scheme?

2. In enumerating the various rules for assignment we did not consider locative assignments like $P \Leftarrow R$ in which both sides are locatives. Explain why not.

3. Although the functions in this book may execute **return** P where P is a locative, the formal result type of a function is never **locative**. If we lift this restriction then the result of a function evaluation might be a legitimate target for assignment; for example, we could write a function *Choose* such that *Choose*(**true**) $\Leftarrow 0$ assigns 0 to A, and *Choose*(**false**) $\Leftarrow 0$ assigns 0 to B. Discuss any modifications to the rules that are necessary in order to incorporate this feature into our language, and write the function *Choose*. (You may wish to think about the programming language Pascal, which has no **return** statement; instead, the value returned by a function is the last value assigned to a variable with the same name as the function.)

Index

As in the text, *italic type* is used to indicate function and procedure names, sans-serif type is used for field names, and **boldface type** is used for literals of the pseudo-programming language (including "built-in" data types).